OXFORD MATHEMATICS

HIGHER

GCSE

Authors

Sue Briggs

Peter McGuire

Derek Philpott

Susan Shilton

Ken Smith

Course Editors

Peter McGuire

Ken Smith

Oxford
University
Press

Acknowledgements

The publisher and authors are grateful to the following for permission to reproduce material.

Illustrators Gecko, Oxford Illustrators, Nick Hawken, Pat Moffett, Ian Dicks, Phillip Reeve

Photographers Mike Dudley, Martin Sookias, Andrew Ward

Photographic Libraries Mary Evans Picture Library, The Science Photographic Library (cover)

Suppliers Eurostar

Every reasonable effort has been made to contact copyright owners, but we apologise for any unknown errors or omissions.

Oxford University Press, Great Clarendon Street, Oxford OX2 6DP

Oxford New York
Athens Auckland Bangkok Bogota Buenos Aires
Calcutta Cape Town Chennai Dar es Salaam
Delhi Florence Hong Kong Istanbul Karachi
Kuala Lumpur Madrid Melbourne Mexico City
Mumbai Nairobi Paris São Paulo Singapore
Taipei Tokyo Toronto Warsaw

and associated companies in
Berlin Ibadan

Oxford is a trade mark of Oxford University Press

© Oxford University Press 1998

First published 1998

ISBN 0 19 914707 8

Printed in Spain by Graficas Estella S.A.

About this book

This book is designed to help you understand and learn the mathematics needed for GCSE. You will also be able to use the book for pre-examination revision, and practice of skills and techniques. Colour is used to help with the organisation of the different parts of the book. In this book you will find:

Contents   This includes a listing of the mathematics in each of the 25 Sections.

Wordfinder   This lists alphabetically, words and mathematical terms that will enable you to refer to specific aspects of mathematics quickly and easily. The colours will help you to decide whether you want to refer to:
- Starting points
- Section
- In Focus
- Exam-style questions

Starting points   This introduces the mathematics you need to be familiar with, before starting on a particular section. There are some questions for you to try out so that you can test what you know already. See page 192 as an example of Starting points.

If you are confident about your grasp of the starting points, you should be able to begin work on the mathematics in the section.

Sections   As you work through each section you will find information in yellow panels. In these panels are:
- explanations of new mathematical ideas, skills and procedures
- worked examples on specific aspects of the mathematics
- methods to help you to use and apply your mathematics

There are many questions for you to answer to consolidate your learning. More difficult questions are numbered in blue – for example, on page 66:

6   a   Calculate the general term for the sequence which starts:
13, 1, ⁻19, ⁻47, ⁻83 …

You will also see that blue text is used at times to stress important points. For example, on page 104: the word eliminate is emphasised.

Within a section the margins of a page give you additional information such as the definitions of mathematical terms.

Words in the margin that link with the main text are coloured red. For example, on page 153: surface area links the definition in the margin and its reference in the main text.

Thinking ahead   This provides an opportunity to try out some questions and discuss ideas that will be introduced in the next subsection.

End points   This is where the work of the section is listed for you. It is one way to check that you have understood the mathematical ideas, skills and techniques which have been taught in that section. See page 206 as an example of End points.

Skills breaks   These provide a variety of questions all linked to the same data. They are one way to revise the mathematics you have learned and already know. You will have to decide on the mathematical skills and techniques you need to answer each of the questions.

In focus pages   Each In focus page offers a set of questions for you to practise and revise individual mathematical skills and techniques.

Exam-style questions   These questions will allow you to become familiar with the style and difficulty you can expect at the Intermediate level of entry.

Answers   You will find the numerical answers to questions at the end of the book.

This is more than just a book of questions: it is a learning package that will help you to make the most of your mathematical talents and expertise. You can be confident that you will be well prepared for your GCSE examination.

⊗ CONTENTS

A note on accuracy

Make sure your answer is given to any degree of accuracy stated in the question, for example 2 dp or 1 sf. Where it is not stated, choose a sensible degree of accuracy for your answer, and make sure you work to a greater degree of accuracy through the problem. For example, if you choose to give an answer to 3 sf, work to at least 4 sf through the problem, then round your final answer to 3 sf.

Examination groups differ in their approach to accuracy. Some say that you should not give your final answer to a greater degree of accuracy than that used for the data in the question, but others state answers should be given to 3 sf.

If you are in any doubt, check with your examination group.

Metric and imperial units

	Metric	Imperial	Some approximate conversions
Length	millimetres (mm) centimetres (cm) metres (m) kilometres (km) 1 cm = 10 mm 1 m = 100 cm 1 km = 1000 m	inches (in) feet (ft) yards (yd) miles 1 ft = 12 in 1 yd = 3 ft 1 mile = 1760 yd	1 inch = 2.54 cm 1 foot ≈ 30.5 cm 1 metre ≈ 39.4 in 1 mile ≈ 1.61 km
Mass	grams (g) kilograms (kg) tonnes 1 kg = 1000 g 1 tonne = 1000 kg	ounces (oz) pounds (lb) stones 1 lb = 16 oz 1 stone = 14 lb	1 pound ≈ 454 g 1 kilogram ≈ 2.2 lb
Capacity	millilitres (ml) centilitres (cl) litres 1 cl = 10 ml 1 litre = 100 cl = 1000 ml	pints (pt) gallons 1 gallon = 8 pt	1 gallon ≈ 4.55 litres 1 litre ≈ 1.76 pints ≈ 0.22 gallons

		Starting points	Section	Focus	Exam-style
Acceleration			277	326	365
Accuracy and limits			93	311	332
Algebraic proof			40	306	
Angles	▪ between lines	31	34	305	357
	▪ in circles		138	323	358
	▪ in polygons		21, 28	305	356, 357
	▪ elevation and depression		257	324	357
Approximation		93	94	311	332
Area	▪ circles	148, 149	150, 152	316	360, 361
	▪ composite shapes		150	316	360, 362
	▪ under a graph		278	326	365
Arc (length)		236	152	316	360
Asymptotes			201, 300	319	345
Average speed		272, 273	274	326	365
Averages		46	50	307	380
Bearings		246	256		368
Bisecting (angles and lines)			76, 77	309	363
Box-and-whisker plots			55	307	
Capacity			153, 156	316	360
Changing the subject of a formula			130 – 133	314	340
Circle	▪ angles in		237	323	358
	▪ area and circumference	148, 149	150, 152	316	360, 361
	▪ theorems		237	323	358
Collecting like terms			32	306	350
Completing the square		292	110, 205	312, 319	345
Compound measures		272	274 – 277	326	365
Cone			158	316	360
Construction	▪ triangles	72	73	309	363
	▪ perpendiculars		77	309	363
	▪ bisectors		77	309	363
Congruent triangles		117	74	309	363
Correlation			268	325	378
Cosine rule			252	324	367 – 369
Cumulative frequency			185	318	382
Cyclic quadrilateral			241	323	358
Data	▪ discrete and continuous		182	318	377
Density			156	316	
Difference of two squares			44, 108	306	
Differences	▪ first and second	59	61, 65	308	351
Dimensions in formulas			164	316	362
Distance–time graphs (travel graphs)			274 – 276	326	365
Enlargement		117	121	313	370
Errors			98	311	
Equations	▪ forming	103	107, 112	312	341, 344
	▪ linear	103	107	312	341
	▪ quadratic		112	312	344
Expressions	▪ forming		43		
	▪ simplifying		32	306	350
Factorising expressions		102, 128, 132	41, 108	306, 312	350, 343
Factors		102	12	304	333
Formulas	▪ rearranging	193	129 – 134	314	340
	▪ types		164	316	360
Fractions		11, 166	13	304	334
Frequency	▪ distributions	47	52	307	377
	▪ polygons		56	307	377
General term – sequences		59	61	308	341
Gradient		192	194	319	345
Graphs	▪ distance–time (travel)	273	274 – 276	326	365
	▪ linear	192	194	319	341
	▪ quadratic		196	319	341
	▪ polynomial		203	319	341
Histograms			181	318	377
Indices		10, 83, 93	84 – 87	310	336
Inequalities		218	220 – 224	321	348
Interest (including compound)			231 – 233	322	335
Interior angles		20	24	305	356
Interquartile range			49	307	380 – 381

Starting points
You need to know about ...

... so try these questions

A Multiples, factors and prime numbers

- The **common multiples** of two numbers are those that are multiples of both.

  Example   Multiples of 4 are: 4, 8, 12, 16, 20, 24, ...
  Multiples of 6 are: 6, 12, 18, 24, 30, 36, ...

  Common multiples of 4 and 6 are: 12, 24, 36, ...
  The **lowest common multiple** of 6 and 4 is 12.

- The **common factors** of two numbers are those that are factors of both.

  Example   Factors of 4 are: 1, 2 and 4.
  Factors of 6 are: 1, 2, 3 and 6.

  Common factors of 4 and 6 are: 1 and 2.
  The **highest common factor** of 4 and 6 is 2.

- A number is **prime** if it has exactly two different factors.

  Example   5 is a prime number: its factors are 1 and 5.

B Writing a number as a product of primes

- The factors of a number that are prime are called **prime factors**.

- A multiplication of prime factors is called a **product of primes**.

- One way to write a number as its product of primes is to break it down into factor pairs until a product of primes is reached.

  Example   Write 63 as a product of primes.

  63
  3 × 21
  3 × 7 × 3

  As a product of primes:
  $63 = 3 \times 3 \times 7$
  $\quad\;\; = 3^2 \times 7$ in index notation.

C Equivalent fractions

- Two fractions equal in value are called **equivalent** fractions, e.g. $\frac{1}{2}$ and $\frac{5}{10}$ are equivalent fractions.

- To find equivalent fractions, multiply or divide the numerator ('top') and denominator ('bottom') by the same number.

  Examples

  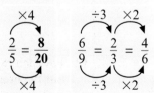

- A fraction in its lowest terms is an equivalent fraction where the numerator and denominator have no common factors except 1.

  Example   In its lowest terms, $\frac{6}{9}$ is written as $\frac{2}{3}$.

A1 Give three common multiples of:
    a 5 and 8   **b** 9 and 12

A2 Find the lowest common multiple of:
    a 2 and 7   **b** 3 and 5
    c 6 and 8   **d** 2 and 4

A3 List the common factors of:
    a 24 and 30   **b** 25 and 30

A4 What is the highest common factor of:
    a 2 and 7   **b** 6 and 8
    c 4 and 8   **d** 36 and 54?

A5 Explain why 1 is not prime.

A6 List all the prime numbers between 30 and 40.

A7 Explain why 2 is the only even prime number.

B1 Write each of these as a product of primes in index notation.
    a 20   **b** 36
    c 385   **d** 504

B2 Evaluate each product of primes:
    a $2^5 \times 3^2 \times 7$
    b $3^3 \times 5 \times 11^2$

C1 Which of these fractions is equivalent to $\frac{4}{10}$?

    $\frac{8}{20}, \frac{7}{13}, \frac{12}{30}, \frac{6}{15}, \frac{2}{5}$

C2 Write three equivalent fractions for:

    a $\frac{6}{8}$ **b** $\frac{2}{9}$

C3 Write each fraction in its lowest terms.

    a $\frac{15}{25}$ **b** $\frac{6}{36}$

D Mixed numbers and improper fractions

◆ An improper fraction is one where the numerator is larger than the denominator ('top-heavy'), e.g $\frac{11}{4}$

◆ An improper fraction is greater than 1, so it can be written as a **mixed number**, a mixture of whole numbers and fractions.

Example $\quad \frac{11}{4} = \frac{8}{4} + \frac{3}{4} = 2\frac{3}{4}$

◆ Any whole number can be written as an improper fraction.

Example $\quad 5 = \frac{5}{1}$

E Calculating with fractions

◆ To **add** or **subtract** fractions:

  ❖ find a common multiple of the denominators.

  ❖ find equivalent fractions with a common multiple as the new denominator

  ❖ add or subtract the fractions.

Example $\quad \frac{3}{4} - \frac{1}{6} = \frac{9}{12} - \frac{2}{12} = \frac{7}{12}$

◆ To **multiply** fractions:

  ❖ multiply the numerators

  ❖ multiply the denominators.

Example $\quad \frac{2}{3} \times \frac{1}{5} = \frac{2}{15}$

◆ Two numbers that multiply together to give 1 are **reciprocals** of each other:

Example The reciprocal of $\frac{3}{4}$ is $\frac{4}{3}$.

◆ Dividing by a fraction has the same effect as multiplying by its reciprocal so, to **divide** fractions:

  ❖ write the division as a multiplication

  ❖ multiply the fractions.

Example $\quad \frac{1}{4} \div \frac{2}{3} = \frac{1}{4} \times \frac{3}{2} = \frac{3}{8}$

F Multiplying out brackets

◆ To multiply out brackets, multiply **every** term inside the brackets.

Example $5(3n - 2) = (5 \times 3n) - (5 \times 2)$
$= 15n - 10$

We say $5(3n - 2)$ and $15n - 10$ are **equivalent expressions** because $5(3n - 2) = 15n - 10$ for **any** value of n.

D1 Write as a mixed number:

    a $\frac{5}{4}$ **b** $\frac{8}{3}$

    c $\frac{40}{12}$ **d** $\frac{20}{4}$

D2 Write as an improper fraction:

    a $2\frac{4}{7}$ **b** $1\frac{1}{2}$

    c $4\frac{5}{8}$ **d** 3

E1 Find the reciprocal of:

    a $\frac{5}{4}$ **b** 3

E2 Give each answer in its lowest terms.

    a $\frac{5}{7} - \frac{3}{7}$ **b** $\frac{1}{3} + \frac{2}{5}$

    c $\frac{2}{3} \times \frac{3}{7}$ **d** $\frac{3}{8} \times \frac{4}{3}$

    e $\frac{3}{4} \div \frac{4}{5}$ **f** $\frac{5}{6} \div 10$

    g $1 \div \frac{4}{5}$ **h** $3 \div \frac{5}{3}$

E3 What is the value of a, in fractional form, when $\frac{1}{a} = \frac{7}{4}$?

F1 For each expression, multiply out the brackets.

    a $3(2x - 1)$ **b** $4(y + 2)$

    c $5(4 - 3a)$ **d** $5(7b + 6)$

Prime products, multiples and factors

Prime products can be used to find highest common factors and lowest common multiples.

Example 1   Find **a** the highest common factor of 72 and 60
                    b lowest common multiple of 72 and 60

As prime products,   **72** $= 2 \times 2 \times 2 \times 3 \times 3$
                      60 $= 2 \times 2 \times 3 \times 5.$

a 2 appears at least twice
3 appears at least once in each prime product:
$2 \times 2 \times 2 \times 3 \times 3$ and $2 \times 2 \times 3 \times 5.$

So the **highest common factor** is $2 \times 2 \times 3 = 12.$

b 2 appears at most three times in a prime product $(2 \times 2 \times 2 \times 3 \times 3)$
3 appears at most twice in a prime product $(2 \times 2 \times 2 \times 3 \times 3)$
5 appears at most once in a prime product $(2 \times 2 \times 3 \times 5).$

So the **lowest common multiple** is $2 \times 2 \times 2 \times 3 \times 3 \times 5 =$ **360.**

Exercise 1.1
Multiples, factors and primes

1 **a** Find the highest common factor of 240 and 168.
    b Find the lowest common multiple of 45 and 60.

2 **a** Choose two prime numbers.
    b Find their highest common factor and lowest common multiple.
    c Investigate for different pairs of prime numbers.

> A product is the result of a multiplication.
>
> For example, the product of 3 and 6 is 18.

3 For any pair of numbers, Sue thinks there could be a rule that links the product, the highest common factor and the lowest common multiple.

She makes a table.

Numbers	Product	HCF	LCM
12, 70	840	2	420
7, 24			
4, 36			
70, 110			

> HCF is shorthand for highest common factor.
>
> LCM is shorthand for lowest common multiple.

    a Copy and complete the table.
    b For any pair of numbers, find a rule that links the product, the highest common factor and the lowest common multiple.
    c Use your rule to find the lowest common multiple of 24 and 36.

4 Two numbers have a highest common factor of 8 and a lowest common multiple of 160. Find all pairs of numbers that fit this description.

5 Four flatmates wash their hair regularly: Di every 2 days, Pete every 3 days, Alison every 4 days, and Jake every 5 days.
All four people wash their hair on 1 June.
What is the next date when they will all wash their hair?

6 Each edge of a cuboid-shaped box measures a whole number of centimetres.
The areas of the three different faces are $120 \, \text{cm}^2$, $96 \, \text{cm}^2$ and $80 \, \text{cm}^2$.
Find the volume of the box.

> It may help to find a rule that gives the number of factors a number has from its prime product.

7 **a** Write 84 as a product of primes.
    b List the factors of 84 as products of primes.
    c How many factors has 84?
    d For whole numbers less than 1000, find the number with the most factors.

Fractions

♦ One way to add or subtract fractions with different denominators is to use the **lowest common multiple** of the denominators as the new denominator.

Example $\quad \frac{5}{6} - \frac{1}{4} = \frac{10}{12} - \frac{3}{12} = \frac{7}{12}$

♦ One way to deal with mixed numbers is to convert to **improper fractions** before doing any calculation.

Example 1 $\quad \frac{1}{4} \times \frac{1}{5} = \frac{5}{4} \times \frac{1}{5} = \frac{5}{20} = \frac{1}{4}$

Exercise 1.2
Fractions

1 Give each answer as a fraction in its lowest terms.

   a $\frac{3}{4} + \frac{1}{10}$ **b** $1\frac{2}{3} \times 2\frac{1}{4}$ **c** $3\frac{1}{8} - 1\frac{3}{16}$ **d** $1\frac{1}{5} \div \frac{3}{10}$

2 Find the value of these in fractional form when $p = \frac{1}{6}$, $q = \frac{3}{8}$ and $r = \frac{1}{4}$.

   a $\dfrac{q - p}{r}$ **b** $pq + r$ **c** $\dfrac{p}{pq + r}$ **d** $\left(\dfrac{q}{r}\right)^2$

3 Find the value of x in each equation.

   a $3\frac{3}{4} = \dfrac{5x}{8}$ **b** $\frac{3}{5} + \dfrac{x}{10} = \frac{9}{10}$ **c** $\dfrac{x}{4} - \frac{1}{3} = \frac{5}{12}$ **d** $\dfrac{x}{9} \div 2\frac{1}{3} = \frac{2}{7}$

4 If $\dfrac{1}{a} = \dfrac{1}{b} - \dfrac{1}{c}$

   what is the value of a, in fractional form, when $b = 2$ and $c = 5$?

> A fraction with a numerator of 1 is called a unit fraction.
>
> $\frac{1}{2}$, $\frac{1}{13}$ and $\frac{1}{21}$ are examples of unit fractions.
>
> Do not include $\frac{1}{1}$ as a unit fraction.

5 What is the value of k if $\dfrac{k}{k} - \dfrac{k}{12} = \dfrac{k}{24}$?

6 Explain why it is not possible to find two unit fractions that add to give a number greater than 1.

7 Joe claims that, when n is a positive integer, the value of the expression

   $\dfrac{n^5}{5} + \dfrac{n^3}{3} + \dfrac{7n}{15}$ is a positive integer.

   Show that Joe's claim is true for values of n from 1 to 5.

> Joe's claim is true for **all** positive integers.

8 These are the first three lines in a sequence of sums:

   a What is the sum of the fractions on:
      i the 3rd line
      ii the 8th line
      iii the nth line?
   b Why can the sum of the fractions on any line never be greater than 1?

$\frac{1}{2} + \frac{1}{4} = \frac{3}{4}$

$\frac{1}{2} + \frac{1}{4} + \frac{1}{8} = \frac{7}{8}$

$\frac{1}{2} + \frac{1}{4} + \frac{1}{8} + \frac{1}{16} =$

> Questions **9 – 12** may take some time using trial and improvement.
>
> Try to find a simpler strategy to solve each problem.

9 Find two different unit fractions that add to give $\frac{2}{7}$.

10 Find three different unit fractions that add to give 1.

11 **a** Show that the sum and product of 3 and $1\frac{1}{2}$ are equal.

    b Find another pair of fractions whose sum and product are equal.

12 We can use each digit from 1 to 9 once to make a fraction equivalent to $\frac{1}{4}$:

$$\frac{3942}{15768} = \frac{1}{4}$$

Use each digit from 1 to 9 once to find a fraction equivalent to $\frac{1}{2}$.

We can use these rules for fractions when we work with algebraic fractions.

◆ To find equivalent algebraic fractions, multiply or divide the numerator and denominator by the same number or expression.

Example

$$\frac{n}{n^2} = \frac{1}{n}$$

$\div n$

◆ To add or subtract algebraic fractions with the same denominator, add or subtract the numerators.

Example $\quad \dfrac{5}{x+1} - \dfrac{2}{x+1} = \dfrac{3}{x+1}$

◆ To multiply algebraic fractions, multiply the numerators and multiply the denominators.

Example $\quad \dfrac{3}{x} \times \dfrac{2}{y} = \dfrac{6}{xy}$

◆ To divide algebraic fractions, use the rule that dividing by a fraction has the same effect as multiplying by its reciprocal.

Example $\quad \dfrac{5}{x+1} \div \dfrac{1}{x-1} = \dfrac{5}{x+1} \times \dfrac{x-1}{1} = \dfrac{5(x-1)}{x+1}$

Exercise 1.3
Fractions and algebra

1 Which of these is equivalent to $\dfrac{x+y}{8}$?

(K) $\dfrac{x}{4} \times \dfrac{y}{2}$ $\qquad$ (L) $\dfrac{x}{8} + \dfrac{y}{8}$ $\qquad$ (M) $\dfrac{x}{4} + \dfrac{y}{4}$ $\qquad$ (N) $\dfrac{x}{8} \div \dfrac{1}{y}$

2 Sort these into four pairs of equivalent expressions.

(P) $\dfrac{2}{3}$ $\qquad$ (Q) $\dfrac{2}{x} \div \dfrac{x}{3}$ $\qquad$ (R) $\dfrac{4}{x} + \dfrac{2}{x}$ $\qquad$ (S) $\dfrac{2x}{3x}$

(T) $\dfrac{8}{x}$ $\qquad$ (U) $\dfrac{6}{x^2}$ $\qquad$ (V) $\dfrac{4x}{3} \times \dfrac{6}{x^2}$ $\qquad$ (W) $\dfrac{6}{x}$

Example
As a single fraction,
$\dfrac{3x}{4} \times \dfrac{2}{y}$ is $\dfrac{6x}{4y}$.

In its simplest form,
$\dfrac{6x}{4y}$ is $\dfrac{3x}{2y}$.

3 Write each of these as a single fraction. Give each answer in its simplest form.

a $\quad \dfrac{n}{3} \times \dfrac{1}{n^2}$ $\qquad$ b $\quad \dfrac{3}{x} + \dfrac{5}{x}$ $\qquad$ c $\quad \dfrac{a}{10} - \dfrac{b}{10}$ $\qquad$ d $\quad \dfrac{p}{8} + \dfrac{3p}{8}$

e $\quad \dfrac{m}{4} \div \dfrac{n}{3}$ $\qquad$ f $\quad \dfrac{7v}{8} - \dfrac{3v}{4}$ $\qquad$ g $\quad \dfrac{z}{5y} \times \dfrac{y}{3}$ $\qquad$ h $\quad \dfrac{c}{6} \div \dfrac{c}{12}$

4 Copy and complete:

a $\quad \dfrac{x}{5} - \dfrac{2}{5} = \dfrac{x-2}{\square}$ $\qquad$ b $\quad \dfrac{2}{m} \times \dfrac{n}{\square} = \dfrac{n}{3m}$ $\qquad$ c $\quad \dfrac{y}{x} + \dfrac{z}{\square} = \dfrac{y+z}{x}$

d $\quad \dfrac{6}{\square} \div \dfrac{1}{n^2} = 6n$ $\qquad$ e $\quad \dfrac{3t}{10} + \dfrac{\square}{10} = \dfrac{t}{2}$ $\qquad$ f $\quad \dfrac{2}{b+3} \div \dfrac{1}{\square} = \dfrac{2(b-2)}{b+3}$

5 Sort these into four pairs of equivalent expressions.

(A) $\dfrac{x}{3}$ $\qquad$ (B) $\dfrac{1}{x+1}$ $\qquad$ (C) $\dfrac{3}{3(x+1)}$ $\qquad$ (D) $\dfrac{x}{x(x-1)}$

(E) $\dfrac{3}{x+1}$ $\qquad$ (F) $\dfrac{1}{x-1}$ $\qquad$ (G) $\dfrac{3x}{9}$ $\qquad$ (H) $\dfrac{3(x-1)}{(x+1)(x-1)}$

To add or subtract algebraic fractions with **different** denominators, find equivalent fractions with the same denominator.

Examples

♦ $\dfrac{y}{3} + \dfrac{y}{4}$

$$\overset{\times 4}{\dfrac{y}{3} = \dfrac{4y}{12}} \quad \text{and} \quad \overset{\times 3}{\dfrac{y}{4} = \dfrac{3y}{12}}$$
$$\underset{\times 4}{} \qquad \underset{\times 3}{}$$

So $\dfrac{y}{3} + \dfrac{y}{4} = \dfrac{4y}{12} + \dfrac{3y}{12}$

$$= \dfrac{4y + 3y}{12} = \dfrac{7y}{12}$$

♦ $\dfrac{2}{a} - \dfrac{3}{b}$

$$\overset{\times b}{\dfrac{2}{a} = \dfrac{2b}{ab}} \quad \text{and} \quad \overset{\times a}{\dfrac{3}{b} = \dfrac{3a}{ab}}$$
$$\underset{\times b}{} \qquad \underset{\times a}{}$$

So $\dfrac{2}{a} - \dfrac{3}{b} = \dfrac{2b}{ab} - \dfrac{3a}{ab} = \dfrac{2b - 3a}{ab}$

♦ $\dfrac{1}{p + 1} + \dfrac{1}{p - 2}$

$$\overset{\times (p - 2)}{\dfrac{1}{p + 1} = \dfrac{(p - 2)}{(p + 1)(p - 2)}} \quad \text{and} \quad \overset{\times (p + 1)}{\dfrac{1}{p - 2} = \dfrac{(p + 1)}{(p + 1)(p - 2)}}$$
$$\underset{\times (p - 2)}{} \qquad \underset{\times (p + 1)}{}$$

So $\dfrac{1}{p + 1} + \dfrac{1}{p - 2} = \dfrac{(p - 2)}{(p + 1)(p - 2)} + \dfrac{(p + 1)}{(p + 1)(p - 2)}$

$$= \dfrac{(p - 2) + (p + 1)}{(p + 1)(p - 2)} = \dfrac{2p - 1}{(p + 1)(p - 2)}$$

Exercise 1.4
Adding and subtracting
algebraic fractions

1 a Which of these is not equivalent to $\dfrac{5}{c}$?

A $\quad \dfrac{15}{3c}$ B $\quad \dfrac{5(c + 1)}{c(c + 1)}$ C $\quad \dfrac{5c^3}{c^2}$ D $\quad \dfrac{5a}{ac}$

b Write as a single fraction $\dfrac{5}{c} + \dfrac{7}{3c}$.

2 Sort these into four pairs of equivalent expressions.

E $\quad \dfrac{10x}{21}$ F $\quad \dfrac{x}{6} + \dfrac{x}{30}$ G $\quad \dfrac{x}{5}$ H $\quad \dfrac{x}{10}$

I $\quad \dfrac{3x}{8} - \dfrac{x}{3}$ J $\quad \dfrac{3x}{10} - \dfrac{x}{5}$ K $\quad \dfrac{x}{24}$ L $\quad \dfrac{x}{3} + \dfrac{x}{7}$

3 Write each of these as a single fraction in its simplest form.

a $\dfrac{2m}{3} + \dfrac{m}{12}$ **b** $\dfrac{3p}{4} - \dfrac{p}{8}$ **c** $\dfrac{q}{2} + \dfrac{r}{5}$ **d** $\dfrac{s}{t} - \dfrac{s}{2}$

e $\dfrac{4}{x} - \dfrac{5}{y}$ **f** $\dfrac{6}{f} + \dfrac{5}{2f}$ **g** $\dfrac{1}{p + 3} + \dfrac{1}{p - 1}$ **h** $\dfrac{2}{z} - \dfrac{1}{z + 6}$

4 Copy and complete:

a $\dfrac{\square}{x} - \dfrac{5}{3x} = \dfrac{19}{3x}$ **b** $\dfrac{\square}{x} + \dfrac{2}{x + 5} = \dfrac{5(x + 3)}{x(x + 5)}$

c $\dfrac{\square}{x + 1} + \dfrac{3}{x} = \dfrac{3}{x(x + 1)}$ **d** $\dfrac{1}{x + 1} + \dfrac{\square}{x - 2} = \dfrac{3x}{(x + 1)(x - 2)}$

Thinking ahead to ...
using algebraic fractions

A This is a sequence of pairs of calculations.

$$\frac{2}{3} - \frac{2}{5} = \frac{4}{15} \qquad \frac{2}{3} \times \frac{2}{5} =$$

$$\frac{2}{4} - \frac{2}{6} = \qquad \frac{2}{4} \times \frac{2}{6} =$$

$$\frac{2}{5} - \frac{2}{7} = \qquad \frac{2}{5} \times \frac{2}{7} =$$

... ...

a Copy and complete these calculations.
b Write down some more pairs of calculations in this sequence.
c Comment on the results of these calculations.

Using algebraic fractions

◆ For the above calculations, the numerator of each fraction is 2 and the denominator of the second fraction is always 2 more than the first.

◆ So if the first fraction is $\frac{2}{n}$, then the second fraction is $\frac{2}{n+2}$.

◆ Subtract: $\dfrac{2}{n} - \dfrac{2}{n+2} = \dfrac{2(n+2)}{n(n+2)} - \dfrac{2n}{n(n+2)} = \dfrac{2n+4}{n(n+2)} - \dfrac{2n}{n(n+2)}$

$$= \dfrac{2n+4-2n}{n(n+2)} = \dfrac{4}{n(n+2)}$$

◆ Multiply: $\dfrac{2}{n} \times \dfrac{2}{n+2} = \dfrac{4}{n(n+2)}$

◆ Both calculations give the result $\dfrac{4}{n(n+2)}$.

So we have shown that for any pair of fractions of the form $\frac{2}{n}$ and $\frac{2}{n+2}$ the results of subtracting them and multiplying are equal.

Exercise 1.5
Using algebraic fractions

1 This is a sequence of pairs of calculations.

$$\frac{3}{4} - \frac{3}{7} = \frac{9}{28} \qquad \frac{3}{4} \times \frac{3}{7} =$$

$$\frac{3}{5} - \frac{3}{8} = \qquad \frac{3}{5} \times \frac{3}{8} =$$

$$\frac{3}{6} - \frac{3}{9} = \qquad \frac{3}{6} \times \frac{3}{9} =$$

... ...

a Complete the calculations above to show that the results are equal for each of these three pairs.
b Explain why we can write any pair of fractions in this sequence in the form $\frac{3}{n}$ and $\frac{3}{n+3}$.
c Use algebra to show that, for **any** pair of calculations in this sequence the results will be equal.

2 a Find some pairs of **unit** fractions that subtract and multiply to give equal results.
b Describe a rule that you think is true for these pairs of unit fractions.
c Use algebra to show that your rule is true.

3   Find a rule that links **any** pair of fractions that subtract and multiply to give the same result.

4   a   Show that $\frac{1}{20} + \frac{1}{5} = \frac{1}{20} \div \frac{1}{5}$.

    b   Find some more pairs of unit fractions that add and divide to give the same result.

    c   Find a rule that you think links the fractions for all these pairs.

    d   Use algebra to show that your rule is true.

5   a   Which fraction gives the same result when added to or multiplied by $\frac{3}{2}$?

    b   Investigate to find rules for pairs of fractions that add and multiply to give the same result.

The Harmonic Triangle

> The Harmonic Triangle was used by Leibniz, a German mathematician and philosopher. It has many interesting properties.

This is part of the first line of the Harmonic Triangle.

$$1 \quad \frac{1}{2} \quad \frac{1}{3} \quad \frac{1}{4} \quad \frac{1}{5} \quad \frac{1}{6} \quad \frac{1}{7} \quad \frac{1}{8} \quad \frac{1}{9}$$

◆ Each fraction in the second line is found by subtracting a pair of fractions in the first line, the fraction directly above and the fraction on its right:

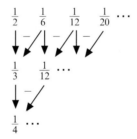

$$1 - \frac{1}{2} = \frac{1}{2}$$
$$\frac{1}{2} - \frac{1}{3} = \frac{1}{6}$$
$$\frac{1}{3} - \frac{1}{4} = \frac{1}{12}$$
$$\dots$$

◆ Each fraction in the remaining lines can be found in the same way:

$$1 \quad \frac{1}{2} \quad \frac{1}{3} \quad \frac{1}{4} \quad \frac{1}{5} \quad \frac{1}{6} \quad \frac{1}{7} \quad \frac{1}{8} \quad \frac{1}{9}$$

$$\frac{1}{2} \quad \frac{1}{6} \quad \frac{1}{12} \quad \frac{1}{20} \quad \dots$$

$$\frac{1}{3} \quad \frac{1}{12} \quad \dots$$

$$\frac{1}{4} \quad \dots$$

Exercise 1.6
The Harmonic Triangle

1   Complete a Harmonic Triangle starting with the fractions 1 to $\frac{1}{9}$. This has been started in the above diagram.

2   Use your triangle to find two pairs of values for x and y so that $\frac{1}{x} - \frac{1}{y} = \frac{1}{72}$.

3   The fractions in the second line form a sequence.

    a   What is the 10th term in this sequence?

    b   Show that $\frac{1}{n} - \frac{1}{n+1}$ is an expression for the nth term in this sequence.

    c   Why must every fraction in the second line be a unit fraction?

4   a   Explain why we can write any pair of adjacent fractions in the second line in the form $\frac{1}{k(k+1)}$ and $\frac{1}{(k+1)(k+2)}$.

    b   Show that every fraction in the third line of the triangle must be a unit fraction.

End points

You should be able to ...   ... so try these questions

A Use multiples and factors to solve problems

A1 **a** Find the highest common factor of 105 and 126.
  b Find the lowest common multiple of 105 and 126.

A2 Two numbers less than 100 have 6 as their highest common factor and 672 as their lowest common multiple.
What are the two numbers?

A3 An area for an art exhibit is in the shape of a rectangle 36 feet by 84 feet. Posts are to be placed along the edges and at the corners so that ropes of equal length can be fastened between them.

What is the smallest number of posts that can be used?

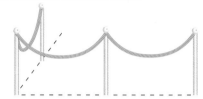

B Calculate with fractions

B1 When $x = \frac{1}{3}$, $y = \frac{5}{6}$ and $z = 1\frac{2}{3}$, calculate, in fractional form, the value of:
  a $2xy$ **b** $y - xz$ **c** $\dfrac{x + y}{z}$

B2 If $\dfrac{1}{p} = \dfrac{1}{q} + \dfrac{2}{r}$

what is the value of p, in fractional form, when $q = 3$ and $r = 4$?

B3 The first eight fractions in the second line of the Harmonic Triangle are:

$\frac{1}{2}$ $\frac{1}{6}$ $\frac{1}{12}$ $\frac{1}{20}$ $\frac{1}{30}$ $\frac{1}{42}$ $\frac{1}{56}$ $\frac{1}{72}$

Fractions from this line can be added to form this sequence:

$\frac{1}{2} + \frac{1}{6} = \frac{2}{3}$

$\frac{1}{2} + \frac{1}{6} + \frac{1}{12} =$

$\frac{1}{2} + \frac{1}{6} + \frac{1}{12} + \frac{1}{20} =$

...

  a Write down the first four complete lines of this sequence of sums.
  b **i** Without calculating, what do you think is the sum of the fractions on the 7th line?
      ii Check your result by adding.

C Use algebraic fractions

C1 Write each of these as a single fraction in its simplest form.
  a $\dfrac{2x}{3} - \dfrac{x}{6}$ **b** $\dfrac{y}{4} \times \dfrac{3}{y}$ **c** $\dfrac{z}{3} \div \dfrac{1}{9}$

  d $\dfrac{3}{a} - \dfrac{7}{b}$ **e** $\dfrac{5}{c} - \dfrac{4}{c+1}$ **f** $\dfrac{1}{d+6} + \dfrac{1}{d-5}$

Some points to remember

- Lowest common multiple = Product ÷ Highest common factor.

- To add and subtract fractions (including algebraic), first find equivalent fractions with the same denominator.

- Dividing by a fraction has the same effect as multiplying by its reciprocal.

Starting points
You need to know about ...

... so try these questions

A Naming angles and triangles

♦ Any angle less than 90° is an **acute angle**.

♦ Any angle equal to 90° is a **right angle**.

♦ Any angle between 90° and 180° is an **obtuse angle**.

♦ Any angle between 180° and 360° is a **reflex angle**.

♦ Any triangle which has:
  ❖ three sides of equal length
  ❖ three equal angles (60°)
  is an **equilateral triangle**.

♦ Any triangle which has:
  ❖ two sides of equal length
  ❖ two equal angles
  is an **isosceles triangle**.

♦ Any triangle which has no sides of equal length and no equal angles is a **scalene triangle**.

♦ Any triangle which has one right angle is a **right-angled triangle**.

B Angle sums

♦ Angles at a point on a straight line add up to 180°.

♦ Angles round a point add up to 360°.

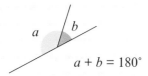

$a + b = 180°$

$c + d + e = 360°$

♦ Vertically opposite angles are equal.

♦ Angles in a triangle add up to 180°.

$x + y + z = 180°$

C Parallel lines

At each point where a straight line crosses a set of parallel lines there are two pairs of vertically opposite angles.

Parallel lines are marked with arrows.

Equal angles are marked with the same colour.

A1

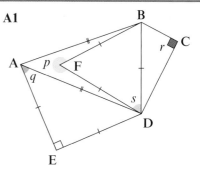

a What type of angle is:
  i p **ii** q **iii** r?
b What type of triangle is:
  i BFD   **ii** BCD?
c Which triangles are isosceles?

B1 In the diagram above calculate:
a the size of angle s
b angle p
c angle $A\hat{D}E$.

B2 On this diagram, angles marked with the same letter are equal in size.

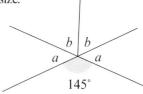

a Work out angles a and b.
b Explain why a triangle can only have one obtuse angle.

C1

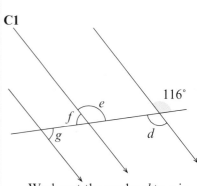

Work out the angles d to g in this diagram.

D Quadrilaterals

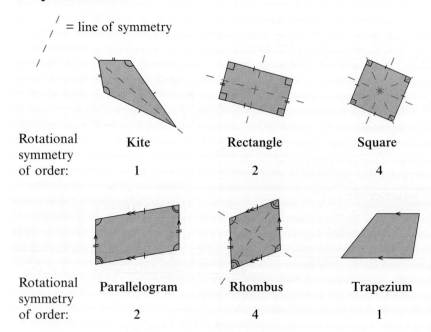

| / = line of symmetry |

	Kite	Rectangle	Square
Rotational symmetry of order:	1	2	4

	Parallelogram	Rhombus	Trapezium
Rotational symmetry of order:	2	4	1

E Polygons

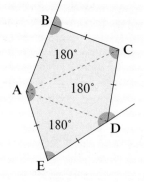

- In ABCDE:
  - the **interior angles** are marked in red
  - the angles marked in blue are not interior angles.

- The **sum of the interior angles** of a polygon with n sides is: $(n – 2) \times 180°$
  So for ABCDE the sum of interior angles is: $(5 – 2) \times 180°$
  $$= 3 \times 180°$$
  $$= 540°$$

- In a **regular polygon** all the sides are equal and the interior angles are equal.

- ABCDE is an **irregular polygon** The sides are all equal but the interior angles are not.

Name of polygon	Number of sides	Sum of interior angles	Interior angle of a regular polygon
Triangle	3	180° ——÷3—▶ 60°	
Quadrilateral	4	360° ——÷4—▶ 90°	
Pentagon	5	540° ——÷5—▶ 108°	
Hexagon	6	720° ——÷6—▶ 120°	
Heptagon	7		
Octagon	8		
Nonagon	9		
Decagon	10		

Another expression for the **sum of the interior angles** of a polygon with n sides is: $(180° \times n) – 360°$

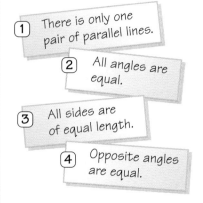

D1 Name all the quadrilaterals that fit each of these labels.

1. There is only one pair of parallel lines.

2. All angles are equal.

3. All sides are of equal length.

4. Opposite angles are equal.

D2 Draw a trapezium with one line of symmetry.

E1 What is the sum of the interior angles of an octagon?

E2 Calculate the angle a in this pentagon.

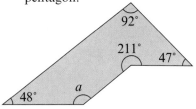

E3 Calculate the interior angle of a regular heptagon to the nearest degree.

E4 A dodecagon has 12 sides.
  a What is the sum of the interior angles of a dodecagon?
  b Calculate the interior angle of a regular dodecagon.

Angles in triangles

To calculate an angle you may need to work out some other angles first.

Example

Calculate the angle $E\hat{G}F$.

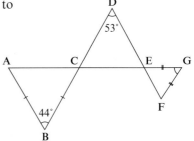

◆ You should sketch a diagram and label each angle that you calculate.

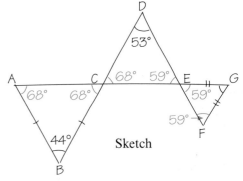

Sketch

△ stands for triangle

An angle can be written in different ways.

For example:
$D\hat{C}E$ is the same angle as $D\hat{C}G$ and $E\hat{C}D$
$D\hat{E}C$ is the same angle as $D\hat{E}A$ and $C\hat{E}D$.

You may not need to calculate all the intermediate angles.

To calculate $E\hat{G}F$

Calculation ...	**... Reason**
$A\hat{C}B = C\hat{A}B...$	...ABC is an isosceles △
$\quad = (180° - 44°) \div 2$	
$\quad = 68°$	
$D\hat{C}E = 68°...$	...Vertically opposite ACB
$D\hat{E}C = 180° - (68° + 53°)...$	...Angle sum of △
$\quad = 59°$	
$F\hat{E}G = 59°...$	...Vertically opposite DEC
$G\hat{E}F = E\hat{F}G...$	...EFG is an isosceles △
$E\hat{G}F = 180° - (59° \times 2)...$	...Angle sum of △

So the angle $E\hat{G}F = 62°$

Exercise 2.1
Angles in triangles

1 a Which is the easiest angle to calculate in this diagram?

b Calculate the angles a to f in this diagram.

c In what order did you calculate the angles? Explain why.

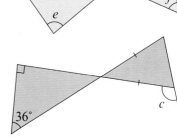

2

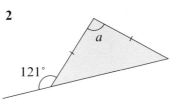

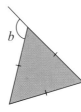

You will need to work out some other angles first.

Calculate the angles a, b and c in these diagrams.
Give a reason for each calculation.

Parallel lines

In each of these diagrams a straight line crosses two parallel lines.

- In each diagram a pair of **corresponding angles** is labelled. Corresponding angles are equal.

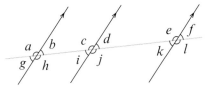

- In each diagram a pair of **alternate angles** is labelled. Alternate angles are equal.

Exercise 2.2
Angles in parallel lines

1 a List five pairs of corresponding angles in this diagram.
  b List three pairs of alternate angles.

> To find corresponding angles in a diagram you could look for an F shape which may be upside down and/or back to front.
>
> To find alternate angles in a diagram you could look for a Z shape which may be back to front.

2 Sketch these diagrams. Work out the angles a, b and c. You may need to calculate some other angles first.

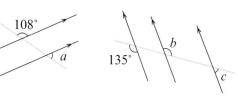

3 In this diagram AS, BR and NQ intersect to make the triangle DPO. CE, FI, JM and NQ are parallel.
  a List three pairs of corresponding angles along the line:
      i AS   **ii** BR
  b Explain why DĜH and DĤI are not corresponding angles.
  c List three pairs of alternate angles in this diagram.

> Give a reason for each calculation that you do.

  d Calculate each of these angles.
      i HD̂G   **ii** AD̂C
      iii GK̂L   **iv** HL̂K
      v QP̂L   **vi** NÔR

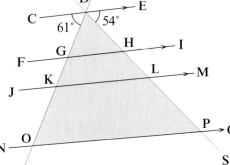

4 In each of these diagrams there is one pair of parallel lines.

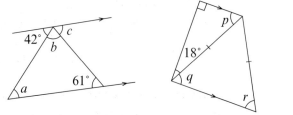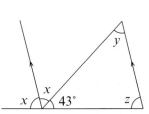

Sketch these diagrams and calculate each of the angles marked with a letter.

5 a Work out each of these angles in ABCD.
  i AB̂D   **ii** AD̂B
  iii BD̂C   **iv** BĈD
 b Which two lines are parallel?
 c What is the mathematical name
   for ABCD?
 d Explain why ABCD is not a rhombus.

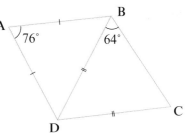

Properties of polygons

Exercise 2.3
Properties of quadrilaterals

1 AB and CD are plastic strips joined by red and yellow elastic bands.
ABCD is a parallelogram; its diagonals intersect at M.
You can stretch the parallelogram if you fix AB and pull CD sideways.

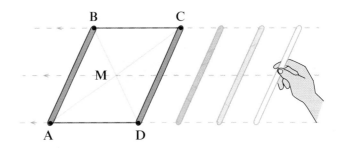

Below are some diagrams of the parallelogram as it is stretched.
ABC′D′ is a rhombus.

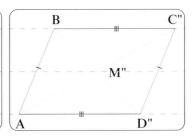

 a Trace the angles AB̂C, AB̂D and CB̂D.
 b Use your tracings to find out what happens to each of
   these angles as the parallelogram is stretched.
   i AB̂C   **ii** AB̂D   **ii** CB̂D
 c What happens to AM̂B as the parallelogram is stretched?
 d What type of angle is each of these?
   i AM̂B   **ii** AM̂′B   **ii** AM̂″B

> The interior angles of ABCD
> are marked in green.

> If you bisect a line or
> angle, you cut it into
> 2 equal parts.
>
> If two lines bisect each
> other, they are both cut
> into two equal lengths.

2

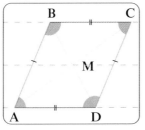
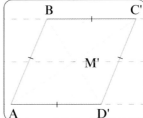
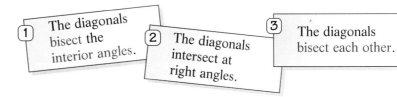

Which of these statements do you think is always true:

 a for a parallelogram   **b** for a rhombus?

On an isometric grid the lines intersect to form equilateral triangles.

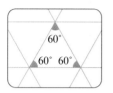

3 This kite is drawn on an isometric grid.
The interior angles of ABCD are marked in green.
The diagonals are marked in red and intersect at M.

a Calculate the interior angles of ABCD.

b Which angle is equal to:

   i BÂC   **ii** CÂD?

c What type of angle is AM̂B?

d List three pairs of equal lengths in ABCD.

e Do the diagonals of ABCD bisect each other?

f Which is the line of symmetry for ABCD?

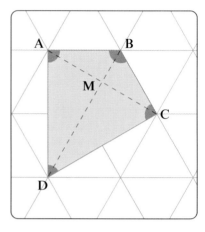

Exercise 2.4
Properties of polygons

1 These polygons are drawn on a seven-dot isometric grid.

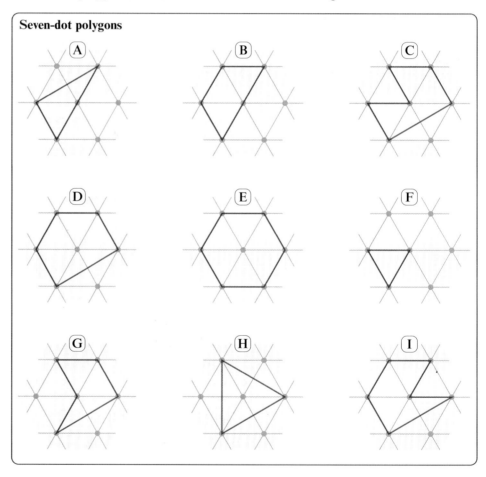

Seven-dot polygons

The sum of the interior angles for a polygon with n sides is

$$(n - 2) \times 180°$$

a On an isometric grid draw each of the polygons A to I.

b Give a mathematical name for each polygon.

c **i** List all the interior angles of each polygon.

   ii Check that the sum of the interior angles is correct for each polygon.

2 Each of these cards matches some of the seven-dot polygons A to I.

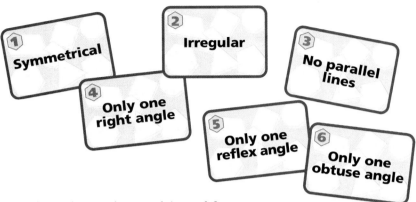

a Which polygons does card 4 match?

b Which cards match polygon C?

c Which card matches:

    i the largest number of polygons

    ii the smallest number of polygons?

d Draw another seven-dot polygon to match each card.
Some polygons may match more than one card.

e Which of the cards would match a regular pentagon?

> Do not count any that are
> a rotation or reflection
> of another polygon.

3 How many different seven-dot polygons is it possible to draw?

Exercise 2.5
Property puzzle

1

Property puzzle	No reflex angles	More than one obtuse angle	No line of symmetry
Only one pair of parallel lines	a	b	c
Regular	d	e	f
More than one acute angle	g	h	i

Use the polygons A to I.

You can:
- only use each polygon once
- put one polygon in each cell.

Fill as many cells as possible.

You can put polygon A in cell ⓘ
because it has
no line of symmetry
and two acute angles.

You can also put it in cell ⓖ.

a   **i** Which polygons can you put in cell ⓗ?

    ii In which cells can you put polygon F?

b   **i** Solve the puzzle

    ii How many cells can you fill?

    iii Which cell can you never fill? Explain why.

c Rearrange the labels in the table so that you can fill all the cells.

Tessellations

♦ Shapes tessellate if they fit together with no gaps and no overlaps.
A tessellation can be continued in any direction.

You can use translations, reflection and rotations of shapes in a tessellation
Using polygon G you can:

❖ fit 6 polygons together to make a hexagon

❖ repeat the hexagon to make this tessellation.

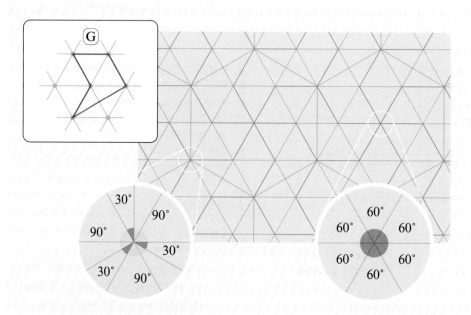

♦ At each vertex of the tessellation the angles add up to 360°.

Exercise 2.6
Tessellations

1 These are three seven-dot polygons on an isometric grid.

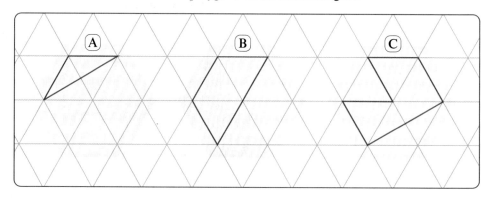

You need to use equilateral grid paper.

a i Draw a tessellation of polygon A.
   ii Check that the total of the angles at each vertex is 360°.
b Draw two different tessellations of polygon B.
c Draw a tessellation of polygon C.

2 a Calculate the interior angle of a regular decagon.
   b Will regular decagons tessellate on their own?
      Explain your answer.

3 Explain why regular octagons will not tessellate on their own.

4 Decide whether each of these will tessellate on their own.

  a regular hexagons   **b** regular heptagons

  Explain your answers.

5 Explain why it is possible to draw a tessellation using:

  a any triangle   **b** any quadrilateral.

Exercise 2.7
Combined tessellations

1 This is a tessellation using three different polygons J, K and L.

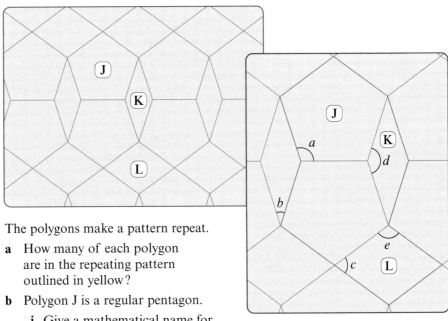

The polygons make a pattern repeat.

  a How many of each polygon
   are in the repeating pattern
   outlined in yellow?

  b Polygon J is a regular pentagon.

   i Give a mathematical name for
    polygons K and L.

   ii Calculate the angles *a* to *e*.

2 Each of these tessellations uses two different polygons.

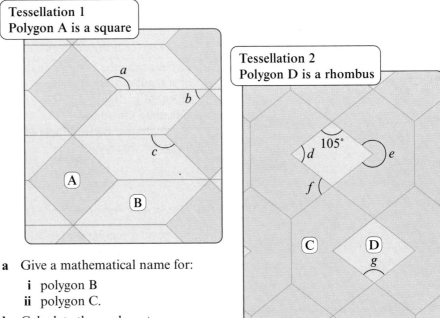

  a Give a mathematical name for:
   i polygon B
   ii polygon C.

  b Calculate the angles *a* to *g*.

Angles in polygons

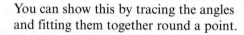

◆ At each vertex of a polygon the angle between an extended side and the adjacent side is called **an exterior angle**.

In ABCDE:

❖ the exterior angles are marked in orange
❖ the interior angles are marked in blue.

◆ The sum of the exterior angles of any polygon is 360°.

In ABCDE:
$a + b + c + d + e = 360°$

You can show this by tracing the angles and fitting them together round a point.

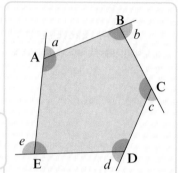

◆ At each vertex the sum of the interior angle and exterior angle is 180°.

Exercise 2.8
Exterior angles of polygons

1 For this polygon:

 a calculate each exterior angle
 b check that the total of the exterior angles is 360°.

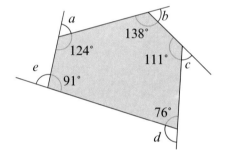

2 A dodecagon has 12 sides.
In this regular dodecagon one side is extended to form the angle p.

 a Explain why the exterior angles of a regular dodecagon are all equal to 360° ÷ 12.
 b Calculate the angle p.
 c Calculate the interior angle of a regular dodecagon.

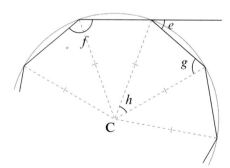

3 This is part of regular nonagon drawn inside a circle with centre C.
One side of the nonagon is extended to form the angle e.
Calculate the angles e to h.

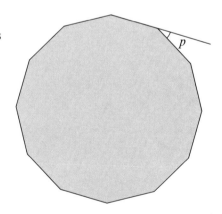

Exercise 2.9
Triangles investigation

You can mark eight points that are equally spaced on the circumference of a circle if you:
- draw a circle on square grid paper
- mark in lines that are vertical, horizontal and at 45° to the horizontal.

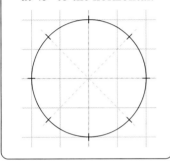

1 This eight-point circle has the points A to H equally spaced on the circumference.
Δ ABD is drawn by joining three of the points.

This is how a student calculated the exterior angle at A for Δ ABD.

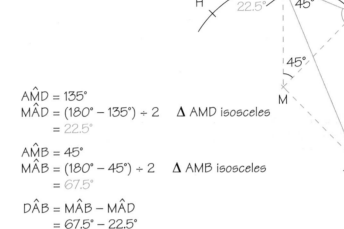

To find the exterior angle at A

$\hat{AMD} = 135°$
$\hat{MAD} = (180° − 135°) ÷ 2$ Δ AMD isosceles
$= 22.5°$

$\hat{AMB} = 45°$
$\hat{MAB} = (180° − 45°) ÷ 2$ Δ AMB isosceles
$= 67.5°$

$\hat{DAB} = \hat{MAB} − \hat{MAD}$
$= 67.5° − 22.5°$
$= 45°$

So the exterior angle at A is **135°**

a Explain why $\hat{AMD}$ is 135°.
b For triangle ABD:
    i explain why the exterior angle at A is 135°
    ii calculate the exterior angles at B and D
    iii check that the total of the exterior angles is 360°.

2 Triangle ACF is also drawn on an eight-point circle.

a For triangle ACF:
    i calculate each interior angle
    ii calculate each exterior angle.
b How many different triangles is it possible to draw in an eight-point circle?

Do not count any that are reflections or rotations of another polygon.

c What different exterior angles are possible for triangles drawn on an eight-point circle?

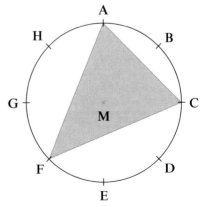

End points

You should be able to ...

... so try these questions

A Calculate angles in parallel lines

A1 Calculate the angles *a*, *b* and *c* in this diagram.

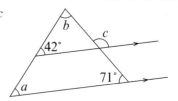

B Use the properties of polygons

B1 Polygons A to E are drawn on an equilateral grid.

   a Which of these polygons:
     i is a regular polygon
     ii has only one obtuse angle?
   b Give a mathematical name for each of the polygons A to E.

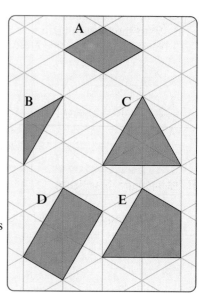

C Decide whether shapes will tessellate

C1 **a** Show how each of these polygons will tessellate on their own.
   b Show how two of these polygons will tessellate together.

D Calculate angles in polygons

D1 For each of the polygons B and E:
   a calculate the interior angles
   b calculate the exterior angles.

D2 What is the exterior angle of a regular octagon?

Some points to remember

- For a polygon with *n* sides:
  - the sum of the interior angles is $(n-2) \times 180°$
  - the sum of the exterior angles is 360°
  - each exterior angle of a regular polygon is $360° \div n$.

- Examples of quadrilaterals

	Square	Rectangle	Kite	Rhombus	Parallelogram
The diagonals:					
• bisect the interior angles	✓	✓	✗	✓	✗
• bisect each other	✓	✓	✗	✓	✓
• intersect at 90°.	✓	✓	✓	✓	✗
Number of lines of symmetry	4	2	1	2	0
Order of rotational symmetry	4	2	1	4	2

Starting points

You need to know about ...

... so try these questions

A Multiplying out brackets

♦ To multiply out brackets, multiply every term inside the bracket by the term outside.

Example 1

$2(3a^2 + 4a - 6) = (2 \times 3a^2) + (2 \times 4a) - (2 \times 6)$
$= 6a^2 + 8a - 12$

We say that $2(3a^2 + 4a - 6)$ and $6a^2 + 8a - 12$ are **equivalent expressions** because:

$2(3a^2 + 4a - 6) = 6a^2 + 8a - 12$ for any value of a.

Example 2

$2(3a - 4b - 2) + 4(2a - 6) = 6a - 8b - 4 + 8a - 24$
$= 14a - 8b - 28$

So $14a - 8b - 28$ is equivalent to $2(3a - 4b - 2) + 4(2a - 6)$

B Algebraic fractions

♦ To find equivalent algebraic fractions, multiply or divide the numerator and denominator by the same number or expression.

Example

$$\overbrace{}^{\div\, n}$$
$$\frac{n^2}{3n} = \frac{n}{3}$$
$$\underbrace{}_{\div\, n}$$

♦ To add or subtract algebraic fractions with different denominators:
  ❖ find equivalent fractions with the same denominator
  ❖ add or subtract the numerators.

Example 1 $\dfrac{2}{p + 3} + \dfrac{3}{p}$

$= \dfrac{2p}{(p + 3)p} + \dfrac{3(p + 3)}{(p + 3)p}$

$= \dfrac{2p + 3(p + 3)}{(p + 3)p}$

$= \dfrac{5p + 9}{(p + 3)p}$

Example 2 $\dfrac{2}{a} - \dfrac{5}{3a}$

$= \dfrac{6}{3a} - \dfrac{5}{3a}$

$= \dfrac{1}{3a}$

♦ To multiply algebraic fractions, multiply the numerators and multiply the denominators.

Example

$$\frac{x}{2} \times \frac{5}{x - 1} = \frac{5x}{2(x - 1)}$$

♦ To divide algebraic fractions, use the rule that dividing by a fraction has the same effect as multiplying by its reciprocal.

Example

$$\frac{3}{x + 1} \div \frac{2}{y} = \frac{3}{x + 1} \times \frac{y}{2} = \frac{3y}{2(x + 1)}$$

A1 Which of these expressions is equivalent to $5a + 7$?

   A $2(3a + 5)$

   B $3(a + 2) + 2(a + 2)$

   C $4(2a + 1) + 3(1 - a)$

   D $5(2a + 1) + 2(1 - a)$

A2 Simplify the expression
$3(4a - 2b) + 2(3b - 6a + 2)$

B1 Write each of these as a single fraction, in its simplest form.

  a $\dfrac{2}{(p + 2)} + \dfrac{4}{p}$ **b** $\dfrac{8p}{9} \times \dfrac{3}{2p}$

  c $\dfrac{1}{p} - \dfrac{1}{(p + 5)}$ **d** $\dfrac{5p}{8} \div \dfrac{3p}{16}$

B2 Sort these into three pairs of equivalent expressions.

A	B
$\dfrac{3a + 2b}{6}$	$\dfrac{a + 1}{a} \times \dfrac{3a}{2b}$

C	D
$\dfrac{2a^2b}{12a}$	$\dfrac{3}{a} - \dfrac{3}{a + 1}$

E	F
$\dfrac{a + 1}{b} \times \dfrac{a + 1}{2b}$	$\dfrac{a + 2}{2} + \dfrac{b - 3}{3}$

G	H
$\dfrac{a}{2} \div \dfrac{3}{b}$	$\dfrac{1}{a + 1} \div \dfrac{a}{3}$

B3 Copy and complete:

  a

$$\frac{\square}{p} + \frac{4}{p + 2} = \frac{7p + 6}{p(p + 2)}$$

  b

$$\frac{3}{p - 1} + \frac{\square}{p + 4} = \frac{5p + \square}{(p - 1)(p + 4)}$$

Using brackets

◆ You can use brackets to write an expression for the shaded area in each of these rectangles.

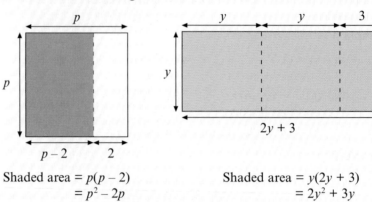

Shaded area = $p(p - 2)$
= $p^2 - 2p$

Shaded area = $y(2y + 3)$
= $2y^2 + 3y$

Exercise 3.1
Using brackets

1 For each of these rectangles write an expression for the shaded area:
  a with brackets **b** without brackets.

For some of the shaded rectangles you will need to find an expression for a missing dimension first.

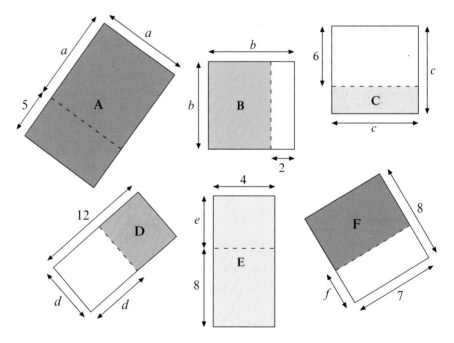

2 For each of P, Q and R write an expression for the shaded area:
  a with brackets **b** without brackets.

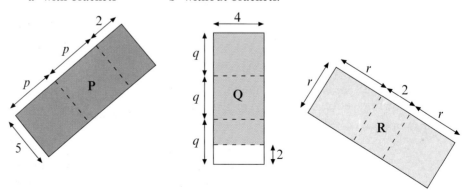

3   Write an expression for the width of rectangles A to E.

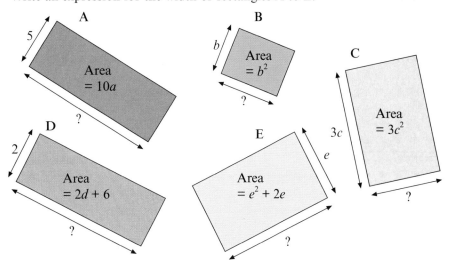

4   Copy and complete these.
   a $4x + 12 = 4(\square + \square)$ b $6p - 4 = 2(\square - \square)$
   c $2a + 8 = \square(a + \square)$ d $10 - 5q = \square(2 - \square)$
   e $3t^2 - 4t = \square(\square - \square)$ f $6s^2 + 7s = \square(\square + 7)$

Multiplying terms and simplifying

♦   When you subtract a bracket each term must have the correct sign.

Example 1	Example 2	Example 3
$30 - (5 + 2)$	$30 - (5 - 2)$	$30 - 2(3 + 5)$
$= 30 - 5 - 2$	$= 30 - 5 + 2$	$= 30 - (6 + 10)$
$= 23$	$= 27$	$= 30 - 6 - 10$
		$= 14$

Example 4	Example 5	Example 6
$5x - (x + 3)$	$5x - (4 - x)$	$5x - 3(y - 4)$
$= 5x - x - 3$	$= 5x - 4 + x$	$= 5x - (3y - 12)$
$= 4x - 3$	$= 6x - 4$	$= 5x - 3y + 12$

Exercise 3.2
Subtracting brackets

1   Multiply out and simplify:
   a $3b - 5(2 - b)$ b $12 - 3(2x - 4)$ c $6c - 3(c + 4)$
   d $6y - 5(3 - y)$ e $6 - 2(a + 3)$ f $5a - 2(7 - b)$

2   Which of these expressions is equivalent to $2 - x$?
   A $2(x + 4) - 3(x + 2)$ B $2(x + 3) - (3x - 4)$
   C $3(x - 2) - 2(x - 4)$ D $5(x - 2) - 3(2x - 4)$

3   Simplify each of these expressions.
   a $2(3a + 3) - (a + 1)$ b $3(x + 4) - (2x - 3)$
   c $2(2a + 3) - 3(4 - a)$ d $2(x + 4) - 3(2x - 1)$
   e $5(x - 3) - 2(4 + x)$ f $5(3x + 2) - 2(4x + 3)$
   g $2(x - 3) - (x + 3)$ h $3(3x + 2y) - 2(y - 4x)$

In any term the letters are usually written in alphabetical order.

For example:

$2ba$ is usually written as $2ab$

$4n^2m$ is usually written as $4mn^2$.

♦ You can **multiply terms** by grouping numbers, and each of the letters.

Example 1

$2m \times 3n$
$= 2 \times m \times 3 \times n$
$= 2 \times 3 \times m \times n$
$= 6mn$

Example 2

$2ab \times a$
$= 2 \times a \times b \times a$
$= 2 \times a \times a \times b$
$= 2a^2b$

Example 3

$2p \times 3p^2$
$= 2 \times p \times 3 \times p \times p$
$= 2 \times 3 \times p \times p \times p$
$= 6p^3$

The letters in each term are usually written in alphabetical order.

♦ **Like terms** must have exactly the same letters in them.

Example 1

$2p^2r = 2 \times p \times p \times r$
$8p^2r = 8 \times p \times p \times r$
So $2p^2r$ and $8p^2r$ are like terms.

Example 2

$3pr^2 = 3 \times p \times r \times r$
$2pr^2 = 2 \times p \times p \times r$
So $2p^2r$ and $3pr^2$ are **not** like terms.

♦ To **simplify an expression** collect together any **like terms**.

These **can be simplified** by collecting like terms.
$2a^2b + 3ab^2 + 4a^2b = 6a^2b + 3ab^2$
$2x^2 + 2x + 3x^2 - x + 4 = 5x^2 + x + 4$

These **will not simplify** as there are no like terms.
$2a^2b + 3ab^2$
$2x^2 + 4x + 3$

Exercise 3.3
Multiplying terms and simplifying

1 Multiply these terms.

a $3a \times 2b$ b $p \times 3q$ c $4y \times 5x$ d $5q \times 6p$
e $x \times 2x$ f $ab \times a$ g $2xy \times y$ h $2ab \times 3a$
i $2p^2 \times 3q$ j $a^3 \times a^2$ k $2b^2 \times 3b$ l $5c^3 \times 2b$

2 Find four pairs of equivalent terms.

A $(2b^2)^3$ B $6b^5$ C $3b^2 \times 2b^4$ D $5b^5$ E $8b^6$

F $3b^2 \times 2b^3$ G $6(b^4)^2$ H $6b^6$ I $6b^8$

3 Multiply out these brackets.

a $a(b + 4)$ b $m(2n + 3p)$ c $2x(3y + 2z)$
d $c(a + c)$ e $p(p - q)$ f $4a(a - b)$
g $a(2b - 4c)$ h $2a(3a + 4b)$ i $4p(2q - 3p)$
j $2pq(3p + 2q)$ k $4xy(x - 2y)$ l $3xy(x^2 - y^2)$

4 Simplify these where possible.

a $4x^2 + x - 2x^2$ b $5a + 2ab - a + 3ab$
c $x^2 + x^3 - 2x$ d $4a - 3b + 7a + 5b$
e $4p^2 - pq + 6q + pq$ f $ab + 2a - ab + 4a$

5 Which of these expressions is equivalent to $2a^2b - 3ab - 5ab^2$?

A $2a(ab + b) + 5b(ab - a)$ B $ab(2a - 2) - a(b - 5b^2)$

C $a(b + 2ab) - ab(4 + 5b)$

6 Multiply out and simplify:

a $2(2a + 3b) + 5(a + 4b)$ b $2(2x + 4y) + 3(2x - y)$
c $x(x - 3) - x(x + 4)$ d $2x(3x + 2y) + x(4x - y)$
e $ab(a + b) + ab(a - b)$ f $3a(ab + b) - 2b(ab - b)$

7 Simplify these expressions.

   a $2a(3a - b) + 4b(2a + 3b)$ **b** $5xy(2x + 4y) + 3x(2xy - 2y)$
   c $pq(2p - 3q) - 2p(3pq - 2q^2)$ **d** $2mn(3m - 4n) - 4m^2(2n - 3m)$

8 Write each of these as a single fraction in its simplest form.

   a $\dfrac{3}{x + 1} + \dfrac{2}{2x + 1}$ **b** $\dfrac{4}{x + 2} - \dfrac{3}{x + 1}$

   c $\dfrac{5}{x - 3} - \dfrac{2}{x + 4}$ **d** $\dfrac{3x}{x + 2} - \dfrac{2}{x + 4}$

Thinking ahead to ...
common factors

A In this triangle puzzle:

   ◆ the numbers in squares on each side
      are multiplied to give the numbers in
      circles

   ◆ the numbers in the circles are added
      to give the total.

      Copy and complete triangles 1 and 2.

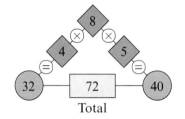

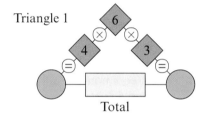

Triangle 1

Triangle 2

B

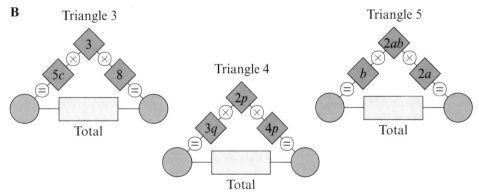

Triangle 3

Triangle 4

Triangle 5

For each of the triangles 3, 4 and 5,
write an expression for the total.

C Copy and complete these triangle puzzles.

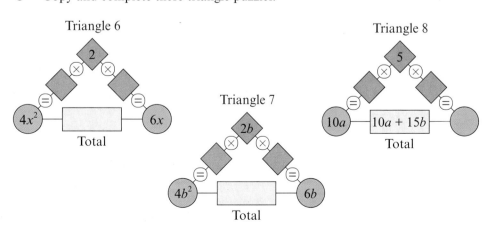

Triangle 6

Triangle 7

Triangle 8

Common factors

> The factors of a number are all **whole numbers**.

♦ A whole number can be written as a product of factors.

Examples
$48 = 12 \times 4$ $72 = 12 \times 6$
$48 = 2 \times 24$ $72 = 2 \times 36$
…   …
12 and 2 are common factors of 48 and 72.

♦ A term can be written as a product of factors.

Examples
$3a^2 = 3 \times a^2$ $6ab = 3 \times 2ab$
$3a^2 = a \times 3a$ $6ab = a \times 6b$
…   …
3 and a are common factors of $3a^2$ and $6ab$.

♦ To **factorise an expression** look for a common factor of the terms and write the expression using brackets.

Example

$$3a^2 + 6ab = 3(a^2 + 2ab) = 3a(a + 2b)$$

| $3 \times a^2$ | $3 \times 2ab$ | | $a \times a$ | $a \times 2b$ |

So 3 is a common factor of $3a^2$ and $6ab$

So a is a common factor of a^2 and $2ab$

So $3a^2 + 6ab = 3a(a + 2b)$

This is **factorised fully** as there are no other common factors.

Exercise 3.4
Common factors

1 Factorise these fully.

a	$2x + 14$	**b**	$8x - 10y$	**c**	$5x + xy$	**d**	$pq + 7p$
e	$6d + 4de$	**f**	$6ab + 9a$	**g**	$2a - 8ab$	**h**	$3a^2 + 12a$
i	$15xy + 20yz$	**j**	$a^2b + ab^2$	**k**	$12c^2d - 15cd$	**l**	$25x^2y + 15yz$

> When you factorise an expression, check that the two expressions are equivalent by multiplying out the bracket.
>
> **Example**
>
> Factorise $3ab^2 + 6a^2$
> $3ab^2 + 6a^2 = 3a(b^2 + 2a)$
>
> Check
>
>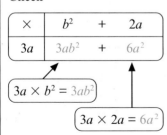

2 Draw a complete solution for triangles L and M.

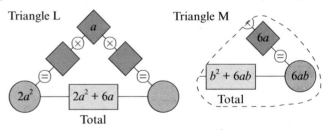

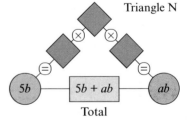

3 a In triangle N what term, other than 1, can be in the top square?
  b Draw a complete solution for triangle N.

4 Draw a complete solution for triangles O and P.

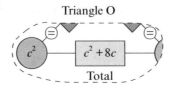

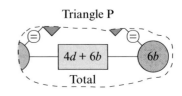

In these puzzles do not use the number 1 in the top square.

5 a Draw two different solutions for triangle Q.

b How many different solutions are there for triangle Q?

Triangle Q

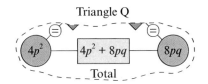

Total

6 How many different solutions are there for triangle R?

Triangle R

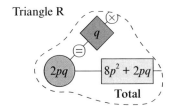

Total

7 Factorise these fully.

   a $5x + 10y + 20$ **b** $6a - 9b + 12c$ **c** $2x^2 + 3x + xy$

   d $14x - 28y + 21z$ **e** $2x^2 + 8xy + 6x$ **f** $6ab^2 + 2a^2b + 5ab$

Thinking ahead to ...
multiplying two brackets

The total area of this shape is $43 \times 28 \, \text{cm}^2$.

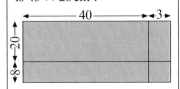

One way to find the area is:

♦ split the shape into 4 rectangles

♦ find the area of each rectangle in cm²
   $20 \times 40 = 800$
   $20 \times 3 = 60$
   $8 \times 40 = 320$
   $8 \times 3 = 24$

♦ add the areas.
The total area is $1204 \, \text{cm}^2$.

There is more than one correct expression.

A Using brackets the area of this shape can be written as $(x + 3)(x + 2)$.

This shape is split into four rectangles.

Find an expression for:

a the area of each rectangle

b the total area of the shape.

B Shapes P and Q are split into rectangles.

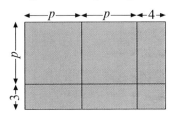

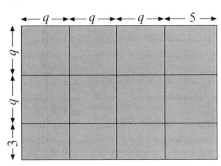

For each of the shapes P and Q write an expression for the total area:

a with brackets   **b** without brackets in its simplest form.

C Shape R is split into four rectangles.

a Which of these is an expression for the shaded area?

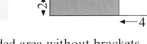

  A $n(n + 2) - 4n$ **B** $(n + 2)(n - 4)$

  C $n(n + 2) - 4(n + 2)$ **D** $(n - 2)(n - 4)$

  E $n(n - 4) + 2(n - 4)$ **F** $n(n + 2) - 8$

b Write and simplify an expression for the shaded area without brackets.

Multiplying two brackets

♦ You can multiply out brackets from $(2n + 3)(3n + 4)$ like this:

   ❖ $(2n + 3)(3n + 4) = (2n + 3) \times (3n + 4)$

   ❖ Work in a table:

$\times$	$2n$	$+3$
$3n$	$6n^2$	$9n$
$+4$	$8n$	12

   ❖ The total is: $6n^2 + 9n + 8n + 12$
    which simplifies to: $6n^2 + 17n + 12$

   ❖ So, $(2n + 3)(3n + 4) = 6n^2 + 17n + 12$ for any value of n.

   ❖ $(2n + 3)(3n + 4)$ and $6n^2 + 17n + 12$ are equivalent expressions.

Exercise 3.5
Multiplying out brackets

1   Which of these expressions is equivalent to $(n + 1)(n + 8)$?

    A $n^2 + 8n + 8$ **B** $2n + 9$ **C** $n^2 + 9n + 8$ **D** $2n + 8$

2   **a**   Which of these expressions gives the area of this rectangle?

    A $n^2 + 10n + 7$ **B** $n^2 + 10n + 10$

    C $n^2 + 7n + 7$ **D** $n^2 + 7n + 10$

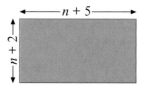

    b   Explain your answer.

3   For each of these, multiply out the brackets and simplify.

    a $(a + 1)(a + 3)$ **b** $(d + 5)(d + 9)$ **c** $(3e + 1)(e + 7)$
    d $(2a + 1)(5a + 4)$ **e** $(2b + 3)(3b + 5)$ **f** $(2c + 7)(3c + 2)$

4   For each of these, multiply out the brackets and simplify.

$(x + 1)^2 = (x + 1)(x + 1)$

    a $(x + 1)^2$ **b** $(x + 2)^2$ **c** $(x + 3)^2$

Comment on any pattern you see in your results.

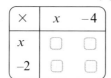

So $(x - 4)(x - 2) =$ ⬚

5   Copy and complete:

6   **a**   This shaded square is surrounded by four rectangles,
        each x cm by 3 cm, where $x > 3$.
        Write an expression for the area
        of the shaded square:
        i   with brackets
        ii   without brackets.

    b   Write an expression for the shaded
        square if the rectangles are:
        i x cm by 4 cm, where $x > 4$
        ii x cm by 5 cm, where $x > 5$
        iii x cm by y cm, where $x > y$.
        Write each answer without brackets
        and simplify.

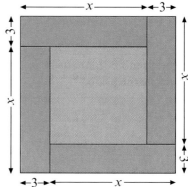

7 Copy and complete:

×	$2x$	-5
$3x$	☐	$-15x$
$+1$	☐	☐

So $(2x - 5)(3x + 1) =$ [   ]

8 For each of these, multiply out the brackets and simplify.
   a $(z + t)(2z + t)$ **b** $(3k + m)(2k + 5m)$ **c** $(2c + 3d)(c + 7d)$
   d $(3p - q)(2p + 5q)$ **e** $(f - g)(5f - 3g)$ **f** $(3w - v)(7w + v)$

9 Find four pairs of equivalent expressions.

   A $(2a + 3)(a - 2)$ B $(2a - 3)(a + 2)$ C $(2a - 1)(a + 6)$

   D $(2a - 1)(a - 6)$ E $2a^2 - 13a - 6$ F $2a^2 + a - 6$

   G $2a^2 - 13a + 6$ H $2a^2 + 11a - 6$ I $2a^2 - a - 6$

10 For each of these, multiply out the brackets and simplify.
   a $(z + t)(z - t)$ **b** $(2k + m)(2k - m)$ **c** $(2c - 3d)(2c + 3d)$
   d $(3p - q)(3p + q)$ **e** $(5f + 3g)(5f - 3g)$ **f** $(7w - v)(7w + v)$

   Comment on any pattern you see in your results.

11 Which of these expressions J to N gives the area shaded in this square?

   J $(a - 3b)^2$ K $a^2 - 6ab + 9b^2$

   L $6ab + a^2$ M $a^2 - 9b^2$

   N $(a - 3b)(a + 3b)$

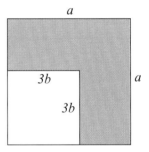

> There is more than one correct expression.

12 a Multiply out and simplify:
   i $(x + 1)^2$ ii $(x + 1)^3$ iii $(x + 1)^4$
   b Look at the pattern in the coefficients.
   Use it to write down $(x + 1)^6$ without brackets (in its simplest from).

13 Write each of these without brackets and simplify.
   a $a(a - 2)(a + 5)$ b $(p - 3)(p - 4)(p + 2)$
   c $2q(2q + 3)(q - 7)$ d $(x + 5)(2x - 1)(x + 2)$

Thinking ahead to ...
algebraic proofs

A a Copy and complete these questions which follow a pattern.

$(3 \times 4) \quad - \quad (1 \times 6) =$ ☐
$(4 \times 5) \quad - \quad (2 \times 7) =$ ☐
$(5 \times 6) \quad - \quad (3 \times 8) =$ ☐

⋮   ⋮   ⋮

$(☐ \times ☐) - (100 \times ☐) =$ ☐

b Describe what happens to the answers in the pattern.
c Write an expression for the nth question in this pattern.

Algebraic proof

♦ Algebra can be used to prove that some statements are true.

Example Prove that the answer to every line in this pattern is 6.

❖ For any value of n, the nth line in this pattern can be written as:
$(n + 2)(n + 3) - n(n + 5)$

$$3 \times 4 - 1 \times 6$$
$$4 \times 5 - 2 \times 7$$
$$5 \times 6 - 3 \times 8$$
$$\cdots$$

❖ This can be simplified:
$$(n + 2)(n + 3) - n(n + 5) = (n^2 + 5n + 6) - (n^2 + 5n)$$
$$= n^2 + 5n + 6 - n^2 - 5n$$
$$= 6$$

This proves that for any value of n the answer will be 6.

Exercise 3.6
Algebraic proof

1 For each of these patterns:

a copy and complete the examples

A
$$2 \times 3 - 1 \times 4 =$$
$$3 \times 4 - 2 \times 5 =$$
$$4 \times 5 - 3 \times 6 =$$
$$\vdots \qquad \vdots$$

B
$$2 \times 2 - 1 \times 3 =$$
$$3 \times 3 - 2 \times 4 =$$
$$4 \times 4 - 3 \times 5 =$$
$$\vdots \qquad \vdots$$

C
$$4 \times 5 - 1 \times 8 =$$
$$5 \times 6 - 2 \times 9 =$$
$$6 \times 7 - 3 \times 10 =$$
$$\vdots \qquad \vdots$$

b write an expression for the nth line

c prove that every line of the pattern gives the same answer and state the answer.

2 Each of these is an expression for the nth line of a pattern.

D $(n + 1)(n + 6) - n\,(n + \square) =$

E $(n + 2)(n + \square) - n\,(n + 5) =$

F $(n + \square)(n + 4) - n\,(n + 9) =$

a For each of the expressions D, E and F:
  i find the missing number
  ii calculate the answer for the pattern.

b In expression G below, a, b and c are constants.

G $(n + a)(n + b) - n\,(n + c) =$

  i Write a relationship that connects a, b and c?
  ii What is the answer for this pattern?

3 For each of these patterns:

a copy and complete the examples

A
$$3 \times 4 - 1 \times 8 =$$
$$4 \times 5 - 2 \times 9 =$$
$$5 \times 6 - 3 \times 10 =$$
$$\vdots \qquad \vdots$$

B
$$3 \times 5 - 1 \times 8 =$$
$$4 \times 6 - 2 \times 9 =$$
$$5 \times 7 - 3 \times 10 =$$
$$\vdots \qquad \vdots$$

C
$$1 \times 6 - 3 \times 3 =$$
$$2 \times 7 - 4 \times 4 =$$
$$3 \times 8 - 5 \times 5 =$$
$$\vdots \qquad \vdots$$

b write an expression for the nth line

c describe what happens to the answers in each pattern.

4 Write some lines in a pattern for which the answer to the nth line is:

a $n + 4$　　b $n - 2$　　c $10 - n$

Factorising

> To factorise an expression is to write it as a **multiplication** of its factors.
> For example:
> $x^2 + 5x + 4$ factorises to give
> $\quad (x + 4)(x + 1)$
> or $(x + 1)(x + 4)$

Example The expression $n^2 + 2n - 8$ has no common factor but it can be factorised. This is one way to factorise $n^2 + 2n - 8$.

❖ Think about a table that gives a total of $n^2 + 2n - 8$ and fill in the parts you are sure about.

×	n
n	n^2
	-8

❖ Try values that give -8 in the correct position.

❖ So $n^2 + 2n - 8 = (n + 4)(n - 2)$ or $(n - 2)(n + 4)$

❖ The total for this table is $n^2 - 2n - 8$ which **is not** what you want.

×	n	-4
n	n^2	$-4n$
$+2$	$2n$	-8

❖ The total for this table is $n^2 + 2n - 8$ which **is** what you want.

×	n	$+4$
n	n^2	$4n$
-2	$-2n$	-8

Exercise 3.7
Factorising

1 Factorise these expressions.

a $x^2 + 8x + 7$ **b** $p^2 + 9p + 8$ **c** $t^2 + 10t + 9$
d $m^2 + 8m + 12$ **e** $n^2 + 6n + 9$ **f** $a^2 + 13a + 36$

2 Copy and complete these statements.

a $x^2 + 6x + \square = (x + 4)(x + 2)$ **b** $q^2 + 6q + \square = (q + 5)(q + 1)$
c $r^2 + \square r + 10 = (r + 5)(r + 2)$ **d** $y^2 - \square y + 10 = (y - 1)(y - 10)$
e $t^2 + 7t + 12 = (t + 4)(\square\square\square)$ **f** $p^2 - 7p - 8 = (p + 1)(\square\square\square)$

3 Which pair of expressions multiply to give $x^2 + 3x - 4$?

| $x + 1$ | $x - 1$ | $x + 2$ | $x - 2$ | $x + 4$ | $x - 4$ |

4 Which pair of expressions multiply to give $x^2 - 6x + 8$?

| $x + 4$ | $x - 1$ | $x + 2$ | $x - 2$ | $x - 8$ | $x - 4$ |

5 Factorise these expressions.

a $p^2 + 2p - 3$ **b** $m^2 + 3m - 10$ **c** $t^2 - 4t - 5$
d $r^2 - 3r - 28$ **e** $x^2 - 8x + 15$ **f** $n^2 - 7n + 6$
g $t^2 - t - 12$ **h** $b^2 - 4b - 12$ **i** $x^2 + 4x - 12$

6 Which pair of expressions multiply to give $x^2 - 16$?

| $x - 16$ | $x - 8$ | $x - 4$ | $x + 1$ | $x + 4$ | $x + 2$ |

7 Factorise these expressions.

a $t^2 - 9$ **b** $r^2 - 25$ **c** $16p^2 - 1$
d $9x^2 - 4$ **e** $x^2 - y^2$ **f** $x^2 - 9p^2$

8 Which of these cannot be factorised as in the Example above?

A $x^2 + x + 15$ **B** $x^2 + 9x + 20$ **C** $x^2 - 6x + 12$

♦ You can use a table to factorise expressions like $2n^2 - 7n + 3$, where the **coefficient** of n^2 is not equal to 1.

❖ Think about a table that gives a total of $2n^2 - 7n + 3$ and fill in the parts you are sure about.

×	n	
$2n$	$2n^2$	
		$+3$

❖ Try values that give $+3$ in the correct position, and give a negative coefficient of n.

×	n	-1
$2n$	$2n^2$	$-2n$
-3	$-3n$	$+3$

❖ The total for this table is $2n^2 - 5n + 3$ which **is not** what you want.

×	n	-3
$2n$	$2n^2$	$-6n$
-1	$-n$	$+3$

❖ The total for this table is $2n^2 - 7n + 3$ which **is** what you want.

❖ So $2n^2 - 7n + 3 = (n - 3)(2n - 1)$ or $(2n - 1)(n - 3)$

Exercise 3.8
Factorising

1 Which pair of expressions multiply to give $2x^2 + 7x + 6$?

$\boxed{2x + 6}$ $\boxed{2x + 3}$ $\boxed{2x + 2}$ $\boxed{2x + 1}$ $\boxed{x + 1}$ $\boxed{x + 2}$ $\boxed{x + 3}$ $\boxed{x + 6}$

2 Factorise these expressions.

a	$3x^2 - 10x + 3$	**b**	$4y^2 + y - 3$	**c**	$4p^2 - 11p - 3$
d	$4x^2 - x - 3$	**e**	$3x^2 + 8x - 3$	**f**	$3a^2 + 10a + 3$
g	$5n^2 - 11n + 2$	**h**	$3x^2 - x - 4$	**i**	$3x^2 - 4x + 1$

3 This puzzle has been completed but the clues are missing.

Algebra Puzzle

	1 $+ 9x^2$		**2** $+ 1$	$+ 4x$	**3** $+ 4x^2$	
4 $+ x^2$	$- 1$		$+ x^2$		$- 1$	
$- 4x$		**5** $+ 3x^2$	$- 2x$	**6** $- 5$		
7 $+ 3$	$+ 4x^2$	$+ 8x$		**8** $- 4x$	$- 1$	**9** $+ 5x^2$
	10 $+ 4$	**11** $- 5x$	$+ x^2$			$+ x$
	12 $- 9$		$+ x^2$		**13** $+ x^2$	$- 4$
	14 $+ 4x^2$	$- x$	$- 14$		$- 49$	

Clues

Across
2 $(2x + 1)(2$
4 $(x - 1)$
5 $(x +$
7 $(2$
8
10
13
14

Down
1
2
3
4
5
6
9
11
12
13

For every clue find a pair of brackets that multiply to give the correct expression.

a Write a full set of clues for this puzzle.
b Make up your own puzzle like this.

4 For each of these find the numerical value of a and b such that for all values of x:

    a $x^2 - 12x + a = (x - b)^2$ **b** $x^2 - ax + 9 = (x - b)^2$

    c $9x^2 - ab + 1 = (3x - b)^2$ **d** $x^2 - ax + a = (x - b)^2$

5 Find a common factor and factorise each of these expressions fully.

    a $3x^2 - 9x + 6$ **b** $6x^2 + 21x + 15$ **c** $6x^2 + 16x - 6$

    d $14x^2 - 21x - 14$ **e** $3x^2 - 6x + 3$ **f** $4x^2 - 4$

6 **a** Factorise fully $n^3 - n$.

    b Show that $n^3 - n$ is even for all integer values of n.

7 Factorise these fully.

    a $x^2 + 2xy + y^2$ **b** $4x^2 + 8xy + 4y^2$ **c** $9x^2 - 16y^2$

> If there is a common factor in all the terms, take that out first then factorise.
>
> **Example**
>
> $2x^2 + 10x + 8$
> $= 2(x^2 + 5x + 4)$
> $= 2(x + 1)(x + 4)$
> This is factorised fully.

Using factorisation

Exercise 3.9
Using factorisation

1 Three consecutive numbers are added together.

    a If the smallest number is p, write each other number in terms of p.

    b **i** Write an expression for the sum of the three numbers.

        ii Simplify the expression.

        iii Explain why this shows that the sum of three consecutive numbers is always a multiple of 3.

2 **a** Evaluate the expression $n^2 + n - 6$ for:

        i $n = 1$ **ii** $n = 2$ **iii** $n = 3$ **iv** $n = 4$

    b Factorise $n^2 + n - 6$.

    c Explain why this shows that the value of $n^2 + n - 6$ is even for any value of n.

3 Show that $n^2 - 6n + 9 \geq 0$ for all values of n.

4 Kim puts this cross anywhere on this size 8 grid. She multiplies the corner numbers in pairs and finds the difference.

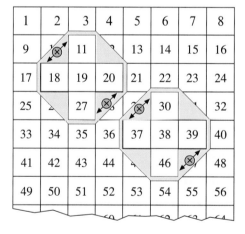

Example

$20 \times 27 - 11 \times 18 = 342$

$39 \times 46 - 30 \times 37 = 684$

    a **i** If the number in the centre of the cross is y, write each of the corner numbers in terms of y.

        ii Write an expression for the difference of the products.

        iii Show that the difference will be $18y$ for all possible values of y.

    b Kim uses the same cross on a size n grid.

        i Write the corner numbers in terms of n and y.

        ii Write an expression for the difference of the products.

        iii What would be the difference for a cross with $y = 16$ on a size 9 grid?

5 Show that the product of three consecutive numbers must be a multiple of 6.

> Because the cross cannot be placed on the edge of the grid some values of y are not possible.
>
> **Example**
>
> On the 8 grid these values of y are not possible:
> 1, 2, 3, 4, 5, 6, 7, 8, 9, 16, 17, 24, 25, … .

Exercise 3.10
Using the difference of
two squares

1 The expression $a^2 - b^2$ is called the difference of two squares.

  a Factorise $a^2 - b^2$.

  b Use this to find the value of:

    i $98^2 - 2^2$ **ii** $47^2 - 3^2$

| Do not use your calculator |
| for this exercise. |

2 **a** Copy and complete this sequence of lines.

  b Describe any patterns that you notice.

  c Write an expression for the nth line
     in this sequence and simplify it.

  d Write down the exact value of:

    i $1234^2 - 1233^2$

    ii $123123123123^2 - 123123123122^2$

$$2^2 - 1^2 =$$
$$3^2 - 2^2 =$$
$$4^2 - 3^2 =$$
$$5^2 - 4^2 =$$
$$6^2 - 5^2 =$$
$$\vdots \quad \vdots$$

3 **a** Use algebra to explain the pattern
    in these answers.

  b Use the pattern to write down
    the value of:

    i $128^2 - 123^2$

    ii $307^2 - 302^2$

$$6^2 - 1^2 = 35$$
$$7^2 - 2^2 = 45$$
$$8^2 - 3^2 = 55$$
$$9^2 - 4^2 = 65$$
$$\vdots \quad \vdots \quad \vdots$$

♦ Some algebraic fractions can be simplified by factorising.

Example

$$\frac{x^2 + 5x + 6}{x^2 + 2x - 3} = \frac{(x+3)(x+2)}{(x+3)(x-1)} = \frac{(x+2)}{(x-1)}$$

with $\div (x+3)$ cancelled from top and bottom.

Exercise 3.11
Factors in algebraic fractions

1 **a** Find the value, in fractional form, of:

$$\frac{n - 6}{n^2 - 5n - 6}$$

  when:

  i $n = 1$ **ii** $n = 2$ **iii** $n = 3$

  b Describe any patterns that you notice.

  c **i** Factorise and simplify the fraction.

    ii Use this to explain any patterns you found.

2 **a** Simplify each of these fractions as far as possible.

    i $\dfrac{2n + 6}{2n^2 + 4n - 6}$ **ii** $\dfrac{n^2 - n - 6}{n^2 - 3n}$

    iii $\dfrac{n^2 + 5n}{2n + 10}$ **iv** $\dfrac{2n^2 - 4n}{n^2 - 5n + 6}$

  b Give the value of each fraction when $n = 50$.

3 **a** Express $\dfrac{x^2 + 3}{3} + \dfrac{x(x + 9)}{6}$ as a single fraction and simplify.

  b Show that the value of this is an integer for all integer values of x.

End points

You should be able to ...   ... so try these questions

A   Multiply out brackets

A1   Simplify these expressions.
    a $2(2b - 4) + 6(4 + 3b)$ **b** $4(2b - 4) + 6(5 + 3b)$
    c $3ab(b - a) + 7ab(b + a)$ **d** $3xy(x - 3) - 7xy(y + 4)$

A2   Which of these expressions is equivalent to $(t + 5)(t - 3)$?

    A $t^2 + 8t + 15$ **B** $t^2 + 8t - 15$ **C** $t^2 + 2t - 15$

A3   For each of these, multiply out the brackets and simplify.
    a $(a + 1)(a + 8)$ **b** $(b + 4)^2$ **c** $(5c + 2)(c + 3)$
    d $(d + 2)(d - 1)$ **e** $(2e + 5)(3e - 10)$ **f** $(f - 7)(3f - 2)$

A4   These questions follow a pattern.
    a   Write the next three lines of this pattern. $(2 \times 7) - (1 \times 5)$
    b   What is the answer to the 20th line $(3 \times 8) - (2 \times 6)$
       of this pattern? $(4 \times 9) - (3 \times 7)$
    c   Write an expression for nth line   ...
       of this pattern.
    d   Prove that the answer to any line of
       this pattern will be a multiple of 3.

B   Factorise expressions

B1   Factorise these fully.
    a $8p + 4q$ **b** $6a - 12b$ **c** $a^2 + ab$
    d $7m + 3mn$ **e** $8xy + 10y$ **f** $4ab + 6a^2$
    g $3xy^2 - 5x^2y$ **h** $4pq - 6p^2q$ **i** $2g^2h - 5h^2$

B2   **A** $\boxed{k + 2}$ **B** $\boxed{k - 7}$ **C** $\boxed{k - 2}$ **D** $\boxed{k + 14}$ **E** $\boxed{k + 7}$ **F** $\boxed{k - 1}$

    Which pair of expressions multiply to give:
    a $k^2 + 5k - 14$ **b** $k^2 - 9k + 14$ **c** $k^2 + 13k - 14$?

B3   Factorise these expressions.
    a $x^2 + 12x + 11$ **b** $x^2 + 9x + 14$ **c** $x^2 + 4x - 5$
    d $x^2 + x - 6$ **e** $x^2 - x - 20$ **f** $x^2 - 5x + 6$
    g $x^2 - 100$ **h** $2x^2 - 11x + 15$ **i** $9x^2 - 16$
    j $5x^2 + 4x - 1$ **k** $x^2 - 4y^2$ **l** $4x^2 - 4xy + y^2$

B4   Find two pairs of equivalent expressions.

    A $\boxed{\dfrac{1}{a + 1} + \dfrac{2}{a}}$ **B** $\boxed{\dfrac{3a + 6}{a^2 + 2a}}$ **C** $\boxed{\dfrac{3}{a - 1} - \dfrac{3}{a + 1}}$

    D $\boxed{\dfrac{2a^2}{5a^3} \times \dfrac{15a}{2a}}$ **E** $\boxed{\dfrac{15a}{a^2 - 1} \times \dfrac{2}{5a}}$ **F** $\boxed{\dfrac{2}{a - 1} \div \dfrac{a - 1}{3}}$

B5   **a**   Simplify $\dfrac{x^2 + 8x + 16}{3x - 12}$ as far as possible.

       b   For what values of x is $\dfrac{x^2 - 8x + 16}{3x - 12}$ positive?

Starting points
You need to know about ...

... so try these questions

A Types of data

- There are two main types of data:
  - data that is divided into **categories**, such as:
    make of car, colour of car
  - data that is **numerical**, such as:
    number of people in car,
    length of car.

TRAFFIC SURVEY		
Car	Make of car	Number of people in car
A	Peugeot	1
B	Ford	3
C	Vauxhall	1
D	Ford	2
E	Rover	2

B Finding averages and the range

- For data in categories, you can only find one average:
  - the **mode** (the **modal** category is the most common).

  Red Blue Yellow Blue Green Black Red Blue

  The modal colour is **Blue**.

- For numerical data, you can find several averages and the range:
  - the **mode** is the most common value (or values)
  - the **range** is the difference between the highest and lowest values

  87 43 101 56 87 67   Mode = **87**
                                   Range = **58** (101 – 43)

  - the **median** is the middle value when the data is in order
    (for an **even** number of values, take the median as halfway
    between the middle pair of values)

  43 56 67 ┆ 87 87 101

  Median = **77**

  - the mean is the total of all the values divided by the number
    of values.

  $$\frac{87 + 43 + 101 + 56 + 87 + 67}{6}$$ Mean = **73.5**

C Deciding which average to use

- The **mean** is the most widely used average.
  It is not a sensible average to use for data with **extreme values**,
  values which are much smaller or much greater than the others.

  G.T. Small & Son – Monthly Salaries (£)

870	870	870	870	1050	1050
1050	1210	1210	1210	2080	2330

  Mean = £1222.50
  Median = £1050
  Mode = £870

  10 of the 12 salaries are smaller than the mean, so
  the **median** is the more sensible average to use.

- The **mode** can also be a poor choice of average.
  For this data, it is a poor choice because it is the lowest salary.

B1

X: 15 42 33 37 84 42 50
   81 29 26 67 15 19 55

Y: 38 25 106 78 44 62
   13 90 25 31 25

For each set of data, find:
a the mode
b the median
c the mean
d the range.

B2

Mode 3 and 7
Median 6
Mean 6

These are averages for a set of
data with 8 values.
List what the values might be.

C1

S. Fry & Partners
Weekly Wages (£)

112 285 285 340 340
340 372 372 388

Find:
a the modal wage
b the median wage
c the mean wage
d For each average wage:
  i decide whether it is
     sensible to use or not
  ii if you think it is not
     sensible, explain why.

D Finding averages from a frequency table

- For data in categories:

  ❖ the **mode** is the category with the highest frequency.

Make of car	Ford	Rover	Vaux.	Others
Frequency	9	6	2	7

The modal make of car is **Ford**.

- For numerical data:

  ❖ the **mode** is the value (or values) with the highest frequency
  ❖ the **range** is the difference between the highest and lowest values

No. of people in car	1	2	3	4	5
Frequency	3	10	6	3	2

Mode = **2** people
Range = **4** people
(5 − 1)

  ❖ the **median** is the middle value when the data is in order

1 1 1 2 2 2 2 2 2 2 2 2 | 2 3 3 3 3 3 3 4 4 4 5 5

Median = **2** people

  ❖ the **mean** is the total of all the values divided by the total frequency.

Number of people in car	Frequency		Total number of people
1	3	1 × 3	3
2	10	2 × 10	20
3	6	3 × 6	18
4	3	4 × 3	12
5	2	5 × 2	10
	24		63

Mean = $\frac{63}{24}$ = **2.6** people (to 1 dp)

E Constructing pie charts

Make of car	Ford	Rover	Vaux.	Others	Total
Frequency	9	6	2	7	24

- For a percentage pie chart, calculate the percentage in each category:
  ❖ there are 2 Vauxhall cars out of 24, so
  100 ÷ 24 × 2 = 8.3% (to 1 dp)

- For an angle pie chart, calculate the angle for each category:
  ❖ there are 9 Ford cars out of 24, so
  360 ÷ 24 × 9 = 135°.

	Freq	Sector	Size
Ford	9	37.5%	135°
Rover	6	25%	90°
Vauxhall	2	8.3%	30°
Others	7	29.2%	105°
Totals	24	100%	360°

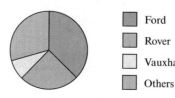

- Ford
- Rover
- Vauxhall
- Others

NUMBER OF CHILDREN IN CAR

1	0	1	2	1	1	0	0
4	1	0	1	0	0	2	0
2	0	3	0	0	2	0	1

COLOUR OF CAR

Red	Blue	Green	White
Silver	Red	White	Black
Black	Green	Red	Blue
Black	Blue	Blue	Silver
Red	White	Blue	Brown
Blue	Black	Brown	Red

D1 Present the colour-of-car data in a frequency table.

D2 Find the modal colour of car.

D3 Present the number-of-children-in-car data in a frequency table.

D4 Find:
- **a** the modal number of children in a car
- **b** the range of the number of children in a car.

D5 Find:
- **a** the median number of children in a car
- **b** the mean number of children in a car.

E1 Use your frequency table from Question **D1** to calculate:
- **a** the percentage for each colour
- **b** the angle for each colour.

E2 Draw a pie chart to show the colour of car data.

F Diagrams that present data

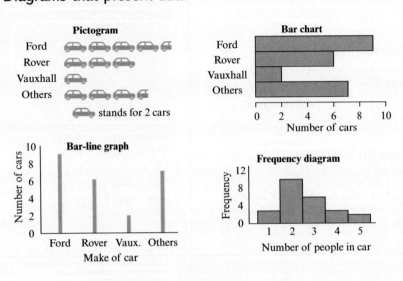

Pictogram

Ford
Rover
Vauxhall
Others

🚗 stands for 2 cars

Bar chart

Ford
Rover
Vauxhall
Others

Number of cars

Bar-line graph

Number of cars

Ford   Rover   Vaux.   Others
Make of car

Frequency diagram

Frequency

Number of people in car

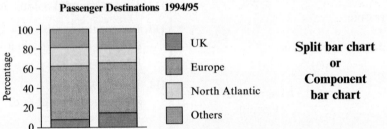

Passenger Destinations 1994/95

Percentage

Gatwick   Heathrow
Airport

■ UK
■ Europe
□ North Atlantic
■ Others

**Split bar chart
or
Component
bar chart**

Passenger changes 1989 - 1995

— Gatwick   — Heathrow

Percentage change

1989 1990 1991 1992 1993 1994 1995
Year

**Line
graph**

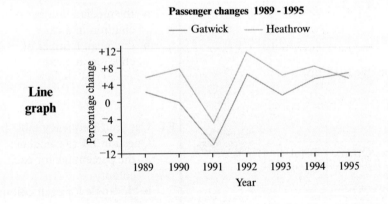

**Main Passenger Destinations
Scottish Airports 1994/95**

■ Glasgow   ■ Edinburgh   □ Aberdeen

UK

Europe

0   10   20   30   40   50   60   70   80
Number of flights (000's)

**Comparative
bar chart**

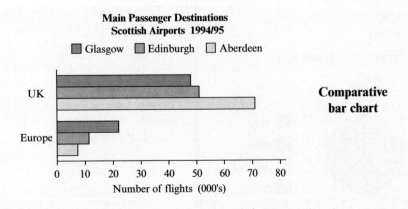

Use your frequency tables from Questions **D1** and **D3** to answer Questions **F1** to **F4**.

F1   Draw a bar-line graph to show the colour-of-car data.

F2   Draw a frequency diagram to show the number-of-children-in-car data.

F3   Draw a pictogram to show the colour-of-car data.

F4   Draw a bar chart to show the colour-of-car data.

F5

Southampton to Channel Islands 1994/95		
	Number of passengers (000's)	Number of flights (000's)
Jersey	156	4.0
Guernsey	100	3.4
Alderney	31	2.9
Totals	287	10.3

Calculate the percentage of passengers going to:
a   Jersey   **b**   Guernsey
c   Alderney

F6   Calculate the percentage of flights going to each of the three islands.

F7   Draw a split bar chart to show the two sets of data.

F8

% change in no. of passengers					
	1990	1991	1992	1993	1994
Glasgow	11.0	ˉ3.1	12.4	7.4	8.8
Edinburgh	5.3	ˉ6.1	8.4	7.2	10.3

Draw a line graph to show this data for Glasgow and Edinburgh.

F9

NUMBER OF FLIGHTS 1994/95 (000's)		
	Heathrow	Gatwick
UK	75	33
Europe	252	111
North Atlantic	40	19
Others	47	21

Draw a comparative bar chart to show this data.

10-ring target

A These are Viv's scores in 12 arrows at a 10-ring target.

Ring score	1	2	3	4	5	6	7	8	9	Total
Frequency	1	0	0	2	1	3	4	0	1	12

a Calculate the range of the scores.
b Explain why the range is not a sensible measure of spread for Viv's scores.

Calculating the interquartile range

Because the spread of the middle 50% of the data is measured, the interquartile range is not affected by any extreme values in the data.

♦ The **interquartile range** of a set of data measures how spread out the middle 50% of the data is.

♦ To calculate the interquartile range:

Ring score	1	2	3	4	5	6	7	8	9	Total
Frequency	1	0	0	2	1	3	4	0	1	12

You can divide the data into four quarters by first dividing it into two halves.

The end values are the medians of the two halves.

❖ list the data in order

   1 4 4 5 6 6 6 7 7 7 7 9

❖ divide the data into four quarters

   1 4 4 ⋮ 5 6 6 ⋮ 6 7 7 ⋮ 7 7 9

❖ find the end values of the middle 50% of the data

   1 4 4 ⋮ 5 6 6 ⋮ 6 7 7 ⋮ 7 7 9
          4.5   **7**
   Lower quartile   **Upper quartile**

❖ calculate the difference between the upper and lower quartiles.

   Interquartile range = 7 − 4.5
                       = 2.5

Exercise 4.1
Interquartile range

1 These are the scores for three archers.

Ring score	2	3	4	5	6	7	8	Total
Frequency	1	0	3	2	5	3	2	16

William

Bryony

Ring score	4	5	6	7	8	9	Total
Frequency	2	4	3	3	0	2	14

Ring score	2	3	4	5	6	7	8	9	10	Total
Frequency	1	1	2	3	5	3	0	3	2	20

Daniel

A set of data presented in a frequency table is called a **frequency distribution**.

a i For each archer list the data.
ii Calculate the interquartile range of their scores.

b Which archer is the most consistent?
Explain your answer.

Thinking ahead to ...
calculating the
mean deviation

A   In a competition, archers fire ten arrows in each round.
Kate and Bob each have a mean round score of 61 in eight rounds.

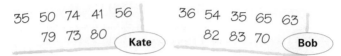

35 50 74 41 56
79 73 80 **Kate**

36 54 35 65 63
82 83 70 **Bob**

Whose round scores do you think are the more consistent?
Explain your answer.

Calculating the mean deviation

Another name for a
measure of spread is a
measure of dispersion.

◆ The range and interquartile range give only a rough idea about how spread
out values are within a set of data, because not all the values are considered.

◆ A more accurate measure of spread is given by the **mean deviation**,
i.e. the mean distance of the values from their mean.

To calculate the mean deviation:
❖ calculate the mean of the values
❖ calculate the **deviation** for each value
i.e. the positive difference between the value and the mean
❖ calculate the mean of the deviations.

Example   Calculate the mean deviation of Kate's scores shown above

The mean, $\bar{x}$, can be
written in shorthand as
a formula:

$$\bar{x} = \frac{\Sigma x}{n}$$

where Σx is the total of
the values
and n is the number
of values.

x		Deviation
35	61 − 35	26
41	61 − 41	20
50	61 − 50	11
56	61 − 56	5
73	73 − 61	12
74	74 − 61	13
79	79 − 61	18
80	80 − 61	19
488		124

$\frac{488}{8} = 61$ $\frac{124}{8} = \textbf{1.55}$

Mean score ($\bar{x}$)   Mean deviation

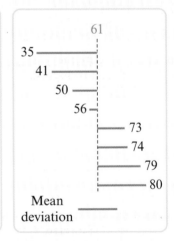

35
41
50
56
73
74
79
80

61

Mean
deviation

Exercise 4.2
Mean deviation

1 **a** Calculate the mean deviation of Bob's scores from Question **A** above.
   b Do you think he is more consistent or less consistent than Kate?
Explain your answer.

2 These archers were knocked out at different rounds of the competition.

56 61 67 49
58 48 **Zöe**

65 58 72 71 54
68 41 53 **Matt**

54 51 56 69 61 74
71 64 76 **Javed**

Another word used to
describe spread or
dispersion is variation.

   a **i** Which archer was the most consistent?
      ii Which archer showed the most variation in their round scores?
   b Explain your answers.

44 50 53 ?

3 The largest of these four round scores is missing.
The mean round score is between 50 and 53, and the mean deviation is 4.25.
Calculate the missing round score.

Calculating the standard deviation

♦ The most widely used measure of dispersion is the **standard deviation**.

To calculate the standard deviation:
* ❖ calculate the mean of the values
* ❖ calculate the **squared deviation** for each value
  i.e. the square of the difference between the value and the mean
* ❖ calculate the square root of the mean squared deviation.

Example   Calculate the standard deviation of Kate's scores.

x		Squared Deviation $(x - \bar{x})^2$
35	$(35 - 61)^2$	676
41	$(41 - 61)^2$	400
50	$(50 - 61)^2$	121
56	$(56 - 61)^2$	25
73	$(73 - 61)^2$	144
74	$(74 - 61)^2$	169
79	$(79 - 61)^2$	324
80	$(80 - 61)^2$	361
488		124
$\frac{488}{8} = 61$		$\sqrt{\frac{2220}{8}} = \textbf{1.67}$ (to 3 sf)
Mean score ($\bar{x}$)		Standard deviation

The standard deviation, σ, can be written as a formula:

$$\sigma = \sqrt{\frac{\Sigma f(x - \bar{x})^2}{n}}$$

where σ is the Greek
letter 'sigma'
$\Sigma(x - \bar{x})^2$ is the
total of the
squared deviations

and n is the number
of values

Exercise 4.3
Standard deviation

1 a Use the data from Exercise **4.2** Question **2** to calculate the standard deviation of each archer's scores.
   b List the archers in order of consistency.

2 a Use the data from Exercise **4.2** Question **1** to calculate the standard deviation of Bob's scores.
   b Copy and complete this table.
   c What do you notice about the statistics in your table ?

	Kate	Bob
Mean deviation	15.5	
Standard deviation	16.7	

   d Explain why this happens with these particular sets of data.

A 'statistic' is any quantity that describes a set of data – for example, the mean, the standard deviation, etc.

3 a Calculate the mean of Paula's round scores.
   b i Calculate their standard deviation.
      ii Check your answer using the alternative formula.

35 45 50
60 75 (Paula)

An alternative formula for the standard deviation is:

$$\sigma = \sqrt{\frac{\Sigma x^2}{n} - \bar{x}^2}$$

where Σx^2 is the total of the squares of each value

4 a Increase each of Paula's round scores by 20%, and list them.
   b Calculate their mean and standard deviation.
   c Describe the effect of the percentage increase on these statistics.

5 Describe the effect on the mean and standard deviation of increasing each of Paula's round scores by 15.

6 Investigate the effect on the mean and standard deviation of decreases in Paula's round scores.

Thinking ahead to ...
calculating the
standard deviation of a
frequency distribution

A   These are Bob's scores from his two best rounds in the competition.

Ring score	5	6	7	8	9	10
Frequency	1	0	1	3	4	1

Round 6

Round 7

Ring score	6	7	8	9	10
Frequency	2	2	0	3	3

For each round:

a   list Bob's scores
b   calculate the standard deviation of the scores.

Calculating the standard deviation of a frequency distribution

♦ To calculate the standard deviation of a frequency distribution:

❖ calculate the mean of all the values
❖ calculate the squared deviation for each different value
❖ multiply each squared deviation by its frequency
❖ calculate the square root of the mean squared deviation.

Example   Calculate the standard deviation of Bob's Round 6 scores.

The standard deviation, σ, can be written as a formula:

$$\sigma = \sqrt{\frac{\Sigma f(x-\bar{x})^2}{\Sigma f}}$$

where $\Sigma f(x-\bar{x})^2$ is the total of the squared deviations
and Σf is the total frequency.

Score x	Frequency f	Total score fx	Squared deviations $(x-\bar{x})^2$	$f(x-\bar{x})^2$
5	1	5	10.24	10.24
6	0	0	4.84	0
7	1	7	1.44	1.44
8	3	24	0.04	0.12
9	4	36	0.64	2.56
10	1	10	3.24	3.24
	10	82		17.60

$$\frac{82}{10} = 8.2 \qquad \sqrt{\frac{17.60}{10}} = \mathbf{1.33} \text{ (to 3 sf)}$$

Mean score ($\bar{x}$)   Standard deviation

Exercise 4.4
Standard deviation of a
frequency distribution

1   a   Use this method to calculate the standard deviation of Bob's Round 7 scores from Question **A** above.
    b   In which round do Bob's scores show less variation? Explain.

2

Ring score	2	3	4	5	6	7	8	9	Total
Frequency	11	8	5	3	3	4	6	10	50

Paula

Ring score	2	3	4	5	6	7	8	9	10	Total
Frequency	4	5	7	11	13	10	6	3	1	60

Zoe

Ring score	2	3	4	5	6	7	8	9	10	Total
Frequency	6	10	12	9	6	9	11	10	7	80

Matt

a   Draw a frequency diagram to show:
    i Paula's scores   ii Zoe's scores   iii Matt's scores.
b   Calculate the standard deviation of each archer's scores.
c   Comment on the shape of your frequency diagrams and your answers for the standard deviations.

Comparing sets of data

◆ One way to compare sets of data is to compare two types of statistic:

a an average

b a measure of dispersion.

Example Compare Zoe's and Matt's round scores using the mean and the standard deviation.

56 61 67 49
     58 48
Zöe

65 58 72 71 54
68 41 53
Matt

Use the statistical function on your calculator to check these values for the mean and the standard deviation.

	Zoe	Matt
Mean	56.5	60.25
Standard deviation (to 3 sf)	6.60	10.0

a Matt's round scores are higher on average.

b Zoe is more consistent because her scores show less variation than Matt's scores.

Exercise 4.5
Comparing sets of data

1

42 61 54 53 67
        72 78
Zeta

48 44 52 61 45
79 56 75
Carlo

a Calculate the mean round score for each archer.

b Calculate the standard deviation of each set of scores.

c Use the mean and the standard deviation to compare the sets of data.

2

Ring score	4	5	6	7	8	Total
Frequency	5	5	7	6	2	25

Dean

Leah

Ring score	3	4	5	6	7	8	Total
Frequency	1	3	7	6	2	1	20

Ring score	3	4	5	6	7	Total
Frequency	7	9	4	3	7	30

Jack

Compare these distributions using the mean and the standard deviation.

3

Ring score	3	4	5	6	7	8	9	10	Total
Frequency	3	7	4	1	1	0	0	2	18

Eliza

Ring score	2	3	4	5	6	7	8	Total
Frequency	1	4	3	4	2	1	1	16

Sam

When you compare data which has extreme values, using the median and the interquartile range can give a better comparison.

a **i** For each archer list the scores.

ii Find the median score

iii Calculate the interquartile range of the scores.

b Use the median and interquartile range to compare the two distributions.

Thinking ahead to ...
using cumulative frequencies
to find the median

A

Ring score	5	6	7	8	9	10	Total
Frequency	3	2	4	0	3	3	15

Salim

Ring score	5	6	7	8	9	Total
Frequency	7	8	13	18	14	60

Emily

a i List all Salim's scores.
  ii Find Salim's median score.
b i List all Emily's scores.
  ii Find Emily's median score.

Using cumulative frequencies to find the median

◆ The median can be found without listing all the data.

◆ To find the median using cumulative frequencies:
  ❖ calculate the cumulative frequencies
  ❖ use the total frequency to decide where the median is
  ❖ find the middle value.

The cumulative frequencies are the running totals of the frequencies.
For example: 7 + 8 = 15.

Example Find the median of Emily's scores.

Ring score	Frequency	Cumulative Frequency
5	7	7
6	8	15
7	13	28
8	18	46
9	14	60

The total frequency is 60, so the median score is halfway between the 30th largest and the 31st largest.

The 28th largest score is 7.

All the scores between the 29th and 46th largest are 8.

The final cumulative frequency here is 60: check it is equal to the total frequency.

The 30th and 31st largest scores are both 8, so
Median score = **8**

Exercise 4.6
Finding the median using cumulative frequencies

1

Ring score	3	4	5	6	7	8	Total
Frequency	7	10	5	1	6	11	40

Lee

Ring score	4	5	6	7	8	Total
Frequency	11	7	8	9	10	45

Faith

Ring score	1	2	3	4	5	6	7	8	9	Total
Frequency	2	4	2	3	1	4	7	9	7	39

Aqib

Ring score	1	2	3	4	5	6	7	8	9	10	Total
Frequency	6	9	5	4	2	5	6	4	3	4	48

Tegan

Find each archer's median score.

2

Ring score	4	5	6	7	8	9	10
Cumulative Frequency	7	18	31	40	48	62	80

Jake

a Explain why Jake's median score is 7.5.
b Explain why the interquartile range of this distribution is 3.

Thinking ahead to ...
box-and-whisker plots

A A survey of three fast food restaurants recorded the number of chips in a serving. A sample of 80 servings was taken from each restaurant.

Restaurant	Number of chips													Total
	32	33	34	35	36	37	38	39	40	41	42	43	44	
X	1	2	3	5	9	13	14	12	8	5	4	3	1	80
Y	4	6	11	14	13	11	8	6	4	3	0	0	0	80
Z	1	1	2	6	9	13	15	13	10	6	2	1	1	80

a i Which restaurant do you think gives more chips in a serving?
ii Explain your answer.

b i Find the median number of chips for each restaurant.
ii Calculate the interquartile range for each distribution.

Drawing box-and-whisker plots

◆ A **box-and-whisker plot** shows a frequency distribution by using:

❖ the lowest and highest values
❖ the median
❖ the lower and upper quartiles.

Example

Draw a box-and-whisker plot for these chips from restaurant W.

Number of chips	34	35	36	37	38	39	40	41	42	43
Frequency	1	2	4	7	12	14	16	15	7	2
Cumulative frequency	1	3	7	14	26	40	56	71	78	80

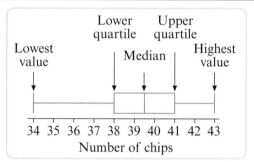

Exercise 4.7
Drawing box-and-whisker plots

1 Copy this box-and-whisker diagram on squared paper. Use the data from Question **A** to draw a box-and-whisker plot for each restaurant.

2 Write a short report that compares the number of chips per serving from the four fast food restaurants.

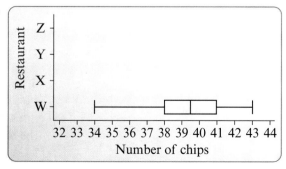

Comparing frequency distributions

- You can compare frequency distributions by considering their shape:
  - this distribution can be described as **skewed**
    (the larger frequencies are nearer to one end than the other)

A **frequency polygon** is a line graph which shows the frequencies that make up a distribution.

You can compare two or more distributions on the same diagram by plotting the frequency polygons.

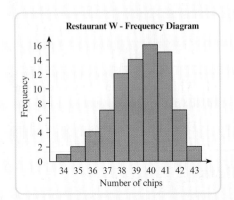

- this distribution can be described as **bell-shaped**
  (the frequencies are larger in the middle, and tail off towards each end).

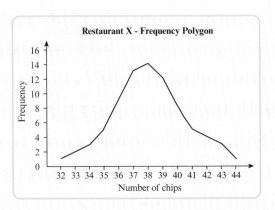

Exercise 4.8
Comparing distributions

1 **a** Draw the frequency polygon for restaurant X on squared paper.
    b Draw a frequency polygon for restaurant Z on the same diagram.
    c Compare the two distributions.

2 **a** Draw the skewed frequency polygon for restaurant W, starting the scale on the horizontal axis at 32 chips.
    b Draw a frequency polygon for restaurant Y on the same diagram.
    c Compare the two distributions.

A skewed distribution that has the 'hump' nearer to

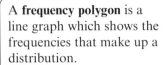

the right-hand end is **negatively skewed**.

When the 'hump' is nearer to the left-hand end,

the distribution is **positively skewed**.

3 For this distribution, the mean number of chips is less than the median number, which is less than the modal number.

  a For each of the other 3 restaurants:
    i calculate the mean number of chips
    ii draw a similar diagram.

  b Describe the link between the shape of a distribution and the mean, the median, and the mode.

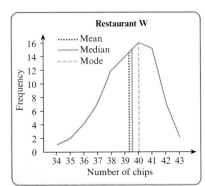

Misleading diagrams

♦ Statistical diagrams can be misleading in several ways, including:

  ❖ when the vertical axis does not start at 0

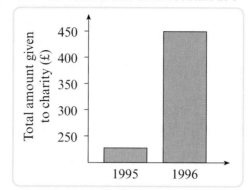

The vertical axis starts at £200.

This gives the impression that the amount given in 1996 was 10 times the amount given in 1995, not 2 times.

  ❖ when enlargements of a shape are used.

The 1996 note is 2 times the height *and* 2 times the width of the 1995 note.

This gives the impression that the amount given in 1996 was 4 times the amount given in 1995.

Exercise 4.9
Misleading diagrams

1 Draw a misleading diagram to show this revenue data by using:

  a a vertical scale which does not start at 0
  b enlargements of a shape.

WD *Wilton Dale Films*		
	1994	**1996**
Revenue (£m)	6.1	18.3

2 Draw a misleading diagram to show this data for number of visitors.

WD *Wilton Dale Theme Parks*			
	1994	**1995**	**1996**
Number of visitors (000's)	24	36	72

3

A

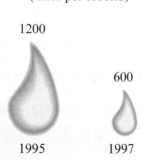

Wyvern Water
Water Wastage
(litres per second)

1200

600

1995   1997

B

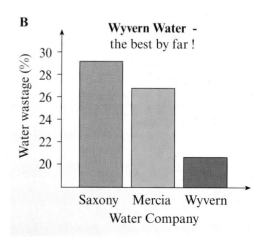

Explain why each of these diagrams is misleading.

End points

You should be able to ...　　... so try these questions

A Calculate the mean deviation and the standard deviation

A1 For Mel's round scores, calculate:
　a the mean
　b the mean deviation
　c the standard deviation.

43　64　67　58　62
　69　83　78　**Mel**

B Understand the effect of adjusting a set of data on the mean and standard deviation

B1 Jason scores 5 less than Mel in each round.
Give the mean and standard deviation of Jason's round scores.

Ring score	5	6	7	8	9	10	Total
Frequency	6	9	13	14	11	7	60	**Robin**

C Calculate the standard deviation of a frequency distribution

C1 Calculate the mean and standard deviation of Robin's scores.

D Compare sets of data

D1 **a** Copy and complete this table using your answers to Question **C1**.
　b Use the statistics in your table to compare Robin and Tina.

	Robin	Tina
Mean		7.42
Standard deviation		1.30

E Find the median and the interquartile range of a frequency distribution

E1 For Robin's scores, find:
　a the median
　b the interquartile range.

F Draw a box-and-whisker plot

F1 Draw a box-and-whisker plot for Robin's scores.

G Recognise when diagrams used to present data are misleading

G1

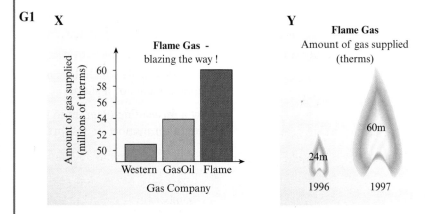

Explain why each of these diagrams is misleading.

Some points to remember

- If you adjust each value in a set of data by a **certain percentage**, the mean and the standard deviation of the data are both adjusted by the same percentage.

- If you adjust each value in a set of data by a **fixed amount**, the mean of the data is adjusted by the same amount but the standard deviation is left unchanged.

- When comparing data which has extreme values, using the median and interquartile range can give a better comparison than using the mean and standard deviation.

Starting points

You need to know about ...

... so try these questions

A Continuing a sequence

◆ A **sequence** of numbers usually follows a pattern or rule.

◆ Each number in a sequence is called a **term**.

For example, in the sequence: 3, 5, 7, 9, 11, ... , the 3rd term is 7.

◆ A sequence can often be continued by finding a pattern in the **differences**.

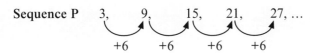

Sequence P   3,   9,   15,   21,   27, ...

     +6   +6   +6   +6

❖ In Sequence P, the **first difference** is 6 each time.

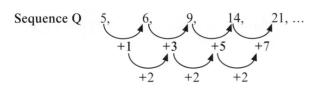

Sequence Q   5,   6,   9,   14,   21, ...

    +1   +3   +5   +7

    +2   +2   +2

❖ In Sequence Q, the **second difference** is 2 each time.
So continue the sequence by adding 9, then 11, and so on.

B A rule for a sequence

These are the first three matchstick patterns in a sequence.

  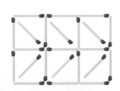

Pattern 1   Pattern 2   Pattern 3

◆ The number of matches in each pattern can be shown in a table.

Pattern number (n)	Number of matches (m)
1	9
2	16
3	23
4	30

❖ The pattern number goes up by 1 each time. (+1 each)

❖ The number of matches goes up by 7 each time. (+7 each)

❖ So a rule that links the number of matches (m) with the pattern number (n) begins $m = 7n$ ...

❖ A rule that fits all the results in the table is $m = 7n + 2$

◆ This rule can be used to calculate the number of matches in **any** pattern,
for example: in Pattern 10 there are $(7 \times 10) + 2 = 72$ matches.

A1 Find the 6th and 7th term in:
  a sequence P
  b sequence Q.

A2 What is the 10th term in this sequence?

    4, 7, 10, 13, 16, ...

A3 For each sequence, find the next three terms.
  a 2, 8, 14, 20, 26, ...
  b 2, 5, 11, 20, 32, ...
  c 2, 3, 9, 20, 36, ...

A4 **a** What are the second differences in this sequence?

    7, 16, 31, 52, ...

  b What is the 5th term?

B1 These are the first three patterns in a sequence.

Pattern 1

Pattern 2

Pattern 3

  a Draw pattern 5.

  b How many matches are in pattern 9?

  c Make a table for the first five patterns in this sequence.

  d Which of these rules fits the results in your table?

    $m = 4n + 2$ $m = 5n + 1$

        $m = 6n - 1$

Sequences and mappings

These equilateral triangles are the first three in a sequence of shapes.

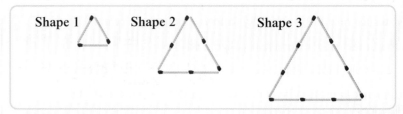

♦ Data for this sequence can be shown in a table.

Shape number	1	2	3	4
Number of matches	3	6	9	12

♦ The data can also be shown in a **mapping diagram** like this.

Shape number	Number of matches
1	→ 3
2	→ 6
3	→ 9
4	→ 12 ...

♦ The number of matches is 3 times the shape number.
For example, the 50th shape in the sequence uses 150 matches.

Using n to stand for the shape number,
the rule for the mapping diagram can be written: $n \longrightarrow 3n$

Exercise 5.1
Sequences and mappings

1 These are the first three patterns in a sequence.

Copy and complete the mapping diagram for the sequence.

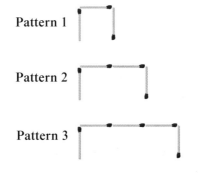

Pattern number	Number of matches
1	→ 3
2	→ ☐
3	→ ☐
4	→ ☐
.	.
20	→ ☐
.	.
n	→ ☐

2 These patterns of touching squares are the first four in a sequence.

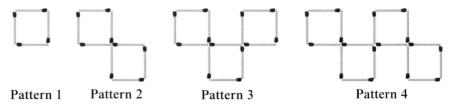

Pattern 1   Pattern 2   Pattern 3   Pattern 4

a Draw a mapping diagram for the first six patterns of touching squares.
b Find a rule for the sequence in the form $n \longrightarrow ....$, where n is the pattern number.
c Use your rule to calculate the number of matches in the 100th pattern.
d Which pattern would use 620 matches?
e Each touching square now has one extra match added as a diagonal. Which pattern will now use 620 matches?

Thinking ahead to ...
finding rules

A These are the first three patterns in sequence A.

Sequence A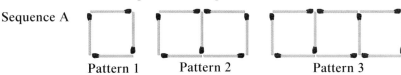

Pattern 1   Pattern 2   Pattern 3

How many matchsticks are in the 100th pattern?
Explain how you worked it out.

Finding rules

Example **Find a rule for the number of matches (*m*) in the *n*th pattern in sequence A above.**

♦ **Method 1** Look at how the patterns are made.

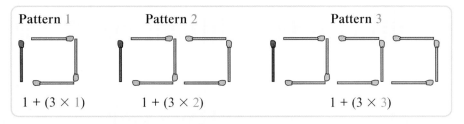

Pattern 1	Pattern 2	Pattern 3
$1 + (3 \times 1)$	$1 + (3 \times 2)$	$1 + (3 \times 3)$

❖ So a rule for the number of matches (*m*) in the *n*th pattern is **$m = 1 + 3n$**

♦ **Method 2** Look at differences.

Pattern
number (*n*)   3*n*   Number of matches (*m*)

1 —— 3 ——▶ 4	⎫ +3
2 —— 6 ——▶ 7	⎬ +3
3 —— 9 ——▶ 10	⎬ +3
4 ——12——▶ 13	⎬ +3
5 ——15——▶ 16	⎭

❖ The pattern number goes up by 1 each time.

❖ The number of matches goes up by 3 each time so there is a linear rule that begins $m = 3n ...$.

Examples of linear rules are:

$m = 4n + 3$
$y = 2 - 5x$
$a = 3b - 1$

Rules such as $m = n^2 + 1$ and
$y = \dfrac{5}{x} - 6$ are non-linear.

❖ Compare 3*n* with the number of matches.

❖ The number of matches is 1 more than 3*n* each time.

❖ So a rule for the number of matches (*m*) in the *n*th pattern is **$m = 3n + 1$**.

Exercise 5.2
Finding rules

1 These triangle patterns are the first three in sequence B.

Sequence B

Pattern 1   Pattern 2   Pattern 3

a Find a rule for the number of matches (*m*) in the *n*th triangle pattern. Explain your method.
b Use your rule to find the number of matches in the 8th pattern.
c Check your answer by drawing the 8th pattern and counting the matches.

2 Sequence C

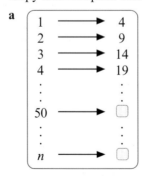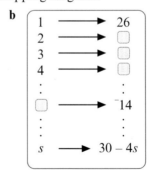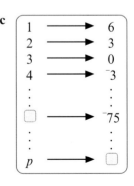

Pattern 1   Pattern 2   Pattern 3

a For sequence C, find a rule for the number of matches (m) in the nth pattern.
Explain your method.

b Calculate the number of matches in the 40th pattern.

c Which pattern uses exactly 129 matches?

3 Sequence D

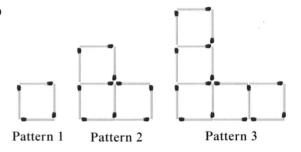

Pattern 1   Pattern 2   Pattern 3

a For sequence D, find a rule for the number of matches (m) in the nth pattern.
Explain your method.

b How many of matches are in the 100th pattern?

4 This mapping diagram fits a sequence of matchstick patterns.

Pattern number (n)	Number of matches (m)
1	→ 6
2	→ 10
3	→ 14
4	→ 18
5	→ 22

a Draw a sequence of matchstick patterns that fits this mapping diagram.

b Find a rule for the number of matches (m) in the nth pattern.

> Any letter can stand for the shape number.
>
> For example, the rule
> $n = \longrightarrow 3n + 2$
>
> can also be written as:
> $p = \longrightarrow 3p + 2$
>
> or
> $s = \longrightarrow 3s + 2$
>
> and so on.

5 Copy and complete each mapping diagram.

a
1	→ 4
2	→ 9
3	→ 14
4	→ 19
⋮	
50	→ ☐
⋮	
n	→ ☐

b
1	→ 26
2	→ ☐
3	→ ☐
4	→ ☐
⋮	
☐	→ ¯14
⋮	
s	→ $30 - 4s$

c
1	→ 6
2	→ 3
3	→ 0
4	→ ¯3
⋮	
☐	→ ¯75
⋮	
p	→ ☐

Thinking ahead to ...
finding the *n*th term

A [7, 9, 11, 13, 15, 17, ...]

    a Write the next two terms in this sequence.
    b Find the 12th term.
    c What is the 50th term?

The *n*th term of a sequence

Example Find an expression for the *n*th term in the sequence
7, 9, 11, 13, 15, …

♦ The sequence can be displayed in a table like this:

Term number (n)	1	2	3	4	5
Term	7	9	11	13	15

♦ The first difference for the terms is 2 each time.
So there is a linear expression for the *n*th term that begins **2*n* ... .**

♦ Comparing the sequence with the sequence $n \longrightarrow 2n$

Term number (n)	1	2	3	4	5
$2n$	2	4	6	8	10

shows that each term is 5 more than $2n$.
So an expression for the *n*th term of the sequence
7, 9, 11, 13, 15, … is **2*n* + 5**.

Exercise 5.3
Finding the *n*th term

1 A 6, 9, 12, 15, 18, ...   B 1, 6, 11, 16, 21, ...
    C 13, 23, 33, 43, 53, ...   D 2, 10, 18, 26, 34, ...

For each of the sequences A to D:
  a find an expression for the *n*th term
  b use your expression to calculate the 50th term.

2 A student has tried to find the *n*th term of this sequence.

[5, 8, 11, 14, 17, ...

nth term is n + 3 ✗]

  a Explain the mistake you think has been made.
  b Find a correct expression for the *n*th term of this sequence.

3 The 2nd term of a sequence is 7.
Which of these could not be an expression for the *n*th term?

[$3n + 1$]   [$11 - 2n$]   [$n + 5$]   [$n + 7$]   [$5n - 3$]

4 List the first 5 terms of the sequence whose *n*th term is $4 - 3n$.

5 Find an expression for the *n*th term of each of these sequences.
  a 20, 18, 16, 14, 12, …
  b 22, 12, 2, ¯8, ¯18, …
  c ¯1, ¯3, ¯5, ¯7, ¯9, …
  d 10, 5, 0, ¯5, ¯10, …

Thinking ahead to ...
non-linear rules

A   These are the first three shapes in a sequence.

Shape 1   Shape 2   Shape 3

a   Draw the next shape in the sequence.
b   How many small squares are in shape 20?

Sequences with non-linear rules

> The general term of the sequence is an algebraic expression which gives the number of squares when you substitute in the shape number.

Example   **Find a general term for the number of squares in the sequence above**

♦ Look at the differences.

The first differences are not the same each time so there is no linear expression.

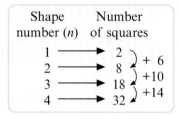

♦ Try looking at how the shapes can be made.

Each shape can be cut into two square shapes.

Shape 1: $2 \times (1 \times 1) = 2$ squares

Shape 2: $2 \times (2 \times 2) = 8$ squares

Shape 3: $2 \times (3 \times 3) = 18$ squares
.
.
.
Shape n: $2 \times (n \times n) = 2n^2$ squares

So a general term for the number of squares in the nth shape is $2n^2$.

Exercise 5.4
Looking at how
shapes can be made

1   For each sequence, find a general term for the number of squares and show with a diagram the way this links with how the shapes can be made.

a   Shape 1   Shape 2   Shape 3

b   Shape 1   Shape 2   Shape 3

c   Shape 1   Shape 2   Shape 3

2   How many squares are in the nth shape for this sequence?

Shape 1   Shape 2   Shape 3

Thinking ahead to ...
looking at differences

A These patterns are the first four in a sequence.

Pattern 1

Pattern 2

Pattern 3

Pattern 4

How many triangles or △ are in pattern 20?

Looking at differences

It is not easy to find a general term for the number of triangles in the triangle sequence by looking at how the patterns can be made.

◆ Look at the second differences. They are the same each time, so the general term will involve n^2.

Pattern number (n)	n^2	Number of triangles		
1	1	3	+3	
2	4	6	+5	+2
3	9	11	+7	+2
4	16	18	+9	+2
5	25	27		+2

u_n means the value of term n.

◆ Compare n^2 with the number of triangles.
   The number of triangles is 2 more than n^2 each time.

So a general term u_n for the sequence of triangles is $n^2 + 2$

◆ Other sequences may be based on the n^2 sequence.
   For example, consider the sequence 8, 17, 32, 53, 80, ...

Term number	1	2	3	4	5	...
Term	8	17	32	53	80	
1st differences		9	15	21	27	
2nd differences			6	6	6	

Here the second differences are all 6, which is three times those for n^2, so the sequence is based on $3n^2$.

Comparing the sequence with the sequence for $3n^2$ shows that each term is 5 more so the general term for the sequence is $u_n = 3n^2 + 5$.

Exercise 5.5
Looking at differences

1 These matchstick patterns are the first three in a sequence.

Pattern 1 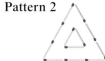 Pattern 2 Pattern 3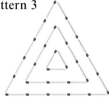

a Find a general term for the number of matches.
   Start your general term as $u_n = ...$
b Calculate the number of matches in pattern 85.

2 Here is a sequence of numbers. $\boxed{0, 3, 8, 15, 24, \ldots}$

   a What is the next term in this sequence?

   b Find an expression for the nth term in the sequence.

3   A 4, 7, 12, 19, 28, ...   B 4, 16, 36, 64, 100, ...

     C 6, 13, 20, 27, 34, ...   D 6, 9, 14, 21, 30, ...

     E 24, 21, 16, 9, 0, ...   F ⁻24, ⁻21, ⁻16, ⁻9, 0, ...

   For each of the sequences A to F:

   a write down the next two terms

   b find a value for the nth term.

4 For the sequence which starts 4, 28, 68, 124, 196, ... find:

   a the next two terms

   b the general term u_n

   c an expression for u_{n+1}.

5   A 3, 9, 19, 33, 51, ...   B 1, 10, 25, 46, 73, ...

     C 11, 32, 67, 116, 179, ...   D 2, 17, 42, 77, 122, ...

     E ⁻5, 1, 11, 25, 43, ...   F ⁻5, 4, 19, 40, 67, ...

   For each of the sequences A to F:

   a find the general term u_n

> u_{10} means the value of term 10.

   b calculate u_{10}.

6 **a** Calculate the general term for this sequence: $\boxed{13, 1, ⁻19, ⁻47, ⁻83, \ldots}$

   b Calculate u_{20}.

7 The sequence below shows a series of symmetrical models made from cubes.

Sequence Z

Model number	1	2	3	4	5	6	7
No. of cubes	1	6	15				

   a Finish the table for the sequence of the number of cubes in the first seven models.

   b By examining the differences find the general term u_n for the number of cubes.

   c How many cubes will there be in model 100?

This table shows the number of exposed faces in each model.

Model number	1	2	3	4	5
No. of exposed faces	6	22	46		

   d Find a general term, u_n for the number of exposed faces in this sequence.

Generalising other sequences

◆ Some sequences are generated by multiplying by one number each time. For example, a term in the sequence 3, 9, 27, 81, … is obtained by multiplying each previous term by 3.

The general term u_n for this sequence is 3^n.

Term number (n)	1	2	3	4	5 …	n
Term	3^1	3^2	3^3	3^4	3^5	3^n

Sequences like this where subsequent terms are multiplied by the same value are known as **geometric sequences**.

> Any number to the power of 0 is 1, so $3^0 = 1$

◆ Other sequences can be based on the one above.
For instance, the sequence 1, 3, 9, 27, … has the general term u_n as 3^{n-1}. In this case the multiplier between terms is still 3.

◆ Where a sequence is given only in fractions treat it as two separate sequences, one for the numerator and another for the denominator.

For example, the sequence $\dfrac{2}{5}, \dfrac{3}{11}, \dfrac{4}{29}, \dfrac{5}{83}, \dfrac{6}{245}, \dots$

has the general term $\dfrac{n+1}{3^n + 2}$.

Exercise 5.6
Generalising sequencies

1 Find the general term for each of these geometric sequences.

  a 2, 4, 8, 16, 32, …   **b** 1, 3, 7, 15, 31, …

  c 1, 2, 4, 8, 16, …   **d** $\dfrac{1}{4}, \dfrac{1}{2}, 1, 2, 4, \dots$

  e $1, \dfrac{1}{3}, \dfrac{1}{9}, \dfrac{1}{27}, \dfrac{1}{81}, \dots$ **f** $\dfrac{1}{4}, \dfrac{1}{16}, \dfrac{1}{64}, \dfrac{1}{256}, \dots$

2 Find the general term for these fractional sequences:

  a $\dfrac{1}{99}, \dfrac{2}{98}, \dfrac{3}{97}, \dfrac{4}{96}$ **b** $\dfrac{1}{4}, \dfrac{4}{8}, \dfrac{9}{16}, \dfrac{16}{32}, \dots$

  c $\dfrac{3}{1}, \dfrac{6}{8}, \dfrac{9}{27}, \dfrac{12}{64}$ **d** $\dfrac{2}{3}, \dfrac{5}{5}, \dfrac{10}{9}, \dfrac{17}{17}, \dots$

3 The general term for the sequence 4, 16, 64, 256, … is 4^n.
Use this to find the general term for the sequences:

  a 196, 184, 136, ¯56, …   **b** 256, 64, 16, 4, 1, …

4 Morag is finding the general term for the sequence 4, 10, 18, 28, 40, … .
This is her working.

The general term for the sequence

> ¯1, 0, 3, 8, 15, …

can be found in a similar way.

1st number	4 = 1 × 4
2nd number	10 = 2 × 5
3rd number	18 = 3 × 6
4th number	28 = 4 × 7
So	$u_n = n \times (n + 3)$
	$= n^2 + 3n$

  a Show how the first five terms can be built up by Morag's method.

  b Write the general term for the sequence in the form $u_n = \dots$.

5 The first five numbers of the triangle number sequence are:

> 1, 3, 6, 10, 15, …

  a Show how the terms can be built up.

  b Find a general term for the sequence.

Iterative sequences

An iterative process is one which is repeated many times. The output from one calculation is put back as the input for the next.

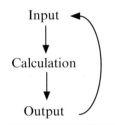

Input

Calculation

Output

You should keep the full value of u_2 (1.714 728 5714 …) in your calculator when you calculate u_3.

♦ The next term in a sequence can often be found by doing a calculation to the term before. For instance, the sequence 7, 11, 15, 19, … is formed by adding 4 to the term before.
This sequence can be written as an iterative sequence as: $u_{n+1} = u_n + 4$
Here u_1 is 7, so $u_2 = u_1 + 4 = 7 + 4 = 11$, $u_3 = u_2 + 4 = 11 + 4 = 15$, and so on.

Example

Give the first five terms of the sequence given by $a_{n+1} = \dfrac{12}{a_n + 4}$, where $a_1 = 3$.

Here $a_1 = 3$ so the second term, $a_2 = \dfrac{12}{a_1 + 4} = \dfrac{12}{3 + 4} = 1.714\,285\,714\ldots$

and $a_3 = \dfrac{12}{1.71\,428\,5714\ldots + 4} = 2.1$ and $a_4 = \dfrac{12}{2.1 + 4} = 1.967\,213\,115\ldots$

and $a_5 = \dfrac{12}{1.967\,213\,115\ldots + 4} = 2.010\,989\,011\ldots$

So the first five terms of the sequence are 3, 1.71 428 5714 …, 2.1, 1.967 213 115 … , 2.010 989 011 …

♦ In the sequence above, a_n gets closer and closer to the value 2 as n gets larger. This sequence is said to be **convergent** as it homes in on one value. The value 2 is said to be the **limit** of the sequence.

♦ For some sequences, the terms do not converge to a limit. For example, $b_{n+1} = 3b_n - 6$ with $b_1 = 4$ gives the sequence 4, 6, 12, 30, 84, … Sequences which do not home in to a limit are known as **divergent** sequences.

Exercise 5.7
Iterative sequences

Write each term to 4 sf but leave all the figures on your calculator while doing the working.

1   List the first five terms of each of these sequences where $u_1 = 1$.

   a $u_{n+1} = \dfrac{u_n}{5} - 1$ **b** $u_{n+1} = 4(u_n + 5)$

   c $u_{n+1} = \dfrac{8}{u_n - 2}$ **d** $u_{n+1} = 2u_n^2 - u_n$

2   For the rule $h_{n+1} = \dfrac{2h_n + 12}{h_n}$ calculate h_4 and h_6, where $h_1 = 4$.

3   A sequence is defined by the rule $u_{n+1} = 0.5\left(u_n + \dfrac{9}{u_n}\right)$, where $u_1 = 1$.

   What do you think is the value of u_n as n becomes larger?

4   **a**   For the sequence $p_{n+1} = \sqrt{\dfrac{p_n + 1}{p_n}}$, where $p_1 = 1$, find p_6.

   b   Does the sequence diverge or converge?
          Explain your answer.

5   The third term of a sequence is 193.
    The sequence is produced with the iterative formula $a_{n+1} = 5a_n + 3$.
    What is the first term?

6   The nth term of a sequence is given by $s_{n+1} = 2s_n - 2s_n^2$, where $s_1 = 0.8$.
    a   Calculate s_2.
    b   What is the limit of the sequence?

End points

You should be able to ...   ... so try these questions

A Find a rule that fits a sequence of patterns

A1 These are the first three matchstick patterns in a sequence.

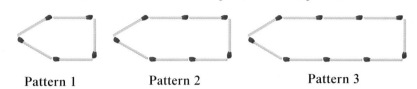

Pattern 1   Pattern 2   Pattern 3

a Find a rule for the number of matches (m) in the nth pattern. Explain your method.

b Use your rule to find the number of matches in the pattern 246.

B Find a general rule for a sequence of numbers or fractions

B1 A 2, 5, 10, 17, 26, ...   B 6, 7, 8, 9, 10, ...
         C 9, 12, 15, 18, 21, ...   D 5, 20, 45, 80, 125, ...
         E 5, 2, ⁻3, ⁻10, ⁻19, ...   F ⁻49, ⁻46, ⁻41, ⁻34, ⁻25 ...
         G ⁻1, 11, 31, 59, 95, ...   H 4, 13, 28, 49, 76

For each of the sequences A to F:
a find a general term, u_n
b calculate u_{20}.

B2 Find the general term for each of these geometric sequences.
a 27, 81, 243, 729, ...   **b** 8, 16, 32, 64, ...
c 4, 6, 10, 18, ...   **d** 1, 13, 61, 253, ...

B3 Find the general term for each of these fractional sequences.
a $\frac{2}{2} \ \frac{4}{5} \ \frac{8}{10} \ \frac{16}{17} \ \frac{32}{26}$ **b** $\frac{3}{3} \ \frac{5}{12} \ \frac{7}{27} \ \frac{9}{48} \ \frac{11}{75}$

C Find terms or limits in iterative sequences

C1 **a** List the first four terms in the sequence $p_{n+1} = p_n^2 + 5$, where $p_1 = 4$.
b Does the sequence diverge or converge ?

C2 **a** For the rule $k_{n+1} = \dfrac{6}{k_n - 5}$, where $k_1 = 1$:

calculate k_2 and k_3.

b To what limit does the sequence converge?

Some points to remember

◆ It is often possible to find a rule for the nth pattern in a sequence of patterns by looking at how each pattern can be made.

◆ In a sequence: ❖ if the first differences are k each time, there is a simple linear expression for the nth term that begins kn ... .

  ❖ if the second differences are the same non-zero number each time, there is an expression for the nth term that involves n^2.

◆ In a sequence where the terms are fractions treat the numerators and denominators as separate sequences.

◆ In a **divergent** sequence the terms will become larger or smaller but do not home in on a fixed limit.
A sequence which approaches a limit after a number of terms is said to be **convergent**.

Decorum Design

DDC is the favourite shop for trade and private buyers who want a new look for bathrooms, kitchens and bedrooms. Here are some of our items but come to the shop to see our full range.

■ WALLPAPER – rolls

width 53 cm, length 10 metres.

FLORAL DESIGN £5.49 per roll.

£4.97 each for 12 rolls or more

ANTIQUE EMBOSSED £7.99 per roll

WALLPAPER PASTE £4.99 – covers 10 sq metres

> TRY OUR ANTIQUE EMBOSSED PAPERS TO COVER THAT TATTY WALL

ALL PAINT PRICES REDUCED BY 20% FOR NEXT THREE WEEKS

■ EMULSION PAINTS – Top quality own brand

BRILLIANT WHITE	1 litre	£3.42
	2 (1/2) litre	£8.45
	5 litre	£16.99
PASTEL SHADES	2 (1/2) litre	£11.99
	5 litre	£19.49

A litre tin will cover about 8 m² with a single coat. Two coats needed over very dark surfaces.

When calculating how much paint to order, do not subtract the area of doors and windows.

■ WALL TILES – imported Italian and French

JARDIN RANGE – Box of 10 tiles £1.79

ASSISI RANGE – Box of 10 tiles £1.99

150 mm × 150 mm

JARDIN

150 mm × 150 mm

ASSISI

For those who have not caught up with metric units yet.

1 foot = 0.3048 metres   1 inch = 25.4 millimetres

All prices include VAT at 17.5%

TILE-FIX CEMENT – £7.99 a tub, covers 4 sq. metres

FORRET – Box of 10 wall tiles £2.14

BENETIA – Box of 10 tiles £2.14

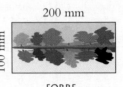

200 mm × 100 mm

FORRE

100 mm × 200 mm

BENETIA

■ FLOOR TILES

QUARRY TILES – terracotta, 120mm x 120 mm, 31p each

CERAMIC REGULAR SHAPED TILES – choice of patterns

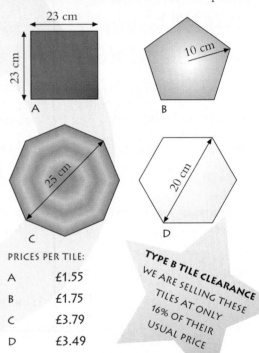

23 cm × 23 cm — A

10 cm — B

25 cm — C

20 cm — D

PRICES PER TILE:

A	£1.55
B	£1.75
C	£3.79
D	£3.49

TYPE B TILE CLEARANCE WE ARE SELLING THESE TILES AT ONLY 16% OF THEIR USUAL PRICE

We also sell small square tiles to fit with our type C tile. Pack of ten £5.75

TILE CEMENT – 12 kg bag – £17.89 – enough for 10 square metres of floor.

COLOURED GROUT £7.69 per tub – enough for 15 square metres of floor.

When calculating what to order, allow one complete tile for every part of a tile you need.

■ DESIGN SERVICE

We offer a free design service for bathrooms and kitchens. Just give us your plans to a scale of 1:50 and we will calculate how much paint, wallpaper or tiling you need.

1 Spencer decides to tile the wall above a bath with Jardin style tiles.
He wants to cover an area 2.5 m by 65 cm.
a How many tiles will he need to buy?
b What will this cost him (including Tile-Fix)?
c What is the total cost ex-VAT?

2 **a** Give a mathematical reason why the type B floor tiles are being sold off so cheaply.
b What is the reduced price of one type B tile?

3 Mike uses Decorum's design service to calculate the number of quarry tiles he should buy for a floor which is 3.82 metres by 4.15 metres.
a Make a scale drawing of the floor to the correct scale.
b Calculate the number of tiles he needs.
c Decorum allow for 5 % of the tiles breaking. How many should Mike buy?

4 For type D tiles:
a What is the mathematical name of the shape?
b What is the size of an internal angle?
c Why does the shape tessellate?
d What is the length of a side?

5 Steve's floor is 3.95 metres by 2.37 metres, and he wants to tile it with type A tiles. He works out that the area of the floor is 9.36 m^2 and that the area of one tile is 0.0529 m^2.
He says the number of tiles he needs is: $9.36 \div 0.0529 = 177$ tiles
a What is wrong with Steve's method?
b How many tiles does he really need?
c What is the cost including grout and cement?

6 Which size tin of brilliant white paint is the best value for money? Explain your answer.

7 The dimensions of a floor are given as 13 ft 6 inches by 11 ft 10 inches.
Calculate the ex-VAT cost of tile cement and grout for this floor.

8 Decorum are thinking of selling smaller bags of tile cement. They have chosen a 5 kg size as most useful. If they price it at the same unit cost as the 12 kg bag, at what price should they sell it?
Give your answer to the nearest penny.

9 **a** What is the mathematical name of the shape of the type C floor tile?
b Calculate the size of an internal angle of this shape.
c Type C shapes will tessellate with squares. Calculate the dimensions of these squares.

10 Type C tiles will also tessellate with isosceles triangles. Draw and cut out an accurate scale model of a type C tile. Use this as a template to show how these will tessellate with triangles.

11 The $2\frac{1}{2}$ litre size can of paint is 18 cm high.
Show that the diameter of this can, to the nearest millimetre is 133 mm.

12 Type B tiles would be of more use if the shop also sold another different-shaped tile.
Draw what you think this tile shape could be.

13 The contents of a tub of Tile-Fix cement weigh 3.5 kg.
New regulations state that:
"Wall tile cement must be applied at a rate of **at least** 885 gm/m^2".
a Does the information given by Decorum Design meet the new regulations?
Explain your answer.
b The £7.99 tub of Tile-Fix is discontinued.
Decorum Design sell a new tub to cover 5 m^2 at a price of £10.49.
  i Is this an increase or decrease in price?
  ii Give any change in price as a percentage of the £7.99 price, to the nearest whole number.

14 Type A floor tiles are 6 millimetres thick.
The contents of a box of 25 tiles weighs 17.8 kg.
Calculate the weight of 1 cm^3 of tile to 1 dp.

15 Sally is asked to find the area of one type C floor tile. She measures a side to be 96 mm.
This is her working:

> Tile shape made up of 8 triangles.
> Area of one triangle is given by:
> $\quad 0.5 \times 9.6 \times 12.5 = 60$
> Area of tile is given by:
> $\quad 60 \times 8 = 480$
> Area of tile is 480 cm^2.

a Explain why Sally's calculation must be wrong.
b Calculate the area of a type C tile.
Give your answer correct to the nearest cm^2.

16 For a display, type D floor tiles are to be cut so that each tile gives two rhombus-shaped parts and two parts in the shape of an equilateral triangle.
a Sketch a type D tile and show how it can be cut to give the shapes for the display.
b Explain why each rhombus shape is more than 25% of the tile.
c Give the area of one isosceles triangle shape as a percentage of a tile (to 1 dp).

Starting points
You need to know about ...

... so try these questions

A Some mathematical terms

◆ Lines AB and CD are **perpendicular** to line XY because they would meet XY at right angles.

XY is also **perpendicular** to AB and CD.

AB and CD are **parallel**.

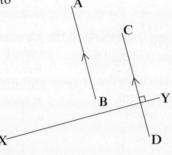

◆ These are some different types of triangle.

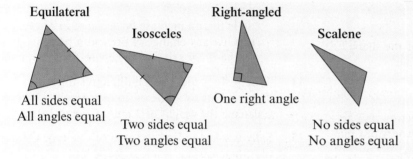

Equilateral	Isosceles	Right-angled	Scalene
All sides equal All angles equal	Two sides equal Two angles equal	One right angle	No sides equal No angles equal

B Congruent shapes

◆ Shapes are said to be congruent if they have the same shape or size or if they are reflections of each other.
Example Triangles A and B are **congruent** to each other.

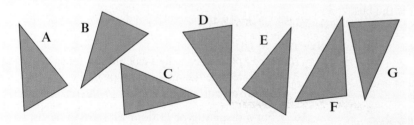

C Constructing a triangle, given all three sides

Example
Construct a triangle ABC where
AB = 4.4 cm, BC = 3.8 cm and CA = 3.2 cm.

◆ Make a rough sketch first.
◆ Draw a base line (say BC).
◆ Draw the locus of points 3.2 cm from C (red arc).
◆ Draw the locus of points 4.4 cm from B (blue arc).
◆ Where the arcs cross is point A
◆ Draw the triangle ABC.

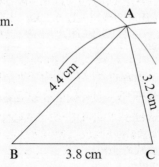

A1 a Draw a straight line PQ which is at an angle of 30° to the horizontal.
b Now draw another straight line RS which you **estimate** to be perpendicular to PQ.
c i At what angle is your RS to the horizontal?
ii What angle do you think this should be?

A2 Can a triangle be both:
a isosceles and scalene
b right-angled and scalene
c isosceles and right-angled
d equilateral and right-angled?

B1 Which of the triangles C to G is not congruent to triangle A?

B2 Draw another triangle which is congruent to triangle A.

B3 If two quadrilaterals both have sides of 12 cm, 13 cm, 14 cm and 15 cm are they necessarily congruent?
Explain your answer.

C1 Draw a triangle PQR, where PR = 8 cm, PQ = 6 cm and RQ = 9 cm.

C2 Draw a triangle RST, where RS = 7.5 cm, ST = 7.5 cm and TR = 12.2 cm.
What type of triangle is this?

C3 A triangular field is 350 metres by 840 metres by 760 metres. Use a scale of 1:100 000 to construct a scale drawing of the field.

Constructing triangles from other data

> ◆ You can construct a triangle when you are not given the length of all three sides. You might be given **one side and two angles**.

> **Example**   Draw △ ABC, where AB = 5 cm, ∠B = 55°, and ∠A = 43°.

> **Stage** 1   Make a rough sketch.
> 2   Make the side you know (AB) the base and draw it.
> 3   At A, draw an angle of 43° with a protractor.
> 4   At B, draw an angle of 55°.

△ABC means Triangle ABC.

∠B means angle B.

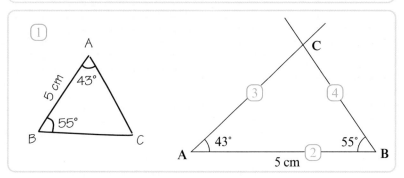

> ◆ You might be given **two sides and one angle**.

> **Example**   Draw △ RST, where RT = 6.5 cm, RS = 4.5 cm and ∠R = 46°.

> **Stage** 1   Make a rough sketch.
> 2   Make the long side (RT) the base, and draw it.
> 3   At R, draw an angle of 46° and mark S, 4.5 cm from R.
> 4   Draw the last side TS.

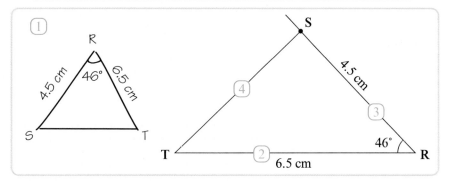

Exercise 6.1
Constructing triangles

1   Construct these triangles:

a   △ DEF, where DF = 6 cm, EF = 5 cm and ∠F = 69°
b   △ GHI, where GI = 7.2 cm, ∠G = 53° and ∠I = 42°
c   △ JKL, where JK = 8 cm, ∠J = 25° and ∠K = 125°
d   △ MNP, where NP = 6.3 cm, MP = 5.2 cm and ∠P = 131°.

2   Construct △QRS, where RQ = 8.3 cm, ∠R = 35° and ∠S = 68°.
You will need to calculate another angle first.

3   Construct these triangles to decide which two look identical:

a   △ IJK, where JK = 5.5 cm, IJ = 8 cm and ∠J = 50°
b   △ LMN, where LM = 8 cm, ∠L = 60° and ∠M = 50°
c   △ PQR, where PR = 6.5 cm, QR = 7.5 cm and ∠R = 70°.

Two of the triangles in
Question **3** are almost
identical but they cannot
be referred to as congruent
unless they **are** identical.

Thinking ahead to ...
congruent triangles

A   **a** Construct a triangle BCD where CD = 8.5 cm,
         BD = 9.4 cm and ∠B = 54°.

   b What is the length BC on your triangle?

   c Construct a different triangle which still meets all the conditions in
      Part **a** but has a different length for side BC.

Congruent triangles

SSS stands for the data
which is equal for both
triangles: Side, Side, Side

The order of the letters is
important, so SAS shows
that the angle is between
the two known sides
(i.e. the included angle):

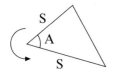

◆ There are four sets of conditions which can help you decide if two triangles
are congruent.

  1 The **three sides** of one are equal
     to the three sides of the other.
     This can be referred to as SSS.

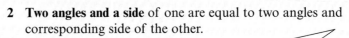

  2 **Two angles and a side** of one are equal to two angles and
     corresponding side of the other.

     This is known as **ASA**
     (or **AAS**).

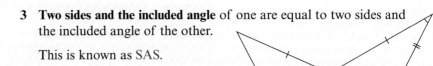

  3 **Two sides and the included angle** of one are equal to two sides and
     the included angle of the other.

     This is known as SAS.

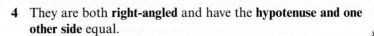

  4 They are both **right-angled** and have the **hypotenuse and one
     other side** equal.

     This is known as **RHS**.

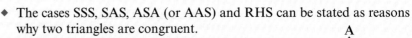

◆ The cases SSS, SAS, ASA (or AAS) and RHS can be stated as reasons
why two triangles are congruent.

  Example Name a triangle which is congruent
            to △BAD and state the case for
            congruence.

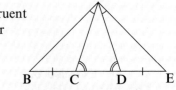

Note that when you name
two shapes which are
congruent you must state
the letters in the
corresponding order.

i.e. △BAD is congruent to
△EAC, but △BAD is not
congruent to △AEC.

∠BAD = ∠EAC since ∠CAD is common to both angles.
BD = CE, since CD is common to both lengths.

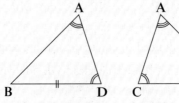

Therefore △BAD is congruent to △EAC. The case for congruence is AAS.

Exercise 6.2
Congruent triangles

1 In each of the following diagrams name a triangle which is congruent to △ABC and state the case for congruence.

a

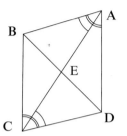

b

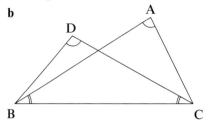

c

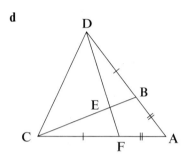

d

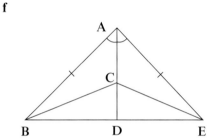

e

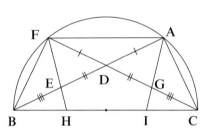

f

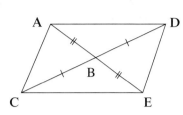

2 Simon said that the following two triangles were definitely congruent. He said there was a new case for congruence, **ASS**, which fitted them.

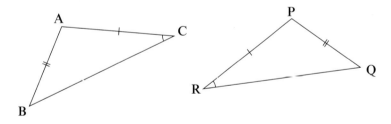

a Although the triangles might be congruent, explain why they need not necessarily be so.
b Construct a pair of triangles which match ASS but which are not congruent.

3 Sketch a pair triangles for each of these, state if the two are not necessarily congruent or certainly congruent and, if they are, the case for congruence.

a In △DEF and △GHI: DF = GI, DE = GH, EF = HI.
b In △ABC and △EFD: AB = DE, BC = EF, ∠ABC = ∠DEF.
c In △LMN and △RST: LN = RT, ∠LMN = ∠RTS, ∠LNM = ∠TSR.
d In △PQR and △STU: PR = ST, QR = TU, ∠QPR = ∠TSU = 90°.
e In △BCD and △EFG: BC = EG, BD = FG, ∠BCD = ∠FEG.
f In △RST and △UVW: ∠RTS = ∠VUW, VW = SR, ∠RST = ∠UVW.

Thinking ahead to ...
bisecting an angle

A pedestrian area is edged by two buildings which meet at an angle of 36°.
The plans say trees must be planted an equal distance from both buildings.

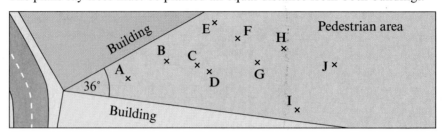

A   Which crosses on the diagram mark where trees could be planted?

'Equidistant from' means 'the same distance from'.

B   Draw two lines which meet at an angle of 36°.
Mark the locus of all points which are equidistant from both lines.

Bisecting an angle

To bisect an angle means to draw a line which cuts it in two equal parts from its vertex.

It is useful to be able to bisect an angle without measuring it.
You can do this using a pair of compasses.

Stage 1
Draw an angle ABC.

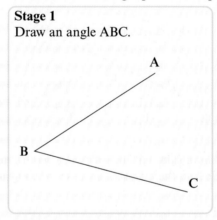

Stage 2
With centre B draw an arc so it cuts AB and BC at D and E.

Stage 3
With centre D, draw an arc.
With centre E, draw an arc.

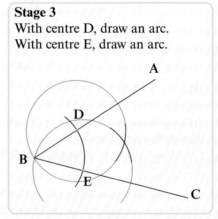

Stage 4
Draw the bisector BF.

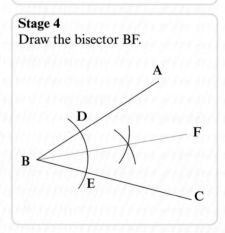

Exercise 6.3
Bisecting an angle

1   Use a protractor to draw each angle then bisect it using compasses.
a 44°   **b** 100°   **c** 146°   **d** 90°

2   Use compasses to draw an equilateral triangle with sides of 8 cm.
What size is each angle?
Bisect one of the angles. What angle have you made?

Thinking ahead to ...
perpendicular bisectors

A Draw a straight line and mark two points, A and B, 6 cm apart.

B Draw a circle at A and another with the same radius at B.

When two lines cross they are said to *intersect*.

C Draw larger circles with equal radii at A and B. If they *intersect*, mark the points of intersection.

D Continue by drawing larger circles and marking the points of intersection.

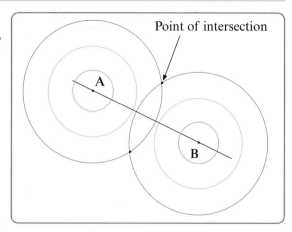

E a Draw the locus of all points of intersection of equal-sized circles.
  b Describe the link between this locus and the line AB.

Perpendicular bisectors

A line which cuts a straight line exactly in half at right angles is called a **perpendicular bisector**.

Example

To construct the perpendicular bisector of the line EF.

♦ Draw the line EF.

♦ With centre E draw an arc with a radius greater than half of EF.

♦ With centre F draw another arc with the same radius.

♦ Join the two points of intersection.

N marks the midpoint of EF.

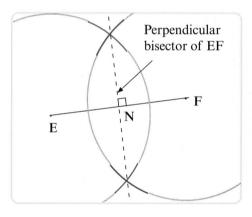

Exercise 6.4
Perpendicular bisectors

1 a Draw a line AB, 6 cm long. Construct the perpendicular bisector of AB.
  b Mark any point on the bisector and measure its distance to A and to B.
  c What can you say about the distance of any point on the bisector from A and from B?

2 Draw the perpendicular bisectors of lines with these lengths:

  a 10 cm   b 7.7 cm   c 4.6 cm

  Check that both sides are equal in length and that you have right angles.

3 a Draw this triangle.
  b Construct the perpendicular bisector of each side.
  c Where do all three bisectors intersect?
  d Does this happen for other triangles?

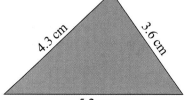

4 **a** Draw a circle of radius 6 cm and mark its centre C.
    b Draw a chord (AB).
    c Construct the perpendicular bisector
       of the chord.
    d Draw two more chords and bisect them.
    e What do you notice about where the
       bisectors intersect?

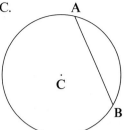

Meeting conditions

> Rules that have to be met such as 'the tap must be the same distance from A and B' are known as conditions.

Constructions such as bisecting angles or lines can be used for making scale drawings where conditions have to be met.

Example

A water tap is to be put in a large garden but it must meet these conditions:
1 It must be the same distance from the two greenhouses, A and B.
2 It must be the same distance from the grape vine wires as from the hedge.

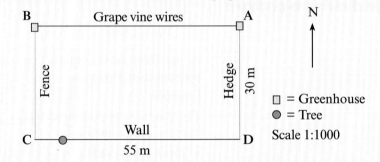

☐ = Greenhouse
● = Tree
Scale 1:1000

Where must the tap be placed? How far is it from the tree?

To meet condition **1** you draw the perpendicular bisector of BA.
This line is the locus of all points equidistant from B and A.
To meet condition **2** you bisect angle BAD.
This line is the locus of all points equidistant from line BA and line AD.

Where the two loci intersect both conditions are met, so the tap must be at this point.

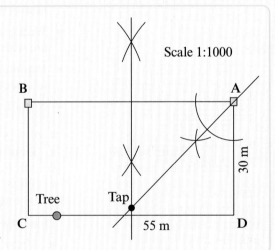

Exercise 6.5
Meeting conditions

1 **a** On the scale diagram above measure the distance in centimetres between
       the tap and the tree.
    b What is this actual distance in the garden?

2 Make a scale drawing to show where the tap will be if:
    condition **1** stays the same
    condition **2** says the tap must be equidistant from the wall and the hedge.

3 An Olympic javelin field has lines which make an angle of 29° to each other.
A thrower aims the javelin so that it flies equidistant from both lines.
The thrower hopes to reach the club record of 88 metres.

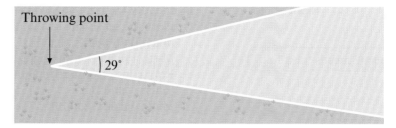

This diagram only approximates to how a true javelin field is marked out. The throwing point actually lies on an arc about 2 metres wide which comes at the end of a 36 metre run-up.

a Make a scale drawing of the field for throws up to 100 metres.
Use a scale of 1:1000.
b Mark the locus of all points 88 metres from the throwing point.
c Construct the locus of points equidistant from the sidelines.
d Mark where the thrower hopes the javelin will land.

4 Two lighthouses are 3.6 miles apart on a straight coastline.
A ferry sails into port by keeping the same distance from both lighthouses.
A fishing boat sails so that it is always 3 miles from the coast.

a Make a scale drawing of the coast to show the position of the lighthouses. Use a scale of 1 cm to 0.5 miles.
b Show and label the course taken by the fishing boat.
c Construct and label the course taken by the ferry.
d Mark the point where there is the greatest risk of a collision.

5 Coastguard A is 14 km due west of coastguard B along a stretch of straight coastline.
A ship S can be seen on a bearing of 030° from A and on a bearing of 300° from B.

a Use a ruler and compasses only to make a scale drawing of the situation. Use a scale of 1 cm to represent 2 km.
b From your drawing find the distance of the ship from coastguard B.

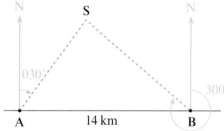

c The ship sails into shore so that its path bisects the angle ASB.
Construct this path and find its distance from A when it docks.

To construct an angle of 60° without a protractor you can construct an equilateral triangle.

To construct an angle of 30°, first construct a 60° angle, as above, then bisect it.

To draw a perpendicular from a point X to a line AB:
◆ draw an arc from X to intersect AB in two places
◆ from each intersection draw equal arcs on the other side of AB
◆ join the intersection of these arcs to X.

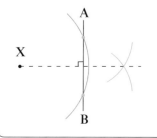

6 **a** Construct a quadrilateral PQRS where RSP = 90°,
QR = 8.4 cm, RS = 9 cm, SP = 6 cm and PQ = 5.4 cm.
b Bisect angles RSP and SPQ, and let these bisectors meet at point T.
c Construct the perpendicular from T to meet PS at N.
d Draw a circle with radius TN and centre T.
Which sides of the quadrilateral does your circle touch?

7 A buoy is moored 1000 metres from a long straight harbour wall.
A small boat sails so that it is always the same distance from the buoy as from the wall. Investigate the path of the boat with the help of a scale drawing.

The locus of a right angle

Exercise 6.6
Right angles

'Adjacent' means 'next to'.

1 **a** Draw a line AB which is 8 centimetres long.
b Identify the right angle on a set square.
Place the set square so that the sides adjacent to the right angle touch both points A and B.
Mark a point P at the right-angled vertex.
c Rotate the set square to another position so adjacent sides touch A and B.
Mark the new point P.

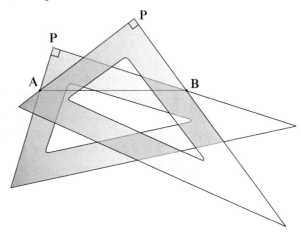

d Mark the locus of all positions of P as you rotate the set square 360°.
What shape is this locus?

2 **a** Draw a circle of any size.
b Draw in a diameter and label it RS.
c Join point R to any point, C, on the circumference of the circle.
d Join C to S.
e Measure angle RCS. What do you notice?
f For any diameter RS and any point on the circumference C, what can you say about the triangle RCS?

3 In this circle point H is the centre and lines AG and GC are equal in length.
Name six angles in the diagram which must be right angles.

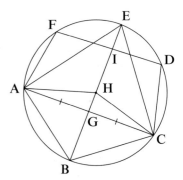

4 The cross-section of a roof is semicircular in shape.

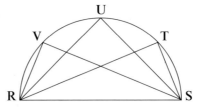

Beam RV is 12 metres long and beam VS is 26 metres.
Beam RU is equal in length to US.

a Use what you know about the angles in a semicircle to calculate the diameter RS to 1 dp.
b Calculate the length of RU to 1 dp.

End points

You should be able to ...   ... so try these questions

A Construct and draw triangles when you are given their sides or angles

A1 Construct △ABC where AB = 7 cm, AC = 6 cm and BC = 6 cm.

A2 Draw △DEF, where ∠EDF = 92°, ∠DFE = 47° and DF = 4.5 cm.

A3 Draw △PQR, where PQ = 7.4 cm, QR = 4.3 cm and ∠Q = 123°

A4 Draw two different triangles STU which each have TU = 6 cm, ∠SUT = 40° and ST = 4.3° cm.

B Construct and use perpendicular bisectors

B1

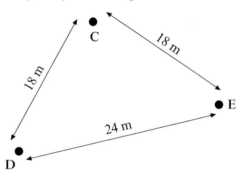

a Draw the parallelogram ABCD with BĈD about 40°.
b Construct perpendicular bisectors for the sides BC and AD.
c What can you say about the gradients of the two bisectors?

B2

Two dogs are tied at points D and E, 24 metres apart.
A cat at point C wishes to pass between the dogs so that it is always the same distance from each one.
Make a scale drawing and construct the path the cat must take.
Use a scale of 1 cm to 3 metres.

C Construct and use the bisectors of an angle

C1 Draw an angle of 110° with a protractor.
Construct the bisector of the angle.

C2 Construct △ABC where AB = 4.3 cm, BC = 6.8 cm and AC = 5.9 cm.
Bisect each of the angles.
What do you notice about where the bisectors intersect?

D Recognise and state the conditions for congruence

D1 For each pair of triangles, state if they are congruent or not necessarily congruent. For those that are congruent state their case for congruence.

a    **b**

c   **d**

e    **f**

E **Draw loci from some conditions given**

E1 This garden is the shape of a trapezium with the dimensions given.

Trees are at the midpoints of sides AD and DC.

A new bush is to be planted:
- equidistant from each fence
- equidistant from each tree.

B ←——— 8.3 m ———→ A

Fence

Tree

9.6 m

80° Fence Tree

C ←——— 10 m ———→ D

Make a scale drawing of the garden and show by construction the position of the bush. Use a scale of 1 : 100.

Some points to remember

- To construct an angle of 90°, draw a line and construct its perpendicular bisector.

- When asked to construct something do not rub out the construction lines when you finish.

- To construct an angle of 60°, construct an equilateral triangle.

- The perpendicular bisector of any chord will pass through the centre of the circle.

- All angles in a semicircle which are made by the diameter and a point on the circumference are right angles.

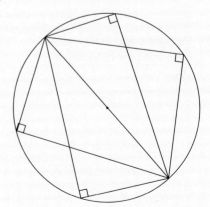

Starting points
You need to know about ...   ... so try these questions

A Fractions and decimals

- In recurring decimal notation, dots are placed over the first and last of the set of recurring digits.

  For example: $0.236666666 \ldots = 0.23\dot{6}$
  $0.236363636 \ldots = 0.2\dot{3}\dot{6}$
  $0.236236236 \ldots = 0.\dot{2}3\dot{6}$

- We can multiply recurring decimals by powers of 10.

  For example: if $n = 0.3232323232 \ldots$
  then $10n = 3.2323232323 \ldots$
  $100n = 32.3232323232 \ldots$ and so on.

- Any fraction is equivalent to a terminating or recurring decimal.

  For example: $\frac{3}{4} = 3 \div 4 = 0.75$
  $\frac{11}{30} = 11 \div 30 = 0.366666 \ldots = 0.3\dot{6}$

B Index notation

- We say 5^4 is **5 to the power 4** or **5 raised to the power 4**.

  $5^4 = 5 \times 5 \times 5 \times 5 = 625$ (4 is the **index**)

- Numbers raised to a **negative power** are defined so that:

  $x^{-y} = \frac{1}{x^y}$ e.g. $5^{-2} = \frac{1}{5^2} = \frac{1}{25} (= 0.04)$

So, the division pattern in this table is continued:

5^3	5^2	5^1	5^0	5^{-1}	5^{-2}	5^{-3}	5^{-4}
125	25	5	1	$\frac{1}{5}$	$\frac{1}{25}$	$\frac{1}{125}$	$\frac{1}{625}$

$\div 5$ $\div 5$ $\div 5$ $\div 5$ $\div 5$ $\div 5$ $\div 5$

C Square roots and cube roots

- The **square roots** of 9 are 3 and $^-3$ because, 3 squared is $3^2 = 3 \times 3 = 9$ and $(^-3)$ squared is $(^-3)^2 = ^-3 \times ^-3 = 9$

  Where a square root can be positive or negative, you should give the positive root unless stated otherwise.

  'The square root of 9 is 3' can be written $\sqrt{9} = 3$ or $\sqrt[2]{9} = 3$.

  Examples of square roots are:
  - $\sqrt{1.44} = 1.2$
  - $\sqrt{1\frac{7}{9}} = \sqrt{\frac{16}{9}} = \frac{4}{3}$

- The **cube root** of 64 is 4, because 4 cubed is $4^3 = 4 \times 4 \times 4 = 64$

  This can be written $\sqrt[3]{64} = 4$.
  Examples of cube roots are:
  - $\sqrt[3]{729} = 9$
  - $\sqrt[3]{(^-8)} = ^-2$

A1 Use recurring decimal notation to write these recurring decimals.
a $0.777777 \ldots$
b $0.12323232323 \ldots$
c $4.56666666 \ldots$

A2 If $n = 0.565656 \ldots$, what is:
a $10n$ b $100n$ c $1000n$?

A3 Convert these fractions to decimals, using recurring decimal notation where necessary.
a $\frac{1}{4}$ b $\frac{1}{3}$ c $\frac{6}{11}$
d $\frac{17}{30}$ e $\frac{3}{8}$

B1 Write these in index notation.
a 3 raised to the power 5
b 4 to the power $^-3$

B2 Evaluate as an integer or in fractional form:
a 3^4 b 3^{-2} c 4^0
d 5^{-1} e 2^9 f $(^-6)^2$
g $(\frac{2}{3})^2$ h $(^-\frac{1}{4})^2$

C1 What is the value of:
a the square root of 169
b the cube root of 1000
c the square root of 6.76
d the cube root of 9.261?

C2 Evaluate correct to one decimal place:
a $\sqrt[2]{12}$ b $\sqrt[2]{105}$ c $\sqrt[2]{6.7}$

C3 Evaluate:
a $\sqrt{49}$ b $\sqrt[3]{3.375}$
c $\sqrt[3]{(^-1000)}$

C4 Evaluate in fractional form:
a $\sqrt{\frac{1}{25}}$ b $\sqrt{\frac{49}{100}}$ c $\sqrt{1\frac{11}{25}}$

C5 Explain why any number has no more than one cube root.

Roots

It is also true that

$(^-1.2)^4 = 2.0736$ so a fourth root of 2.0736 is $^-1.2$.

If a root can be positive or negative, give the positive root as your answer (unless stated otherwise).

♦ As well as square and cube roots, there are fourth, fifth, sixth, ... roots.

Examples

❖ $3^5 = 3 \times 3 \times 3 \times 3 \times 3 = 243$ so a fifth root of 243 is 3.
This can be written: $\sqrt[5]{243} = 3$.

❖ $1.2^4 = 1.2 \times 1.2 \times 1.2 \times 1.2 = 2.0736$ so a fourth root of 2.0736 is 1.2
This can be written: $\sqrt[4]{2.0736} = 1.2$

❖ $\frac{1}{2}^6 = \frac{1}{2} \times \frac{1}{2} \times \frac{1}{2} \times \frac{1}{2} \times \frac{1}{2} \times \frac{1}{2} = \frac{1}{64}$ so a sixth root of $\frac{1}{64}$ is $\frac{1}{2}$.
This can be written: $\sqrt[6]{\frac{1}{64}} = \frac{1}{2}$.

♦ Sometimes a root cannot be written exactly as a decimal or fraction.

Example Find $\sqrt[5]{20}$ correct to 1 dp using trial and improvement.
$2^5 = 32$ (> 20 so 2 is too big)
$1.5^5 = 7.59375$ (< 20 so 1.5 is too small)
$1.9^5 = 24.76099$ (> 20 so 1.9 is too big)
$1.8^5 = 18.89568$ (< 20 so 1.8 is too small)
$1.85^5 \approx 21.66999$ (> 20 so 1.85 is too big)

The solution lies between 1.8 and 1.85 so $\sqrt[5]{20} = 1.8$ (to 1 dp).

Exercise 7.1
Roots

1 Calculate:

a $\sqrt[4]{16}$ b $\sqrt[6]{11.390625}$ c $\sqrt[5]{1}$

2 Which of these are integers?

a $\sqrt[3]{8}$ b $\sqrt[4]{12}$ c $\sqrt[6]{600}$ d $\sqrt[5]{32}$

3 Evaluate these, giving each answer as a fraction.

a $\sqrt[3]{\frac{27}{64}}$ b $\sqrt[5]{\frac{32}{243}}$ c $\sqrt[7]{\frac{1}{78125}}$

4 Evaluate $\sqrt[4]{10}$ correct to 1 decimal place.

5 Find the value of x when:

a $\sqrt[4]{x} = 3.5$ b $\sqrt[x]{1.728} = 1.2$ c $\sqrt[3]{x} = ^-4.5$

6 Copy and complete:

a $\sqrt[2]{6^4} = 6$ b $\sqrt[3]{2^6} = 2$ c $\sqrt[4]{5^8} = 5$

7 a Solve:
   i $\sqrt[x]{x^x} = 16$ ii $\sqrt[x]{x^x} = 216$
 b Make up two more problems like this that give integer values for x.

Using positive and negative indices

To multiply powers of the same number, **add** the indices.

Example 1

$3^2 \times 3^4$

$= 3^{2+4}$

$= 3^6$

$3^2 \times 3^4$

$= (3 \times 3) \times (3 \times 3 \times 3 \times 3)$

$= 3^6$

Example 2

$3^{-2} \times 3^4$

$= 3^{2+4}$

$= 3^2$

$3^{-2} \times 3^4 = \frac{1}{3^2} \times 3^4$

$= \frac{3 \times 3 \times 3 \times 3}{3 \times 3}$

$= 3^2$

To divide powers of the same number, **subtract** the indices.

Example 1
$$\frac{4^5}{4^2}$$

$$\frac{4^5}{4^2} = \frac{4 \times 4 \times 4 \times 4 \times 4}{4 \times 4}$$

$= 4^{5-2}$ $= 4^3$

$= 4^3$

Example 2
$$\frac{2^3}{2^7}$$

$$\frac{2^3}{2^7} = \frac{2 \times 2 \times 2}{2 \times 2 \times 2 \times 2 \times 2 \times 2 \times 2} = \frac{1}{2 \times 2 \times 2 \times 2} = \frac{1}{2^4}$$

$= 2^{3-7}$ $= 2^{-4}$

$= 2^{-4}$

To raise a power of a number to another power, **multiply** the indices.

Example 3
$(3^2)^3$

$(3^2)^3 = (3 \times 3) \times (3 \times 3) \times (3 \times 3)$

$= 3^{2 \times 3}$ $= 3^6$

$= 3^6$

Exercise 7.2
Multiplying and dividing

1 Give the answer to each of these in index notation.

   a $6^2 \times 6^3$ **b** $5^5 \times 5^{-1}$ **c** $(7^2)^4$ **d** $\dfrac{3^5}{3^4}$ **e** $\dfrac{2^8}{2^{-3}}$ **f** $(5^3)^{-2}$

2 Copy and complete these calculations.

   a $7^3 \times 7^{\square} = 7^8$ **b** $4^{\square} \times 4^5 = 4^5$ **c** $3^{-4} \times 3^{\square} = 3^2$

   d $\dfrac{5^7}{5^{\square}} = 5^{-3}$ **e** $\dfrac{2^{\square}}{2^4} = 2$ **f** $(7^3)^{\square} = 7^{15}$

Algebraic expressions involving indices can be simplified using the rules for indices.
For example:

$x^2 \times x^3 = x^{3+2} = x^5$

$\dfrac{a^7}{a^2} = a^{7-2} = a^5$

3 Simplify:

   a $x^5 \times x^3$ **b** $x^8 \div x^2$ **c** $(x^2)^5$ **d** $\dfrac{x^4}{x^2}$ **e** $\dfrac{x^5}{x}$ **f** $\dfrac{x^7}{x^9}$

4 Copy and complete:

   a $(t^{\square})^4 = t^{12}$ **b** $(q^5)^{\square} = q^{-5}$ **c** $(p^2)^{\square} = \dfrac{1}{p^8}$

5 To what power must x^2 be raised to give:

   a x^{10} **b** x^{-4} **c** $\dfrac{1}{x^2}$?

6 A student has made mistakes in trying to simplify some expressions.

   a $a^2 \times a^4 = a^8$ ✗   **b** $a^{10} \div a^2 = a^5$ ✗

   c $a^3 \div a^{12} = a^9$ ✗   **d** $(a^4)^3 = a^7$ ✗

   Explain the mistakes, and simplify each expression correctly.

7 Solve these equations.

   a $2^x \times 2^x = 2^{16}$ **b** $(7^x)^x = 7^{36}$ **c** $\dfrac{3^x}{3^{4x}} = \dfrac{1}{27}$

8 Simplify these expressions as far as you can.

   a $\dfrac{4p^3 \times p^2}{2p^4}$ **b** $\dfrac{2q \times 3q^5}{5q^2}$ **c** $\dfrac{4r^5 \times 6r^2}{12r^3}$

Thinking ahead to ...
fractional indices

According to the rules for multiplying powers:

* $25^{\frac{1}{2}} \times 25^{\frac{1}{2}} = 25^{\frac{1}{2} + \frac{1}{2}} = 25^1 = 25$

* $27^{\frac{2}{3}} \times 27^{\frac{2}{3}} \times 27^{\frac{2}{3}} = 27^{\frac{2}{3} + \frac{2}{3} + \frac{2}{3}} = 27^2 = 729$

A   What do you think could be the value of:

   a $25^{\frac{1}{2}}$ **b** $27^{\frac{2}{3}}$?

B   What value does your calculator give for $16^{\frac{1}{4}}$?

Fractional indices

Fractional powers are defined so that rules for calculating with integer indices can also be used with fractional indices.

Example 1

* $9^{\frac{1}{2}} \times 9^{\frac{1}{2}} = 9^{\frac{1}{2} + \frac{1}{2}} = 9^1 = 9$, so $9^{\frac{1}{2}} = \sqrt[2]{9} = 3$

* $8^{\frac{1}{3}} \times 8^{\frac{1}{3}} \times 8^{\frac{1}{3}} = 8^{\frac{1}{3} + \frac{1}{3} + \frac{1}{3}} = 8^1 = 8$, so $8^{\frac{1}{3}} = \sqrt[3]{8} = 2$

In general, $x^{\frac{1}{n}} = \sqrt[n]{x}$

Example 2

* $8^{\frac{2}{3}} \times 8^{\frac{2}{3}} \times 8^{\frac{2}{3}} = 8^{\frac{2}{3} + \frac{2}{3} + \frac{2}{3}} = 8^2 = 64$

   so, $8^{\frac{2}{3}} = \sqrt[3]{8^2} = \sqrt[3]{64} = 4$

* $16^{\frac{3}{4}} \times 16^{\frac{3}{4}} \times 16^{\frac{3}{4}} \times 16^{\frac{3}{4}} = 16^{\frac{3}{4} + \frac{3}{4} + \frac{3}{4} + \frac{3}{4}} = 16^3 = 4096$

   so $16^{\frac{3}{4}} = \sqrt[4]{16^3} = \sqrt[4]{4096} = 8$

In general, $x^{\frac{m}{n}} = \sqrt[n]{x^m}$

Example 3

* $9^{-\frac{1}{2}} \times 9^{\frac{1}{2}} = 9^{-\frac{1}{2} + \frac{1}{2}} = 9^0 = 1$, so $9^{-\frac{1}{2}} = \frac{1}{9^{\frac{1}{2}}} = \frac{1}{\sqrt{9}} = \frac{1}{3}$

In general, $x^{-\frac{m}{n}} = \frac{1}{x^{\frac{m}{n}}} = \frac{1}{\sqrt[n]{x^m}}$

Exercise 7.3
Fractional indices

1   Find four matching pairs of equal value.

   a $16^{\frac{1}{2}}$ **b** $^-2$ **c** $\frac{1}{2}$ **d** $512^{\frac{1}{3}}$

   e $4^{-\frac{1}{2}}$ **f** 8 **g** 4 **h** $(^-32)^{\frac{1}{5}}$

2   Evaluate these as integers or in fractional form.

   a $36^{\frac{1}{2}}$ **b** $125^{\frac{1}{3}}$ **c** $81^{\frac{1}{4}}$

   d $49^{-\frac{1}{2}}$ **e** $8^{-\frac{1}{3}}$ **f** $1^{-\frac{1}{5}}$

3   From the list of fractions, $\frac{2}{9}, \frac{3}{2}, \frac{1}{3}, \frac{2}{3}, \frac{1}{9}$, which one is equivalent to:

   a $\left(\frac{4}{9}\right)^{\frac{1}{2}}$ **b** $\left(\frac{1}{27}\right)^{\frac{1}{3}}$?

4 Find four pairs of equivalent expressions.

A $x^{-\frac{5}{3}}$ B $\dfrac{1}{\sqrt[5]{x^3}}$ C $x^{\frac{3}{5}}$ D $\sqrt[3]{x^5}$

E $\dfrac{1}{\sqrt[3]{x^5}}$ F $\sqrt[5]{x^3}$ G $x^{-\frac{3}{5}}$ H $x^{\frac{5}{3}}$

5 Sort these into four pairs of equal value.

A $64^{\frac{1}{2}}$ B 512 C 32 D $4^{\frac{5}{2}}$

E $216^{\frac{2}{3}}$ F 8 G 36 H $16^{\frac{9}{4}}$

6 Which of these fractions is equivalent to $32^{-\frac{2}{5}}$?

A $\frac{1}{4}$ B $-\frac{64}{5}$ C $\frac{5}{64}$ D $-\frac{1}{4}$

7 Evaluate these as integers or in fractional form.

A $125^{\frac{2}{3}}$ B $81^{\frac{3}{4}}$ C $243^{\frac{2}{5}}$

D $64^{\frac{7}{6}}$ E $4^{-\frac{3}{2}}$ F $27^{-\frac{4}{3}}$

8 A $x^{\frac{1}{3}}$ B 9^x C x^2 D $x^{\frac{1}{2}}$ E $x^{\frac{3}{4}}$ F $x^{\frac{2}{3}}$

a Which of these expressions gives an integer value when:
  i $x = 9$ **ii** $x = 64$ **iii** $x = 16$?
b Find a value for x that gives an integer value for all six expressions.

9 What is the value of p when $(p^{\frac{2}{3}})^{\frac{3}{2}} = 243$?

10 A number y is such that $y^{\frac{1}{2}} = \frac{1}{3}$. Find the value of:

a $y^{\frac{3}{2}}$ **b** y^{-1}

Exercise 7.4
Solving equations

1 Solve:

a $64^{\frac{1}{x}} = 4$ **b** $7^{2y} = \frac{1}{49}$ **c** $1024^{\frac{1}{5}} = 2^z$

d $32^a = 2$ **e** $125^b = \frac{1}{5}$ **f** $2^{2c+1} = \frac{1}{128}$

g $3 \times 4^p = 96$ **h** $\dfrac{8^q}{4} = 4$ **i** $8 \times 16^r = 1$

2 In this puzzle, the solution to each clue is the solution of an equation.
Copy and complete the puzzle.

Across

2 $3721^{-\frac{1}{2}} = \frac{1}{x}$

3 $y^{\frac{2}{5}} = 16$

6 $z^{\frac{2}{3}} = 121$

8 $v^{-\frac{1}{3}} = \frac{1}{3}$

Down

1 $w^{-2} = \frac{1}{100}$

2 $a^{\frac{1}{6}} = 2$

3 $\left(\frac{1}{b}\right)^{\frac{1}{2}} = \frac{1}{4}$

4 $c^{\frac{3}{5}} = 27$

5 $k^{-\frac{3}{4}} = \frac{1}{27}$

6 $m^{-1} = \frac{1}{17}$

7 $n^{-\frac{4}{5}} = \left(\frac{1}{2}\right)^4$

Thinking ahead to ...
square roots

A   Use your calculator to decide which of these are false.

Ⓐ $\sqrt{20} = \sqrt{10} \times \sqrt{2}$

Ⓑ $\sqrt{20} = \sqrt{17} + \sqrt{3}$

Ⓒ $\sqrt{20} = 2 \times \sqrt{5}$

Ⓓ $\sqrt{20} = \dfrac{\sqrt{40}}{\sqrt{2}}$

Ⓔ $\sqrt{20} = \sqrt{25} - \sqrt{5}$

Simplifying square roots

The rules for multiplying and dividing square roots also apply to other roots.

For example:

$a^{\frac{1}{3}} \times b^{\frac{1}{3}} = (a \times b)^{\frac{1}{3}}$

$a\sqrt{b} = a \times \sqrt{b}$

For example:

$2\sqrt{11} = 2 \times \sqrt{11}$

Expressions such as $5 + 2\sqrt{6}$ are said to be in **surd form**. They include roots that are not equivalent to integers or fractions.

Greek mathematicians thought of numbers such as $\sqrt{2}$ and $\sqrt{3}$ as absurd.

Rules for multiplying and dividing square roots are:

◆ $\sqrt{a} \times \sqrt{b} = \sqrt{ab}$

Example

$\sqrt{9} \times \sqrt{16} = 3 \times 4$
$\qquad\qquad = 12$

$\sqrt{9 \times 16} = \sqrt{3 \times 3 \times 4 \times 4}$
$\qquad\quad = \sqrt{(3 \times 4) \times (3 \times 4)}$
$\qquad\quad = 3 \times 4$
$\qquad\quad = 12$

So $\sqrt{9} \times \sqrt{16} = \sqrt{(9 \times 16)}$
$\qquad\qquad\qquad = \sqrt{144}$
$\qquad\qquad\qquad = 12$

◆ $\dfrac{\sqrt{a}}{\sqrt{b}} = \sqrt{\dfrac{a}{b}}$

Example

$\dfrac{\sqrt{100}}{\sqrt{4}} = \dfrac{10}{2} = 5$

$\sqrt{\dfrac{100}{4}} = \sqrt{\dfrac{10}{2} \times \dfrac{10}{2}}$
$\qquad = \dfrac{10}{2} = 5$

So $\dfrac{\sqrt{100}}{\sqrt{4}} = \sqrt{\dfrac{100}{4}} = \sqrt{25}$

So some expressions involving square roots can be simplified.

Example

◆ $(2\sqrt{11})^2 = (2 \times \sqrt{11}) \times (2 \times \sqrt{11})$
$\qquad\qquad = 2 \times 2 \times \sqrt{11} \times \sqrt{11}$
$\qquad\qquad = 4 \times 11$
$\qquad\qquad = 44$

◆ $\sqrt{20} = \sqrt{4} \times \sqrt{5}$
$\qquad\quad = 2\sqrt{5}$

◆ $(\sqrt{2} + \sqrt{3})^2 = 2 + \sqrt{6} + \sqrt{6} + 3$
$\qquad\qquad\qquad = 5 + 2\sqrt{6}$

×	$\sqrt{2}$	+	$\sqrt{3}$
$\sqrt{2}$	2		$\sqrt{6}$
$+\sqrt{3}$	$\sqrt{6}$		3

Exercise 7.5
Simplifying square roots

In this exercise, do not use a calculator unless stated otherwise.

1 a Which of these is not equivalent to $\sqrt{24}$?

Ⓐ $2\sqrt{6}$

Ⓑ $4\sqrt{6}$

Ⓒ $\sqrt{8} \times \sqrt{3}$

Ⓓ $\sqrt{4} \times \sqrt{7}$

Ⓔ $\dfrac{\sqrt{27}}{\sqrt{3}}$

b Check your results with a calculator.

2

Ⓐ $(\sqrt{5} + \sqrt{2})^2$

Ⓑ $(\sqrt{5} \times \sqrt{2})^2$

Ⓒ $\dfrac{\sqrt{54}}{\sqrt{6}}$

Ⓓ $\dfrac{\sqrt{100}}{\sqrt{5}}$

Ⓔ $\sqrt{6} \times \sqrt{2}$

Ⓕ $\sqrt{8} \times \sqrt{2}$

Ⓖ $(\sqrt{12} - \sqrt{3})^2$

Ⓗ $(4\sqrt{5})^2$

For each of these expressions:

a decide if it gives an integer value
b explain how you made your decision.

3 Sort these into five pairs of equal value.

A $\sqrt{3} \times \sqrt{5}$

B $\sqrt{8}$

C $\sqrt{2} \times \sqrt{2}$

D $2\sqrt{2}$

E $(\sqrt{2} + \sqrt{8})^2$

F 2

G $(\sqrt{3} - 1)^2$

H $\sqrt{15}$

I $4 - 2\sqrt{3}$

J 18

> When simplifying surds, write square roots in the form $\sqrt[a]{b}$ so that a and b are integers and b is as small as possible.

4 Simplify as far as you can, giving answers in surd form where necessary.

a $\sqrt{40}$

b $\sqrt{7} \times \sqrt{3}$

c $\dfrac{\sqrt{90}}{\sqrt{10}}$

d $\sqrt{2} \times \sqrt{32}$

e $\sqrt{3} \times \sqrt{15}$

f $(3\sqrt{5})^2$

g $(2 + \sqrt{7})^2$

h $(\sqrt{6} + \sqrt{12})^2$

i $(3 + \sqrt{5})(1 - \sqrt{2})$

j $(\sqrt{8} - \sqrt{2})^2$

k $(3\sqrt{2} + \sqrt{15})^2$

l $(2\sqrt{3})^4$

5 Find the value of:

a $(8 \times 10^{21})^{\frac{1}{3}}$

b $2^{\frac{1}{4}} \times 8^{\frac{1}{4}}$

c $\dfrac{54^{\frac{1}{3}}}{2^{\frac{1}{3}}}$

Rational and irrational numbers

- ◆ Any number that can be written as $\dfrac{a}{b}$, where a and b are integers, is called a **rational number**. Examples of rational numbers are: $\frac{3}{4}$, $\frac{9}{2}$, 0, 7.

- ◆ Any recurring decimal can be written as a fraction and is therefore rational.

   Example   Write the decimal $0.121212\ldots$ as a fraction.

   > $0.121212\ldots$ consists of a set of **two** recurring decimals so it is multiplied by 100.

   If $n = 0.121212\ldots$ Equation 1
   then $100n = 12.121212\ldots$ Equation 2
   Subtracting 1 from 2 gives: $100n - n = 12.121212\ldots \; - 0.121212\ldots$
   $$99n = 12$$
   $$n = \frac{12}{99} = \frac{4}{33}.$$

> All numbers are either rational or irrational.

- ◆ Any number that cannot be written as a fraction is called **irrational**. An irrational number in decimal form does not recur or terminate.

   Any root that cannot be simplified to an integer or a fraction is an irrational number.
   Examples of irrational numbers are: $\sqrt{2}$, $\sqrt[3]{4}$, $\sqrt{\frac{3}{5}}$.

Exercise 7.6
Rational and irrational numbers

1 Write each of these recurring decimals as a fraction in its lowest terms.

a $0.454545\ldots$

b $0.888888\ldots$

c $0.387387\ldots$

d $0.\dot{6}$

e $0.\dot{0}\dot{3}$

f $0.\dot{4}2857\dot{1}$

2 For each number, decide whether it is rational or irrational.

a $\sqrt{5}$ **b** $\sqrt[4]{9}$ **c** $0.\dot{2}\dot{7}$ **d** $\sqrt{2\frac{1}{4}}$ **e** $\sqrt[3]{2\frac{1}{4}}$ **f** $\sqrt[5]{\frac{1}{32}}$

3 $p^3 = 8$, $q^3 = 9$, $r^3 = 3\frac{3}{8}$, $s^3 = 0.027$

Which of the numbers p, q, r, s are irrational ?

4 Show that each of these recurring decimals is rational by writing it as a fraction in its lowest terms. Explain your methods clearly.

a $0.0\dot{6}$ **b** $5.0\dot{6}$ **c** $0.1\dot{6}$ **d** $0.8\dot{3}$ **e** $0.02\dot{3}$ **f** $0.0\dot{2}\dot{3}$

In these tables:
Rat stands for rational and
Irr stands for irrational

Expressions that combine rational and irrational numbers will have rational or irrational values.

Two numbers can be added, subtracted, multiplied or divided.
Rules to decide if the result is rational or irrational are given in these tables.

+/–	Rat	Irr
Rat	Rat	Irr
Irr	Irr	Either*

×/÷	Rat	Irr
Rat	Rat	Irr
Irr	Irr	Either*

*In most cases, adding or subtracting two irrationals gives an irrational result. Sometimes, however, the result is rational –
for example:

♦ $\sqrt{2} - \sqrt{2} = 0$
♦ $(1 + \sqrt{5}) + (1 - \sqrt{5}) = 2$

Multiplying or dividing two irrational numbers gives a rational **or** irrational result.

For example: $\sqrt{2}$, $\sqrt{3}$ and $\sqrt{8}$ are all **irrational** numbers.

♦ $\sqrt{2} \times \sqrt{3} = \sqrt{6}$ is **irrational** but
♦ $\sqrt{2} \times \sqrt{8} = \sqrt{16} = 4$ is **rational**.

Exercise 7.7
Rational or irrational?

1 For each of the following, decide whether it is rational or irrational.

   a $\sqrt{5} + 1$ **b** $\sqrt{3} - \sqrt{2}$ **c** $\sqrt{7} \times \sqrt{7}$

   d $\dfrac{\sqrt{12}}{\sqrt{2}}$ **e** $\sqrt{2} \times \sqrt{18}$ **f** $\dfrac{\sqrt{18}}{\sqrt{2}}$

   g $4^{-1} + 4$ **h** $12^{\frac{2}{3}} + 5$ **i** $5^0 + 5^{-1} + 5^{-2}$

2 n is an integer greater than 5.
   Write down a possible value for n so that $\sqrt{5} \times \sqrt{n}$ is:

   a rational   **b** irrational.

3 If $f = \sqrt{2}$, $g = 2\sqrt{5}$ and $h = \sqrt{10}$, determine whether each of the following expressions are rational or irrational.

   a $h - f$ **b** $(h - f)^2$ **c** $\dfrac{fg}{h}$

   d f^3 **e** $fg + h$ **f** $(fg + h)^2$

An example of an irrational number that is not a root is π.
π^n is irrational for all values of n except 0.

So, for example, π^2 and $\pi^{\frac{1}{2}}$ are irrational numbers.

4 Decide whether each of the following expressions is rational or irrational.

   a $\pi + 3$ **b** π^3 **c** $\sqrt{\pi}$

   d 2π **e** $\dfrac{2\pi}{\pi}$ **f** $\dfrac{\pi}{4}$

5 A number y is irrational. For each of these, decide whether the expression is **(i)** always rational or **(ii)** always irrational, or **(iii)** could be rational or irrational.

   a $3y$ **b** y^2 **c** $\dfrac{5}{y} + 8$

6 Give a number between 4 and 5 that is irrational.

7 Find a number between 3 and 4 that has a rational square root.

8 x and y are both rational numbers.

   a Explain why $x = \dfrac{a}{b}$ and $y = \dfrac{c}{d}$ for some integers a, b, c and d.

   b Show that the following must be rational numbers.

      i xy ii $x + y$ iii $\dfrac{1}{x}$

Lengths and areas can be rational or irrational.

Example   Find the perimeter and area of triangle ABC, giving any
irrational lengths in surd form.
State whether each length is rational or irrational.

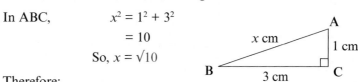

In ABC, $x^2 = 1^2 + 3^2$
                       $= 10$
        So, $x = \sqrt{10}$

> $\sqrt{10}$ is the exact value for x.
> Writing x correct to a
> number of decimal places
> does not give its exact value.

Therefore:

◆ Perimeter of ABC = $1 + 3 + \sqrt{10}$
                           $= 4 + \sqrt{10}$ cm

which is **irrational**.

◆ Area of   ABC = $(1 \times 3) \div 2$
                         $= \frac{3}{2}$ cm²

which is **rational**.

Exercise 7.8
Length and area

1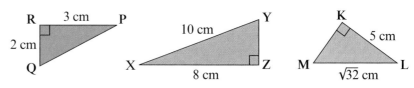

a Find the perimeter of triangle PQR, giving your answer in surd form.
b Which of these triangles has:
  i a rational perimeter   **ii** a rational area?

2 Triangle ABC is isosceles.

a Calculate the height of triangle ABC.
b Write down the exact value of:
  i $\sin \theta$ **ii** $\cos \theta$ **iii** $\tan \theta$

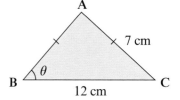

3 A circle passes through the vertices of a square as shown.
AB = 2 metres.
AC passes through the centre of the circle.

Write down exact values for each of these
and state whether they are rational or irrational:

a the diameter of the circle
b the perimeter of the square
c the circumference of the circle
d the area of the circle.

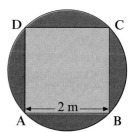

4 The midpoints of a square of side 8 cm
are joined to form another square.
This is repeated so that a pattern of
squares is formed.
Each square is labelled at one vertex.

a Calculate the perimeter of:
  i square 4   **ii** square 5.
b Which squares in this pattern
have an irrational perimeter?
Explain how you decided.
c Explain why the area of any square in this pattern is rational.

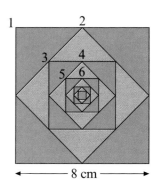

End points

You should be able to ...   ... so try these questions

A   Evaluate roots

A1   Evaluate:

    a $\sqrt[5]{243}$ **b** $\sqrt[3]{216}$ **c**   the fourth root of 16

B   Use rules for multiplying and dividing powers

B1   Copy and complete:

    a $2^4 \times 2^{\square} = 2^{12}$ **b** $\dfrac{3^4}{3^{\square}} = \dfrac{1}{3^2}$ **c** $(7^2)^{\square} = 7^6$

B2   Simplify:

    a $2x^3 \times x^4$ **b** $\dfrac{x^6}{x^2}$ **c** $(3x^3)^4$

C   Work with indices

C1   Evaluate these as integers or in fractional form.

    a $100^{\frac{1}{2}}$ **b** $64^{\frac{2}{3}}$ **c** $32^{-\frac{3}{5}}$

C2   Solve these equations.

    a $27^x = 3$ **b** $6^x = \dfrac{1}{36}$ **c** $81^x = \dfrac{1}{3}$

D   Simplify square roots

D1   Simplify these as far as you can.

    a $\sqrt{2} \times \sqrt{5}$ **b** $\sqrt{32}$ **c** $(3\sqrt{7})^2$ **d** $(\sqrt{3} - \sqrt{2})^2$

E   Decide if a number is rational or irrational

E1   Write the recurring decimal 0.272727 ... as a fraction.

E2   Decide, giving reasons, whether each of these is rational or irrational.

    a $\sqrt{8}$ **b** $7^{-3} + 7^{-2}$ **c** $6^{\frac{1}{4}}$

    d $(\sqrt{2} + \sqrt{8})^2$ **e** $(\sqrt{5} - \sqrt{3})^2$ **f** $\sqrt{6\frac{1}{4}}$

E3   This pattern consists of a set of six right-angled triangles as shown. Each triangle is labelled.

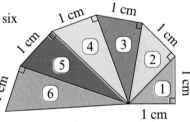

    a   In surd form, how long is the hypotenuse in:

      i   triangle 1

      ii   triangle 2?

    b   Which of the triangles has a hypotenuse of rational length ?

    c   If the pattern was continued, would the length of the hypotenuse in triangle 16 be rational or irrational? Explain your answer.

Some points to remember

Rules for indices:

    ♦ $a^m \times a^n = a^{m+n}$ ♦ $a^{-m} = \dfrac{1}{a^m}$

    ♦ $a^m \div a^n = a^{m-n}$ ♦ $a^{\frac{m}{n}} = \sqrt[n]{a^m}$

    ♦ $(a^m)^n = a^{mn}$

Rules for square roots   ♦ $\sqrt{a} \times \sqrt{b} = \sqrt{ab}$ ♦ $\sqrt{\dfrac{a}{b}} = \dfrac{\sqrt{a}}{\sqrt{b}}$

A **rational** number is a number that can be written in the form $\dfrac{a}{b}$, where a and b are integers.

Starting points

You need to know about ...

... so try these questions

A Decimal places for rounding

♦ Numbers can be approximated to a set number of decimal places.

Examples

32.3743 to 2 decimal places (2 dp) is **32.37**.
32.3753 to 2 dp is **32.38** (5, or greater, in this position rounds the 7 up).

34.496 to 2 dp is **34.50** (the 6 makes 49 one larger, i.e. 50).

102.49981 to 3 dp is **102.500** (3 places after the point must be shown).

B Significant figures for rounding

♦ Rounding to a set of significant figures is another form of approximating. This is the most natural way to round.

Examples

32.3743 to 2 significant figures (2 sf) is **32**.
32.5743 to 2 sf is **33** (5, or greater, in this position rounds the 2 up).

34.496 to 3 sf is **34.5**.

0.0002756 to 2 sf is **0.00028**.

346534.7945 to 3 sf is **347000** and to 7 sf is **346534.80**.

C Calculating with indices

♦ When two index numbers are multiplied their powers are added.
Examples
$$6^5 \times 6^3 = 6^8$$
$$10^8 \times 10^{-3} = 10^5$$
$$4^{-6} \times 4^{-3} = 4^{-9}$$

♦ When two index numbers are divided their powers are subtracted.
Examples
$$6^7 \div 6^2 = 6^5$$
$$10^{-5} \div 10^2 = 10^{-7}$$

♦ When an index numbers is itself raised to a further power the powers are multiplied.
Example
$$(10^3)^4 = 10^{12}$$
$$(8^{-3})^2 = 8^{-6}$$

D Standard form

♦ Very large numbers or very small ones are often expressed in standard form. The first part is a number between 1 and 10 and the second part is a power of ten.

Examples

Number	In standard form
15000000	1.5×10^7
0.00000000254	2.54×10^{-9}
523800	5.238×10^5
0.04	4×10^{-2}
146.356	1.46356×10^2

A1 Round each number to 2 dp.
  a 23.4671   b 4.1627
  c 142.855   d 12.2962

A2 Round each number to 1 dp.
  a 56.48932   b 0.33928
  c 5.9642   d 599.999

B1 Round each number to 2 sf.
  a 146   b 15.634
  c 3425.7   d 6.2521
  e 0.35726   f 1097423

B2 Round each number to 1 sf.
  a 32.87   b 167.2
  c 0.04914   d 473524
  e 96.65   f 0.000086

C1 Calculate the following leaving your answers in index notation.
  a $8^7 \times 8^3$ b $6^6 \div 6^4$
  c $10^6 \div 10^8$ d $10^{-4} \times 10^2$
  e $4^{-4} \times 4^{-6}$ f $10^{-6} \div 10^{-8}$
  g $(5^2)^4$ h $(6^4)^{-3}$

D1 Write each number in standard form.
  a 345000   b 0.00417
  c 42.97   d 4 million
  e 0.0000023   f 6413.234

D2 Convert these standard form numbers to normal numbers.
  a 6.74×10^3
  b 1.5×10^{-4}
  c 6.5241×10^2
  d 2×10^{-7}

Limits of accuracy

> The tolerance is the amount by which a value may vary.

> The sign $\pm$ means **plus or minus**. So D is 74 miles, plus or minus 3 miles.

- Any measurement is only approximate because it is only as accurate as the instrument used to make it.

- Measurements are often given as having a certain tolerance.
  You may measure the distance between Bristol and Oxford as 74 miles but mean it is 74 miles with a tolerance of 3 miles because your mileometer can have an error of 3 miles (i.e. the distance is between 71 and 77 miles).

  This can be written as $D = 74 \pm 3$ or as $71 \leqslant D \leqslant 77$
  where D is the distance in miles.

  The numbers 71 and 77 are known as the **bounds** between which the distance can lie.

- Because of the problem of accuracy, measured values are rounded to a certain number of decimal places or significant figures.

  Example A pencil measured as 12.6 cm to the nearest millimetre can have a true length anywhere between 12.55 cm and 12.65 cm.

  The value 12.55 is known as the **lower bound** and 12.65 as the **upper bound**.

Exercise 8.1
Limits of accuracy

1 Steve buys a piece of material of length 3 metres, correct to the nearest centimetre. What is the minimum length of the material?

2 Alison has a piece of wood of length 15.6 cm, correct to the nearest millimetre. What are:
   a the maximum length it could be
   b its minimum length?

3 Australia has a land area of 7 700 000 km² to the nearest 100 000 km².
   a What is the upper bound for the land area.
   b State the lower bound.
   c Write an inequality in L for the range of values for the land area.

4 The thickness t of a sheet of steel is given as 0.17 mm $\pm$ 0.01 mm.
   Write an inequality in t for the range of values the thickness can have.

Errors or approximations for measured values are often increased when these measurements are used in a calculation.

> In Example 1 the length and width are both given correct to 3 sf but, surprisingly, the answer is only accurate to 2 sf.
>
> A volume would be even more inaccurate as three lengths are multiplied – but it is interesting to consider how an answer can be less accurate than 1 sf!

Example 1 A machine can cut card to the nearest millimetre.
A card is to be cut 12.2 cm wide by 16.5 cm long.
What are the maximum and minimum areas the card can have?

> The width can lie between 12.15 cm and 12.25 cm and the length between 16.45 and 16.55 cm.
>
> So **the maximum area of card = 12.25 × 16.55 = 202.7375 cm²**
> and **the minimum area of card = 12.15 × 16.45 = 199.8675 cm²**.

In this case, the maximum and minimum areas only appear similar when they are both given to 2 sf (i.e. area = 200 cm² to 2 sf).

Example 2

A cylinder has a volume of 640 cm³ correct to 2 sf.
Ezra measures its height h to the nearest millimetre as 9.3 cm.
Between what bounds does the radius r of the cylinder lie?

> The volume of the cylinder is given by $V = \pi r^2 h$
>
> Rearranging gives $r^2 = \dfrac{V}{\pi h}$
>
> **For upper bound**   **For lower bound**
>
> $r^2 = \dfrac{645}{\pi \times 9.25}$ $r^2 = \dfrac{635}{\pi \times 9.35}$
>
> $r^2 = 22.195\,662\,33\,\ldots$ $r^2 = 21.617\,837\,19\,\ldots$
>
> $r = 4.711\,227\,264\,\ldots$ cm $r = 4.649\,498\,596\,\ldots$

Note that for the upper bound, the greatest value of V is taken but the smallest value of h is used – because dividing by a smaller number gives a larger answer.

Here, the difference between the upper and lower bounds for r is about 6 hundredths of a centimetre.

Exercise 8.2
Accuracy in calculations

1 A box of cornflakes weighs 805 grams. The empty box weighs 55 grams. Both weights are only accurate to the nearest 5 grams.
Calculate:

  a the maximum weight of cornflakes in the box
  b the minimum weight of cornflakes.

2 Twelve volumes of an encyclopedia are placed on a shelf.
Volumes 1 to 6 are each 3.5 cm wide and volumes 7 to 12 are each 4.3 cm wide, all measurements being to the nearest millimetre.

  a What is the lower bound for the width of all twelve volumes?
  b Calculate the difference between the upper and lower bounds.

3 A triangular field has the measurements shown. Each side has been measured to the nearest metre.

  a Calculate the range of possible values for the length L of the hedge to the nearest metre.
    Express this as an inequality in L.
  b Calculate the lower bound for the angle θ.

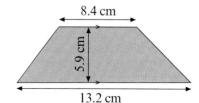

4 A rectangular badminton court measures 13.40 metres by 6.10 metres where measurements are taken correct to two decimal places.

Calculate the upper and lower bounds for:
  a the area of the court
  b the perimeter of the court.

5 The area of a trapezium is given by $A = \dfrac{h(a + b)}{2}$

where h is the perpendicular height and a and b are the lengths of the parallel sides.

Calculate the range of values for the area of this trapezium if all the measurements are given correct to 1 dp.

Using significant figures to estimate answers

One way to check if a calculation gives an answer of about the right size is to round each of the numbers to 1 sf.

Example
Here are some answers given by four students when they had to calculate the value of **43183.5 × 184.23** without using a calculator.

a 795 569.6   **b** 79 556 962   **c** 7 955 696   **d** 79 557

Which answer is likely to be most accurate?

> A value which is of the correct order of magnitude is about the right size.

To 1 sf these numbers become $40\,000 \times 200$
which is $40\,000 \times 2 \times 100$
$= 80\,000 \times 100$
$= \mathbf{8\,000\,000}$

Answer **c** (7 955 696) is about the same order of magnitude as 8 000 000 so it is most likely to be most accurate.

Exercise 8.3
Estimating answers

1   Work out estimates of the answers to each of these.
Show all the stages you use.

a	31.2 × 241.45	**b**	5677 × 3.764
c	54 856 × 83.42	**d**	542 × 52
e	56 234 ÷ 82.5	**f**	62 381.23 ÷ 578.23
g	452 ÷ 2.34	**h**	28 536 ÷ 0.9623

2   A theatre sells 562 tickets at £28.50 each.

a   Roughly what is their income from ticket sales?
b   Why does rounding both numbers to 1 sf give too large an estimate?

> Population density means the average (mean) number of people to each square kilometre.

3   France has a land area of 549 619 km².
In 1990 the population was 56 304 000.
Estimate the population density in people per km².

4   When the numbers in 341.2 × 14.25 are rounded to 1 sf and then multiplied the estimate is much smaller than the true answer.
For the problem 156 ÷ 34.7 the estimate is much larger.
Explain why.

5   For each of these problems, say if rounding all numbers to 1 sf makes estimates too large, too small, or about the right size.

a	56.5 × 1763.2	**b**	184 ÷ 19.6
c	491.432 × 2061.4	**d**	445 × 84 632
e	2265 ÷ 27.7	**f**	6834 ÷ 14.23
g	453 782 + 242 565	**h**	7452.3 − 2837.324

6   For the problem 342 561 + 453, why is rounding to 1 sf not helpful?

7   In problems which only use addition and subtraction, when is rounding to 1 sf useful for finding an estimate?

Working with numbers less than 1

Example 1   Estimate the value of **342 × 0.052**.

> Approximating to 1 sf, this becomes 300 × 0.05.
> The answer to this estimate will be smaller than 300.
> One way to work out the value is to look for patterns.
>
> 300 × 5 = 1500
> 300 × 0.5 = 150
> 300 × 0.05 = 15   **So the estimate is 15**.

Example 2   Estimate for the value of **26 ÷ 0.0056**.

> To 1 sf this is: 30 ÷ 0.006.
> 30 ÷ 6   = 5
> 30 ÷ 0.6   = 50
> 30 ÷ 0.06   = 500
> 30 ÷ 0.006   = 5000   **So the estimate is 5000.**

Exercise 8.4
Calculating and
estimating answers

1   **a**   Calculate 342 × 52 without a calculator.
  b   Use the example above to help decide what 342 × 0.052 is.

2   Estimate the value of 45 × 0.0023. Show all the stages you use.
  Calculate the exact answer and check it with your estimate.

3   Estimate then calculate the values of these.

  a $346.3 \div 0.04$ **b** 26.23×0.67 **c** $876.2 \times 0.000\,23$

  d $2.448 \div 0.0018$ **e** $\dfrac{2567.245 \times 0.032}{54.23}$ **f** $\dfrac{78.4567 - 7.64}{0.0421}$

4   Estimate the volumes of these cuboids. Show the rounding you do.

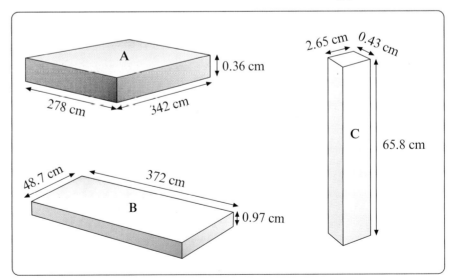

5   A cuboid is 113.6 cm long, 0.42 cm deep and has a volume of 18.42 cm³.
  Estimate its width.

Errors in calculations

Rounding at the start of a calculation is fine for a rough check, but for an accurate answer you should only round at the end.

Example   What error is produced in the value of P when numbers are rounded to 1 dp before the calculation $P = 3.342 \times 12.437 \times 1.629$?

Using the values given: $\quad P = 3.342 \times 12.437 \times 1.629$
$$= 67.708\,495\,57$$
Rounding all numbers to 1 dp at the start:
$$P = 3.3 \times 12.4 \times 1.6$$
$$= 65.472$$
The error made by rounding to 1 dp is $67.708\,495\,57 - 65.472$.
Error = 2.236 495 57

This error is known as the absolute error.
It is often more useful to consider **percentage error** which is given by:

$$\text{Percentage error} = \frac{\text{Absolute error}}{\text{True value}} \times 100$$

In the case above: Percentage error $= \dfrac{2.236\,495\,57}{67.708\,495\,57} \times 100$

$$= \textbf{3.3\%} \text{ (to 1 dp)}$$

The absolute error is less useful because it does not take into account the size of the true value.

For example, an error of 2 cm in a length of 6 cm is more significant than an error of 2 cm in a length of 306 cm.

An error of 3.3% would be very large if you were dealing with, for instance, the capacity of a fuel tank for a rocket. In other situations, such as for the volume of a compost heap, it would not be significant.

Exercise 8.5
Percentage error

1   For $P = 3.342 \times 12.437 \times 1.629$:
   a   round all the numbers to 2 dp and calculate the value of P using the rounded values
   b   calculate the absolute error and percentage error this gives
   c   round the numbers to the nearest whole number and calculate the percentage error this gives in the value of P.

2   Through history different approximations have been used for the value of π:
   a   Egypt $\left(\frac{16}{9}\right)^2$
   b   China $\frac{355}{113}$
   c   Rome $\frac{25}{8}$
   d   Greece $3\frac{1}{7}$

   Calculate the percentage error each of these approximations gives compared with the value of π given by your calculator.
   Which is the most accurate approximation?

Note that the value of π given by your calculator is also an approximation because π is an irrational number: a non-repeating, infinitely long number.

3 **a** Use a calculator to work out the value of R where $R = \dfrac{3.06 \times (9.81)^3}{257 + 312}$

   b **i** Write down a calculation which could be done mentally to find the value of R.

      ii What value does this give for R?

   c Calculate the percentage error that this approximation gives.

4 The volume of a cylinder is calculated using the height h and the base radius r.

When the cylinder is measured, each measurement of h and r is subject to a maximum percentage error of 3%.

What maximum percentage error will the volume be subject to?

Calculating with numbers in standard form

Calculations with very large numbers can be estimated by approximating each part to a number of significant figures and then using standard form.

Example 1 The land area of Australia is $7\,682\,300\,km^2$ and its population is $16\,260\,400$. Singapore has a land area of $580\,km^2$ and a population of $2\,645\,400$.

How do the population densities compare?

> For Australia:
> Rounding to 2 sf gives populations $16\,000\,000$ and area as $7\,700\,000\,km^2$.
>
> $$\text{Population density} = \frac{\text{Population}}{\text{Land area}} = \frac{1.6 \times 10^7}{7.7 \times 10^6} = 0.21 \times 10 \text{ (to 2 sf)}$$
>
> $$= 2.1 \text{ people per kilometre}^2.$$
>
> For Singapore:
> Rounding to 2 sf gives population as $2\,600\,000$ and area as $580\,km^2$.
>
> $$\text{Population density} = \frac{2.6 \times 10^6}{5.8 \times 10^2} = 0.45 \times 10^4 \text{ (to 2 sf)}$$
>
> $$= 4500 \text{ people per kilometre}^2.$$
>
> Singapore therefore has a population density over 2000 times as great as that of Australia.

> When powers of ten are divided their indices are subtracted. For example:
>
> $$10^7 \div 10^6 = 10^1 \text{ or } 10$$
> $$10^6 \div 10^2 = 10^4$$

Example 2 The mass M of Jupiter is $1.25 \times 10^{27}\,kg$ and it has a radius of $71\,942\,km$. Use this formula to find its density.

$$\text{Density} = \frac{M}{\frac{4}{3}\pi r^3}$$

> When powers of ten are raised to a further power the indices are multiplied. For example:
>
> $$(10^4)^3 = 10^{12}$$

> $$\text{Density} = \frac{1.25 \times 10^{27}}{\frac{4}{3} \times \pi \times (7.2 \times 10^4)^3} = \frac{3 \times 1.25 \times 10^{27}}{4 \times \pi \times (7.2)^3 \times 10^{12}}$$
>
> $$= 0.000\,799\,51 \times 10^{15}.$$
>
> $$= \mathbf{8 \times 10^{11}\ kg\ km^{-3}\ (2\ sf).}$$

Exercise 8.6
Using standard form

1 When lightning strikes the Earth there is a lead stroke which travels down at about $1.6 \times 10^2\,km$ per second and a brighter return stroke which flashes up at about $1.4 \times 10^5\,km$ per second.

How many times faster is the return stroke than the lead stroke?

2   The Earth is approximately 1.5×10^8 km from the Sun.
Light travels at about 3×10^5 km per second.

How long does it take light from the Sun to reach the Earth?

3   The Earth can be considered to have a circular orbit around the Sun of
radius 149 600 000 km. Earth travels through space at 107 244 km per hour.

   a   Approximate the speed and radius to 3 sf and write
each in standard form.
   b   Use your figures to find roughly how long in hours the Earth
takes to make one orbit. What do we call this length of time?

4   A ream of paper is a stack of 500 sheets.
Each sheet of paper is 0.000 096 metres thick.

   a   Write 500 and 0.000 096 in standard form.
   b   Use your answers to part **a** to calculate the height of a ream of paper.

5   The mass of one atom of carbon is about 2×10^{-23} grams and the mass
of an oxygen atom is 2.66×10^{-23} grams.
A molecule of carbon dioxide gas (CO_2) has two atoms of oxygen and
one atom of carbon.

   a   Calculate the mass of one carbon dioxide molecule.
   b   Calculate the number of molecules in 1 gram of carbon dioxide gas.

6   The Amazon river discharges 1.05×10^{13} litres of water per minute
into the Atlantic.
There are estimated to be about 5.74×10^9 people alive today.

COLD BATHS FOR EVERYONE EVERY MINUTES

How long would it take the Amazon to fill a bath of 80 litres for every
person on Earth?

7   The largest gasholder in the world is at Simmering near Vienna.
It is shaped like a cylinder, stands 84 metres tall, and holds 3×10^5 cubic
metres of gas.
Calculate the diameter of the gasholder in metres giving your
answer in standard form.

8   4×10^4 tonnes of cosmic dust are estimated to fall on the Earth each year.
The Earth has a diameter of about 1.3×10^7 metres.

   a   Taking the Earth as a sphere, estimate its surface area giving your
answer in standard form to 2 sf.
   b   How much cosmic dust falls on each square metre of the
Earth's surface each year?

The volume V of a cylinder
is given by:

$$V = \pi r^2 h$$

where h is its height and r
is its base radius.

The surface area A of a
sphere is given by:

$$A = 4\pi r^2$$

where r is its radius.

End points

You should be able to ...   ... so try these questions

A Understand upper and lower bounds

A1 A cylinder has a diameter of 6.7 cm and a height of 9.8 cm, both measurements given to the nearest millimetre.
  a What is the upper bound of the diameter?
  b What is the lower bound of the cylinders height?
  c Calculate the range of values for the volume of the cylinder.
  d Calculate the upper bound for the curved surface area of the cylinder.

B Use significant figures to estimate answers

B1 By rounding numbers to 1 significant figure estimate the value of each of these:
  a 6453×48.734 **b** $765.27 \div 0.000\,342$
  c $\dfrac{4.645 \times 0.000\,32}{34.82}$ **d** $\dfrac{0.259 \times 0.422}{0.000\,872}$

C Calculate percentage errors in calculations

C1 To work out an estimate for A in the problem below Sonia rounds every number first to 1 sf then does the calculation in her head.

$$A = \frac{(4.653 + 3.842)^3 \times 106.3}{45.2175}$$

  a What is Sonia's estimate of the answer?
  b What percentage error does she make?

D Calculate with numbers in standard form

D1 The Strahov sports stadium in Prague can hold 2.4×10^5 spectators. If the average mass of a spectator is 5.4×10^{-2} tonnes calculate the total mass of the spectators when the stadium is full.

Some points to remember

- When a number is written as say 8.6 correct to 1 decimal place its true value can actually lie anywhere between 8.55 and 8.65.
  8.55 is known as the **lower bound** and 8.65 as the **upper bound**.

- One method to calculate an estimate of the answer to a calculation is to round every number to 1 sf at the start. Beware: it is not sensible to give these answers to more than 1 sf.

- The percentage error is given by: Percentage error $= \dfrac{\text{Absolute error}}{\text{True value}} \times 100$

Starting points

You need to know about ...

A Expanding brackets

Expressions are often written including brackets.
By multiplying the terms you can remove, or expand, the brackets.

To remove the brackets from the expression $(y + 4)(y - 5)$ you can:

♦ Use a table

×	y	$+4$
y	y^2	$+4y$
-5	$-5y$	-20

The table gives: $y^2 + 4y - 5y - 20$
Simplified gives: $y^2 - y - 20$
So removing the brackets we have: $(y + 4)(y - 5) = y^2 - y - 20$

♦ Multiply each term in the second bracket by each term in the first bracket.

This gives:
$$(y + 4)(y - 5) = y(y - 5) + 4(y - 5)$$
$$= y^2 - 5y + 4y - 20$$
$$= y^2 - y - 20$$

With a systematic approach you can deal with more than two brackets.
Remove the brackets from the expression $(n + 2)(n - 3)(2n + 1)$:
$$(n + 2)(n - 3)(2n + 1) = (n + 2)(2n^2 - 5n - 3)$$
$$= 2n^3 - 5n^2 - 3n + 4n^2 - 10n - 6$$
$$= 2n^3 - n^2 - 13n - 6$$

B Factorising quadratic expressions

To factorise an expression is to find two, or more, other expressions which when multiplied together produce the original expression.

♦ As $(y + 4)(y - 5) = y^2 - y - 20$
we say that $(y + 4)$ and $(y - 5)$ are factors of $y^2 - y - 20$
Factorising $y^2 - y - 20$ gives: $y^2 - y - 20 = (y + 4)(y - 5)$

♦ You can factorise expressions like $3n^2 + 2n - 8$ where the coefficient of n^2 is greater than 1.
Factorising $3n^2 + 2n - 8$ gives: $3n^2 + 2n - 8 = (3n - 4)(n + 2)$

♦ In general terms if you think of a quadratic expression as:
$$ax^2 + bx + c$$

Factorising gives:

$$\text{(factor of } ax + \text{ factor of } c)(\text{factor of } ax + \text{ factor of } c)$$

We must ensure that the factors of a and the factors of c are chosen so that they can be combined to give the value of b.

Factorising the expression $5x^2 - 8x - 4$ gives:

$$5x^2 - 8x - 3 = (5x + 2)(x - 2)$$

The factors of 5 are 5×1, the factors of 4 are 4×1, or 2×2
A total of $^-8$ cannot be made combining 5 and 1 with 4 and 1.
Combining 5 and 1 with 2 and 2 we have:

$$5 \times {}^-2 = {}^-10, 1 \times 2 = 2 \text{ and } {}^-10 + 2 = {}^-8$$

A1 Expand the brackets and simplify these expressions.
 a $(y + 3)(y + 5)$
 b $(k - 4)(k + 3)$
 c $(n + 3)(n - 9)$
 d $(w - 5)(w - 4)$
 e $(v - 8)(v + 8)$

A2 Remove the brackets and simplify these expressions.
 a $(2n + 3)(n - 4)$
 b $(w - 8)(3w + 2)$
 c $(3y - 4)(4y - 3)$
 d $(2k - 3)^2$
 e $(3v + 1)(v^2 - 3)$

A3 Remove the brackets and simplify these expressions.
 a $2y(y - 3)(y + 2)$
 b $3x(x + 1)^2$
 c $(x + 1)(x - 3)(x + 5)$
 d $(2n - 1)(2n - 3)(n + 1)$
 e $(x + 2)^3$
 f $(k - 3)(4 - 2k)(k + 2)$

B1 Factorise these expressions.
 a $y^2 + 9y + 14$
 b $k^2 - 3k - 40$
 c $x^2 + 4x - 12$
 d $w^2 + 5w - 36$
 e $x^2 - 11x + 24$
 f $y^2 - 9y + 8$
 g $p^2 + 7p - 60$
 h $b^2 + b - 72$
 i $x^2 - 16x + 48$
 j $n^2 - 25$
 k $y^2 - 100$
 l $a^2 - b^2$
 m $4y^2 - 36$
 n $16x^2 - 36y^2$
 o $100a^2 - b^4$

C Solving linear equations

Linear equations can be solved by manipulating the terms of the equation so that the unknown is equated to a value.

Manipulation can be thought of as keeping the equation balanced. This can be seen when the equation $5x - 8 = 3x + 5$ is solved.

$$5x - 8 = 3x + 5$$
[+8] $5x = 3x + 13$
[−3x] $2x = 13$
[÷2]   **$x = 6.5$**

Manipulation can also involve dealing with brackets or fractions.
Dealing with brackets.

Solve the equation $3(4x + 1) = 5(x - 3)$
[Remove the brackets] $12x + 3 = 5x - 15$
[−3] $12x = 5x - 18$
[−5x] $7x = {^-}18$
[÷7]   **$x = {^-}2.57$** (2 dp) or $x = \frac{^-18}{7}$

Dealing with fractions.

Solve the equation $\frac{3}{4}(x - 2) = \frac{1}{2}(3x - 4)$
[Multiply each side by 4] $3(x - 2) = 2(3x - 4)$
[Remove the brackets] $3x - 6 = 6x - 8$
[+6] $3x = 6x - 2$
[−6x] ${^-}3x = {^-}2$
[÷ ${^-}3$]   **$x = 0.67$** (2 dp) or $x = \frac{2}{3}$

D Forming linear equations from problems

A problem given in words can often be solved by creating and solving a linear equation. This will be possible if one unknown is chosen and any other unknowns expressed in terms of the one unknown.

This can be seen when this problem is solved.

Lisa is 4 years younger than her sister Emma and 19 years older than her daughter Nicole. Together their ages total 96. How old is each of them?

Let Lisa be n years old.
Emma is 4 years older than Lisa i.e. $n + 4$
Nicole is 19 years younger than Lisa i.e. $n - 19$

Their ages total 96, so we have:
$$n + n + 4 + n - 19 = 96$$
$$3n - 15 = 96$$
[+15] $3n = 111$
[÷3] $n = 37$

This gives:

Lisa (n) is   **37 years old**
Emma ($n + 4$) is   **41 years old**
Nicole ($n - 19$) is   **18 years old**

You can check your answer to this sort of problem, as follows.

The total of the three ages is:
$$37 + 41 + 18 = 96$$
and 96 is the total for the ages given in the problem.

C1 Solve these linear equations.
   a $9y + 5 = 5y - 13$
   b $y - 8 = 11y - 42$
   c $3(4x - 5) = 9$
   d $28 = 7(3x - 5)$
   e $19 - 4x = 3(2x - 7)$

C2 Solve these linear equations.
   a $5(4x + 2) = 3(2x - 6)$
   b $8(2 - 3n) = 4(2n + 1)$
   c $7(w + 3) = 12(w - 7)$
   d $2(3k + 3) = 9(5k - 8)$
   e $6(9v - 2) = 5(6v + 8)$

C3 Solve these linear equations.
   a $\frac{2}{3}(3y + 1) = 18$
   b $\frac{3}{5}(3u - 4) = 12$
   c $\frac{5}{8}(2k + 4) = 15$
   d $\frac{1}{4}(8h - 12) = 21$
   e $\frac{7}{10}(4a - 5) = 2.1$

C4 Solve these linear equations.
   a $\frac{3}{5}(2w - 1) = \frac{1}{3}(3w - 6)$
   b $\frac{2}{3}(k + 1) = \frac{3}{4}(2k - 3)$
   c $\frac{1}{2}(8n - 4) = \frac{1}{3}(4n - 5)$

D1 A rectangle is 6 centimetres longer than it is wide.
The rectangle has a perimeter of 48 cm.

Write and solve an equation to find the length and width of the rectangle.

D2 In a game a player was asked to think of a number and add seven, then to multiply the answer by three.
The player answered 81.

Write and solve an equation to find the number the player first thought of.

D3 Three buses took fans to a match. Bus A carried 9 more fans than bus B. Bus C carried 3 fewer fans than bus A.

The three buses carried a total of 147 fans.

Write and solve an equation to find the number of fans on each bus.

Thinking ahead to ...
solving simultaneous
linear equations

A   In a cafe, two teas and 4 coffees cost £4.60.
From this information:

a   Calculate the cost of one tea and two coffees. Explain your method.
b   Calculate the cost of three teas and six coffees. Explain your method.
c   Explain why the cost of six teas and eight coffees cannot easily be calculated.

B   In a shop:
1 cola and 3 bags of crisps cost £1.52
2 colas and 4 bags of crisps cost £2.48.
Find the cost of:

a   3 colas and 7 bags of crisps   **b**   1 cola and 1 bag of crisps
c   1 bag of crisps   **d**   1 cola.

Solving simultaneous linear equations

When a linear relationship between two variables can be expressed by two or more different equations, you can find the value of each variable by solving the equations simultaneously.

One way to solve these equations is algebraically, the most common being a combination of elimination and substitution.

Example

Find the values of a and b that satisfy the equations:

$$2a + b = 19$$
$$3a + 4b = 26$$

♦ Label the equations (1) and (2):

$$2a + b = 19 \text{ ... (1)}$$
$$3a + 4b = 26 \text{ ... (2)} -$$

♦ Eliminate one variable by making the coefficients of a or b the same in both equations.
In this case multiply equation (1) by 4 (to eliminate b)

$$8a + 4b = 76 \text{ ... (3)}$$
$$3a + 4b = 26 \text{ ... (2)}$$

> The coefficients of b are now 4 in each of the equations (3) and (2).

♦ Subtract (2) from (3) to eliminate b

$$5a = 50$$

♦ Find the value of a:

$$a = 10$$

♦ Substitute the value of a in one equation

$$2a + b = 19$$
$$2(10) + b = 19$$
$$20 + b = 19$$
$$b = {}^-1$$

♦ Check your solution in one other equation
When $a = 10$ and $b = {}^-1$

$$3a + 4b = 26 \text{ ... (2)}$$

LHS gives $3(10) + 4({}^-1) = 26 = $ RHS

Exercise 9.1
Solving simultaneous
equations

1   Solve each pair of equations simultaneously to find values for x and y.

a $x + 4y = 42$
   $2x + 5y = 57$

b $11x + 3y = 91$
   $3x + y = 25$

c $5x + 7y = 44$
   $x + 3y = 12$

d $5x + 3y = 7$
   $4x + y = 7$

e $12x + 5y = {}^-9$
   $5x + y = {}^-7$

f $8x + y = 20$
   $11x + 4y = 17$

2 To find a value of m and n that satisfies these equations:

$$2m + 3n = 28 \ldots (1)$$
$$3m + 4n = 37 \ldots (2)$$

a Multiply equation (1) by 3.
b Multiply equation (2) by 2.
c Subtract and find a value for n that satisfies both equations.
d Substitute for n in one equation to find a value for m.
e Check your solutions are correct.

In these equations the only way to make the coefficients of one variable the same, is to multiply each equation by a different value.

This means that you create two new equations which you can label (3) and (4).

3 Solve each pair of equations.

a $2v + 3w = 40$
   $5v + 2w = 34$

b $3v + 2w = 3$
   $6v + 10w = 24$

c $4v + 2w = 8$
   $3v + 7w = {}^-5$

d $3v + 5w = 19$
   $2v + 4w = 14$

e $2v + 3w = 3$
   $3v + 5w = 4$

f $8v + 4w = 16$
   $3v + 3w = 3$

g $6v + 3w = 9$
   $4v + 5w = 3$

h $11v + 2w = 17$
   $2v + 3w = 11$

i $7v + 4w = 1$
   $2v + 3w = 4$

Sometimes to eliminate one variable when the coefficients are the same you have to add two equations.

Example

Find the values of x and y that satisfy the equations:

$$6x - 2y = 18 \ldots (1)$$
$$5x + 3y = 1 \ldots (2)$$

♦ Make the coefficients of y the same by multiplying: (1) $\times$ 3 and (2) $\times$ 2

$$18x + 6y = 54 \ldots (3)$$
$$10x + 6y = 2 \ldots (4)$$

♦ Eliminate y by adding: (3) + (4)

$$28x = 56$$

♦ Find x

$$\boldsymbol{x = 2}$$

♦ Substitute $x = 2$ in (1)

$$6(2) - 2y = 18$$
$$12 - 2y = 18$$
$$-2y = 6$$
$$\boldsymbol{y = {}^-3}$$

♦ Check $x = 2$ and $y = {}^-3$ in equation (2)

$$5x + 3y = 1 \ldots (2)$$

$$\text{LHS} = 5(2) + 3({}^-3) = 1 = \text{RHS}$$

Exercise 9.2
Solving simultaneous equations

1 Solve each pair of equations.

a $a - b = 8$
   $4a + b = 42$

b $5b + 2a = 29$
   $b - 2a = 1$

c $3a - b = 15$
   $4a + 2b = 10$

d $b + 3a = 2$
   $3b - a = 26$

e $5a + 2b = 17$
   $2a - 3b = 3$

f $7a + 5b = 22$
   $3a - 2b = 26$

g $3a + 2b = 4$
   $2a - 3b = 7$

h $5a - 2b = 24$
   $2a - 7b = 22$

i $7a + 3b = 15$
   $5a - 4b = 23$

j $4a + 5b = 13$
   $3a + 2b = 8$

k $3a - 4b = 18$
   $2a - 5b = 19$

l $5b + 3a = 17$
   $7b - 4a = 32$

2 Find values for k and n that satisfy $5k - n = 15$ and $3k - n = 5$.

In some cases you will need to rearrange one or more of the equations before you can begin to solve them simultaneously.

3 Find a value for m and n that satisfy the equation $5m - 2n = 28$, and also the equation $7m - 37 = 5n$.

4 Solve each pair of equations.

a $5x = 16 + 2y$
$2x = 3y + 2$

b $4y = x + 17$
$3y - 4x = 3$

c $5x = 7 + 3y$
$2x = 4y$

d $5y = 7 - 3x$
$7x = 3 - 5y$

e $3y = 17 - 4x$
$5x = 7y + 32$

f $3x = 13 - 2y$
$59 + 6y = 5x$

g $7y = 3x - 5$
$5y - 2 = 4x$

h $y + 31 = 9x$
$5x - 27 = 3y$

i $12x = 13 - 11y$
$5x + 8y = 2$

j $x = y + 8$
$29 + 4y = 3x$

k $4y = 5 - 3x$
$12 = 5y - 2x$

l $7y = 7 - 7x$
$11 - 2x = 5y$

Solving problems with simultaneous equations

From some problems you can create two equations with the variables. Solving the equations simultaneously will produce values that satisfy the problem.

Example

Two groups of friends met in a cafe. One group bought three teas and four coffees, this cost them a total of £5.35. The other group paid a total of £5.80 for five teas and three coffees.
Find the price charged in the cafe for coffee and tea.

◆ Decide on the variables:
    let the price of coffee be c (pence)
    and the price of tea be t (pence)

For ease of working you may prefer to work with integer values.

Here the 535 is the total for the first group in pence.

◆ Create two different equations.

    for the first group $3t - 4c = 535$
    the second group $5t + 3c = 580$

◆ Solve the equations:

$$3t + 4c = 535 \quad \dots (1)$$
$$5t + 3c = 580 \quad \dots (4)$$

Multiply (1) by 3 and (2) by 4 to eliminate c:

$$9t + 12c = 1605 \dots (3)$$
$$20t + 12c = 2320 \dots (4)$$

Subtract: (4) − (3)

$$11t = 715$$

Find t $\mathbf{t = 65}$

Substitute $t = 65$ in (1)

$$3t + 4c = 535 \quad \dots (1)$$
$$3(65) + 4c = 535$$
$$195 + 4c = 535$$

Find c $4c = 340$
         $\mathbf{c = 85}$

◆ Check in equation (2) $5t + 3c = 580$
LHS = 5(65) + 3(85) = 325 + 255 = 580 = RHS

The charge for coffee was 85 pence, and for tea was 65 pence.

Exercise 9.3
Solving problems

1 Two groups visited Waterworld. The first group of four adults and three children paid a total of £38 for their tickets. The second group of five adults and two children £40.50 for their tickets.
What are the charges for adult and child tickets at Waterworld?

When you check your answers it is always best to use the original word problem.

This is because you may have created an incorrect equation. This will not be shown up if you substitute your solutions in anything other than the original word problem.

2 Crispers is a snack food sold in bags of two sizes: regular and jumbo.
Three regular bags and four jumbo bags weigh a total of 264 g.
Five of each size weigh a total of 350 g.
Find the weight of each size of Crispers.

3 A bag contains 89 marbles. Some are large; some are small.
Each small marble weighs 2 g, and each large marble weighs 5 g.
The total weight of the marbles in the bag is 256 g.
a Write two different equations that describe this situation.
b Solve your equations to find the number of each marble type in the bag.

4 Mina pays her gas bill with a mixture of £5 and £10 notes.
Her gas bill is for £155, and she pays with a total of 22 notes.
How many of each type of note does she use to pay the bill?

5 A parking meter takes 10 p and 20 p coins. The meter was emptied and found to contain 380 coins with a total of £63.70.
How many of each type of coin were in the meter?

6 Two numbers are such that when you add three times one number to five times the other number a total of 46 is produced. The difference between the two numbers is 2.
What are the two numbers?

7 The line $y = mx + c$ passes through the points (3,10) and (5, 18).
Find the values of m and c.

8 A promoter sold 28 500 tickets for a pop concert. A standing ticket cost £8, and a ticket for a seat cost £12.50. All the tickets were sold and ticket sales produced a total of £283 350.
How many of each type of ticket were sold?

9 The line $mx + y = c$ passes through the points (2, 2) and (⁻1, 11).
a Find values of m and c.
b Give the equation of the line and one other point that lies on the line.

10 The curve $y = ax^2 + bx + c$ passes through the points (3, 13), (1, ⁻1) and (0, ⁻5).
a Find values for a, b, and c
b Give the equation of the curve.

11 The curve $y = ax^2 + bx + c$ passes through the points (1, 0), (0, 1) and (⁻1, 6).
a Find values for a, b, and c.
b Give the equation of the curve.

12 The curve $y - bx = ax^2 + c$ passes through the points (2, 6), (⁻1, 0),(⁻2, 10).
a Find values for a, b, and c.
b Give the equation of the curve.

13 Print Express print T-shirts. They have two printing machines: machine A prints 64 T-shirts an hour, and machine B prints 44 T-shirts an hour.
Print Express have an order for 1430 T-shirts and only a total of 25 hours to complete the printing.
For how many hours should they print T-shirts on each machine?

14 Two numbers are such that a half the larger number added to two thirds of the smaller number gives a total of sixteen.
What are the two numbers if they have a difference of ten?

Solving quadratic equations by inspection (factors)

Quadratic equations must have a term like x^2. Often they will have a term like $3x$ and a term which is a numerical value.

In general, quadratic equations have two different solutions or roots.

Example

- Solve the equation $\qquad\qquad\qquad\qquad x^2 + 5x - 14 = 0$

- Factorise $\qquad\qquad\qquad\qquad\qquad (x + 7)(x - 2) = 0$

  Here we have a situation where two brackets are multiplied to give an answer of zero. This is only possible if either, or both, of the brackets is equal to zero.

  In this case if $(x + 7)(x - 2) = 0$
  then: either $(x + 7) = 0$ or $(x - 2) = 0$
  which means $x = {}^-7$ or $x = 2$

- Solving the equation $\qquad\qquad\qquad x^2 + 5x - 14 = 0$
  gives $\qquad\qquad\qquad\qquad\qquad\mathbf{x = {}^-7 \text{ or } x = 2}$

Exercise 9.4
Solving quadratic equations by inspection

1 Solve these quadratic equations.

a $y^2 + 5y + 4 = 0$	**b** $y^2 + 9y + 18 = 0$	**c** $y^2 + 5y - 24 = 0$
d $x^2 + 6x - 7 = 0$	**e** $x^2 + 5x - 36 = 0$	**f** $x^2 + 2x - 63 = 0$
g $w^2 - 7w - 44 = 0$	**h** $w^2 - 8w - 105 = 0$	**i** $w^2 - 9w - 112 = 0$
j $a^2 - 8a + 15 = 0$	**k** $a^2 - 12a + 35 = 0$	**l** $a^2 - 11a + 30 = 0$
m $b^2 - 7b + 10 = 0$	**n** $b^2 + 31b + 84 = 0$	**o** $b^2 - 13b - 30 = 0$
p $c^2 + 7c - 60 = 0$	**q** $c^2 - 14c + 45 = 0$	**r** $c^2 + 12c - 45 = 0$
s $h^2 + h - 210 = 0$	**t** $h^2 - 2h - 399 = 0$	**u** $h^2 - 17h + 42 = 0$
v $n^2 + 3n - 180 = 0$	**w** $n^2 - 15n + 56 = 0$	**x** $n^2 - 9n - 136 = 0$

The basis of solving quadratics in this way is being able to factorise the quadratic equation that is given.
Remember that the equation might not be in the form: $ax^2 + bx + c = 0$

Example

Solve the equation $\qquad\qquad\qquad\qquad x^2 + 9x = 0$

- Factorise $\qquad\qquad\qquad\qquad\qquad\qquad x(x + 9) = 0$
  which means $\qquad\qquad\mathbf{x = 0 \text{ or } x = {}^-9}$

Example

- Solve the equation $\qquad\qquad\qquad\qquad x^2 - 49 = 0$

- Factorise $\qquad\qquad x^2 - 49$ is known as a difference of two squares the squares being x^2 and 49 (i.e. 7^2)

  $\qquad\qquad\qquad\qquad\qquad\qquad x^2 - 49 = 0$
  gives $\qquad\qquad\qquad\qquad (x + 7)(x - 7) = 0$
  which means $\qquad\qquad\mathbf{x = {}^-7 \text{ or } x = 7}$

> Factorising a difference of two squares always produces a result in the same format.
>
> Factorising $a^2 - b^2$ gives $(a + b)(a - b)$

Exercise 9.5
Solving quadratic equations

1 Solve these quadratic equations.

a $y^2 + 8y = 0$	**b** $y^2 - 5y = 0$	**c** $y^2 - 18y = 0$
d $h^2 - 100 = 0$	**e** $h^2 - 25 = 0$	**f** $h^2 - 81 = 0$

2 Solve these quadratic equations.

   a $x^2 - 12x = 0$ **b** $x^2 + 79x = 0$ **c** $3x^2 + x = 0$

   d $4x^2 - x = 0$ **e** $x^2 - 169 = 0$ **f** $x^2 - x = 0$

   g $5x^2 - 2x = 0$ **h** $4x^2 + 5x = 0$ **i** $7x^2 + 2x = 0$

Quadratic equations, where the coefficient of (say) x^2 is greater than 1, can also be solved by factorising.

Example

Solve the equation $6x^2 - 17x + 12 = 0$

◆ Factorise $(3x - 4)(2x - 3) = 0$

              which means   **$x = \frac{4}{3}$ or $x = \frac{3}{2}$**

Exercise 9.6
Solving quadratic equations

1 Solve these quadratic equations.

   a $12x^2 - 5x - 2 = 0$ **b** $6x^2 - 13x - 5 = 0$ **c** $4x^2 - 4x - 3 = 0$

   d $10y^2 - 3y - 1 = 0$ **e** $9y^2 + 9y - 4 = 0$ **f** $6y^2 - 7y + 2 = 0$

   g $9h^2 + 3h - 2 = 0$ **h** $14a^2 - 12a - 2 = 0$ **i** $12a^2 + 2a - 4 = 0$

   j $5c^2 - 11c + 2 = 0$ **k** $6c^2 + 16c - 6 = 0$ **l** $3c^2 - 16c + 16 = 0$

   m $4w^2 - 4w - 24 = 0$ **n** $6w^2 - 16w + 8 = 0$ **o** $12w^2 - 22w - 4 = 0$

2 Solve these equations.

   a $12x^2 - 6x = 0$ **b** $4x^2 - 12x = 0$ **c** $56x^2 + 14x = 0$

   d $5y^2 = 8y$ **e** $16y^2 = 8y$ **f** $25y^2 - 1 = 0$

   g $k^2 - \frac{1}{16} = 0$ **h** $3k^2 - 27k = 0$ **i** $5k = k^2$

   j $w^2 = w$ **k** $w^2 - \frac{1}{9} = 0$ **l** $3w^2 - 4w = 0$

   m $c^2 = 31c$ **n** $42c^2 - 18c = 0$ **o** $16c^2 - 9 = 0$

Solving quadratic equations using the formula

If a quadratic equation cannot be solved by factorising, a formula can be used to provide the solutions.

To solve the equation $ax^2 + bx + c = 0$ for x this formula is used:

$$x = \frac{^-b \pm \sqrt{(b^2 - 4ac)}}{2a}$$

> In the formula:
> a is the coefficient of the term in x^2
>
> b is the coefficient of the term in x
>
> c is the numerical or (constant) value.

Example

Solve the equation $3x^2 + 4x - 1 = 0$

◆ Using the formula:
   matching coefficients we have $a = 3, b = 4, c = ^-1$

> When you use the formula you need to check that:
> $b^2 - 4ac$
> gives a positive result.
>
> If $b^2 - 4ac$ gives a negative answer then $\sqrt{}$(negative) is not real. We say the equation has no real roots, so no solution is found.

The formula gives $x = \dfrac{^-4 \pm \sqrt{16 - (4 \times 3 \times ^-1)}}{(2 \times 3)}$

                      $x = \dfrac{^-4 \pm \sqrt{16 - (^-12)}}{6} = \dfrac{^-4 \pm \sqrt{28}}{6}$

                      $x = \dfrac{^-4 \pm 5.292}{6}$

So $x = \dfrac{^-4 + 5.292}{6} = \textbf{0.22}$ (2 dp) or $x = \dfrac{^-4 - 5.292}{6} = ^-\textbf{1.55}$ (2 dp)

Exercise 9.7
Solving quadratic
equations using the
formula

1 Use the formula to solve these quadratic equations.
Give your answers correct to two decimal places (2 dp).

a $2x^2 + 3x - 4 = 0$ b $4x^2 + 3x - 5 = 0$ c $x^2 + 3x - 5 = 0$
d $y^2 + 5y + 3 = 0$ e $2y^2 + 7y + 1 = 0$ f $5y^2 + 8y + 1 = 0$
g $3p^2 - 5p + 1 = 0$ h $4p^2 - 8p + 2 = 0$ i $3p^2 - 3p - 3 = 0$
j $2w^2 + w - 5 = 0$ k $3w^2 - w - 8 = 0$ l $5w^2 - 5w + 1 = 0$
m $2a^2 + 2a - 3 = 0$ n $6a^2 + a - 6 = 0$ o $4a^2 - a - 4 = 0$
p $8c^2 + 8c - 1 = 0$ q $5c^2 + 8c + 1 = 0$ r $7c^2 + 9c + 1 = 0$
s $4 - 3n - 2n^2 = 0$ t $3 + 5n - n^2 = 0$ u $12 + 6n - 2n^2 = 0$

2 Solve these equations giving your answers correct to 2 dp.

a $x(2x + 3) = 7$ b $1 = x(7 - 3x)$ c $x(4x + 5) = 4$

Solving quadratic equations by completing the square

Another way to solve a quadratic equation that cannot be factorised is by
completing the square. This might be quicker than using the formula.

Example

Solve the equation $x^2 + 6x - 1 = 0$

Check that $b^2 \geq 4ac$ for
the equation.
If $b^2 < 4ac$ then:
$(b^2 - 4ac)$ is negative and
the equation will have no
solution.

♦ The equation cannot be factorised, but $b^2 \geq 4ac$ so it can be solved.

♦ If we look for a complete square which includes $x^2 + 6x$ we
must start with $(x + 3)^2$.

The diagram shows that $(x + 3)^2$ gives:
$x^2 + 6x + 9$

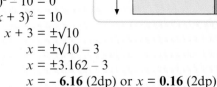

We have:
$x^2 + 6x + 9 = (x + 3)^2$
$x^2 + 6x = (x + 3)^2 - 9$

When we replace $x^2 + 6x$ the original
equation becomes:
$$(x + 3)^2 - 9 - 1 = 0$$
$$(x + 3)^2 - 10 = 0$$
$$(x + 3)^2 = 10$$
[√ each side] $x + 3 = \pm\sqrt{10}$
$$x = \pm\sqrt{10} - 3$$
$$x = \pm 3.162 - 3$$
$$x = -\mathbf{6.16} \text{ (2dp) or } x = \mathbf{0.16} \text{ (2dp)}$$

Exercise 9.8
Solving quadratic
equations by completing
the square

1 **a** Show that $x^2 + 10x - 5$ can be solved using the square of $(x + 5)$.
b Solve $x^2 + 10x - 5 = 0$ by completing the square.

2 Explain why $x^2 + 5x + 9 = 0$ cannot be solved.

3 Solve $x^2 + 8x - 3 = 0$ by completing the square.

4 By completing the square, where possible, solve these equations.

a $x^2 + 12x - 2 = 0$ b $x^2 + 6x - 8 = 0$ c $x^2 + 14x - 1 = 0$
d $x^2 + 4x + 5 = 0$ e $x^2 + 6x + 27 = 0$ f $x^2 + 8x + 6 = 0$

Accuracy
Give your answers correct
to 2 dp.

5 Solve $x^2 + 3x - 5 = 0$ by drawing a diagram and completing the square.

6 Complete the square to solve these equations.

a $x^2 + 5x - 4 = 0$ b $x^2 + 7x - 2 = 0$ c $x^2 + 3x + 1 = 0$

Rearranging quadratic equations before solving them

A quadratic equation might be written in such a way that it does not look like your expectation of a quadratic equation.

Example

Solve the equation $(2x + 1)^2 = 3x(x - 1) + 9$

- Remove the brackets
$$(2x + 1)(2x + 1) = 3x(x - 1) + 9$$
$$4x^2 + 4x + 1 = 3x^2 - 3x + 9$$
$$x^2 + 7x - 8 = 0$$

- The quadratic equation $\mathbf{x^2 + 7x - 8 = 0}$
can then solved by an appropriate method.

Example

Solve the equation $x + 6 = \dfrac{27}{x}$

- Remove the fraction by $x^2 + 6x = 27$
multiplying each term by x

- The quadratic equation $\mathbf{x^2 + 6x - 27 = 0}$
can then be solved by an appropriate method.

Example

Solve the equation $\dfrac{x + 3}{4} = \dfrac{3}{x - 1}$

- Remove the fractions $(x + 3)(x - 1) = 12$
- Remove the brackets $x^2 + 2x - 3 = 12$
- The quadratic equation $\mathbf{x^2 + 2x - 15 = 0}$
can then be solved by an appropriate method.

Example

Solve the equation $2x + 3 = \sqrt{(x^2 - 1)}$

- Remove the $\sqrt{}$ by squaring $(2x + 3)^2 = x^2 - 1$
- Remove the bracket
$$(2x + 3)(2x + 3) = x^2 - 1$$
$$4x^2 + 12x + 9 = x^2 - 1$$
$$3x^2 + 12x + 10 = 0$$

- The quadratic equation $\mathbf{3x^2 + 12x + 10 = 0}$
can then be solved by an appropriate method.

These are just some forms of manipulation you might use when faced with an equation you need to rearrange.

Exercise 9.9
Rearranging and solving quadratic equations

1 Rearrange and solve these equations. Give solutions correct to 2 dp.

a $x - 5 = \dfrac{36}{x}$ **b** $x(x - 7) = 60$ **c** $(x - 1)^2 = 64$

d $y = \dfrac{27}{(y + 6)}$ **e** $2y + 5 = \sqrt{(y^2 - 2)}$ **f** $y + 5 = \dfrac{6}{y}$

g $\dfrac{w - 2}{2} = \dfrac{7}{w - 3}$ **h** $\dfrac{w + 4}{2} = \dfrac{1}{2w - 1}$ **i** $36 = \dfrac{1}{w^2}$

j $\dfrac{4}{v^2} = 100$ **k** $3v^2 = 5v$ **l** $3v + 4 = \dfrac{5}{v} - 3$

m $\dfrac{3}{a} - 5 = 4a + 1$ **n** $\dfrac{2}{a - 1} + \dfrac{3}{a + 2} = 4$ **o** $100a = \dfrac{1}{a}$

Creating and solving quadratic equations from problems

Some problems enable you to create a quadratic equation which you can solve to find an answer. While a quadratic equation will have two solutions it is possible that only one of them will be appropriate as an answer.

Example

A rectangle is 5 metres longer than it is wide. The rectangle has an area of $456\,m^2$. Calculate the length of a diagonal of the rectangle.

♦ Show the situation on a diagram.

Let the width of the rectangle be w.
The length of the rectangle is $w + 5$
AB is a diagonal of the rectangle.

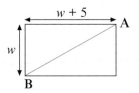

♦ Create and solve equation in w.

The area of the rectangle is $456\,m^2$
i.e.
$$w(w + 5) = 456$$
$$w^2 + 5w = 456$$
$$w^2 + 5w - 456 = 0$$
$$(w - 19)(w + 24) = 0$$
$$w = 19 \text{ or } w = {}^-24$$

The width of the rectangle is 19 m (the width cannot be ⁻24 m).
The length of the rectangle is 24 m (i.e. 19 + 5).

♦ To find the length of the diagonal AB.
By Pythagoras' rule:
$AB^2 = 19^2 + 24^2$
$AB^2 = 937$
$AB = \sqrt{937} = 30.6$ (1 dp)
The length of a diagonal of the rectangle is 30.6 m (1 dp).

Exercise 9.10
Solving problems using quadratic equations

1 The width of a rectangle is 12 cm less than its length. The rectangle has an area of $448\,cm^2$.

  a Write and solve an equation to find the dimensions of the rectangle.
  b Calculate the length, to 2 dp, of a diagonal of the rectangle.

2 Two positive numbers multiplied together give 432.
  One number is greater than the other number by six.
  Find the two numbers.

3 A rectangle has a perimeter of 126 cm. The length of a diagonal of the rectangle is 45 cm.

  Write and solve an equation to find:

  a the length of the rectangle
  b the area of the rectangle.

4 In triangle ABC the base is 4 cm longer than its height. ABC has an area of $117\,cm^2$.

  Calculate the size of $\hat{ABC}$ to 2 dp.

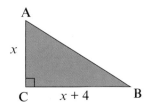

5 Use the formula $p = vt + 0.5gt^2$ to find values for t to 2 dp when $p = 20$, $v = 6$ and $g = 1$.

6 The base of a right-angled triangle is 9 cm longer than the height of the triangle. The area of the triangle is 486 cm².

   a Calculate the length of the base and the height of the triangle.

   b Calculate the perimeter of the triangle.

7 The diagram shows a trapezium ABCD which has a height w. The lengths of AB and CD are given in terms of w. The area of ABCD is 93.5 cm².

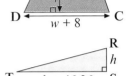

   a Write and solve an equation to find a value for w.

   b The trapezium ABCD has the same area as triangle RST. Calculate the length of RT to 2 dp.

   c Calculate the size of RTS to 2 dp.

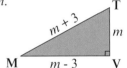

8 Two positive numbers differ by 4, and when multiplied give 2752.25 Write and solve an equation to find the two numbers.

9 In triangle TVM all the sides are given in terms of m.

   a Show that $m^2 = 12m$

   b Calculate the area of TVM.

   c Show that, to the nearest degree, $\angle$MTV = 37°.

10 A concrete beam used to construct a bridge is in the shape of a cuboid. The beam is 2.8 metres longer than it is wide, and is 2.5 metres high. The volume of the beam is given as $52.7\,m^3$.

   a Show that the beam is more than 6 metres long.

   b If the width of the beam is y metres show that the total surface area of the beam (S) is given by the equation:

$$S = 2y^2 + 15.6y + 14$$

Solving quadratic equations by iteration

Section 5 (page 68) of this book explains iterative sequences.

Some iterative sequences converge to a limit of the sequence.
This limit can be said to be the root of (solution to) an equation represented by the sequence.

Example

The equation $x^2 + 4x - 12 = 0$ can be rearranged to read as $x = \dfrac{12}{x + 4}$

This can be written as an iterative sequence given by $x_{n+1} = \dfrac{12}{x_n + 4}$

As the number of terms in the sequence becomes very large, x_{n+1} becomes almost identical to x_n.

As this is the case x_n can be replaced by x_{n+1}.

If you choose to start with x_0 = zero
The first term of the sequence x_1 is 3 $[12 \div (0 + 4)]$
The next term of the sequence x_2 is 1.714 2857... $[12 \div (3 + 4)]$
The next term x_3 is 2.1 $[12 \div (1.71 \ldots + 4)]$
The next term x_4 is 1.967 2131 $[12 \div (2.1 + 4)]$
The sequence is converging on the value 2, as n gets larger, i.e. $x_n = 2$.

So, $x = 2$ is one solution to the equation $x^2 + 4x - 12 = 0$.

Exercise 9.11
Iterative solutions to
quadratic equations

1   **a**   Show that $x^2 + 5x - 84 = 0$ can be rearranged to read $x = \dfrac{84}{x+5}$.

b   Show that the sequence given by $x_{n+1} = \dfrac{84}{x_n + 5}$ converges.

c   Give a solution to the equation $x^2 + 5x - 84 = 0$.

2   **a**   Show that the sequence given by $x_{n+1} = \dfrac{84}{x_n + 6}$ can be used to solve the equation $x^2 + 6x - 55 = 0$.

b   What is the value of x_n as n becomes very large?

c   Give a solution to the equation $x^2 + 6x - 55 = 0$.

3   By considering an iterative sequence find a solution to these equations.

   a $x^2 + 10x - 56 = 0$ **b** $x^2 + 3x - 108 = 0$ **c** $x^2 + 2x = 168$
   d $x^2 = 21 - 4x$ **e** $20 - x^2 = 8x$ **f** $x^2 + x = 72$

Iterative sequences, providing they converge, can provide a solution of a quadratic equation. As most quadratic equations have two solutions this iterative process needs to be able to give both roots if it is to be a useful way of finding solutions.

Example

To solve $x^2 + 4x - 12 = 0$

the sequence $x_{n+1} = \dfrac{12}{x_n + 4}$ gave a solution $x = 2$

The equation $x^2 + 4x - 12 = 0$

can also be rearranged to give $x = \dfrac{12 - x^2}{4}$

Consider the sequence $x_{n+1} = \dfrac{12 - x_n^2}{4}$

If $x_0 = 0$:
The first term of the sequence x_1 is 3.
The next terms are : 0.75, 2.85 …, 0.95 …, 2.77 …, 1.07 …, 2.70 …, … .
This sequence also converges to the value 2.

The equation $x^2 + 4x - 12 = 0$
can also be rearranged to give $x = \dfrac{12}{x} - 4$

Consider the sequence $x_{n+1} = \dfrac{12}{x_n} - 4$

> Each time the equation is rearranged in a different form, a different sequence can be generated.
>
> To find both roots of a quadratic equation by iteration you need to generate two sequences that converge to different values.

If $x_0 = 1$:
The next term of the sequence is 8.
The next terms are: ⁻2.5, ⁻8.8 …, ⁻5.36 …, ⁻6.23 …, ⁻5.92 …, ⁻6.02 …, … .
This sequence converges to the value ⁻6.
So $x = ⁻6$ is also a solution to the equation $x^2 + 4x - 12 = 0$.

For $x^2 + 4x - 12 = 0$ the solutions are: $x = 2$ and $x = ⁻6$.

Exercise 9.12
Solving quadratic equations
by iterative methods

1   **a**   Rearrange the equation $x^2 + 7x - 60 = 0$ in as many different ways as you can.

b   Solve $x^2 + 7x - 60 = 0$ using iteration.

2   Use iteration to solve these equations.

   a $x^2 - 4x - 21 = 0$ **b** $x^2 - 10x - 24 = 0$ **c** $x^2 + x - 240 = 0$

End points

You should be able to ... ... so try these questions

A Solve simultaneous linear equations

A1 Solve these equations for x and y.
  a $5x - 3y = 21$
      $2x + 5y = {}^-4$
  b $2x - 3y = {}^-3$
      $7x - 2y = {}^-19$

B Solve problems with simultaneous equations

B1 Two groups of people bought tickets on the Cliff Railway. The first group of five adults and two children paid a total of £29.30. The second group of two adults and three children paid a total of £17.55.
Find the charges for adult and child tickets for the Cliff Railway.

C Solve quadratic equations by inspection

C1 Solve these quadratic equations.
  a $x^2 + 5x - 24 = 0$
  b $x^2 - 8x - 65 = 0$
  c $x^2 - 15x + 36 = 0$
  d $2x^2 - 2x - 12 = 0$

D Solve quadratic equations using the formula

D1 Solve quadratic equations using the formula.
Solve these quadratic equations to 2 dp.
  a $x^2 + 6x - 2 = 0$
  b $x^2 - 9x + 3 = 0$
  c $2x^2 + 5x - 1 = 0$

E Solve quadratic equations by completing the square

E1 By completing the square solve the equation $x^2 + 5x - 3 = 0$.

F Create and solve quadratic equations for problems

F1 A rectangle has an area of 570 cm². The rectangle is 23 cm longer than it is wide.
Write and solve an equation to find the dimensions of the rectangle.

G Use iteration to solve quadratic equations

G1 Use iteration to solve these equations.
  a $x^2 + 5x - 6 = 0$
  b $x^2 - 8x + 15 = 0$

Some points to remember

◆ When you are solving simultaneous equations you may have to rearrange one or both of them at the start.

◆ Check when starting to solve a quadratic equation that $b^2 \geq 4ac$.

◆ When creating equations to solve word problems do not introduce more unknowns than you need. Always try to express one unknown in terms of another unknown.

◆ You can always check a solution to an equation by substitution.

Starting points

You need to know about ...   ... so try these questions

A The equation of a straight line

♦ You can use the coordinates of points on a line to find the equation of the line.

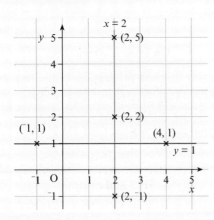

A1

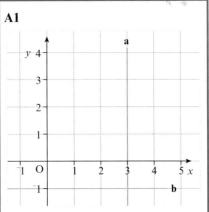

Write down the equation of the lines **a** and **b**.

B Reflections

♦ To describe a reflection you must give the mirror line.
On a grid you can give the equation of the mirror line.

Example

B is the image of A after a reflection in $y = {}^-x$.

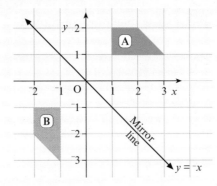

B1 a Copy this diagram.

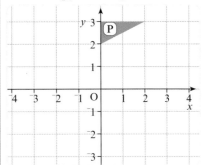

b Draw the image of P after a reflection in:
   i $y = x$ **ii** $x = {}^-1$

C Rotations

♦ To describe a rotation you must give:
  ❖ the angle and direction of rotation
  ❖ the centre of rotation.

♦ On a grid you can give the coordinates of the centre.

Example

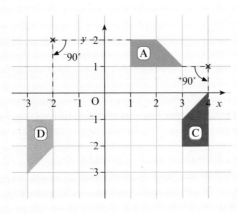

  ❖ C is the image of A after a rotation of $^+90°$ (90° anticlockwise) about (4, 1).
  ❖ D is the image of A after a rotation of $^-90°$ (90° clockwise) about ($^-2$, 2).

C1

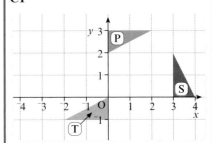

a Triangle S is the image of P after a rotation about (3, 3). What is the angle of rotation?

b Triangle T is the image of P after a rotation of 180°. Give the coordinates of the centre of rotation.

D Translations

- ◆ A translation only changes the position of a shape.

- ◆ On a grid you can use a vector to describe a translation.

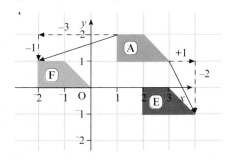

Example

- ❖ A is translated on to E by the vector $\begin{pmatrix} 1 \\ -2 \end{pmatrix}$.

- ❖ A is translated on to F by the vector $\begin{pmatrix} -3 \\ -1 \end{pmatrix}$.

E Enlargements

- ◆ To describe an enlargement you must give:
  - ❖ the centre of enlargement
  - ❖ the scale factor (SF).

Example

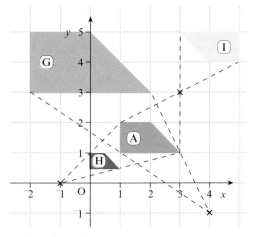

G is an enlargement of A with centre (4, ⁻1) and SF 2.

H is an enlargement of A with centre (⁻1, 0) and SF $\frac{1}{2}$.

I is an enlargement of A with centre (3, 3) and SF ⁻1.

- ◆ If the SF is **greater than 1**, or **less than ⁻1**, the image is **larger** than the object.

- ◆ If the SF is **between 0 and 1**, or **between ⁻1 and 0**, the image is **smaller** than the object. (Although the image is smaller, it is still called an enlargement!)

- ◆ If the scale factor is **negative**, the image is on the opposite side of the centre of enlargement and upside down.

F Congruence and similarity

- ◆ Of the four main types of transformation, enlargement is the only one that changes the **size** of the object (unless the SF is ⁻1 or 1).

  - ❖ Under either reflection, rotation, or translation: the object and image are always **congruent**, i.e. they have the same shape and size.

  - ❖ Under enlargement: the object and image are only **similar**, i.e. they have the same shape but are different in size.

D1 These translations map P on to U and V.

Object	Translation	Image
P	$\begin{pmatrix} 2 \\ 0 \end{pmatrix}$	U
P	$\begin{pmatrix} -1 \\ 3 \end{pmatrix}$	V

On your diagram from Question **B1**, draw and label the image of P after each of these translations.

E1 Copy this diagram and enlarge triangle P with:
  a SF 2 and centre (⁻1, 4)
  b SF $\frac{1}{2}$ and centre (0, 5)
  c SF ⁻1.5 and centre (2, 2.5).

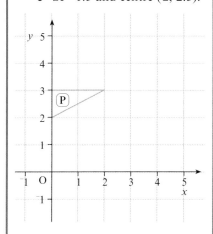

F1 a In this tessellation which shapes are congruent to U?

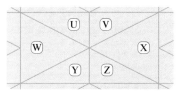

  b Explain why the triangle made by W, Y, and Z is similar to triangle U.

Thinking ahead to ...
combined transformations

A **a** Draw triangle A on axes with
‾5 ≤ x ≤ 5 and ‾5 ≤ y ≤ 5.

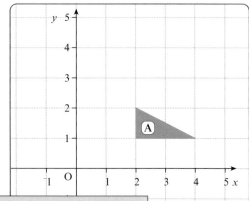

b These transformations map
triangle A on to B, C, D, E
and F.

Object	Transformation	Image
A	Reflection in the line y = x	B
A	Reflection in the line x = 1	C
A	Rotation of 180° about the origin	D
A	Rotation of ‾90° about the point (1, 0)	E
A	Translation $\begin{pmatrix} ^-4 \\ 2 \end{pmatrix}$	F

Draw and label the images B, C, D, E and F.
c Describe a transformation that maps B on to C.
d Describe a transformation that maps:
  i D on to E   **ii** E on to C   **iii** F on to E.

Combined transformations

♦ To describe a mapping you
can use a combination of
transformations.

Example

To map F on to G you can use:

a rotation of ‾90° about (1, 0)

followed by

a translation $\begin{pmatrix} ^-4 \\ 2 \end{pmatrix}$

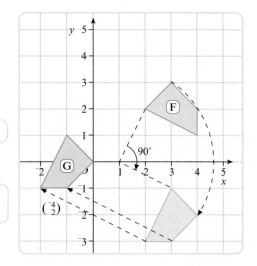

Exercise 10.1
Combined transformations

Use axes with:
‾5 ≤ x ≤ ⁺6 and
‾5 ≤ y ≤ ⁺5

1 H is the image of F after:

a translation $\begin{pmatrix} ^-4 \\ 2 \end{pmatrix}$

followed by

a rotation of ‾90° about (1, 0)

a Draw and label F and its image H.
b Compare G and H and comment on any differences.

2 These transformations map the quadrilateral F on to J and K.

	Transformations		
Object	First	Second	Image
F	Rotate 180° about (2, 1)	Rotate ⁺90° about (2, 1)	J
F	Rotate ⁺90° about (2, 1)	Rotate 180° about (2, 1)	K

> Use the same axes as you drew for Question **1**.

a Draw and label the images J and K.
b Compare J and K and comment on any differences.

3
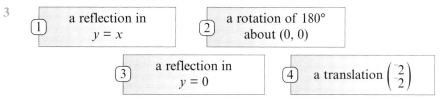

Sort the transformations 1 to 4 into two pairs so that:

> in each pair the transformations are commutative.

> A pair of transformations are commutative if the image of an object is the same whichever transformation you use first.

Draw diagrams to explain your answers.

◆ Combined transformations can be equivalent to a single transformation.

Example

A rotation of ⁻90° about (0, 3) maps F on to G.
So

> a rotation of ⁻90° about (1, 0)

followed by

> a translation $\begin{pmatrix} ^-4 \\ 2 \end{pmatrix}$

is **equivalent to the single transformation**

> a rotation of ⁻90° about (0, 3)

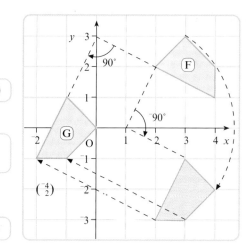

Exercise 10.2
Equivalent transformations

1 These transformations map the quadrilateral F on to L, M and N.

	Transformations		
Object	First	Second	Image
F	Reflect in y = 1	Reflect in y = x	L
F	Rotate 180° about (1, 1)	Translate $\begin{pmatrix} 0 \\ 2 \end{pmatrix}$	M
F	Reflect in y = ⁻1	Rotate ⁻90° about (1, ⁻1)	N

> Use axes with:
> ⁻5 ⩽ x ⩽ 5 and
> ⁻5 ⩽ y ⩽ 5

a On a new diagram draw and label the images L, M and N.
b What single transformation maps F on to:
    i L   **ii** M   **iii** N?

Exercise 10.3
Tessellations from
transformations

This is part of a tessellation. Each tile is a transformation of tile P.

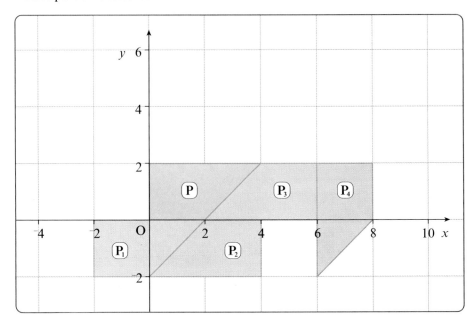

1   **a**   Draw these tiles on axes with $^-4 \leqslant x \leqslant 10$ and $^-4 \leqslant y \leqslant 8$.
    b   Describe a single transformation that maps P on to:
        i P_1 **ii** P_2 **iii** P_3

2   In this table each pair of transformations maps tile P on to P_4.
    a   For each mapping describe the second transformation fully.

	Object	Image	Transformations First	Second
i	P	P_4	Rotate $^-90°$ about (2, 0)	
ii	P	P_4	Rotate 180° about (1, 4)	
iii	P	P_4	Reflect in y = x	

    b   Describe another pair of transformations that maps P on to P_4.

3   These transformations map tile P on to P_5, P_6 and P_7.

	Transformations		
Object	First	Second	Image
P	Rotate $^-90°$ about (2, $^-2$)	Reflect in x = 5	P_5
P	Reflect in y = x	Translate $\begin{pmatrix} ^-2 \\ 0 \end{pmatrix}$	P_6
P	Rotate $^+90°$ about (0, 2)	Reflect in x = 1	P_7

    a   On your diagram draw the images P_5, P_6 and P_7.
    b   Describe a pair of transformations that map P_5 on to P.
    c   Draw four more tiles to continue the tessellation.

Enlargements

Exercise 10.4
Enlargements

1 This is part of a tessellation of tiles arranged in the shape of a Greek cross.

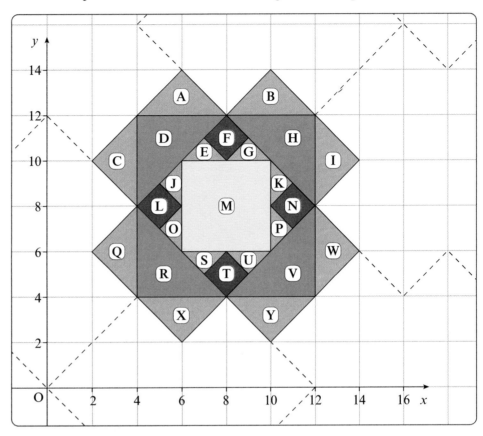

You could put tracing paper over your drawing for each question.

If you draw lines through corresponding points on the object and image, they will meet at the centre of enlargement.

a Copy the diagram and label the tiles A to Y.

b What is the image of E after an enlargement with centre (4, 8) and SF 2?

c Find the scale factor and centre for each of these enlargements.

Object	Image	SF	Centre
S	Y		
Y	U		
E	A		
Q	W		

d Explain why tile T will not map on to M with just an enlargement.

e This table gives a pair of transformations for three mappings. Describe fully the second transformation for each of these mappings.

For an enlargement give the scale factor and the coordinates of the centre.

For a translation give the vector.

For a reflection give the equation of the mirror line.

For a rotation give the angle of rotation and the coordinates of the centre.

	Object	Image	Transformations	
			First	Second
i	G	W	Enlarge SF 2 with centre (8, 8)	
ii	Q	E	Rotate ⁻90° about (6, 6)	
iii	A	S	Enlarge SF $\frac{1}{2}$ with centre (4, 8)	

Exercise 10.5
Drawing enlargements

1   Draw the triangle A on
    axes with:
    $^-6 \leqslant x \leqslant 10$
    $^-6 \leqslant y \leqslant 10$.

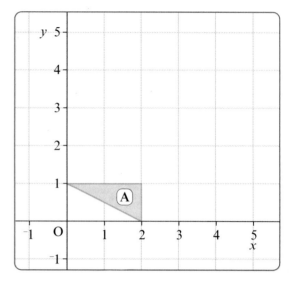

For an enlargement:
the distance from the centre
to a point on the object
multiplied by the scale factor
gives the distance from the
centre to the corresponding
point on the image.

2   These transformations map the triangle A on to B_1, B_2, B_3 and B_4.

Object	First transformation	Second transformation	Image
A	Enlarge SF 2 with centre (0, 0)	Translate $\begin{pmatrix} 1 \\ 2 \end{pmatrix}$	B_1
A	Rotate $^-90°$ about (2, 0)	Enlarge SF 2 with centre ($^-1$, 0)	B_2
A	Enlarge SF 2 with centre ($^-1$, 0)	Translate $\begin{pmatrix} 4 \\ 4 \end{pmatrix}$	B_3
A	Rotate $^+90°$ about (0, 1)	Enlarge SF 2 with centre ($^-3$, $^-2$)	B_4

a   On your diagram draw and label the images B_1, B_2, B_3 and B_4.
b   Describe a single transformation that will map B_1:
    i   on to B_2 **ii**   on to B_3 **iii**   on to B_4.
c   What single transformation maps A:
    i   on to B_1 **ii**   on to B_3.

3   In this table each pair of transformations maps B_2 on to A.
    For each mapping describe the second transformation fully.

Object	Image	First transformation	Second transformation
a B_2	A	Rotate $^+90°$ about (5, 0)	
b B_2	A	Rotate $^+90°$ about (5, 2)	

4 Each tile in this pattern is also a transformation of A.

   a Copy this pattern on axes with:
$$^-6 \leqslant x \leqslant 10$$
$$^-6 \leqslant y \leqslant 10$$

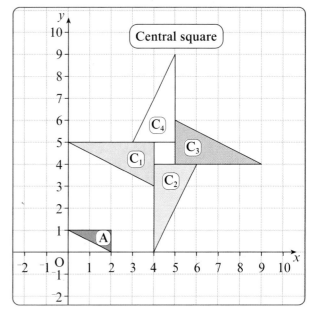

> You do not need more than two transformations for each mapping.

   b In a table show what transformations map A on to each triangle in this pattern.

   c **i** Make another pattern using four triangles.
      ii In a table to show what transformations map A on to each triangle in your pattern.
     iii Pass your table to a partner and ask them to draw your pattern.

5

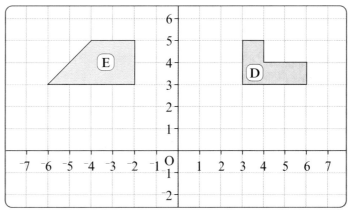

   a Copy these shapes on axes with: $^-12 \leqslant x \leqslant 12$
$$^-7 \leqslant y \leqslant 10$$

   b On your diagram, draw and label the images D_1 and E_1.

Transformations			
Object	First	Second	Image
D	Enlarge SF 2 with centre (O, 1)	Rotate 180° about (O, 1)	D_1
E	Enlarge SF $^-$1.5 with centre (O, 1)	Enlarge SF $^-$1.5 with centre (O, 1)	E_1

   c Describe a single transformation that maps:
     i D on to D_1 **ii** E on to E_1.

   d Describe a single transformation that maps:
     i D_1 on to D   **ii** E_1 on to E.

Thinking ahead to ...
inverse transformations

A a Draw hexagon R on axes with:
$^-7 \leqslant x \leqslant 7$ and $^-7 \leqslant y \leqslant 7$.

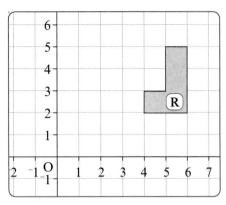

b Describe the effect on R of each of these pairs of transformations.

	Transformations	
Object	First	Second
R	Enlarge SF $^-2$ with centre (2, 1)	Enlarge SF $^-0.5$ with centre (2, 1)
R	Rotate $^-90°$ about (1, 0)	Rotate $^-270°$ about (1, 0)

Inverse transformations

♦ If a combination of two transformations maps the object on to itself then each transformation is the **inverse** of the other.

Exercise 10.6
Inverse transformations

1 Describe the inverse transformation of:

a
Translation
$\begin{pmatrix} 1 \\ ^-2 \end{pmatrix}$

b
Rotation
$^-90°$
about
(1, 0)

c
Enlargement
SF 2
with centre
($^-1$, 2)

2 a Describe the inverse transformation of:
Reflection
in
$y = ^-x$

b What is special about the inverse transformation of any reflection?

3 a Draw the triangle S on axes with:
$^-1 \leqslant x \leqslant 5$
$^-5 \leqslant y \leqslant 5$.

b On your diagram, draw and label the images S_1 and S_2.

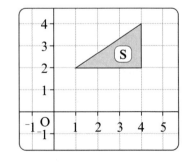

$\boxed{S_1}$ Rotation 180° about (3, 0)

$\boxed{S_2}$ Enlargement SF $^-1$ with centre (3, 0)

c Describe two inverse transformations of   Rotation 180° about (x, y)

End points

You should be able to ... ... so try these questions

A Use combined transformations

A1 **a** Draw shape E on axes with:
$^-12 \leqslant x \leqslant 6$ and $^-6 \leqslant y \leqslant 6$.

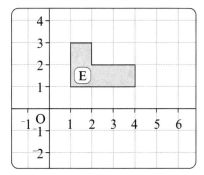

b On your diagram, draw and label the images K, L and M.

	Transformations		
Object	First	Second	Image
E	Enlarge SF $^-2$ with centre $(^-1, 0)$	Enlarge SF 0.5 with centre $(3, ^-4)$	K
E	Reflect in $y = ^-x$	Reflect in $y = 0$	L
E	Rotate 180° about $(0, 0)$	Rotate 180° about $(0, ^-2)$	M

c What single transformation maps E on to:
i K **ii** L **iii** M ?

d These transformations map K on to L, M and E.
Describe the second transformation.

			Transformations	
	Object	Image	First	Second
i	K	L	Rotate $^-90°$ about $(^-1, ^-3)$	
ii	K	M	Reflect in $x = 0$	
iii	K	E	Translate $\begin{pmatrix} 2 \\ 2 \end{pmatrix}$	

e **i** What single transformation maps K on to L?
ii Describe two single transformations that each maps K on to M.

B Identify inverse transformations

B1 Describe the inverse transformation of each of these.

a
Enlargement
SF 0.25
with centre
$(3, ^-1)$

b
Rotation
$^-270°$
about
$(0, 2)$

c
Translation
$\begin{pmatrix} 0 \\ ^-3 \end{pmatrix}$

B2 Describe the inverse transformation of:
Reflection in $y = x + 1$

Toujours Paris

Ile de la Cité

This boat-shaped island in the River Seine is where Paris was first inhabited by Celtic tribes over 2000 years ago. It is where Notre Dame is situated. This cathedral is a superb example of French medieval architecture and is particularly known for its wonderful stained glass rose windows.

The width of this South Window is 13 metres.

In the Ile de la Cité you will also find Point Zéro. This is a geometer's mark from which all distances in France are measured.

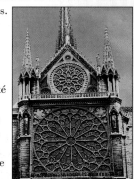

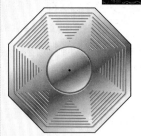

Each side of the shape is 12 cm long.

Paris au Quotidien

Arrondissements: Il faut le savoir, Paris est divisé en 20 arrondissements se déroulant en spiraleà partir du 1er (le quartier du Louvre).

Banques: Ouvertes en général du lundi au vendredi de 9h à 16h30, quelques (rares) agences le samedi. Les Caisses d'Epargne ouvrent plus souvent le samedi et ferment le lundi.

Change: On ne peut pas tout prévoir à l'avance; vous pourrez changer vos devises dans les gares, les aéroports, les grandes agences de banque, les points change (ouverts tard le soir), ainsi qu'à notre bureau d'accueil des Champs-Elysées.

Daily Life in Paris

Districts: You should know that Paris is divided into 20 districts numbered in a circular direction, starting with the 1st district (the Louvre area).

Banks: They are generally open from Monday to Friday from 9 am to 4.30 pm, some (rare) branches on Saturday. The savings banks are more often open on Saturday and closed on Monday.

Exchange: You cannot foresee everything; you can therefore change your foreign currency in railway stations, airports, major bank branches, exchange offices (open late in the evening), as well as in the visitors office on the Champs-Elysées.

Eiffel Tower Factfile – 1996

- Built in 1889 for the Universal Exhibition
- Built by Gustave Eiffel (1832–1923)
- Built from pig iron girders
- Total height 320 metres
- The world's tallest building until 1931
- Height to 3rd level is 899 feet
- There are 1652 steps to the third level
- Two and a half million rivets were used
- The tower is 15 cm higher on a hot day.
- Its total weight is 10100 tonnes
- 40 tons of paint are used every 4 years
- On a clear day it is possible to see Chartres Cathedral, 72 km away to the South West.
- The tower is visited by about $5\frac{1}{2}$ million people every year

Admission charge   56 Francs

DAY TRIPS BY EUROSTAR

Waterloo Station (London) to Paris
Celebrate that special occasion in style with a day trip to Paris!

ADULT   £
CHILD (4–11 YRS) £

Entry fees in Paris – 1996

Eiffel Tower	56 FF
Louvre	45 FF
Pompidou Centre	35 FF
Picasso Museum	28 FF
Museum of Modern Art	27 FF
Versailles Palace	45 FF
Parc de la Villette	45 FF
Cluny Museum	28 FF

Paris Lucky dip – Superb value !

In the hat are four tickets to the: Eiffel Tower, Picasso Museum, Versailles Palace and the Museum of Modern Art. Pick two tickets at random from the four. Entry fee – only 83 Francs.

83 FF

Datafile

Population of Paris (in 1982)   2 188 918
In 1996, £1 sterling was equivalent to 7.54 French Francs.
1 metre = 3.281 feet
1 kilometre = 0.62 miles

1   a   How many lines of symmetry has the South
        Window of Notre Dame?
    b   What is the order of rotational symmetry of the
        South Window?
    c   Draw a window shape where the number of
        lines of symmetry is not equal to the order of
        rotational symmetry.

2   The South Window is surrounded by a frame with
    the cross-section below.

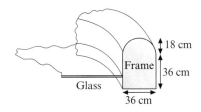

    a   Calculate the area of the window inside the
        frame.
    b   Calculate the area of the frame's cross-section.
    c   Calculate the approximate volume of the frame
        in cubic metres.

3   For Point Zéro in the Ile de la Cité, the outer
    polygon is a regular octagon.
    a   Calculate the size of an exterior angle.
    b   Calculate the size of an interior angle.

4   a   Calculate the distance across the octagon from
        one flat face to the opposite one.
    b   Calculate the total area of Point Zéro.

5   How many tons of paint will have been used on the
    tower from when it was built up to the year 2000?

6   a   How much higher than the third level is the
        total height of the tower?
        Give your answer to the nearest metre.
    b   From a point 2000 metres away what is the
        angle of elevation to the topmost point on the
        Eiffel Tower, to the nearest degree?
    c   The spire of Notre Dame reaches 90 metres
        from the ground and is 4.3 km as the crow
        flies from the Eiffel Tower.
        What is the angle of depression from the third
        level of the Eiffel Tower to the tip of Notre
        Dame's spire? Give your answer to 2 sf.

7   The ratio of steps to the third level, to steps to the
    first level is about 9 to 2.
    About how many steps are there to the first level?

8   Calculate the approximate percentage that the
    tower grows on a hot day.

9   What is the approximate bearing of Paris from
    Chartres?

10 a   In 1996, what was the Eiffel Tower entry fee
        equivalent to in £ Sterling?
    b   By 1997 one French Franc had changed in
        value to 10.6 pence. What effect did this
        change have on the entry fee in £ sterling?

11 Compare the French and English text in the extract
    on Daily Life in Paris.
    What is the relative frequency of a vowel
    in each language? (Vowels are a, e, i, o, and u.)

12 Compare the French and English extracts.
    Which language uses the longest words?
    Explain how you decided.

13 For the Paris Lucky Dip use the following
    shorthand:
    E – Eiffel Tower   *P* – Picasso Museum
    V – Versailles Palace *M* – Museum of Modern Art
    a   What is the probability that a pair of tickets is
        picked which includes the Versailles Palace?
    b   What is the probability of picking P and M?
    c   Give the probability of picking a pair of tickets
        i   worth more than the entry fee
        ii worth less than the entry fee.
    d   Is the seller likely to make a profit or loss on
        every hundred entries? Give your reasons.

Paris Special

Enclosed are tickets for:
2 adults and 3 children
Total charge £465

Paris Special

Enclosed are tickets for:
3 adults and 1 child
Total charge £386

14 These two bills were for Eurostar day trips to Paris.
    Calculate:
    a   the cost of an adult's ticket **and** a child's ticket
    b   the total cost for 1 adult and 2 children.

Starting points
You need to know about ...

... so try these questions

A Solving equations in one unknown

- where the unknown is on both sides of the equation

$$5c - 4 = 3c - 8$$
[−3c] $$2c - 4 = {}^-8$$
[+4] $$2c = {}^-4$$
[÷2] $$c = {}^-2$$

- where brackets are involved

$$3(4p + 5) = 5(3p - 4)$$
$$12p + 15 = 15p - 20$$
[−15] $$12p = 15p - 35$$
[−15p] $${}^-3p = {}^-35$$
[÷ ${}^-3$] $$p = \frac{35}{3} = 11.66 \ldots$$

- where fractions are involved

$$\tfrac{2}{3}(w + 1) = \tfrac{3}{4}w - 3$$
[× both sides by 12] $$8(w + 1) = 9w - 3$$
$$8w + 8 = 9w - 36$$
[−8] $$8w = 9w - 44$$
[−9w] $${}^-w = {}^-44$$
w = 44

B Factorising expressions

- when a numerical factor can be identified
  factorise $$12a - 9x + 18y$$
  i.e. **3(4a − 3x + 6y)**

- when an algebraic factor can be identified
  factorise $$a^2b + ab^2 - ac$$
  i.e. **a(ab + b² − c)**

- when more than one factor can be identified
  factorise $$15xy - 20x^3 + 5xy^2 + 10x^2y^3$$
  i.e. **5x(3y − 4x² + y² + 2xy³)**

- when there is a need to factorise more than once
  factorise $$6ab + 3ac + 10bx + 5cx$$
  $$3a(2b + c) + 5x(2b + c)$$
  i.e. **(2b + c) (3a + 5x)**

C Dealing with powers and roots

- when powers are involved

$$x^2 = 3a^2b - 4c$$
[√ both sides] **x = √(3a²b − 4c)**

- when roots are involved

$$\sqrt{c} = 3xy + b$$
[square both sides] **c = (3xy + b)²**

A1 Solve these equations:
  a $7d - 8 = 3d + 14$
  b $3y + 9 = 2y - 5$
  c $5(2x + 1) = 41 + x$
  d $3(3p + 4) = 2(p + 27)$
  e $5(4 - x) = 3(2x + 1)$
  f $3(k - 1) = 2(1.5 - 3k)$
  g $8(n + 5) = 4(3n - 8)$
  h $15(g - 3) = 10(2g + 1)$

A2 Solve these equations:
  a $\tfrac{2}{3}c - 1 = 4$
  b $\tfrac{3}{4}x + 1 = 2x$
  c $3 - \tfrac{1}{2}x = x - 15$
  d $\tfrac{3}{5}(v + 1) = \tfrac{3}{10}v$
  e $\tfrac{1}{2}(w - 3) = \tfrac{2}{3}(2w - 1)$
  f $\tfrac{1}{2}(4a + 2) = \tfrac{3}{4}(a - 6)$
  g $\tfrac{3}{2}(x - 1) = \tfrac{5}{4}(2x - 6)$
  h $\tfrac{3}{8}y + 2 = \tfrac{1}{3}y - 3$

B1 Factorise these expressions:
  a $6bc - 15ax + 3by$
  b $18a^2 + 24b^2c$
  c $3a^2x - 5ay^2 + 6ab - ac$
  d $axy - a^2x^2 + ax^2y - abx$
  e $6c^2d - 15bcd$
  f $8axy^2 + 12abx - 20a^2x + 16ax$
  g $6ax - 2bx + 9ac - 3bc$
  h $4a^2b + 8ax - 3abx - 6x^2$
  i $6ax^2 - 3x^3y + 4ay - 2xy^2$
  j $2ab^2c - 2b^3cy - a^2bc + ab^2cy$

C1 Write each of these as an equation in x:
  a $x^2 - 3 = 4a$
  b $3x^2 = 5c + 1$
  c $5 + \sqrt{x} = 3a - 2$
  d $\sqrt{(ax)} = 7$
  e $5\sqrt{x} = 4a$

Thinking ahead to ...
changing the subject
of formulas

A A cook book gives this formula to find
the time to cook a piece of lamb.

> Allow 30 minutes per pound
> and an extra 20 minutes.

  a How long would it take to
cook 6 pounds of lamb?

  b What weight of lamb would be cooked in 1 hour and 50 minutes?

Changing the subject of formulas

The formula that links cooking time (T) with weight (W) can be written as:

> The subject of a formula is
> the variable that is to be
> calculated.

$$T = 30W + 20$$ $T =$ is the subject of this formula

♦ With the formula you to calculate a value for T for a value of W.

♦ To calculate W for a value T, we need to make W the subject of the formula.

> Addition 'undoes'
> subtraction and vice versa.
> For example:
>
>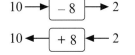

Flowchart method for changing the subject of a formula

♦ Draw a flowchart
for the formula.

$$W \xrightarrow{} \boxed{\times 30} \xrightarrow{30W} \boxed{+20} \xrightarrow{30W + 20} T$$

♦ Reverse the flow
chart to rearrange
the formula.

$$W \xleftarrow{\frac{T-20}{30}} \boxed{\div 30} \xleftarrow{T-20} \boxed{-20} \xleftarrow{} T$$

$$W = \frac{T - 20}{30}$$

> Multiplication 'undoes'
> division and vice versa.
> For example:
>
>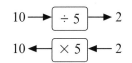

Algebraic method for changing the subject of a formula

♦ T is the subject

$$
\begin{array}{c}
-20 \\
\div 30
\end{array}
\left(
\begin{array}{c}
T = 30W + 20 \\
T - 20 = 30W \\
\dfrac{T - 20}{30} = W
\end{array}
\right)
\begin{array}{c}
-20 \\
\div 30
\end{array}
$$

♦ W is the subject $W = \dfrac{T - 20}{30}$

Exercise 11.1
Changing the subject
of formulas

1 The formula that gives the cost in pence (c) of placing an advertisement in a
local paper, where n is the number of words is:

$$c = 15n + 50$$

  a Calculate the cost of a 65 word advert.

  b **i** Make n the subject of the formula.

    ii How many words are in an advert that costs £19.85?

  c For £10, what is the maximum number of words in an advert?

2 A formula for the sum (S) of the interior angles of a polygon is:

$$S = 180(n - 2) \text{ where } n \text{ is the number of sides}$$

  a Calculate the sum of the interior angles of a heptagon.

  b **i** Make n the subject of the formula.

    ii The sum of the interior angles of a polygon is 3240°.
How many sides does the polygon have?

  c Explain why it is not possible to draw a polygon where the sum of the
interior angles is 600°.

3   When a metal rail of length w metres is increased in temperature by $t°$C it increases in length. The new length x metres is given by the formula:

$$x = w(1 + kt), \quad \text{where } k \text{ has a value of } 0.0008$$

a   The temperature of a rail 55 metres in length is increased by 21°C.
   i   Calculate the length of the rail after the temperature increase.
   ii With an increase in temperature of 21° does the length of the rail increase by more that 15%. Explain your answer.

b   i   Make t the subject of the formula.
   ii What increase in temperature increases the rail length by 1.342 metres?

4   The surface area (S) of a cylindrical axle is given by the formula:

$$S = 2\pi r(r + h) \text{ where } r \text{ is the radius, and } h \text{ the length.}$$

a   Calculate the value of S, to 4 sf, when $r = 22.5$ cm and $h = 2.2$ metres.
b   i   Make h the subject of the formula.
   ii An axle has a radius of 15 cm, and a surface area of 3016 cm^2. Calculate the length of the axle to 2 sf.

5   Make y the subject of each of these formulas:

a $5x = 3(2y - 1)$ b $3(y - 4) = 2a$ c $2(a - y) = 3x$
d $2(3y + 1) = 3(a - 2)$ e $4(3y - 1) = x^2 + 2$ f $5a^2 + 3 = 4 - 2y$
g $2(3a - 5y) = p - 3y$ h $x(4 - y) = 2x + 1$ i $2a(3 - 4y) = x^2$
j $3x(y - 5) = a - 9x$ k $0.5c(4 - 6y) = x^2 + 5c$ l $x(3x - y) = 2 - 7x^2$
m $p^2 - 1 = 1.5(ay - 3)$ n $axy + 5a = 3 + 4a$ o $15 + x^2y = 4 - 3a$
p $a^2(b + 2y) = 5$ q $x^2 - 4 = 3a(y - a)$ r $at(t - y) = t^2 + 1$
s $dt(3 + ay) = t + 2$ t $h(r^2 - 2y) = \pi d$ u $3\pi + 2ay = a^2r$

Changing the subject of formulas that involve fractions

Example 1

♦ An approximate formula to convert kilometres to miles is: $m = \dfrac{5}{8}k$

   ❖ Making k the subject gives a formula
   for converting miles to kilometres.

$$m = \dfrac{5}{8}k$$

$$[\times 8] \quad 8m = 5k$$

$$[\div 5] \quad \dfrac{8m}{5} = k$$

   ❖ So $k = \dfrac{8m}{5}$

Example 2

♦ A formula that links t and a is given as: $\dfrac{3t}{4} = \dfrac{5}{a - 1}$

   ❖ for subject a: [× both sides by 4] $3t = \dfrac{4 \times 5}{a - 1}$

[× both sides by $(a - 1)$] $3t(a - 1) = 20$
$3at - 3 = 20$
$[+3] \qquad\qquad\qquad\qquad\qquad 3at = 23$
$[\div 3t] \qquad\qquad\qquad\qquad\quad a = 23 \div 3t$

$$a = \dfrac{23}{3t}$$

> Multiplying both sides by 4, and then $(a - 1)$ produces an equation with no fractions. In this way manipulation is easier.

This is just one way to rearrange the above formula so that it reads $a = \ldots$.
Different rearrangements may have more, or fewer, steps.

Exercise 11.2
Rearranging formulas
with fractions

For these questions, round each answer to 2 dp.

Remember manipulation is made easier if you can produce an equation with no fractions involved.

1 A formula for converting kilograms (k) to pounds (p) is: $p = \dfrac{11}{5}k$

  a How many pounds are equivalent to 8 kilograms?
  b Make k the subject of the formula.
  c Convert 3 pounds to kilograms.

2 The formula for the area (A) of a triangle with base length b and height h is:

$$A = \frac{1}{2}bh$$

  a Make h the subject of the formula.
  b Find the height of a triangle with area $100 \, cm^2$ and base length 2.5 cm.

3 Temperature in °F can be converted to °C using this formula:

$$C = \frac{5(F - 32)}{9}$$

  a Convert 68°F to °C.
  b Rearrange the formula to give a formula to convert ˚C to °F.
  c Convert 24° C to °F.

4 Make y the subject of each formula:

  a $z = \dfrac{3}{4}y$ **b** $m = \dfrac{1}{3}xy$ **c** $d = \dfrac{1}{2}(y + 4)$ **d** $k = \dfrac{4}{7}(y - h)$

5 When d metres are travelled in t seconds,
a formula for average speed (s) in km/h is: $s = \dfrac{18d}{5t}$

  a In 1992, Linford Christie ran 100 metres in 9.96 seconds.
     What was his average speed in $km \, h^{-1}$?
  b Make d the subject of the formula.
  c Make t the subject.

6 When the temperature at ground level is G°C and the height above the ground in metres is h, the approximate temperature $T(°C)$ is given by:

$$T = G - \frac{h}{300}$$

  a The temperature at ground level is 26° C. Calculate the temperature outside a jet flying at 15 000 metres above ground.
  b Make h the subject of the formula.
  c Calculate h when $G = 20$ and $T = ^-30$.

7 A formula for the area (A) of a
trapezium is given as: $A = \dfrac{h(b + c)}{2}$.

Calculate a value for c when:
$A = 250.25$, $b = 12.40$, and $h = 17.50$.

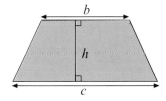

8 Make w the subject of each formula:

  a $\dfrac{5}{3w} = 2x$ **b** $\sin 32° = \dfrac{3}{4w}$ **c** $\dfrac{w}{3} - 5a = 4b$

  d $t = \dfrac{a}{w - b}$ **e** $\dfrac{a^2}{2w} = 0.5b$ **f** $\dfrac{c^2 - b}{2w} = 2ab$

  g $\dfrac{3}{2w + 3} = 4a$ **h** $\dfrac{3}{w - 1} = 2c$ **i** $\dfrac{\tan 50°}{2w + 1} = 3c$

  j $\dfrac{3}{aw + 2} = y^2$ **k** $5x = \dfrac{3}{2}(w + 5a - b)$ **l** $a \sin 2x = \dfrac{\cos 3x}{2w + 1}$

  m $y = \dfrac{a}{w + a} - 2y$ **n** $\dfrac{1}{a} = \dfrac{1}{w}$ **o** $\dfrac{1}{2}k^2 = \dfrac{3w}{2c - 1}$

  p $\dfrac{a}{w - 1} = \dfrac{3}{5}$ **q** $\dfrac{2}{3}k = 4b + \dfrac{1}{2w - 3}$ **r** $\dfrac{\cos 135°}{w - 2} = \sin 65°$

Rearranging formulas when factorising is involved

Example

♦ A formula that links b, c, and w is:

$$2b + 3 = \frac{b + c}{w}$$

❖ Make b the subject: [× both sides by w]

$$w(2b + 3) = b + c$$
$$2bw + 3w = b + c$$
$$2bw - b = c - 3w$$

[Factorise]

$$b(2w - 1) = c - 3w$$

[÷ both sides by $(2w - 1)$]

$$\mathbf{b = \frac{c - 3w}{2w - 1}}$$

Exercise 11.3
Using factorising

1 A formula for the surface area (S) of this cuboid is: $S = 2bw + 2ab + 2aw$

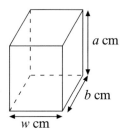

  a Make w the subject of the formula.
  b Make a the subject of the formula.
  c When $w = 4.50\,\text{cm}$ and $a = 6.40\,\text{cm}$ the surface area is $136.08\,\text{cm}^2$.
    Calculate a value for b in this cuboid.

2 The diagram shows a circular play area centre O and radius W metres.
  Part of the area is to be fenced, shown in the diagram as a red line.
  A formula for the length of fencing (P) is:

$$P = 2w + \frac{\pi w}{2}$$

  a Rearrange the formula so that w is the subject.
  b The length of fencing used was 89.27 metres.
    Calculate, to 2 sf, the diameter of the play area.

3 This is a block of packaging material with a rectangular slot cut through it.
  A formula for the volume V of packaging material in the block is: $V = abc - 2abd$

  a **i** Rearrange the formula to make b the subject.
    ii Calculate a value for b when:
      $V = 1602.25\,\text{cm}^3$, $a = 6.50\,\text{cm}$, $c = 25.00\,\text{cm}$, and $d = 4.00\,\text{cm}$.
  b Calculate a value for a when:
    $V = 4212.00\,\text{cm}^3$, $b = 18.00\,\text{cm}$, $c = 32.50\,\text{cm}$, and $d = 6.50\,\text{cm}$.

4 Rearrange each of these formulas to make h the subject:

  a $3ac = 4ah - hy$

  b $3h = 4x + 2ah$

  c $3xh + 5 = 2x + ah$

  d $ah + b^2 - c^2h = 4$

  e $3(5 - 2h) = a^2(3h + 2)$

  f $h(3x^2 + h) = 2h$

  g $\frac{3}{4}ht = 2x + ch$

  h $\frac{3x + 2h}{h} = a - 3$

  i $k = \frac{h - x^2}{3 - 2h}$

  j $\frac{3h}{4} - 2y = a^2hy$

  k $5 - \frac{2}{3h} = 2a + ax - 1$

  l $3 = \frac{k}{2h} + m^2 - n$

  m $2f^3 + \frac{x}{h} = a - 1$

  n $3w \sin 42° = \frac{3}{4}hw$

  o $\frac{3}{h} + \frac{1}{a} = k$

  p $\frac{2h}{3} = \frac{2}{3}(y + 1)$

  q $\tan 55° + bc = \frac{3}{5}a^2h$

Rearranging formulas with squares and roots

Example 1

Four square photographs, of side x, are placed in a square mount of side c as shown in the diagram.

a Write a formula for the area (A) of mount that is still visible.

b Rearrange the formula to make x the subject.

i A formula for the area (A) is: $A = c^2 - 4x^2$

ii A formula for area is: $A = c^2 - 4x^2$

$$[+ 4x^2] \qquad 4x^2 + A = c^2$$
$$[-A] \qquad 4x^2 = c^2 - A$$
$$[\div \text{ both sides by 4}] \qquad x^2 = \frac{(c^2 - A)}{4}$$

$$[\sqrt{\ } \text{ both sides}] \qquad x = \frac{\sqrt{(c^2 - A)}}{4} = \frac{\sqrt{(c^2 - A)}}{\sqrt{4}} = \frac{\sqrt{(c^2 - A)}}{2}$$

Example 2

> To square both sides, you square the *expression* on each side. This is not simply squaring each *term* on both sides.

Make y the subject of the formula: $\sqrt{(y + 3a)} = a - 2$

$$[\text{square both sides}] \qquad y + 3a = (a - 2)^2$$
$$y + 3a = a^2 - 4a + 4$$
$$[-3a] \qquad \mathbf{y = a^2 - 7a + 4}$$

Exercise 11.4
Dealing with squares and roots

1 When an object is dropped, a formula for the approximate distance (d metres) travelled in a time of t seconds is:

$$d = \left(\tfrac{49}{10}\right)t^2$$

The Sears tower in Chicago is 443 metres high.
About how long will it take an apple to fall from the top to the ground?

2 A formula for velocity (v) is : $v^2 = u^2 + 2as$
 a Show why a formula for u is: $u = \sqrt{(v^2 - 2as)}$
 b Calculate a value for u, to 1 sf, when: $v = 14$, $a = 3.5$, and $s = 18$

3 The formula for the volume (V) of a right cone of radius r, and height h is: $V = \left(\tfrac{1}{3}\right)\pi r^2 h$.
Rearrange the formula to make r the subject.

4 A formula for the volume (V) of a sphere of radius r is : $V = \left(\tfrac{4}{3}\right)\pi r^3$.
 a Make r the subject of the formula.
 b Calculate the radius of a sphere which has a volume of $100\,\text{cm}^3$.

5 A formula for the area (A) of a triangle is: $A = \sqrt{s(s - a)(s - b)(s - c)}$

Rearrange the formula to make b the subject.

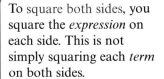

> $p^3 = p \times p \times p$
>
> If $y = p^3$ then the **cube root** of y is p.
>
> $\sqrt[3]{y} = p$

6 Rearrange each formula to make b the subject:
 a $b^2 + 3a - 4 = y^2$ **b** $3y = x - 2ab^2$ **c** $b^2 x = y - 1$
 d $ab^2 - 3x = 4 - 2x$ **e** $4x = 2a(b^2 - 5)$ **f** $3x + 4a = 2a(1 - b^3)$
 g $ab^2 = \dfrac{(x - 1)}{b}$ **h** $b^2 = \dfrac{(b^2 - c)}{2a}$ **i** $\sqrt{(3b - 1)} = a$
 j $2a = \sqrt{(b - 2)}$ **k** $w = \sqrt{(ab^2 + 3)}$ **l** $bc = \sqrt{(b^2 + 1)}$
 m $2\sqrt{(a^2 - b^2)} = xy$ **n** $\pi\sqrt{(a + b)} = r$ **o** $k = 2\pi\sqrt{\dfrac{b}{y}}$
 p $\sqrt{(2b - x)} = \sqrt{(a + c)}$ **q** $c - 3 = \sqrt{(2b + 1)}$ **r** $2\sqrt{(b - x)} = x - 2$

Evaluating non-linear formulas

♦ For the formula, $a = (b + 5)(b - 1)$, find the value of a when $b = 3$.
$$a = (3 + 5) \times (3 - 1)$$
$$= 8 \times 2$$
$$= 16$$

♦ For the formula, $y = x^2 + 4x + 1$, find the value of y when $x = 7$.
$$y = 7^2 + (4 \times 7) + 1$$
$$= 49 + 28 + 1$$
$$= 78$$

Exercise 11.5
Evaluating non-linear
formulas

1 Stopping distance is the distance a vehicle travels as it brakes to a halt. A formula that gives the stopping distance of a car on a dry road is:

$$d = \frac{v^2}{200} + \frac{v}{5},$$

where d is the stopping distance (metres) and v the speed (km h^{-1}).

Calculate the stopping distance of a car travelling at 110 km h^{-1} on a dry road.

> **Accuracy**
> For these questions, give answers correct to 2 dp when no other degree of accuracy is stated.

2 The net for a square-based box is made by cutting four square corners from a 12 cm square piece of card as shown.

A formula for the volume ($V \text{cm}^3$) of the box is:
$$V = 4x(x^2 - 12x + 36)$$
where x is the length shown on the diagram.

a Find the volume of the box when $x = 1.5$
b Calculate V when $x = 4$.
c What value for x gives the box with the greatest volume?

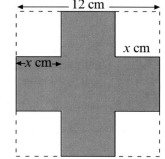

12 cm

x cm

←x cm→

> To calculate the greatest volume think about using a graph, or a spreadsheet.

3 A $\boxed{y = x^2 + 5x - 8}$ B $\boxed{y = x^2 + 3x + 2}$ C $\boxed{y = x^3 - 3x^2 - x + 2}$

D $\boxed{y = (x + 1)(x + 2)}$ E $\boxed{y = (x - 2)(x + 9)}$ F $\boxed{y = (x + 3)(x + 1)(x - 3)}$

For each formula find the value of y when:

a $x = 5$ **b** $x = {}^-5$ **c** $x = 2$ **d** $x = {}^-2$ **e** $x = 2.5$ **f** $x = {}^-2.5$

Comment on any patterns in your results.

4 The formula $v = \sqrt{(u^2 + 2as)}$ gives:
the velocity of an object (v) in m/s, for an initial velocity of u m/s, an acceleration (a) in m s^{-2}, and a distance (s) travelled in metres.

a Calculate to 1 dp a value for v when:
   i $u = 30$, $a = 5$ and $s = 6.8$ **ii** $u = 20$, $a = 9.8$ and $s = 2.4$
b Calculate to 2 sf a value for u when:
   i $s = 15.40$, $v = 120.00$ and $a = 3.60$
   ii $v = 100$, $a = {}^-14.50$, $s = 250$
   iii $a = 3\frac{1}{2}$, $v = 18\frac{1}{4}$, and $s = 6\frac{1}{3}$

5 The volume (V) of a sphere of radius r is given by the formula $V = \frac{4}{3}\pi r^3$. The Earth is an approximate sphere of radius 6.4×10^6 metres.

a Calculate an estimate, to 4 sf, for the volume of the Earth.
b Rearrange the formula to give r in terms of V.

End points

You should be able to ...   ... so try these questions

A Rearrange a formula

A1 Rearrange each formula to make x the subject:
  a $3x - a = 5$
  b $a - 4x = 2x + 3$
  c $2(3x + y) = 5$
  d $3(a - xy) = b + 2xy$
  e $3(2 - 3x) = 3(x + bc)$

B Handle formulas where fractions are involved

B1 Make v the subject of each formula:
  a $\frac{3}{4}v = a - x$ **b** $2v + 1 = \frac{3}{5}(a - 3)$

  c $\frac{2a + 3}{v} = 3a^2$ **d** $\frac{2v + 5}{4} = ax + 2y$

  e $\frac{3v + 2a}{3} = \frac{a + v}{5}$ **f** $\frac{3}{b - 2v} = c^2$

  g $\frac{1}{w} + \frac{2}{v} = \frac{3}{x}$

C Recognise when you need to factorise when rearranging a formula

C1 Rearrange each formula to give c in terms of the other variables:
  a $ax^2 + cx = 3$
  b $3x + 2ac = bc - 5x + cy$
  c $2a(a + 3c) = b(1 + cx)$
  d $a^2b - a^2c = 3 - bc + 2a$
  e $3x(w - cx^2) = \frac{c + 2}{3}$
  f $2 + a^2c + cx - cy^2 = ax + c$

D Deal with powers and roots in formulas

D1 In each formula rearrange the terms to make y the subject:
  a $\sqrt{xy} = 5$
  b $(a + x) = \sqrt{(1 + y)}$
  c $\frac{2}{\sqrt{y}} = 2x - 1$

  d $3\sqrt{\frac{y}{a}} = b$

  e $5 = 2\sqrt{(a^2 - y)}$
  f $\sqrt{(1 - ay + by)} = \sqrt{(x^2y - 3)}$
  g $4y^2 + 3 = 2(b - y^2)$
  h $5(3y^2 + a) = a(2 - a)$
  i $\frac{2a + b}{y^3} = 5$

E Evaluate formulas

E1 A formula for the surface area (S) of a cylinder is:
  $S = 2\pi rh + 2\pi r^2$, where r is the radius and h the height.
  a Calculate a value for S when: $r = 5.7$ cm and $h = 12.5$ cm. Give your answer to 3 sf.
  b Calculate a value for h when: $r = 5$ cm and $S = 424$ cm^2. Give your answer to 1 dp.

E2 Given the formula $p = \frac{a + b^2}{3a}$

  Calculate to 2 sf a value for b when: $a = 3.5$, and $p = 5.5$

Starting points
You need to know about ...

... so try these questions

A Writing ratios

◆ A **ratio** compares the size of two or more quantities.

$$3:4 \qquad 1:4:2 \qquad 3\tfrac{1}{2}:\tfrac{1}{2}$$

◆ In the ratio $3:4$, the **number of parts** are 3 and 4.

B Equivalent ratios

◆ The ratios $3:4$ and $6:8$ are **equivalent ratios**.

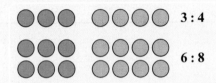

3 : 4

6 : 8

◆ To write an equivalent ratio:
 ❖ multiply or divide each number of parts by the same number.

$$\div2 \overset{\frown}{\underset{\smile}{6:8}} \div2 \qquad \times5 \overset{\frown}{\underset{\smile}{2:3:7}} \times5$$
$$\mathbf{3:4} \qquad \mathbf{10:15:35}$$

◆ A ratio in its **simplest terms**, or **lowest terms**, is written with the smallest whole numbers possible.

$$\times4 \overset{\frown}{\underset{\smile}{1:\tfrac{1}{4}:3}} \times4 \qquad \div3 \overset{\frown}{\underset{\smile}{15:24}} \div3$$
$$\mathbf{4:1:12} \qquad \mathbf{5:8}$$

C Unitary ratios

◆ Two or more ratios can be compared by writing each one as a **unitary ratio** in the form $n:1$ or $1:n$.

A   B   C

3.2"   4"   4.8"

4"   5"   6"

The ratio of **width to height** for each of these photographs is:

A 4:3.2	B 5:4	C 6:4.8
1.25:1	**1.25:1**	**1.25:1**
or **1:0.8**	or **1:0.8**	or **1:0.8**

The ratios are equivalent so the photographs are **in proportion**.

A1 Roughcast is used to cover walls. It is a mix of 3 parts mortar to 1 part gravel.
Write this mix as a ratio of:
a mortar to gravel
b gravel to mortar.

B1 Copy and complete these sets of equivalent ratios.
a $4:1$ **b** $2:5:4$ **c** $9:12$
    $12:?$ $1:?:2$ $?:4$
                                $6:?$

B2

$2:5$	$1:3:2$	$10:20$
$10:25$	$2\tfrac{1}{2}:5$	$1:2:3$
$3:9:6$	$2:1$	$1:2\tfrac{1}{2}$

List the sets of equivalent ratios.

B3 Write each of these ratios in its simplest terms.
a $9:6$ **b** $14:21$
c $4:8:2$ **d** $5:\tfrac{1}{2}$
e $2:1\tfrac{1}{2}:3$

C1

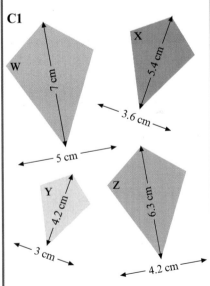

Which of these kites are in proportion?

D Writing ratios as fractions, decimals and percentages

◆ A ratio that compares **two** quantities can be written as a fraction, as a decimal, and as a percentage.

4″

5″

The **width-to-height ratio** is 5 : 4 or:

$$\frac{\text{width}}{\text{height}} = \frac{5}{4} = 1.25 = 125\%$$

❖ the width is $\frac{5}{4}$ of the height

❖ the width is 1.25 times the height

❖ the width is 125% of the height.

E Sharing in a given ratio

◆ An amount can be shared in a given ratio.

Example   Share £140 in the ratio 2 : 1 : 4
❖ find the total number of parts
 2 + 1 + 4 = 7
❖ find the amount for one part
 £140 ÷ 7 = £20
❖ multiply each number of parts by the amount for one part.

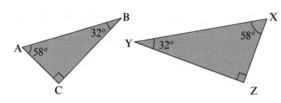

Total
7

2	:	1	:	4	7
×£20		×£20		×£20	×£20
£40	:	**£20**	:	**£80**	£140

F Similar triangles

◆ Triangles that have the same three angles are similar.

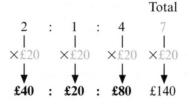

❖ $\hat{A}$ and $\hat{X}$ are **corresponding angles** because they are equal.

❖ AC and XZ are **corresponding sides** because they are opposite corresponding angles

◆ Triangles that are enlargements of each other are similar.

G Reciprocals

◆ Two numbers which multiply together to equal 1 are **reciprocals** of each other.

0.8 is the reciprocal of 1.25 $\frac{4}{5}$ is the reciprocal of $\frac{5}{4}$

1.25 is the reciprocal of 0.8 $\frac{5}{4}$ is the reciprocal of $\frac{4}{5}$

◆ The reciprocal of a number n is $\frac{1}{n}$ or $1 ÷ n$.

$$\frac{1}{0.8} = 1.25 \qquad \frac{1}{1.25} = 0.8$$

D1 Write each of these ratios as:
  i   a fraction
  ii a decimal
  iii a percentage.

  a 5 : 8   **b** 9 : 5
  c 7 : 12   **d** 15 : 11
  e 11 : 18   **f** 17 : 24

E1 Amy, Ben and Zoe are left £150 by their grandmother. They share the money in the ratio of their ages: 5, 3, and 2. Calculate how much each gets.

E2 Liz trains for the 100 m hurdles. She splits her time 3 : 5 between speed work and technique. Calculate how long Liz spends on:
  a technique in 2 hours training
  b speed work in 4 hours training

F1 EFG and JKL are similar.

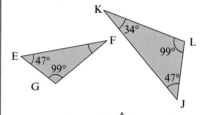

  a Explain why $\hat{F}$ is equal to 34°.
  b Give the corresponding angle to $\hat{G}$.
  c Give the corresponding side to:
    i EG   **ii** KL

G1 Give the reciprocal of:
  a 2   **b** 0.25
  c 3   **d** $1\frac{1}{3}$

Keeping in proportion

◆ When adjusting a recipe, you need to keep the ingredients in proportion.

Example This recipe for Swiss Hot Chocolate serves 2 people.
How much of each ingredient is needed for 5 people?

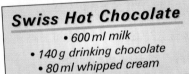

Swiss Hot Chocolate
- *600 ml milk*
- *140 g drinking chocolate*
- *80 ml whipped cream*

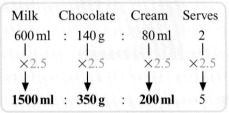

Milk		Chocolate		Cream		Serves
600 ml	:	140 g	:	80 ml		2
×2.5		×2.5		×2.5		×2.5
1500 ml	:	**350 g**	:	**200 ml**		5

> You can keep the multiplier in your calculator memory.

❖ find the **multiplier**:
5 ÷ 2 = 2.5

❖ multiply each amount by the multiplier.

Exercise 12.1
Recipes

1 This recipe serves 6 people.
How much of each ingredient
do you need for 9 people?

Chilled Chocolate Drink
230 g caster sugar • 300 ml water
50 g cocoa • 1200 ml chilled milk

2 This recipe for chocolate fudge makes 36 pieces.
  a How much cocoa is needed to make 72 pieces?
  b How much milk is needed to make 18 pieces?
  c Calculate how much of each ingredient you
    need to make 24 pieces.

> The multipliers here are less than 1.

Chocolate Fudge
- 450 g white sugar
- 150 ml milk
- 150 ml water
- 75 g butter
- 30 g cocoa

3 This recipe makes 24 sweets.
  a Calculate how many drops of
    peppermint essence are needed
    to make 42 sweets.
  b How many egg whites do you
    need to make these 42 sweets?

Chocolate Peppermint Creams
- 230 g icing sugar • 1 egg white
- 4 drops peppermint essence
- 100 g plain chocolate

◆ When you use an equivalent ratio to solve a problem, you are keeping the
number of parts in proportion.

Example

An orange dye is a mix of red and yellow in the ratio 2 : 3.
  a What amount of red is mixed with 480 ml of yellow?
  b How much orange dye is produced?

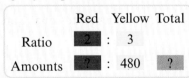

	Red	Yellow	Total
Ratio	2	: 3	
Amounts	?	: 480	?

❖ find the multiplier,
480 ml ÷ 3 = 160 ml

❖ multiply the other number of
parts by the multiplier

❖ find the total of the amounts.

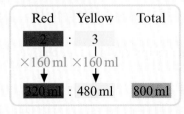

Red	Yellow	Total
2	: 3	
×160 ml	×160 ml	
320 ml	: 480 ml	800 ml

Exercise 12.2
Using equivalent
ratios

1 Calculate:

   a the amount of yellow dye to mix with 210 ml of red dye

   b how much orange dye is produced.

2 Walls can be covered with mortar to protect them from the weather.

   a For a clay wall how much cement is mixed with 1500 kg of sand?

   b For a concrete wall:

      i write the mortar mix as a ratio in its simplest terms

      ii calculate how much concrete is produced with 400 kg of cement.

Wall surface	Mortar mix Cement : Lime : Sand
Clay	$1 : 1 : 6$
Concrete	$1 : \frac{1}{2} : 4\frac{1}{2}$

3 On a map, 4.8 cm stands for a distance of 240 m.

   a What length on the map represents a distance of 315 m?

   b Give the map scale as a unitary ratio.

   c Explain why the total number of parts has no meaning in this ratio.

◆ When one shape is an enlargement of another, each dimension has been multiplied by the same number to keep it in proportion.

   Example I′J′K′L′ is an enlargement of IJKL. Find the height K′ L′.

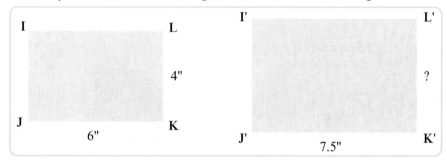

The multiplier is the scale factor of the enlargement.

❖ find the multiplier,
   $7.5 \div 6 = 1.25$

❖ multiply the height KL by the multiplier.

The shapes have the same width-to-height ratio, so they are in proportion.

Width	Height		$\dfrac{\text{Width}}{\text{Height}}$
6″	4″	IJKL	$\frac{6}{4} = 1.5$
×1.25	×1.25		
7.5″	**5″**	I′J′K′∠′	$\frac{7.5}{5} = 1.5$

Exercise 12.3
Enlargement

1

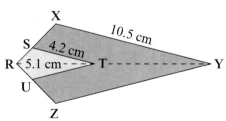

Kite RXYZ is an enlargement of kite RSTU.

   a Calculate the scale factor of the enlargement.

   b Find the length RY.

   c Calculate the ratio:

      i $\dfrac{RT}{ST}$ **ii** $\dfrac{RY}{SY}$

   d Explain why the ratios are equal.

Similar shapes

◆ Two shapes are **similar** if:
 ❖ all corresponding angles are equal, **and**
 ❖ all ratios of lengths of corresponding sides are equal.

These ratios are greater than 1 because lengths in the larger shape have been divided by lengths in the smaller shape.

A ratio is less than 1 if you divide lengths in the smaller shape by lengths in the larger shape.

$$\frac{AB}{PQ} = \frac{BC}{QR} = \frac{CD}{RS} = \frac{AD}{PS}$$

$$= 0.\dot{6}$$

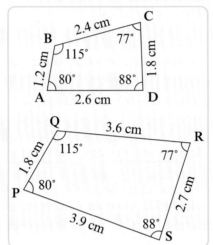

For shapes ABCD and PQRS:

❖ corresponding angles are equal:
 $\hat{A} = \hat{P}, \quad \hat{B} = \hat{Q}, \quad \hat{C} = \hat{R}, \quad \hat{D} = \hat{S}$

❖ ratios of lengths of corresponding sides are equal:

$$\frac{PQ}{AB} = \frac{1.8}{1.2} = 1.5 \qquad \frac{RS}{CD} = \frac{2.7}{1.8} = 1.5$$

$$\frac{QR}{BC} = \frac{3.6}{2.4} = 1.5 \qquad \frac{PS}{AD} = \frac{3.9}{2.6} = 1.5$$

So ABCD and PQRS are similar.

Exercise 12.4
Similar shapes

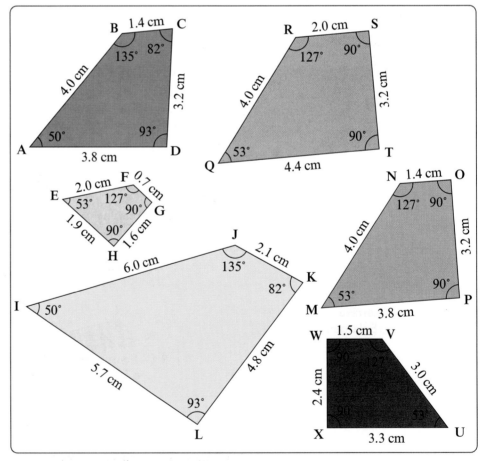

1   **a**   Which shape is similar to EFGH?
   b   Explain why.

2   **a**   List all the pairs of similar shapes.
   b   Give a ratio of the lengths of corresponding sides for each pair.

Finding lengths in similar shapes

♦ You can use a ratio to find a length in the **larger** of two similar shapes.

Example ABC and PQR are similar triangles.
Find the length PQ.

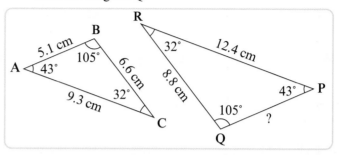

> Dividing a length on the larger shape by a length on the smaller shape gives the ratio greater than 1:
> $$\frac{PR}{AC} = \frac{12.4}{9.3} = 1.\dot{3}$$
>
> The ratio less than 1 is:
> $$\frac{AC}{PR} = \frac{9.3}{12.4} = 0.75$$

❖ Calculate the ratio greater than 1 for any two corresponding lengths. $\quad \dfrac{PR}{AC} = \dfrac{12.4}{9.3} = 1.\dot{3}$

❖ Multiply AB, the corresponding length to PQ, by the ratio.

$$\begin{array}{ccc} AB & \xrightarrow{\times 1.\dot{3}} & PQ \\ 5.1\text{ cm} & & \textbf{6.8 cm} \end{array}$$

♦ To find a length in the **smaller** of two similar shapes:
  ❖ use the same method with the ratio less than 1.

Exercise 12.5
Finding lengths in similar shapes

1

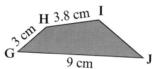

GHIJ and WXYZ are similar.
Find the length:

a YX **b** IJ.

2

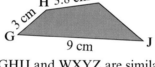

DEF and STU are similar.
Explain why this calculation is wrong.

To find DF: $\quad \dfrac{TU}{FE} = \dfrac{8}{6.4} = 1.25$

So DF = US × 1.25 = 7 cm × 1.25
= 8.75 cm ✗

3 KLNP and QMNO are similar.
Find the length LN.

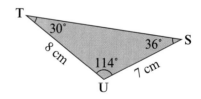

4 LMN and LJK are similar triangles.
  a Find the length JM.
  b Explain why JK and MN are parallel.

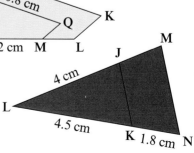

Similar triangles

♦ You need to recognise when triangles are similar.

Example In this diagram, PQ is parallel to ST.

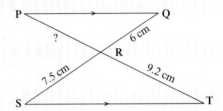

a Explain why triangles PQR and TSR are similar.
b Find the length PR.

> If two triangles have the same three angles then they must be similar.
>
> All ratios of corresponding lengths, therefore, are equal.

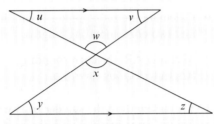

u and z are alternate angles,
v and y are alternate angles,
w and x are opposite angles, so
$u = z$, $v = y$, $w = x$

The triangles have the same three angles, so they are similar.

b The ratio is: $\dfrac{QR}{RS} = \dfrac{6}{7.5} = 0.8$

$$PR = RT \times 0.8$$
$$= 9.2\,\text{cm} \times 0.8$$
$$= \mathbf{7.36\,cm}$$

Exercise 12.6
Similar triangles

1 a Explain why ABD and CAD are similar triangles.
  b Give the corresponding side to:
    i AC   **ii** AD
  c Find the length:
    i AB   **ii** BC

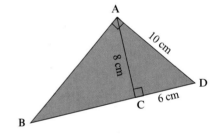

2 a Calculate the ratio:
    i $\dfrac{KM}{NM}$ **ii** $\dfrac{OM}{LM}$
  b Explain why KMO and NML are similar triangles.
  c Find the length KO.

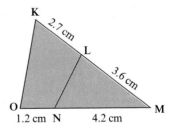

3 a Explain why DEF and GHF are similar triangles.
  b Find the length GH.

4 Explain why enlarging GHF, using centre of enlargement F, does **not** give DEF.

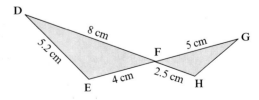

Proportionality

♦ All the shapes in a set of similar shapes must be in proportion.

Example This logo is made up of four similar triangles.
The dimensions of the triangles,
in centimetres, are:

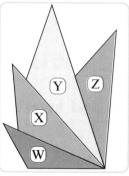

	W	X	Y	Z
Base (b)	4	5	6	4.8
Height (h)	1	1.25	1.5	1.2

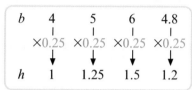

All the ratios $\dfrac{h}{b}$ are the same, 0.25, so h is **proportional to** b.

♦ If one variable, y, is proportional to another variable, x, you can write:

$$y \propto x$$

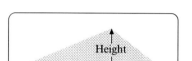
Height
Base

This ratio is a **constant** because it is the same for each pair of values.

The symbol $\propto$ means 'is proportional to'.

Exercise 12.7
Proportionality

1 **a** Draw a graph of h against b.

The four points lie on a straight line.

b Explain why the line, when extended, passes through $(0, 0)$.
c What is the connection between the constant and the gradient of the line?
d Give an equation connecting b and h in the form $h = \dots$.

2 **a** For each of the four similar triangles, calculate the ratio $\dfrac{b}{h}$.

b Give an equation connecting b and h in the form $b = \dots$.

This angle is the angle between the base of each triangle and the horizontal.

3 **a** Draw a graph of a against b.
  b Is a proportional to b?
    Explain your answer.

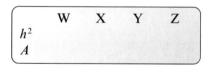

	W	X	Y	Z
Base (b)	4	5	6	4.8
Angle ($a°$)	24°	48°	72°	84°

4 **a** Copy and complete this table.
  b Draw a graph of A against h.
  c Is $A \propto h$?
    Explain your answer.

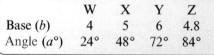

	W	X	Y	Z
Height (h)	1	1.25	1.5	1.2
Area (A)				

5 **a** Copy and complete this table.
  b Draw a graph of A against h^2.
  c Is $A \propto h^2$?
    Explain your answer.

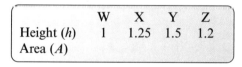

	W	X	Y	Z
h^2				
A				

6 These are the dimensions of another four triangles.

a Draw a graph of h against b.
b Give an equation connecting b and h in the form $h = \dots$.
c Calculate ratios to show that h is not proportional to b.

	A	B	C	D
b	4	4.8	5	6
h	2.5	2.7	2.75	3

7 a Each of these five triangles has an area of $3\,cm^2$.
  i Draw a graph of h against b.
  ii Is $h \propto b$?
  Explain your answer.

	P	Q	R	S	T
Base (b)	3	4	5	6	8
Height (h)	2	1.5	1.2	1	0.75

b i Copy and complete this table.
  ii Draw a graph of h against $\dfrac{1}{b}$.
  iii Is $h \propto \dfrac{1}{b}$?
  Explain your answer.

	P	Q	R	S	T
$\dfrac{1}{b}$					
h	2	1.5	1.2	1	0.75

Direct and inverse proportion

♦ If two variables, x and y, are proportional to each other, $y \propto x$, then they are in **direct** proportion.

> When two variables are directly proportional, an **increase** in one matches an **increase** in the other.

The relationship between the variables can be given as: $y = kx$, where k is a constant.

Example

b	4	5	6	4.8
	↓ ×0.25	↓ ×0.25	↓ ×0.25	↓ ×0.25
h	1	1.25	1.5	1.2

$h = 0.25\,b$

♦ Two variables, x and y, are in **inverse** proportion when one of the variables is in direct proportion to the reciprocal of the other: $y \propto \dfrac{1}{x}$

> When two variables are inversely proportional, an **increase** in one matches a **decrease** in the other.

The relationship between the variables can be given as: $y = \dfrac{k}{x}$ or $xy = k$, where k is a constant.

Example

b	3	4	5	6	8
h	2	1.5	1.2	1	0.75
bh	6	6	6	6	6

$h = \dfrac{6}{b}$ or $bh = 6$

Exercise 12.8
Direct and inverse proportion

1 The dimensions of these metric paper sizes, given in millimetres, are in direct proportion.

	A4	A3	A2	A1	A0
Width (w)	210	297	420	594	841
Height (h)	297	420	594	841	1189

a Calculate the height to width ratio, $\dfrac{h}{w}$, for each size.

b Explain why these ratios are not exactly equal to $\sqrt{2}$.
c Give an equation connecting w and h.

2 The dimensions of the sticky labels in this packet, given in centimetres, are inversely proportional.

Width (w)	18	12	9	7.2	6
Height (h)	2	3	4	5	6

a What is the area of each of the labels?
b Give an equation connecting w and h in the form:
  i $h = \dots$ **ii** $wh = \dots$ **iii** $w = \dots$.

3   The mass of glaze, g grams, needed to glaze a plate is in direct proportion to the square of the plate's diameter, d.

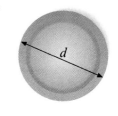

a   Copy and complete this table.

d	5	7	9	10	14
d^2					
g	10	19.6	32.4	40	78.4

b   Give an equation connecting d and g in the form $g = kd^2$.

Finding the constant

◆ To give an equation connecting two variables, you need to find the constant.

'Varies directly as' is another way of saying 'is in direct proportion to' or 'is directly proportional to'.

Example w varies directly as the square of f, and $w = 45$ when $f = 5$.
Give an equation connecting w and f.

Write down the relationship.

Substitute $w = 45$ and $f = 5$ into the formula.

Rearrange the formula to find the constant.

$$w \propto f^2 \quad \text{so} \quad w = kf^2$$
$$45 = k \times 5^2$$
$$45 = 25k$$
$$\frac{45}{25} = k$$

This gives $k = 1.8$, so **$w = 1.8f^2$**

◆ For two variables in inverse proportion, it is easier to use the formula $xy = k$ to find the constant.

'Varies inversely as' is another way of saying 'is in inverse proportion to' or 'is inversely proportional to'.

Example d varies inversely as the positive square root of z, and $d = 2.5$ when $z = 36$.
Give d in terms of z.

$$d \propto \frac{1}{\sqrt{z}} \quad \text{so} \quad d\sqrt{z} = k$$
$$2.5 \times \sqrt{36} = k$$
$$2.5 \times 6 = k$$

This gives $k = 15$, so **$d = \dfrac{15}{\sqrt{z}}$**

Exercise 12.9
Finding the constant

1   m varies inversely as v, and $m = 6$ when $v = 9$.
   a   Write down the relationship between m and v.
   b   Find the constant.
   c   Give an equation connecting m and v.
   d   Calculate m when $v = 4.5$.
   e   Explain what happens to m when v is halved.

2   s varies directly as the positive square root of q, and $s = 28$ when $q = 16$.
   a   Write down the relationship between s and q.
   b   Give an equation connecting s and q.
   c   Calculate s when $q = 36$.

3   p is in inverse proportion to the square of t, and $p = 2.5$ when $t = 6$.
   a   Give an equation connecting p and t in the form $p = \dots$.
   b   Calculate p when $t = 3$.
   c   Explain what happens to p when t is halved.
   d   Rearrange your equation to give t in terms of p.
   e   Calculate t when $p = 3.6$.

4 The number of plates, n, that can be glazed with one bag of glaze powder varies inversely as the square of the diameter, d, of the plate.
One bag glazes 800 side plates, diameter $5''$.

    a Write down the relationship between n and d.
    b Find the constant.
    c Give an equation connecting n and d.
    d Calculate how many plates one bag of powder will glaze for:
        i $10''$ dinner plates   **ii** $14''$ serving plates.

5 The area of cardboard needed to make a box for a basketball, A cm^2, is directly proportional to the square of the diameter of the ball, d cm.
A 26 cm basketball box needs 2366 cm^2 of cardboard.

    a Write down the relationship between A and d.
    b Find the constant.
    c Give A in terms of d.
    d Calculate how much cardboard is needed for a 19 cm basketball box.

6 The length of time, t seconds, that a basketball bounces when dropped varies directly as the square root of the height, h cm, from which it is dropped.
The ball bounces for 16 seconds when dropped from 1 m.

> You need to convert m into centimetres.

    a Give an equation connecting t and h.
    b Calculate the bounce time, to the nearest 0.1 seconds, from a height of 50 cm.

7 The f/stop on this camera lens is inversely proportional to the aperture diameter, a mm.
f8 has an aperture of 5.25 mm.

> The aperture is the adjustable opening in the lens that lets the light in when you take a photograph.

    a Write down the relationship between f and a.
    b Find the constant.
    c Give f in terms of a.
    d Calculate the aperture diameter for f16.

8 The brightness ratio, r, of a camera lens is in inverse proportion to the square of the f/stop.
f4 has a brightness ratio of 0.25.

> The brightness ratio compares how much light is let in at two different apertures.
> For example: an aperture with a brightness ratio of 0.5 lets twice as much light in as an aperture with a brightness ratio of 0.25.

    a Give an equation connecting r and f.
    b Calculate the brightness ratio for f16.
    c Find the f/stop that has a brightness ratio of 1.

9 Chocolate Chunks are cubic pieces of chocolate.
The mass of one piece, m grams, varies directly a the cube of the width, w cm.
The 1.5 cm chunk has a mass of 10.8 grams.

    a Give m in terms of w.
    b Calculate the mass of a 3 cm chunk.
    c The width of two chunks is in the ratio $1:2$.
       Give the ratio of the mass of the two chunks.

End points

You should be able to ...   ... so try these questions

A Keep amounts in the same proportion

A1 This ice-cream recipe serves 8 people.
  a Calculate how much of each of these ingredients you need to serve 20 people.
    i caster sugar   **ii** boiling water
  b How many eggs are needed to serve 6 people?

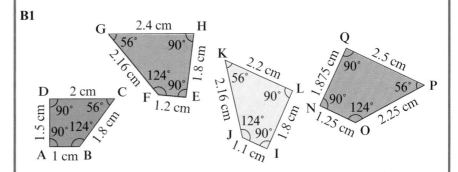

Chocolate Ice Cream
• 150 g caster sugar
• 20 g cocoa • 4 eggs
• 410 g can evaporated milk
• 4 tablespoons boiling water

B Identify similar shapes

B1

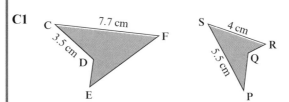

Which of these shapes are similar to ABCD?

C Find lengths in similar shapes

C1

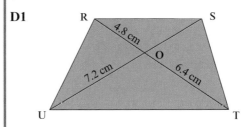

CDEF and PQRS are similar. Find the length:
  a PQ   **b** EF

D Recognise and use similar triangles

D1

RSTU is a trapezium.
  a Explain why triangles ROS and TOU are similar.
  b Find the length OS.

E Understand direct and inverse proportion

E1 The length of time, s seconds, that a tennis ball bounces when dropped is in direct proportion to the square root of the height, h cm, from which it is dropped.
The ball bounces for 18 seconds when dropped from 64 cm.
  a Give an equation connecting s and h.
  b Calculate the bounce time from a height of 1 m.

E2 w varies inversely as q, and $w = 1.2$ when $q = 5$.
  a Give w in terms of q.
  b Calculate w when $q = 10$.
  c Explain what happens to w when q is doubled.
  d Calculate q when $w = 7.5$.

Starting points
You need to know about ...

... so try these questions

A Prisms and pyramids

- This solid has a cross-section which is the same all through the solid. This is known as a **uniform cross-section**.

- Solids with a uniform cross section are known as **prisms**.

- These are other examples of prisms.

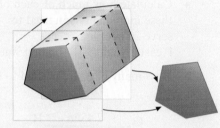

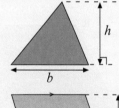

Triangular prism   Pentagonal prism

- A **pyramid** is a solid with a polyhedral base with triangular sides which meet at one vertex.

- These are two examples of pyramids.

Hexagonal pyramid   Square pyramid

B The area of a plane shape

- Area of a triangle $= \frac{1}{2}bh$

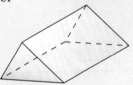

- Area of a parallelogram $= bh$

- Area of a trapezium $= \dfrac{h(a + b)}{2}$

where h is the perpendicular height.

C The area and circumference of a circle

- Area of a circle $= \pi r^2$

- Circumference of circle $= 2\pi r$ or πd

A1 Each of the solids is either a prism or a pyramid.
  a List all the prisms.

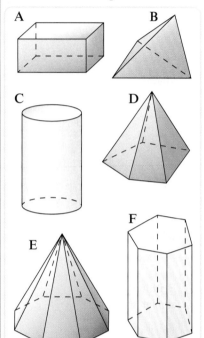

  b Name each solid.

B1 Calculate the areas of these shapes.

a

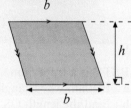

b

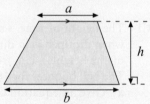

c

C1 Calculate the area of a circle with a diameter of 2.4 m.

C2 A circle has a circumference of 52 cm. What is its radius?

D Volumes and surface areas of prisms

♦ The volume of any prism = Area of uniform cross-section × Depth

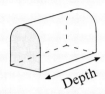

Depth

Example What are the volume and surface area of this prism?

The uniform cross-section is trapezium-shaped.

Area of trapezium = $\dfrac{5 \times (3 + 6)}{2}$

= 22.5 cm²

Volume of prism = 22.5 × 12
= **270 cm³**

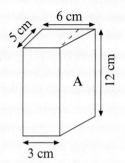

♦ The surface area is the total of the areas of **all the exterior faces**.

To find the area of face A you need to know its width PQ.

By Pythagoras' rule:

$$PQ^2 = PT^2 + TQ^2$$
$$AB = \sqrt{3^2 + 5^2} = \sqrt{34}$$
$$AB = 5.83 \ (2 \ dp)$$

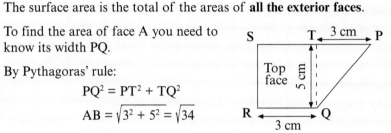

Area of face A = 5.83 × 12 = 70 cm² (2 sf)
Area of left side face = 5 × 12 = 60 cm²
Area of top = 22.5 cm²
Area of bottom = 22.5 cm²
Area of back = 6 × 12 = 72 cm²
Area of front = 3 × 12 = 36 cm²

Surface area of prism = 283 cm² (3 sf)

E The volume and surface area of a cylinder

♦ Volume of cylinder = $\pi r^2 h$

♦ Area of curved surface = $2\pi rh$ or πdh

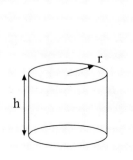
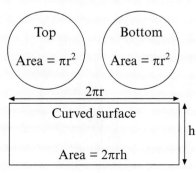

D1 Calculate the volume and surface area of each of these prisms.

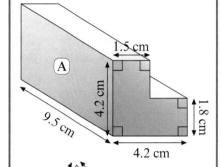

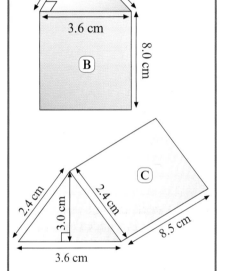

E1 Calculate the volume and total surface area of this cylinder.

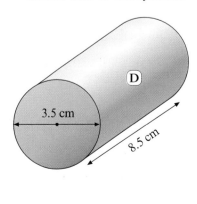

The area of composite shapes

Composite shapes are made up from more than one shape.
Sometimes you can find the area by adding areas; at other times it is easier to subtract.

Example 1

Find the area of ABCDEF.

The area (A) of ABCDEF can be given by:
$$A = (12.4 \times 4.5) + (4.6 \times 4.8)$$
$$= 55.8 + 22.08$$
$$= 77.9 \text{ (1 dp)}$$

The area of ABCDEF is 77.9 cm^2

or

The area (A) of ABCDEF is given by:
$$A = \text{Area of large rectangle} - \text{Area cut out for L-shape}$$
$$A = (12.4 \times 9.3) - (4.8 \times 7.8)$$
$$A = 115.32 - 37.44$$
$$\mathbf{A = 77.9 \text{ (1 dp)}}$$

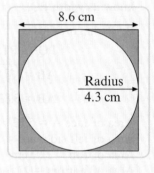

Example 2

Find the shaded area.

The area of the shaded part (A) is given by:
$$A = \text{Area of square} - \text{Area of circle}$$
$$A = (8.6 \times 8.6) - (\pi \times 4.3^2)$$
$$A = 73.96 - 58.09 \ldots$$
$$\mathbf{A = 15.9 \text{ (1 dp)}}$$

The shaded area is 15.9 cm^2.

> The answer is rounded at the end of the calculation.

Exercise 13.1
Working with composite shapes

1 This shows an open-topped magazine holder which is made from card.
The front is cut away so magazines can be removed easily.

a Calculate the area of side R.
b Calculate the total area of card used to make the box.

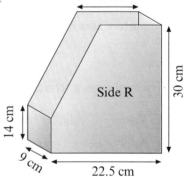

2 This shows how milk bottle tops are cut from a strip of foil.

a Calculate the area of foil wasted by cutting out these five tops.
b Tops are cut from a 7.2 m strip of foil. Calculate the area of wasted foil.

3 This surround is used to frame photographs.
   A circle of radius 4 cm is cut from a rectangle
   of card. Gold lines are printed 1 cm from the
   edge of the circle and the card as shown.

   a Calculate the area of card after the cut out.
   b Is the area of photograph showing more
      or less than $\frac{1}{4}$ of the area of the surround?
      Explain your answer.
   c Calculate the length of gold line on the card.

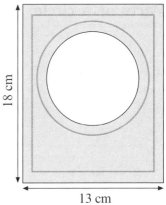

18 cm

13 cm

4 This diagram shows the net of
   a box for playing cards.
   The net was cut from a
   rectangle of card that it
   just fitted.

   a What were the original
      dimensions of the piece
      of card?
   b Calculate the area of the
      glue flap on the right.
   c The box opens at either end.
      Find the area of an
      opening end.
   d Calculate the total area of
      the net.
   e Roughly, what fraction of
      the card is wasted?
      Explain how you decided.

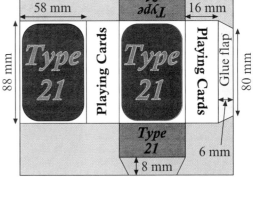

55 mm
58 mm 16 mm
Type 21
88 mm Playing Cards Type 21 Playing Cards Glue flap 80 mm
Type 21
8 mm 6 mm

5 This logo design for a company that makes
   helmets uses two parts of a circle in a
   red square.

   a Calculate the area of the visor in
      the logo. (the blue part).
   b Find the area of the helmet in the logo
      (the yellow part).
   c What percentage of the logo is red.

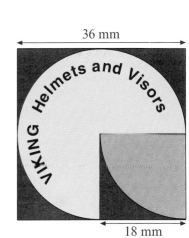

36 mm

VIKING Helmets and Visors

18 mm

6 These are diagrams of filters used in spotlights.
   Blue and yellow filters can
   give blue, yellow and green light.

   Each filter is in a square frame
   of length x.

   Give an expression in x for:

   a the area of the blue filter
   b the non-coloured area in
      the yellow filter frame
   c the area of green where the two filters overlap.

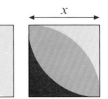

x

Blue filter   Yellow filter   Both filters

Parts of a circle

For some problems you need to calculate the area of a sector of a circle or the length of an arc.

For both of these the ratio of the angle θ to a full circle (360°) is used.

- Area of sector $= \dfrac{\theta}{360} \times$ area of circle

$$= \dfrac{\theta}{360}\pi r^2$$

- Arc length $= \dfrac{\theta}{360} \times$ Circumference

$$= \dfrac{\theta}{360}\pi d$$

Example   A piece of cheese of angle 56° is cut from a round cheese of radius 15 cm. Find its area and perimeter.

Area of sector $= \frac{56}{360} \times \pi r^2$

$\qquad\qquad\qquad = \frac{56}{360} \times \pi \times 15^2$

$\qquad\qquad\qquad = \textbf{110.0 cm}^2$ (to 1 dp)

Arc length $\qquad = \frac{56}{360} \times \pi d$

$\qquad\qquad\qquad = \frac{56}{360} \times \pi \times 30$

$\qquad\qquad\qquad = 14.7\,\text{cm}$

Perimeter $= 15 + 15 + 14.7 = \textbf{44.7 cm}$

Exercise 13.2
Arcs and sectors

1   In each case calculate the area of the sector and its perimeter.

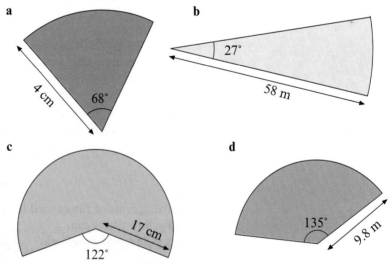

a 4 cm, 68°

b 27°, 58 m

c 17 cm, 122°

d 135°, 9.8 m

2   A baby's bib is made from towelling and is designed around two arcs of circles with the same centre.

   a   Calculate the area of towelling in the bib.

   b   The bib is edged all round with piping. What length of piping is used?

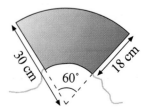

30 cm, 60°, 18 cm

Calculating volumes and surface areas

Exercise 13.3
Volumes and surface
area problems

1 This toy is made from a clear plastic
cuboid filled with blue liquid.
The depth of liquid is 3.5 cm.

  a Calculate the volume of blue liquid in
the cuboid.

  b The toy is turned on to its side.
What is the depth of blue liquid correct
to the nearest 0.1 cm?

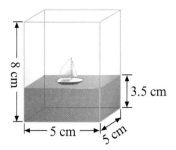

2 This collecting box is in the shape of a cylinder.
The circumference of its base is 29.2 cm
and its capacity is 1120 cm³.
Calculate the height of the box.

3 In a childrens' play area this space under the
swings is dug to a depth of 0.3 m and filled
with bark chippings.

  a Calculate the volume of bark chippings
needed.

  b Forestry Products sell bark chippings in
bags. Each bag costs £5.12 and
contains 0.07 m³ of chippings.

    i How many bags of chippings
should be bought?

    ii What is the total cost of
chippings?

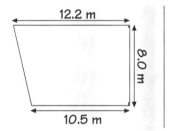

4 The diagram shows the uniform cross-section of an open-air swimming pool.

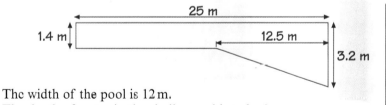

The width of the pool is 12 m.
The depth of water in the shallow end is to be 1 m.

  a Calculate the area of the cross-section.

  b What is the total capacity of the swimming pool?

  c Calculate the volume of water in the pool.

  d The amount of chlorine added to the water
in this pool is 1 millilitre per cubic metre
of water.
How much chlorine, in litres, will be added?

> The surface area of a solid
> is the **total** area of all its
> **exposed** faces, including
> curved ones.

5 A solid spigot is made from a cylinder of
diameter 6 cm and height 4 cm which is fixed
on to a cylinder of diameter 12 cm and
height 8 cm.
Calculate the surface area of the spigot.

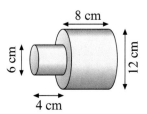

6 Kevin usually makes a fruit cake in a 20 cm square cake tin.
The finished cake has a depth of 8 cm.
Just to be different, he makes a cake of the same volume
in a round tin with a diameter 24 cm.
What is the expected depth of this cake?

7 This competition appeared in a puzzle magazine.

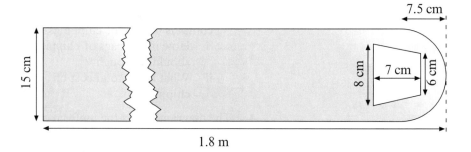

WIN A BOX OF POUND COINS !!

- A cuboid shaped box is full of pound coins.

- The areas of the three different rectangular faces
  are 120 cm², 96 cm² and 80 cm².

- Each edge measures a whole number of centimetres.

FIND THE VOLUME OF THE BOX AND WIN THE MONEY !

a Find the volume of the box described in the competition.
b A pound coin has a diameter of 2.2 cm and a thickness of 0.3 cm.
Estimate how much money is in the box.

8 A concrete post to support a handrail has this symmetrical uniform
cross-section. The post is 16 cm thick.

> Beware: you will need to
> calculate a further
> dimension before you can
> do part **b**.

15 cm

7.5 cm

8 cm 7 cm 6 cm

1.8 m

a Calculate the volume of concrete in the post.
b Calculate its total surface area (not forgetting the handrail cut-out).

9 A slice of cheese is cut from a large cylinder of cheddar.
Each cut passes vertically down through the centre of the end circle.
The slice has an angle of 54°.

a Calculate the area of one end of the
cheese slice.
b Calculate the area of the curved surface.
c What is the total surface area of the
slice of cheese?
d If no other slices have been cut, what is
the surface area of the remainder of the
cylinder of cheese?

54°

8 cm

22 cm

10 A tunnel is cut through a hillside.
The cross-section of the tunnel is shown
where the arc AB is a semicircle.
The tunnel is 540 metres long.

   a Calculate the volume of spoil which
     must be removed.
   b All the interior surfaces are lined with a
     skin of concrete.
     Calculate the internal surface area of
     the tunnel.

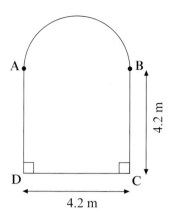

11 The diagram shows a two kilogram weight.
The weight is made from
a hollow cylinder of metal
from which a sector of
angle 30° is cut out.
This cut-out allows the
weight to be slid on to
a pole.

   a Calculate the volume
     of the weight.
   b Calculate the mass of
     metal which is cut
     out from the hollow
     cylinder.

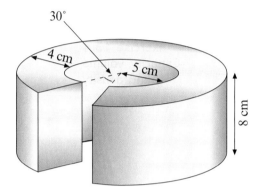

12 a Sketch two cylinders where the sum of the radius and height is 12 cm.
   b Find the volume of each cylinder.
   c When the sum of the radius and height is 12 cm, what do you think
     is the maximum possible volume?

13 A solid is made from a cuboid with
dimensions x, y and z.
A hole of radius r is drilled right through
from one side as shown.

Write and simplify an expression for:

   a the volume of the solid
   b the surface area of the solid.

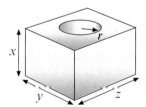

14 In a solid cylinder the height is half the radius.
Write an expression for the radius R in terms of the volume V and the
surface area S.

Capacity, volume and density

♦ For liquids, volume or capacity is often measured in litres (l) or millilitres (ml).

> 1 litre = 1000 millilitres
> 1 millilitre is equivalent in volume to 1 cm³.

♦ Mass (often called weight) is measured in kilograms (kg) or grams (g).

> 1 kilogram = 1000 grams
> 1 ml of water weighs 1 gram.

♦ Density can be measured in grams per cubic centimetre (g/cm³).

$$\text{Density} = \frac{\text{mass in grams}}{\text{volume in cm}^3}$$

Exercise 13.4
Capacity, volume and density

1 Write down one choice from each bracket to complete the sentence.
   a The volume of an orange is about (30 cm³, 300 cm³, 3000 cm³).
   b The capacity of a wine glass is about (75 litres, 7.5 litres, 75 millilitres).
   c The weight of an apple is about (17 grams, 170 grams, 1.7 kilograms).

2 A dairy plans to sell cartons containing 550 ml of milk.

Milk carton designs – External dimensions

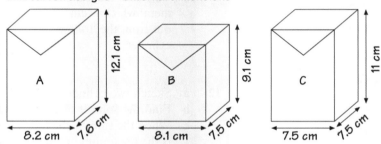

a Which of these cartons do you think the dairy should use?

The waxed cardboard used for the cartons is 1 mm thick.

b Which carton do you now think they should use?
c What is the capacity of carton C?
d What percentage of the capacity of carton C would be airspace if 550 ml of milk were added?
e What volume of waxed card is used to make carton C? Ignore the flaps.
f Find the mass of C if the density of cardboard is 0.86 g/cm³.

Question **2** shows the difference between volume and capacity.
Carton A has a **volume** of 8.2 × 7.6 × 12.1 cm³, but its **capacity** is less than this because of the thickness of the cardboard.

3 The milk tank on a tanker is a cylinder of radius 1.2 m and length 4.8 m. Calculate the capacity of the tank in:
   a cm³   b litres.

4 Each of these pieces of cheese has a uniform cross-section.

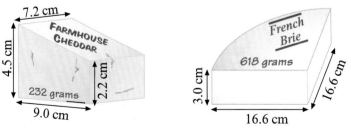

Calculate the volume and density of each piece.

Planes of symmetry

Some solids have **plane symmetry**.
For example, this solid has plane symmetry.

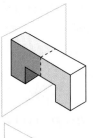

In the mirror, look at half of the solid like this and you see the other half.

So the mirror shows the position of a **plane of symmetry**.

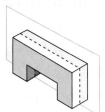

This mirror shows the position of another **plane of symmetry**.

This solid is said to have two **planes of symmetry**.

Exercise 13.5
Properties of solids

1 Each of these solids is made from four cubes.

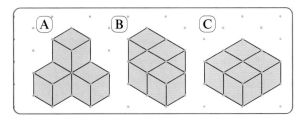

a Which of these solids are prisms?
b How many planes of symmetry has solid B?
c Which solid has exactly 3 planes of symmetry?

2 Draw a prism made from four cubes that has:

a 2 planes of symmetry b 5 planes of symmetry.

3 Each of these nets A to D is for a prism or a pyramid.

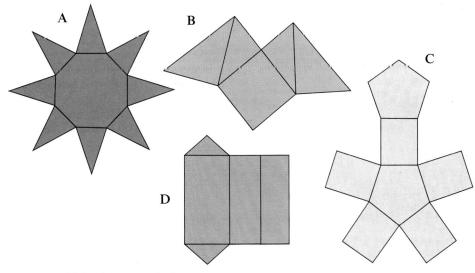

a Which of the nets is for:
   i a prism   ii a pyramid?
b How many planes of symmetry would each assembled solid have?

Pyramids and cones

♦ For any pyramid:

  ❖ **Volume** = $\frac{1}{3}$**Base area** × **Perpendicular height**

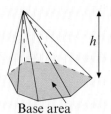

Base area

♦ A cone can be considered as a pyramid but with a circular base (i.e. a polygon base with an infinite number of sides). The base area of a cone of radius r is πr^2.

♦ So for a cone:

  ❖ **Volume of a cone** = $\frac{1}{3}\pi r^2 h$

  ❖ **Curved surface area** = $\pi \times r \times$ **Slant height**

> A right cone or right pyramid is one where the vertex lies directly over the centre of the base.

Example Find the volume and surface area of a right cone with a base diameter of 12 cm and a perpendicular height of 14 cm.

Volume of cone = $\frac{1}{3}\pi r^2 h$

                = $\frac{1}{3} \times \pi \times 6^2 \times 14$

                = **528 cm³** (nearest integer).

To find the slant height (s)

Using Pythagoras' rule: $s = \sqrt{14^2 + 6^2}$

                      = 15.23 cm

Curved surface area = $\pi \times r \times s$

                 = $\pi \times 6 \times 15.23$

                 = 287 cm² (nearest integer).

Surface area = Curved surface area + Area of base

            = 287 + ($\pi \times 6^2$)

            = **400 cm²** (nearest integer).

Exercise 13.6
Pyramids and cones

1 For a cone of height 10 cm and base radius of 4 cm, calculate:

  a the volume

  b the curved surface area

  c the surface area.

2 A pyramid has a perpendicular height of 2.4 m and a square base of length 0.8 m. Calculate the volume of the pyramid.

3 A right hexagonal pyramid has a base which is a regular hexagon of side 4 cm and a perpendicular height of 12 cm.

  a Calculate the area of its base.

  b Calculate its volume.

4 Cone A has a base radius of 5 cm and a height of 10 cm.
Cone B has a base radius of 10 cm and a height of 5 cm.

  a Which cone has the larger volume?

  b Explain why the curved surface areas of cone A is half that of cone B but the volume of A is not half that of B.

The sphere

Archimedes, a Greek mathematician and inventor, was famous for his marvellous machines which were used against the invading Roman army. He was killed in 212 BC by the Romans while defending his home town of Syracuse.

What seems obvious now that a curved surface can have an area was first put forward by Archimedes in about 250 BC. He also discovered the formulas for the surface area and volume of a sphere.

- For a sphere of radius r
  - **Volume = $\frac{4}{3}\pi r^3$**
  - **Curved surface area = $4\pi r^2$**

Example Calculate the volume and curved surface area of a basketball which has a diameter of 26 cm.

> **Volume of basketball = $\frac{4}{3}\pi r^3$**
> $= \frac{4}{3} \times \pi \times 13^3$
> $= 7203\,\text{cm}^3$ (nearest integer).
>
> **Curved surface area = $4\pi r^2$**
> $= 4 \times \pi \times 13^2$
> $= 2124\,\text{cm}^2$ (nearest integer)

Exercise 13.7
Volumes and surface areas of spheres

1 Ball bearing A has a diameter of 1 cm and ball bearing B one of 2 cm.
   a Calculate the surface area of each ball bearing.
   b How many times larger is the surface area of B than A?
   c Calculate the volumes of each one.
   d How many times larger is the volume of B than A?

2 a A ball has a surface area of 3632 cm².
     What is its diameter to the nearest centimetre.
   b A different ball has a volume of 3632 cm³.
     Find its diameter to the nearest millimetre.

3 Saturn has a diameter of 1.2×10^5 km.
   What is its surface area?

4 What are the dimensions of a square piece of card which has the same surface area as a sphere of diameter 14 cm?

5 An Eiffel Tower paperweight is shaped like a hemisphere with a radius of 55 mm.
   a What is its volume?
   b What is its surface area?

55 mm

Archimedes had the diagram in Question **6** carved on his tomb because of its special properties. That's real pride in your work!

6 A sphere of diameter 15 cm fits exactly into a cylinder of height 15 cm and diameter 15 cm.

   Calculate:

   a the curved surface area of the cylinder
   b the curved surface area of the sphere.

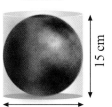

15 cm

15 cm

7 A sphere, diameter d, fits exactly inside a cylinder of diameter d and height d.
   Show why both always have the same curved surface area regardless of the value of d.

Parts of solids and composite solids

A cone or pyramid which has had its vertex cut off by a plane parallel to its base is known as a frustum.

Example What is the volume of this frustum of a cone?

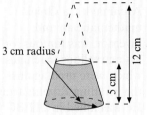

Volume of frustum = Vol. of 12 cm cone − Vol. of 7 cm cone

To calculate the volume of the 7 cm cone you need to know its base radius b.
The easiest way to find this is to consider the similar triangles ABE and ACD.

$$\frac{BE}{CD} = \frac{AB}{AC} \quad \text{so} \quad \frac{b}{3} = \frac{7}{12}$$

$$b = \frac{3 \times 7}{12} = 1.75 \text{ cm}$$

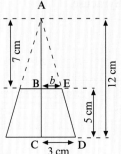

Vol. of frustum $= (\frac{1}{3}\pi \times 3^2 \times 12) - (\frac{1}{3}\pi \times 1.75^2 \times 7)$

$=(\frac{1}{3}\pi \times 108) - (\frac{1}{3}\pi \times 21.4375)$

$=\frac{1}{3}\pi (108 - 21.4375)$

$= \mathbf{90.6\,cm^3}$ (to 1 dp)

◆ Cones, pyramids and spheres can be parts of composite solids.

Example A perfume spray fits tightly inside a clear plastic cube of side 12 cm.
The shape of the spray is a hemisphere that sits on a cylinder.
Calculate the volume of air between the spray and the cube.

Vol. perfume = Vol. hemisphere + Vol. cylinder

$= (\frac{1}{2} \times \frac{4}{3}\pi r^3) + \pi r^2 h$

$= (\frac{4}{6} \times \pi \times 6^3) + (\pi \times 6^2 \times 6)$

$= 144\pi + 216\pi$

$= 360\pi$

$= 1131 \text{ cm}^3$ (nearest integer)

Vol. airspace = Vol. cube − Vol. perfume

$= 12^3 - 1131$

$= 1728 - 1131$

$= \mathbf{597\,cm^3}$

Exercise 13.8
Volume of complex solids

1 A cylindrical pencil is 17.6 cm long and has a radius of 7 mm.
It has 1.5 cm of its length shapened to a point. Calculate:

   a its volume   **b** its surface area.

2 Three spheres of diameter 4 cm sit inside a cuboidal tin with internal dimensions of 12 cm, 16 cm and 14 cm.
The space in the tin is then filled with water and this water is then poured out into a measuring cylinder of radius 4 cm.
How high up the cylinder does the water reach?

3 An ice lolly mould is shaped like an inverted cone of height 9 cm.

Green juice is poured into the mould until it reaches half the height then red juice is added to the top.

a What volume of red juice is added?

b What percentage of the volume of the lolly is green?

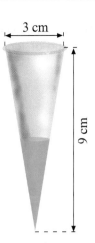

Note that the formula for the volume of a cone still applies to cones which are not right cones, i.e. sloping ones.

4 A model of a clock tower is made from one piece of card.

It is shaped like a square-based pyramid on a square-based prism.

A scale of 1 : 50 is used.

a What is the volume of the clock tower in m³?

b What is the volume of the model in cm³?

c Sketch a possible net for the model.

d Calculate the area of card needed for your net (ignore tabs and other fixings).

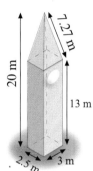

5 A tennis ball can be considered as a hollow sphere of exterior diameter 8 cm with a rubber skin of thickness 2 mm.

a What volume of rubber is used for the ball.

b Four balls are packed tightly end to end in a cylinder of card of thickness 1 mm. (The ends have the same thickness.)

i Calculate the exterior volume of the cylinder.

ii Calculate the air space inside the cylinder (including the air inside the balls) when it contains all four balls.

6 This frustum was made by cutting the top off a right cone. Let h be the height of the original cone in cm.

a Write an expression for the height of the part which was cut off.

b Use similar triangles to show why $5h = 48$, and hence calculate the height of the original cone and the part which was cut off.

c Calculate the volume of the frustum.

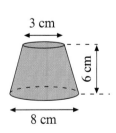

7 Which is the better fit: a square peg in a round hole or a round peg in a square hole, or does it depend on the size?

Thinking ahead to ...
the ratio of lengths areas
and volumes

A Cube A has a side length of 1 cm and cube B has a side length of 2 cm.
  a Calculate the surface areas of both cubes.
  b Calculate the volumes of both cubes.
  c The ratio of the dimensions of the cubes is 1 : 2.
     Calculate:
     i the ratio of the surface areas
     ii the ratio of the volumes.

The ratio of lengths, areas and volumes

♦ As an object is enlarged the ratio of its lengths obviously increases.
  Less obviously, the area and volume will also increase but not in the
  same ratio.

♦ Areas involve multiplying a length by a length, so if the all corresponding
  lengths on an object increase x times, **any** area on the object will increase
  $x \times x$ or x^2 times.

♦ Volumes involve multiplying a length by a length by a length, so if all
  the corresponding lengths on an object increase x times, **any** volume on
  the object will increase $x \times x \times x$ or x^3 times.

♦ This may seem obvious as cubes or cuboids are enlarged. It also applies to
  any **similar** objects such as spheres, cones, or irregular or compound shapes.

Example Two similar wine bottles have base
areas of 30.8 cm² and 50.3 cm².

a Calculate the ratio of the heights of the
two bottles in the form 1 : n.

b The large bottle has a height of 30 cm.
Calculate the height of the small bottle.

c If the large bottle is a standard bottle, is
it true to call the small bottle a 'half bottle'?

Large   Small

a The ratios of the base areas is:
30.8 : 50.3 = 1 : 1.633 1169 (to 7 dp)

so the ratio of corresponding lengths will be   1 : $\sqrt{1.633\,1169}$
                                                = 1 : 1.277 9346

The ratio of the heights of the bottles is 1 : 1.2779 (to 4 dp)

b **The height of the small bottle** = $\dfrac{30}{1.2779}$ = **23.5 cm** (to 3 sf)

c The ratio of lengths is 1 : 1.277 9346
so the ratio of the volumes will be   1 : $(1.277\,9346)^3$
                                     = 1 : 2.087

so the large bottle has roughly twice the capacity of the small one.
so the small bottle can justifyably be called a 'half bottle'.

> It is best not to round these
> ratios too greatly because
> squaring and cubing
> numbers tends to
> exaggerate any errors.

Exercise 13.9
Ratio of areas and volumes

1 Two similar cones have heights of 4 cm and 12 cm.
  a The volume of the larger cone is 353 cm³.
     Calculate the volume of the smaller cone.
  b The surface area of the small cone is 13.8 cm².
     Calculate the surface area of the large one.

2 Two similarly shaped weights have masses of 5 kg and 2 kg.
The 5 kg weight has a base
which is 9 cm across.

a Write the ratio of volumes of
the two weights in the
form $n : 1$.

b How wide is the base of
the 2 kg weight?

3 A newspaper displayed
this chart as part of a
feature on how two
companies donated
money to charity.

a The newspaper
believe they have
displayed the data
accurately, but why is
the chart misleading?

b The £ sign for Cyclone UK is 36 mm tall.
How should the newspaper change Denopt System's £ sign to accurately
reflect the companies' contributions?

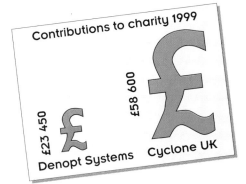

4 This irregular solid of end area 16 cm² and
volume 132 cm³ is enlarged by certain scale factors.
Calculate the following with the
stated scale factors:

a End area, SF 2   **b** Volume, SF 3   **c** End area, SF $\frac{1}{3}$

d End area, SF $1\frac{3}{4}$ **e** Volume, SF $\frac{2}{3}$ **f** Volume, SF 2.

5 A barn with a curved roof has a maximum height of 6 metres and
holds 1740 tons of straw.
A similarly shaped but smaller barn holds half as much straw.

Calculate the maximum height of the smaller barn.

6 Three similar plane shapes, A, B and C, are enlarged.
When A is enlarged by SF 4, B by SF $\frac{1}{2}$ and C by SF 2, the images all
have the same area.

Calculate the scale factor which would enlarge:

     a   shape A on to shape C   b   shape B on to shape C
     c   shape A on to shape B   d   shape B on to shape A
     e   shape C on to shape A   f   shape C on to shape B.

Formulas for length, area and volume

In calculations with length, area and volume:

- ◆ a length added to or subtracted from a length gives a length
- ◆ an area added to or subtracted from an area gives an area
- ◆ a volume added to or subtracted from a volume gives a volume
- ◆ a length multiplied by a length gives an area
- ◆ a length multiplied by a length multiplied by a length gives a volume
- ◆ the square root of an area gives a length
- ◆ to add, subtract, multiply or divide by a number that is not a length does not change whether an expression gives a length, area or volume.

For example, if the letters a, b and c represent lengths:

$3a + b$ represents a **length**: the lengths $3a$ and b add to give a length

$\frac{1}{2}a(b - c)$ represents an **area**: the expression $(b - c)$ is a length; the lengths $(b - c)$ and a multiply to give an area

$5a(b^2 + 3c^2)$ represents a **volume**: the areas b^2 and $3c^2$ add to give an area; the length a and the area $(b^2 + 3c^2)$ multiply to give a volume.

Exercise 13.10
Formulas for length, area and volume

1 In the following expressions, l and w each represent a length.
For each expression, decide if it represents a length, area or volume.

   a $4(l + w)$ **b** $4lw^2$ **c** $lw + w^2$

2 One of these expressions gives the volume of the prism.

$\frac{1}{2}(x + y + z + l)$ $x^2 + yz - l^2$ $2zx + zl$

$\frac{1}{2}lz(x + y)$ $\frac{1}{4}l(x + y + z)$

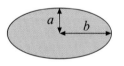

   a Which is the correct expression for the volume of the prism?
   b Give reasons for your answer.

3 One of these expressions gives the perimeter of this shape and one gives the area.

$\pi a^2 b$ πab $\pi b^2 a^2$ $\pi(a + b)$ $\pi b^2(a + 4)$

> π is a number, not a length.

Which is the correct expression for:
   a the perimeter   **b** the area?

4 In the following expressions, r and h each represent a length.
For each expression, decide if it represents a length, area or volume.
Give reasons for each answer.

   a $\frac{1}{4}rh$ **b** $\sqrt{r^2 + h^2}$ **c** $3(r + h) + \pi h$

   d $r^2(r + h)$ **e** $\frac{4}{3}\pi r^3$ **f** $\pi r(r + h)$

5 The letters x, y and z represent lengths.
Explain why $xy + xyz + y(x - z)$ cannot represent a length, area or volume.

End points

You should be able to ...   ... so try these questions

A Calculate areas of composite shapes

A1 Calculate the area of this shape.

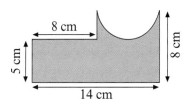

B Understand about planes of symmetry

B1 This solid is made from six cubes.

How many planes of symmetry does it have?

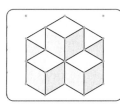

C Calculate volumes, capacities and surface areas of solids

C1 This is a section through a plastic closed tank which holds heating oil. The tank is shaped like a cylinder with a hemisphere at each end. The thickness of the plastic can be ignored.

Calculate:
a the capacity of the tank in m³
b surface area of the tank in m²
c how many litres of oil there are in a full tank.

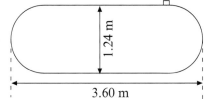

D Understand the effect of scale on area and volume

D1 A large dumb-bell solid has a surface area of 852 cm². A smaller similar solid has a surface area of 284 cm².

a The length of the small solid is 15 cm. What is the length of the larger one?

b The volume of the large solid is 3742 cm³. What is the volume of the smaller one?

E Decide if a formula could be for length, area or volume

E1 Amy knows that some of the following formulas could give the curved surface area (A) of a solid but she has forgotten which ones they are. s and r are lengths on the solid.

a $A = 4\pi r^2 s$ **b** $A = \pi(3r - s)$ **c** $A = 2\pi(r^2 + s^2)$

d $A = 4\pi r s^2$ **e** $A = 3\pi r s$ **f** $A = \dfrac{15\pi r^3}{3s}$

Which formulas cannot be for the surface area? Give your reason in each case.

Some points to remember

- The volume of a cone with base radius r and height h is given by: $V = \frac{1}{3}\pi r^2 h$
- The curved surface area of the cone of slant height s is given by: $A = \pi r s$
- The volume of a sphere of radius r is given by: $V = \frac{4}{3}\pi r^3$
- The surface area of a sphere of radius r is given by: $A = 4\pi r^2$

Starting points
You need to know about ...

... so try these questions

A Theoretical probability

- Theoretical probability can be calculated just by examining possible outcomes.

- It is usually given as a fraction (it must be less than 1).

- **It can only be used when outcomes are equally likely**.

Example 1
What is the probability that this spinner will stop on B?
There are twelve sections of equal size.
Four sections have B on them.
So the probability that the spinner stops on B is $\frac{4}{12} = \frac{1}{3}$.

This can be written as $p(B) = \frac{1}{3}$.

Example 2
In the same way, $p(A \text{ or } B) = \frac{7}{12}$.

This can also be written as $p(A, B) = \frac{7}{12}$.

- Probabilities can be shown on a probability scale from 0 to 1.

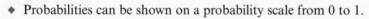

$$0 \qquad \frac{1}{4} \qquad \frac{1}{2} \qquad \frac{3}{4} \qquad 1$$

$$P(B) \qquad P(A,B)$$

B The probability of a non-event

If you know the probability of something happening, then you can also calculate the probability of it **not** happening.

Example
$p(B)$ on the spinner above is $\frac{1}{3}$.

$p(\text{not } B)$ is $1 - \frac{1}{3} = \frac{2}{3}$.

C Multiplication of fractions

In probability, sometimes you need to multiply fractions.

You can think of $\frac{3}{4} \times \frac{2}{5}$ like this:

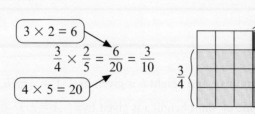

$3 \times 2 = 6$

$$\frac{3}{4} \times \frac{2}{5} = \frac{6}{20} = \frac{3}{10}$$

$4 \times 5 = 20$

- Multiply the numerators.
- Multiply the denominators.
- Then reduce to the simplest terms if you need to.

A1 What is the probability that the wheel will stop on:
  a A   b E   c D?

A2 What are these probabilities for the wheel?
  a $p(B \text{ or } F)$
  b $p(E, A)$
  c $p(A, B \text{ or } C)$
  d $p(a \text{ letter after D in the alphabet})$
  e $p(a \text{ letter of the alphabet})$
  f $p(the letter N)$

A3 Draw a probability scale and label the positions of $p(A)$, $p(C)$, $p(D)$, and $p(A, B, E, F)$.

A4 For a 1 to 6 dice what is the probability that for one roll you will get:
  a a multiple of 3
  b a prime number
  c a factor of 12?

B1 The probability of getting a red colour on a spinner is $\frac{4}{5}$. What is the probability of not getting red?

B2 In a game $p(2 \text{ points})$ is $\frac{1}{4}$ and $p(3 \text{ points})$ is $\frac{1}{8}$. What is $p(\text{not 2 nor 3 points})$?

C1 Multiply these fractions. Give each answer in its simplest terms.
  a $\frac{3}{4} \times \frac{1}{4}$
  b $\frac{5}{8} \times \frac{2}{5}$
  c $\frac{2}{3} \times \frac{6}{7}$
  d $\frac{1}{9} \times \frac{3}{4}$

D Relative frequency

- Relative frequency is a way of **estimating** a probability.

- It can still be used in equally likely situations but is the **only** way when outcomes are not equally likely.

- It is found by experiment (**experimental probability**), by survey, or by looking at data already collected (**empirical probability**).

- It is usually given as a decimal or as a percentage.

Example

This data shows the colour of cars passing a factory gate one morning.

Estimate the probability that, at a random time, a car passing will be red.

Colour	Frequency
Red	68
Black	14
Yellow	2
Green	34
Blue	52
Grey	35
Other	23
Total	228

The relative frequency of red cars is $\frac{68}{228} = 0.30$ (to 2 dp).

So the probability of a red car is 0.30 or 30%.

- This estimate of the probability can then be used to predict the number of red cars that will pass the gate on a different morning.

E Tree diagrams for combined events

- A tree diagram can help to organise data when calculating the probability of several events happening together.

- To find the probability of a particular joint outcome you can multiply the probabilities along the branches that lead to it.

This is a tree diagram for spinning a coin and rolling a 1 to 6 dice.

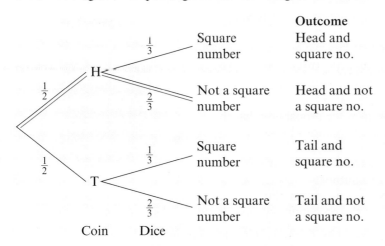

Example

To find the probability of a head **and** a non-square number you multiply the probabilities along the dotted branches.

Probability of a head and non-square no. is $\frac{1}{2} \times \frac{2}{3} = \frac{2}{6}$

D1 What is the relative frequency of blue cars in the survey. Give your answer to 2 dp.

D2 Estimate the probability that, at a random time, a car passing will be:
- **a** not blue
- **b** either yellow or green
- **c** neither green nor red
- **d** either black, grey or blue
- **e** pink.

D3 For which of these are the outcomes not equally likely.

The probability that:
- **a** a dropped matchbox will land face up
- **b** the next sidelight bulb that blows in a car will be in a front light
- **c** a person will catch measles before they are ten
- **d** the next rainstorm is on a Tuesday.

E1 What is the probability of a head and a square number?

E2 What is the probability of a tail and a non-square number?

E3 A red 1 to 6 dice and a blue 1 to 6 dice are rolled.

- **a** Draw a tree diagram to show the probability of a triangle number on the red dice and an even or odd number on the blue one.

- **b** What is the probability of getting a non-triangle number on the red with an even number on the blue dice?

Ways of pairing things

Exercise 14.1
Pairing

When people come down to breakfast
in France the custom is that each
person shakes hands with
everyone else.
This can mean a large number of
handshakes, but exactly how many
depends on the number of people.
Two people shaking hands counts as
one handshake.

There are five members of the Leblanc
family: Angeline, Bruno, Charles,
Danielle and Emmelle.
Here are three of the handshakes that
are made: AB, AD, BE.

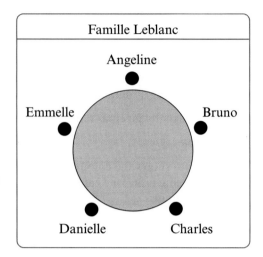

Famille Leblanc

Angeline

Emmelle

Bruno

Danielle

Charles

1 **a** List all the handshakes for the Leblanc family above.
   b Arrange your list so you can be sure you have every handshake.
   c How many handshakes in total?

2 A guest, Frederic, stays overnight with the Leblancs.
   a When they all come down to breakfast list the handshakes made.
   b How many handshakes are made?

3 **a** Draw up a table like this.

No. of people	1	2	3	4	5	6
No. of handshakes	0	1				

   b Describe any patterns you can see in the table.
   c Use your pattern to predict how many handshakes there will be for
        seven people. Check your prediction.

4 Emmelle is going on a trip. She
   wishes to take two books. Her
   bookshelf has five books she has not
   read. She picks two books at random.
   a List all the different pairs of
        books she might pick.
   b What is the probability that she
        picks two books by Sartre?
   c What is the probability that she
        picks two books by the
        same author?
   d What is the probability that she picks at least one blue book?
   e Give the probability of picking two books of different colour.

5 Bruno has eight books on his shelf, four of which are by Sartre.
   He picks two books at random.
   What is the probability that they are both by Sartre?

Dependent and independent events

If one cube is pulled from this bag at random, **replaced**, then another cube is chosen the probability of getting a red is $\frac{3}{9}$ on both occasions.

The same applies to the probability of other colours. This can be represented on a tree diagram like this:

When replacing cubes   Outcomes

	R	RR
$\frac{3}{9}$ R	$\frac{5}{9}$ B	RB
	$\frac{1}{9}$ Y	RY
	$\frac{3}{9}$ R	BR
$\frac{5}{9}$ B	$\frac{5}{9}$ B	BB
	$\frac{1}{9}$ Y	BY
	$\frac{3}{9}$ R	YR
$\frac{1}{9}$ Y	$\frac{5}{9}$ B	YB
	$\frac{1}{9}$ Y	YY

First pick   Second pick

The probability of getting two reds is therefore $\frac{3}{9} \times \frac{3}{9} = \frac{1}{9}$.

In this case the probabilities for the second pick **does not depend** on the first. Events of this type are known as **independent events**.

> Two or more events or outcomes are independent if the happening of one of them has no effect on the other.
>
> Two events or outcomes are dependent if the happening of one of them directly affects the other.

Suppose that when a cube has been picked it is **not replaced** for the second pick. If a red cube is picked first there will be 8 cubes left and only 2 of them will be red. For the second pick the probability of a red will be $\frac{2}{8}$.
The probabilities on the tree diagram will now look like this.

When not replacing cubes   Outcomes

	$\frac{2}{8}$ R	RR
$\frac{3}{9}$ R	$\frac{5}{8}$ B	RB
	$\frac{1}{8}$ Y	RY
	$\frac{3}{8}$ R	BR
$\frac{5}{9}$ B	$\frac{4}{8}$ B	BB
	$\frac{1}{8}$ Y	BY
	$\frac{3}{8}$ R	YR
$\frac{1}{9}$ Y	$\frac{5}{8}$ B	YB
	$\frac{0}{9}$ Y	YY

First pick   Second pick

The probability of getting two reds has now changed to $\frac{3}{9} \times \frac{2}{8} = \frac{1}{12}$.

In this case the probabilities for the second pick **do depend** on the first. Events of this type are known as **dependent events**.

Exercise 14.2
Probabilities for dependent events

1   For the problem above, what is the probability of getting:

   a   two blues when cubes are replaced
   b   two blues when cubes are not replaced
   c   a yellow and a red when cubes are replaced
   d   a yellow and a red when cubes are not replaced?

2   A washing line has these socks hanging on it.

Andy the thief steals two socks from the line at random.

a   What is the probability that the first sock he takes has a white stripe?

b   If one of the socks has a white stripe, what is the probability that the other will also have a white stripe?

c   Draw a tree diagram to show white stripes or no white stripes when two socks are taken from the line.

d   From your diagram calculate the probability that both socks the thief takes have no stripes.

Andy has a pang of conscience and puts the socks back on the line.
His friend, Lisa, then steals two socks from the twelve, also at random.

e   What is the probability that Lisa steals:
   i   two green socks
   ii   a blue sock and a yellow sock
   iii   a pair of the same colour (ignore the stripes)?

Note that these are dependent events. Even if the thief takes both socks at exactly the same instant, in probability terms this is the same as taking one then the other.

Even though a tree diagram can get crowded when dealing with four colours, it can still provide a visual way to organise the data.

For instance you could use a reduced tree diagram such as this for question 2e part i.

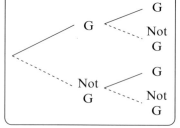

3   A card is picked at random from a pack of nine number cards.
It is not replaced then a second card is picked.
The cards are numbered 2, 3, 4, 5, 6, 7, 8, 9, 10.

a   Copy and complete the reduced tree diagram for picking cards with prime numbers.

b   Calculate the probability that both cards show prime numbers.

c   What is the probability that only one card will have a prime number?

Prime   Prime   Prime / Not prime

Not prime   Prime / Not prime

First pick   Second pick

d   Draw a different tree diagram to help you calculate the probability that the product of the two numbers will be even.

4   Three stable hands decide who mucks out the horses by drawing straws.
There are 3 short straws and 2 long ones.
When a straw has been picked it is not replaced.
Any person picking a short straw must help with mucking out.

What is the probability that:

a   all three people have to muck out

b   no one has to muck out

c   only one person mucks out

d   exactly two people muck out?

5 A charity decides to raise funds by using a scratch card with ten hidden numbers. There are always five 1's, three 3's and two 4's but they are in different positions on each card.
You win if you uncover a total of 5. More than 5 and you lose.

a List all the winning combinations.

A tree diagram has been started to show the winning combinations.

b Why do you think the ends of some of the branches are crossed out and others are ticked?

Note that not every branch need always be shown on a tree diagram. You only need to draw those useful to you.

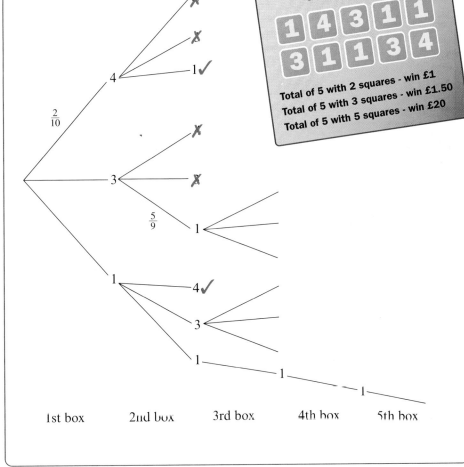

c Copy and complete the tree diagram and the probabilities to show winning combinations.
d Calculate the probability of getting a total of 5 by uncovering:
  i 5 squares **ii** 3 squares **iii** 2 squares?
e Is it true to say there is 'Over 50% chance of winning' with one card? Explain your answer.
f If the charity sells 500 cards, what profit or loss are they likely to make?

Conditional probability

The probability of something happening may depend on what happened earlier. For instance, the probability that a student will be absent from school on one day may be affected by whether the same student was absent the day before. These probabilities are often estimates based on relative frequencies.

> The probability that Jenny goes to the cinema on Friday night is an example of **conditional probability**.

Example

The probability that Jenny goes to the cinema on Friday is 0.27 based on her usual behaviour, but if she buys a video the probability goes down to 0.12. The probability that she buys a video is 0.3

Draw a tree diagram and calculate the probability that Jenny goes to the cinema.

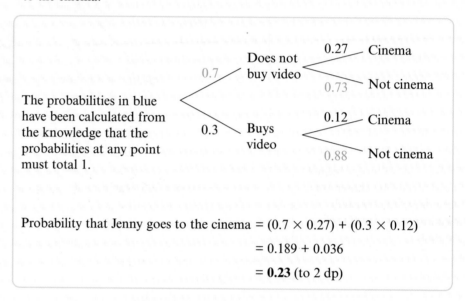

The probabilities in blue have been calculated from the knowledge that the probabilities at any point must total 1.

Probability that Jenny goes to the cinema = (0.7 × 0.27) + (0.3 × 0.12)

$$= 0.189 + 0.036$$

$$= \textbf{0.23} \text{ (to 2 dp)}$$

Exercise 14.3
Conditional probability

1 The probability that a new road needs repair after one year is 0.14.
If the road is not repaired in the first year, the probability that it needs repair in the second year is 0.45.
If it is repaired, the probability drops to 0.33 in the second year.

   a Draw a tree diagram to show the probabilities of repair over the two years.
   b Calculate the probability that the road:
      i does not need repair over the two years
      ii needs repair in the second year.

2 If it is a sunny day, the probability that the following day is sunny is 0.53.
If it is not sunny, the probability for sun the following day drops to 0.13.
Amy has her holiday on Monday, Tuesday and Wednesday.
It is sunny on Monday.

   What is the probability that Amy has:

   a three days of sun   b only one day of sun   c two days of sun?

3 The probability that a person chosen at random is left-handed is 0.08.
If they are left-handed, the probability that they are also left-footed is 0.91.
If they are not left-handed, the probability of being left footed is 0.01.

   Use a tree diagram to calculate the probability that a person chosen at random catches a ball with one hand but kicks it with the other.

When can you add probabilities?

Exercise 14.4
Adding probabilities

This shows the set of males with criminal records in the town of Humbleton.

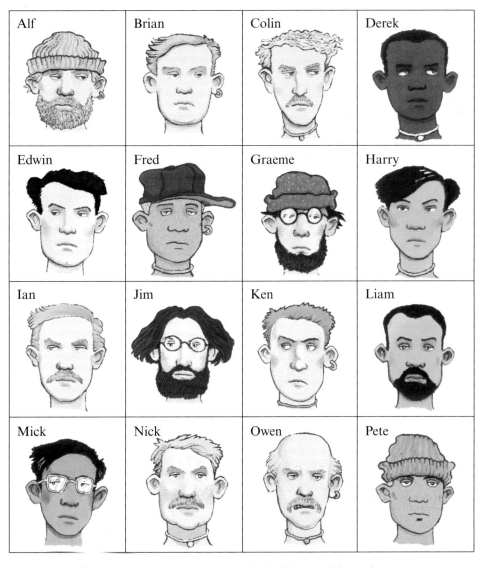

Give your probabilities as fractions and do not cancel them down.

1 What is the probability that a male criminal in Humbleton has:
    a a beard   **b** a necklace   **c** a beard or a necklace?

2 Compare your answers for the probabilities in Question **1**.
    What link can you find between them?

3 What is the probability that a male criminal in Humbleton has:
    a an earring   **b** a moustache?

4 **a** Predict the probability of a criminal having
       either an earring or a moustache.
    b Use the full set above to find the probability that a criminal has
       either an earring or a moustache.
    c Why do you think your prediction may not be the
       same as the true answer?

5 What is the probability that a criminal, chosen at random, has:
    a a hat   **b** a beard   **c** a beard or a hat?

Venn diagrams are named after the mathematician John Venn, who invented them in 1881 for his work on logic.

You can use Venn Diagrams to help you see why you can sometimes add probabilities, but at other times you must not.

Look at those criminals who have:
- dark hair
- earrings.

All those with dark hair are in the red loop and all those with an earring are in the blue loop.

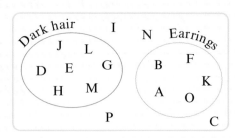

From this you can see that the probability of having dark hair is $\frac{7}{16}$ and of having an earring is $\frac{5}{16}$.

The probability of having either is $\frac{12}{16}$ (which is $\frac{7}{16} + \frac{5}{16}$).

The outcomes 'dark hair' and 'earrings' in Hambleton are said to be mutually exclusive.

Mutually exclusive outcomes are ones that cannot happen together. For instance, if you are born in January in England you cannot also be born in a summer month.

Outcomes which are not mutually exclusive can happen together. For example, if you are born in January you can be a teenager.

But now look at those with:
- a beard
- a moustache.

This time the loops overlap because Alf, Liam and Jim have both beards and moustaches.

The probability of having a beard is $\frac{4}{16}$ and of having a moustache is $\frac{7}{16}$.

The probability of having either is $\frac{8}{16}$ (which is **not** $\frac{4}{16} + \frac{7}{16}$).

A beard and a moustache in Hambleton are not mutually exclusive outcomes.

You can only add probabilities when outcomes are mutually exclusive.

**Exercise 14.5
Probability and
Venn diagrams**

1 a Draw a Venn diagram to show the criminals with a necklace and those with fair hair.
   b Can you add the separate probabilities to find the probability that a criminal has either a necklace or fair hair? Explain your answer.

2 Use your diagram to decide the probability that a criminal has:
   a **either** a necklace **or** fair hair
   b **both** a necklace **and** fair hair
   c **neither** a necklace **nor** fair hair
   d a necklace but not fair hair
   e fair hair but not a necklace.

3 Draw Venn diagrams to help you decide on the probabilities of having:
   a either a hat or an earing
   b either a necklace or dark hair
   c either glasses or fair hair
   d neither glasses nor dark hair.

4 For each of these, describe whether the two parts are mutually exclusive – the probability of:
   a a girl playing hockey in a school or a girl playing basketball
   b a boy playing basketball in a school or a girl playing hockey
   c a driver or a passenger
   d a bus driver or a tall woman
   e a dancer or a mechanic.

Outcomes from a biased dice

This table shows the probabilities of getting each number on a biased 0–9 dice.

Outcome	0	1	2	3	4	5	6	7	8	9
Probability	0.13	0.21	0.05	0.10	0.01	0.25	0.13	0.07	0	0.05

> A biased dice is one where each outcome is not equally likely.

Other probabilities can be found from these probabilities.

Example

What is the probability of getting a number less than 4 in one roll of the dice?

There are four numbers (0, 1, 2, and 3) less than 4.
There is no overlap between them (you can't get a 3 and a 1 in the same roll).
So you can add the probabilities for 0, 1, 2 and 3.

So the probability of a number less than 4 is 0.13 + 0.21 + 0.05 + 0.1 = 0.49.

Take care with some probabilities where outcomes are not mutually exclusive.

Example
What is the probability of getting either a multiple of 3 or an odd number?

> Here you can get a multiple of 3 **and** an odd number in the same roll of the dice.

The numbers 3 and 9 come in both sets but must only be counted once.

So the probabilities to add are those for:

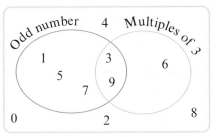

1, 5, 7, 3, 9 and 6.

0.21 + 0.25 + 0.07 + 0.1 + 0.05 + 0.13

So the probability of a multiple of three or an odd number is 0.81.

Exercise 14.6
Outcomes from a biased dice

> Note that 0 is counted as the first even number.

1 What is the probability, with this dice, of getting:
a a number greater than 6
b an even number
c a prime number
d a number which is not prime
e a number which is a multiple of 3 **and** an even number?

2 Use the Venn diagram to calculate the probability of getting in one roll:
a a multiple of three **and** an odd number
b a number which is **neither** a multiple of 3 **nor** an odd number
c a number which **is not** a multiple of 3 but **is** an odd number.

3 Use a Venn diagram to find the probability of getting a number greater than 5 or an even number.

4 **a** Why can you add all the probabilities when you find the probability that in one roll you get a number less than 5 or a number greater than 7?
b Calculate this probability.
c What is the probability of **not** getting a number less than 5 **nor** a number greater than 7?

Using Venn diagrams to find probabilities

Venn diagrams can be very useful when you have to find, for instance, the probability of: (one event **and** another event), (one event **or** another event), (**neither** one event **nor** another) or (one event **but not** another).

Example On Saturday night 20 young people went into town. 12 of these visited Kingston's club, 9 went to Night Owls, and 3 decided not to go to any club.

Calculate:

a p(Kingston's or Night Owls) **b** p(Kingston's and Night Owls)
c p(Kingston's but not Night Owls).

This problem seems strange at first. You know only 20 people went out but $12 + 9 + 3$ appears to make 24 people in town that night.

This must mean 4 people have been counted twice – in other words, they went to both clubs.

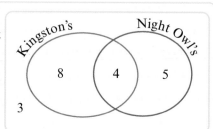

The Venn diagram would therefore look like this.

Therefore:

$$p(\text{Kingston's or Night Owls}) = \frac{(8 + 4 + 5)}{20} = \frac{17}{20}$$

$$p(\text{Kingston's and Night Owls}) = \frac{4}{20}$$

$$p(\text{Kingston's but not Night Owls}) = \frac{8}{20}$$

Exercise 14.7
Venn diagrams and probabilities

1 Liam carried out a survey into what people had for breakfast.

He found that, of the 44 people asked, 20 had English breakfast(E), 6 of these had both cereal(C) and English breakfast, and 5 people did not have either English breakfast or cereal.

a Draw a Venn diagram to show the information.
b Calculate the following probabilities:
   i p(cereal but not English breakfast) **ii** p(cereal or English breakfast)
   iii p(cereal) **iv** p(not cereal nor English breakfast)
c Explain why $p(E) + p(C) \neq p(E \text{ or } C)$.

The symbol $\neq$ means is not equal to …

2 Two hundred TV viewers were asked about the soaps they watched on Monday night. These are some of the findings where E stands for Eastenders, C for Coronation Street and N for Neighbours.

26 watched only N, in total 100 watched E, 8 watched all three, 35 watched E and C, 20 watched E and N but not C, 22 watched C and N, and 29 watched none of the soaps.

a Copy the Venn diagram and fill in the numbers in each region.
b Calculate these probabilities:
   i p(E and N)
   ii p(C)
   iii p(E or N)
   iv p(E and C but not N).

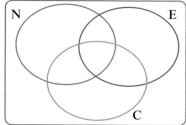

End points

You should be able to ...   ... so try these questions

A Calculate probabilities for
dependent events

A1 A box contains 7 coach bolts, 4 machine bolts and 2 galvanised bolts.
No other bolts are in the box.
Two bolts are taken at random from the box at the same time.
a If one of the bolts taken is a machine bolt, what is the
probability that the other one is also a machine bolt?
b Draw a tree diagram to show the probabilities when two bolts
are taken.
c What is the probability that:
  i both are coach bolts
  ii the two bolts are of different types?

B Understand the effect of
conditional probability

B1 The probability that Claire gets up before 7 am is 0.26.
If she does get up before 7 am, the probability that she has a bath
is 0.68.
If not, the probability of a bath drops to 0.24.
a Draw a tree diagram with the probabilities to show the situation.
b Calculate the probability that Claire has a bath in the morning.

C Decide when you can find a
probability by adding the
separate probabilities

C1 For each of these, describe whether the two parts are
mutually exclusive.
The probability of:
a a 1 to 6 dice giving a multiple of 3 or a square number
b a very large spinner giving a square number or a prime number
c a 1 to 6 dice giving a prime number or an even number
d a 1 to 6 dice giving a square number or a triangular number.

D Use Venn diagrams to help
find probabilities

D1 Amongst a group of 34 jugglers, 12 wore green hats and 19 had
red trousers. The number of jugglers who had neither green hats
nor red trousers was twice the number who had both red hats and
green trousers.
a Draw a Venn diagram to display the information.
b What was the probability that a juggler, chosen at random, had:
  i a red hat but no green trousers
  ii a red hat or green trousers
  iii a red hat and green trousers?

Some points to remember

- You can only calculate theoretical probability where outcomes are equally likely.

- With combined probability questions it is often helpful to draw a tree diagram.
  A reduced tree diagram may be necessary where there are many outcomes at each stage.

- With combined probability questions first establish if the events are dependent
  or independent.

- Where two objects are picked at the same time it is equivalent to two dependent events
  where one happens then the other.

- Before you add separate probabilities check that there is no overlap between the sets.
  A Venn diagram can sometimes help you decide this.

Starting points

You need to know about ...

... so try these questions

A Finding the median and the interquartile range

♦ You can find the median and interquartile range of a set of ungrouped data by listing the data in order.

♦ For a distribution with a large total frequency, using cumulative frequencies is quicker than listing the data.

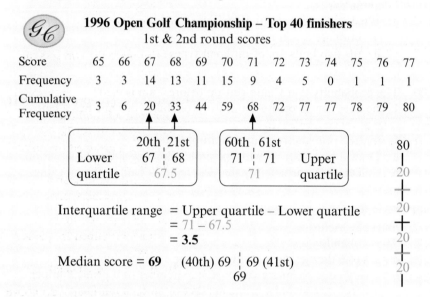

1996 Open Golf Championship – Top 40 finishers
1st & 2nd round scores

Score	65	66	67	68	69	70	71	72	73	74	75	76	77
Frequency	3	3	14	13	11	15	9	4	5	0	1	1	1
Cumulative Frequency	3	6	20	33	44	59	68	72	77	77	78	79	80

	20th	21st		60th	61st	
Lower quartile	67	68		71	71	Upper quartile
	67.5			71		

Interquartile range = Upper quartile – Lower quartile
= 71 – 67.5
= **3.5**

Median score = **69**   (40th) 69 ⁝ 69 (41st)
69

B Calculating the standard deviation of a distribution

♦ To calculate the standard deviation of a frequency distribution:

1996 Open Golf Championship – Top 40 finishers
2nd round scores

Score	65	66	67	68	69	70	71	72	73
Frequency	2	3	6	8	6	8	3	3	1

❖ calculate the mean of all the values

❖ calculate the square root of the mean squared deviation.

Score x	Frequency f	Total score fx	Squared deviation $f(x-\bar{x})^2$
65	2	130	28.125
66	3	198	22.6875
67	6	402	18.375
68	8	544	4.5
69	6	414	0.375
70	8	560	12.5
71	3	213	15.1875
72	3	216	31.6875
73	1	73	18.0625
	40	2750	151.5

$\frac{2750}{40} = 68.75$ $\sqrt{\frac{151.5}{40}} = \mathbf{1.95}$ (to 3 sf)

Mean score ($\bar{x}$)   Standard deviation

1996 Open Golf Championship

Score	Frequency 3rd round	4th round	Score	Frequency 3rd round	4th round
64	1	0	70	4	7
65	0	1	71	3	6
66	2	1	72	3	6
67	0	5	73	3	3
68	5	4	74	3	2
69	6	2	75	3	3

A1 Find the median and interquartile range of:
  a the 3rd round scores
  b the 4th round scores.

A2 Find the median and interquartile range of the 3rd and 4th round scores combined.

1996 Open Golf Championship
Top 40 finishers

Score	Frequency	Score	Frequency
65	1	72	1
66	0	73	4
67	8	74	0
68	5	75	1
69	5	76	1
70	7	77	1
71	6		

B1 **a** Calculate the mean and standard deviation of the 1st round scores.

  b Copy and complete this table using your answer to part **a**.

	1st round	2nd round
Mean		68.75
Standard deviation		1.95

C Comparing sets of data

♦ You can compare sets of data using two types of statistic: an average, and a measure of dispersion.

	3rd round	4th round
Mean	70.55	70.4
Standard deviation (to 3 sf)	2.52	2.56

The 4th round scores are slightly lower on average.
The amount of variation in the scores is almost identical.

♦ When you compare data which has extreme values, the median and the interquartile range can give a better comparison.

D Grouped data

♦ Data that is collected in groups, or grouped to make it easier to present, is called a **grouped frequency distribution**.

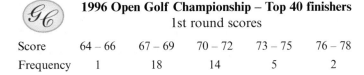

1996 Open Golf Championship – Top 40 finishers
1st round scores

Score	64 – 66	67 – 69	70 – 72	73 – 75	76 – 78
Frequency	1	18	14	5	2

♦ Each group of data is a **class**: the size of a class is the **class interval**.
  ❖ the 64-66 class has a class interval of 3.

♦ You can present grouped data on a **grouped frequency diagram**.

♦ The class with the highest frequency is called the **modal class**:
  ❖ the modal class here is 67–69.

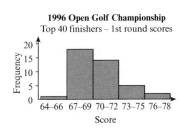

1996 Open Golf Championship
Top 40 finishers – 1st round scores

E Estimating the mean of grouped data

♦ To calculate an estimate of the mean of a grouped frequency distribution:
  ❖ find the **mid-class value** for each class
  ❖ estimate the total for each class
    i.e. multiply the mid-class value by the frequency
  ❖ divide the sum of the estimated totals by the total frequency.

1st round score	Frequency f	Mid-class value m	Total score estimate fm
64 –65	1	65	65
67 – 69	18	68	1224
70 – 72	14	71	994
73 – 75	5	74	370
76 – 78	2	77	154
	40		2807

Estimate of mean score $(\bar{m}) = \frac{2807}{40} = 70.175$

C1 Use the statistics in your table from Question **B1b** to compare the 1st and 2nd round scores.

C2 a Copy and complete this table using your answer to Question **A2**.

	1st & 2nd rounds	3rd & 4th rounds
Mean	69	
Interquartile range	3.5	

b Compare the two sets of data.

D1 Use the ungrouped data above Question **A1**, and classes 64–66, 67–69, 70–72, 73–75, to create a grouped frequency distribution for:
a the 3rd round scores
b the 4th round scores.

D2 For each distribution:
a draw a grouped frequency diagram
b give the modal class.

D3 Use the ungrouped data above Question **A1**, and a class interval of 2 to group the 3rd round scores.

E1 Use your grouped frequency distribution from Question **D1a** to calculate an estimate of the mean of the 3rd round scores.

E2

4th round Score	Frequency f	Mid-class value m
64 – 65	1	64.5
66 – 67	6	66.5
68 – 69	6	
70 – 71	13	
72 – 73	9	
74 – 75	5	
	40	

Copy and complete this working to calculate an estimate of the mean.

Estimating the standard deviation of a grouped frequency distribution

♦ When you calculate an estimate of the mean of grouped data, you are simply calculating the mean of the distribution of mid-class values.

♦ To calculate an estimate of the standard deviation of a grouped frequency distribution:
  ❖ find the mid-class value for each class
  ❖ calculate the mean of all the mid-class values
  ❖ calculate the standard deviation of all the mid-class values.

Example   Estimate the standard deviation of these 4th round scores.

Score	Frequency f	Mid-class value m	Total score estimate fm	Squared deviation estimate $f(m - \bar{m})^2$
64 – 65	5	64.5	322.5	120.05
66 – 67	6	66.5	399	50.46
68 – 69	6	68.5	411	4.86
70 – 71	13	70.5	916.5	15.73
72 – 73	9	72.5	652.5	86.49
74 – 75	1	74.5	74.5	26.01
	40		2776	303.6

$$\frac{2776}{40} = 69.4 \qquad \sqrt{\frac{303.6}{40}} = 2.75 \text{ (to 3 sf)}$$

Estimate of mean score ($\bar{m}$)   Estimate of standard deviation

Exercise 15.1
Estimating the standard deviation

1 In the Example above, the frequency for class 64–65 should have been 1, and the frequency for class 74–75 should have been 5.

  a What effect do you think these mistakes had on the two estimates?
  b Calculate the correct estimates of the mean and the standard deviation.

2

ⓞⓞⓞ   **1996 Olympic Games – Decathlon (Day 1)**
Points scored in each of the 5 events by the top 10 decathletes

Points	700 – 799	800 – 899	900 – 999	1000 – 1099	Total
Frequency	8	23	16	3	50

ⓞⓞⓞ   **1996 Olympic Games – Decathlon (Day 2)**
Points scored in each of the 5 events by the top 10 decathletes

Points	400 – 499	500 – 599	600 – 699	700 – 799	800 – 899	900 – 999	1000 – 1099	Total
Frequency	1	0	8	10	17	10	4	50

The **exact** mid-class value of the 700 – 799 class is 749.5.

You can use the simpler value of 750 because it will only have a small effect on your estimate of the mean, and will have no effect on your estimate of the standard deviation.

  a For each of these distributions, calculate an estimate of:
    i the mean   **ii** the standard deviation.
  b Compare the two distributions.
  c Give the class interval for these distributions.
  d Draw a grouped frequency diagram for day 2.

Histograms

♦ A grouped frequency diagram is also called a **histogram**.

The histogram you drew in Exercise 15.1 Question **2** has **equal** class intervals, i.e. the classes are all the same size.

♦ Data can be collected, or presented, in groups with **unequal** class intervals.

To draw a histogram for a distribution with unequal class intervals:

❖ find the class interval for each class

❖ calculate the **frequency density** for each class i.e. the frequency divided by the class interval

❖ use the frequency density as the height of each bar.

Example Draw a histogram for this grouping of the day 2 scores.

Points	Frequency	Class interval	Calculation	Frequency density
400 – 699	9	300	9 ÷ 300	0.03
700 – 799	10	100	10 ÷ 100	0.10
800 – 849	13	50	13 ÷ 50	0.26
850 – 949	8	100	8 ÷ 100	0.08
950 – 1099	10	150	10 ÷ 150	0.06̇

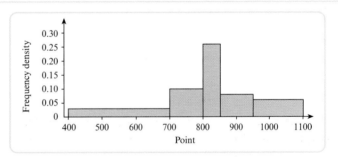

Exercise 15.2
Histograms

1

1996 Olympic Games – Decathlon (Day 1)
Points scored in each of the 5 events by the top 10 decathletes

Points	700 – 799	800 – 849	850 – 899	900 – 949	950 – 999	1000 – 1099	Total
Frequency	8	10	13	8	8	3	50

a Draw a histogram for this distribution.
b The frequencies for three of the classes are the same.
Explain why the height of the bar for the 700–799 class is only half the height of the bars for classes 900–949 and 950–999.

2

Alex Kruger (GB) retired on Day 1 of the Decathlon because of a knee injury.

1996 Olympic Games – Decathlon
Total points scored by each decathlete

Points	6500 – 7499	7500 – 7799	7800 – 7999	8000 – 8099	8100 – 8099	8100 – 8199	8200 – 8299	8500 – 8999
Frequency	2	3	4	3	3	6	4	6

Draw a histogram for this distribution.

Discrete and continuous data

♦ There are two types of numerical data:
  ❖ **discrete** data can only be certain definite values

> **1996 Olympic Games – Decathlon**
> Dan O'Brien (US) – Points scored in each event
>
> 975   952   830   868   967   991   845   910   842   644

This data is discrete because it is not possible to score fractional numbers of points such as 873.5 in a decathlon event.

  ❖ **continuous** data results from measuring and can be any value, including fractional values.

> **1996 Olympic Games – Women's Javelin**
> Tessa Sanderson (GB) – Qualifying throws
>
> 58.86 m   56.80 m   56.64 m

This data is continuous because the distance thrown can be any value, but it is measured and rounded down to the nearest centimetre.

♦ Some data may appear to be continuous, but is actually discrete.

> **1996 Olympic Games – Men's High Jump**
> Steve Smith (GB) – Clearances in Final
>
> 2.25 m   2.32 m   2.35 m

This is discrete data because the bar is only set at certain heights in a high jump competition, e.g. in the men's final, it was not possible to set a height of 2.30 m.

Tessa Sanderson was taking part in her sixth Olympic Games in 1996. She won the Javelin Gold Medal in 1984.

Steve Smith won the Bronze Medal with his jump of 2.35 m.

Exercise 15.3
Discrete and continuous data

Fiona May won the Silver Medal with her jump of 7.02 m.

Great Britain won the Silver Medal in the men's 4 × 400 m relay, and set a new European record time.

1 **A**

> **1996 Olympic Games – Women's Long Jump**
> Fiona May (GB) – Distances jumped in Final
>
> 6.68 m   7.02 m   6.78 m   6.73 m   6.76 m   6.88 m

B

> **1996 Olympic Games – Pole Vault**
> Jean Galfione (GB) – Heights cleared in Final
>
> 5.60 m   5.80 m   5.86 m   5.92 m

C

> **1996 Olympic Games
> 4 × 400 m Men's Relay Final**
> Great Britain
> 400 m split times (seconds)
>
> Iwan Thomas   44.91
> Jamie Baulch   44.19
> Mark Richardson   43.62
> Roger Black   43.87

For each set of data:
a decide whether the values are discrete or continuous
b explain your decision.

2 Gail Devers and Merlene Ottey were given the same time in the final of the women's 100 m.
Their times, to 3 dp, could have been any value between 10.930 and 10.940 seconds.

Explain why it is appropriate in athletics events to round times **up** to the nearest unit, and distances **down** to the nearest unit.

Women's 100 m Final

	Time (s)
Devers	10.94
Ottey	10.94
Torrence	10.96
Sturrup	11.00

3   a   Calculate the mean age of these athletes.

     b   Explain why the exact mean age is in fact 0.5 years greater than your answer.

     c   When age data is given in years, do you think it is discrete or continuous ? Explain your answer.

Great Britain's Men's 4 × 400 m Relay Team Ages at 20th July 1996	
Jamie Baulch	23
Roger Black	30
Mark Richardson	23
Iwan Thomas	22

Using continuous data

◆ When you group continuous data, you need to decide what happens to values at the ends of the classes, the **class limits**.

$$16.5 \leqslant x < 18.0$$
$$18.0 \leqslant x < 18.5$$
⟵ 18.0 ⟶
$$16.5 < x \leqslant 18.0$$
$$18.0 < x \leqslant 18.5$$

A distance of 18.0 m goes into different classes in each grouping because of the different ways the classes are defined.

◆ A common way of showing classes such as:
$16.5 \leqslant x < 18.0$, $18.0 \leqslant x < 18.5$, etc. is $16.5 -$, $18.0 -$, $18.5 -$, etc.
When grouping data using unequal class intervals, you should also show the upper class limit of the final class, e.g. 21.0

1996 Olympic Games – Women's Shot Final					
Distance (metres)	16.5 –	18.0 –	18.5 –	19.0 –	19.5 – 21.0
Frequency	5	13	10	9	4

◆ When age data is given in its usual form, in completed years, you can group it in the same way as discrete data.

Exercise 15.4
Using continuous data

1

1996 Olympic Games – Great Britain's Athletics Team					
Age	18 – 23	24 – 26	27 – 29	30 – 32	33 – 41
Frequency	18	18	19	18	9

Draw a histogram for this distribution.

> The width of the 18 – 23 class is 6 years, and the mid-class value is 21.

2

1996 Olympic Games – Men's Shot Final					
Distance (metres)	19.0 –	19.5 –	20.0 –	20.5 –	21.0 – 22.0	Total frequency
Frequency	5	11	17	8	1	42

  a   Draw a histogram for this distribution.
  b   The mid-class value of the 19.0 – class is 19.25
     List the mid-class values for the other four classes.
  c   Calculate an estimate of:
     i   the mean distance   ii   the standard deviation of the distances.

> You can use the same method to estimate the mean and the standard deviation as you used before for discrete data.

3   For the data from the women's shot final above:

  a   draw a histogram
  b   use the statistical function on your calculator to estimate:
     i   the mean   ii   the standard deviation.

4   Use your answers to Questions **2** and **3** to compare the men and women.

5   This data shows the reaction times of athletes in the sprint events.

> The reaction time is the length of time between the starter's gun firing and the rear foot leaving the starting block.

> s is the abbreviation for seconds.

> Linford Christie (GB), the 100 m Gold Medal winner in 1992, was disqualified after a second false start when his recorded reaction time was 0.086 s.
>
> Scientists believe a reaction time under one-tenth (0.100) of a second is impossible.

Men's 100 m Final

	Reaction time (s)
Bailey	0.174
Fredericks	0.143
Boldon	0.164
Mitchell	0.145
Marsh	0.147
Ezinwa	0.157
Green	0.169
Christie	DISQ

Men's 200 m Final

	Reaction time (s)
Johnson	0.161
Fredericks	0.200
Boldon	0.208
Thompson	0.202
Williams	0.182
Garcia	0.229
Stevens	0.151
Marsh	0.167

110 m Hurdles Final

	Reaction time (s)
Johnson	0.170
Crear	0.124
Schwarthoff	0.164
Jackson	0.133
Valle	0.179
Swift	0.151
Vander-Kuyp	0.167
Batte	0.160

Women's 100 m Final

	Reaction time (s)
Devers	0.166
Ottey	0.166
Torrence	0.151
Sturrup	0.176
Trandenkova	0.151
Voronova	0.133
Onyali	0.174
Pintusevych	0.176

Women's 200 m Final

	Reaction time (s)
Perec	0.174
Ottey	0.194
Onyali	0.231
Miller	0.172
Malchugina	0.198
Sturrup	0.165
Cuthbert	0.175
Guidry	0.207

100 m Hurdles Final

	Reaction time (s)
Engquist	0.132
Bukovec	0.164
Girard-Leno	0.133
Devers	0.189
Rose	0.179
Freeman	0.181
Shekhodanova	0.175
Goode	0.160

1996 Olympic Games – Reaction Times
Semifinals – 100 m, 200 m, 100 m/110 m Hurdles

Reaction time (s)	0.12–	0.14–	0.15–	0.16–	0.17–	0.18–	0.19–	0.21–0.27	Total
Frequency	7	11	13	16	14	16	9	8	94

   a   Group the data for the six finals in the same way as the semifinals data.
   b   Draw a histogram for:
      i   the semifinals   **ii**   the finals.

6   **a**   Copy your grouped frequency distribution for the finals data, and double each of the frequencies.
   b   Draw a frequency polygon to show this distribution by plotting each frequency against its mid-class value.
   c   On the same diagram, draw a frequency polygon for the semifinalists.
   d   Do you think your frequency polygons give a fair comparison of the reaction times in the finals and semifinals ?
      Explain your answer.

> There were exactly twice as many semifinalists as finalists.

7   Use your calculator to estimate the mean and standard deviation for:
   a   the semifinals   **b**   the finals.

8   'Athletes' reaction times are faster in finals than in semifinals'

   a   Do you think this hypothesis is true or false ?
   b   Give reasons for your answer.

9   Investigate the effects of grouping the finals data in different ways.

Drawing a cumulative frequency curve

1996 Olympic Games – Decathlon (Day 2)
Points scored in each of the 5 events by the top 10 decathletes

Points	400 – 499	500 – 599	600 – 699	700 – 799	800 – 899	900 – 999	1000 – 1099	Total
Frequency	1	0	8	10	17	10	4	50

◆ To draw a **cumulative frequency curve**:

   ❖ construct a cumulative frequency table

> If you include a cumulative frequency of 0 in your table then you have a point to start the curve from: (400, 0).

Points	<400	<500	<600	<700	<800	<900	<1000	<1100
Cumulative frequency	0	1	1	9	19	36	46	50

   ❖ plot the cumulative frequencies on a graph
   ❖ join the points with a smooth curve.

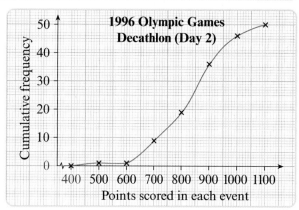

Exercise 15.5
Drawing cumulative frequency curves

1

1996 Olympic Games – Decathlon (Day 1)
Points scored in each of the 5 events by the top 10 decathletes

Points	700 – 799	800 – 849	850 – 899	900 – 949	950 – 999	1000 – 1099	Total
Frequency	8	10	13	8	8	3	50

a Copy and complete the cumulative frequency table below.

Points	<700	<800	<850	<900	<950	<1000	<1100
Cumulative frequency	0						

b Use your table to draw a cumulative frequency curve.

2

> Steve Backley (GB) won the javelin silver medal with the very first throw of the final.

1996 Olympic Games – Men's Javelin Final

Distance (metres)	76 –	80 –	81 –	82 –	84 –	87 – 89
Frequency	6	6	8	13	13	2

a Copy and complete the following cumulative frequency table.

Distance (metres)	<76	<80	<81	<82	<84	<87	<89
Cumulative frequency	0	6					48

b Draw a cumulative frequency curve for the Men's Javelin final.

3 Using your answers to Question **2**, can you think of a way to find the median distance thrown in the final? Explain your method.

Estimating the median and the interquartile range

There were 48 throws in the final, so the **exact** median distance is halfway between the 24th and 25th longest.

It is impossible to find these distances from the table, so you can only **estimate** the median.

♦ A cumulative frequency table shows which class the median is in.

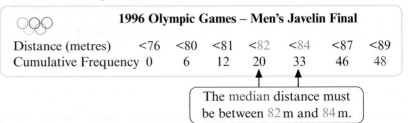

1996 Olympic Games – Men's Javelin Final

Distance (metres)	<76	<80	<81	<82	<84	<87	<89
Cumulative Frequency	0	6	12	20	33	46	48

The median distance must be between 82 m and 84 m.

As you are only estimating distances within the classes, you can divide the 48 throws into four quarters using the **12th**, **24th**, and **36th** longest (cumulative frequencies 12, 24, and 36).

♦ To estimate the median and quartiles from a cumulative frequency curve:

❖ divide the cumulative frequency into four quarters

❖ go across to the curve, then go down and read off each value.

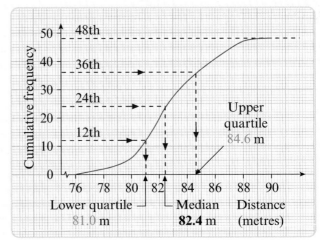

Estimate of median distance   = **82.4 m**
Estimate of interquartile range = 84.6 – 81.0
                                              = **3.6 m**

Exercise 15.6
Estimating the median and interquartile range

1

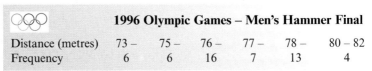

1996 Olympic Games – Men's Hammer Final

Distance (metres)	73 –	75 –	76 –	77 –	78 –	80 – 82
Frequency	6	6	16	7	13	4

a Copy and complete the following cumulative frequency table.

Distance (metres)	<73				<80	<82
Cumulative frequency	0					52

b Draw a cumulative frequency curve for the Men's Hammer final.

2   Use your cumulative frequency curve to estimate:

a the median distance thrown   **b** the interquartile range.

3   Compare the distances thrown in the Men's Hammer final and the men's javelin final.

4 a From page 185, copy the cumulative frequency table and the cumulative frequency curve for the Decathlon (day 2).
b Estimate the median points score.
c Estimate the interquartile range of the scores.

Use cumulative frequencies 12.5, 25, and 37.5 to divide the data into four quarters.

> Use cumulative frequencies 12.5, 25, and 37.5 to divide the data into four quarters.

5 Use your answers to Exercise 15.5, Question **1** to estimate:
  a the median points score on day 1 of the decathlon
  b the interquartile range of the scores.

6 Compare the points scored on days 1 and 2 of the Decathlon.

7

1996 Olympic Games – Women's Javelin Final

Distance (metres)	56 –	58 –	60 –	62 –	64 –	66 – 68	Total frequency
Frequency	7	11	10	10	7	1	46

  a Make a cumulative frequency table for the Women's Javelin final.
  b Draw a cumulative frequency curve.
  c Decide how to divide the data into four quarters.
  d Estimate the median distance thrown and the interquartile range.

Estimating cumulative frequencies

♦ You can estimate cumulative frequencies from a cumulative frequency curve.

Example   Estimate how many Men's Javelin throws were:
  a less than 81.5 m   **b** greater than 85 m

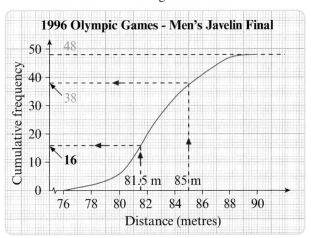

  a Estimated number of throws less than 81.5 m   = **16**

  b Estimated number of throws greater than 85 m = 48 – 38
                                                              = **10**

Exercise 15.7
Estimating cumulative frequencies

1 Use the cumulative frequency curve above to estimate how many throws were less than 83 m.

2 The winning throw in the 1988 Men's Javelin final was 84.28 m. Estimate how many throws were greater than this in 1996.

3

> Jonathan Edwards (GB) won the Silver Medal in the Triple Jump.

1996 Olympic Games – Men's Triple Jump Final

Distance (metres)	15.5 –	16.0 –	16.5 –	17.0 –	17.5 –	18.0 – 18.5
Frequency	1	7	14	6	2	1

  a Draw a cumulative frequency curve for the Men's Triple Jump final.
  b Estimate how many jumps were greater than 16.8 m.

Sampling from a population

♦ A **population** is the name given to any set of data under investigation. If you are investigating a very large population, it may not be possible to collect all the data.

♦ A **sample** is a smaller set of data, chosen from a population, that can be analysed and used to make conclusions about the population.

Exercise 15.8
Sampling from a population

1 The British Team for the 1996 Olympic Games consisted of 500 members. This is the distribution of their ages.

1996 Olympic Games
Ages of Great Britain Team at 20/7/96

Age	16 –	21 –	24 –	27 –	29 –
Frequency	25	54	68	59	63

Age	31 –	34 –	37 –	42 –	52 – 71
Frequency	51	41	47	55	37

Draw a histogram for this age distribution.

2 These are three random samples taken from the 500 members of the Great Britain Olympic Team.

In a random sample, each member of the population has the same chance of being chosen.

One way of choosing a random sample is to:

♦ allocate a number to each member of the population

♦ use a random number table to select the sample.

If the population is listed at random then you could choose a **systematic** sample, e.g. every 10th member on the list is chosen until the sample is complete.

1996 Olympic Games
Great Britain Team

Age	Frequency
19 –	5
24 –	4
29 –	7
39 –	4
49 – 68	5

Sample size 25

1996 Olympic Games
Great Britain Team

Age	Frequency
19 –	8
24 –	13
29 –	12
34 –	3
39 –	5
49 – 68	9

Sample size 50

1996 Olympic Games
Great Britain Team

Age	Frequency
19 –	14
24 –	25
29 –	28
34 –	10
39 –	11
49 –	8
59 – 68	4

Sample size 100

a Draw a histogram for each random sample.
b Compare the shape of your distributions with your answer to Question **1**.

3 For each random sample in Question **2**, use mid-class values of 21.5, 26.5, … etc. to calculate an estimate of:

a the mean   **b** the standard deviation.

The estimates for each sample can be used as estimates of the mean and standard deviation of the population.

4 The actual mean age of the Great Britain Olympic Team was 33.4 years, with a standard deviation of 10.6 years.
Use your answers to Question **3** to describe the effect of the size of sample on the estimates of the mean and standard deviation.

5 The Great Britain Team had 312 competitors and 188 support staff.

a Do you think the mean age of these two groups is likely to be the same? Explain your answer.

b When choosing a random sample of 50, what do you think the advantage might be of choosing random samples of 31 from the competitors and 19 from the support staff?

End points

You should be able to ...   ... so try these questions

OOOO	1996 Olympic Games – Discus Finals					
Distance (metres)	56 –	60 –	62 –	64 –	66 –70	Total
Frequency Women	7	10	13	13	6	49
(of throws) Men	5	8	16	13	3	45

A Use histograms and frequency polygons

A1 Draw a histogram to show the distances thrown in the:
  a Women's Discus final   **b** Men's Discus final.

A2 **a** Draw a frequency polygon for the Women's Discus final.
  b On the same diagram, draw a frequency polygon for the Men's final.
  c Compare the two distributions.
  d Explain why the frequency polygons would not have given a fair comparison if the number of throws in the finals had been 59 and 45.

B Calculate an estimate of the standard deviation of a grouped frequency distribution

B1 (Do **not** use the statistical function on your calculator for this question.) For the Men's Discus final, calculate an estimate of:
  a the mean distance thrown
  b the standard deviation of the distances thrown.

B2 Use your calculator to estimate the mean and standard deviation of the distances thrown in the Women's Discus final.

OOOO	1996 Olympic Games – Men's Long Jump Final						
Distance (metres)	6.4 –	7.2 –	7.6 –	7.8 –	8.0 –	8.2 –	8.4 – 8.6
Frequency	2	3	4	13	13	2	1

OOOO	1996 Olympic Games – Women's Long Jump Final				
Distance (metres)	6.2 –	6.4 –	6.6 –	6.8 –	7.0 – 7.2
Frequency	3	6	9	14	3

C Estimate the median and the interquartile range

C1 **a** Draw a cumulative frequency curve for the Men's Long Jump final.
  b Use your cumulative frequency curve to estimate:
    i the median distance jumped   **ii** the interquartile range.

C2 Use cumulative frequencies 8.75, 17.5, and 26.25 to estimate the median and interquartile range for the Women's final.

D Compare grouped frequency distributions

D1 Compare the distances jumped in the Women's and Men's finals.

D2 Use your answers to Questions **B1** and **B2** to compare the distances thrown in the Women's and Men's Discus finals.

E Estimate cumulative frequencies

E1

OOO	1996 Olympic Games – Women's Triple Jump Final					
Distance (metres)	13.5 –	13.9 –	14.1 –	14.4 –	14.7 –	15.0 – 15.4
Frequency	10	9	12	8	7	1

  a Draw a cumulative frequency curve for the Women's Triple Jump final.
  b Use your curve to estimate how many jumps were:
    i less than 14.0 m   **ii** greater than 14.5 m.

Some points to remember

♦ When you choose a sample from a population, usually the larger the sample the closer its mean and standard deviation are to those of the whole population.

WHEEL GARDEN CENTRE

OUR WATER WHEEL PRODUCES OVER 60% OF THE ELECTRICITY WE USE

Watering cans - plastic			
5 litre	8 litre	10 litre	12 litre
99p	£1.29	£1.69	£1.99
Watering cans - traditional			
1 gallon	1.5 gallon	2 gallon	2.5 gallon
£4. 99	£6.49	£7.99	£9.99

Visit our
Coffee Shop

Rolls of Plastic Sheet

The easy way to stop weeds

15 metres long
and
1650 mm wide

Only £3.75
per roll
while stocks last

Special Offers on Spring bulbs

Traditional Watering Can Roses
Now in stock

£15.99

Cloches

Cloche Frames

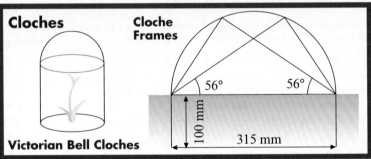

56°   56°

100 mm

315 mm

Victorian Bell Cloches

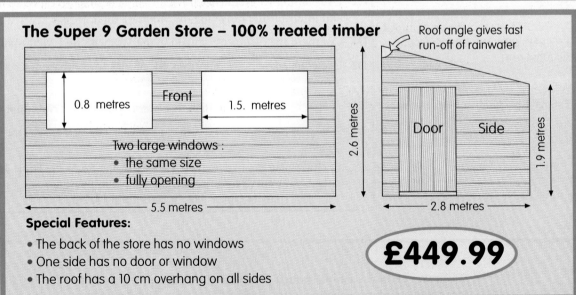

The Super 9 Garden Store – 100% treated timber

Roof angle gives fast
run-off of rainwater

0.8 metres

Front

1.5. metres

Two large windows :
• the same size
• fully opening

5.5 metres

Door   Side

2.6 metres

1.9 metres

2.8 metres

£449.99

Special Features:

• The back of the store has no windows
• One side has no door or window
• The roof has a 10 cm overhang on all sides

1 The plastic sheet is 120 microns thick.
(One micron is $\frac{1}{10\,000}$th of a centimetre.)
  a Give the thickness of the sheet in metres as a number in standard form.
  b Give the volume of the plastic sheet on the roll in m³ in standard form.

2 The plastic sheet is rolled onto a cardboard tube. The inside diameter of the tube is 86 mm and the outside diameter is 94 mm.
  a Calculate the volume of cardboard used to make the tube.
  b The outside of the tube is coated with adhesive. The adhesive is applied at a rate of 135 ml/m², and is supplied in 5 litre cans.
  How many tubes can be coated with adhesive from one can? (There is no wastage.)

3 Calculate, to the nearest millimetre, the length of wire used to make one cloche frame.

4 A four-frame open-ended cloche 2.5 metres long is made by covering four frames, above ground level, with plastic sheet. At either end, an extra 15 mm of sheet is allowed for a seam.
  a How many cloches can be made from one roll of plastic sheet?
  b Calculate the percentage of each roll of sheet that is wasted making these cloches.

5 A Victorian bell-cloche is in the shape of a cylinder surmounted by a hemisphere. The internal dimensions of the cloche are: diameter 28 cm and height 42 cm.
  a Show that the capacity of the bell-cloche is approximately 23 litres.
  b The bell-cloche is made of 9 mm thick glass. Calculate the volume of glass used to make the cloche.
  c If the internal diameter (cm) of a bell-cloche is 2r, and the internal height (cm) is h, show that the capacity C of the cloche is given by:
$$C = \tfrac{1}{3}\pi r^2(h - r)$$
  d Rearrange the formula for capacity C to give a formula for h in terms of r and C.
  e A different bell-cloche has a capacity of approximately 4.5 litres and an internal radius of 32 cm.
  Find the approximate internal height of the cloche.

6 Wheel Garden Centre have a policy that price increases will never be more than 6%.
Next month they will increase the price of plastic sheet to £3.99 per roll.

Is this increase in line with their policy? Explain.

7 In metres the height h of a bucket, painted red, on the water wheel above the pool is given by the equation:
$$h = 4 + 3\sin(30t)$$
where t is the time in seconds after the wheel has been set in motion.
  a Calculate h (to 1dp) for values of t from 0 to 12.
  b Draw a graph to show how the height of the red bucket varies during the first 12 seconds.
  c The floor of the Coffee Shop is 3.7 metres above the pool. In the first 12 seconds when was the red bucket level with the floor of the Coffee Shop?

8 In the Coffee Shop Jim paid £3.29 for three coffees and two teas. Ella paid £4.10 for five teas and 2 coffees.

Write and solve two equations to find the prices of tea and coffee in the Coffee Shop.

9 Packs of spring bulbs are made up with daffodils and tulips in the ratio 5:3.

If there are n bulbs in a pack, give the number of tulip bulbs in terms of n.

10 The outside of the Super 9 store is sprayed with timber preservative (excluding the roof). The preserver is sprayed at a rate of 250 ml/m².

Will 5 litres of preserver cover one store? Explain your answer.

11 Which traditional watering can is the best value for money in your opinion? Explain your answer.

12 The traditional copper watering can 'rose' is the shape of a truncated right cone.
  a Calculate to 2 dp the volume of water needed to fill the rose.
  b Calculate to 1 dp the curved surface area of the rose.

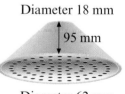

Diameter 18 mm

95 mm

Diameter 62 mm

Starting points

You need to know about ...

... so try these questions

A Linear (straight line) graphs

A linear graph can be identified from its equation.
The equation of all linear graphs is of the form

$$y = mx + c \quad \text{where } m \text{ is the gradient and}$$
c the intercept with the y-axis

Line A has a gradient of $\frac{3}{4}$, and an intercept with the y-axis at $^+1$.

The equation of line A is
$$y = \frac{3}{4}x + 1$$

Line B has a gradient of $\frac{^-5}{2}$, and an intercept with the y-axis at $^-3$.

The equation of line B is:
$$y = \frac{^-5}{2}x - 3$$

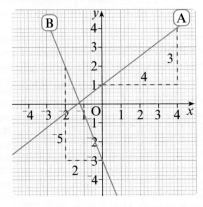

Line A has a **positive gradient** sloping upwards from left to right.
Line B has a **negative gradient** sloping downwards from left to right.

Being able to identify the gradient and intercept with the y-axis from a linear equation enables you to sketch or draw a graph.

To sketch a graph of $y = \frac{2}{3}x - 5$
you can identify that:

the gradient m is $\quad \frac{2}{3}$

the y-intercept c is $\quad ^-5$

The sketch shows a graph of
$$y = \frac{2}{3}x - 5$$

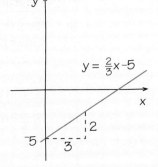

(Note this is a sketch, so no accurate plotting or measuring is needed.)

To draw a graph of $y = \frac{2}{3}x - 5$

you can identify that the gradient is $\frac{2}{3}$, and the y-intercept is $^-5$.

To draw the graph:

♦ draw, graduate, and label a pair of axes
♦ plot the point $(0, ^-5)$, i.e. the y-intercept
♦ from the y-intercept show the gradient,
   i.e. to plot a second point on the graph
♦ draw a straight line passing through the two points
♦ label the linear graph with its equation.

(Note this is drawing a graph, so accuracy is essential.)

A1 Identify the gradient and intercept with the y-axis for these linear graphs.
  a $y = 4x + 3$
  b $y = \frac{1}{5}x - 8$
  c $y = 0.8x + 1.5$
  d $y = \frac{7}{4} + \frac{5}{4}x$
  e $y = 1 - 0.25x$
  f $y = 6x$
  g $y = x$
  h $y = 12$

A2 A linear graph has an intercept with the y-axis at $(0, 3)$ and a gradient of 2.5.

Write the equation of this graph.

A3 A linear graph has a gradient of $^-1$ and an intercept with the y-axis at the point $(0, ^-2)$.

Give the equation of this line.

A4 Sketch each of these linear graphs.
  a $y = 3x + 2$
  b $y = 5x - 4$
  c $y = \frac{3}{5}x + 1$
  d $y = \frac{5}{8}x$
  e $y = 3 - 4x$
  f $y = 0.5 - 1.5x$

A5 Draw each of these linear graphs.
  a $y = \frac{1}{2}x + 1.2$
  b $y = \frac{3}{4} - 2x$
  c $y = 4 + 3x$
  d $y = \frac{3}{4}x$
  e $y = 1.5 - 4x$
  f $y = x - 2$

B Rearranging linear equations

Linear equations may have to be rearranged to put them in the form

$$y = mx + c$$

(Note that rearranging an equation is **not** changing the equation; it is producing an equivalent equation.)

◆ To draw the graph of $3y + 4x = 6$ using the gradient and intercept method, the equation will need to be in the form $y = mx + c$.

Example   To rearrange $3y + 4x = 6$

$$3y + 4x = 6$$
[– 4x from both sides] $3y = {}^-4x + 6$
[÷ both sides by 3] $y = {}^-\frac{4}{3}x + 2$

So $3y + 4x = 6$ and $y = {}^-\frac{4}{3}x + 2$ are equivalent equations.

The graph of $3y + 4x = 6$ has a gradient of ${}^-\frac{4}{3}$ and a y-intercept at (0,2).

◆ Rearranging the linear equation may involve dealing with brackets.

Example   To rearrange $4 = 2(3y - 5x)$

$$4 = 2(3y - 5x)$$
[multiply out bracket] $4 = 6y - 10x$
[+ 10x to both sides] $4 + 10x = 6y$
[÷ both sides by 6] $\frac{4}{6} + \frac{10}{6}x = y$

So $4 = 2(3y - 2x)$ and $y = \frac{5}{3}x + \frac{2}{3}$ are equivalent equations.

◆ Rearranging the linear equation may involve dealing with fractions.

Example   To rearrange $\frac{3}{5}x = \frac{1}{2}y - 1$

$$\frac{3}{5}x = \frac{1}{2}y - 1$$
[multiply both sides by 10] $6x = 5y - 10$
[+ 10 to both sides] $6x + 10 = 5y$
[÷ both sides by 5] $\frac{6}{5}x + 2 = y$

So $\frac{3}{5}x = \frac{1}{2}y - 1$ and $y = \frac{6}{5}x + 2$ are equivalent equations.

◆ Rearranging the linear equation may involve fractions and brackets.

Example   To rearrange $\frac{3}{4}(2y - 3x) = 2$

$$\frac{3}{4}(2y - 3x) = 2$$
[× both sides by 4] $3(2y - 3x) = 8$
[multiply out the bracket] $6y - 9x = 8$
[+ 9x to both sides] $6y = 9x + 8$
[÷ both sides by 6] $y = \frac{3}{2}x + \frac{4}{3}$

So $\frac{3}{4}(2y - 3x) = 2$ and $y = \frac{3}{2}x + \frac{4}{3}$ are equivalent equations.

(Note that when you are dividing both sides of an equation by a value it is better to write the coefficient of x as a fraction rather than a decimal. In this way you can work with a gradient as a fraction.)

B1 Rearrange each of these equations so that they are in the form $y = mx + c$.

a $5y = 3x + 15$

b $2y + 5x = 8$

c $3y - 4x = 3$

d $4 - 2y = 3x$

e $7x - 2y = 1$

f $2(x - 3y) = 6$

g $5 = 4(2x + y)$

h $2(3 - 2y) = 5x$

i $4(2x - 1) = 2y$

j $\frac{2}{3}y - 1 = 3x$

k $4 - \frac{1}{2}x = 5y$

l $1 + \frac{1}{3}x = \frac{3}{4}y$

m $\frac{1}{3}x + \frac{1}{4}y = 3$

n $2 + \frac{3}{5}y = \frac{1}{4}x$

o $\frac{3}{5}(x + 1) = 2y$

p $\frac{2}{3}(x + 2y) = 1$

q $5 = \frac{1}{4}(3x - y)$

r $\frac{5}{8}(y - 2x) = 3$

s $\frac{1}{3}x = \frac{1}{2}(2 - 3y)$

t $\frac{3}{4} = \frac{1}{3}(2y - x)$

Solving simultaneous linear equations graphically

When a linear relationship between two variables can be expressed by two or more different equations, you can find the value of each variable by drawing graphs of each equation and finding a point where the coordinates satisfy both equations (i.e. where the line graphs intersect).

Example

Find values of x and y that satisfy the equations:

$$2x + 3y = {}^-5 \ldots (1)$$
$$x + y = {}^-1 \ldots (2)$$

- To draw graphs using the gradient and intercept the equations need to be in the form $y = mx + c$

To rearrange Equation (1)

$$2x + 3y = {}^-5$$
[i.e.] $$3y = {}^-5 - 2x$$
[i.e.] $$y = \frac{{}^-5}{3} - \frac{2}{3x}$$

To rearrange Equation (2)

$$x + y = {}^-1$$
[i.e.] $$y = {}^-1 - x$$

- Draw graphs of $y = \dfrac{{}^-5}{3} - \dfrac{2}{3x}$ and $y = {}^-1 - x$ on the same pair of axes.

> Linear graphs are of the form $y = mx + c$. This can be rearranged to give:
>
> $$mx = c - y$$
> $$c = y - mx$$
> $$y = c + mx$$
> $$\frac{y - c}{m} = x$$
>
> …
>
> So, $y = \dfrac{{}^-5}{3} - \dfrac{2}{3}x$ is a rearranged form of:
>
> $$y = -\frac{2}{3}x - \frac{5}{3}$$

The graph of

$$y = \frac{{}^-5}{3} - \frac{2}{3x} \text{ has:}$$

a gradient of $\dfrac{{}^-2}{3}$

a y-intercept at $\dfrac{{}^-5}{3}$

The graph of
$y = {}^-1 - x$ has:
a gradient of $^-1$
a y-intercept at $^-1$

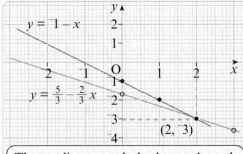

> The two linear graphs both pass through the point $(2, {}^-3)$. The values of x and y at this point must satisfy both equations, i.e. $x = 2$ $y = {}^-3$.

> When the scales for the axes are not given in the question you must decide on appropriate scales.
>
> Having drawn your graphs you may have to extend your axes to find a point that both graphs pass through (point of intersection).

Where the two linear graphs cross, the coordinates give the solution to the equations.
The solutions are $x = 2$ and $y = {}^-3$.

Check the graphical solution by substituting the values in one equation.

Check in Equation (1) for $x = 2$, $y = {}^-3$:
$$\text{LHS} = 2(2) + 3({}^-3) = 4 - 9 = {}^-5 = \text{RHS (solution is correct.)}$$

> It is always a good idea to check the solution to an equation. Finding an error will allow you to rework your solution and not lose marks.

Exercise 16.1
Solving simultaneous equations graphically

1 Solve each pair of equations graphically.

a $x + 4y = 7$
$2x + 5y = 8$

b $5x - 3y = {}^-7$
$3x + y = 7$

c $5x + 7y = 4$
$x + 3y = 4$

d $3x + 2y = 12$
$4x - y = 5$

e $12x + 5y = 9$
$5x - y = {}^-13$

f $8x + y = 7$
$11x + 4y = 7$

2 By drawing two linear graphs find values of x and y that satisfy the two equations $3x + 2y = 5$ and $3y - 3x = 15$.

3 **a** On a pair of axes draw a graph of $y = 3x - 5$.
   b Show that $2(y + 5) = 6x$, and $y = 3x - 5$ are equivalent.
   c Draw another linear graph on your axes and solve these simultaneous equations.
$$2(y + 5) = 6x \dots (1)$$
$$3x - 2y = 4 \dots \quad (2)$$

4 **a** On a pair of axes draw a graph of $3x + y = 9$.
   b By drawing another linear graph on the axes solve the simultaneous equations:
$$3x + y = 9 \dots (1)$$
$$x + 2y = 6 \dots (2)$$

   c Use graphs to explain why this pair of equations
$$y - 3x = 5 \dots \quad (1)$$
$$2y - 4 = 6x \dots (2)$$
   cannot be solved simultaneously.

5 A group of male and female students went on a fell walk.
In total, sixty-three students were in the group.
The number of females was nine more than twice the number of males.
Let x be the number of females in the group and y the number of males.
   a Write two different equations in x and y from the student data.
   b **i** Draw and label a pair of axes with values: $0 \leqslant x \leqslant 63$ and $0 \leqslant y \leqslant 63$
       ii By drawing suitable linear graphs find the number of females and the number of males in the group.

6 A blend of olive oil is made by mixing Extra Virgin and Virgin olive oils.
When making 500 litres of the blended oil the amount of Virgin oil used was 25 litres more than four time the amount of Extra Virgin oil used.
Let x be the number of litres of Extra Virgin oil used and y the number of litres of Virgin oil used.
   a Write two different equations in x and y from the olive oil data.
   b **i** Draw and label a pair of axes with values: $0 \leqslant x \leqslant 500$ and $0 \leqslant y \leqslant 500$.
       ii Draw two linear graphs to find the amount of each type of oil used when 500 litres of the blended oil are produced.

The next 500 litres was a different blend, with the amount of Virgin oil being 40 litres more than six times the amount of Extra Virgin oil.
   c **i** Write a different equation in x and y from the new data.
       ii Draw a third linear graph on the axes to find the amount of each type of oil used in this next blend.

7 Two variables x and y are such that:
$$y = \tfrac{1}{2}(x + 7)$$
$$\text{and} \quad x = \tfrac{1}{3}(29 - 4y)$$

   a On a pair of axes, draw two linear graphs to show the relationship between x and y.
   b Find a value for x, and a value for y, that will satisfy both equations.

8 The equation $2y + 2 = 3x$ is solved simultaneously with a second linear equation in x and y. The solution of $x = 4$ and $y = 5$ satisfies both equations. The graph of the second equation has a y-intercept at $(0, 3)$.
Draw graphs to find the second linear equation.

Quadratic graphs

A quadratic expression in one variable (e.g. n) is an expression where the highest power of the variable is 2 (e.g. n^2).

Quadratic graphs are shown on these axes.

The graph of $y = x^2 + 2x$ can be plotted by calculating values of y for chosen values of x.

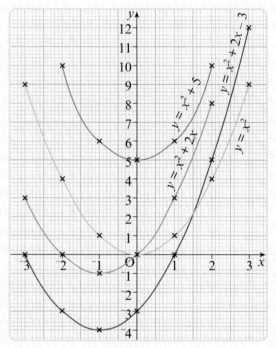

Example

For $y = x^2 + 2x$

when $x = 0$
$$y = (0)^2 + 2(0) = 0$$
when $x = 1$
$$y = (1)^2 + 2(1) = 3$$
when $x = {}^-1$
$$y = ({}^-1)^2 + 2({}^-1) = {}^-1$$

i.e. the graph of $y = x^2 + 2x$ passes through the points:
$(0, 0)$, $(1, 3)$, $({}^-1, {}^-1)$, ...

> The smooth curve of a quadratic graph is known as a **parabola**.

Note that the points should be joined by a smooth curve.

From the graphs drawn on the axes you can note that:

♦ quadratic graphs are symmetrical
graphs such as $y = x^2$, $y = 2x^2$, $y = 0.5x^2$, are symmetrical about the y-axis (the line $x = 0$).

♦ the value of any constant, i.e. not a term in any variable, fixes the y-intercept of the graph.
$y = x^2 + 5$ has a y-intercept at $(0, 5)$; $y = x^2 + 3x - 3$ has a y-intercept at $(0, {}^-3)$.

Exercise 16.2
Quadratic graphs

1 From the graphs above give the line of symmetry of:
   a   the graph of $y = x^2 + 2x + 5$ **b**   the graph of $y = x^2 + 2x$.

2 Draw a pair of axes where ${}^-4 \leqslant x \leqslant 4$, and ${}^-12 \leqslant y \leqslant 28$.
   a   On the axes draw these quadratic graphs.
     $y = x^2$ $y = x^2 + 6$ $y = x^2 - 3x$ $y = x^2 - 3x - 8$
   b   Give the line of symmetry of the graph $y = x^2 - 3x$.
   c   Give the equation of a quadratic graph that has the same line of symmetry as $y = x^2 - 3x$ but has a y-intercept at $(0, {}^-8)$.

3 Draw a pair of axes where ${}^-4 \leqslant x \leqslant 4$, and ${}^-4 \leqslant y \leqslant 32$.
   a   On the axes draw these quadratic graphs and compare them.
     $y = x^2 + 2x$ $y = x^2 + 3x$ $y = x^2 - 2x$ $y = x^2 - 4x$

> You might choose to use a graphical calculator when you have to compare a number of graphs.

   b   What does the coefficient of x tell you about a quadratic graph?

A sketch graph shows the shape of the graph and known data. This data might show x-intercepts and/or y-intercepts, or maybe the relative steepness or tightness of a graph.

Sketching a graph is not the same as drawing a graph. Points are not plotted and graduations on axes do not have to be accurate.

4 Give the line of symmetry and the y-intercept for each of these graphs.

a $y = x^2 + 4x - 3$ b $y = x^2 - x + 2$ c $y = x^2 + 5x$
d $y = x^2 - 6x + 1$ e $y = x^2 + 6x - 2$ f $y = x^2 + 8x + 3$
g $y = x^2 - 7$ h $y = x^2 - 6x + 8$ i $y = x^2 - 7x + 5$

5 This is a sketch graph of $y = x^2$.

a Make a copy of this sketch.
b On your copy sketch and label these graphs.
   i $y = x^2 + 3$
   ii $y = x^2 - 5x$
   iii $y = x^2 - 4x - 5$

6 On a pair of axes, sketch these graphs and label them.

a $y = x^2 - 5x - 6$
b $y = x^2 + x + 4$

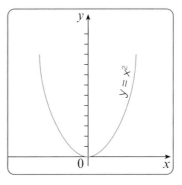

We have considered the effect of the coefficient of x, and the constant value in a quadratic expression, on its graph.

The coefficient of x^2 will also have an effect on a quadratic graph.

Example

When the coefficient of x^2 is not 1.

For the graph of $y = 2x^2$
when $x = 0$, $y = 0$
      $x = 1$, $y = 2$
      $x = 2$, $y = 8$
      $x = {}^-1$, $y = 2$
      $x = {}^-2$, $y = 8$
      ... , ...

So, on the same axes the graph of $y = 2x^2$ is a tighter curve than the graph of $y = x^2$

Example

When the coefficient of x^2 is negative.

For the graph of $y = {}^-x^2$
when $x = 0$, $y = 0$
      $x = 1$, $y = {}^-1$
      $x = 2$, $y = {}^-4$
      $x = {}^-1$, $y = {}^-1$
      $x = {}^-2$, $y = {}^-4$
      ... , ...

When we say the graph is inverted, we could say that it is upside down. We might also say that, in this case it is a reflection in the x-axis, i.e. the line $y = 0$.

So, the graph of $y = {}^-x^2$ is inverted compared with the graph of $y = x^2$.

7 Draw a pair of axes where ${}^-4 \leqslant x \leqslant 4$, and ${}^-10 \leqslant y \leqslant 60$.

a On the axes draw these quadratic graphs.
   $y = {}^-3x^2$ $y = 2 - 4x - x^2$ $y = 3x - 2x^2$ $y = 6x - 8 - 2x^2$
b For the graph of $ax^2 + bx + c$, describe the effect of changes in a, b, or c.

Solving quadratic equations graphically

This is the graph of $y = x^2 + 5x - 6$, for values of x from $^-8$ to $^+6$.

$y = 0$ is the equation of the x-axis.

You can be fairly confident of these values of x as solutions because they are both integer values.

If you are in any doubt, substitute in the equation to check each value.

We can use the graph to solve the equation $x^2 + 5x - 6 = 0$.

The graph of $y = x^2 + 5x - 6$ crosses the graph of $y = 0$ where:
$$x = ^-6 \quad \text{and where} \quad x = 1$$

At $x = ^-6$, and $x = 1$ the two equations must be equal.
So we can write:
$$x^2 + 5x - 6 = 0$$

From the graphs, the values of x that satisfy the equation are:
$$x = ^-6 \text{ or } x = 1$$

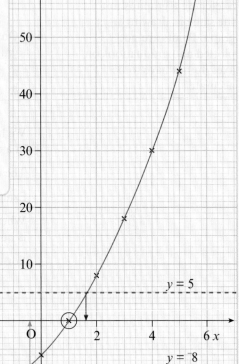

For this graph:

when $x = ^-8$	$y = 18$
$x = ^-7$	$y = 8$
$x = ^-6$	$y = 0$
$x = ^-5$	$y = ^-6$
$x = ^-4$	$y = ^-10$
$x = ^-3$	$y = ^-12$
$x = ^-2$	$y = ^-12$
$x = ^-1$	$y = ^-10$
$x = 0$	$y = ^-6$
$x = 1$	$y = 0$
$x = 2$	$y = 8$
$x = 3$	$y = 18$
$x = 4$	$y = 30$
$x = 5$	$y = 44$
$x = 6$	$y = 60$

These values of x, from the graph, are not integer values. The values are not exact, they are a good approximation. They answer the question, from the graph.

For more accurate solutions, use the values from the graph as a starting point for the trial-and-improvement method.

The graph of $y = x^2 + 5x - 6$ can be used to solve many more equations.

Example From the graph solve $x^2 + 5x - 6 = 5$.
The graph of $y = x^2 + 5x - 6$ crosses the graph of $y = 5$
so we can say: $x^2 + 5x - 6 = 5$
The two equations are equal where $x \approx ^-6.6$ and where $x \approx 1.6$

The solutions for $x^2 + 5x - 6 = 5$ are: $x \approx ^-6.6$ and $x \approx 1.6$

Example From the graph solve $x^2 + 5x - 6 = ^-8$.
The graph of $y = x^2 + 5x - 6$ crosses the graph of $y = ^-8$
so we can say: $x^2 + 5x - 6 = ^-8$

The solutions for $x^2 + 5x - 6 = ^-8$ are: $x \approx ^-4.6$ and $x \approx ^-0.4$

Exercise 16.3
Solving quadratic
equations graphically

1 The graph of $y = x^2 + 5x - 6$ can also be used to solve the equation:
$$x^2 + 5x - 6 = 10$$

  a What other graph would you draw on the axes to solve $x^2 + 5x - 6 = 10$?
  b Explain how you would use the two graphs to solve the equation.
  c From the graph on page 198, solve $x^2 + 5x - 6 = 10$.

2 The graph on page 198 can be used to solve these equations:
$$x^2 + 5x - 6 = 0$$
$$x^2 + 5x - 6 = 5$$
$$x^2 + 5x - 6 = 8$$
$$x^2 + 5x - 6 = 1$$

  a Give two other equations you think can be solved from the same graph.
  b Explain how you would solve your equations.

3 Asif used the same graph to solve $x^2 + 5x - 6 = 22$,
and only found one solution.

  a Explain why.
  b Give the solution you think Asif did find from the graph.
  c Is the other solution greater or less than $x = {}^-8$? Explain.

4 Draw the graph of $y = x^2 - 5x + 6$ for values of x from $^-2$ to $^+6$.

  a Use your graph to solve $x^2 - 5x + 6 = 0$.
  b On your axes draw and label the graph of $y = 4$.
  c Use your graphs to solve $x^2 - 5x + 6 = 4$.
  d Use the graph solve $x^2 - 5x + 6 = 10$.

5 Draw the graph of $y = x^2 - 4x - 5$ for values of x such that $^-3 \leqslant x \leqslant 7$.

  a Use the graph to solve:
    i $x^2 - 4x - 5 = 0$ **ii** $x^2 - 4x - 5 = 11$
  b From the graph solve $x^2 - 4x - 5 = {}^-9$.

6   **a**   **i** Draw the graph of $y = x^2 - 4x + 3$ for x such that $^-3 \leqslant x \leqslant 5$.
    ii Use the graph to solve $x^2 - 4x + 3 = 0$.
  b   **i** For values of x such that $^-3 \leqslant x \leqslant 5$ draw the graph of $y = x^2 + 3$.
    ii On the same axes draw and label a graph of $y = 4x$.
    iii Show that the solutions to $x^2 + 3 = 4x$ are $x = 1$ and $x = 3$.

7 In each of the following draw a graph and solve the equation.

  a For x: $^-6 \leqslant x \leqslant 2$ draw the graph of $y = x^2 + 5x - 4$, and solve:
    i $x^2 + 5x - 4 = 0$ **ii** $x^2 + 5x - 4 = {}^-6$ **iii** $x^2 + 5x = 4$
  b For x: $^-4 \leqslant x \leqslant 2$ draw the graph of $y = x^2 + 3x - 1$, and solve:
    i $x^2 + 3x - 1 = 0$ **ii** $x^2 + 3x + 1 = 0$ **iii** $x^2 + 3x - 1 = 0.5$
  c For x: $^-2 \leqslant x \leqslant 5$ draw the graph of $3 + 4x - x^2$, and solve:
    i $4x - x^2 + 3 = 0$ **ii** $4x + 3 - x^2 = 4$ **iii** $4x - x^2 + 1 = 0$
  d For x: $^-4 \leqslant x \leqslant 2$ draw the graph of $y = 1 - 3x - 2x^2$, and solve:
    i $2x^2 = 1 - 3x$ **ii** $^-3 = 1 - 3x - 2x^2$
  e For x: $^-2 \leqslant x \leqslant 3$ draw the graph of $y = 5x - 2x^2$, and solve:
    i $5x - 2x^2 = 0$ **ii** $5x - 2x^2 + 2 = 0$

8 Draw a suitable graph and solve the equation $(x + 2)^2 - 5 = 0$.

9 For x: $^-2 \leqslant x \leqslant 3$, solve $3x(x - 2) + 1 = 0$ by drawing a graph.

10   **a** Draw a graph to show that if $x(x + 4) = 6$, then $x \approx {}^-5$ or $x \approx 1$.
  b Use graphs to explain that the equations $x(x + 4) = 6$ and $x(x + 4) - 6 = 0$
have the same solutions.

> For x: $^-6 \leqslant x \leqslant 2$ is a
> notation that can be
> interpreted in this way:
>
> for values of x such that,
> x is greater than or equal
> to $^-6$, and less than or
> equal to 2.

In some cases to use a graph to solve an equation is only possible if you can decide on an additional graph to draw on the axes.
Rearranging the equation is one way to decide on additional graphs.

Example

Draw the graph of $y = 2x^2 + x - 4$ for x: $^-2 \leqslant x \leqslant 2$.
Use the graph to find approximate solutions to:

a $2x^2 + x - 4 = 0$ **b** $2x^2 + x = x + 3$ **c** $2x^2 + 1 = x + 2$

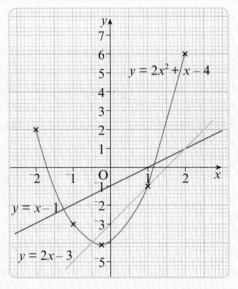

The graph of $y = 2x^2 + x - 4$
is drawn.

a To solve $2x^2 + x - 4 = 0$
From the graph:
$x \approx ^-1.8$, or $x \approx 1.2$

b To solve $2x^2 + x = x + 3$
the equation must be rearranged.

The LHS is $2x^2 + x$.
By subtracting 4 from the LHS
we have $2x^2 + x - 4$ (graph drawn)

So, to solve $2x^2 + x = x + 3$
we subtract 4 from both sides.

$2x^2 + x - 4 = x + 3 - 4$
i.e. $2x^2 + x - 4 = x - 1$

On the axes draw the graph of $y = x - 1$.
Where the curve $2x^2 + x - 4$ and the line $x - 1$ intersect is the solution to the equation $2x^2 + x = x + 3$.

The solution to $2x^2 + x = x + 3$ is $x \approx ^-1.3$, or $x \approx 1.2$

c To solve $2x^2 + 1 = x + 2$

The LHS is $2x^2 + 1$.
By subtracting 5 and adding x LHS is $2x^2 + 1 - 5 + x = 2x^2 + x - 4$.

So, to solve $2x^2 + 1 = x + 2$, we subtract 5 and add x to both sides.

$2x^2 + 1 - 5 + x = x + 2 - 5 + x$
i.e. $2x^2 + x - 4 = 2x - 3$

On the axes we draw the graph of $y = 2x - 3$.
Where the curve $2x^2 + x - 4$ and the line $2x - 3$ intersect is the solution to the equation $2x^2 + 1 = x + 2$.

The solution to $2x^2 + 1 = x + 2$ is $x \approx ^-0.5$, or $x = 1$.

11   **a**   Draw the graph of $y = x^2 - 4x - 2$, for x: $^-3 \leqslant x \leqslant 6$.
       b   Use the graph to find approximate solutions to $x^2 - 5x - 5 = x - 10$.
       c   Find approximate solutions to $x^2 - 2x + 3 = 8 - x$ from the graph.

12   **a**   Draw the graph of $y = 9 - 2x - x^2$, for x: $^-5 \leqslant x \leqslant 3$.
       b   Find approximate solutions to $12 - x = 13 - 5x - x^2$.
       c   Find approximate solutions to $7 + 2x - x^2 = 3 + x$.

13   If you had drawn the graph of $y = 12 - 4x - x^2$, find the equation of each additional line you would draw to solve these.
       a $10 - x^2 = 5x + 6$ **b** $7 - 6x = 15 - 6x - x^2$

14 **a** For x: $^-8 \leqslant x \leqslant 3$ draw the graph of $y = 12 - 4x - x^2$.
    b Use the graph to find approximate solutions to $1 - x = 8 - 7x - x^2$.
    c Find approximate solution to $4 - 3x - x^2 = 1 - 2x$ from the graph.
    d Use the graph to find approximate solutions to $2x + 7 = 4 - x^2 - 2.5x$.

    The graph of $y = 12 - 4x - x^2$ was used to solve an equation and the approximate solutions were given as $x \approx 1.7$ or $x \approx ^-4.7$.

    e Show from the graph that the equation solved was $9 - 4x = 17 - x^2 - 7x$.

15 **a** For x: $^-7 \leqslant x \leqslant 3$, draw the graph of $y = x^2 + 5x - 8$.

    Use the graph to find approximate solutions to these equations.

    b $x(x + 5) = 8$ **c** $5(x - 1) + x^2 = 0$ **d** $x^2 + 5x = 10$
    e $x(x + 7) - 3 = 1 + 7x$ **f** $3(x - 2) = x(x + 11) - 12$

Graphs of reciprocal curves

> If a number could be divided by zero the answer would be infinite.
>
> So $8 \div 0$ is said to be ∞.
>
> Think about $\frac{8}{x}$.
>
> If $x = 1$, $\frac{8}{x} = 8$
>
> $x = 0.01$, $\frac{8}{x} = 800$
>
> $x = 0.001$, $\frac{8}{x} = 8000$
>
> as x approaches zero $\frac{8}{x}$ will approach ∞.
>
> If $x = ^-1, ^-0.01, ^-0.001, \ldots$ then $\frac{8}{x}$ approaches $^-\infty$.

Reciprocal graphs can be identified from their equation.

There will be a term in the form $\frac{n}{x}$.

Example   Draw the graph of $y = \frac{8}{x}$ for x: $^-4 \leqslant x \leqslant 4$

When $x = ^-4$, $y = ^-2$
          $x = ^-3$, $y = ^-2.7$ (1dp)
          $x = ^-2$, $y = ^-4$
          $x = ^-1$, $y = ^-8$
          $x = 0$, y is ∞
          $x = 1$, $y = 8$
          $x = 2$, $y = 4$
          $x = 3$, $y = 2.7$ (1dp)
          $x = 4$, $y = 2$

From these values, the curve is broken at $x = 0$.

Also, as x becomes very large, $\frac{8}{x}$ becomes very small, but

$\frac{8}{x}$ will never equal zero.

So the graph will get very close to each of the axes, but it will never touch either of them.

Here the x-axis ($y = 0$) and the y-axis ($x = 0$) are called asymptotes to the curve.

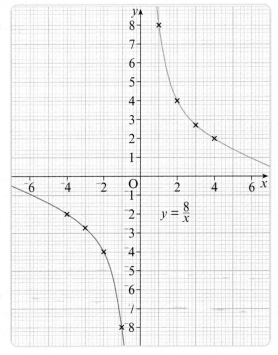

> An asymptote to a curve is a straight line to which a curve continuously draws nearer but without ever touching it.

> Displaying this graph on a graphical calculator will help you to investigate how the graph of a curve approaches an asymptote.

Exercise 16.4
Reciprocal graphs

1 **a** **i** For x: $^-5 \leqslant x \leqslant 5$, draw the graph of $y = \frac{5}{x}$.

       ii Give the equation of any asymptotes to the graph of $y = \frac{5}{x}$.

    b On the same axes draw and label the graph of $y = \frac{5}{2x}$.

2 **a** For x: $^-5 \leqslant x \leqslant 5$ draw the graph of $y = \frac{4}{x} + 3$.

    b Give the equation of any asymptotes to the graph of $y = \frac{4}{x} + 3$.

3   Give the equation of any asymptotes to the curve $y = \dfrac{6}{x} - 8$.

4   **a**   Sketch the curve of $y = \dfrac{6}{x} + 2$.

One asymptote to the curve is the line $x = 0$.

b   On your sketch draw and label the other asymptote with its equation.

5   **a**   For x: $1 \leqslant x \leqslant 12$, draw the graph of $y = \dfrac{12}{x}$.

b   Use the graph to find approximate solutions to these equations.

   i $\dfrac{12}{x} = x + 1$ **ii** $\dfrac{12}{x} = x - 3$ **iii** $x^2 = 12$

6   Draw graphs of $y = \dfrac{20}{x}$, and $y = x$ on the same axes.

From your graphs show that $\sqrt{20} \approx \pm 4.5$.

7   **a**   For x: $1 \leqslant x \leqslant 10$, draw the graph of $y = \dfrac{10}{x} - x$.

b   As the value of x increases, explain what value y will approach.

c   Give the equation of two asymptotes to the graph of $y = \dfrac{10}{x} - x$.

8   Explain why $y = {}^-2x$ is an asymptote to the graph of $y = \dfrac{25}{x} - 2x$.

Include a labelled sketch graph in your explanation.

9   The graph of $y = x + 3$ is an asymptote to a reciprocal graph.
The reciprocal graph passes through the point (1, 12).
a   Give the equation of this reciprocal graph.
b   Draw and label a sketch graph showing both graphs.

10   For x: ${}^-5 \leqslant x \leqslant 4$, draw the graph of $y = \dfrac{6}{x - 4}$.

Reading and interpreting graphs

When a graph is read or interpreted, it is important to remember that any values taken from the graph can only be approximate, say to 1 dp.

Example   For x: $1 \leqslant x \leqslant 10$ draw the graph of $y = \dfrac{15}{x} + x - 5$.

Use the graph to find:
a   the minimum value for y
b   the values of x
when $y = 5.2$.

For the graph, calculate values for y from values for x
i.e. when $x = 1$, $y = 11$
         $x = 2$, $y = 4.5$
         $x = 3$, $y = 3$
         ... ,   ...

From the graph:
a   the minimum value for y
is approximately 2.7
b   when $y = 5.2$, the values of x
are: $x \approx 1.8$, and $x \approx 8.4$

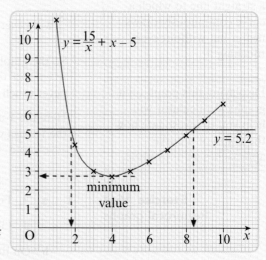

Exercise 16.5
Reading and interpreting
graphs

1   For x: $1 \leqslant x \leqslant 10$, draw the graph of $y = \dfrac{12}{x} + x - 10$. From the graph find:

   i   the minimum value of y **ii**   values of x when $y = {}^-2.5$

2   Draw the graph of $y = 4 - 3x - x^2$.

   a   Use the graph to find an approximate maximum value for y.
   b   Give two values of x for which $y = 2.5$.

3   For x: $^-6 \leqslant x \leqslant 2$, draw the graph of $y = 9 - 5x - x^2$.

   a   From your graph give the approximate maximum value of y.
   b   When $y = 11.5$, give approximate values for x.
   c   Solve the equation $6 - 2x = 9 - 5x - x^2$.
   d   i   Explain why, by drawing the graph of the line $y = x + 15$, you should
           be able to find approximate solutions to $5x + 8 = 2 - x - x^2$.
       ii Find approximate solutions to $5x + 8 = 2 - x - x^2$.
   e   On the same axes draw the graph of $y = x^2 + x + 5$.
       i   What is the approximate minimum value of y?
       ii Use your graphs to solve $x^2 + x + 5 = 9 - 5x - x^2$.
       iii Give an equation for the line joining the points where the two curves
           intersect.

4   Draw the graph of $y = \frac{1}{2}(x^2 - 3x - 5)$ for x: $^-3 \leqslant x \leqslant 4$.

   a   From the graph:
       i   give an approximate minimum value of y.
       ii find approximate values for x when $y = ^-1$.
   b   On the same axes draw the graph of $y = \frac{4}{x} - 6$.
   c   Explain why neither of the curves
       intersect with the line $y = ^-6$.

5   On the same axes draw the graphs of $y = \frac{2x}{3 - x}$, and $y = \frac{1}{2}x^2 + 2$.
   Use x: $^-4 \leqslant x \leqslant 4$.

   a   Use the graphs to solve the equation $2x = (0.5x^2 + 2)(3 - x)$.
   b   Only one curve will intersect with the line $x = 3$.
       Which curve will not intersect? Explain why.

Graphs of higher-order polynomial equations

An equation of higher order than a quadratic has a highest power of the
variable greater than 2, as in the following polynomial equations.
$$3a^3 + 4a \qquad a^3 + a^2 - 1 \qquad y^5 - 4y = 3 \qquad k^6 = 1$$

Example

Draw the graph of $y = x^3 + 2$
for x: $^-3 \leqslant x \leqslant 3$.

> The graph, when drawn,
> will be a smooth curve.

When $x = ^-3$, $y = ^-25$
      $x = ^-2$, $y = ^-6$
      $x = ^-1$, $y = 1$
      $x = 0$, $y = 2$
      $x = 1$, $y = 3$
      $x = 2$, $y = 10$
      $x = 3$, $y = 29$

The graph can be used to solve $x^3 + 2 = 0$
From the graph if $x^3 + 2 = 0$ then $x \approx ^-1.3$

$x^3 + 2 = 0$ is known as a **cubic** equation.

> Remember values read
> from the graph will only be
> approximate.

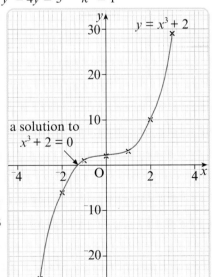

a solution to
$x^3 + 2 = 0$

203

Exercise 16.6
Graphs of polynomial
equations

1 On the same axes draw graphs of $y = x^3 + 4$ and $y = 4 - x^3$.

 a Describe any common features of the graphs.
 b Describe any differences between the graphs.
 c For each graph:
  i describe what happens as x becomes increasingly large.
  ii describe what happens as x becomes increasingly negative.

2 For $x:\ ^-4 \leqslant x \leqslant 3$ draw the graph of $y = x^3 + 2x^2$.

 a From your graph solve the equation $x^3 + 2x^2 = 0$.
 b By drawing an additional graph, find an approximate solution to the equation $12x + 5 = 2x^2 + x^3$.
 c i On the same axes draw the graph of $y = 4x^2 - x^3$ for $x:\ ^-2 \leqslant x \leqslant 4$.
  ii Use your graph to solve $4x^2 - x^3 = 0$.
  iii Find approximate values for x when $y = 7$.
  iv Find an approximate value for y when $x = ^-1.5$.

3 Draw the graph of $y = x^3 - 3x^2$ for values of x from $^-3$ to 4.

 a Use your graph to find an approximate value for x when $y = 8$.
 b Find values for x when $x^3 - 3x^2 = ^-4$.

 For $x:\ ^-3 \leqslant x \leqslant 4$, the equation $x^3 - 3x^2 = n$ is satisfied by only one value of n.

 c List a range of values for n that give one solution only to $x^3 - 3x^2 = n$.

4 Draw the graph of $y = \frac{1}{2}(x^3 - 3x - 8)$ for values of x from $^-4$ to 4.

 Use the graph to find:

 a an approximate value for y, when $x = 3.4$
 b an approximate value for x when $y = ^-9$
 c an approximate solution to the equation $\frac{1}{2}(x^3 - 3x - 8) = 0$
 d three approximate values of x that satisfy $\frac{1}{2}(x^3 - 3x - 8) = 5x - 2$.

5 Draw the graph of $y = x^3 - x^2 - 4x + 4$ for $x:\ ^-3 \leqslant x \leqslant 4$.

 a Use the graph to solve $x^3 - x^2 - 4x + 4 = 0$.
 b When $x = ^-1.5$ give an approximate value for y.
 c Find three approximate values for x that give $x^3 - x^2 - 4x + 4 = 2$.

6 The width of a rectangle is given as w (cm), and the length as $w + 8$ (cm). An expression for the area A (cm^2) of the rectangle is $A = w(w + 8)$.

 a Draw a graph of $A = w(w + 8)$ for values of w from zero to 8. (Plot w on the horizontal axis.)
 b From the graph find approximate dimensions of the rectangle when the area is:
  i 55 cm^2　　ii 18 cm^2　　iii 100 cm^2
 c What is the approximate area of the rectangle when $w = 3.8$ cm?
 d If the rectangle has an area of 75 cm^2, find the value of w to 1.dp.

7 The dimensions of a rectangle of area A (cm^2) are given in this way.

 ◆ let the width of the rectangle be w (cm)
 ◆ the length is 4 cm less than twice the width of the rectangle.

 a Write an expression for the area of the rectangle.
 b Draw a graph of A against w, for values of $w:\ 0 \leqslant w \leqslant 8$.
 c From the graph, give the approximate dimensions of the rectangle when the area is:
  i 35 cm^2　　ii 62 cm^2　　iii 80 cm^2
 d What is the approximate area of the rectangle when the width is 5.6 cm?
 e Give the dimensions of the rectangle (to 1 dp) when the area is 44 cm^2.

Sketching graphs by completing the square

If you can write a quadratic expression as a complete square, it can help to sketch the graph.

Example

Sketch the graph of $y = x^2 + 4x + 1$.

Completing the square gives:
$$y = (x + 2)^2 - 4 + 1$$
i.e. $y = (x + 2)^2 - 3$

> A full explanation of completing the square can be found on page 110 of this book.

For the graph of $y = (x + 2)^2 - 3$
$(x + 2)^2$ cannot be negative,
so the minimum value of y
is when $(x + 2) = 0$, i.e. $x = {}^-2$

When $x = {}^-2$, $y = {}^-3$, so,
the minimum point is $({}^-2, {}^-3)$.

The intersect with the y-axis
is where $x = 0$ i.e.
when $x = 0$, $y = 1$
so, the y-intercept is at $(0, 1)$.

The graph can now be sketched.

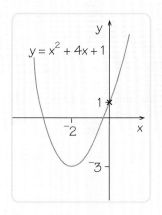

Exercise 16.7
Sketching graphs by completing the square

1 For the graph of $y = x^2 + 6x - 2$:
   a Rearrange the equation by completing the square.
   b What is the minimum value of y? Explain your answer.
   c Give the coordinates of the intercept with the y-axis.
   d Sketch the graph of $y = x^2 + 6x - 2$.

2 For the graph of $y = x^2 + 10x + 4$:
   a Show that the minimum value of y is $^-21$.
   b Sketch the graph of $y = x^2 + 10x + 4$.

3 Sketch the graph of $y = x^2 + 14x - 5$.

4 Sketch the graph of $y = x^2$ $8x$ 6.

5 a On the same axes sketch the graphs of $y = x^2 + 8x + 4$, and $y = x - 9$.
   b Explain, with the help of your sketch graphs, why you cannot find a value for x that satisfies $x^2 + 8x + 4 = x - 9$.

6 Explain why you cannot use completing the square to help sketch the graph of $y = 6x - 10 - x^2$.

7 The diagram shows a sketch of a quadratic graph in the form:
   $$y = ax^2 + bx + c$$
   Find an equation for the graph that is sketched and list values for a, b, and c.

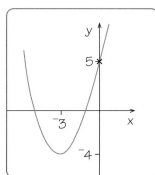

End points

You should be able to ...   ... so try these questions

A Solve simultaneous linear equations graphically

A1 By drawing suitable graphs solve these equations for x and y.

   a $5x - 3y = 13$
      $2x + 5y = {}^-1$

   b $2x - 3y = 3$
      $7x - 2y = 19$

A2 Two groups of people bought tickets on the Cliff Railway. The first group of five adults and two children paid a total of £32. The second group of two adults and three children paid a total of £20.50.

By drawing suitable linear graphs, find the charges for adult and child tickets for the Cliff Railway.

B Work with, and solve equations from quadratic graphs

B1 Give the equation of the line of symmetry of the graph $y = x^2 - 4x$.

B2 Solve these quadratic equations by drawing suitable graphs.

   a $x^2 + 2x - 8 = 0$
   b $x^2 - 3x - 7 = 3$
   c $x^2 - x + 12 = 16$
   d $2x^2 - 2x - 12 = 0$

B3 **a** Draw the graph of $y = 2x^2 + x - 5$.

Use the graph of $y = 2x^2 + x - 5$ together with any additional graphs you choose to draw to solve these equations.

   b $2x^2 + 4x - 9 = 5x - 5$
   c $5x + 7 = 2x^2 + 5x + 1$
   d $2x - 5 = 2x^2 + 5x - 7$

C Draw and interpret reciprocal graphs

C1 For x: ${}^-5 < x < 5$ draw the graph of $y = \dfrac{6}{x} - 2$.

C2 For x: ${}^-6 \leqslant x \leqslant 4$ draw the graph of $y = \dfrac{2}{x} + 5$.

Give the equation of any asymptotes to the graph of $y = \dfrac{2}{x} + 5$.

C3 Sketch the curve of $y = \dfrac{5}{x} + 4$.

On your sketch draw and label any asymptotes.

D Read and interpret graphs

D1 For x: $1 \leqslant x \leqslant 10$, draw the graph of $y = \dfrac{12}{x} + x - 8$.

   a From the graph find an approximate minimum value for y.
   b Give approximate values for x when $y = {}^-0.6$.

D2 For x: ${}^-6 \leqslant x \leqslant 2$ draw the graph of $y = 8 - 5x - x^2$.

   a From the graph give an approximate maximum value for y.
   b When $y = 3.8$ give two approximate values for x.
   c Use the graph and any suitable additional graph find values of x that satisfy the equation $2x + 4 = 9 - x - x^2$.

D3 The width of a rectangle is given as w (cm) and the length as $w + 6$ (cm). An expression for the area A (cm^2) of the rectangle is given as $A = w(w + 6)$.

a Draw a graph of $A = w(w + 6)$ for values of w from zero to 10. (Plot w on the horizontal axis.)

b From the graph find approximate dimensions of the rectangle when the area is:

   i 58 cm^2 **ii** 32 cm^2.

c Calculate the approximate area of the rectangle when $w = 5.4$ cm.

d If $A = 35$ cm^2, calculate a value for w correct to 1 dp.

E Sketch graphs and use completing the square

E1 On the same axes sketch and label these graphs.

   a $y = x^2 + 3x + 1$

   b $y = 2x + 3$

E2 Sketch and label these graphs on the same axes.

   a $y = x^2 - 4$

   b $y = 4 - x^2$

   c $y = 4 - 3x - x^2$

E3 On the same axes sketch and label these graphs.

   a $y = \dfrac{9}{x} + 1$

   b $y = x^3 + 4$

   c $y = 4 - x^3$

E4 For the graph of $y = x^2 + 8x - 7$.

   a Show that the graph has a minimum value of $^-23$.

   b Sketch the graph of $y = x^2 + 8x - 7$.

E5 The diagram shows a sketch of a quadratic graph in the form

$$y = ax^2 + bx + c$$

Find an equation for the graph and list values for a, b, and c.

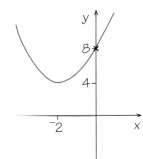

Some points to remember

- The equation of any graph gives you data about the graph before you plot any points or sketch a line on a pair of axes. This data can indicate shape, intersects with axes and any maximum or minimum values.

- The graphs of curves should be drawn as a smooth curve, with axes clearly graduated, points accurately plotted and the final curve labelled with its equation.

- Data that you read from a graph is only an approximation. For more exact values use trial and improvement starting with any approximate value read from a graph.

Starting points
You need to know about ...   ... so try these questions

A Trigonometric ratios

♦ These are definitions of three
trigonometric ratios (trig ratios).

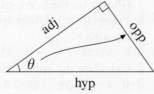

$$\sin \theta = \frac{\text{opp}}{\text{hyp}} \qquad \cos \theta = \frac{\text{adj}}{\text{hyp}} \qquad \tan \theta = \frac{\text{opp}}{\text{adj}}$$

$$\text{opp} = \text{hyp} \times \sin \theta \qquad \text{adj} = \text{hyp} \times \cos \theta \qquad \text{opp} = \text{adj} \times \tan \theta$$

♦ These trig ratios can be used to calculate sides or angles in
right-angled triangles.

Example   In $\triangle ABC$ $AB = AC = 5\,cm$ and $BC = 6\,cm$.
Calculate the angle $C\hat{A}B$.

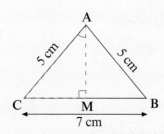

$\triangle ABC$ is isosceles.
$$CM = MB = 3.5\,cm$$
$$C\hat{A}M = B\hat{A}M$$

In $\triangle AMC$:
$$\sin C\hat{A}M = \frac{CM}{AC} = \frac{3.5}{5} = 0.7$$
$$C\hat{A}M = 44.42\ldots°$$
$$C\hat{A}B = 88.9° \text{ to 1 dp.}$$

B Graphs of $y = \sin x$ and $y = \cos x$

♦ This diagram shows the graphs of $y = \sin x$ and $y = \cos x$
for values of x from 0° to 90°.

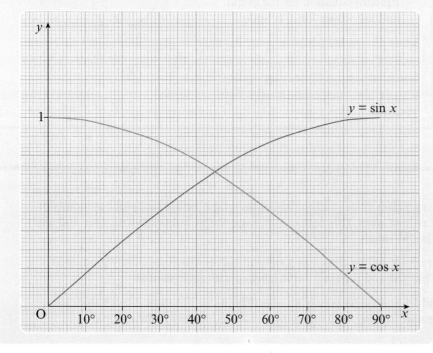

A1 The points B and C lie on the
circumference of a circle with
centre O.

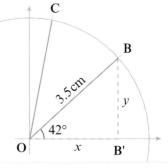

a Calculate, correct to 2 dp:
  i the coordinates of B
  ii the area of $\triangle OBB'$
b C is the point (0.88, 3.39).
Calculate the angle between
OC and the horizontal axis,
correct to 1 dp.

A2 Calculate the area of a regular
pentagon of side 8 cm.

A3 If $\tan \theta = \frac{3}{4}$ find the value of:
  a $\cos \theta$ **b** $\sin \theta$.

Use the graphs of $y = \sin x$
and $y = \cos x$ to answer
Questions **B1 – B3**.

B1 Estimate the value of:
  a $\cos 40°$
  b $\sin 40°$

B2 Estimate the angle x for
each of these:
  a $\sin x = 0.4$
  b $\cos x = 0.4$

B3 Find the angle x for each
of these:
  a $\sin 20° = \cos x$
  b $\cos 48° = \sin x$
  c $\cos x = \sin x$

Notation for trigonometric ratios

◆ $y = \cos 4x$ can also be written as $y = \cos (4x)$ to show that you need to find the value of $4x$ before finding the cosine.

When $x = 10$ $y = \cos 4x$
$$= \cos (4 \times 10)°$$
$$= \cos 40°$$
$$= 0.766 \text{ (3 sf)}$$

◆ $y = 4 \cos x$ can also be written as $y = 4 \times \cos x$

When $x = 10$ $y = 4 \cos x$
$$= 4 \times \cos 10°$$
$$= 3.94 \text{ (3 sf)}$$

◆ In the same way
$y = \sin 3x$ can be written as $y = \sin (3x)$ and
$y = 3 \sin x$ can be written as $y = 3 \times \sin x$

Exercise 17.1
Evaluating trigonometric functions

1 Evaluate these expressions, correct to 2 dp, when $x = 20$.

   a $2 \sin x$ **b** $\sin 3x$ **c** $\cos 2x$
   d $3 \cos 2x$ **e** $2 \sin 4x$ **f** $5 \cos 3x$

2 If $y = 4 \cos 3x$:

   a   find the value of y when
     i $x = 5$ **ii** $x = 7.5$ **iii** $x = 12.35$
   b   for what value of x does
     i $y = 0$ **ii** $y = 2$?

Polar and cartesian coordinates

◆ Polar coordinates give the position of a point in a plane by stating:
   ❖ its distance, r from a fixed point, the pole
   ❖ the angle, θ measured anticlockwise, between a line drawn from the pole to the point and a fixed line, the polar axis.
These are written (r, θ) the distance followed by the angle, for example $(4, 50°)$.

◆ Cartesian coordinates give the position of a point in a plane by stating
   ❖ its distance from two perpendicular axes, for example $(6, 5)$.

Example   This diagram shows the position of a boat at S on a radar screen with rings 10 km apart.

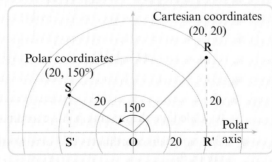

The cartesian coordinates for R are $(20, 20)$ °
   In $\triangle ORR'$
   $ROR = 45°$
     $= \sqrt{800}$
     $= 28.28 \text{ (2dp)}$
So the polar coordinates for R are $(28.28, 45°)$.

Exercise 17.2
Using polar and cartesian coordinates

1 The polar coordinates of S are $(20, 150°)$.

   a   Explain why the cartesian coordinates for S are $(^-20 \cos 30°, 20 \sin 30°)$.
   b   Calculate the cartesian coordinates of S.

2 Each of the points A to D on the radar screen shows the position of an aeroplane. The rings are 10 km apart.
AOD and BOC are straight lines.

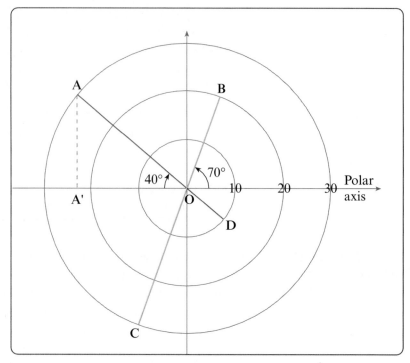

a Explain why the polar coordinates for the point A are (30, 140°).

b Calculate these distances, correct to 2 dp.
   i OA′   **ii** AA′.

c Give the cartesian coordinates of A.

d For each of the points B, C and D:
   i give the polar coordinates
   ii calculate the cartesian coordinates correct to 2 dp.

> For the cartesian coordinates each distance is given correct to 2 dp.

> It may help to mark each position on a sketch.

3 For three other aeroplanes the polar coordinates and cartesian coordinates are given below. For two more aeroplanes only the cartesian coordinates are given.

a Match each of the polar coordinates to its cartesian coordinates.

Polar coordinates	Cartesian coordinates
(13, 225°) (40, 114°)	(⁻16.27, 36.54)
	(⁻9.19, ⁻9.19)
	(21.53, ⁻22.30)
(25, 291°)	(⁻16.19, 3.24)
	(8.96, ⁻23.34)

b Calculate the missing polar coordinates, to the nearest whole number.

4 The cartesian coordinates of point A are (x, y), and the polar coordinates are (r, θ).

   a Write an expression for r in terms of x and y.
   b Write the cartesian coordinates in terms of r and θ.
   c If $r = 1$, what are the cartesian coordinates in terms of θ?

Trigonometric functions for any angle

> A unit circle is a circle of radius 1 unit.

◆ For any angle the values of $\sin \theta$ and $\cos \theta$ are defined as the cartesian coordinates of the point on a unit circle with polar coordinates $(1, \theta)$.

Example Find the value of cos 128° and sin 128°.

The point A lies on a unit circle so the coordinates of A are (cos 128°, sin 128°).

So   cos 128° = ⁻OA′
$\qquad$ sin 128° = AA′

In △ OAA′:
$\qquad$ OA′ = 1 × cos 52°
$\qquad\quad$ = cos 52°
$\qquad\quad$ = 0.616
$\qquad$ AA′ = 1 sin 52°
$\qquad\quad$ = sin 52°
$\qquad\quad$ = 0.788

So the coordinates of A are (⁻0.616, 0.788)

So, cos 128° = ⁻0.616 and sin 128° = 0.788

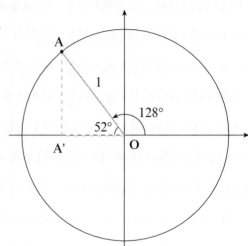

Exercise 17.3

Evaluating trigonometric functions for any angle

> You do not need to use a calculator for this exercise.
>
> It may help to sketch a unit circle for each question.

1 Find another angle whose cosine = ⁻0.616.

2 Draw a diagram to find the value of:
$\quad$ **a** cos 308° $\qquad\qquad$ **b** sin 308°.

3 Use diagrams to explain why:
$\quad$ **a** sin 21° = sin 159° $\qquad$ **b** sin 201° = ⁻sin 21°
$\quad$ **c** cos 5° = cos 355° $\qquad$ **d** cos 185° = ⁻cos 5°.

4 The value of cos 36° is 0.809 (3sf). What is the value of:
$\quad$ **a** cos 144° $\qquad$ **b** cos 324° $\qquad$ **c** cos 216°?

5 **a** Sort these into pairs that have the same value.

$\qquad$ sin 53° $\qquad\qquad$ sin 233° $\qquad\qquad$ sin 127°

$\qquad$ cos 233° $\qquad\qquad$ cos 127° $\qquad\qquad$ sin 307°

$\quad$ **b** Find the value for each pair correct to 3 sf.

6 For what values of θ, from 0° to 360°, is:
$\quad$ **a** $\cos \theta < 0$ $\qquad$ **b** $\sin \theta < 0$

7 A negative angle is measured clockwise from the polar axis.
$\quad$ **a** Draw a diagram above to find the value of $\cos \theta$ and $\sin \theta$ for:
$\qquad$ **i** $\theta = ⁻90°$ $\qquad\qquad$ **ii** $\theta = ⁻52°$
$\quad$ **b** Find a negative value for θ which satisfies:
$\qquad$ **i** $\sin \theta = \sin 54°$ $\qquad$ **ii** $\sin \theta = \sin 100°$ $\qquad$ **iii** $\cos \theta = \cos 200°$

8 **a** Explain why cos 450° = 0.
$\quad$ **b** Give three values of θ for which $\sin \theta = 1$.

Graphs of $y = \sin x$ and $y = \cos x$

♦ The diagram shows the graphs of $y = \sin x$ and $y = \cos x$ for $0° \leqslant x \leqslant 360°$

♦ If you use your calculator to find $\sin x$ for values of x from $0°$ to $90°$, you can use the symmetry of the graph to find other solutions.

Example **Solve $\sin x = \sin 20°$ and $\sin x = {}^-\!\sin 20°$ for $0° < x < 360°$**

From a calculator $\sin 20° = 0.34$ (2 dp), so $^-\!\sin 20° = {}^-0.34$ (2dp).

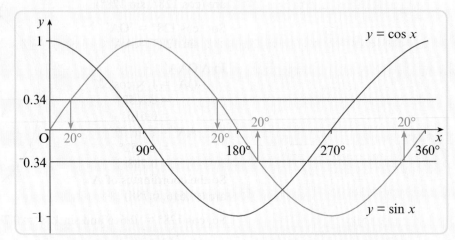

Solve $\sin x = \sin 20°$

From a calculator:
$$\sin 20° = 0.34 \text{ (2 dp)}$$
$$\sin x = 0.34$$

From the graph:
$$x = 20°$$

or $x = 180° - 20°$
$$x = 160°$$

Solve $\sin x = {}^-\!\sin 20°$

From a calculator:
$$\sin 20° = 0.34 \text{ (2 dp)}$$
so $^-\!\sin 20° = {}^-0.34$ (2dp)

From the graph:
$$x = 180° + 20°$$
$$x = 200°$$

or $x = 360° - 20°$
$$x = 340°$$

Exercise 17.4
Using the graphs of
$y = \sin x$ and $y = \cos x$

> To avoid marking the page put tracing paper over the graph each time you use it.

1 What is the maximum and minimum value for:

   a $\sin x$ **b** $\cos x$?

2 For what values of x, between $0°$ and $360°$, is $\sin x = 0.5$?

3 Solve each of these for values of x between $0°$ and $360°$.

   a **i** $\cos x = \cos 40°$ **ii** $\cos x = {}^-\!\cos 35°$ **iii** $\sin x = {}^-\!\sin 72°$?

   b **i** $\sin x = 0.9$ **ii** $\cos x = {}^-0.9$?

   c **i** $\cos x < 0.5$ **ii** $\sin x < {}^-0.5$ **iii** $\cos x = \sin x$

      iv $\cos x < \sin x$

4 Two solutions for $\cos x = 0.5$ are $x = 60°$ and $x = 300°$.

   a Find two other solutions with $x > 300°$.

   b Give another solution with $x \leqslant 0°$.

5 One solution for $\sin x = 1$ is $x = 90°$.

   Find another solution with:

   a $x > 90°$ **b** $x \leqslant 0°$.

> A symbol that represents a constant is a number with a fixed value.

6 Find a value of the constant k so that each of these is true for all values of x.

   a $\sin (x + k) = \cos x$ **b** $\sin (x + k) = {}^-\!\cos x$

An example which shows that a statement is false is called a counter-example.

Finding a value for which a statement is true does not prove that it is true for all values of x.

7 Three of these statements are false for some values of x.
a Give a counter-example for the three statements that are false.

A $\sin (180° - x) = \sin (180° + x)$
B $\cos x = \sin (90° + x)$
C $\sin (x + x) = \sin x + \sin x$
D $\cos x = \cos (90° + x)$
E $\cos x = \cos (360° - x)$

b Explain how you know that the other two statements are true for all values of x.

Transformations of the graphs of $y = \sin x$ and $y = \cos x$

Exercise 17.5
Drawing trigonometric graphs

We say the movement is modelled by this equation because it does not describe the movement exactly but it is reasonably accurate.

1 The movement of the tip of the needle in this sewing machine can be modelled by the equation

$$h = 9 \cos \theta$$

where:

θ(in degrees) $= 6t$,
t is the time in milliseconds (thousandths of a second) that the machine has been running.
h is the height above the footplate in millimetres.

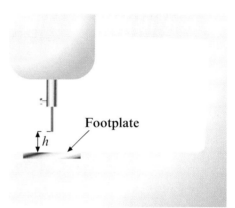

Footplate

These are some values for $h = 9 \cos \theta$.

$t = 0 \quad h = 9 \times \cos (6 \times 0)°$
$\qquad = 9 \times \cos 0°$
$\qquad = 9$

$t = 10 \quad h = 9 \times \cos (6 \times 10)°$
$\qquad = 9 \times \cos 60°$
$\qquad = 4.5$

a Copy and complete this table for values of $h = 9 \cos \theta$ over the first 100 milliseconds.

t (ms)	0	10	20	30	40	50	60	70	80	90	100
h (m)	9	4.5									

b i Explain why the graph should be a smooth curve.
   ii Draw the graph of $h = 9 \cos \theta$.
c At what height above the footplate did the tip of the needle start?
d Each time the tip of the needle returns to its maximum height above the footplate it completes one stitch.
   i How long does the machine take to complete one stitch?
   ii For how long is the needle below the footplate on each stitch?
e How many stitches will the machine complete in one second?

Use the same pair of axes as you used for Question **1b**.

2 The movement of the tip of the needle on another sewing machine can be modelled by the equation

$$h = 12 \cos \theta$$

a Sketch the graph of $h = 12 \cos \theta$
b Does this machine complete stitches at the same rate?
c What is the difference between the two machines?

◆ Each of the graphs below is a transformation of the graph of $y = \sin x$.

A   **A graph of $y = \sin x + 2$**

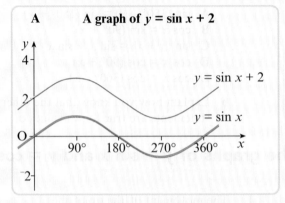

x	$y = \sin x + 2$	
0°	$\sin 0° + 2$	$= 2.00$
45°	$\sin 45° + 2$	≈ 2.71
90°	$\sin 90° + 2$	$= 3.00$
135°	$\sin 135° + 2$	≈ 2.71
180°	$\sin 180° + 2$	≈ 2.00
225°	$\sin 225° + 2$	≈ 1.29
...	...	

B   **A graph of $y = 2 \sin x$**

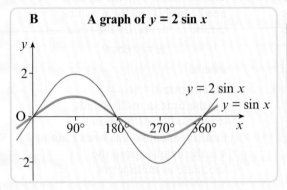

x	$y = 2 \sin x$	
0°	$2 \times \sin 0°$	$= 0.00$
45°	$2 \times \sin 45°$	≈ 1.41
90°	$2 \times \sin 90°$	$= 2.00$
135°	$2 \times \sin 135°$	≈ 1.41
180°	$2 \times \sin 180°$	$= 0.00$
225°	$2 \times \sin 225°$	$\approx ^-1.41$
...	...	

C   **A graph of $y = \sin 2x$**

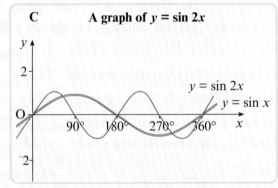

x	$y = \sin 2x$	
0°	$\sin (2 \times 0)°$	$= 0.00$
45°	$\sin (2 \times 45)°$	$= 1.00$
90°	$\sin (2 \times 90)°$	$= 0.00$
135°	$\sin (2 \times 135)°$	$= ^-1.00$
180°	$\sin (2 \times 180)°$	$= 0.00$
...	...	

Exercise 17.6
Sketching and using
trigonometric graphs

1   Using the diagrams above:
   a   state the maximum and minimum values of y on each graph
   b   describe the link between the graphs of $y = \sin x$ and:
      i $y = \sin x + 2$ **ii** $y = 2 \sin x$ **iii** $y = \sin 2x$.

It may help to sketch the
graph of $y = \cos x$ first.

2   **a**   For the values $0 \leqslant x \leqslant 360°$ sketch the graphs of:
      i $y = \cos x - 2$ **ii** $y = 3 \cos x$ **iii** $y = \cos 3x$.
   b   For each graph state the maximum and minimum values of y.

3   What are the maximum and minimum values of y for:
   a $y = \sin 4x$ **b** $y = 5 \cos x$ **c** $y = \sin x - 4$
   d $y = \cos 2x + 1$ **e** $y = 2 \sin x - 2$ **f** $y = 3 \sin 2x + 2$.

4   On one pair of axes sketch the graph of:
   a $y = \sin 3x$ **b** $y = 2 \sin 3x$ **c** $y = 2 \sin 3x - 4$.

5   Each of these graphs is a transformation of $y = \sin x$ or $y = \cos x$.

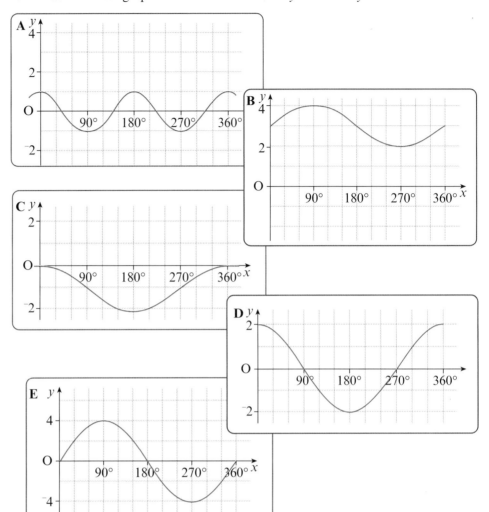

These are the five equations for the graphs above.

$$y = a \sin x \qquad\qquad y = \cos x + a \qquad\qquad y = a \cos x$$

$$y = \sin x + a \qquad\qquad y = \cos ax$$

For each graph:
a   write down the matching equation
b   find value of a in its equation.

> In each equation a is a constant.

6   For the graph of $y = a \sin bx + c$, where a, b and c are constants, write an expression for the maximum value of y.

7   Sketch the graphs of:
a $y = \cos (x + 45°)$ **b** $y = \cos (x - 45°)$.

> These are some values for
> $y = \cos (x + 45°)$:
>
> | x | $y = \cos (x + 45°)$ |
> |---|---|
> | 0 | $\cos (0 + 45°) \approx 0.71$ |
> | 45 | $\cos (45° + 45°) = 0.00$ |

8   Explain why the graph of $y = \sin (x + 90°)$ and $y = \cos x$ are the same.

9   Which of these gives the same graph as $y = \cos x$?
   A $y = \sin (x + 90°)$ B $y = \sin x - 90°$ C $y = \cos (x + 360°)$
   D $y = \sin x + 90°$ E $y = \sin (x - 90°)$ F $y = \cos x + 1$.

> $\sin x \times \sin x$ can be written as $(\sin x)^2$ but it is usually written as $\sin^2 x$.
>
> Similarly $\cos x \times \cos x$ can be written as $\cos^2 x$.

10   Sketch the graphs of:
   a $y = \sin^2 x$ **b** $y = \cos^2 x$ **c** $y = \sin^2 x + \cos^2 x$.

The graph of $y = \tan x$

◆ You can write $\tan x$ in terms of $\sin x$ and $\cos x$.

For values of x in the first quadrant

$$\frac{\sin x}{\cos x} = \frac{\text{opp}}{\text{hyp}} \div \frac{\text{adj}}{\text{hyp}}$$

$$= \frac{\text{opp}}{\text{hyp}} \times \frac{\text{hyp}}{\text{adj}}$$

$$= \frac{\text{opp}}{\text{adj}}$$

$$= \tan x$$

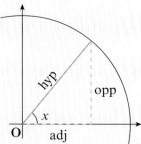

So $\dfrac{\sin x}{\cos x} = \tan x$ for $0 \le x < 90$

This can be extended to values of x in the other quadrants.

◆ This is a graph of $y = \tan x$ for $^-90° < x < 450°$

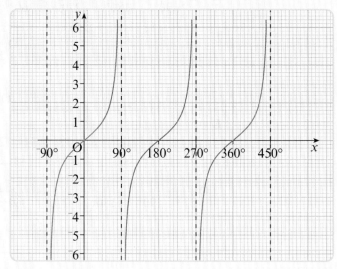

Exercise 17.7

Using the graph of
$y = \tan x$

1 Explain why the value of $\tan 100°$ is negative.

2 Solve each of these for values of x between 0° and 360°.
   a i For what acute angle x does $\tan x = 1$?
   ii Give another value of x that satisfies this equation.
   b Give two values of x that satisfy the equation $\tan x = ^-1$.

3 Explain why:
   a $\tan 56° = \tan 236°$ b $\tan 304° = \tan (^-56)°$.

4 a Use your calculator to find a value for x such that $\tan x \approx 1.1918$.
   b Use the graph to find other values of x which satisfy this equation.

5 Give three values of x between $^-90°$ and 450° for which:
   a $\tan x = \tan 60°$ b $\tan x = ^-\tan 25°$ c $\tan x = ^-\tan 32°$

6 a Use your calculator to find the value of:
   i $\tan 89°$ ii $\tan 89.5°$ iii $\tan 89.9°$ iv $\tan 89.99°$
   b Use your calculator to find the value of:
   i $\tan 91°$ ii $\tan 90.5°$ iii $\tan 90.1°$ iv $\tan 90.01°$
   c Why do you think your calculator does not give a value for $\tan 90°$?
   d Lines drawn at $^-90°$, 90°, 270° and 450° are called asymptotes.
      At what value of x would the next asymptote occur?

End points

You should be able to ...   ... so try these questions

A Use polar and cartesian coordinates

A1 These are the cartesian and polar coordinates for some points.
For one of the points only the polar coordinates are given.
a Match each of the cartesian coordinates to its polar coordinates.

Cartesian coordinates	Polar coordinates
(⁻1.50, 3.60) (6.00, ⁻1.75)	(10.00, 105.25°) (6.25, 343.74°)
(⁻0.60, ⁻0.80)	(1.00, 233.13°) (3.90, 112.62°)

b Calculate the missing cartesian coordinates.

B Solve trigonometric equations

B1 Solve each of these for $0° \leqslant x \leqslant 360°$.
a $\cos x = \cos 70°$ **b** $\cos x = {}^-\cos 70°$
c $\tan x = {}^-\tan 40°$ **d** $\sin x = {}^-\sin 28°$.

B2 Sort these into pairs that have the same value.

$\cos 41°$ $\cos 139°$ $\cos 229°$ $\cos 319°$ $\cos 131°$ $\cos 221°$

C Transform trigonometric graphs

C1 Sketch the graph of:
a $y = 3 \cos x$ **b** $y = \sin 3x$
c $y = \sin x + 4$ **d** $y = 2 \cos x - 3$

C2 Which of these equations matches this graph?
A $y = \sin 2x$
B $y = \cos x + 2$
C $y = \cos (x + 2°)$
D $y = \sin (x + 90°) + 2$
E $y = 2 \cos x + 2$

Give reasons for your answers.

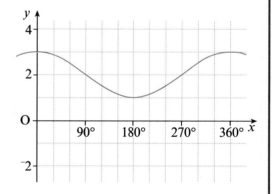

Some points to remember

◆ The graphs of $y = \sin x$ and $y = \cos x$

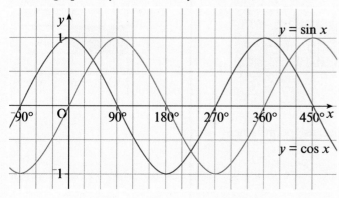

◆ The graph of $y = \tan x$

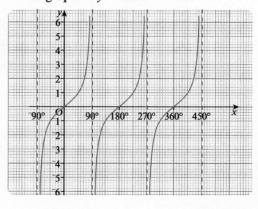

Starting points
You need to know about ...   ... so try these questions

A Inequalities that describe a set of integers or range of values

♦ The inequality signs: > **greater than**
                          < **less than**
                          ⩾ **greater than or equal to**
                          ⩽ **less than or equal to**
can be used to define a range of values for a variable.
For instance $^-3 < c \leqslant 4$ means the variable c can have any value greater than $^-3$ but less than or equal to 4.
Values for c such as $^-2$, 3.2, $^-1\frac{1}{2}$ are all acceptable.

This is sometimes called the **solution set** for c.

♦ The solution set
$^-3 < c \leqslant 4$
can be shown on a
number line like this.

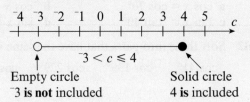

Empty circle   Solid circle
$^-3$ **is not** included   4 **is** included

♦ Sometimes only integer values are considered. Two different inequalities can then describe the same set of integers.

For instance, both these solution
sets have the integers
0, 1, 2, 3, 4, 5

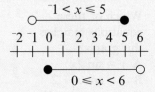

B Identifying and showing simple regions on a graph

♦ The conditions satisfied by two or more inequalities can be shown by a region on a graph.

Example
Sketch the region where $x > 4$ **and** $^-5 \leqslant y \leqslant 2$.

♦ The region where $x > 4$ is shown by the red shaded area and where $^-5 \leqslant y \leqslant 2$ by the blue one. Where both regions overlap both conditions are satisfied.

♦ Sometimes the region which meets
the condition is shaded in (as here).
At other times you will be asked to
shade in the region not wanted.
Check carefully.

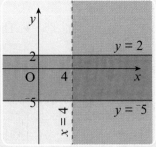

♦ Note that the red boundary line for x is dotted because points where $x = 4$ are not included in the inequality $x > 4$.

The blue lines for y are solid because $y = 2$ and $y = ^-5$ are included in $^-5 \leqslant y \leqslant 2$.

A1 a Show the inequality
$^-2 \leqslant x < 5$ on a number line.
b Which of these values for x
satisfy the inequality:
2, $^-5$, 5, $^-2$, 1.634, $^-4$, $4\frac{3}{4}$?

A2 For each of these, what integer
values of n satisfy the
inequality?
a $4 < n \leqslant 9$
b $^-2 \leqslant n \leqslant 3$
c $71 > n \geqslant 68$
d $^-4 \geqslant n > ^-12$

A3 Which one of these inequalities
describe a different set of
integer values from the others?
$^-4 \leqslant h < 6$, $^-5 < h < 6$,
$^-4 \leqslant h \leqslant 5$, $^-4 < h < 6$,
$^-5 < h \leqslant 5$

A4 Write two different inequalities
involving g which are satisfied
by these integers: $^-3$, $^-2$, $^-1$, 0, 1.

A5 Write a single inequality to
show those integers common to
all three of these inequalities.
$^-5 < f \leqslant 8$ $^-24 \leqslant f < 7$
$^-3 \leqslant f \leqslant 7$

B1 Sketch graphs to show the
regions satisfied by each pair
of inequalities.
a $2 \leqslant x < 5$ $y \geqslant 3$
b $x < ^-4$ $3 \leqslant y < 7$
c $^-3 < x \leqslant 3$ $^-8 \leqslant y \leqslant ^-1$

B2 What two inequalities are
satisfied by the shaded region
on this sketch graph?

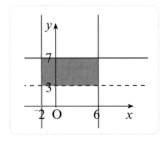

C The graphical link between a linear equation and an inequality

Example

Show the region on a graph where both the inequalities $y > 10 - 2x$ and $y \leq 2x - 1$ are satisfied.

♦ Lightly draw the linear graphs of $y = 10 - 2x$ and $y = 2x - 1$ to show the **boundaries** of the regions.

♦ Decide if the lines should be dotted or solid.

$y = 2x - 1$ is solid since points on the line are included in $y \leq 2x - 1$.

$y = 10 - 2x$ is dotted since points on the line are not included.

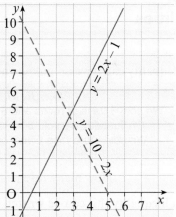

♦ For each boundary line in turn, choose a point P on one side of it, e.g. (6, 7). Substitute P's coordinates into the inequality and check if the inequality is true or not for that point.

Substituting into $y \leq 2x + 1$ gives $7 \leq (2 \times 6) + 1$
$7 \leq 13$ true:
so for this side of the line $y \leq 2x + 1$ is true.

Then choose a point to check which side of its boundary line the other inequality applies to.

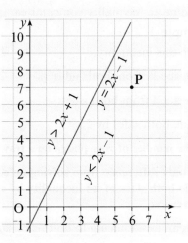

♦ Shade out the regions where the inequalities are **not true**.

The part of the graph **not shaded** meets both conditions.

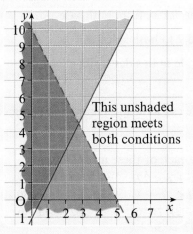

This unshaded region meets both conditions

C1 Show the region on a graph where both the inequalities $y \geq x + 1$ and $y < 8 - \frac{1}{2}x$ are satisfied. Shade out the regions **not required**.

C2 Use a graph to show the region where all of these inequalities are satisfied:
$$y < x + 2$$
$$y \geq x$$
$$^-1 \leq x < 4$$

C3 What two inequalities describe the unshaded region?

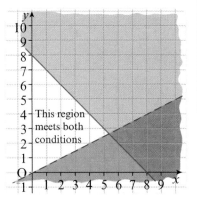

This region meets both conditions

Thinking ahead to ...
solving inequalities

A Start with the inequality **8 > 4** which is true.
Do each of the following operations to the inequality and state if the result is still true.

a Add 7 to both sides.   **b** Subtract 5 from both sides.
c Multiply both sides by 8.   **d** Divide both sides by 2.
e Add ⁻8 to both sides.   **f** Multiply both sides by ⁻3.
g Divide both sides by ⁻2.

Rearranging and solving inequalities

♦ An inequality can have an unknown on both sides – for instance:

> ### Danfield Nurseries
> We sold 5 trays of roses and 3 single rose plants on Monday.
> On Tuesday we sold 3 trays and 13 single rose plants.
> We sold more rose plants on Monday than on Tuesday.

> How many rose plants are on a tray?

As an inequality this can be written as $5x + 3 > 3x + 13$ where x is the number of rose plants on a tray.

♦ To solve an inequality you can treat it like an equation.

Example 1

Solve this inequality: $5x + 3 > 3x + 13$

Subtract $3x$ from both sides: $2x + 3 > 13$

Subtract 3 from both sides: $2x > 10$

Divide both sides by 2: $x > 5$

So the number of rose plants on a tray must be greater than 5, i.e. at least 6.

♦ **The only difference from solving an equation is that if you multiply or divide both sides of an inequality by a negative value the inequality signs will reverse.**

You can avoid having to do this by keeping the coefficient of x positive.

Example 2

Solve this inequality $3x - 8 \leqslant 5x - 2$

Subtract $3x$ from both sides $⁻8 \leqslant 2x - 2$

Add 2 to both sides $⁻6 \leqslant 2x$

Divide both sides by 2 $⁻3 \leqslant x$

So $x \geqslant ⁻3$

So x can have any values greater than or equal to ⁻3.

> When you rearrange an inequality try to keep the number in front of the variable positive. (i.e. try to keep the coefficient of x positive).
>
> **Example**
>
> Solve
> $$3x - 8 \leqslant 5x - 2$$
>
> Subtract $3x$ from both sides. Do not subtract $5x$ or you will get $⁻2x - 8 \leqslant ⁻2$ and will have the problem of dividing through by ⁻2 and changing the sign.

Exercise 18.1
Solving inequalities

1 Solve each of these inequalities.

   a $3y + 6 < 27$ **b** $13 \geqslant s + 5$ **c** $5p - 3 \geqslant 27$
   d $10 < 2b + 3$ **e** $2 \geqslant 6a + 50$ **f** $5x - 2 > 40$
   g $8 - 3k \geqslant ⁻6$ **h** $22 \leqslant 4a - 6$ **i** $13 - 4d > 33$
   j $⁻32 \geqslant 3a + 7$

> Where there are brackets,
> multiply them out first.

> For inequalities like
> $^-9 < 2x + 1 < 5$ treat them as
> two separate inequalities,
> e.g. $^-9 < 2x + 1$
> and $2x + 1 < 5$
>
> So $^-5 < x < 2$

2 Solve each of these inequalities.

a	$2a - 5 \geq 6 - a$	**b**	$2k - 6 > 7k + 8$
c	$3x + 7 > x - 11$	**d**	$2n - 2 \leq 4n - 9$
e	$3q + 5 < 1 - 2q$	**f**	$6 < 2(2k - 1)$
g	$7h + 3 > 13h + 5$	**h**	$2(3c - 2) < 11$
i	$7h - 4 < 5(4 - 3h)$	**j**	$2 - 4(2 - 3p) \geq 5(p + 2)$

3 Rearrange these inequalities into the form $A < x < B$, where A and B are integers.

a	$^-3 < x + 1 < 2$	**b**	$^-7 < 2x - 3 < 7$
c	$^-14 < 1 - x < 2$	**d**	$6 < 2 - 4x < 14$

Inequalities with squared terms

♦ Where an inequality involves an index power, the range of values for the variable may be continuous or have several separate parts.

Example 1 For which values of x is $x^2 < 9$ true?

> Since $x^2 = 9$ has two solutions $x = 3$ and $x = ^-3$ the inequality
> $x^2 < 9$ has two values between which x must lie $^-3 < x < 3$.
> This is a continuous range between $^-3$ and 3.
>
>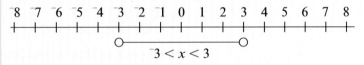
> $^-3 < x < 3$

Example 2 For which values of x is $x^2 > 9$ true?

> Here the inequality $x^2 > 9$ has two values outside of which x
> must lie so $x < ^-3$ or $x > 3$
> This is not a continuous range but two separate parts.
>
>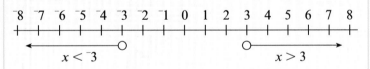
> $x < ^-3$ $x > 3$

Exercise 18.2
Inequalities with
squared terms

1 Solve each of these inequalities to give the range of values for the variable.

a	$d^2 \geq 36$	**b**	$17 > g^2$
c	$a^2 + 7 \leq 56$	**d**	$4 + 2h^2 > 36$
e	$64 - 3t^2 < 16$	**f**	$14 - 4c^2 \geq 6 - 2c^2$
g	$3c^2 - 8 \geq 1 - 6c^2$	**h**	$2(f^2 + 2) < 4(2f^2 - 5)$

2 What set of integers satisfies each of these inequalities?

a	$k^2 \leq 36$	**b**	$5 + b^2 < 30$
c	$1 - 2d^2 > d^2 - 47$	**d**	$5 \geq 4(x^2 - 5)$
e	$7s^2 - 45 < 5(s^2 - 6.5)$	**f**	$3(x^2 - 3) \geq 2(3x^2 - 7)$

3 Why is there no value of h which satisfies $2h^2 + 40 < 0$?

4 Which of these inequalities has no solution?

a	$34 + 2d^2 > 6$	**b**	$34 - 2d^2 > 6$
c	$34 + 2d^2 < 6$	**d**	$34 - 2d^2 < 6$

5 What set of integers satisfies the inequality $14p - 4p^2 > 0$?

Linear programming

> The optimum solution is the best possible solution which meets all the conditions imposed.
> It is often the solution which gives the maximum profit.

Some mathematical problems can be described by a set of inequalities and the optimum solution found by examining regions on a graph.
This is known as linear programming.

Example

A poultry keeper wants to keep ducks and turkeys in the same run.
Each duck needs $3\,m^2$ and each turkey needs $17\,m^2$ of run space. The run can have a maximum area of $100\,m^2$. The keeper wants fewer than 20 birds and she wants to spend £60 or more for a discount from her supplier.
At discount prices, a duck £3.60 and a turkey costs £4.80.
Let d the number of ducks and t be the number of turkeys.

a Write three different inequalities from the conditions above.
b Draw a graphs of t against d to show the inequalities.
c The profit from a duck is £3 and from a turkey is £7.
How many of each bird should she buy for maximum profit?

---

a For the space needed: $17t + 3d \leqslant 100 \ ... \ (1)$

   For the total number of birds: $d + t < 20 \qquad ... \ (2)$

   For the cost: $360d + 480t \geqslant 6000$
     divide both sides by 120 $3d + 4t \geqslant 50 \ ... \ (3)$

b The regions for these inequalities can be drawn by looking at where each boundary line crosses the t and d axes.
    For (1), when $d = 0$, $t = 5.88$ and when $t = 0$, $d = 33.3$
    For (2), when $d = 0$, $t = 20$ and when $t = 0$, $d = 20$
    For (3), when $d = 0$, $t = 12.5$ and when $t = 0$, $d = 16.7$

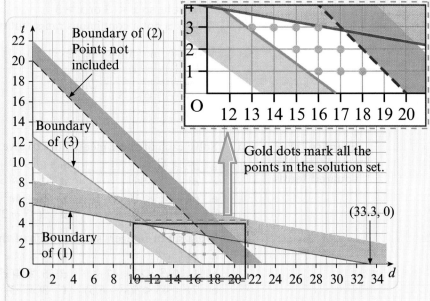

> The largest or smallest values of the profit will lie at one vertex (corner) of the region which meets the other conditions. This means it is only necessary to test points nearest the vertices.

c At the point (13, 3) the profit is $(13 \times £3) + (3 \times £7) = £60$
   At the point (16, 3) the profit is $(16 \times £3) + (3 \times £7) = £69$
   At the point (17, 0) the profit is $(17 \times £3)$ $= £51$
   At the point (19, 0) the profit is $(19 \times £3)$ $= £57$

So 16 ducks and 3 turkeys gives the maximum profit of £69.

Exercise 18.3
Linear programming

1 For the turkey and duck problem:
  a Why is the point (19, 1) not in the solution set, i.e. not shown as a gold dot?
  b Why is the point (16.5, 2.5) not in the solution set?
  c The point (13, 3) appears to be in the solution set.
     How can you be certain that it is in the solution set?
  d What profit is represented by the point (17, 2)?

2 Seascape Ferries have two types of ferry, Viking and Neptune.
   They have 7 Vikings and 8 Neptunes in their fleet.
   A Viking carries 80 cars and 3 lorries and a Neptune 50 cars and 6 lorries.
   On one day Seascape must transport at least 600 cars and at least 45 lorries.

  a If v Vikings and n Neptunes are used, explain why:
     i for lorries: $3v + 6n \geqslant 45$ or $v + 2n \geqslant 15$ **ii** for cars: $8v + 5n \geqslant 60$
  b Give two other inequalities which apply.
  c Draw a graph of v against n and show the region which meets all
     the conditions.
     Mark with dots all the possible combinations in the solution set.
  d What is the smallest number of ferries that can be used?
     How many of each type could be used?

3 Canfield Exhibition Hall hire out stands to exhibitors.
   There are prominent stands by the entrance, each with an area of $8\,\text{m}^2$,
   and stands in the centre with an area of $10\,\text{m}^2$.
   The charge is £280 a day for an entrance stand and £120 for a centre one.
   The total area for all stands is $120\,\text{m}^2$ and the rental per day must be at
   least £1680.
   The manager has calculated the ratio of centre stands to entrance stands.
   Let E be the number of entrance stands and C the number of centre stands.

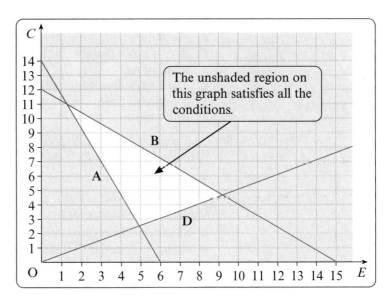

The unshaded region on this graph satisfies all the conditions.

  a From the information given, write an inequality which applies to:
     i the stand areas   **ii** the rental.
  b What do you think are the equations of lines A and B on the graph?
  c Line D shows the boundary of the ratio of large stands to entrance stands.
     Write an inequality which describes this ratio.
  d The number of visitors to the hall is in direct proportion to the
     number of stands. How many centre stands and entrance stands should
     there be for the maximum number of visitors?

4   A rectangular hen run of length L and width W is to be made from one roll of fencing which surrounds the perimeter.
The run has dimensions which must lie within certain limits.
The unshaded region of this graph shows the sizes of run that meet all the conditions.

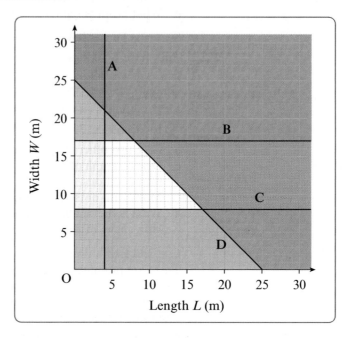

a   What are the equations of lines A, B, C and D on the graph?
b   Write down an inequality for the length of the run.
c   Write an inequality for the width.
d   Write an inequality that links L and W.
e   From the graph, what length of fencing must there be on a roll?
f   Why is it not possible in this case to mark dots for all the points in the solution set?
g   The keeper decided to make the run as long as possible within the other conditions. Calculate the maximum length, showing how you reached your answer.

5   At a concert Celine Kale decides to sing x rock numbers and y ballads.
A rock number lasts for 5 minutes and a ballad for 4 minutes.

a   Show on a graph her possible repertoire if she sings for exactly:
    i   40 minutes   ii   60 minutes.   iii   80 minutes.

Celine decides to sing for between 40 minutes and 80 minutes.

b   Shade out the regions on your graph that do not meet this condition.
c   If she sings exactly 8 ballads, what are the maximum and minimum number of rock numbers that she can sing?
d   If she sings 6 rock numbers, what are the limits on the number of ballads she can sing?
e   If Celine decides to sing the same number of each type of song, what are the maximum and minimum numbers of songs she will sing at the concert?

End points

You should be able to ...   ... so try these questions

A Find integer values which satisfy an inequality

A1 For each of these what integer values of g satisfy the inequality?

    a $^-2 < g < 0$ **b** $^-5 \leqslant g < 4$

    c $7 \geqslant g \geqslant 4$ **d** $^-56 \geqslant g > {}^-60$

    e $d^2 < 16$ **f** $4c^2 - 6 \geqslant 6c^2 - 32$

B Solve an inequality to find the range of values for x

B1 Solve these inequalities.

    a $5x \leqslant 30$ **b** $12 < 4f$

    c $4a + 5 \geqslant 53$ **d** $5k + 28 > 3$

    e $3(4s - 2) \leqslant 42$ **f** $7d - 10 > 5 - 3d$

    g $x^2 > 100$ **h** $2x^2 - 6 \leqslant 2$

C Draw a region to illustrate where several inequalities are satisfied

C1 On a graph with values of x and y between 0 and 12 show the region where the inequalities $y \geqslant x + 3$ and $y \leqslant 12 - 3x$ are both satisfied.

D Use linear programming to find an optimum solution to a problem

D1 Cinema 2 can seat up to 200 people and the owners need takings per performance of at least £720 to make a profit.

The majority of seats are standard grade at £4 each and the remainder are luxury grade at £5 each. For different performances there are different numbers of standard and luxury seats, but there are never more than three times as many standard seats as luxury seats.

Let S be the number of standard seats and L the number of luxury seats.

a Which of these conditions fits the data given?

    $S < L$ $S \leqslant L$ $S = L$ $S > L$ $S \geqslant L$

b Write an inequality for:

    i the seating capacity of the cinema

    ii the seats that have to be sold to make a profit

    iii the ratio of standard to luxury seats.

c Draw a graph of L against S with axes from 0 to 200 to show the region which satisfies all the conditions.

d What is the maximum possible takings on one performance?

Some points to remember

    ◆ Always check carefully to see if $\geqslant$ rather than $>$, or $\leqslant$ rather than $<$, is used.

    ◆ When you solve an inequality you can treat it like an equation except that:

        ❖ if you multiply or divide both sides by a negative value you must reverse the signs.

    ◆ Often in linear programming you have to find the optimum solution to a further condition. In this case test the points nearest to the vertices of the region which matches the other conditions.

Starting points
You need to know about ...

... so try these questions

A Writing fractions as decimals and percentages

◆ To write a fraction as a decimal:
  ❖ divide the numerator by the denominator.

$$\frac{3}{8} = 3 \div 8 = 0.375 = 37.5\%$$ $$\frac{5}{6} = 5 \div 6 = 0.8\dot{3} = 83.\dot{3}\%$$

B Calculating a percentage of a given amount

To calculate a percentage of a given amount:

◆ Multiply the amount by the appropriate decimal.
  For instance, to calculate **65%** of 420 kg
$$420 \times \mathbf{0.65} = 273$$
  So 65% of 420 kg is 273 kg

C Writing one number as a percentage of another

Compare the numbers 18 and 36:
◆ 18 is half of 36 or $18 \div 36 = 0.5$
◆ 18 is 50% of 36 or $0.5 \times 100 = 50\%$
As a single calculation: $(18 \div 36) \times 100 = 50\%$
This method can be used with any two numbers p and t

To **calculate p as a percentage of t: $(p \div t) \times 100$**

Example
Jenny and Bruce walked from John O'Groats to Lands End,
a distance of 868 miles. By the end of Day 4 they had walked
113 miles. What percentage of the total distance is this?

To calculate **113** as a percentage of 868
$$(\mathbf{113} \div 868) \times 100 = 13.018 \ldots$$
They had travelled 13.0% (1 dp) of the total distance.

D Interpreting a calculator display in calculations with money

Interpreting a calculator display correctly, is important.
When you calculate 24% of £15 the display shows:

The calculation is in pounds so the answer is **£3.60**

When you calculate 24% if £1.50 the display shows:

The calculation is in pounds so the answer is **£0.36**
It is more likely that the answer will be given as **36 pence**.

A1 Write each of these as a decimal and as a percentage:

a $\frac{3}{4}$ **b** $\frac{5}{8}$ **c** $\frac{8}{5}$ **d** $\frac{5}{4}$

e $\frac{6}{5}$ **f** $\frac{13}{20}$ **g** $\frac{8}{32}$ **h** $\frac{19}{6}$

B1 Calculate:
  a 55% of 650 miles
  b 72.5% of £400
  c 46% of 3450
  d 28% of £415
  e 4.5% of 360 metres
  f 38% of £4.50
  g 0.5% of £25
  h 8% of 3 miles.

C1 Calculate, giving your answer correct to 2 dp:
  a 52 as a percentage of 80
  b 85 as a percentage of 184
  c 1.5 as a percentage of 12
  d 15 as a percentage of 12
  e 0.75 as a percentage of 25.

C2 Of a total bill for £65.70, only £9.20 of this was for parts.

  Calculate the charge for parts as a percentage of the total bill (correct to 2 sf).

D1 In each of these, interpret your calculator display appropriately.
  a Calculate 16% of £85 (answer in pounds)
  b Calculate 14% of 4 cm (answer in millimetres).
  c Find 44% of 3.5 kg (answer in grams).
  d Find 9% of £2.27 (answer in pence).
  e What is 78% of 65 mm:
    i in millimetres
    ii in centimetres?

Thinking ahead to ...
percentage changes

Often percentages are used to describe
a change in an amount.
For example, in supermarkets special offers
can be shown as:

Extra 15% FREE !

For the customer:

A How much extra do you get free?
Is it more or less than a quarter of the
amount for the normal price?

B What fraction would you use to
describe the extra free amount?

C How many ml of the product are in the special offer pack?

Percentage changes

For an increase by a certain percentage, a final value can be found in this way.

Example
Toothpaste is sold in tubes containing 150 ml.
In a special offer, 12% extra toothpaste is in the tube for the same price.
How much toothpaste is in the special offer tube?

> Think of the toothpaste in this way: 100% of the contents is 150 ml.
>
> The special offer tube has 12% extra, so it must contain: 112% of 150 ml.
>
> 112 % as a decimal is 1.12
>
> To calculate 112% of 150: $150 \times 1.12 = 168$
>
> The special offer tube contains **168 ml** of toothpaste.

Similarly you can decrease by a given percentage.

Example
A fast food store decided to decrease by 18% the weight of packaging for
their regular meals, which weighed 40 grams.
Calculate the weight of the new packaging.

> Think of the packaging in this way: 100% of the contents weighs 40 g.
>
> The new packaging weighs 18% less, so it must weigh 82% of the 40 grams.
>
> 82% as a decimal is 0.82
>
> To calculate 82% of 40: $40 \times 0.82 = 32.8$
>
> The new regular meal packaging weighs **32.8 grams**.

Exercise 19.1
Percentage changes

1 In a special offer, the 440 gram of coffee in a jar is to be increased by 15%.

    a What percentage of the 440 grams of coffee are in the special offer jar?
    b Calculate the amount of coffee in the special offer jar.

2 **a** Increase 350 kg by 18%.   **b** Increase 447 km by 16%.
    c Increase 4.50 metres by 22%.   **d** Increase £35 000 by 8%.
    e Increase £27.50 by 32%.   **f** Increase 25800 tonnes by 17%.
    g Increase 3 500 000 litres by 9%.   **h** Increase 0.6 cm by 15%.

3   In 1992 in the USA there were a total of 143 081 443 registered cars.
By the year 2010 it is estimated that this total will increase by 44%.
Estimate the number of registered cars in the USA in 2010.

4   A crisp manufacturer sells 25 gram bags of crisps. They decide to increase
the weight of crisps in a bag by 4%. Give the new weight of crisps per bag.

5   **a**   Decrease 380 kg by 18%.   **b**   Decrease 416 km by 27%.
     c   Decrease 22 metres by 4%.   **d**   Decrease £338 000 by 14%.
     e   Decrease £25.50 by 28%.   **f**   Decrease 28600 tonnes by 42%.
     g   Decrease 5 300 000 by 11%.   **h**   Decrease 1.6 cm by 25%.

6   Anya grows strawberries for supermarkets.
Last year she used a total of 1560 kilograms of fertilizer.
Next year, she wants to decrease the amount of fertilizer used by 6%.

How much fertiliser would you expect to be used next year?
Give your answer correct to the nearest kilogram.

7   The car ferry Vista was built to carry a maximum of 1210 cars.
New safety rules mean that the number of cars must be reduced by 7%.

   a   What is the maximum number of cars for the Vista with the new rules?
   b   Explain the degree of accuracy you used, and why.

8   Before a bypass was built, an estimated 41 000 cars a day passed through
the town of Ashington.
The bypass was supposed to reduce the cars in Ashington by 35%.

   a   Estimate how many cars passed through Ashington, per day, after the
       bypass had been built.
   b   How many fewer cars per day is this?

9   Last year the fishing boat Emma K landed 9210 kg of shellfish.
This year they expect shellfish landings to be reduced by 17%.

How much shellfish does the Emma K expect to land this year?

> Depreciate means to lose value.

10   A manufacturer buys a machine for £56 800. The machine is expected to
depreciate by 12% in the first year and by 8.5% each future year.
What will be the value of the machine after ten years to the nearest £1?

11   Baz paid £2685 for a new keyboard. The salesman told him to expect that,
at the end of every year, the value of the keyboard would fall by 15% of its
value at the start of that year.

What do you expect to be the value of the keyboard at the end of five years?

12   Last year a company spent £3.4 million on advertising. Next year they
have set a target of saving 3.5% on advertising spending.

Next year, how much do they expect to spend on advertising?

13   In 1997 Wyvern Water lost water from their underground pipes at the rate of
600 litres per minute. Between 1998 and the end of 2004 they have a
programme of repairs that will save, on average, 4.8% per year, on water loss.

In total, how much water do Wyvern Water expect to lose in 2005?

14   Each year for five years, a company plans to use 20% less paper.
Will they use no paper in five years time? Explain your answer.

Looking ahead to ...
percentages and VAT

> VAT is short for:
> **value-added tax.**
>
> VAT is a tax added to the price of goods or services. It was introduced on 1 April 1973 at a standard rate of 10%.
>
> On 18 June 1979 the standard rate was increased to 15%.
>
> On 1 April 1994 the standard rate was increased to 17.5%.

Shopkeepers, traders, and customers have had to calculate VAT since 1973.

When it was first introduced at 10%, one quick method was: "Divide by 10 and add it on."

When VAT was increased to 15%, a quick method was: "Divide by 10, half the answer, and add both amounts on."

A   What quick method can you think of to calculate VAT at 17.5%?

B   In 1995 Ria fitted a stair carpet and charged £200 + VAT at 17.5%. What was the total charge to fit the carpet?

C   Peter bought a cycle tyre and was charged £12.50 + VAT at 17.5%.
  i What did he pay in total for the tyre?
  ii Explain any rounding you did when calculating the total.

Percentages and VAT

To calculate the total price of goods or services including VAT is the same as: increasing the cost price by the percentage VAT.

Example   A garden shed is advertised for: **£114.99** + VAT at 17.5%
Calculate the total charge for the shed.

> This example is with VAT at 17.5%.
>
> In all questions that involve VAT you must use the standard rate of VAT at the time.
>
> If you are unsure, ask for the rate of VAT.

> Think of the total charge (cost price + VAT) for the shed in this way:
>
> The total charge for the shed is: **117.5%** of its cost price
>
> To calculate 117.5% of £114.99:
> $$114.99 \times 1.175 = 135.113$$
>
> The total charge for the shed (including VAT) is:
>
> **£135.11** (to the nearest penny)

Exercise 19.2
Calculating with VAT

1   The cost of these items is given without VAT (ex VAT). Calculate the charge, including VAT, for each item.

a camera £16	**b** trainers £44.25	**c** bike £185
d toaster £19.40	**e** pen 72 pence	**f** TV £368.42
g fridge £262	**h** mower £24.55	**i** CD £9.35
j video £188.70	**k** battery 34 pence	**l** pencil 11 pence

> Traders have to charge VAT. The VAT is then paid by the traders to the Customs and Excise.
>
> These payments are made every three months.

2   Jenny was told that repairs to her car would be £245.
When she paid she found that the £245 did not include VAT.

  a How much did she pay, including VAT?
  b How much VAT was added to her bill?

3   To hire a coach for a hockey tour cost £675 + VAT.
The cost of the coach was shared equally by the 23 people on the tour.

Calculate to the nearest fifty pence how much each person on the tour had to pay for the hire of the coach.

4   Fraser needs four new tyres for his car. He has a maximum of £150 in total to spend on the tyres. All tyre prices are given ex VAT.

To the nearest 10 pence, what is the most Fraser can pay for a tyre ex VAT.

Reverse percentages

> When you divide by 117.5, you are calculating 1%.
>
> You then multiply by 100% to calculate the 100%.
>
> This is for VAT at 17.5%
>
> Check on the current rate of VAT to find the number to divide by to calculate 1%.

Calculating the original value of something, before an increase or decrease took place, is called 'calculating a reverse percentage'.

Example   The total price of a bike (inc. VAT at 17.5%) is £146.85
Calculate the cost price of the bike ex VAT.

The total price of the bike = 117.5% of the ex VAT price
146.85 = 117.5 × ex VAT price
146.85 ÷ 1.175 = the ex VAT price
124.978... = the ex VAT price

The price of the bike ex VAT is £124.98 (to the nearest penny)

Exercise 19.3
Calculating reverse percentages

1   These prices include VAT, calculate each price ex VAT.
Give your answers correct to the nearest penny.

a   CD player £135.50   b   camera £34.99   c   ring £74.99
d   trainers £65.80   e   TV £186.75   f   phone £14.49
g   calculator £49.99   h   PC £799.98   i   tent £98.99

2   Ella bought a pair of climbing boots for £45.60 in a sale that gave '20% off!'.

a   What was the non-sale price of the boots?
b   How much did Ella save buying the boots in the sale?

3   When Mike sold his bike for £35, he said he made a profit of about 45%.
To the nearest pound, how much did Mike pay for the bike?

4   A 675 gram box of cereal is said to hold 35% more than the regular box.
How many grams of cereal are in the regular box?

5   The Bay Point Hotel charges £65.45 per person per night for bed and breakfast. This charge includes VAT.
How much does the hotel take per person per night, at this charge?

6   In 1997 Reynards Fast Foods made a profit of £146 455.
The profits for 1997 were 6.5% above the profits made in 1996.
Calculate the profit made in 1996, correct to the nearest £5.

7   A light-bulb manufacturer makes clear and pearl light-bulbs.
Each week they make 45 360 clear bulbs, which is 64% of the total production of the bulbs made in a week.

a   What is the total number of bulbs produced in a week?
b   How many pearl bulbs are produced in a week?
c   For each week give the ratio in its lowest terms, of clear bulbs made : pearl bulbs made.

8   Asif and Nina make and sell vegetarian snack foods. They sell at prices to give them a profit of 315%. Last year their total sales were £26 855.

a   To the nearest pound, how much profit did they make last year?
b   Write a formula that they might use to calculate their profit (p) from their total sales (s).

9   In 1996, a total of 126 788 people visited the Butterfly Sanctuary.
This was estimated to be 14% fewer visitors than 1995.
Give an estimate of the total number of visitors in 1995.
Explain the degree of accuracy you worked to.

10   Write a formula to calculate the cost of an item without VAT (c) from the price of the item with VAT (p).

Percentages and interest

Interest is explained in the *Oxford Mathematics Study Dictionary* in this way:

> Interest The interest is the amount of extra money paid in return for having the use of someone else's money.

When you borrow, or save money with a Bank, Building Society, the Post Office, a Credit Union, or a finance company, interest is *charged* or *paid*.

Interest is: *charged* on money you borrow and *paid* on money you save.

Interest is: *charged* or *paid* pa, at a fixed rate, e.g. 6% pa.

Simple interest is a type of interest not often used these days.

pa means *per annum*, or each year.

♦ Simple interest is fixed to the sum of money you originally borrow or save.

Simple interest can be calculated using this *simple interest formula*:

> In words, the formula is:
>
> $I = P \times R \times T$ **I**nterest = **P**rincipal × **R**ate × **T**ime
>
> **P**rincipal is the amount of money you borrow or save.
> **R**ate is the interest rate pa. **as a decimal**.
> **T**ime is for how long, usually in years.

> **Example**
> Calculate the interest charged on a loan of £750, for 4 years at 7% pa.
> Using the formula gives:
> $I = P \times R \times T$, with $P = 750$, $R = 0.07$ (7% = 0.07) and $T = 4$
> $I = 750 \times 0.07 \times 4$
> $I = 210$
> **The interest charged on this loan is £210.**
>
> (If the £750 had been saved for 4 years at 7% pa,
> **the interest paid on the savings would be £210.**)

Exercise 19.4
Calculating with simple interest

1 Calculate the simple interest charged, or paid for each of these:
   a £450 borrowed for 6 years with interest at 12% pa
   b £280 saved for 8 years with a rate of interest of 3% pa
   c £1500 saved for 15 years at 6% pa interest
   d £6000 borrowed for 10 years at an interest rate of 17% pa

2 To buy new kit a band borrows £3500 over 10 years at 17% interest pa.
   a Calculate the amount of interest paid on the loan.
   b At the end of the loan, how much in total will have been paid for the kit?

3 A new bridge will cost an estimated £44 million, and take six years to build. If, at the start, all £44 million is borrowed at a simple interest rate of 8.5%, estimate the total cost of the bridge.

4 A sum of £350 was saved for six years. Over this time the simple interest earned was a total of £96.60. Calculate the rate of interest paid.

Compound interest

> Compound interest is used by banks, building societies, credit card companies and high street shops.

Compound interest is either *charged* or *paid*, but not just on the original sum.

Example

Calculate the interest on £100 saved for 2 years at 4%.

- ◆ At the end of year 1, the total is £104 (£100 + £4 interest)
- ◆ At the end of year 2, the total is £108.16 (£104 + £4.16 interest)

In short, compound interest includes interest on interest already *paid* or *charged*.

Working year-by-year, you can calculate compound interest and see that it builds to a greater total than simple interest over the same period of time.

Example

Calculate the interest on £480 saved for 3 years at 7%.

- ◆ Interest paid at the end of year 1 is: **£33.60** (£480 × 0.07)
  Interest for year 2 will be calculated on £513.60 (£480 + £33.60)
- ◆ Interest paid is: **£35.95** (£513.60 × 0.07)
  Interest for year 3 will be calculated on £549.55
- ◆ Interest paid is: **£38.47**
  The total interest paid is: £33.60 + £35.95 + £38.47 = **£108.02**

> **Exercise 19.5**
> Calculating with compound rates

1 Calculate the total interest paid on these savings at compound interest:

a	£350 for 3 years at 9% pa	**b**	£1400 for 4 years at 3% pa
c	£3600 for 5 years at 6% pa	**d**	£12 250 for 3 years at 4% pa
e	£4050 for 2 years at 12% pa	**f**	£35 250 for 2 years at 9.5% pa
g	£565 for 3 years at 10.5% pa	**h**	£185 for 4 years at 0.3% pa
i	£45 000 for 4 years at 7.2% pa	**j**	£1224 for 2 years at 2.3% pa.

2 Shelley won £5000, and put it in a savings scheme for five years.
The savings scheme pays interest at 6.8% pa compound.

   a Calculate the total interest paid on her savings.

   b At the end of five years what was the total in Shelley's saving scheme?

3 Roughly how long must a sum of money be saved at 8% pa compound, for the value of the savings to double? Explain your answer.

4 On average, the price of new cars has increased by 3.8% pa over the last five years. At this rate, what would you expect a model that cost £18 955 five years ago to be priced at today to the nearest £1?

5 The world population of a species of bird is estimated to be decreasing at the rate of 18% pa. There were estimated to be 4200 birds in 1995.

   a If the rate of decrease remains the same, estimate the year in which the species would become extinct. Explain your answer.

In 1995 a programme was put in place to halt the decrease, and increase the world population of the species by 4% pa.

   b If this rate remains the same, when would you expect the population of this species to reach 6000? Explain your answer.

> Check that your formula works by using it with Questions **2**, **3**, and **4** above.

6 The sum of £A is saved in a scheme that pays interest at r% pa compound. Write, and simplify, an expression for the total vaule of the savings at the end of five years.

Here the rate of interest is:

given as a percentage but used as a **decimal** for calculations.

There is a compound interest formula.

♦ For a principal of £150, invested at a rate of 6% for a period of 4 years

At the end of year 1, the value of the principal is:

$$150 \times 1.06$$

At the end of year 2, the value of the principal is:

$$150 \times 1.06 \times 1.06 \quad \text{or} \quad 150 \times 1.06^2$$

At the end of year 3:

$$150 \times 1.06^2 \times 1.06 \quad \text{or} \quad 150 \times 1.06^3$$

At the end of year 4:

$$150 \times 1.06^3 \times 1.06 \quad \text{or} \quad 150 \times 1.06^4$$

The total for the interest £I is therefore: $I = (150 \times 1.06^4) - 150$

For any principal, a general formula can be used. This is based on:

Interest £I, on a principal sum £P, invested at r%, for n years.

The compound interest can be found by using this formula:

$$I = [P \times (1 + r)^n] - P$$

Exercise 19.6
Using the compound interest formula

1 Calculate the total interest paid on a principal of £8500 invested for twelve years at a rate of 4% pa compound.

2 W&J claim that the value of their Unit Trust is likely to grow by 8.5% pa compound for the next five years.

If you invest £15 250 with the W&J Unit Trust, what would you expect your investment to be worth at the end of five years?

3 Two sisters, Rhian and Celine, were each left £2500 in a will.

Rhian decided to spend £5 per week on the National Lottery, and at the end of three years she had won a total of £1216.50.

Celine decided to invest her share at an interest rate of 7.5% pa compound.

Who do you think made the best decision? Explain your answer.

4 A building society offered the following terms for a minimum saving of £25 000 over a 10-year period.

For the first three years interest is paid at 5.8% pa compound
For the next four years interest is paid at 6.6% pa
For the remaining time interest is paid at 7.2% pa

At the end of ten years, what will be the value of a £25 000 investment?

5 A village is given a grant of £185 000 to build a new village hall. Once the grant is given it cannot be invested for more than five years.

The village hall committee decide to invest the grant in total for five years, at the end of which they would need **at least** £232 000 in the account.

a What is the lowest rate of interest (1 dp) they need for this investment? Explain your answer.

b How will your figures change for a maximum period of four years?

6 After investing £P for a period of time (n years) the total value of the investment at r% is £T.

Write a formula for T in terms of P, r, and n.

Buying on credit

Here the deposit is an amount you must pay in cash.

The deposit paid can be an amount of money (£30), or a percentage of the full price, e.g. 20% deposit.

There are rules for buying on credit. These can be changed by governments, and it may be possible to buy on credit with no deposit.

If you buy on credit, you pay a deposit on purchase and the remainder you pay off with a loan.
The total for the loan is paid off in a number of equal *instalments*.

Example

This advert is for a colour television.

only **£179.99**

CREDIT PLAN: **You pay £20 deposit the balance at 23% compound interest in 24 equal instalments (2 years)**

Calculate the monthly instalment for this credit plan.

The amount of the loan is £159.99 (i.e. £179.99 – £20 deposit)
With interest the total to be repaid on the loan is £242.05
With 24 instalments, each instalment $= £242.05 \div 24$
$\qquad\qquad\qquad\qquad\qquad\qquad\qquad = £10.085 \ldots$
The monthly instalment will be £10.09 (to the nearest penny)

Exercise 19.7
Buying on credit

1   With the same Credit Plan as for the television above, calculate the monthly instalment for a washing machine costing £399.99 over three years.

2   Eric bought a camcorder advertised for £469.99.
He paid no deposit, was charged interest at 26% pa compound, and had the loan over 4 years (48 equal instalments).
   a   Calculate the total Eric will pay for the camcorder.
   b   Calculate the monthly instalment.

3   Dinah decides to buy a second-hand car priced at £6995.
She is allowed £1150 for her old car and takes out a loan for the difference.
The interest rate is 13.5% pa compound, and the loan is over 30 months.
   a   Calculate her monthly instalment.
   b   How much, in total, will this *new* car have cost Dinah?

4   An extension to an hotel has to be carpeted.
The total floor area is 586m^2, and the carpet costs £34.99 ex VAT per m^2.
The hotel pays a deposit of £8 500, and borrows the remainder of the money over five years at an interest rate of 14.2% pa compound.
   a   How much in total will the hotel pay for the carpet?
   b   What will the hotel have paid for each square metre of carpet?

5   Copy and complete this repayment table for up to 60 months.

Repayment table Interest rate 9.6% pa (compound)					
Amount borrowed	Repayments (months)				
	12	24	36	48	60
£100					
£500					
£1000					
£2000					
£5000					
£10000					

End points

You should be able to ...   ... so try these questions

A Calculate percentage changes

A1 Increase 480 km by 16%.

A2 A CJ regular size cola is 380 ml.
CJ decide to increase the size of their regular cola by 12%.
To the nearest millilitre, give the size of the larger regular cola.

A3 Decrease £55.80 by 6%. Give your answer to the nearest penny.

A4 In 1992, there were a total of 42 154 breakdowns on a motorway section.
In 1993 the total number of breakdowns fell by an estimated 7%.
Estimate the number of breakdowns in 1993, on this motorway section.

A5 A new magazine sold 835 000 copies the first week it was published.
The magazine is expected to increase sales by 4% per week on average.

   a Geoff estimates sales at the end of week six to be 1 002 000 copies.
Explain why his calculated estimate is wrong.

   b After how many weeks, provided sales are on target, do you expect circulation to be more than 1.5 million copies?

B Work with VAT

B1 A fridge/freezer is advertised for £849.99 ex VAT.
Calculate the price of the fridge/freezer with VAT.

B2 To the nearest penny, the VAT (at 17.5%) added to a bill was £84.88.
Calculate the total for the bill including VAT.

C Calculate reverse percentages

C1 In 1996 Buslinks *UK* made a profit of £2.42 million pounds. This was a increase of 6.5% on the profits for 1995.
Calculate the profits for 1995 correct to 4 sf.

C2 Jetstream have been providing charter flights to Spain for three years.
In their third year they flew a total of 425 620 passengers to Spain.
This was an increase of 8% on their second year, which was an increase of 3.5% on their first year.
Estimate the total number of passengers they flew to Spain in their first year.

D Calculate simple interest

D1 Calculate the simple interest on £235 invested at 4.5% for 7 years.

D2 Asif had savings of £650 for a period of 5 years. He was paid simple interest, and at the end of the 5 years he had £796.25 in the account.
Calculate the rate of interest he was paid.

E Calculate compound interest

E1 Calculate the interest paid on a principal of £45 250 invested for 6 years at 4.25% pa compound.

Some points to remember

♦ Working with a calculator it is easier if you think of, and use, percentages as decimals.

♦ Check that your answer to a calculation is of the right size, and to a sensible degree of accuracy.

♦ When you are calculating interest, paid or charged, make sure you know whether it is at a rate of simple interest, or compound interest.

Starting points
You need to know about ...

... so try these questions

A The terminology for parts of a circle

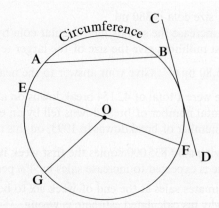

In this circle with centre O:

AB is a **chord**	A chord is a straight line that joins two points on the circumference of a circle.
CD is a **tangent**	A tangent to a circle is a straight line which touches the circle at one point only.
EF is a **diameter**	A diameter is a chord that passes through the centre.
Circumference	The circumference is the distance measured around the curved edge of a circle.
OG is a **radius**	A radius is any straight line from the centre to the circumference.

The curved part of the circle between
A and B is known as an **arc**.
There are two **arcs** AB:
the larger is the **major arc**
the smaller is the **minor arc**.

The chord AB divides the circle
into two **segments**.
There are two segments created by the
chord AB: the **major segment** and the **minor segment**.

AB, PR, and GH are all chords.
The **perpendicular bisector** of
each chord has been drawn to
show that:
**The perpendicular bisector of
any chord passes through the
centre of its circle.**

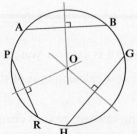

A1 ◆ Draw a circle, centre O with a radius of 4 cm.
  ◆ Mark any point P on your page 8 cm from O.
  ◆ From P draw two tangents to the circle.
  ◆ Label the point where one tangent touches the circle A, and where the other tangent touches B.
  a Measure the distance PA and PB.
  b What do you notice?
  c Is this the case for other points P?
  ◆ Join PO.
  d Measure angles APO and BPO.
  e What do you notice?
  f Is this always the case for other points P?
  ◆ Draw in the lines OA and OB.
  g Measure angles OAP and OBP.
  h What do you notice?
  i Is this always the case?
  ◆ Draw in the chord AB.
  j Is OP the perpendicular bisector of AB? Give reasons for your answer.

A2 Draw any circle centre O. The chord AB is such that the ratio
minor arc AB : major arc AB
is 1:2.
  a Mark a position for A and B on your circle.
  b Explain how you were able to fix points for A and B.

A3 a Draw around a circular object. By drawing and bisecting chords find the centre of the circle you have drawn.
  b Two straight lines meet at right angles at B so that AB = 4 cm and BC = 6 cm. AB and BC are chords of the same circle, centre O. Find the distances OA, OB and OC.

Angles in the same segment

For a chord AB and any point C on the circumference of a circle, joining A to C, and B to C gives angle ACB.

Angle ACB is said to be subtended by the chord AB.

In this circle, AB is a chord. The points C, D, and E are other points on the circle.

The angles ACB, ADB, and AEB are all:

* subtended by the chord AB
* at the circumference of the circle
* in the same segment
  (in this case the major segment).

A geometrical property of the circle is that:
the angles ACB, ADB, and AEB are all equal in size.
The general statement is:
Angles subtended at the circumference by the same chord in the same segment are equal.

The angle subtended at the centre

In this circle, centre O, AB is a chord and C is a point on the circumference.
Angle ACB is:

* subtended by the chord AB
* at the circumference of the circle.

Angle AOB is:

* subtended by the chord AB
* at the centre of the circle.

A geometrical property of the circle is that:
the angle AOB is twice the angle ACB ($A\hat{O}B = 2 \times A\hat{C}B$).

The general statement is:
For the same chord, the angle subtended at the centre is twice the angle subtended at the circumference in the major segment.

When the angle subtended at the centre is in the minor segment:

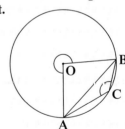

The general statement is:
For the same chord, the angle subtended at the circumference is half the reflex angle subtended at the centre.

Angles in a semicircle

When a chord becomes a diameter, then each segment is a semicircle. The angle subtended at the circumference in a semicircle is a right angle.

In this case $P\hat{G}T = P\hat{F}T = 90°$

The general statement is:
Any angle subtended at the circumference in a semicircle is a right angle.

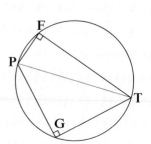

Secant

Any straight line that cuts across a circle at two points is called a **secant**.

A tangent is a special case of a secant as the two cuts become a single point of contact.

The two cuts are said to become **coincident**, giving a single point.

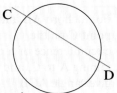

Tangents to a circle

From any fixed point (P) outside a circle, two tangents can always be drawn to that circle, in this case PS and PT.
From point P to the point where either tangent touches the circle, is the same distance, i.e. PS = PT.

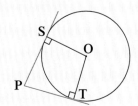

The general statement is:
From any point P, outside the circle, two tangents to the circle can be drawn the distance from P to the point of contact being the same for each tangent.

A radius drawn to the point of contact of a tangent is at right angles to the tangent.

In this case: $\hat{PSO} = \hat{PTO} = 90°$

The general statement is:
The angle between a radius, drawn to the point of contact of a tangent, and the tangent is a right angle.

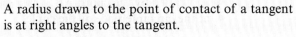

Any chord (ST) drawn in a circle creates two segments. One of these two segments can be described as being **alternate** to the other.

When a tangent (PT) is drawn at one end of the chord, then an angle is created between the tangent and the chord ($P\hat{T}S$).

This angle, measured on one side of the chord, is equal to the angle in the alternate segment ($S\hat{C}T$).

In this case $P\hat{T}S = S\hat{C}T$

The general statement is:
The angle between a chord an a tangent, at its point of contact, is equal to the angle subtended at the circumference in the alternate segment.

In this circle, CD is a secant. A tangent to the circle from C has a point of contact at E.

There is a relationship between distances such that:

$$CE^2 = CA \times CD$$

This is called the secant/tangent rule.

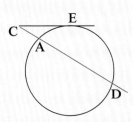

Exercise 20.1
Using circle properties

1 a Name two angles subtended at the circumference by the chord AC.
   b Name two angles subtended at the circumference by the chord CD.
   c What is the size of $\hat{CAD}$?
   d What is the size of $\hat{CEA}$?
   e BC is a tangent to the circle.
   What is the size of $\hat{BCA}$?
   Explain the reason for your answer.

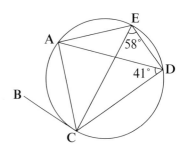

2 In this diagram, the circle has centre O.
   BE is a chord, AB a tangent, and $\hat{BDE} = 37°$.

   a What is the size of $\hat{EOB}$?
   Explain your answer.
   b What is the size of $\hat{BCE}$?
   c What is the size of $\hat{ABO}$?
   Explain the reason for your answer.
   d What is the size of $\hat{OBE}$?
   Explain the reason for your answer.
   e What is the size of $\hat{EBA}$?

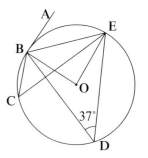

3 In the diagram, the circle is centre O.
   ED is a chord.

   a Name an angle at the circumference in the major segment subtended by ED.
   b Calculate the size of $\hat{EOD}$ (reflex).
   c Calculate the size of $\hat{DFE}$.
   d Calculate the size of $\hat{OED}$.
   Give the reason for your answer.

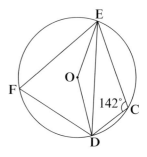

4 In the diagram, the circle has centre O.
   DE is a diameter, FE is a chord, and FC a tangent.

   a Calculate the size of $\hat{FGE}$.
   Explain the reasons for your answer.
   b Calculate the size of $\hat{OEF}$.
   Explain the reasons for your answer.
   c Explain why $\hat{EFC}$ is 41°.
   d DEH is 29°. Calculate the size of $\hat{HDE}$.
   Explain your answer.

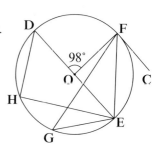

5 In the diagram, the circle has centre O.
   GC is a diameter and DF a tangent.

   DF = 7.2 cm and CF = 2.8 cm.

   a Calculate the length GF.
   b Calculate the length CE.
   c Calculate the area of triangle GCE.

6   In the diagram, the circle has centre O.
    The radius of the circle is b cm.

    a   Write an expression in a for:
        i $D\hat{O}C$ ii $O\hat{C}D$
    b   By considering the angles at O:
        i   Write an equation in a for the
            sum of the angles at the centre.
        ii Solve your equation, and
            calculate the size of $C\hat{A}D$, $D\hat{O}C$ and $O\hat{D}C$.
    c   Write an expression in b for the length OB.
    d   Calculate the size of $C\hat{F}D$. Explain your calculation.

7   In the diagram the circle has centre O.
    DE is a diameter.

    a   Give an expression for each of
        these angles:
        i $A\hat{E}C$ ii $A\hat{C}B$ iii $A\hat{O}C$
    b   Write an expression for $C\hat{A}B$.
    c   Write an expression for $A\hat{D}C$.
        Explain your answer.
    d   AE = EC. Write an expression for $B\hat{C}E$.
    e   AD = DC. Write an expression $D\hat{C}A$.

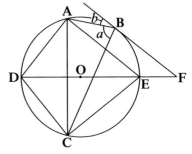

8   a   What is the value of b?
        Explain your answer.
    b   Find a value for a.
        Give reasons for your answer.
    c   Explain why $A\hat{D}E$ is 68°.
    d   Explain why $O\hat{D}A = 27°$.
    e   If AB and DE are parallel, calculate
        the size of $A\hat{D}B$.

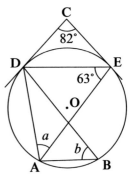

9   In the diagram the circle has a centre O.
    There is a tangent to the circle at C.

    Write and simplify an expression for the
    size of $B\hat{A}D$.

    Explain each step of your thinking, and the
    circle properties you use.

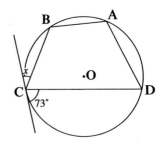

The cyclic quadrilateral

RSTU is a cyclic quadrilateral.
A quadrilateral is said to be cyclic when:

♦ the four vertices of the quadrilateral lie
on the circumference of the same circle.

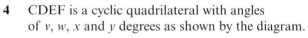

The other property all cyclic quadrilaterals
have is that:

♦ the angles at opposite vertices are
supplementary.

Supplementary angles are a
pair of angles that, when
added together, give a total
of 180°.

As RSTU is cyclic then: $R\hat{S}T + T\hat{U}R = 180°$

and $S\hat{R}U + U\hat{T}S = 180°$

Exercise 20.2
Cyclic quadrilaterals

1   Explain why all rectangles are cyclic quadrilaterals.

2   Is it possible to draw a parallelogram that is cyclic?
Explain your answer.

3   Apart from the rectangle, what other quadrilateral is always cyclic?
Explain your answer with diagrams.

4   CDEF is a cyclic quadrilateral with angles
of v, w, x and y degrees as shown by the diagram.
   a   If $p = 15°$, explain why:
$v + x = 12p$
   b   If v, w, x and y are such that:
$w : y = 2 : 7$ and $v : x = 13 : 17$
find values for v, w, x, and y.

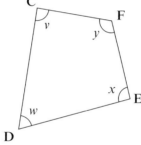

5   In the diagram the circle has centre O. The size of $N\hat{K}L$ is given as a.
Use circle properties to explain why
$N\hat{K}L$ and $L\hat{N}M$ are supplementary.

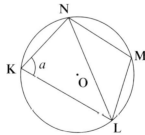

6   In the diagram the circle has centre O.
Calculate $F\hat{G}H$.

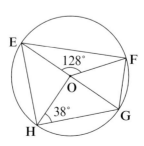

7   In the diagram the circle has centre O.
    A tangent is drawn to the circle at G.

    a   Write and solve an equation in x to find
        the size of angles:
        i $H\hat{E}G$ **ii** $H\hat{F}G$.
        Explain your answer.
    b   Calculate the size of $G\hat{O}H$.
    c   Could HOGF be a cyclic quadrilateral?
        Give two reasons for your answer.

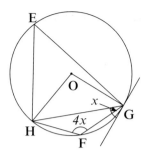

8   In the diagram, O is the centre of the circle and
    FB is a chord.
    The ratio $B\hat{C}E : B\hat{F}E$ is $3 : 5$

    a   Calculate the size of:
        i $B\hat{C}E$ **ii** $B\hat{F}E$ **iii** $F\hat{B}C$
    b   Calculate the size of $F\hat{O}C$.
        Explain your answer.

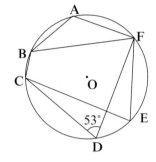

9   In the diagram O is the centre of the circle.
    AB is a chord and DC = DA.
    Angle $A\hat{O}B$ is v degrees.

    a   Write an expression in v for each of these angles:
        i $B\hat{C}A$ **ii** $O\hat{B}A$ **iii** $D\hat{C}B$
    b   Explain why an expression for $D\hat{A}B$ is:
        $135° - \frac{1}{2}v$
    c   Show that an expression for $D\hat{E}B$ is:
        $\frac{1}{2}(90° + v)$

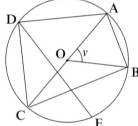

10 In the diagram O is the centre of the circle.
    BD is a tangent to the circle.

    a   Give the size of $C\hat{E}A$.
        Explain your answer.
    b   Calculate $C\hat{D}E$.
        Give reasons to support your calculations.

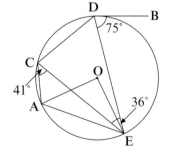

11 In the diagram O is the centre of the circle.
    Tangents are drawn to the circle from B.

    a   What is the size of $E\hat{D}A$?
        Give reasons for your answer.
    b   Is AOCB a cyclic quadrilateral?
        Explain your answer.
    c   Calculate $O\hat{C}A$.
        Give reasons for your answer.
    d   Explain why $D\hat{E}O + D\hat{A}O = 105°$.

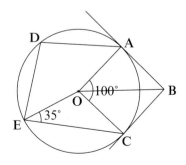

End points

You should be able to ...   ... so try these questions

A Identify angles in the same segment

A1 **a** What is the size of DÂB?
       b What is the size of EÂC?
A2 Give an angle that is the same size as:
       a EÂD   **b** CÊB

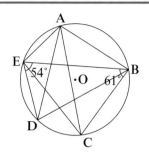

B Link angles at the centre and at the circumference on the same chord

B1 Calculate the size of:
       a AB̂C   **b** AD̂C

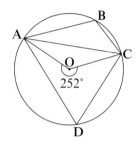

C Work with angles in a semicircle

C1 In the circle the centre is O and CÂB = 28°
       Calculate the size of AĈB.
       Explain your calculation.

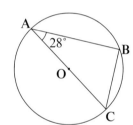

D Solve problems when tangents are involved

D1 Calculate the size of DÂE.
       Explain your working.
D2 Calculate the size of DÊA.
       Give reasons for your answer.
D3 Calculate the size of DÂO.
       Explain your answer.

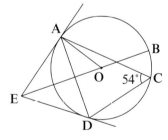

E Use the secant/tangent relationship

E1 Write an expression for the length of:
       a TP   **b** SC
       When TP = 7.4 cm, and SC = 9.1 cm
       c To 1 sf, calculate the length CP.

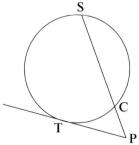

F Use the properties of cyclic quadrilaterals

F1 List the properties of all cyclic quadrilaterals.
F2 The angles of a cyclic quadrilateral are given as $3k$, $4k$, $5k$, and $6k$.
       a On a diagram show possible positions of these angles.
       b Write and solve an equation in k to find the size of each angle.

Southampton Evening Chronicle   *Monday 15 April 1912*

TRAGEDY AT SEA

IT IS WITH great regret that we bring you the news that last night at 10:40 pm the 'unsinkable liner' the Titanic hit an iceberg on her way to New York. The Titanic later sank at 2:20 am with the loss of many lives. It was the liner's maiden voyage and on board were 331 first class passengers, 273 second class 712 third class and a full crew – only 32.2 % of those on board survived. Each first-class passenger had paid £870 for the privilege of making the voyage in this luxury floating palace. To reassure the passengers the orchestra was still playing as the liner was going down and many passengers were so sure the ship could not sink that they refused to board the lifeboats.

The captain had been given repeated warnings of icebergs ahead but chose to steam on at 22.5 knots. It was calm weather with good visibility but the lookouts had not been issued with binoculars. The iceberg is thought to have had a height of about 100 feet showing above the water and a weight of about 500 000 tons. The sea water temperature was only 28° Fahrenheit and this took its toll on those jumping overboard. It is thought that the capacity of the lifeboats was insufficient for the number of people on board.

Survivors were picked up by the liner Carpathia which had heard the SOS when it was 58 miles away. The Carpathia steamed at a staggering 17.5 knots to reach the sinking Titanic. The ship's engineer said this was 25% faster than her usual speed.

HOW FAIR WAS THE RESCUE?

Reports coming in give the final casualty figures from the Titanic. There was not enough lifeboat space for all on board because the Titanic was considered to be the first unsinkable ship. The owners White Star admit that lifeboats could only hold 33% of the full capacity of the liner and 53% of those on board on that fateful night. Breaking the survival figure down by class we find 203 first-class, 118 second-class and 178 third-class passengers were rescued. Nearly a quarter of all crew were saved. Analysis of these figures is taking place to see if all people on board had an equal chance of being rescued.

Strange BUT *true*

Fourteen years before the disaster, and before the Titanic had been built, a story was published which described the sinking of an enormous ship called the Titan after it had hit an iceberg on its maiden voyage.

The comparisons between ships is even more amazing.

	Titan (Fiction 1898)	*Titanic* (True 1912)
Flag	British	British
Month of sailing	April	April
Displacement (tons)	70 000	66 000
Propellers	3	3
Max. speed	24 knots	24 knots
Length	800 feet	882 feet
Watertight bulkheads	19	15
No. of lifeboats	24	20
No. on board (inc crew)	2000	2208
What happened?	Starboard hull split by iceberg	Starboard hull split by iceberg
Full capacity	3000	

Distances at sea are measured in nautical miles and ships' speeds are given in knots.
1 nautical mile is 1852 metres.
1 knot is a speed of 1 nautical mile/hour.

1 Calculate approximately how many people died in the tragedy.

2 If all those who survived were in lifeboats, what was the mean number of people per boat?

3 In 1912 the price of a small house was about £200. In 1996 the same house would cost about £68 000. If fares on a cruise liner increased in the same ratio what would have been the first class ticket price in 1996?

4 About $\frac{1}{9}$th of the volume of an iceberg is above water level.
   The part of the iceberg showing above the water line can be approximated to a cone with base diameter of 85 metres.
   a Estimate the volume of the iceberg showing in cubic metres. Take 1 foot as 0.305 metres.
   b The density of an iceberg is about 950 kg per metre^3.
      Estimate the total mass (in tonnes) of the iceberg that the Titanic hit.

5 a What was the Carpathia's usual speed?
   b At 17.5 knots, how long would it take the Carpathia to steam the 58 nautical miles to the Titanic?
   c The Carpathia received the SOS message at 12:30 am. Approximately how long after the Titanic sank did she arrive at the scene?

6 You can convert a temperature from °Celsius (C) to °Fahrenheit (F) with this formula:
   $$F = \frac{9}{5}C + 32$$
   a Make C the subject of the formula.
   b Calculate a water temperature of 28 °F in degrees Celsius.
   c An approximation to convert °F to °C is "Subtract 30 from the temperature in °F then halve the result."
      For a temperature of 28 °F find the percentage error that this approximation gives.

7 Show, with working, that the statement

   Nearly a quarter of all crew were saved

   is correct.

8 a How many people could the lifeboats have held in total?
   b Use your answer to part **a** to calculate an approximate value for the full capacity of the Titanic.

9 Calculate the relative frequency of survival for:
   a first-class passengers
   b second-class passengers
   c third-class passengers.

10 Calculate the total percentage of the passengers aboard who were rescued.

11 What is the displacement of the Titanic to 1 sf?

12 A nautical mile is defined as "the length of arc along the equator subtended by an angle of $\frac{1}{60}$ of a degree at the centre of the Earth". The Earth has a diameter of about 12 756 kilometres.

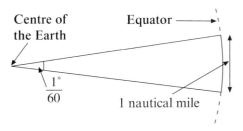

Show that a nautical mile is about 1850 metres.

13 The Titanic had cranes, known as "derricks", for lifting the cargo on to the ship. This diagram shows a derrick in one position. The tower and part of the cable are vertical.

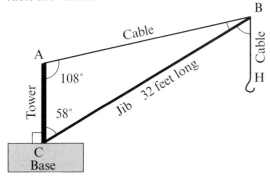

   a What is the angle ABH? Give your reasons.
   b Calculate the length AB on the derrick.
   c Calculate how high point B is above point A?

At the enquiry after the sinking, White Star, the owners, said that in the previous ten years they had carried 21 79 594 passengers with the loss of only 2 lives.

14 Give the number of passengers carried to:
   a 1 sf   b 4 sf

15 In the ten years between 1981 and 1990 about 1.2×10^7 people from the UK crossed the Atlantic by plane. With the same death rate as White Star gave, roughly how many people would have died in that time?

Starting points
You need to know about ...

... so try these questions

A Bearings

- All bearings are:
  - measured clockwise from North
  - written using three figures.

Example

The bearing of B from A is 105°.
The bearing of A from B is 285°.

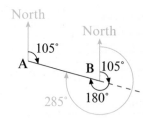

- You can fix a position by:
  - giving a bearing and distance from one point
  - giving a bearing from two different points.

Example

The point B is on a bearing of 105° from A and is 10 km from A.

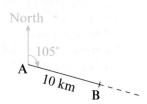

Example

The point C is on a bearing of 078° from A and on a bearing of 320° from B.

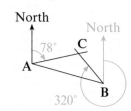

B Pythagoras' rule

- In any right-angled triangle, the area of the square on the hypotenuse is equal to the sum of the area of the squares on the other two sides.

  AB is the hypotenuse,
  so $AB^2 = AC^2 + BC^2$

  i.e. $AB = \sqrt{(AC^2 + BC^2)}$

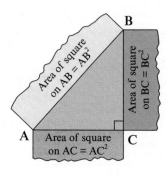

C Trigonometric ratios

- The trigonometric ratios can be used to calculate sides or angles in right-angled triangles.

- Each trig ratio can be written in different ways.

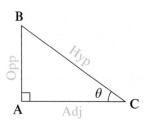

$$\sin \theta = \frac{Opp}{Hyp} \qquad \cos \theta = \frac{Adj}{Hyp} \qquad \tan \theta = \frac{Opp}{Adj}$$

$$Opp = Hyp \times \sin \theta \qquad Adj = Hyp \times \cos \theta \qquad Opp = Adj \times \tan \theta$$

A1 This diagram shows some towns on a radar screen positioned at H.

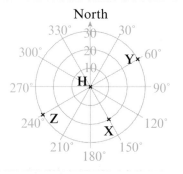

a What is the bearing of:
  i   Y from H
  ii H from Y
  iii Z from Y ?

b Estimate the bearing of X from Y.

c The rings on the screen are 10 km apart. Point P is due North of X and on a bearing of 030° from H. How far from H is P?

B1 a From the radar screen above sketch and label ΔXHY.

b Calculate the distance XY to the nearest 0.1 km.

C1 Using triangle XHY above calculate the angle $H\hat{X}Y$ to the nearest degree.

C2 Z is south and west of H.

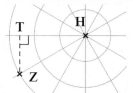

Calculate, to the nearest km:
a how far Z is west of H
b how far Z is south of H.

D Sine cosine of angles from 0° to 180°

◆ Graph y = sin x and y = cos x from 0° to 180°

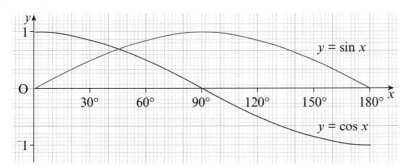

E Constructing triangles

◆ To construct a triangle with sides of *a* cm, *b* cm and *c* cm.

❖ draw one line as the base e.g. *a*

❖ with one end of the base as centre:

❖ draw an arc of radius *b*

❖ with the other end of the base as centre draw an arc of radius *c*

❖ join the ends of base to the intersection of the arcs to give the triangle.

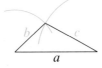

◆ To construct a triangle when you know two sides *v* and *t*, and one non-included angle 54°.

❖ draw one side as the base e.g. *v*

❖ at one end of the base measure and draw an angle of 54°

❖ with the other end of the base as centre draw an arc of radius *t*

❖ where the arc and the line at 54° to the base intersect is the third vertex of the triangle.

F Triangles

◆ When sides of a triangle are labelled, it is normal to use a small letter that matches the label of the opposite vertex.

For example:
side ST is labelled *w*.

◆ The largest angle is always opposite the largest angle.

For example:
largest angle SWT, longest side *w*, or ST.

◆ Angle SWT is called:
the **included angle** between sides SW and WT.

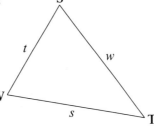

D1 Solve each of these for:
$0 \leqslant \theta \leqslant 360°$.

Give the answer to the nearest degree.

a **i** $\sin \theta = 0.5$

ii Explain why there are two possible values.

b $\cos \theta = ^-0.2$

c $\cos \theta = 0.2$

d $\cos \theta = \sin \theta$

E1 **a** Construct a triangle with sides of length 6 cm, 4 cm and 8 cm.

b Measure the largest angle.

E2 **a** Construct two different triangles ABC with $A = 42°$ AB = 8 cm and BC = 6 cm.

b For each of your triangles measure the angle B.

F1 In triangle PQR $p = 8$ cm, $q = 4$ cm and $R = 90°$. Calculate the size of the smallest angle to the nearest degree.

F2 In triangle DEF $f = 5$ cm, $d = 6$ cm and $E = 58°$. Calculate, to the nearest millimetre, the shortest distance from F to the line DE.

247

The area of a triangle

The included angle for two sides of a triangle is the angle between those two sides.

Example

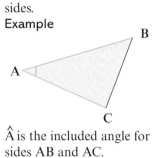

$\hat{A}$ is the included angle for sides AB and AC.

♦ The area of any triangle can be written in terms of two sides and the included angle.

Area of $\triangle ABC = \frac{1}{2}ah$

Using $\triangle CAO$ $h = b \sin C$

So the area of $\triangle ABC = \frac{1}{2}ab \sin C$

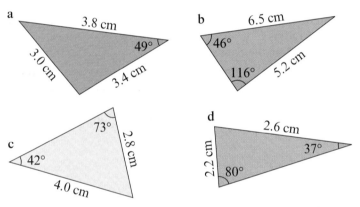

In the same way you can write:

Area of $\triangle ABC = \frac{1}{2}bc \sin A$ (*A* is the included angle for sides BA and CA)

Area of $\triangle ABC = \frac{1}{2}ca \sin B$ (*B* is the included angle for sides CB and AB)

Exercise 21.1
The area of a triangle

Accuracy
For this exercise:
♦ give each length and area correct to 2 sf
♦ give each angle to the nearest degree.

1 Calculate the area of each of these triangles.

a 3.8 cm   49°   3.0 cm   3.4 cm

b 6.5 cm   46°   116°   5.2 cm

c 73°   42°   2.8 cm   4.0 cm

d 2.6 cm   37°   2.2 cm   80°

2 Triangle DEF is isosceles with DE = EF = 4 cm and $D\hat{E}F = \theta$.

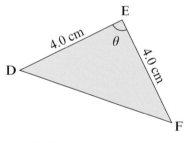

   E   4.0 cm θ 4.0 cm   D   F

a Find the area of $\triangle DEF$ when $\theta = 48.5°$.

b **i** For what values of θ is the area 4 cm²?
    ii Explain why there are two possible values for θ.

c What value of θ gives the maximum area of $\triangle DEF$?

3 In triangle JKL, JK = 5 cm, KL = 6 cm.

a For what values of *K* is the area of $\triangle JKL = 10.8$ cm²?
b Calculate the maximum area of $\triangle JKL$?

4 Jamie drew $\triangle PQR$ with PQ = 3.4 cm, PR = 2.8 cm and QPR = 52°.
He drew lengths to the nearest millimetre and angles to the nearest degree.

a Find the maximum and minimum length of PQ.
b Calculate the maximum and minimum area possible for $\triangle PQR$.

5 In this diagram triangle ABC is equilateral, with sides of length a.

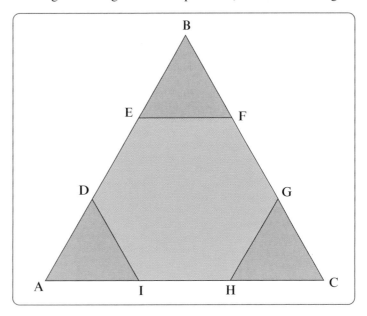

Each of the fractional
answers in Question **5**
is rational.

a Give the area of $\triangle$ ABC in terms of a.

b DEFGHI is the largest regular hexagon that can be drawn inside $\triangle$ ABC.
  i Write the length of EF in terms of a?
  ii Write the area of the hexagon as a fraction of the area of $\triangle$ ABC.
    Give the fraction in its simplest terms.

c DFH is the largest equilateral triangle drawn inside DEFGHI.
  Write the area of $\triangle$ DFH as a fraction of:
  i the area of DEFGHI   **ii** the area of $\triangle$ ABC.

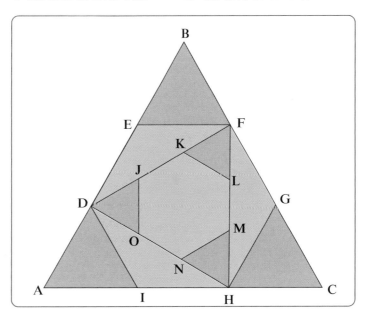

d JKLMNO is the largest hexagon that can be drawn inside DFG.
  Write the area of JKLMNO as a fraction of the area of $\triangle$ ABC.

e You can continue this sequence of regular triangles and hexagons.
  Taking $\triangle$ ABC as the first triangle, and DEFGHI as the first hexagon:
  i what fraction of $\triangle$ ABC is the area of the nth triangle?
  ii what fraction of $\triangle$ ABC is the area of the nth hexagon?

6 Investigate the areas of a similar sequence of squares and regular octagons
drawn inside each other.

Sine rule

◆ The **sine rule** links the sides and angles of a triangle.
This is one way to prove the **sine rule**.

In $\triangle ABD$ $h = c \sin A$
In $\triangle BCD$ $h = a \sin C$
Therefore $a \sin C = c \sin A$

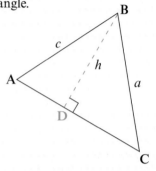

This can be rearranged to give the **sine rule**.

$$\frac{a}{\sin A} = \frac{c}{\sin C} \quad \text{and} \quad \frac{\sin A}{a} = \frac{\sin C}{c}$$

In the same way you can show that:

$$\frac{b}{\sin B} = \frac{c}{\sin C} \quad \text{and} \quad \frac{\sin B}{b} = \frac{\sin C}{c}$$

and $$\frac{a}{\sin A} = \frac{b}{\sin B} \quad \text{and} \quad \frac{\sin A}{a} = \frac{\sin B}{b}$$

Exercise 21.2
The sine rule

1 **a** Which of these expressions is true for $\triangle PQR$?

$\boxed{A}$ $\dfrac{p}{\sin Q} = \dfrac{q}{\sin P}$ $\boxed{B}$ $r = \dfrac{\sin P \times q}{\sin Q}$

$\boxed{C}$ $p \sin P = q \sin Q$ $\boxed{D}$ $p \sin R = r \sin P$

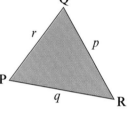

2 Copy and complete these statements for $\triangle LMN$.

a $m = \dfrac{7.6 \times \sin \square}{\sin \square}$

b $\sin L = \dfrac{\square \times \sin \square}{\square}$

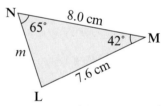

◆ The sine rule can be used to calculate the length of a side in a triangle,
given any two angles and the length of one side.

> It may help to label the
> sides from the vertices first.

> In some triangles you will
> need to calculate the
> missing angle before you
> can use the sine rule.

Example   In triangle RST calculate the length of RS.

❖ Use the angle sum of a triangle for the missing angle.
$S = 180° - (53° + 48°) = 79°$
❖ Use the sine rule to calculate a side.

$$\frac{t}{\sin T} = \frac{s}{\sin S}$$

$$t = \frac{s \times \sin T}{\sin S} = \frac{6.5 \times \sin 48°}{\sin 79°} = 4.9 \text{ to 1 dp}$$

So the length of RS is 4.9 cm (1 dp).

Exercise 21.3
Calculating lengths
using the sine rule

1 **a** Find the sequence of key presses on your calculator to calculate the
length of RS.
b Calculate the length of ST correct to 1 dp.

Accuracy
For this exercise give each answer correct to 1 dp.

2 In these triangles calculate the length of the side marked with a letter.

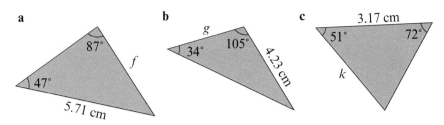

a

87°

47°

f

5.71 cm

b

g

34°

105°

4.23 cm

c

3.17 cm

51°

72°

k

3 Triangle PQR is isosceles with PQ = 8 cm and QPR = 56°.

a Draw two different triangles, and show that QR has two possible lengths.

b Calculate the two possible lengths for QR.

Use the full calculator value for each calculation

4 In triangle TUV the angle $T = 104°$, $U = 37°$ and TU = 5 cm. Calculate the area of Δ TUV.

5 To construct Δ XYZ Eamonn drew XZ, to the nearest millimetre, and angles X and Z to the nearest degree.

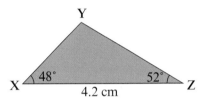

Y

48°   52°

X   4.2 cm   Z

a What is the largest possible value of X?

b Explain why the smallest possible value of Y is 79°.

c Calculate the maximum possible length of YZ.

♦ With the sine rule, given two sides and one opposite angle, a second angle in the triangle can be calculated.

On some formula sheets the sine rule is only given as:

$$\frac{a}{\sin A} = \frac{b}{\sin B} = \frac{C}{\sin C}$$

For each problem use one pair of expressions.
For instance

$$\frac{a}{\sin A} = \frac{c}{\sin C}$$

can be rearranged to give:

$$\frac{\sin A}{a} = \frac{\sin C}{c}$$

Example   Calculate angle B in Δ ABC

❖ Use the sine rule with the two sides given.

In Δ ABC $\dfrac{\sin C}{3.7} = \dfrac{\sin 24°}{4.8}$

$\sin C = \dfrac{3.7 \times \sin 24°}{4.8}$

$\sin C = 0.313\,52° \ldots$

$C = 18.2718° \ldots$

B

3.7 cm

A   24°

4.8 cm

C

❖ Calculate the required angle:
$B = 180° - (24 + 18.2718\ldots)°$
$B = 137.73°$ (2 dp)

Exercise 21.4
Using the sine rule to calculate angles

1 Calculate the angle θ in each of these triangles.

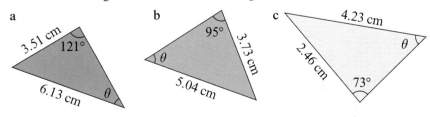

a

3.51 cm

121°

6.13 cm θ

b

95°

θ

3.73 cm

5.04 cm

c

4.23 cm

θ

2.46 cm

73°

Accuracy
For this exercise give each answer correct to 1 dp.

2 This pentagon is right-angled at A and E.

   a The angle $B\hat{D}C = 37°$.
      Calculate the angle $A\hat{B}C$.

   b Calculate the area of ABCDE.

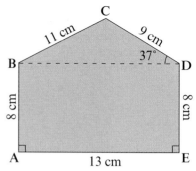

> Use the full calculator value in each calculation.

3 In triangle ABC, AC = 6.2 cm, AB = 5.1 cm and C = 28°.
This diagram shows that in $\triangle$ ABC, there are two possible positions for **B**, shown as B_1 and B_2.

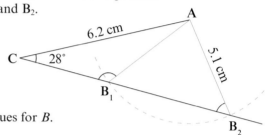

   a Use the sine rule to find the value of sin *B*.

   b Calculate two possible values for *B*.

4 **a** Sketch two possible triangles for each of these.

     i In triangle XYZ XZ = 8.3 cm, XY = 7.3 cm and Z = 58°

     ii In triangle XYZ XZ = 9.2 cm, YZ = 8.0 cm and X = 43°.

   b Give two possible values for *Y* in each of these triangles.

Cosine rule

♦ The cosine rule links an angle and three sides of a triangle.
This is one way to prove the **cosine rule**.

In $\triangle CAD$ $h^2 = b^2 - p^2$

In $\triangle BCD$ $a^2 = h^2 + (c - p)^2$
$$a^2 = b^2 - p^2 + (c - p)^2$$
$$a^2 = b^2 - p^2 + c^2 - 2cp + p^2$$
$$a^2 = b^2 + c^2 - 2cp$$
$$a^2 = b^2 + c^2 - 2c \times b \cos A \qquad (\text{in } \triangle CAD, p = b \cos A)$$

This gives the **cosine rule**:
$$a^2 = b^2 + c^2 - 2bc \cos A$$

The cosine rule gives an expression for one side in terms of **the opposite angle** and the other two sides of the triangle.

♦ The cosine rule can be rearranged to give an expression for the cosine of one angle in terms of the lengths of the sides.

$$a^2 = b^2 + c^2 - 2bc \cos A$$
$$2bc \cos A = b^2 + c^2 - a^2$$
$$\cos A = \frac{b^2 + c^2 - a^2}{2bc}$$

Exercise 21.5
The cosine rule

1 **a** Copy and complete these for $\triangle DEF$.

    i $d^2 = e^2 + f^2 - 2ef \cos \square$

    ii $f^2 = e^2 + \square - 2e\square \cos \square$

b Which of these is true for $\triangle DEF$?

    i $\quad e^2 = d^2 + f^2 - 2de \cos E$

    ii $\quad e^2 + d^2 - f^2 = 2de \cos F$

    iii $\quad \cos D = \dfrac{e^2 + f^2 - d^2}{2ef}$

    iv $\quad \cos E = \dfrac{e^2 + f^2 - d^2}{2df}$

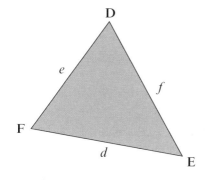

2 In this diagram AB is the diameter of the circle.

Use the cosine rule to explain why:

    a $\quad AB^2 > AC^2 + CB^2$

    b $\quad AB^2 = AD^2 + DB^2$

    c $\quad AB^2 < AE^2 + EB^2$

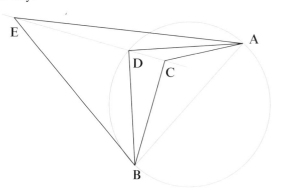

◆ The cosine rule can be used to calculate the length of a side in a triangle given the length of two sides and the included angle.

Example

Calculate the length of PQ in triangle PQR.

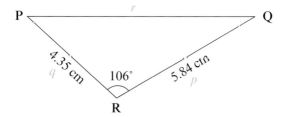

From the vertices label the sides p, q and r.

Use the cosine rule to calculate the length of the side.

$$r^2 = p^2 + q^2 - 2pq \cos R$$
$$r^2 = 4.35^2 + 5.84^2 - 2 \times 4.35 \times 5.84 \times \cos 106°$$
$$r^2 = 67.032\,683 \ldots$$
$$r = 8.2 \ (1dp)$$

♦ Given the lengths of all three sides, any angle of a triangle can be calculated using the cosine rule.

Example Calculate the angle *F* in triangle EFG.

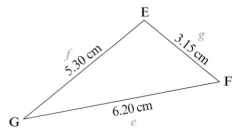

From the vertices label the sides *e*, *f* and *g*.

Use the cosine rule to calculate the angle.

$$\cos F = \frac{e^2 + g^2 - f^2}{2eg}$$

$$\cos F = \frac{6.20^2 + 3.15^2 - 5.30^2}{2 \times 6.20 \times 3.15}$$

$$\cos F = 0.519\,0092\ldots$$

Therefore *F* = 58.7° (1 dp)

Exercise 21.6
Calculating angles using the cosine rule

1   For triangle EFG above:
   a   list the correct sequence of key presses to evaluate *F*.
   b   explain why there is only one possible value for *F*.

2   In each of these triangles find the side or angle marked in blue.

> **Accuracy**
> For this exercise give each length and area correct to 3 sf.

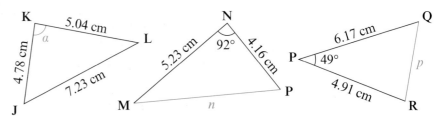

3   Find the largest angle in a triangle with sides of 8 cm, 12 cm, and 15 cm.

4   Calculate the area of a triangle with sides of length 6 cm, 9 cm and 10 cm.

5   Triangle ACE is one triangle that can be drawn by joining the vertices of ABCDE, a regular pentagon of side 4 cm.
   a   What is the size of:
      i $A\hat{B}C$
      ii $C\hat{A}B$
      iii $C\hat{A}E$?
   b   Calculate the length of AC.
   c   Calculate the perimeter of △ACE.
   d   Calculate the area of the △ACE.
   e   How many different triangles can you draw by joining the vertices of ABCDE?

> Use the full calculator value in each calculation.

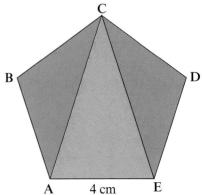

6 FGHIJKLMN is a regular nonagon. Each side is 6 cm.

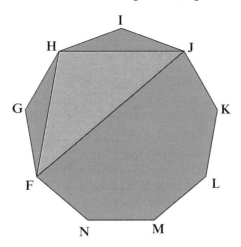

a FHJ is one triangle that can be drawn
joining the vertices of the nonagon.
Calculate the area and perimeter of Δ FHJ.

b How many different triangles can you draw
by joining vertices of FGHIJKLMN?

c For the triangles that can be drawn inside FGHIJKLMN:
  i Do you think the triangle with the largest perimeter
    also has the largest area?
  ii Find the largest possible perimeter.
  iii Calculate the largest possible area.

7 Investigate the area and perimeter of triangles, drawn by joining
the vertices, in other regular polygons.

8 Any polygon is cyclic if all its vertices lie
on the circumference of a circle.
This circle is called its circumcircle.

This is a regular decagon.

The radius of its circumcircle is 5 cm
and its centre is at O.

a Calculate the area of the decagon.
b Calculate the perimeter of the decagon.

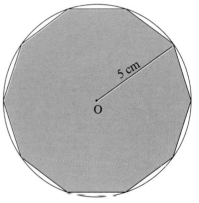

9 Calculate the area of regular dodecagon
with a circumcircle of radius 8 cm.

10 a A regular polygon (with n sides) has a circumcircle of radius r.
Write an expression for the area of the polygon in terms of r and n.

b If the radius of the circumcircle is 1 cm, calculate the area
of the regular polygon when:
  i $n = 20$ **ii** $n = 40$ **iii** $n = 100$ **iv** $n = 1000$

What do you notice about the area?

11 Find the radius of the circumcircle of a regular hexagon of perimeter 54 cm.

The circumcircle of a shape
is a circle that passes
through all its vertices.
Example
This is the circumcircle of
triangle ABC.

A dodecagon is the name
given to a 12-sided
polygon.

Bearings

Exercise 21.7
Calculating bearings and
distances

Accuracy
For this exercise:
♦ give each distance
correct to 4 sf
♦ round each angle
to the nearest degree.

1 This diagram shows the position
of three lighthouses.
Braydon is 56 km from Alington
on a bearing of 071°.
Caster is 78 km from Alington
on a bearing of 216°.

a What is the bearing of
Alington from Caster?
b Calculate the distance from
Braydon to Caster.
c Calculate the bearing of
Braydon from Caster.

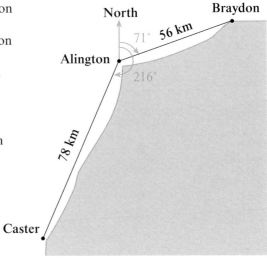

2 This diagram shows the route taken
by a boat which starts at P.
The boat sails on a bearing of 143°
for 24 km to a buoy at Q, then sails
due south for 18 km to a buoy at R.

a What is the bearing of P from Q?
b Calculate:
  i the distance between P and R
  ii the bearing of R from P.
c **i** How far is Q east of P?
  ii How far is Q south of P?
d How far is Q east of PR?

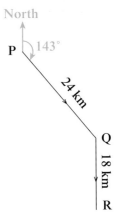

3 A boat starts at A and sails on a bearing of 048° for 12.6 km to B, where it
changes course to a bearing of 154° to sail 18.5 km to C.

Calculate how far C is due east of the starting point A.

4 From his boat Salamander Harry fixes the position of two other boats.
Enya is at a distance of 2300 metres on a bearing of 146°.
Cosmos is at a distance of 4200 metres on a bearing of 062°.

a Calculate the distance (in a straight line) between Enya and Cosmos.
b What is the bearing of Cosmos from Enya.

5 The boat Wija sails due north between two headlands A and B. The bearing
of B from A is 303°. From W, the bearing of A is 055°, and B 329°.

Wija is 3.4 Km from A and 7.5 km from B, calculate the distance AB.

6 Two boats leave harbour at the same time.
One sails on a bearing of 308° at a speed of 18 knots, the other on a bearing
of 204° at a speed of 22 knots.
What is the distance between the boats after 30 minutes?

Angles of elevation and depression

◆ From a point A the angle of elevation of a point B is the angle between the horizontal and the line of sight from A to B.

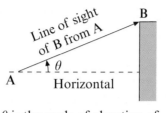

θ is the angle of elevation of B from A.

◆ From a point A the angle of depression of a point C is the angle between the horizontal and the line of sight from A to C.

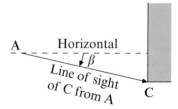

β is the angle of depression of C from A.

Exercise 21.8
Angles of elevation and depression

Accuracy
For this exercise round your answers to 2 dp.

1 Jan uses a theodolite at T to measure the distance and the angle of elevation or depression to points A and B.

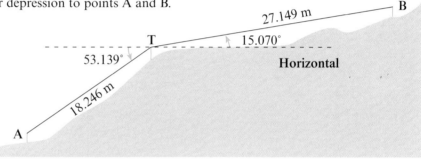

The angle of depression of A from T is 53.139° and TA is 18.246 metres.
The angle of elevation from T to B is 15.070° and TB is 27.149 metres.

a What is the obtuse angle AT̂B?

b Calculate:
  i the distance AB
  ii the angle of depression from B to A
  iii the angle of elevation from A to B.

2 This diagram shows a loading ramp used for ferries. It is supported by cables that are fed out from a tower and fixed half way along the ramp at A.
The ramp must be fixed so that it is horizontal at high tide.
The maximum angle of depression allowed, at low tide, on the ramp is 18°.

a At which of these ports could this ramp be used?

Harbour	Tidal range
Arden	4.28 m
Jameston	2.86 m
Daleen	3.85 m
Palter	3.54 m

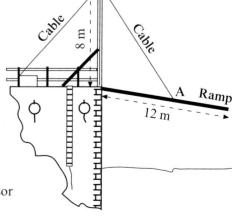

b A sensor is to be fitted to the cable sounding an alarm when the slope reaches 18°.
How far from A should the sensor be fixed?

257

3-D coordinates

♦ A vertical line is perpendicular to any line drawn in the horizontal plane.

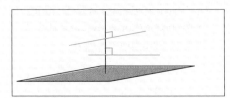

♦ A horizontal line is perpendicular to any line drawn in the vertical plane.

Exercise 21.9
Three-dimensional coordinates

1 This cuboid is drawn on three perpendicular axes, marked in centimetres, with the origin at O.

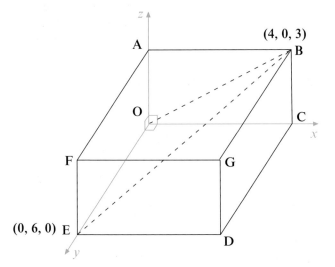

Accuracy
For this exercise give your answers correct to 2 dp.

a The coordinates of B are (4, 0, 3) and E is the point (0, 6, 0). Give the coordinates of these vertices.

  i D   **ii** G   **iii** A

b Explain why the line OB is perpendicular to OE
c Which of these lines is perpendicular to GC?

> GD   GE   OC   GO   GF   CA

For each problem look for a triangle which includes the required angle or side in which you can find, or know enough information.

d Calculate the length of OB.
e **i** Show that the length of the diagonal EB can be written as:

$$EB = \sqrt{EO^2 + OC^2 + CB^2}$$

  ii Write a different expression for the length of EB.
  iii Calculate the length of EB.

f Calculate the angle between the line BE and the base OCED.

2 ABGF is one face of this cuboid.

   a **i** Calculate the length of AG.
      ii P is the mid-point of AG.
         Give the coordinates of P.

   b A pyramid is formed by joining
      P to the points A, C, D and E.

      Calculate the volume
      of the pyramid ABCDEP.

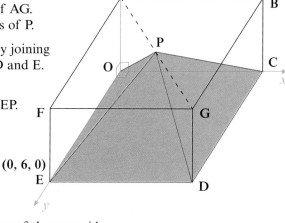

   c Triangle EPD is one face of the pyramid:
      i Calculate the length of the slant height PD.
      ii Calculate the angle between PD and the base OCDE.

Three-dimensional trigonometry

When you work in 3-D, it is essential to identify
angles correctly.

The diagram shows a pyramid.
The vertical height is shown by WY.
(The line WY is perpendicular to the base.)

> Perpendicular indicates
> that two lines are at right
> angles to each other.

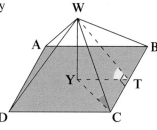

Identifying angles:

The angle between a side (WCB) and the base is angle WTY
where WT is perpendicular to BC.

The angle between the edge CW and the base is angle WCY.

Note that angle WTY and angle WCY are **not** the same size.

Exercise 21.10
Three-dimensional
trigonometry

1 The diagram shows a pyramid where the
vertical height OP = 7.6 cm.

The base of the pyramid is a rectangle where,
KL = 12.4 cm, and LM = 10.5 cm.

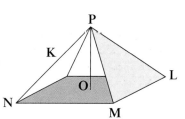

   a Calculate the length KM.
   b Calculate the length PM.
   c Calculate the angle between the edge PM
      and the base KLMN.
   d Calculate the angle the edge PN makes with the edge of the base MN.
   e On a sketch, show the angle between the side PLM and the base.
   f Calculate the angle between the side PLM and the base KLMN.
   g Calculate the surface area of the pyramid.
   h What is the volume of the pyramid?

2 In a pyramid R, the angle between each edge and the base is the same.
What can you say about the shape of the base of pyramid R?
Explain your answer including a sketch.

3   The diagram shows an 8 cm cube.
Cutting through the midpoints, B, C and D of three edges forms a pyramid
ABCD which has a triangular base.

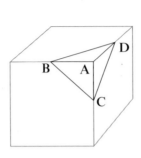

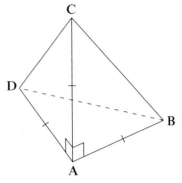

a   Calculate the volume of the pyramid cut from the cube.
b   What is the angle between the edge BC and the base ABD?

The pyramid is placed to stand on the cut face, Δ BCD.

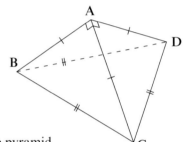

c   Calculate the length of each side
of the base BCD.
d   What is the angle BCD?
e   Calculate the area of ΔBCD.
f   Calculate the perpendicular height of the pyramid.
g   Calculate the angle between the line AB and the base BCD.

4   The diagram shows a pyramid cut from a cube. The cut is through the points
F, G and H, where EF = 2 cm, EG = 3 cm, and EH = 4 cm.

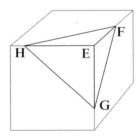

The pyramid is stood on the cut face, Δ FGH.

Calculate:

a   the volume of pyramid EFGH
b   the area of the cut face FGH
c   the height of the pyramid.

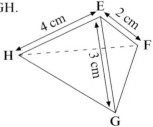

End points

You should be able to ...   ... so try these questions

A Use the sine rule

A1 In triangle RST calculate:

    a the length RS

    b the length of RT.

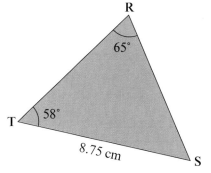

A2 In triangle CDE calculate:

    a angle DEC

    b the length of ED.

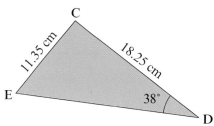

B Calculate the area of a triangle

B1 In Δ EFG calculate:

    a the size of angle GEF

    b the length EG

    c the area of triangle EFG.

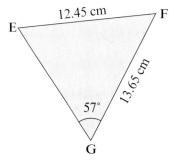

C Use the cosine rule

C1 Using the cosine rule in Δ RST, calculate:

    a the size of angle TRS

    b the size of angle RST.

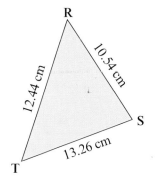

C2 Using the cosine rule in Δ KLM calculate:

    a the length of KL

    b the size of angle MKL.

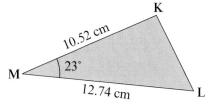

D Use bearings

D1 A boat sails from point A for 4.5 kilometres on a bearing of 072° to point B. From B the boat sails on a bearing of 134° to point C. C is 10 kilometres due east of A.

Calculate how far the boat sailed from point B to point C.

D2 Two boats leave harbour at the same time:

Seeker Me sails at a speed of 15 knots on a bearing of 192°.

Bold Over sails at a speed of 18 knots on a bearing of 316°.

Calculate the distance between the two boats after 150 minutes.

E Use an angle of elevation or depression

E1 From the top of a church tower, an observer notes that the church gate and a signpost are in line.

The gate is 65 metres from the base of the tower and at an angle of depression of 60° from the top of the tower.

The angle of depression of the signpost from the top of the tower is 18°.

Calculate the distance between the gate and the signpost.

E2 A radio mast is 75 metres tall is erected on level ground.

A camera is to be installed, at ground level, 20 metres from the base of the mast.

Calculate the angle of elevation of the camera if it is to monitor the top of the radio mast.

F Solve three-dimensional problems

F1 The diagram is of a growing unit sold by a garden centre.

The unit is in the shape of a square base with four triangular frames on top, in the shape of a pyramid.

When in position the triangular frames are at an angle of 55° to the base.

Calculate the full height of the growing unit.

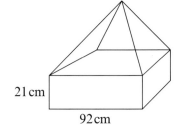

21 cm

92 cm

Some points to remember

For any triangle ABC

- ◆ Sine rule

$$\frac{a}{\sin A} = \frac{b}{\sin B} = \frac{c}{\sin C}$$

$$\frac{\sin A}{a} = \frac{\sin B}{b} = \frac{\sin C}{c}$$

- ◆ Cosine rule

$$a^2 = b^2 + c^2 - 2bc \cos A$$

$$\cos A = \frac{b^2 + c^2 - a^2}{2bc}$$

- ◆ Area of △ABC

$$\tfrac{1}{2}ab \sin C$$

Starting points
You need to know about ...
... so try these questions

A Investigations using data

◆ The reason for carrying out an investigation using data is to either test a **hypothesis** or answer a **question**.
The start of an investigation into sleep could be:
    Hypothesis – most people sleep at least 7 hours a night
    Question   – how long do people sleep at night?

◆ You can carry out an investigation in four stages:

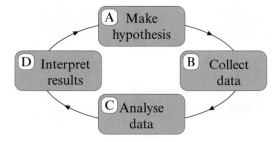

    A, make a hypothesis (or ask a question)
    B, collect the data you need
    C, analyse the data you have collected
    D, use the results of your analysis to decide
       whether the hypothesis is true or false.

◆ Stage D may give you an idea for a follow-up investigation.
For example, the start of a follow-up into sleep could be:
    Hypothesis – people need more sleep in the winter
    Question   – is there a link between sleep and time of year?

B Collecting data

◆ A **data collection sheet** is any form or table used to collect data.

To the BDA,
10 Queen Anne Street, London W1M 0BD
Tel: 0171-323 1531

A charity helping people with diabetes and supporting diabetes research.

I enclose a cheque/postal order*
payable to the BDA £ _____

Debit my Access/Visa* card
by the amount of   £ _____
Card number ☐☐☐☐☐☐☐☐☐☐☐☐☐☐☐☐
Expiry data ☐☐☐☐
    Please send me more information
    and membership details

Name _____
Address _____
Signature _____
*Delete which is inapplicable   Reg. Charity no. 215199

Body Matters			
Name	Length of thumb (cm)	Length of foot (cm)	Height (cm)
Sam			
Wasim			
Liz			
Shane			
Des			
Linda			
Dean			
Nisha			

◆ A **questionnaire** collects data by asking questions.

Sleep Questionnaire

1 What is your name?   _____

2 How old are you?   _____ years

3 What time do you usually go to bed? _____

◆ A data collection sheet or questionnaire is also called a **survey**.

A1 a Make your own hypothesis about sleep.
   b Decide what data you need to collect to test your hypothesis.

B1 Design a data collection sheet to use for a traffic survey.

C Types of question

◆ You can use different types of questions on a questionnaire:

❖ multi-choice questions

> **7** What do you sleep on ?
>
> *Please tick one box only*   ☐ Back   ☐ Front   ☐ Side

❖ multi-choice questions with a scale

> **8** How heavy a sleeper are you ?   HEAVY ——————▶ LIGHT
>
> *Please tick one box only*   Very Fairly Average Fairly Very
>
> ☐   ☐   ☐   ☐   ☐

❖ branching questions

> **9** Do you suffer from regular sleepless nights ?
>
> *Please tick one box only*   ☐ Yes   ☐ No
>
> *If your answer is* NO *then go to Question 12*

❖ questions with more than one answer.

> **12** What helps you get a good night's sleep ? ☐ A hot drink just before bed
> *Put a 1 in the box for the most helpful,* ☐ Eating just before bed
> *a 2 for the next most helpful,* ☐ Exercise during the evening
> *and so on* ☐ Relaxation breathing
>   ☐ Other *(please state)*
>   _____

D Using a scatter diagram

◆ You can use a scatter diagram to investigate if there is a link between two sets of data.

Question – does the time taken to get to sleep depend on the amount of light in the room?

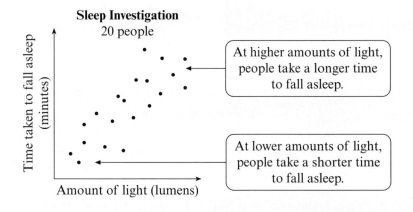

Sleep Investigation
20 people

Time taken to fall asleep (minutes)

Amount of light (lumens)

At higher amounts of light, people take a longer time to fall asleep.

At lower amounts of light, people take a shorter time to fall asleep.

The time taken to fall asleep does depend on the amount of light: as the amount of light increases, the time taken to fall asleep also increases.

C1 Design a questionnaire about sleep which includes different types of question.

D1

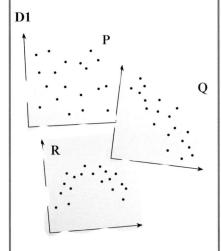

P

Q

R

Match each scatter diagram to each pair of sets of data.

a Time taken to get to sleep against Time since drank coffee

b Amount of sleep against Room temperature

c Amount of sleep against Height of bed off floor

Designing and criticising questions

◆ When you create a questionnaire, your questions must be carefully designed to:

  ❖ make them easy to answer
  ❖ make sure the answers give you the data you need.

Poor question

| How much sleep did you get last night? |
| ☐ Less than average |
| ☐ About average |
| ☐ More than average |

This question is **not clear**: the words used need to be more exact.
(Different people are likely to have different ideas of what is meant by 'average'.)

Improved question

| How much sleep did you get last night? |
| ☐ Less than 8 hours |
| ☐ About 8 hours |
| ☐ More than 8 hours |

| Do you agree that we need at least 8 hours sleep each night? |

This is a **leading** question: it leads people into giving a certain answer.
(The question seems to expect the answer 'Yes'.)

| Do you think we need at least 8 hours sleep each night? |
| ☐ Yes   ☐ No |
| ☐ Not sure |

| What do you sleep on? |

This question is **ambiguous**: it could have more than one meaning.
(The question is meant to be about sleeping position, but could be answered 'a bed'!)

| What do you sleep on? |
| ☐ Back |
| ☐ Front |
| ☐ Side |

Exercise 22.1
Designing and criticising questions

1 **a** Explain why this question is not clear.
   b Write an improved question.

| When do you usually go to bed? |
| ☐ Early   ☐ Late |

2 **a** Explain why this is a leading question.
   b Write an improved question.

| You get a worse night's sleep on a soft bed, don't you? |

3 **a** Explain why this question is ambiguous.
   b Write an improved question.

| Where do you sleep best? |

4

Leisure Centre Survey

1 Do you agree that the town needs a new leisure centre? ☐ Yes ☐ No

2 Would you be a frequent user of the centre? ☐ Yes ☐ No

3 Would you use the courts? ☐ Yes ☐ No

4 How much would you be prepared to pay to use the pool? ☐ Less than £1.50
                                                              ☐ More than £2.50

This questionnaire has been written to survey local people about a new leisure centre.

a Criticise each of the questions.
b Write an improved question for each one.

Experiments

♦ A survey asks people to give an opinion about something, or asks about facts which are easy to remember.

Example

> ### TV Survey
>
> 1 What is your favourite TV channel? ☐ BBC1 ☐ BBC2 ☐ ITV
> ☐ Channel 4 ☐ Channel 5
>
> 2 Did you watch TV last night? ☐ Yes ☐ No

♦ The data needed for some investigations can only be collected:

❖ over a period of time

> How much time do you spend in a week watching each TV channel?

❖ by designing an experiment.

> People take longer to get to sleep the more light there is in the room.

The data collection sheet used for these types of investigation can be called an **observation sheet**.

Exercise 22.2
Experiments

> To design your experiment:
> ❖ decide what data you need
> ❖ decide how to collect it
> ❖ design an observation sheet.

1 Design an observation sheet to collect data on how much time people spend in a week watching each TV channel.

2 Design an experiment to answer this question.

> *Body Matters*
> How many times do people blink in a day?

3 a Carry out your experiment.
   b Analyse the data you collect.
   c Interpret your results to answer the question.

4 Design an experiment to test this hypothesis.

> *Body Matters*
> Taller people do not have as good a sense of balance as shorter people.

5 a Carry out your experiment.
   b Analyse the data you collect.

6 Do you think the hypothesis is true or false? Explain why.

Thinking ahead to ...
sampling

A Rachel is investigating how much sleep students in her school get each night.

This is the distribution of students in the school.

	Yr 7	Yr 8	Yr 9	Yr 10	Yr 11	Total
	150	155	161	140	146	752

Rachel decides to take a random sample of 150, i.e. about 20%.

Which of these possible selections do you think will give the best sample? Explain your answer.

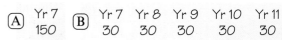

	Yr 7				
(A)	150				

	Yr 7	Yr 8	Yr 9	Yr 10	Yr 11
(B)	30	30	30	30	30

	Yr 7	Yr 8	Yr 9	Yr 10	Yr 11
(C)	30	31	32	28	29

Stratified random sampling

◆ When you choose a random sample from a population, the sample should model the characteristics of the population as closely as possible.

◆ If you think there are certain groups, or strata, within the population that are likely to give very different responses, then you can model this by taking a random sample from each group: a **stratified random sample**.

◆ The size of the sample you take from each group, or stratum, should be proportional to the size of the group in the population.

Example Show how a sample of 150 is chosen from this population, taking into account the students' year group and gender.

	Yr 7	Yr 8	Yr 9	Yr 10	Yr 11	Total
Boys	69	74	85	74	76	378
Girls	81	81	76	66	70	374
Total	150	155	161	140	146	752

Number of Yr 7 girls in sample = $\frac{81}{752} \times 150 = \mathbf{16}$

Number of Yr 11 boys in sample = $\frac{76}{752} \times 150 = \mathbf{15}$

Exercise 22.3
Sampling

1 Copy and complete the following table to show how the stratified random sample is chosen for the example above.

	Yr 7	Yr 8	Yr 9	Yr 10	Yr 11	Total
Boys					15	
Girls	16					
Total						150

2 The Great Britain Team for the 1996 Olympic Games had 500 members: 312 competitors and 188 support staff.
Show how a stratified random sample of 120 members is chosen.

3 The gender breakdown of the Great Britain Olympic Team was:

	Competitors	Support Staff	Total
Male	189	132	321
Female	123	56	179
Total	312	188	500

a Show how a stratified random sample of 120 members is chosen.
b What is the quickest way to calculate how many females would be in a stratified random sample of 75 members?
Explain your answer.

4 a What was the total population of the UK in 1995?
b Calculate how many people from each country would be in a stratified random sample of 500 000.

1995 UK Population (milions)			
England	Northern Ireland	Scotland	Wales
48.9	1.7	5.1	2.9

Make sure that the number of people in your sample adds up to 500 000.

Correlation

◆ You can describe the link between two sets of data using the term **correlation**.

Sleep Experiment 1
Does the length of time you take to fall asleep depend on how light the room is?

These results show **positive** correlation: an *increase* in one set of data tends to be matched by an *increase* in the other set.

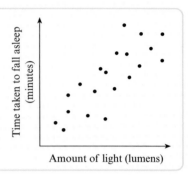

The result of experiment 2 may not be what you expect. It happens because sleep is part of your daily rhythm of sleeping and waking.

Going to bed late means that you will soon reach your time for waking, and vice versa.

A daily rhythm, like this sleep/wake example, is called a **circadian rhythm**.

Sleep Experiment 2
Does the length of time you sleep depend on the length of time since you last slept?

These results show **negative** correlation: an *increase* in one set of data tends to be matched by a *decrease* in the other set.

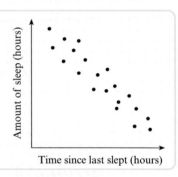

Exercise 22.4
Correlation

1

Mean semi-detached house prices in towns near London – 2nd Quarter 1996												
Distance from London (miles)	44	66	41	75	86	47	68	36	62	77	57	53
Mean house price (£000's)	93	78	98	72	63	97	71	104	86	64	78	88

a Draw these axes: horizontal 0 to 90, vertical 50 to 130.
b Plot the house price data on your diagram.
c Is the correlation positive or negative?

2

A negative number of dioptres shows short-sightedness; a positive number of dioptres shows long-sightedness.

Eye Tests for 10 people										
Pressure in eye (mmHg)	12.1	11.7	15.2	19.1	11.2	18.9	15.9	17.3	13.0	16.6
Refractive power of lens (dioptres)	3.6	¯3.9	5.1	10.4	¯6.4	3.0	¯6.9	6.5	¯8.4	0.8

a Draw these axes: horizontal 10 to 20, vertical ¯12 to 12
b Plot the eye test data on your diagram.
c Is the correlation positive or negative?

This is called drawing a line **by eye** or **by inspection**.

3 For each of your scatter diagrams, draw a line through the middle of the plots, like this:

4 Which scatter diagram did you find it easier to draw the line on? Explain why.

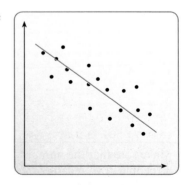

Using a line of best fit

♦ A line drawn through the middle of the plots on a scatter diagram is called a **line of best fit**. The stronger the correlation, the easier it is to draw this line.

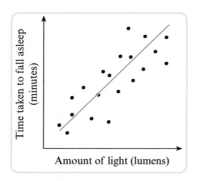

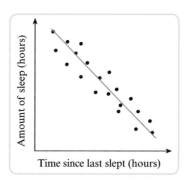

This is **moderate** positive correlation because the plots are well scattered around the line of best fit.

This is **strong** negative correlation because the plots are quite close to the line of best fit.

♦ When it is not possible to draw a line of best fit, there is no link between the two sets of data: there is **no correlation**.

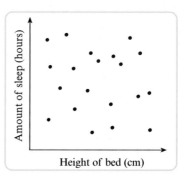

Exercise 22.5
Describing correlation

1 Use this scatter diagram to describe the correlation between income and percentage of income given to charity.

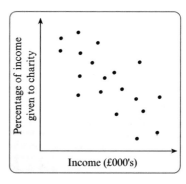

2 Use your scatter diagram from Exercise 23.3 Question **1** to describe the correlation between distance of town from London and mean house price.

3 Use your scatter diagram from Exercise 23.3 Question **2** to describe the correlation between pressure in eye and refractive power of lens.

4 Design an experiment to answer this question:
'Is there any correlation between your fathom and your height?'

5 **a** Carry out your experiment.
b Plot the data you collect on a scatter diagram.
c Draw a line of best fit.
d Use your scatter diagram to describe any correlation.

Your fathom is the distance between the ends of your fingers when your arms are stretched as wide as possible. This distance is roughly six feet for an adult.

Estimating values from a line of best fit

♦ It is possible to estimate values from a line of best fit.

Example

a Estimate the height of a person with head circumference 56 cm.
b Estimate the head circumference of a person 195 cm tall.

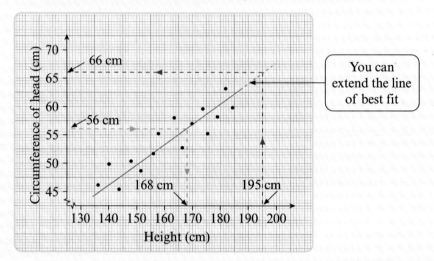

a Estimated height of person with head circumference 56 cm = **168 cm**
b Estimated head circumference of person 195 cm tall = **66 cm**

Exercise 22.6
Estimating values

Use your scatter diagram from Exercise 22.4 Question **1** for Questions **1** to **3**.

1 Estimate the distance from London of a town with a mean house price of:
 a £90 000 b £65 000

2 Estimate the mean house price for a town:
 a 70 miles from London b 55 miles from London

3 Extend your line of best fit to estimate:
 a the distance from London of a town with a mean house price of £120 000
 b the mean house price for a town 25 miles from London.

4

Natural Births – Length of Pregnancy & Weight of Baby									
Length of pregnancy (days)	271	287	283	274	271	279	263	276	283	270
Weight of baby (kg)	2.5	4.2	3.8	3.3	4.5	3.4	2.9	4.1	4.3	3.5

This data has been collected to test the hypothesis:
'A longer pregnancy leads to a heavier baby.'
Plot this data on a scatter diagram.

5 a Draw a line of best fit on your scatter diagram.
 b Describe the correlation between length of pregnancy and weight of baby.
 c Use your line of best fit to estimate:
  i the length of pregnancy for a baby that weighs 3.5 kg
  ii the weight of a baby with a length of pregnancy of 280 days.

6 Do you think it would make sense to extend this line of best fit?
Give reasons for your answer.

End points

You should be able to ...   ... so try these questions

A Design and criticise questions for a questionnaire

A1

Bypass Survey

1 Are you a local?   ☐ Yes   ☐ No
2 What do you think of the traffic in the village? _____
3 Do you agree that the village needs a bypass? ☐ Yes   ☐ No

a Criticise each of these questions.
b Write an improved question for each one.

B Design experiments

B1 Design an experiment to answer this question.

Body Matters
How long can people hold their breath for?

C Choose a stratified random sample

C1

1991 Population of capital Cities (000's)			
Belfast	Cardiff	Edinburgh	London
279	272	402	2343

Calculate how many people from each capital city would be in a stratified random sample of 10 000.

Petrol Cars – Size of Engine & Petrol Consumption											
Size of engine (litres)	1.6	2.6	1.2	4.0	2.5	1.1	3.2	4.0	3.2	1.8	2.4	3.5
Petrol consumption (mpg)	45	37	40	22	43	48	29	29	33	39	32	25

D Use a scatter diagram and line of best fit to describe correlation

D1 a Draw axes: horizontal 0 to 6.0,   vertical 0 to 50
       b Plot the petrol car data on your diagram.
       c Draw a line of best fit.
       d Describe any correlation between size of engine and petrol consumption.

E Estimate values from a line of best fit

E1 Use your scatter diagram to estimate:
       a the petrol consumption of a car with a 3.0 litre engine
       b the engine size of a car with petrol consumption of 40 mpg.

E2 Extend your line of best fit to estimate:
       a the petrol consumption of a car with a 5.0 litre engine.
       b the engine size of a car with petrol consumption of 20 mpg.

Some points to remember

◆ When you choose a stratified random sample, check that the sum of the sample sizes from each stratum equals the total sample size.

◆ When you draw a line of best fit on a scatter diagram, make sure the line goes through the middle of the points.

◆ In some cases, it does not make sense to extend the line of best fit on a scatter diagram.

Starting points

You need to know about ...

... so try these questions

A Calculations with time, distance and speed

Speed = Distance ÷ Time

Time = Distance ÷ Speed

Distance = Speed × Time

Example 1   How long does it take a car travelling at an average speed of 54 mph to cover a distance of 350 miles?

Time = Distance ÷ Speed

= 350 ÷ 54

= 6.48 hours (to 3 sf)

= **6 hours 29 minutes** (to the nearest minute)

(since 0.48 hours is 0.48 × 60 = 28.8 minutes)

Example 2   An arrow from a long bow flew a distance of 196 metres in 2 seconds. What was its average speed in mph?

Speed = Distance ÷ Time

= 196 ÷ 2   = 98 metres per second

= 98 × 60 × 60   = 352 800 metres per hour

= 352 800 ÷ 1000   = 352.8 km per hour

= 352.8 ÷ 1.609   = **219.3 mph** (1 mile = 1.609 km)

A1   What is 0.68 hours to the nearest minute?

A2   A car made the journey from Doncaster to Oxford (135 miles) in 2 hours 52 minutes. What was its average speed? Give your answer to 2 sf.

A3   How long does it take a hot air balloon to fly 100 metres at a speed of 41 m min^{-1}? Give your answer in minutes and seconds.

A4   Convert the following:

   a   14 metres per second into miles per hour

   b   38 miles per hour into metres per second.

B The area of a trapezium

Area = $\frac{1}{2}(a + b)h$

where h is the perpendicular height.

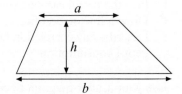

Example   Find the area of this trapezium.

First identify the dimensions a, b and h:

$a = 12$ cm

$b = 25$ cm

$h = 14$ cm

Note that the lengths 15 cm and 16 cm are not used.

Area = $\frac{1}{2}(a + b)h$

= $\frac{1}{2}$ × (12 + 25) × 14

= 0.5 × 37 × 14

= 259

The area of the trapezium is 259 cm².

B1   What is the area of this trapezium?

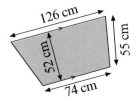

B2   Calculate the area of this trapezium in square units.

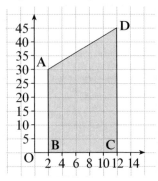

C Using distance–time graphs

This graphs shows journeys made by four people on one day.
They all travelled on the same road.

Joe left home in his Citröen and got back home some time after 4 pm.

Sally took the Jeep and stopped at a friends for lunch then continued her journey.

Ravi drove without a break all day on his Honda motorbike.

Charlie pedalled non-stop on his Claude Butler bike.

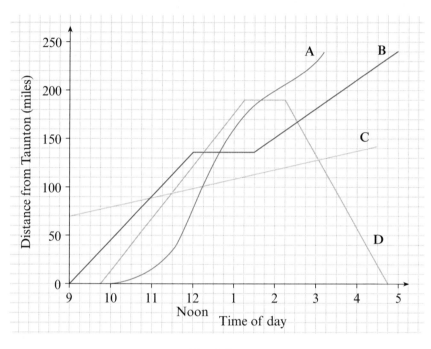

$$\text{Average speed} = \frac{\text{Total distance}}{\text{Total time}}$$

The total time includes any breaks.

Example 1   Calculate the average speed of A over the journey.

$$\text{Average speed} = \frac{240}{(10\,\text{am to }3{:}15\,\text{pm})}$$

$$= \frac{240}{525} \quad (5\,\text{h }15\,\text{min is }5.25\,\text{h})$$

$$= \textbf{45.7 mph}$$

Example 2   Calculate the average speed of D over the day.

$$\text{Average speed} = \frac{(190 + 190)}{(9{:}45\,\text{to }4{:}45)}$$

$$= \frac{380}{7}$$

$$= \textbf{54.3 mph}$$

C1   Identify the line on the graph for each person's journey. Give reasons for your answers.

C2   Which two journeys finished at the same place? Explain your answer.

C3   Which two journeys started at the same time?

C4   At what time did D's journey start?

C5   At noon how far away from Taunton was:
a A   **b** B
c C   **d** D?

C6   How long did Sally spend at her friend's house? How can you tell?

C7   Who did not start at Taunton? How far was this person from Taunton at 9 am?

C8   How far from Taunton was A when overtaking C?

C9   From the graph:
D passed C twice.
a At what times did they pass?
b What was the difference about the directions on the two occasions?

C10   Calculate C's average speed over the whole journey.

C11   What was B's average speed over the whole journey?

C12   How does B's speed, up to noon, compare with B's speed after 1:30 pm? Give your reasons.

C13 a   Who appears to reach the highest top speed at any time on their journey?
b   Roughly when was this?
c   Why is it impossible to tell for certain from the graph?

Finding speeds from distance–time graphs

This distance–time graph shows journeys taken by four people who arrange to meet in Haddington. Julie and Simon are having problems with their cars.

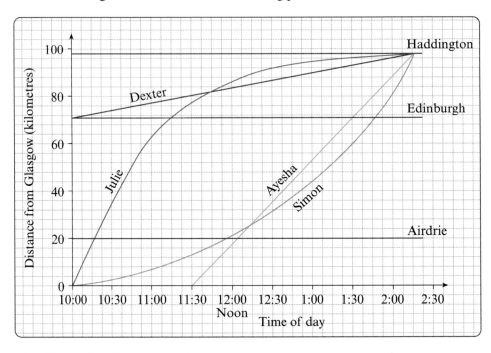

Exercise 23.1
Speeds from graphs

You may see
kilometres per hour
in any of these forms

kph
km h⁻¹
km/h

1 Where does Dexter start from?

2 **a** What was Dexter's average speed in kilometres per hour?
    b How do you think Dexter was travelling?

3 **a** At what time did Ayesha start her journey?
    b What was her average speed in km h⁻¹?

4 Describe how the speeds during Julie's and Simon's journeys differed from each other.

5 What was the average speed over the journey for:
    a Simon
    b Julie?

6 How did Simon's, Ayesha's and Julie's speeds compare when they passed Airdrie?

7 At what time was Simon travelling at roughly the same speed as
    a Ayesha
    b Dexter?
    Explain how you decided.

8 How far from Glasgow was Julie when she was travelling at roughly the same speed as:
    a Ayesha
    b Dexter?

9 At roughly what time were Simon and Julie travelling at the same speed?

10 Julie and Simon passed the same point on the road at the same speed. How far from Glasgow is this point?

During a normal car journey the speed will vary greatly depending on road conditions as this graph shows.

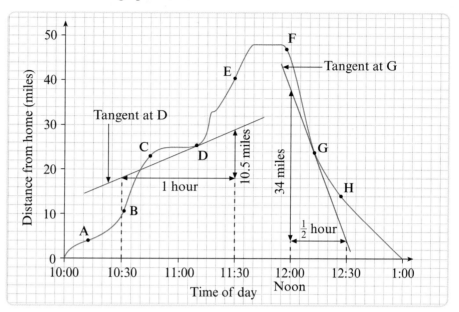

It is possible to estimate the speed at any point from a distance–time graph by drawing a tangent at the point and finding its gradient.

Example 1   Find the speed at point D.

◆ Draw the tangent at D

◆ Calculate the gradient:

$$\text{Gradient} = \frac{\text{Difference in distance coordinates}}{\text{Difference in time coordinates}} = \frac{10.5}{1}$$

$$= 10.5$$

The speed at point D was 10.5 mph *away* from home.

Example 2   Find the speed at point G.

◆ Draw the tangent at G

◆ Calculate the gradient:

$$\text{Gradient} = \frac{^-34}{0.5}$$

$$= \,^-68$$

The speed at point G was 68 mph *towards* home.

A tangent to a curve is a straight line which touches the curve at a point.

Tangent at point P

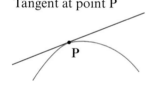

When a distance–time graph has a negative gradient it simply means that the vehicle or person is approaching.

Exercise 23.2
Finding speeds
from gradients

For Question **2**, answers on gradients read from a graph can only be approximate.

---

1 Trace the graph and the axes.
Carefully mark on the points A, B, C, E, F and H in the correct place.
Draw tangents and calculate the speed of the vehicle at each point.

2 **a** At what time in the journey was the vehicle travelling the fastest?
   b What speed was this?
   c Why do you think this journey proved very expensive for the driver?

3 Describe how the vehicle's speed varied over the whole journey, and give some likely road conditions to explain why this might have happened.

The link between distance–time and speed–time graphs

A distance–time graph can give an indication of changing speed when the changing gradient of the curve is considered. It is also possible to draw a speed–time graph from it. Here are two graphs of the same short bicycle journey.

On this distance–time graph some tangents have been drawn to show the speed at these points. It is possible, though, to draw a tangent at any point on the curve. There are an infinite number of tangents possible.

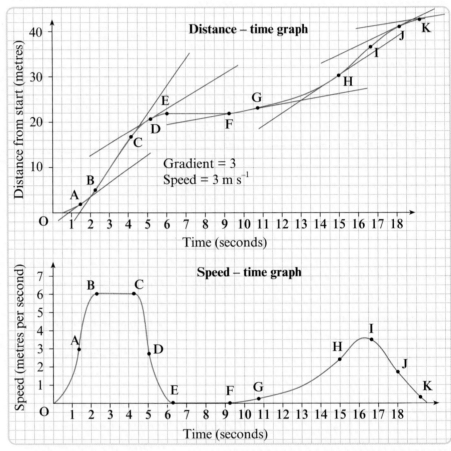

You may see
metres per second
in any of these forms:

m per s
m/s
m s^{-1}

At any point on the distance–time graph a gradient can be drawn and the speed calculated. For example, at point A (after about 1.3 seconds) the speed of the bike is 3 metres per second. Point A can therefore be plotted on the distance–time graph as a speed of 3 m s^{-1} after 1.3 seconds. The more points at which the gradient is found, the more accurate will be the speed–time graph.

Exercise 23.3
Reading a
speed–time graph

1 How can you tell from the distance–time graph that the bike is travelling faster at point B than at point A?

2 What does a horizontal line indicate on:

   a a distance–time graph   **b** a speed–time graph?

3 The following questions are about the speed–time graph, but you may need to look at the corresponding points on the distance–time graph.

   a Why does the graph show a speed of zero between points E and F?
   b Why are the speeds equal at points B and C?
   c Why is the second peak on the graph lower than the first peak?
   d Give two labelled points where the bike is:
      i accelerating (speeding up)   **ii** decelerating (slowing down).

Acceleration from a speed–time graph

This is a speed–time graph for a delivery van travelling between two houses.

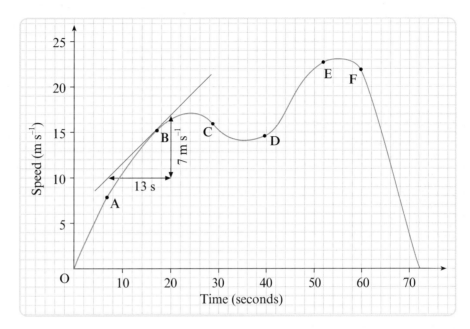

Acceleration or deceleration are the rate at which the speed changes over time. They are described as:

a speed per a time in units such as

metres per second per second written as **m s⁻²**

Where the curve is rising the van is accelerating (the speed is increasing) and where it is falling the van is decelerating. The acceleration or deceleration at any point can be found by drawing a tangent to the curve.

Example Estimate the acceleration at point B.

$$\text{Gradient} = \frac{\text{Difference in speed coordinates}}{\text{Difference in time coordinates}} = \frac{7}{13}$$

$$= 0.54$$

So the acceleration at point A is about 0.5 metres per second per second.

It is difficult to be more accurate than 1 sf when giving gradients of tangents. The gradient at point C is negative, which indicates that the car is decelerating.

Exercise 23.4
Finding acceleration from speed–time graphs

1 Use tracing paper to help you draw tangents at points A to F above and then estimate the acceleration or deceleration at each point.

2 When the van is neither accelerating nor decelerating what is the gradient of the tangent to the speed–time graph?

3 Which of these statements are true?

a When the acceleration is least, the van is going most slowly.
b When the speed is increasing most rapidly, the acceleration is greatest.
c When the van is decelerating, it is going more slowly than when it is accelerating.
d The maximum acceleration is when the van is travelling at 23 m s⁻¹.

4 This table shows the speed of a car at different time intervals.
It started from rest.

Time (s)	1	2	3	4	5	6
Speed (m s⁻¹)	2	6	11	16	20	22

a Draw a speed–time graph.
b Use your graph to estimate the car's acceleration after 4 seconds.

Thinking ahead to ...
area under a graph

On a speed–time graph no lines can be truly vertical because speed cannot change instantly. Here the lines appear vertical because the changes take place in a few seconds but the time scale on the graph is in hours.

The green line on this graph shows the speed of a hill walker over a day.

She started at 8:30 am.

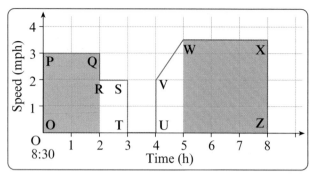

A a At what speed did the walker travel for the first two hours?
   b How many miles did she cover in the first two hours?
   c How many squares are in the rectangle shaded red?

B Between what times did the walker stop for lunch?

C a How many miles did the walker cover between points W and X?
   b How many squares are in the blue shaded rectangle?

D a What does the line VW on the graph tell you?
   b How many squares are under the line VW?
   c How many miles do you think she covered after lunch?

Area under a graph

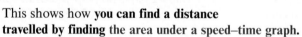

The symbol ≡ means
is equivalent to.
It is like the = sign but means the two sides are not quite the same type of quantity.

The area under a speed–time graph is the area between the line which shows the journey and the time axis.

On a speed–time graph the vertical axes represents speed, and the horizontal axis represents time.

The shaded region under the line is almost a rectangle with an area of:

Vertical dimension × Horizontal dimension
    So Area of rectangle ≡ Speed × Time

But Distance = Speed × Time
    So Distance = Area under the line.

In this case the distance travelled in the first 5 hours is 5 × 60 = 300 km.

This shows how **you can find a distance travelled by finding** the area under a speed–time graph.

Example How far did this lorry travel between 8 am and noon?

The area of the small red rectangle represents 20 × 1 = 20 kilometres.

There are $14\frac{1}{2}$ of these rectangles under the graph.

Therefore

Distance travelled = 14.5 × 20
                  = 290

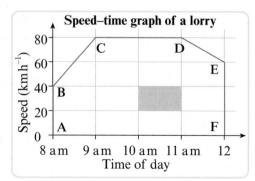

The lorry travelled 290 kilometres between 8 am and noon.

Exercise 23.5
Area under a graph

Graphs of this sort only approximate to real journeys. No lines can be truly vertical and few vehicles keep up a steady speed or a steady increase in speed over any length of time. With a different time scale the start of the same journey might really look like this.

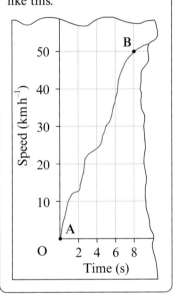

This is an approximate speed–time graph for a minicab over 8 hours of a day.

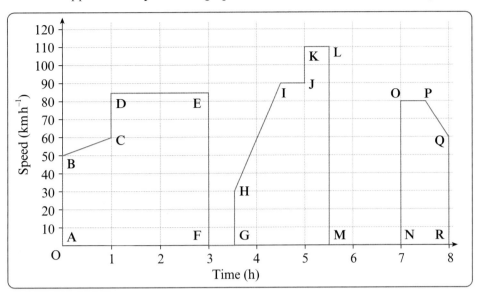

1 a For how long in total was the cab stationary?
   b At which points did the cab start accelerating?
   c What was the average acceleration between points H and I in $km\,h^{-2}$?
   d What was the average deceleration between points P and Q?

2 Between points A and F what distance was travelled?

3 Estimate the distance travelled by the cab over the whole day?

4 a Over which period of 60 minutes did the cab cover the greatest distance?
   b What distance was this?

5 This is a log from a police patrol vehicle:

8 am	Started shift	
8 am to 9 am	Motorway patrol	65 mph
9 to 9:30 am	Hot pursuit – steady speed	115 mph
9:30 to 10 am	Observing traffic flow	stationary
10 to 1 am	Ambulance escort	40 mph
1 to 1:30pm	Steadily slowing from 40 mph to standstill.	
1:30 to 2 pm	Lunch	
2 to 2:30 pm	Motorway patrol	65 mph
2:30 to 4 pm	Speed monitoring	70 mph
4 to 5 pm	Convoy escort	50 mph
5 to 6:30 pm	Return trip to station	70 mph
6:30 pm	Garaged vehicle	

a Draw an approximate speed–time graph to show the speed of the police vehicle over the day.
b By finding the area under the graph, estimate how many miles the vehicle travelled after lunch.
c How far did the vehicle travel over the whole day?
d i What was the average speed of the vehicle over the whole day?
   ii Draw a dotted line on your graph to represent this average speed.
   iii During which times of the day was the vehicle moving at less than its average daily speed?

279

Trapezium Rule

Speed–time graphs are usually curved because changes in speed do not occur instantly. Then it is less easy to find the area under the curve.

Using the **Trapezium Rule**, you can find an estimate for the area under a curve by splitting it into trapeziums of equal width.

Example This shows a 12–second interval of a speed–time graph for an object. Find the distance travelled in the 12 seconds by estimating the area under the curve.

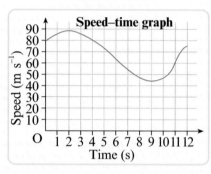

You usually have to choose how many trapeziums to split the area into. It is best to choose a width for each trapezium that fits easily into the total width under the graph.

Using 4 trapeziums for the estimate:

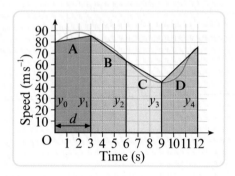

Area of A $= \frac{1}{2}(y_0 + y_1)d = 0.5 \times (80 + 85) \times 3 = 247.5$

Area of B $= \frac{1}{2}(y_1 + y_2)d = 0.5 \times (85 + 64) \times 3 = 223.5$

Area of C $= \frac{1}{2}(y_2 + y_3)d = 0.5 \times (64 + 46) \times 3 = 165.0$

Area of D $= \frac{1}{2}(y_3 + y_4)d = 0.5 \times (46 + 75) \times 3 = 181.5$

Total = 817.5

Distance is about 820 metres (to 2 sf)

Using 6 trapeziums for the estimate:

Area of A = 0.5 × (80 + 89) × 2 = 169

Area of B = 0.5 × (89 + 80) × 2 = 169

Area of C = 0.5 × (80 + 63) × 2 = 143

Area of D = 0.5 × (63 + 47) × 2 = 110

Area of E = 0.5 × (47 + 47) × 2 = 94

Area of F = 0.5 × (47 + 75) × 2 = 122

Total = 807

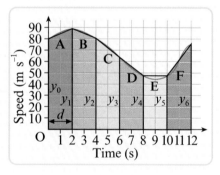

You may need tracing paper for Exercise 23.6.

Distance is about 810 metres (to 2 sf)

Exercise 23.6
Trapezium rule

1 **a** Trace or copy the speed–time graph.
   b Divide the area under the curve into three trapeziums and calculate an estimate for the distance travelled in 12 seconds.

2 Using another copy of the graph, estimate the distance travelled when you use only two trapeziums.

3 **a** How do you think the number of trapeziums under the graph affects the accuracy of the estimate?
   b What is a disadvantage of having very few trapeziums?
   c What is a disadvantage of having a very large number of them?
   d How many trapeziums do you think gives a sensible estimate in the above speed–time graph?

4   This speed-time graph shows is for a 4-minute ride at a fairground.

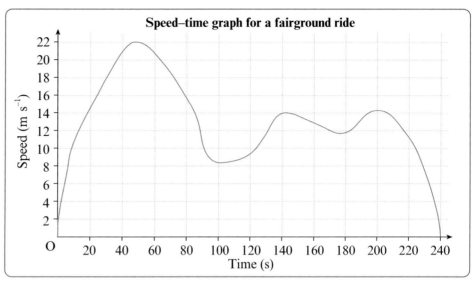

Speed–time graph for a fairground ride

The trapeziums on the extreme left- and right-hand sides will have one vertical dimension as zero. They are, in fact, triangles.

a   Trace or copy the graph and axes accurately.
b   By splitting the area under the graph into trapeziums of width 60 seconds, estimate the distance covered over the four minutes.
c   **i**   What do you think is a sensible width to use for the trapeziums?
    ii   Use this width and give an accurate estimate of the total distance travelled.
d   Estimate the distance travelled in the time interval between 80 seconds and 130 seconds.
    Explain how you made your estimate.

5   This is a speed–time graph showing the speed of an arrow over a 20-second interval.

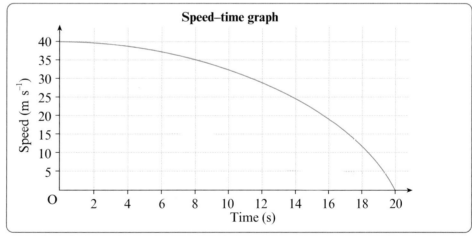

Speed–time graph

Choose a sensible number of trapeziums to estimate the distance travelled by the arrow over this time interval.

6   This table shows the speed of a drivebelt as it starts up.

Time (s)	0	3	6	9	12	15	18	21	24	28	32
Speed (m s^{-1})	0	2	6	11.5	19	26	29	30.2	31	31.5	32

a   Draw the speed–time graph for a point on the belt.
b   Use your graph to estimate the distance travelled by a point on the belt in the first 32 seconds.

Areas under other graphs

Compound measures are measures which need more than one unit such as:

Kilometres per hour
People per square mile
Pence per kilogram
Kilometres per litre
Passengers per car

The area under a speed–time graph represents distance but the area under some other graphs which involve compound measures can also have a meaning.

Example

This graph shows the power output from a motor over 80 seconds. Estimate the energy (in joules) used by the motor in this time.

The area of the shaded square represents 20 joules of energy because:

Width × Height = Area

so

10 seconds × 2 joules per second = 20 joules

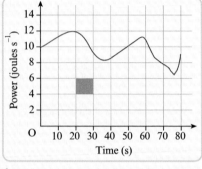

There are about 38 squares under the graph so the total energy used is about 38 × 20 = 760 joules.

The motor used about 760 joules of energy over the time.

Exercise 23.7
Graphs with compound measures

1 This graph shows the rate at which water flowed from an irrigation pipe.

  a Describe what the area of the shaded square represents.
  b Estimate the total amount of water delivered in 24 minutes.

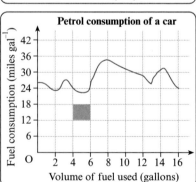

2 This graph shows how the petrol consumption of a car varied over a journey from Carlisle to Penzance. The car used 16 gallons of petrol in total.

  a Describe what the area of the shaded square represents.
  b Estimate how far Carlisle is from Penzance.
  c What was the average rate of petrol consumption?

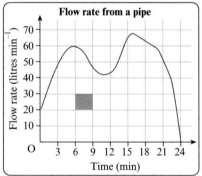

3 Measurements of water flow (in cubic metres per hour) were taken hourly after a sluice gate was opened on the Somerset Levels to lower the level of the River Tone. These are the results.

Rate of flow, f (m³ h⁻¹)	950	640	470	340	250	160	120	90
Time since opening, t (h)	1	2	3	4	5	6	7	8

  a Draw a graph of f against t for $1 \leqslant t \leqslant 8$.
  b Use the Trapezium Rule to estimate the volume of water which flowed in the time interval between $t = 1$ and $t = 8$.

End points

You should be able to ...   ... so try these questions

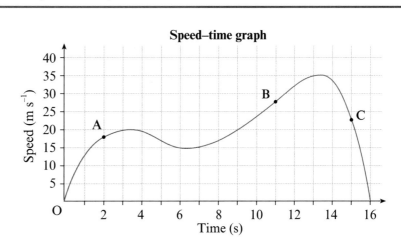

A Interpret a speed–time graph

A1 At what times was this vehicle travelling at 18 m s⁻¹?

A2 Give two times when the vehicle was starting to accelerate.

A3 At which times was the vehicle stationary ?

A4 Describe what the vehicle was doing 4 seconds from the start.

B Estimate acceleration or deceleration from a speed–time graph

B1 Estimate the acceleration of the vehicle at points A and B.

B2 Estimate the deceleration at point C.

B3 At which points was the vehicle neither accelerating nor decelerating ?

B4 At what time did the vehicle have the greatest acceleration ?

C Estimate the distance travelled from a speed–time graph

C1 Estimate how far the vehicle travelled in the first two seconds.

C2 Use the Trapezium Rule to estimate how far the vehicle travelled altogether.

C3 What was the average speed of the vehicle over the whole time?

Some points to remember

- The gradient of a distance–time graph gives a measure of its speed at the point where the tangent is drawn.

- The gradient of a speed–time graph gives a measure of its acceleration (positive gradient) or deceleration (negative gradient).

- Acceleration (and deceleration) are given in units such as m s⁻² (metres per second per second) or km h⁻² (kilometres per hour per hour).

- The area under a speed–time graph gives the distance travelled.

Starting points

You need to know about ...

... so try these questions

A Using vectors to describe a translation

- A vector can be used to describe the movement in a translation.

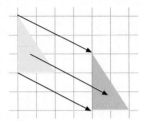

Every point on the triangle has moved 4 squares right and 2 squares down.

The vector which describes this translation is: $\begin{pmatrix} 4 \\ ^-2 \end{pmatrix}$

A1 Copy triangle ABC and translate it using the vector:

a $\begin{pmatrix} 3 \\ ^-1 \end{pmatrix}$ **b** $\begin{pmatrix} 5 \\ 2 \end{pmatrix}$

c $\begin{pmatrix} ^-2 \\ ^-3 \end{pmatrix}$ **d** $\begin{pmatrix} ^-4 \\ 2 \end{pmatrix}$

B Resultant vectors

- The total effect of two or more vectors can be shown as a single vector called the **resultant**.
  So if you translate,
  first by $\begin{pmatrix} 3 \\ 1 \end{pmatrix}$ then by $\begin{pmatrix} ^-5 \\ 3 \end{pmatrix}$,
  the resultant vector is given by:
  $\begin{pmatrix} 3 + ^-5 \\ 1 + 3 \end{pmatrix} = \begin{pmatrix} ^-2 \\ 4 \end{pmatrix}$

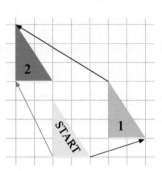

B1 Give the resultant vector for each of these combined translations.

a $\begin{pmatrix} 3 \\ 1 \end{pmatrix} \begin{pmatrix} 2 \\ ^-2 \end{pmatrix}$

b $\begin{pmatrix} ^-2 \\ ^-4 \end{pmatrix} \begin{pmatrix} 3 \\ 2 \end{pmatrix}$

c $\begin{pmatrix} 2 \\ 5 \end{pmatrix} \begin{pmatrix} 0 \\ ^-2 \end{pmatrix} \begin{pmatrix} ^-3 \\ 1 \end{pmatrix}$

C Using algebra

- Expressions that include negative coefficients can be factorised in two ways.
  To factorise $6y - 2x$:

  $6y - 2x$ or $6y - 2x$
  $= 2(3y - x)$ $= ^-2(^-3y + x)$
  $= ^-2(x - 3y)$

- Expressions that include fractional coefficients can be factorised.

  To factorise: $\frac{1}{2}x + y$ $\frac{1}{2}(x - y) + x$

  $\frac{1}{2}x + y$ $\frac{1}{2}(x - y) + x$
  $= \frac{1}{2}(x + 2y)$ $= \frac{1}{2}x - \frac{1}{2}y + x$
               $= 1\frac{1}{2}x - \frac{1}{2}y$
               $= \frac{1}{2}(3x - y)$

C1 Copy and complete:
a $4x - 2y = 2(\square)$
b $4x - 2y = ^-2(\square)$
c $9y - 3x = ^-3(\square)$
d $9y - 3x = 3(\square)$

C2 Factorise:
a $x + \frac{1}{2}y$
b $\frac{1}{3}x - y$
c $x + \frac{1}{2}(x + y)$
d $\frac{1}{3}(x - y) + x$
e $2x + \frac{2}{3}(y - 2x)$
f $2y - \frac{2}{3}(x + y)$

D Ratios and fractions of straight lines

- A straight line can be divided into two parts, like this:

  A ___1___ X _____2_____ B

  Point X divides line AB in the ratio 1 : 2, and AX is $\frac{1}{3}$ of the line.

  AX : AB = 1 : 2   AX = $\frac{1}{3}$AB

P _____3_____ Y _1_ Q

D1 Give these ratios.
a PY : YQ **b** QY : YP

D2 What fraction of PQ is:
a YQ **b** PY ?

Defining vectors

♦ A **vector** is something that can be defined by two quantities:
  ❖ its **size**
  ❖ its **direction**.

♦ A vector can be placed anywhere in a plane, and is usually represented by a straight line:
  ❖ the size of the vector is the length of the line,
  ❖ the direction of the vector is how the line is pointing, in the direction of the arrow.

Other ways of writing the vector **z** include:

$$\underline{z} \quad \underset{\sim}{z} \quad \bar{z} \quad \tilde{z}$$

♦ The **negative** of a given vector is a vector that is:
  ❖ equal in size but
  ❖ opposite in direction.

♦ A **scalar multiple** of a given vector is found by:
  ❖ multiplying its size by a single number
  ❖ leaving its direction unchanged.

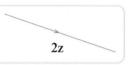

♦ When a vector is placed on a coordinate grid, it can also be represented by a **column vector**.

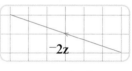

$$z = \begin{pmatrix} 3 \\ 1 \end{pmatrix} \qquad {}^{-}z = \begin{pmatrix} {}^{-}3 \\ 1 \end{pmatrix} \qquad {}^{-}2z = \begin{pmatrix} {}^{-}6 \\ 2 \end{pmatrix}$$

Exercise 24.1
Vectors on a grid

Use these vectors for this exercise.

$$p = \begin{pmatrix} 1 \\ 3 \end{pmatrix} \qquad q = \begin{pmatrix} 4 \\ 1 \end{pmatrix} \qquad r = \begin{pmatrix} {}^{-}1 \\ 2 \end{pmatrix}$$

1   Draw vectors **p**, **q**, and **r** on a coordinate grid.

2   Write each of these as a column vector, and draw it on a coordinate grid.
    a ⁻p   b 2q   c 3r   d ⁻2p   e ⁻3r

3   This diagram shows the effect of the combined translation, **q** then **p**. Give the resultant vector.

4   a Draw a diagram to show the combined translation, **p** then **q**.
    b Give the resultant vector.

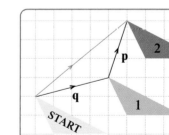

5   Write down what you notice about the effect of combined translations.

6   This diagram shows the effect of the combined translation, **q** then ⁻**r**.

    a Give the resultant vector.
    b Explain how you can find the resultant from column vectors **q** and **r**.

Adding vectors

◆ You can add vectors by combining them end to end, so that their direction 'follow on' from each other.

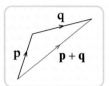

Example

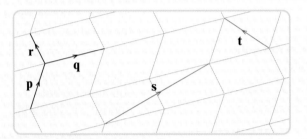

Give **s** and **t** in terms of **p**, **q**, and **r**.

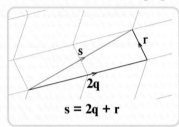

s = 2q + r

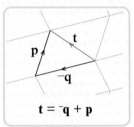

t = ⁻q + p

Exercise 24.2
Adding vectors

1 a This sketch to show **x** = **q** + **r** is incorrect.
   Explain why.
b Make a sketch to show the correct **x**.

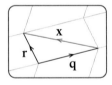

2 Give each of these vectors in terms of **p**, **q**, and **r**.

a 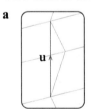 **b**  **c**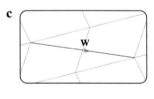

Adding vectors is commutative because, however you combine them, the resultant is the same.

3 a Explain why this diagram shows that adding vectors is commutative:
   p + **q** = **q** + **p**
b Make a sketch to show that:
   ⁻**q** + **p** = **p** + ⁻**q**

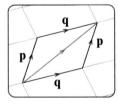

Adding vectors is associative because, however pairs of vectors are grouped, the resultant is the same.

4 a Sketch this diagram.
b Label your sketch to show that adding vectors is associative:
   p + (**q** + **r**) = (**p** + **q**) + **r**

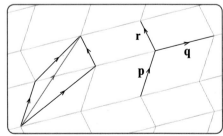

Subtracting vectors

♦ Adding a negative vector can be written as a subtraction.

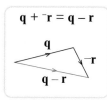

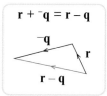

♦ In general, vectors **a** – **b** and **b** – **a** are:
 ❖ the same in size,
 ❖ opposite in direction.

Therefore, **b** – **a** is the negative vector of **a** – **b**.

$$^-(\mathbf{a} - \mathbf{b})$$
$$= {}^-\mathbf{a} + \mathbf{b}$$
$$= \mathbf{b} + {}^-\mathbf{a}$$
$$= \mathbf{b} - \mathbf{a}$$

Exercise 24.3
Subtracting vectors

1 Show that **p** – **q** is the negative vector of **q** – **p**:
 a using a sketch **b** using algebra

2 Make a sketch to show the vector (**p** – **q**) – **r**.

3 Make a sketch to show:
 a **q** – **r** **b** **p** – (**q** – **r**)

4 Use algebra to explain why subtracting vectors is not associative:

p – (**q** – **r**) is not equal to (**p** – **q**) – **r**.

5

Give vectors **r**, **s**, and **t** in terms of **p** and **q**.

6 **a** Sketch a large grid like the one in Question **5**.
 b Use your grid to draw:
  i 3**p** – 2**q** **ii** 2**q** – 3**p** **iii** 3**p** – **q** **iv** 6**p** + 2**q**
 c Use algebra to explain why 3**p** – **q** and 2**q** – 6**p** are parallel vectors.

7 These vectors include three pairs of parallel vectors.

$$\boxed{{}^-2\mathbf{p} - \mathbf{q}} \quad \boxed{2\mathbf{p} - \mathbf{q}} \quad \boxed{2\mathbf{q} - \mathbf{p}} \quad \boxed{2\mathbf{p} + 4\mathbf{q}} \quad \boxed{2\mathbf{q} - 4\mathbf{p}} \quad \boxed{2\mathbf{p} + \mathbf{q}} \quad \boxed{\mathbf{p} + 2\mathbf{q}}$$

List each pair.

8 **a** Give each side of this parallelogram of vectors in terms of **p** and **q**.
 b Add your vectors.
 c Explain your answer.

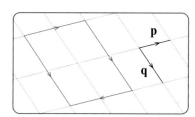

Vectors in space

♦ You can refer to a vector by labelling each end.

Example $\overrightarrow{KL}$ is a vector with:

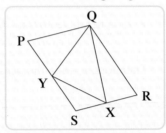

❖ size equal to the distance from K to L
❖ direction from K to L.
$\overrightarrow{LK}$ is the same size as $\overrightarrow{KL}$, and opposite in direction.

♦ This notation is useful when giving a vector as a **vector sum**.

Example

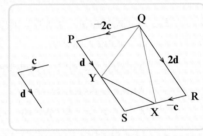

$$\overrightarrow{PY} = \overrightarrow{PQ} + \overrightarrow{QY}$$
$$\overrightarrow{PS} = \overrightarrow{PQ} + \overrightarrow{QR} + \overrightarrow{RS}$$
$$\overrightarrow{YX} = \overrightarrow{YQ} + \overrightarrow{QX}$$

etc.

♦ You can use vector sums to give other vectors.

Example

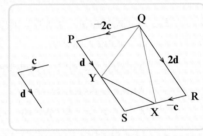

Y is the midpoint of PS;
X is the midpoint of SR.

Give $\overrightarrow{QY}$ and $\overrightarrow{QX}$ in terms of **c** and **d**.

$$\overrightarrow{QY} = \overrightarrow{QP} + \overrightarrow{PY} \qquad \overrightarrow{QX} = \overrightarrow{QR} + \overrightarrow{RX}$$
$$= {}^-2\mathbf{c} + \mathbf{d} \qquad\qquad = 2\mathbf{d} + {}^-\mathbf{c}$$
$$= \mathbf{d} - 2\mathbf{c} \qquad\qquad = 2\mathbf{d} - \mathbf{c}$$

Exercise 24.4
Vectors in space

1 a Give $\overrightarrow{YQ}$ in terms of **c** and **d**.

b Use $\overrightarrow{YX} = \overrightarrow{YQ} + \overrightarrow{QX}$ to show that $\overrightarrow{YX} = \mathbf{c} + \mathbf{d}$.

2 a Give the resultant vector for:

  i $\overrightarrow{EH} + \overrightarrow{HD}$

  ii $\overrightarrow{EF} + \overrightarrow{FG}$

  iii $\overrightarrow{HG} + \overrightarrow{GD} + \overrightarrow{DE}$

  iv $\overrightarrow{EF} + \overrightarrow{FD} + \overrightarrow{DG}$

b List three vector sums that each give the vector $\overrightarrow{FH}$.

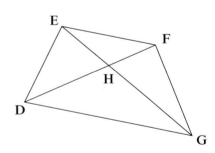

3 a Use $\overrightarrow{FG} = \overrightarrow{FE} + \overrightarrow{ED} + \overrightarrow{DG}$ to show that $\overrightarrow{FG}$ is equal to **q** – **p**.

b Z is the midpoint of FG, so:
$\overrightarrow{FZ} = \frac{1}{2}(\mathbf{q} - \mathbf{p})$

  i Show that:
  $\overrightarrow{EZ} = \frac{1}{2}(3\mathbf{q} - \mathbf{p})$

  ii Give DZ in terms of **p** and **q**.

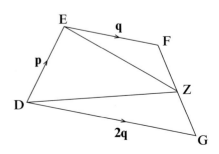

Using vectors

Plane geometry is the study of the properties and relationships of points and lines in two-dimensional space.

◆ You can use vectors to prove facts in plane geometry.

Example

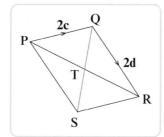

PQRS is a parallelogram.
T is the midpoint of PR:
$PT = \frac{1}{2}PR$

Prove that T is also the midpoint of QS.

$$\overrightarrow{PR} = \overrightarrow{PQ} + \overrightarrow{QR}$$
$$= 2\mathbf{c} + 2\mathbf{d}$$
$$= 2(\mathbf{c} + \mathbf{d})$$
So $\frac{1}{2}\overrightarrow{PR} = \mathbf{c} + \mathbf{d}$

Writing $\overrightarrow{QS}$ and $\overrightarrow{QT}$ in terms of **c** and **d**:

$$\overrightarrow{QS} = \overrightarrow{QR} + \overrightarrow{RS} \qquad \overrightarrow{QT} = \overrightarrow{QP} + \overrightarrow{PT}$$
$$= 2\mathbf{d} + {}^-2\mathbf{c} \qquad\qquad = \overrightarrow{QP} + \frac{1}{2}\overrightarrow{PR}$$
$$= 2\mathbf{d} - 2\mathbf{c} \qquad\qquad = {}^-2\mathbf{c} + \mathbf{c} + \mathbf{d}$$
$$= 2(\mathbf{d} - \mathbf{c}) \qquad\qquad = \mathbf{d} - \mathbf{c}$$

The distance QS is twice the distance QT so,
T must be the midpoint of QS.

Exercise 24.5
Using vectors

1   D is the point so that $PD = 3\mathbf{d} - \mathbf{c}$.
    Use $\overrightarrow{QD} = \overrightarrow{QP} + \overrightarrow{PD}$ to prove that
    D lies on an extension of QS.

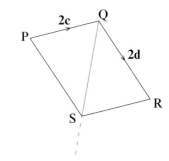

2   In this diagram $DH = \frac{2}{3}DF$.

    a Give these in terms of **p** and **q**.

    i $\overrightarrow{DH}$ **ii** $\overrightarrow{EG}$

    b Prove that $EH = \frac{1}{3}EG$.

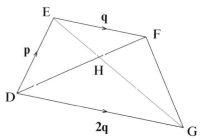

3   OJMN is a parallelogram.
    K is the midpoint of JM.
    The ratio KL : LN is 1 : 2.

    a Give these in terms of **x** and **y**.

    i $\overrightarrow{KN}$ **ii** $\overrightarrow{KL}$

    b Prove that the ratio OL : LM is 2 : 1.

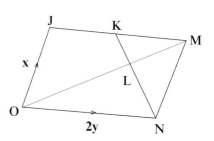

Using parallel vectors

> Other uses of vectors in plane geometry include:
> > to prove that lines are parallel,
> > to prove that points are collinear.

Points are collinear when they all lie in the same straight line.

Example

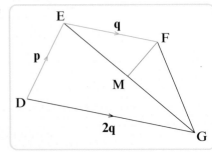

M is the midpoint of EG.

a Prove that MF is parallel to DE.

b If N is the midpoint of DG, prove that N, M, and F are collinear.

$$\overrightarrow{GE} = \overrightarrow{GD} + \overrightarrow{DE}$$
$$= {}^-2q + p$$
$$= p - 2q$$
$$\text{So} \quad \tfrac{1}{2}\overrightarrow{GE}$$
$$= \tfrac{1}{2}(p - 2q)$$

a $\overrightarrow{MF} = \overrightarrow{ME} + \overrightarrow{EF}$

$= \tfrac{1}{2}\overrightarrow{GE} + \overrightarrow{EF}$

$= \tfrac{1}{2}(p - 2q) + q$ $\overrightarrow{MF}$ is in the same direction as $\overrightarrow{DE}$,

$= \tfrac{1}{2}p - q + q$ so MF must be parallel to DE.

$= \tfrac{1}{2}p$

b $\overrightarrow{NF} = \overrightarrow{ND} + \overrightarrow{DE} + \overrightarrow{EF}$ $\overrightarrow{NF}$ is in the same direction as $\overrightarrow{MF}$.

$= {}^-q + p + q$ As point F lies on NF and MF, the

$= p$ points N, M, and F must be collinear.

Exercise 24.6
Using parallel vectors

1 In this diagram,
OV = 2ON and OW = 2OP.
Prove that VW is parallel to NP,
and twice its size.

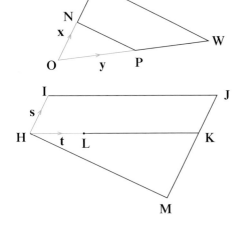

2 HIJK is a parallelogram,
and HL = $\tfrac{1}{3}$HK.
The ratio JK:KM is 1 : 2.

Prove that points I, L, and M
are collinear.

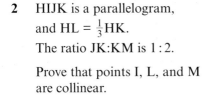

3 In this diagram,
OU = $\tfrac{1}{4}$OT,

OX = $\tfrac{1}{2}$OS,

UW = $\tfrac{1}{2}$US,

V is the midpoint of TS.

Prove that:

a XW is parallel to OT,
b V, W, and X are collinear.

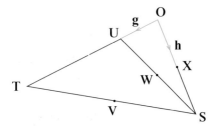

End points

You should be able to ...   ... so try these questions

A Add and subtract
column vectors

$$r = \begin{pmatrix} 2 \\ 1 \end{pmatrix} \qquad s = \begin{pmatrix} 1 \\ 4 \end{pmatrix} \qquad t = \begin{pmatrix} {}^-2 \\ 2 \end{pmatrix}$$

A1 Write each of these as a column vector, and draw it on squared paper.

  a 2s   **b** ⁻3r   **c** r + s   **d** s – t   **e** 2t – r   **f** 2s + t

B Recognise when
vectors are parallel

B1 These vectors include two pairs of parallel vectors.

  3r + s   3s – r   2r + 6s   6r + 2s   2r – 6s

  List each pair.

B2 Use algebra to explain why **2s – t** and **3t – 6s** are parallel vectors.

C Add and subtract
vectors in space

C1 **a** Write CD as a vector sum.
  b Use your vector sum to give
    CD in terms of **p** and **q**.

C2 M is the midpoint of CD.

  a Show that BM = $\frac{1}{2}$(**4p + q**)
  b Give AM in terms of **p** and **q**.

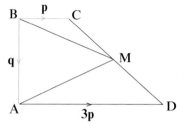

D Use vectors to prove
facts in plane geometry

D1 OPQR is a quadrilateral.
EFGH is another quadrilateral, formed
by joining the midpoints of each side.

  a Give these in terms of **u**, **v**, and **w**.
    i $\overrightarrow{RQ}$ **ii** $\overrightarrow{PG}$
  b Prove that $\overrightarrow{EH} = \overrightarrow{FG}$.
  c Prove that EFGH is a parallelogram.

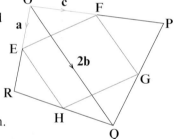

D2 XYZ is a triangle.
L, M, and N are the midpoints of each
of the sides.
The ratio YW:WM is 2:1

  a Give these in terms of **c** and **d**.
    i $\overrightarrow{YM}$ **ii** $\overrightarrow{YW}$ **iii** $\overrightarrow{YZ}$
  b Prove that X, W, and N are collinear.

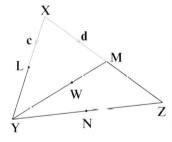

Some points to remember

♦ A vector can be represented in different ways, for example: $\overrightarrow{AB}$ **a** $\begin{pmatrix} x \\ y \end{pmatrix}$

♦ Adding vectors is:
  ❖ commutative   **a + b = b + a**
  ❖ associative   **a + (b + c) = (a + b) + c**

♦ Subtracting a vector has the same effect as adding its negative vector.

Starting points

You need to know about ...

... so try these questions

A Finding a linear rule from a set of data

The speed of a moving object is measured at different times.

Time t (seconds)	0	1	2	3	4	5
Speed v (m s^{-1})	2.4	3.0	3.6	4.0	4.6	5.2

◆ To test for a linear rule, draw a graph of v against t.

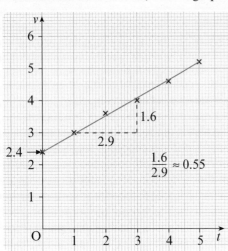

◆ The points lie approximately on a straight line.

◆ To 2 significant figures, the gradient is 0.55 and the y-intercept is 2.4.

◆ So a rule that fits the data approximately is:
$v = 0.55t + 2.4$

A1

A

x	0	1	2	3	4
y	4.1	4.3	4.9	5.5	5.6

B

x	2	4	6	8	10
y	2.1	1.9	19	50	97

C

x	1	2	4	5	9
y	12	18	30	36	60

For each table of values:
a Draw a graph of y against x.
b i Decide if y and x could be linked by a linear rule.
ii Find an approximate equation for any linear rule.

B Sketching quadratic graphs

◆ It is easier to find the minimum or maximum point of a quadratic graph when its equation is given in completed square form.

Example Sketch the graph of $y = (x + 3)^2 - 4$.

◆ When $x = {}^-3$, $(x + 3)^2 = 0$, so the minimum value of y occurs when $x = {}^-3$.

◆ When $x = {}^-3$, $y = ({}^-3 + 3)^2 - 4 = {}^-4$, so the minimum point is $({}^-3, {}^-4)$.

◆ The graph of $y = x^2$ is mapped to the graph of $y = (x + 3)^2 - 4$ by a translation of $\begin{pmatrix} {}^-3 \\ {}^-4 \end{pmatrix}$

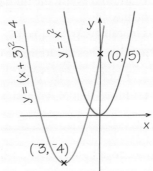

B1 For each equation, sketch a graph and show clearly the coordinates of the minimum or maximum point and the y-intercept.
a $y = (x + 2)^2 + 3$
b $y = (x - 1)^2 + 5$
c $y = (x + 3)^2$
d $y = (x + 5)^2 - 1$
e $y = (x - 8)^2 - 4$

B2 What translation maps the graph of $y = x^2$ to the graph of $y = (x - 6)^2 + 5$?

C Function notation

◆ A rule that maps one number to another is called a function.

Example $f(x) = x^2 + 6$ is a function.
Calculate the value of $f(3)$.
$f(3) = 3^2 + 6 = 9 + 6 = 15$
We say '3 maps to 15' and '15 is the image of 3'.

C1 A function f is defined so that $f(x) = 3x^2 - 5$.
a Calculate the value of:
  i $f(4)$ ii $f({}^-1)$
  iii $f(2.5)$ iv $f(0)$
b Find a value for x so that $f(x) = {}^-3.31$.

Matching graphs

> A symbol that is used for a constant represents a number whose value is fixed.

- The equation of this curve is of the form $y = kx^2 + c$, where k and c are constant.
- The point $(0, 0.5)$ is on the curve so, for these values of x and y:
$$y = kx^2 + c$$
$$0.5 = k \times 0^2 + c$$
$$0.5 = c$$

So the equation is of the form:
$$y = kx^2 + 0.5$$

- The point $(2, 2.9)$ is also on the curve so, for these values of x and y:
$$y = kx^2 + 0.5$$
$$2.9 = k \times 2^2 + 0.5$$
$$2.4 = 4k$$
$$0.6 = k$$

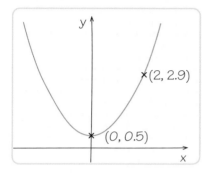

So the equation of the curve is: $y = 0.6x^2 + 0.5$

Exercise 25.1
Matching graphs

1

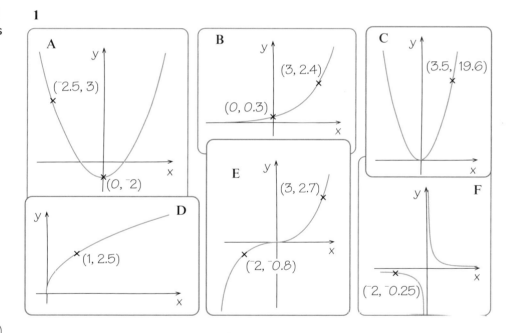

> In all equations in this exercise, p, q and k are constants.

$$y = kx^2 \qquad y = kx^2 + p \qquad y = \frac{k}{x} \qquad y = qx^k \qquad y = k\sqrt{x} \qquad y = pq^x$$

Each equation above matches one of the graphs.

   a For each graph:
     i Write down its matching equation.
     ii Find the value of each constant in its equation.
   b Explain why the equation of curve D could not be of the form $y = qx^4$.

2 The equation of a curve is of the form $y = px^2 + q$.
   The curve passes through the points $(1.5, 15.3)$ and $(^-0.5, 3.3)$.
   Find the values of p and q.

3 A curve has an equation of the form $y = kq^x$.
   It passes through the points $(1, 2)$ and $(2, 8)$.
   Find the values of k and q.

Looking for relationships

Many different equations give curved graphs; for example:
$C = ar^3 + b$, $C = ax + b$.

For circular tables, the cost could be linked to the area (πr^2) of the table so $C = ar^2 + b$ is a likely rule.

If possible, use the table to check your answers are sensible.

♦ This shows the cost of some circular tables.

Radius r (m)	0.4	0.6	0.8	1.0	1.2	1.4
Cost C (£)	175	210	260	320	395	480

♦ Graph C against r to test for a linear rule.

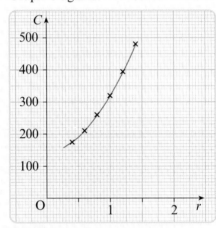

♦ Points on the graph of C against r lie on a curve, so any rule linking C and r is not linear.

♦ C and r could be linked by an equation of the form $C = ar^2 + b$

♦ Graph C against r^2 to test for a rule of the form $C = ar^2 + b$

r^2	0.16	0.36	0.64	1.0	1.44	1.96
C	175	210	260	320	395	480

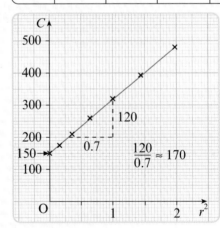

♦ The points lie approximately on a straight line.

♦ To 2 significant figures the gradient is 170 and the y-intercept is 150.

♦ So a rule that fits the data approximately is: $C = 170r^2 + 150$

Exercise 25.2
Finding non-linear rules

1 A stone is dropped and the distance it has fallen is measured at different times.

Time t (seconds)	1	2	3	4	5
Distance fallen d (metres)	5	20	44	78	123

a Draw a graph of d against t^2.
b Explain why your graph shows that a rule of the form $d = kt^2 + p$ approximately fits the data.
c Find a rule of the form $d = kt^2 + p$ that approximately fits the data.
d Use your rule to estimate how far the stone had fallen after 2.5 seconds.
e About how long did it take the stone to fall 100 metres?

2 This table shows the cost of some circular rugs.

Radius r (m)	0.5	1.0	1.5	2.0	2.5	3.0
Cost C (£)	85	145	245	385	565	785

a Draw a graph of C against r^2.
b Use your graph to find a rule that links C and r.
c Estimate the cost of a rug with a radius of 4.5 m.

3 For pendulums of different lengths,
these are the times taken to complete 100 swings.

Length of pendulum l (cm)	Time for 100 swings t (seconds)
5	45
10	63
15	77
20	89
25	100
30	110
35	118
40	126
45	134
50	141

a Draw a graph of t against $\sqrt{l}$.
b Explain why your graph shows that a rule of the form $t = k\sqrt{l}$ approximately fits the data.
c Find the value of k correct to 2 significant figures.
d Estimate how long a pendulum of length 60 cm would take to complete 100 swings.

4 The table below gives information about the planets in our Solar System.

Planet	Average distance from the Sun, R (millions of miles)	Speed at which it travels through space, V (mph)	Time taken to go once round the Sun, T (days)
Earth	93	66 641	365
Jupiter	484	29 216	4329
Mars	142	53 980	687
Mercury	36	107 132	88
Neptune	2794	12 147	60 150
Pluto	3674	10 604	90 670
Saturn	887	21 565	10 753
Uranus	1784	15 234	30 660
Venus	67	78 364	225

Hypotheses are statements that are thought to be true but have not yet been proved.

These are some hypotheses about relationships between R, V and T, where p, q and n are constants.

$\boxed{A}$ $V \approx \dfrac{p}{\sqrt{R}}$ $\boxed{B}$ $V \approx n\sqrt{T}$ $\boxed{C}$ $T \approx q\sqrt{R^3}$

a Draw suitable straight-line graphs to show which hypotheses are correct.
b Find the value of the constants in the correct hypotheses.

Transforming graphs

Exercise 25.3
Transforming graphs

1

Each straight line continues
for ever.

a Which line is the image of $y = 2x + 3$ after a translation of $\begin{pmatrix} 1 \\ -3 \end{pmatrix}$?

b Give three different translations that map $y = 2x - 2$ to $y = 2x + 3$.

c Which line is the image of $y = 2x + 3$ after a rotation of $^-90°$ about $(0, 3)$?

d Describe a reflection that maps $y = \frac{1}{2}x - 3$ to $y = ^-\frac{1}{2}x + 3$.

2 **a** On a set of axes, draw graphs of:

   i $y = 2x + 1$ **ii** $y = ^-3x - 4$ **iii** $y = \frac{1}{2}x - 1$.

b For each line, find the equation of the image after reflection in the y-axis.

c Without drawing, give the equation of the image of $y = 4x - 3$ after reflection in the y-axis. Explain your method.

3 Give the equation of the image of $y - x = 8$ after reflection in the y-axis.

4 **a** On a set of axes, draw graphs of:

   i $y = x + 1$ **ii** $y = ^-2x + 3$ **iii** $y = \frac{1}{4}x - 1$.

b For each line, find the equation of the image after reflection in the x-axis.

c Without drawing, give the equation of the image of $y = ^-5x + 1$ after reflection in the x-axis. Explain your method.

5 **a** Find three different translations that map $y = x - 1$ to $y = x + 5$.

b Describe the link between p and q when $y = x - 1$ is mapped.

   to $y = x + 5$ after a translation of $\begin{pmatrix} p \\ q \end{pmatrix}$.

6 What is the equation of the image of $y = 3x + 1$ after a translation of $\begin{pmatrix} v \\ w \end{pmatrix}$?

7 Find the image of $y = kx + l$ after a translation of $\begin{pmatrix} a \\ b \end{pmatrix}$.

◆ If a function f is defined so that $f(x) = x^2$, then $y = x^2$ can be written as $y = f(x)$.

◆ Other equations can be expressed in terms of this function f, and their graphs can be drawn.

Example 1
Draw a graph for the equation $y = f(x) + 2$.

Graph of $y = f(x) + 2$ and $y = f(x)$

x	$y = f(x) + 2$		y
⁻3	$f(⁻3) + 2 = (⁻3)^2 + 2$	$=$	11
⁻2	$f(⁻2) + 2 = (⁻2)^2 + 2$	$=$	6
⁻1	$f(⁻1) + 2 = (⁻1)^2 + 2$	$=$	3
0	$f(0) + 2 = (0)^2 + 2$	$=$	2
1	$f(1) + 2 = (1)^2 + 2$	$=$	3
2	$f(2) + 2 = (2)^2 + 2$	$=$	6
3	$f(3) + 2 = (3)^2 + 2$	$=$	11

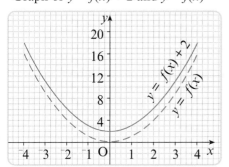

Example 2
Draw a graph for the equation $y = f(x + 2)$.

Graph of $y = f(x + 2)$ and $y = f(x)$

x	$y = f(x + 2)$		y
⁻3	$f(⁻3 + 2) = f(⁻1) = (⁻1)^2$	$=$	1
⁻2	$f(⁻2 + 2) = f(0) = 0^2$	$=$	0
⁻1	$f(⁻1 + 2) = f(1) = 1^2$	$=$	1
0	$f(0 + 2) = f(2) = 2^2$	$=$	4
1	$f(1 + 2) = f(3) = 3^2$	$=$	9
2	$f(2 + 2) = f(4) = 4^2$	$=$	16
3	$f(3 + 2) = f(5) = 5^2$	$=$	25

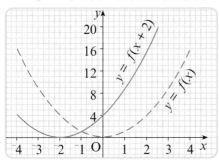

Exercise 25.4
Using function notation

1 A function g is defined so that $g(x) = 2x - 1$.
On one set of axes, draw graphs of:

   a $y = g(x)$ **b** $y = g(x) + 5$ **c** $y = g(x + 5)$

2 A function h is defined so that $h(x) = x^2 + 3$.

   a On one set of axes, draw graphs of:
      i $y = h(x)$ **ii** $y = h(x - 2)$ **iii** $y = h(x) - 2$
   b Describe a transformation that maps $y = h(x)$ to $y = h(x - 2)$.

3 This is the graph of a function $y = g(x)$.

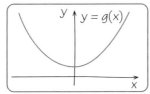

Which of these could be the graph of $y = g(x) - 4$?

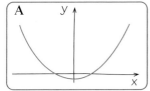

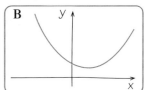

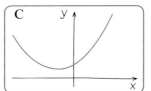

4 A function f is defined so that $f(x) = x^2$.

    a On one set of axes, draw graphs of:

        i $y = f(x)$ **ii** $y = f(x + 3)$ **iii** $y = f(x + 3) + 2$

    b Describe a transformation that maps $y = f(x)$ to $y = f(x + 3) + 2$.

5 A student makes the following statement:

> For any function f, a translation of $\begin{pmatrix} ^-4 \\ 5 \end{pmatrix}$ will map the
>
> graph of y = f(x) to y = f(x − 4) + 5. ✗

    Explain what is wrong with this statement.

6 Two functions are defined so that $g(x) = x^2 + 1$ and $h(x) = x - 4$

    a On one set of axes, sketch graphs of:

        i $y = g(x)$ **ii** $y = h(x)$

        iii $y = {}^-g(x)$ **iv** $y = {}^-h(x)$

    b **i** Describe a transformation that maps $y = g(x)$ to $y = {}^-g(x)$ and also maps $y = h(x)$ to $y = {}^-h(x)$.

        ii Do you think this transformation will map $y = f(x)$ to $y = {}^-f(x)$ for any function f? Explain your answer fully.

> Your sketches should show:
> ◆ the shape of the graph
> ◆ the coordinates of any y-intercepts.

7 A function k is defined so that $k(x) = 4x - 5$.

    a On one set of axes, draw graphs of $y = k(x)$ and $y = k({}^-x)$.

    b Describe a transformation that maps $y = k(x)$ to $y = k({}^-x)$.

    c Do you think this transformation will map $y = k(x)$ to $y = k({}^-x)$ for any function k? Explain your answer fully.

8 For $g(x) = x^2$, explain why the graphs of $y = g(x)$ and $y = g({}^-x)$ are the same.

9 This is a sketch of the graph of a function $y = p(x)$.

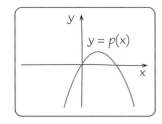

    Which of the sketches below could be the graph of:

    a $y = {}^-p(x)$ **b** $y = p({}^-x)$?

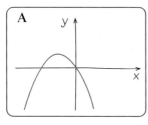 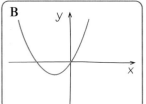 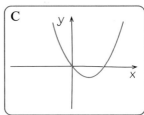

10 A function g is defined so that $g(x) = x^2 - 3$.

    a Draw sketch graphs of:

        i $y = g(x)$ **ii** $y = g(2x)$ **iii** $y = 2g(x)$.

        iv $y = \left(\frac{1}{4}\right)g(x)$ **v** $y = g\left(\frac{1}{4}x\right)$ **vi** $y = {}^-g(2x)$

    b Comment on your results.

11 Sketch $y = f(x)$ where $f(x) = x^2$.

    On separate diagrams, sketch graphs of:

    a $y = {}^-f(x) + 5$ **b** $y = f({}^-3x)$ **c** $y = f\left(\frac{1}{2}x\right) - 4$

12 This is a sketch graph of the
function $y = f(x)$ where $f(x) = x^2 - 4x + 5$.

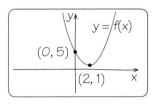

For the following sets of equations and
graphs, match each equation to a graph.

a $y = f(^-x)$ **b** $y = f(x + 5)$ **c** $y = f(2x)$

d $y = f\left(\frac{1}{2}x\right)$ **e** $y = {}^-f(x) + 10$ **f** $y = f(x - 3) - 2$

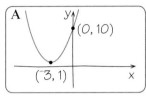
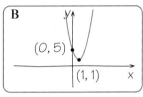
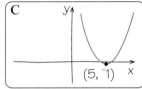

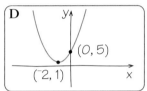
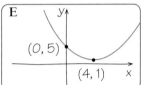
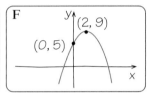

Using graphs only

This is part of the graph of a function $y = f(x)$.
From this you can draw other related graphs.

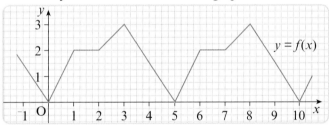

Example   Draw the graph of $y = f(2x)$ for $0 \leqslant x \leqslant 5$.

In this example, you can only
find values for $y = f(2x)$
from the graph of $y = f(x)$.

One way to draw the graph is to
find values for $y = f(2x)$.

♦ Choose some values for x and
find the corresponding y values.

x	$y = f(2x)$	y
0	$f(2 \times 0) = f(0)$	$= 0$
1	$f(2 \times 1) = f(2)$	$= 2$
2	$f(2 \times 2) = f(4)$	$= 1.5$
3	$f(2 \times 3) = f(6)$	$= 2$
4	$f(2 \times 4) = f(8)$	$= 3$
5	$f(2 \times 5) = f(10)$	$= 0$

♦ Plot the points.

♦ Decide how the graph of $y = f(2x)$ is
linked to the graph of $y = f(x)$.
(Find more values for y if needed:
e.g. for $x = 0.5$, $y = f(1) = 2$
for $x = 1.5$, $y = f(3) = 3$.)

When transforming graphs,
draw the transformed graph
on axes that use the same
scales as the original graph.

♦ Draw the graph.

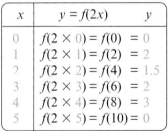

Exercise 25.5
Transforming graphs

1 Using the graph of $y = f(x)$ above, draw the graph of:

a $y = f(x + 2)$ for $0 \leqslant x \leqslant 5$ **b** $y = 2f(x)$ for $0 \leqslant x \leqslant 5$.

2 The graph of $y = p(x)$ is drawn for $^-2 \leqslant x \leqslant 6$.

a For $0 \leqslant x \leqslant 3$ draw graphs of:

i $y = \frac{1}{2}p(x)$

ii $y = p(x - 2)$

iii $y = -p(x)$

iv $y = p(2x)$

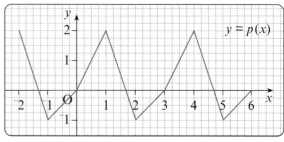

b Describe the transformation that maps the graph of $y = p(x)$ to $y = ^-p(x)$.

c Find two values of x for which $p(x + 2) = 0$.

3 The graph of $y = g(x)$ is drawn for $^-5 \leqslant x \leqslant 5$.

a For $^-4 \leqslant x \leqslant 4$ draw graphs of:

i $y = g(x) + 3$

ii $y = g(x + 1) - 2$

iii $y = g(-x)$

iv $y = g\left(\frac{x}{2}\right)$.

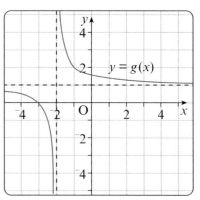

> It may help to work out where the asymptotes will be first.

b Which transformation maps the graph of $y = g(x)$ to $y = g(x + 1) - 2$?

c Find a value of x for which $g(x) = ^-g(x)$.

4 This is the graph of $y = h(x)$.

a Estimate values of x for which:

i $h(x) = 2$

ii $h(^-x) = -2$

iii $h(x + 3) = 3$.

b Sketch graphs of:

i $y = h\left(\frac{x}{3}\right)$

ii $y = ^-h(x) - 1$

iii $y = h(x - 1) + 1$.

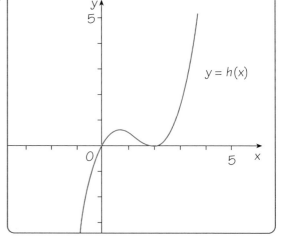

5 The graph of $y = k(x)$ is drawn for $0 \leqslant x \leqslant 4$.

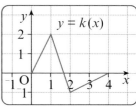

Write down, in terms of k, the equation of each graph below.

A

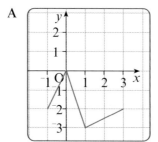

B

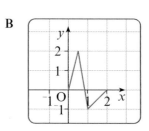

End points

You should be able to ...   ... so try these questions

A Calculate constants in equations from coordinates on graphs

A1 The equation of this curve is of the form $y = pq^x$, where p and q are constants.

Find the value of p and q.

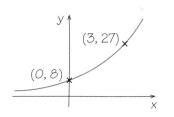

B Find rules by drawing linear graphs

B1 This table shows the cost of some square tablecloths.

Width (x m)	0.6	0.8	1.0	1.2	1.4	1.6
Cost (£ C)	7.50	8.50	9.80	10.40	13.25	15.40

a Draw a graph of C against x^2.
b It is claimed that C and x are linked by a formula of the type:

$$C = ax^2 + b$$

  i Explain why your graph supports this claim.
  ii Estimate the values of a and b.
c Estimate the cost of a tablecloth that is 1.5 m wide.

C Transform graphs of functions

C1 This is the graph of a function $y = f(x)$ for $^-4 \leqslant x \leqslant 6$.

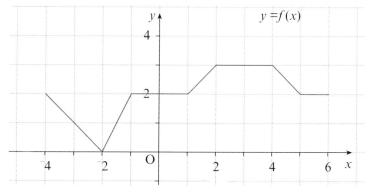

a For $0 \leqslant x \leqslant 4$, draw the graph of:

  i $y = f\left(\dfrac{x}{2}\right)$ ii $y = f(x + 1)$ iii $f(^-x)$.

b Write down, in terms of f, the equation of this graph.

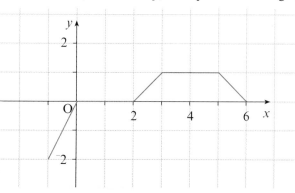

Bananananananananananananananananananananana
On 30 April 1988 in Selinsgrove Pennsylvania USA a banana split was made which was 7.32 km long.

On 31 May 1682 there was a cloudburst in Oxford which gave 24 inches of water in less than a quarter of an hour.
A slight shower!

Jo's always on hand
In 1900 Johann Hurlinger of Austria walked 871 miles from Vienna to Paris on his hands. His average speed was 1.58 mph and he walked for 10 hours each day.

OH! WHAT A LITTLE ONE-WHEEL
In March 1994 in Las Vegas Peter Rosendahl of Sweden rode a unicycle 20 centimetre high for a distance of 3.6 metres. The wheel diameter was only 2.5 cm.

Up the pole!
Mellissa Sanders lived in a hut at the top of a pole in Indianapolis USA for two years starting on 10 October 1986. Her hut measured 1.8 metres wide by 2.1 metres deep.

Stacks of cards!
In 1995 Brian Berg of Spirit Lake Iowa USA built a tower of playing cards with 83 stories. The tower was 4.88 metres high. In 1978 James Warnock of Canada held the previous record with 60 stories.

Number types
On 14 October 1993 Mikhail Shestov set a record when he had typed the numbers 1 to 795 on a PC by the time 5 minutes was up. He had made no errors.

Unique cycle on unicycle
Takayuki Koike of Japan rode 100 miles on a unicycle in a record time of 6 hours, 44 minutes and 21 seconds on 9 August 1987.

Rail Trick
The Katoomba Scenic Railway in New South Wales in Australia is the steepest railway in the world. Its gradient is 1 in 0.8 but it is only 310 metres long. The ride takes about 1 minute 40 seconds and carries about 420 000 passengers a year.

The circumference of the Earth at the equator is 40 075 km and its mass is 5880 000 000 000 000 000 000 tons.
Weight watchers

Piece on earth
A jigsaw with 1500 wooden pieces was made for the photograph on the cover of the BEEB magazine. The jigsaw was assembled in 1985 by students from schools in Canterbury. It measured 22.31 metres by 13.79 metres.

Tall stories
The tallest man in the world was Robert Wadlow from Alton Illinois in the USA who was 8 feet 11.1 inches tall. The tallest man in Scotland was Angus Macaskill from the Western Isles who was 7 feet 9 inches tall. The highest mountain in the USA is Mount McKinley at 20 320 feet and the highest one in Scotland is Ben Nevis at 4408 feet.

Can beans be hasbeens?
Baked beans were first introduced into the UK in 1928. By 1992 they were selling at the rate of 55.8 million cans per year.

The swift hare and the XJ tortoise
In 1992 the Jaguar XJ220 set the land speed record for a road car of 217 miles per hour.
The spine-tailed swift has been recorded as flying at 220 miles per hour. Will this mean that Brands Hatch is converted for spine-tailed swift racing?

Can can or cannot
A square based pyramid tower of 4900 cans was built by 5 adults and 5 children at Dunhurst School, Petersfield on 30 May 1994 in a time of 25 minutes 54 seconds.

Barmy salami
A salami is usually about 9cm in diameter and about 35cm long, but at Flekkefjord in Norway in July 1992 a giant salami was made which had a circumference of 63.4 cm and was 20.95 metres long.

AMAZING FACTS
p9

1   Calculate the height of James Warnock's tower of cards in 1978.

2   Give the weight of the Earth in standard form.

3   Give the circumference of the Earth to:
    a   4 significant figures   **b**   3 significant figures.

4   **a**   Calculate the volume of the Earth in km³.
    b   Calculate the Earth's density in tons/km³.

5   For Peter Rosendahl's mini unicycle give:
    a   the height of the bike in metres
    b   the distance he travelled in millimetres
    c   the number of revolutions the wheel would make over a journey of 100 miles.

6   How many days was it between when Mellissa Sanders came down from her pole hut and Mikhail Shestov set his number typing record?

7   Convert the height of water that fell on Oxford in less than a quarter of an hour to metres.

8   If the Canterbury jigsaw had been out in the Oxford rain, what volume of water would have landed on it?

9   Taking 1 mile as 1.609 km, what was the average speed of Takayuki Koike's unicycle ride:
    a   in miles per hour   **b**   in metres per second?

10 How long would it take Taayuki Koike to unicycle along the length of the Selinsgrove banana split if he always unicycles at the same average speed?

11 How many of the giant banana splits would fit end to end round the equator? Give your answer in standard form to a suitable degree of accuracy.

12 A salami is roughly shaped like a cylinder. Use this to calculate the approximate surface area of a normal salami.

13 **a**   Calculate the diameter of the Flekkefjord salami in centimetres.
    b   Calculate the volume of the Flekkefjord salami in cm³.
    c   The density of salami is about 1.01 g/cm³. Calculate the mass (weight) of the giant salami in kg.

14 If the capacity of Mellisa Sanders's hut on a pole was 6.62 metres³, what was its approximate surface area in meters²? Give your answer to 3 sf.

15 Give the ratio of the length of the giant salami to the length of the giant banana split in the form $1:n$, to the nearest whole number.

16 **a**   What is the ratio
    tallest man : highest mountain
    in the form $1:n$ for:
    i   the USA   **ii**   Scotland?
    b   If this ratio for Scotland were the same as for the USA, how high would the tallest man in Scotland have been, to the nearest foot?

17 For the numbers 1 to 12, fifteen digits are used.
    a   How many digits are in the numbers 1 to 100?
    b   How many digits had Mikhail Shestov typed in by the time five minutes was up?
    c   What was Mikhail Shestov's typing speed in digits per second (to nearest whole number)?

18 For how many days was Johann Hurlinger walking on his hands when he travelled between Paris and Vienna?

19 **a**   At what angle does the Katoomba Scenic Railway climb?
    b   How many metres does the railway rise over its entire length?
    c   What is the average speed of the train in km per hour?

20 The spine-tailed swallow and the Jaguar XJ220 race together at their maximum speeds over a course of 240 miles. How long will the swallow have to wait for the Jaguar at the finish line?

21 A baked bean can has a diameter of 7.4 cm and a height of 10.5 cm.
    a   What was the total volume of the cans in the Petersfield tower in m³?
    b   In 1992 what volume of beans was eaten. Give your answer in metres³ to 2 sf in standard form.

22 The pyramid of cans in Petersfield had one can on the top layer and each can in the stack rested on four cans below. One can is 10.5 cm tall. Calculate:
    a   the total number of cans in the top three layers
    b   the number of stories in the Petersfield pyramid
    c   the height of the tower in metres.

23 Imagine that as baked bean cans are bought in the UK they are emptied then lined up end to end round the equator. After roughly how long would they encircle the Earth?

24 Lands End to John O'Groats is 886 miles.
    a   How many giant salamis long is this?
    b   If the giant salami was rolled along this distance, how many rotations would it make?

25 Give the ratio
    Banana split : Stab an Alp plant in a basin
    in its simplest terms.
    Hint: think of a bananagram!

Fractions

1 For each of the following pairs of numbers, find:
  - **i** the highest common factor
  - **ii** the lowest common multiple.

  a 2 and 7   **b** 25 and 30
  c 28 and 63   **d** 10 and 100
  d 36 and 126   **f** 660 and 1260

2 Give each answer as a fraction in its lowest terms. Write fractions greater than 1 as mixed numbers.

  a $\frac{1}{4} + \frac{1}{9}$ **b** $2\frac{1}{2} - 1\frac{1}{3}$ **c** $\frac{3}{5} + \frac{1}{10}$

  d $3\frac{1}{5} - 2\frac{3}{10}$ **e** $\frac{2}{3} - \frac{1}{24}$ **f** $1\frac{1}{2} + \frac{4}{9}$

  g $1\frac{5}{12} + 2\frac{7}{8}$ **h** $\frac{3}{4} - \frac{1}{22}$ **i** $5\frac{1}{4} - 3\frac{5}{8}$

3 Give each answer as a fraction in its lowest terms. Write fractions greater than 1 as improper fractions.

  a $\frac{2}{3} \times 2\frac{1}{2}$ **b** $\frac{5}{6} \div \frac{2}{3}$ **c** $\frac{3}{4} \div \frac{1}{2}$

  d $1\frac{1}{3} \times 2\frac{1}{4}$ **e** $3\frac{4}{5} \div \frac{3}{4}$ **f** $\frac{8}{9} \times \frac{9}{10}$

  g $4\frac{1}{6} \div \frac{3}{5}$ **h** $\frac{1}{2} \times \frac{2}{5} \times \frac{3}{10}$

4 Find the value of these, in fractional form, when $x = \frac{1}{3}$, $y = \frac{2}{5}$ and $z = \frac{3}{10}$.

  a $5(x + y)$ **b** $\frac{x}{z}$ **c** $z^2 x$

  d $\frac{y - z}{x}$ **e** $\frac{1}{x} + \frac{1}{y}$ **f** $\frac{z}{y - x}$

5 Find the value of these, in fractional form, when $p = 2$, $q = \frac{1}{4}$ and $r = \frac{2}{3}$.

  a pqr **b** $(r - q)^2$ **c** $q(p - r)$

  d $\frac{q}{p}$ **e** $\frac{1}{p} + \frac{1}{q}$ **f** $\frac{1}{p - q}$

6 If $\frac{1}{f} = \frac{2}{g} + \frac{3}{k}$

  what is the value of f, in fractional form, when:

  a $g = 4$ and $k = 8$ **b** $g = 3$ and $k = 5$
  c $g = 6$ and $k = 7$ **d** $g = 5$ and $k = 2$

7 Find two different unit fractions that add to give:

  a $\frac{2}{3}$ **b** $\frac{1}{4}$ **c** $\frac{1}{9}$

8 In a magic square, the sums of the numbers in each row, column and diagonal are equal.

Square A

$\frac{3}{2}$	$\frac{1}{3}$	
$\frac{2}{3}$		
$\frac{5}{6}$		

Square B

$2\frac{1}{4}$	$\frac{1}{2}$	$2\frac{2}{3}$
2	$1\frac{11}{12}$	$1\frac{5}{6}$
$1\frac{1}{6}$	$3\frac{1}{3}$	$1\frac{1}{4}$

  a Copy and complete Square A so that it is a magic square.
  b Square B is not a magic square. How could you change one of the fractions to make a magic square?

9 Find four pairs of equivalent expressions.

  Ⓐ $\dfrac{x}{x(x + 5)}$ Ⓑ $\dfrac{x + 5}{x(x + 5)}$ Ⓒ $\dfrac{2}{x + 5}$

  Ⓓ $\dfrac{1}{x + 5}$ Ⓔ $\dfrac{1}{x(x + 5)}$ Ⓕ $\dfrac{3}{x}$

  Ⓖ $\dfrac{4}{2(x + 5)}$ Ⓗ $\dfrac{1}{x}$ Ⓘ $\dfrac{3x}{x^2}$

10 Write each of these as a single fraction. Give each answer in its simplest form.

  a $\frac{x}{3} + \frac{x}{9}$ **b** $\frac{2}{x} \times \frac{x}{5}$ **c** $\frac{7}{x} - \frac{4}{x}$

  d $\frac{7x}{3} \div \frac{x}{9}$ **e** $\frac{2x}{5} - \frac{x}{10}$ **f** $\frac{3}{x} + \frac{1}{3x}$

  g $\frac{x}{2} + \frac{y}{7}$ **h** $\frac{3}{x} - \frac{1}{x + 4}$ **i** $\frac{x}{4} - \frac{y}{2}$

  j $\frac{5}{x} \times \frac{x}{x - 1}$ **k** $\frac{x}{x + 2} \div \frac{x}{x - 1}$ **l** $\frac{1}{x} + \frac{2}{y}$

  m $\frac{4}{x} + \frac{1}{x - 1}$ **n** $\frac{1}{x} - \frac{x}{y}$ **o** $\frac{1}{x + 4} \div \frac{1}{x - 1}$

  p $\frac{2}{x + 1} + \frac{3}{x + 2}$ **q** $\frac{2}{x + 1} + \frac{3}{x + 2}$

  r $\frac{5}{x + 3} + \frac{1}{x + 3}$ **s** $\frac{2}{x} - \frac{1}{x + 2}$

  t $\frac{1}{x - 1} + \frac{5}{x + 2}$ **u** $\frac{5}{x + 1} + \frac{1}{y + 2}$

11 Copy and complete:

  a $\dfrac{\square}{x} - \dfrac{3}{x - 3} = \dfrac{3(x - 6)}{x(x - 3)}$

  b $\dfrac{1}{x + 1} + \dfrac{\square}{x - 1} = \dfrac{2(5x + 4)}{(x + 1)(x - 1)}$

Properties of shapes

1

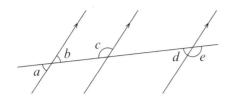

  a If $a = 47°$, calculate angles b to e.
  b If $a = 51.5°$, calculate the angles b to e.
  c If $e = 169°$, calculate angles a to d.

2 These polygons are drawn on a grid of parallel lines. The diagonals of PQRS are marked in red.

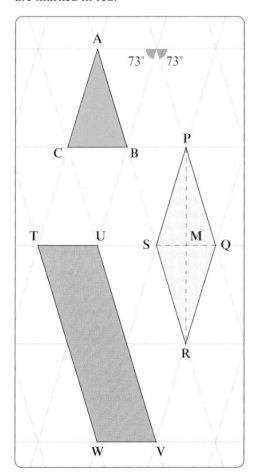

  a Work out each interior angle of ΔABC.
  b What type of triangle is ABC?
  c Work out each interior angle of:
    i PQRS   **ii** TUVW.
  d Explain why PQRS is a rhombus.
  e Explain why TUVW cannot be a rhombus.
  f The diagonals of PQRS intersect at M. Work out each of these angles:
    i PM̂Q   **ii** PQ̂M   **iii** MQ̂R
    iv QR̂M   **v** SR̂M

3 These quadrilaterals are on an isometric grid.

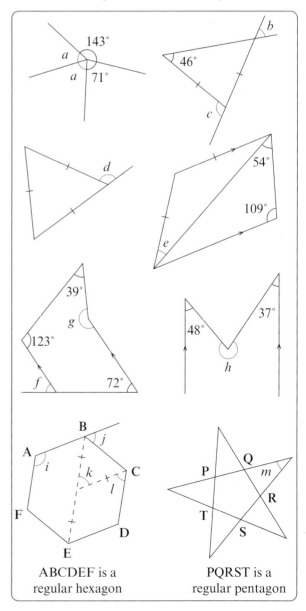

  a Show how each of these quadrilaterals will tessellate on its own.
  b Show how they will tessellate together.

4 Calculate the angles a to m in the diagram below.

ABCDEF is a regular hexagon

PQRST is a regular pentagon

Manipulation

1 Multiply these terms.

   a $mn \times mn$ **b** $pq \times 4p$ **c** $9b \times 2a^2$

   d $a^3 \times g^3$ **e** $4p \times 5p^2$ **f** $7a^3 \times 4b$

2 Multiply out these brackets.

   a $6(4a - 3b)$ **b** $p(n - p)$ **c** $s(s + t)$

   d $6m(n - m)$ **e** $5x(x + y)$ **f** $u(4u + 3)$

   g $p(5q + 3r)$ **h** $3n(4m + 7n)$ **i** $9a(3b + a)$

3 Simplify these.

   a $8n + 4m - 6n + 3m$ **b** $12a^2 - a + 9a^2$

   c $b^3 + 2b - b^3$ **d** $8x - 4xy - 2y + 6xy$

   e $p + 8q - 5q + 3p$ **f** $8p^2 + 3pq + 5q^2 - pq$

   g $4m^2 + mn - 6n + nm$ **h** $x + 2xy + x - 4xy$

4 Which of these expressions is equivalent to
$4a(2ab + 3a) + a(5b - a) + 4b(2a^2 + 5a)$?

   A $35a^2b + 11a^2$

   B $12a^2b + 14ab + 7a^2$

   C $41ab + 10a$

   D $16a^2b + 11a^2 + 25ab$

5 Multiply these out and simplify

   a $x(6x - 2) + 2x(5x + 3)$

   b $8x(2y + 3x) + x(6x - 3y)$

   c $6(p + 2q) - 3(4p + 2q)$

   d $4(3a + b) - (3a - 2b)$

   e $p(5p - 4) - 2(2p^2 - 3)$

6 Write each of these as a single fraction.

   a $\dfrac{3}{p + 1} + \dfrac{5}{p - 1}$ **b** $\dfrac{5}{p + 4} - \dfrac{3}{p + 2}$

   c $\dfrac{1}{2p + 1} + \dfrac{3}{3p - 2}$ **d** $\dfrac{p + 4}{3} - \dfrac{p - 3}{6}$

7 Write an expression for the width of rectangles A and B.

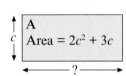

A Area $= 2c^2 + 3c$, height c, width $?$

B Area $= 6a + 8ab$, height $2a$, width $?$

8 Factorise these fully.

   a $7p + 3pq$ **b** $m + 3mn$ **c** $8pq + 4q$

   d $3y - 12xy$ **e** $2b^2 + 10b$ **f** $18ab + 24bc$

   g $x^2y - 2xy$ **h** $9a^2b + 6ab^2$ **i** $12m^2n - 9mn$

9 Multiply out these brackets and simplify.

   a $(w + 2)(w + 6)$ **b** $(y + 9)(y + 5)$

   c $(x - 3)^2$ **d** $(v - 2)(v - 3)$

   e $(b - 3)(b - 5)$ **f** $(b - 3)(b - 5)$

   g $(h + 5)(h - 5)$ **h** $(t - 3)(t + 3)$

10 Multiply out these brackets and simplify.

   a $(2w - 3)(2w + 3)$ **b** $(2p + 1)^2$

   c $(5x + 6)(3x - 2)$ **d** $(3g - 7)(4g - 5)$

11

$x + 1$	$x + 2$	$x + 3$	$x + 4$	$x + 6$	$x + 12$

Which pair of expressions multiply to give:

   a $x^2 + 7x + 12$ **b** $x^2 + 8x + 12$ **c** $x^2 + 7x + 6$

   d $x^2 + 5x + 6$ **e** $x^2 + 13x + 12$ **f** $x^2 + 6x + 8$?

12 Factorise the following expressions.

   a $x^2 + 4x + 4$ **b** $x^2 + 9x + 20$ **c** $x^2 + 3x - 4$

   d $x^2 + 2x - 15$ **e** $x^2 - x - 6$ **f** $x^2 - 11x + 10$

   g $x^2 - 2x - 8$ **h** $x^2 - 3x + 2$ **i** $x^2 - 4x + 4$

13 Simplify each of these

   a $\dfrac{3x - 6}{x^2 + x - 6}$ **b** $\dfrac{6(x - 3) - 2(x - 3)}{x^2 + 3x - 18}$

14

$x - 6$	$x - 3$	$x - 2$	$x + 1$	$x + 2$	$x + 3$

Which pair of expressions multiply to give:

   a $x^2 + x - 6$ **b** $x^2 - 2x - 3$ **c** $x^2 - 5x + 6$

   d $x^2 - 4$ **e** $x^2 + 5x + 6$ **f** $x^2 - 9$?

15 Factorise these fully.

   a $3x^2 + 13x + 12$ **b** $3x^2 - 15x + 12$

   c $2x^2 - 9x + 4$ **d** $6x^2 - 3x - 3$

   e $3x^2 - 6x$ **f** $9x^2 - 25y^2$

16 Find the values of p and q such that for all values of x:

   a $x^2 - px + 16 = (x - q)^2$ **b** $x^2 - 6x + p = (x - q)^2$

17 Write each of these as a single fraction in its simplest form.

   a $\dfrac{4}{p - 3} + \dfrac{3}{p + 1}$ **b** $\dfrac{2}{(a - b)^2} - \dfrac{3}{2(a - b)}$

   c $\dfrac{15p^2}{8a} \div \dfrac{10p}{12a^3}$ **d** $\dfrac{2}{p + 1} \times \dfrac{3}{p - 1}$

18 **a** Factorise $p^2 - q^2$.

   b In the equation $p^2 - q^2 = 149$, p and q are positive integers.

      i Explain why there is only one solution.

      ii Explain why $(p - q)$ must equal 1.

      iii Find the value of p and q.

19 Use the difference of two squares to calculate the exact value of:
$132\,413\,241\,324^2 - 132\,413\,241\,323^2$

20 Copy and complete:
$$\dfrac{\square\square\square}{x + 1} + \dfrac{3}{x} = \dfrac{x^2 + 5x + 3}{x(x + 1)}$$

Comparing data

1 These are the round scores from a competition.

| 60 | 68 | 52 | 68 |
| 64 | 72 | 64 | **Dina** |

| 57 | 61 | 59 |
| 68 | 61 | 75 | **Cian** |

| 58 | 59 | 63 | 65 | 57 |
| 70 | 68 | 74 | **Joe** |

For each set of scores, calculate:

a the mean
b the mean deviation
c the standard deviation.

2 If Joe had scored 15 less in each round, what would the mean and standard deviation of his scores have been?

3 Dina improved each of her round scores by 25% in the next competition.
Give the new mean and standard deviation.

4

Ring score	2	3	4	5	6	7	8	9
Frequency	2	1	3	2	3	6	4	3	**Sally**

Ring score	2	3	4	5	6	7	8	9
Frequency	1	1	3	7	14	13	6	7

Gavin

a For each distribution, calculate:
　　i the mean
　　ii the standard deviation
b Compare the two distributions.

5

Peggy

Ring score	2	3	4	5	6	7	8
Frequency	1	0	2	3	5	4	1

Ring score	3	4	5	6	7	8	9
Frequency	2	4	5	4	6	0	1

Toby

Ring score	2	3	4	5	6	7	8	9
Frequency	2	1	3	2	3	6	4	3

Sue

a For each distribution:
　　i find the median
　　ii calculate the interquartile range.
b Compare the three distributions.

	Number of chips								
Restaurant	34	35	36	37	38	39	40	41	Total
P	8	10	14	9	6	5	4	4	60
Q	8	7	5	9	12	11	8	0	60
R	0	3	5	10	12	14	10	6	60

6 For each restaurant:
　a find the median number of chips
　b calculate the interquartile range
　c draw a box-and-whisker plot.

7 **a** Draw frequency polygons for restaurant P and restaurant R on the same diagram.
　b Compare the two distributions.

8

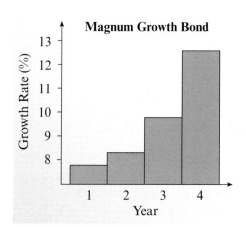

Magnum Growth Bond

Vector Videos
Total Sales (000's)

Explain why each of these diagrams is misleading.

9

𝒲𝒟	*Wilton Dale Theme Parks*	
	1994	**1996**
A Number of injuries	21	14
B Number of rides	6	15

Draw a misleading diagram to show each of these sets of data.

Sequences

1 Each diagram shows the first three patterns in a sequence.

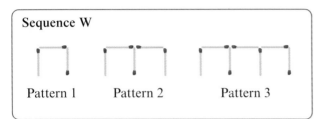

Sequence W

Pattern 1   Pattern 2   Pattern 3

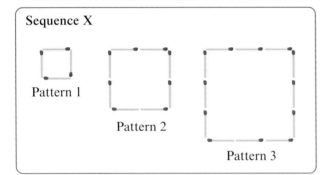

Sequence X

Pattern 1

Pattern 2

Pattern 3

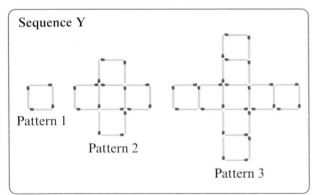

Sequence Y

Pattern 1

Pattern 2

Pattern 3

For each sequence:

 a Draw the 4th pattern.

 b Find the general term for the sequence.
   Write it in the form $a_n = \dots$.

 c Use the general term to calculate the number
   of matches in the 10th pattern.

2 Copy and complete each mapping diagram.

a
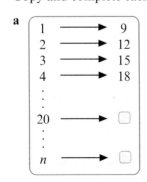

1 ⟶ 9
2 ⟶ 12
3 ⟶ 15
4 ⟶ 18
⋮
20 ⟶ ☐
⋮
n ⟶ ☐

b
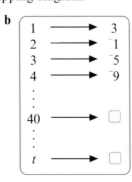

1 ⟶ 3
2 ⟶ ‾1
3 ⟶ ‾5
4 ⟶ ‾9
⋮
40 ⟶ ☐
⋮
t ⟶ ☐

3 These are the first three patterns in a sequence.

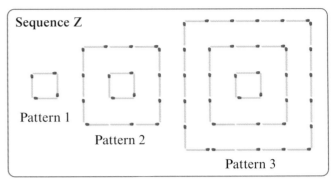

Sequence Z

Pattern 1

Pattern 2

Pattern 3

 a Find a rule for the number of matches in
   the nth pattern in the form $n \longrightarrow \dots$.

 b Show how you found your rule.

4 **A** 1, 4, 7, 10, 13, …
    B 2, 5, 10, 17, 26, …
    C 2, 7, 12, 17, 22, …
    D 3, 12, 27, 48, 75, …
    E 11, 8, 3, ‾4, ‾13, …
    F ‾898, ‾895, ‾890, ‾883, ‾874, …
    G ‾1, 2, 7, 14, 23, …
    H ‾2, 7, 22, 43, 70, …
    I 6, 12, 22, 36, 54, …
    J 5, ‾1, ‾11, ‾25, ‾43, …

For each of the sequences A to H:

 a Find the general term, g_n.

 b Calculate g_{30}.

5 Give the general term for each of these geometric
   sequences.

 a 16, 32, 64, 128, 256, …

 b 5, 7, 11, 19, 35, …

 c 1, 2, 4, 8, 16, …

 d 2, 0, ‾4, ‾12, ‾28, …

 e $\frac{1}{3}$, 1, 3, 9, 27, …

 f 24, 18, 0, ‾54, ‾216, …

6 For each of the following sequences where $u_1 = 1$:

 a Calculate u_4.

 b State if the sequence diverges or converges and
   any limit it approaches?

 A $u_{n+1} = u_n(u_n + 4)$

 B $u_{n+1} = \dfrac{u_n + 1}{2}$

 C $u_{n+1} = \dfrac{u_n + 2}{u_n}$

 D $u_{n+1} = \dfrac{9u_n + 5}{2u_n}$

Constructions and loci

1 Construct these triangles accurately.
Show all your construction lines.

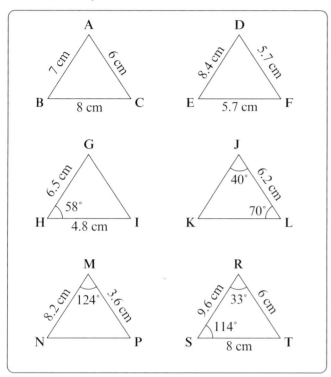

2 Copy each line full size and contruct a
perpendicular bisector of it.

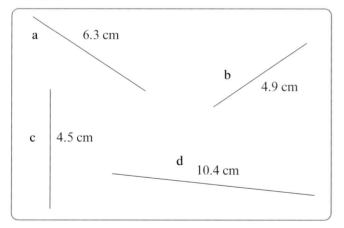

3 Draw each angle accurately and construct its
bisector.

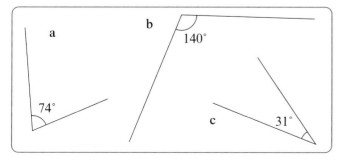

4 For each pair of triangles, state if they are congruent
or not necessarily so and, if congruent, state the case
of congruence.

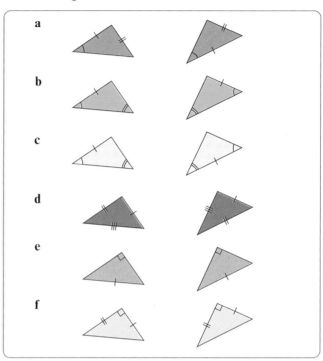

5 A field for the village fete is shaped as a triangle
with these dimensions.

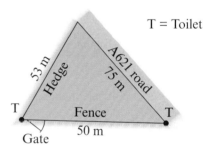

Colonel Briggs Shilton has set out these conditions
for the position of the drinks tent.

| Condition 1 | The tent must be equidistant from the hedge and the fence. |
| Condition 2 | The distance from each toilet to the tent must be equal. |

a Construct a scale drawing of the field to a
scale of 1 to 1000.
b Find by construction the position of the tent.
c Why is this position not a sensible one?
d Give some different conditions which you think
puts the tent in a better position.

Rationals and irrationals

1 Which of these are not integers?

   a $\sqrt[4]{40}$ **b** $\sqrt[5]{7776}$ **c** $\sqrt[3]{3}$

   d $\sqrt[3]{^-1}$ **e** $\sqrt[5]{10}$ **f** $\sqrt[9]{1}$

2 Evaluate:

   a $\sqrt[3]{64}$ **b** $\sqrt[6]{0.046\,656}$

   c $\sqrt[5]{(^-243)}$ **d** $\sqrt[5]{1.610\,51}$

3 Evaluate correct to 1 decimal place:

   a $\sqrt[3]{15}$ **b** $\sqrt[6]{20}$ **c** $\sqrt[4]{24}$

4 Evaluate as a fraction:

   a 4^{-3} **b** $\sqrt[4]{\frac{81}{625}}$ **c** $\sqrt[3]{\frac{1}{343}}$

5 Find the value of x when:

   a $\sqrt[5]{x} = 1.3$ **b** $\sqrt[x]{10.4976} = 1.8$

   c $\sqrt[x]{512} = 2$ **d** $\sqrt[7]{x} = {}^-0.000\,0128$

6 Give the answer to each of these using index notation.

   a $4^5 \times 4^3$ **b** $3^2 \times 3^{-3}$ **c** $2^4 \times 2^{-4}$

   d $(2^3)^4$ **e** $(6^7)^{-2}$ **f** $6^5 \div 6^3$

   g $6^3 \div 6^5$ **h** $(6^{-2})^7$

7 To what power must 2^3 be raised to give:

   a 2^9 **b** 2^{-6} **c** $\frac{1}{2^3}$?

8 Simplify as far as you can:

   a $y^2 \times y^3$ **b** $(y^6)^5$ **c** $(3y^2)^4$

   d $3y^5 \times 4y^2$ **e** $\frac{y^5}{y^4}$ **f** $\frac{4y^3}{2y^7}$

   g $\frac{2y^3 \times 6y^5}{4y^2}$ **h** $\frac{4y \times 3y^4}{6y^7}$ **i** $\frac{11y^5}{2y^2 \times 5y^3}$

9 Find two sets of equivalent expressions.

   Ⓐ $3^{\frac{2}{5}}$ Ⓑ $\frac{1}{\sqrt{3^5}}$ Ⓒ $3^{\frac{5}{2}}$ Ⓓ $\sqrt[5]{3^2}$

   Ⓔ $\sqrt{3^5}$ Ⓕ $\frac{1}{\sqrt[3]{3^2}}$ Ⓖ $3^{\frac{5}{2}}$ Ⓗ $3^{\frac{2}{5}}$

10 Evaluate these as integers or in fractional form.

   a $49^{\frac{1}{2}}$ **b** $81^{\frac{1}{2}}$ **c** $27^{\frac{1}{3}}$

   d $343^{\frac{1}{3}}$ **e** $1^{\frac{1}{4}}$ **f** $625^{\frac{1}{4}}$

   g $243^{-\frac{1}{5}}$ **h** $(^-1024)^{\frac{1}{5}}$ **i** $32^{\frac{1}{5}}$

   j $16^{-\frac{1}{2}}$ **k** $216^{-\frac{1}{3}}$ **l** $729^{-\frac{1}{6}}$

   m $343^{\frac{2}{3}}$ **n** $256^{\frac{3}{4}}$ **o** $32^{\frac{2}{5}}$

   p $64^{\frac{5}{6}}$ **q** $512^{\frac{2}{3}}$ **r** $625^{\frac{3}{4}}$

   s $32^{\frac{3}{5}}$ **t** $243^{\frac{4}{5}}$ **u** $729^{\frac{5}{6}}$

   v $27^{\frac{4}{3}}$ **w** $64^{-\frac{2}{3}}$ **x** $256^{-\frac{3}{4}}$

   y $243^{-\frac{3}{5}}$ **z** $64^{-\frac{5}{2}}$

11 Solve these equations.

   a $121^{\frac{1}{x}} = 11$ **b** $3^x = \frac{1}{27}$ **c** $27^x = 3$

   d $729^{\frac{1}{x}} = 3$ **e** $2^{3x+1} = 16$ **f** $3^{2x-1} = \frac{1}{81}$

   g $125^x = 25$ **h** $81^x = 729$ **i** $x^{\frac{4}{3}} = 16$

   j $25^x = \frac{1}{5}$ **k** $343^x = \frac{1}{49}$ **l** $x^{-\frac{2}{5}} = \frac{1}{16}$

12 Simplify as far as you can:

   a $(\sqrt{6})^2$ **b** $(\frac{1}{5}\sqrt{5})^2$ **c** $\sqrt{2} \times \sqrt{7}$

   d $\sqrt{5} \times \sqrt{20}$ **e** $(\sqrt{3} + \sqrt{5})^2$ **f** $(\sqrt{7} - \sqrt{2})^2$

   g $\sqrt{14} \div \sqrt{7}$ **h** $(2\sqrt{5} + 1)^2$ **i** $(\sqrt{11} - 3)^2$

13 Write each of these recurring decimals as a fraction in its lowest terms.

   a $0.333333 \dots$ **b** $0.363636 \dots$

   c $0.010101 \dots$ **d** $0.126126 \dots$

   e $0.\dot{5}$ **f** $0.\dot{0}\dot{9}$

   g $0.\dot{8}5714\dot{2}$ **h** $0.\dot{2}\dot{7}$

14 Write down:

   a a rational number between 1 and 2

   b an irrational number:

     i between 3 and 4   **ii** between 29 and 30

   c a number between 1 and 2 that has a rational square root.

15 Decide, giving reasons whether each of the following expressions is rational or irrational.

   a $\sqrt{2} + \sqrt{5}$ **b** $\sqrt{7} \times \sqrt{5}$ **c** 6^{-1}

   d $\sqrt{10} - 1$ **e** 3π **f** $\pi + 2$

   g $4^{\frac{1}{3}}$ **h** $\sqrt{\pi}$ **i** $8^{-\frac{2}{3}}$

16

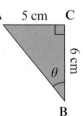 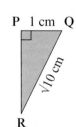 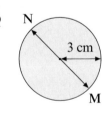

   a Which of these lengths are rational?

     i AB   **ii** PR   **iii** MN

     iv the perimeter of triangle ABC

     v the circumference of the circle

   b Which of these trigonometric ratios are irrational?

     i $\sin \theta$ **ii** $\cos \theta$ **iii** $\tan \theta$

Approximation and Errors

1 Round each number to the degree of accuracy stated:

   a 5.674   (2 dp)
   b 12.652   (1 dp)
   c 12.652   (1 sf)
   d 2143   (nearest ten)
   e 15.77777   (4 sf)
   f 93747656   (5 sf)
   g 15.986   (2 sf)
   h 456.21345 (1 sf)

2 By approximating each number to 1 sf calculate approximate answers to each of these.

   a 84.3×452.53
   b 4.876×37.71
   c 5683.2×0.0372
   d 458.12×518
   e $734.6 \div 2.316$
   f $0.005\,682\,43 \div 7.8931$
   g $419\,52 + 77442$
   h $\dfrac{34.6296 + 87.3}{0.003\,21}$

   i $\dfrac{6834 \times 1939.453}{54.26}$

   j $\dfrac{45.95 \times (2.943\,56)^2}{(0.067)^2}$

3 Work out approximate answers by rounding each part first to 1 sf then calculate the percentage error produced by doing this.

   a 56.6×21.5
   b 4924×3.7
   c $246.3 \div 9.67$
   d $54.27 \times (21.6)^3$
   e $\dfrac{17.63 \times 1839}{(54.64)^2}$

4 State both the upper and lower bound for each number when it is given correct to the degree of accuracy stated.

   a 5.6   given to 1 dp
   b 54   given to nearest whole number
   c 690   given to nearest ten
   d 56.372   given to 3 dp
   e 65.00   given to 2 dp
   f 100   given to 1 sf
   g 100   given to 2 sf
   h 160000   given to 4 sf
   i 12.90   given to 3 sf
   j 16 million given to nearest ten thousand
   k 1000.00   given to 2 dp
   l 7.0001   given to 5 sf

5 The dimensions of a large room are shown on this plan and are given correct to the nearest ten centimetres.

9.7 m   6.2 m

   a Calculate the range of values that the perimeter could have.
   b Calculate the upper and lower bounds for the floor area.
   c The floor is to be covered with carpet at £11 per square metre (to the nearest pound).
      Calculate the range of values for the cost of the carpet used.

6 A scooter covers a distance of 1320 metres (to the nearest ten metres) in 60 seconds (to the nearest 10 seconds).
   Calculate the range of values for its speed in metres per second.

7 The volume V of a sphere is given by $V = \frac{4}{3}\pi r^3$ where r is its radius.
   A spherical gas tank has a radius of 3.2 metres, to the nearest ten centimetres.

   Calculate the upper and lower bounds for the volume of the tank.

8 Convert these numbers into standard form.

   a 435000   **b** 12 million
   c 0.000321   **d** 54,267 45
   e 654×10^6 **f** 654×10^{-4}

9 Convert these into ordinary numbers.

   a 5.23×10^3 **b** 1.5×10^{-6}
   c 1.094×10^{-1} **d** 3×10^{-2}

10 Calculate the value of each of these giving your answers in standard form.

   a $(3.42 \times 10^3)^2 \times (1.35 \times 10^{-2})$
   b $\dfrac{(4 \times 10^3) + (5 \times 10^2)}{2 \times 10^{-5}}$

   c $\dfrac{(4.2 \times 10^{-4}) - (4.2 \times 10^{-5})}{(4.2 \times 10^3) - (4.2 \times 10^2)}$
   d $(9 \times 10^{-2})^3 - (9 \times 10^3)^{-2}$
   e $(9 \times 10^{-2})^3 - (9 \times 10^{-3})^2$

Solving equations algebraically

1 Solve these equations.

   a $3(2x - 5) = 12$ **b** $4(5x + 1) = 3(4x + 12)$

   c $5(6x + 9) = 12x$ **d** $3(x + 1) = 9(5x - 9)$

   e $\frac{2}{3}(x - 1) = 8$ **f** $\frac{4}{5}(2x + 3) = 14$

   g $\frac{3}{4}(2x - 4) = 2(x + 5)$

   h $\frac{2}{3}(x - 1) = \frac{3}{5}(x + 4)$

   i $\dfrac{5}{2x - 1} = 10$

   j $\dfrac{3}{x - 1} = \dfrac{5}{2x - 3}$

   k $\dfrac{3(2x - 1)}{4} = \dfrac{2(6x + 3)}{5}$

2 The perimeter of a rectangle is 86 cm.
The long side is 9 cm longer than the short side.

   Write and solve an equation to find the dimensions of the rectangle.

3 Remove the brackets from these expressions.

   a $(x + 3)(x - 5)$ **b** $(2x - 1)(x - 3)$
   c $(4 - 5x)(3x + 2)$ **d** $(x - 3)(3 - 4x)$
   e $(x + 4)(x - 4)$ **f** $(2x - 3)(2x + 3)$
   g $x^2(x - 4)$ **h** $2x(x^2 + 3x - 8)$
   i $3x(x^3 + 5x^2 + 4x - 1)$
   j $(x + 3)(x^2 + 6x - 7)$
   k $(x - 5)(3 + 5x - x^2)$
   l $(x^2 + 8x - 15)(4 + x)$
   m $(x + 1)(x + 2)(x - 3)$

4 Solve each pair of simultaneous equations.

   a $2x + 3y = 9$ **b** $4x - 3y = 5$
       $5x - 4y = 11$ $5x + 7y = 17$

   c $6x + 3y = 3$ **d** $8x - 3y = 30$
       $5x + 2y = 3$ $5x - 2y = 19$

   e $7x - 2y = \ ^-11$ **f** $3x + 9y = 15$
       $3x + 5y = 7$ $4x + 5y = 6$

   g $2x + 7y = 29$ **h** $3x - 5y = 10$
       $3x - 4y = \ ^-29$ $5x - 7y = 6$

   i $4x + y = \ ^-11$ **j** $13x - 7y = 66$
       $3x + 5y = \ ^-21$ $9x + 15y = 6$

5 Two numbers are such that when you add three times the first number to three times the second number the answer is 3. The difference between the first and second numbers is 9.

   What are the two numbers?

6 Gareth pays for a holiday with a mixture of £5 and £10 notes. the holiday costs £365 and this is paid with a total of 55 notes.

   How many of each type of note were used to pay for the holiday?

7 A shop sells two types of calculator: Scientific and Graphical.
Customer A orders 35 Scientific and 72 Graphical calculators at a total cost of £1228.15
Customer B orders 124 Scientific and 15 Graphical calculators at a total cost of £1242.05

   Calculate the price of each type of calculator.

8 A bag contains a mixture of 5 pence and 20 pence coins. There are 2250 coins in the bag. If the monetary value of the coins in the bag is £183.30, how many of each type of coin is in the bag?

9 A bag contains large and small marbles, and there are 378 marbles in the bag.
Each small marble weighs 2.5 g and each large marble weighs 4.8 g. The total weight of the marbles in the bag is 1.4349 kg.

   Calculate how many of each type of marble is in the bag.

10 Solve these quadratic equations by factorising.

   a $x^2 + 5x - 84 = 0$ **b** $x^2 - 8x + 7 = 0$
   c $x^2 + 3x - 54 = 0$ **d** $x^2 - 15x + 36 = 0$
   e $x^2 + 8x + 12 = 0$ **f** $x^2 - 4x - 320 = 0$
   g $x^2 - 11x - 60 = 0$ **h** $x^2 - 14x + 48 = 0$
   i $x^2 + 6x = 135$ **j** $x^2 - 8x = 65$
   k $x^2 + 20 = 9x$ **l** $x^2 + 28 = 16x$
   m $x^2 = 3x$ **n** $x^2 - 64 = 0$
   o $x^2 - 196 = 0$ **p** $x^2 - 10\,000 = 0$
   q $2x^2 - 5x - 3 = 0$ **r** $2x^2 + 6x - 20 = 0$
   s $3x^2 + x - 2 = 0$ **t** $3x^2 + x - 4 = 0$
   u $6x^2 - x - 2 = 0$ **v** $6x^2 + 35x - 6 = 0$
   w $8x^2 + 14x - 4 = 0$ **x** $18x^2 + 3x - 6 = 0$

11 Solve these equations to 2 dp.

   a $x^2 - 5x + 3 = 0$ **b** $x^2 + 6x - 2 = 0$
   c $x^2 + 8x + 1 = 0$ **d** $x^2 - 3x - 1 = 0$
   e $x^2 + x - 5 = 0$ **f** $x^2 + 2x - 7 = 0$
   g $x^2 - 3x - 2 = 0$ **h** $x^2 + 6x - 8 = 0$
   i $x^2 - 4x - 3 = 0$ **j** $x^2 - x - 3 = 0$
   k $x^2 + 6x + 3 = 0$ **l** $x^2 + x - 1 = 0$
   m $2x^2 + 3x - 6 = 0$ **n** $3x^2 + x - 3 = 0$
   o $4x^2 + x - 1 = 0$ **p** $7x^2 + 3x = 5$

12 Solve these equations using iteration.

   a $x^2 + 6x - 16 = 0$ **b** $x^2 - 6x + 5 = 0$
   c $x^2 - 4x - 32 = 0$ **d** $x^2 + 2x - 15 = 0$

Transformations

1 Draw the pentagon A on axes with:
$^-12 \leqslant x \leqslant 6$ and
$^-6 \leqslant y \leqslant 6$.

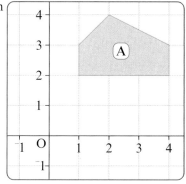

2 Draw the image of A after:

  a an enlargement SF $^-2$ with centre ($^-1$, 1)

  b an enlargement SF $\frac{1}{2}$ with centre (7, $^-4$).

3 These transformations map A on to B, C, D, E and F.

Object	Transformation	Image
A	Rotate $^+90°$ about (0, 0)	B
A	Rotate $^-90°$ about (1, 1)	C
A	Reflect in x = 5	D
A	Rotate $^+90°$ about (6, 2)	E
A	Reflect in y = $^-$x	F

  a **i** On a new diagram, on axes with:
      $^-6 \leqslant x \leqslant 10$ and $^-6 \leqslant y \leqslant 6$
    ii draw and label the images B, C, D, E and F.

  b Describe the transformation that maps:
    i C on to A   **ii** D on to A.

  c Describe the inverse of the transformation that maps:
    i A on to E   **ii** A on to F.

  d For each of these mappings which pentagon is the image of B?

	Object	Transformation	Image
i	B	Enlarge SF 1 with centre (0, 1)	
ii	B	Reflect in y = 0	
iii	B	Translate $\begin{pmatrix} 8 \\ ^-4 \end{pmatrix}$	

  e Describe a transformation that maps C on to E.

4

	Transformations		
Object	First	Second	Image
A	Rotate $^+90°$ about (0, 1)	Reflect in y = 0	G
A	Reflect in y = 0	Rotate $^+90°$ about (0, 1)	H

  a On a new diagram draw the images G and H.

  b What single transformation maps G on to H?

  c In the table below, each pair of transformations maps G on to H.
    Describe each of the second transformations.

	Object	Image	First transformation	Second transforma
i	G	H	Translate $\begin{pmatrix} 6 \\ 0 \end{pmatrix}$	
ii	G	H	Rotate $^-90°$ about (1, $^-2$)	
iii	G	H	Rotate 180° about (0, $^-1$)	

5 These transformations map A on to J, K L and M.

	Transformations		
Object	First	Second	Image
A	Enlarge SF 2 with centre (0, 1)	Reflect in y = 1	J
A	Reflect in x = 1	Enlarge SF 2 with centre (5, 0)	K
A	Enlarge SF 2 with centre (5, 0)	Reflect in x = 4	L
A	Enlarge SF $^-2$ with centre (5, 0)	Reflect in x = 2	M

  a **i** Draw A on a new diagram with axes:
      $^-10 \leqslant x \leqslant 14$ and $^-10 \leqslant y \leqslant 10$.
    ii Draw and label images J, K, L and M.

  b What single transformation maps:
    i J on to M **ii** L on to J **iii** J on to K?

6 Give three different types of transformation that are their own inverse.

Using formulas

1 Rearrange each formula to make x the subject:

  a $3x + 5a = 4$ **b** $2(3 - x) = a + 1$

  c $3(a - 2x) = b$ **d** $3x - 1 = 2(a - 2x)$

  e $3a(x + a) = 2a$ **f** $5(1 - 2x) = 3(x - a)$

  g $3a^2x - 1 = n + 2$ **h** $y(2 + ax) = 1 - 3y$

  i $ay + ax = 2 - y^2$ **j** $c^2(3a - ac + bx) = 1$

  k $wx - wy = 2bc$ **l** $n(2a + ax - c) = ab$

  m $b^2(a - 3x) = a^2b$ **n** $\pi(3a - xy) = 2a(\pi - 1)$

  o $w(3x - 4) = w - 1$ **p** $3a + 1 = 2a(a - x)$

  q $a(1 - ax) = 5a$ **r** $2(3 - 2ax) = a(1 + 3x)$

  s $h = ab + 0.5cx$ **t** $ac(w^2 - 3x) = acx$

2 The formula or the cost ($£C$) of hiring a bicycle for n days is: $C = 5.75 + 2.4n$

Zina paid £32.15 to hire a bike while on holiday. For how many days hire was this?

3 The cost ($£C$) of hiring a car for n days travelling t miles is: $C = 21n + 0.15(t - 120n)$

  a Calculate the cost of hiring a car to travel a total of 1654 miles over four days.

  b **i** Make t the subject of the formula.

    ii £145.50 was paid for 6 days hire. Calculate the number of miles travelled.

  c The hire charge is a fixed price per day, plus so much a mile travelled. A number of free miles are allowed each day. From the formula:

    i What is the fixed price per day?

    ii What is the charge per mile?

    iii How many free miles are allowed a day? Explain your answer.

4 Make n the subject of each formula:

  a $\frac{1}{3}n = a + 2$ **b** $\frac{3n}{5} = 2(1 - x)$

  c $\frac{1}{n} = \frac{2}{a}$ **d** $\frac{3x - 2}{2n} = 2a$

  e $\frac{3n}{a^2 - b} = \frac{1}{2}$ **f** $2x + 3 = \frac{3}{5}(n - 1)$

  g $\frac{2}{n - 3} = ax$ **h** $\frac{a}{2n} = \frac{3}{5}$

  i $x^2 = \frac{3}{2n - 1}$ **j** $w = \frac{x^2}{3 - n}$

  k $\frac{a}{n \cos 30°} = b$ **l** $\frac{a}{x^2} = \frac{3}{2n}$

  m $\frac{2}{3n - 4} = a^2$ **n** $\frac{1}{n} = \frac{2}{a + 1}$

  o $\frac{a}{b} = \frac{c}{n}$ **p** $\frac{bn}{3n - 2a} = 5$

  q $\cos 30° = \frac{3}{n}$ **r** $a = \frac{x}{n - b}$

  s $x^2 = \frac{2n - 3}{5}$ **t** $\frac{a}{n} + \frac{1}{n} = w$

5 Given the formula: $\frac{a}{2n} = b + c$

Explain why $n \neq \frac{1}{2}a - \frac{1}{2}(b + c)$ it is not correct.

6 Rewrite each of these as a formula in p.

  a $px - py = 3$ **b** $pt^2 = 1 + 3p$

  c $3p - 2 = ap + c$ **d** $2(3 - 2p) = a(p - 1)$

  e $2(3p - 5) = a^2p$ **f** $\frac{2p + 3}{p + 1} = ab$

  g $3 = \frac{p - 2x}{p}$ **h** $ap + ax = b^2p + y$

  i $2a(3p - y) = p$ **j** $p \sin x + p \sin y = w$

  k $3pw + 1 = p - 3$ **l** $a^2bp + 1 = b^2p$

  m $1 + 2cp = ap + b$ **n** $3n(p + b) = a(p - 2b)$

  o $3a + \frac{1}{p} = bc$ **p** $\frac{2}{3}(p + 1) = 2(1 - ap)$

  q $\frac{1}{4}(2p + 1) = an$ **r** $b(3 + ap) = \frac{1}{3}c^2n$

  s $\frac{2}{5}p + a = py$ **t** $a^2p + 2 = \frac{1}{2}(p + 2)$

7 The surface area S of a cylinder is: $S = 2\pi rh + 2\pi r^2$

Rearrange the formula to make π the subject.

8 A formula for the cost ($£C$) of supplying and laying n paving slabs is:

$C = 1.85n + y(n - 50)$ with a materials fee of y

  a Make n the subject of the formula.

  b What do you think is the cost of one slab? Explain your answer.

9 Rewrite each formula with v as the subject:

  a $\sqrt{v} = (1 + x)$ **b** $3a = \sqrt{(1 - v)}$

  c $2x = \sqrt{3v}$ **d** $\sqrt{(2v - 3)} = a - b$

  e $a^2 = 3\sqrt{v} - 1$ **f** $2x - 1 = \sqrt{5v}$

  g $4 = \sqrt{(v - 3a^2)}$ **h** $x + 3 = \frac{1}{\sqrt{v}}$

  i $y^2 = v^2 + 1$ **j** $2v^2 + 1 = ax$

  k $3v^2 + av^2 = 4$ **l** $3x - v^2 = v^2y$

  m $ab + av^2 = bv^2$ **n** $3(2 - v^2) = a(v^2 - 2)$

  o $a^2 + 1 = \frac{1}{v^2}$ **p** $kv^2 + 1 = a^2(v^2 - k)$

  q $\frac{1}{3v^2} = 2a - 1$ **r** $\frac{1}{v} = \frac{v}{x + 2}$

10 A formula for the area A of a disc of inner radius r and outer radius R is: $A = \pi(R^2 - r^2)$

  a Make r the subject of the formula.

  b A disc has an outer radius of 7.5 cm, and an area of 91.8 cm². To 1 sf, what is the inner radius of the disc?

11 A formula linking t, a, and g is given as: $t = 2\pi\sqrt{\frac{a}{g}}$

Make g the subject of the formula.

Ratio and Proportion

1 This recipe makes 25 biscuits.

> **Chocolate Biscuits**
> 50 g icing sugar • 225 g margarine
> 100 g plain chocolate • 225 g flour

Calculate how much of each ingredient is needed to make:

a 45 biscuits   **b** 10 biscuits

2 Tropical Fruit Juice is a mix of pineapple and grapefruit in the ratio 5:2. Calculate:

a the amount of pineapple juice to mix with 180 ml of grapefruit juice

b how much Tropical Fruit Juice is produced.

3 On a map, 3.6 cm stands for a distance of 108 m.

a What length on the map stands for 87 m?

b Give the map scale as a unitary ratio.

c Explain why the total number of parts has no meaning in this ratio.

4
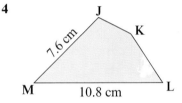

EFGH is an enlargement of JKLM.

a Calculate the scale factor of the enlargement.

b Find the length HG.

c Calculate the ratio: **i** $\dfrac{MJ}{ML}$ **ii** $\dfrac{HE}{HG}$

d Explain why the ratios are equal.

5
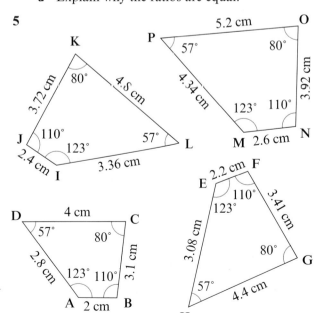

Which of these trapeziums are similar to ABCD?

6
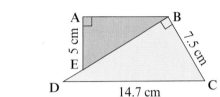

PQRS and WXYZ are similar.
Find the length: **i** QR   **ii** WZ

7
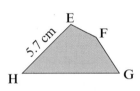

AB and DC are parallel.

a Explain why ABE and BDC are similar triangles.

b Give the corresponding side to: **i** AB **ii** AE

c Find the length BE.

8
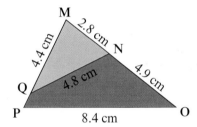

a Calculate the ratio: **i** $\dfrac{PO}{QN}$ **ii** $\dfrac{MO}{QM}$

b Explain why MOP and MQN are similar triangles.

c Find the length PQ.

9 z is in direct proportion to the square of p, and $z = 21.6$ when $p = 6$.

a Write down the relationship between z and p.

b Find the constant.

c Give an equation connecting z and p.

d Calculate z when $p = 5$.

e Rearrange your equation to give p in terms of z.

f Calculate p when $z = 86.4$.

10 Chunkie is a chocolate bar that comes in four different sizes of square prism. Each bar has the same mass of chocolate.
The length of a bar, l cm, is inversely proportional to the square of its width, w cm². The 1.5 cm bar is 16 cm long.

a Give an equation connecting l and w.

b Calculate the length of a 2.5 cm Chunkie.

c Calculate the width of a Chunkie 25 cm long.

Working in 3D

1 Each of these solids is made from three cubes.

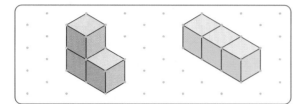

How many planes of symmetry has each solid?

2 **a** Draw a solid made from five cubes with 1 plane of symmetry.
b Draw a solid made from six cubes with 3 planes of symmetry.

3 How many planes of symmetry has:
a a cuboid with no square faces
b a cube?

4 Each prism P and Q has a capacity of one litre.

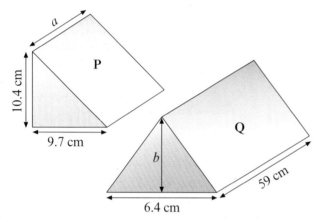

Find the values of a and b correct to 1 dp.

5 Calculate the area of the shaded ring.

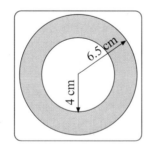

6 This is a company logo. Calculate:
a its total area
b its perimeter.

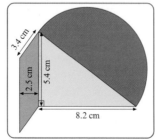

7 A cylindrical cheese has a sector of angle 135° cut out vertically from one end.

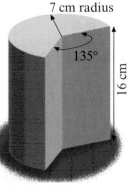

a Calculate the volume of the remaining piece of cheese.
b Calculate the surface area of the piece removed.

8 A bubblegum display cabinet is shaped like a frustum of a cone with a hemisphere on top.

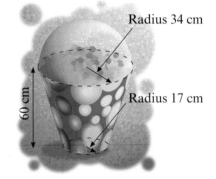

a Calculate the volume of the cabinet.
b Calculate its surface area.

9 The capacity of a hollow Russian doll is 1024 cm³.
A smaller similar doll from the set has a capacity of 640 cm³.
The height of the larger doll is 16 cm.

Calculate the height of the smaller doll?

10 In the following expressions, r, h and l each represent a length.
Decide if each expression represents:
a length, area, volume or none of these.
Give reasons for each answer.

a $4h$ **b** h^2
c rh **d** rhl
e $2(h + l)$ **f** πr^2
g $hl + r$ **h** $\frac{1}{3}rh^2$
i $\sqrt{h^2 + l^2}$ **j** $\pi rh - 3l^2$
k $r^3 + h^2 + rl$ **l** $h^3 + rl^2$
m $5(rh + hl + rl)$ **n** $\pi rh(h + l)$
o $2h(r - l)$ **p** $\frac{4}{3}\pi(r + h)$

Probability

1   A 1 to 6 dice is rolled.
What is the probability of getting:

   a   a multiple of 4
   b   a prime number which is a factor of 6
   c   a square number or a triangle number?

2   **a**   If you have six cards with the numbers 1 to 6 on them what is the probability of getting a Fibonacci number by picking a card
   b   If you have each of the first six Fibonacci numbers on six cards what is the probability of picking a card with 1 on it?

3   You roll two dice at the same time.
What is the probability of getting:

   a   a total of 3
   b   a total score of 8
   c   a 3 on only one dice
   d   a 5 on both dice
   e   a total which is not 6?

4   In an experiment an object could land in three ways, on a face, on an edge or on a side. These are the results from a number of trials: face 68, edge 25, side 18. Calculate an estimate of the probability that the object will land:

   a   on a face
   b   not on a side
   c   on a side or a face.

5   Dom's top drawer has 2 red T-shirts, 3 blue ones and 1 yellow one. The draw below has 3 red socks 4 blue socks and 2 yellow ones. Dom is unconcerned with fashion and always picks his clothes from a drawer at random.

   a   He picks a T-shirt and one sock.
      What is the probability that:
      i   they are both blue
      ii   one is yellow and one red
      iii   they are the same colour?

   b   He picks two socks.
      What is the probability that:
      i   they are both red
      ii   they are different colours
      iii   neither of them are blue?

   c   He picks three socks.
      What is the probability that he has a pair the same colour amongst them?

   d   He picks a T-shirt and two socks.
      What is the probability that:
      i   they are all blue
      ii   they are all the same colour?

6   Parveen is a disc jockey. She has 18 reggae and 14 jungle CDs to play. She chooses the CD to play at random and only plays any single once.

   a   Draw a tree diagram to show the probabilities when she plays the first three CDs in her programme.

   b   What is the probability that the first three CDs Parveen plays:
      i   are all reggae CDs
      ii   include exactly two jungle CDs
      iii   include only one reggae CD
      iv   have no two of the same type played consecutively.

   c   Parveen plays five CDs in the first twenty minutes of her programme. What is the probability that they are:
      i   all jungle
      ii   all the same type?

7   The probability that snow will fall on the roof of the Weather Centre in London on a day in December is 0.07. If snow falls on one day, the probability that it will snow on the next day increases to 0.15.

   a   Draw a tree diagram to show the probabilities for two consecutive days in December.
      What is the probability that:
      i   there will be snow on both days
      ii   there will be snow on only one day
      iii   there will be no snow on either day?

   b   For three consecutive days in December calculate the probability that there will be snow:
      i   on only one day
      ii   on all three days
      iii   on exactly two days.

8   Amongst a group of 30 British students, 18 speak some French and 14 speak some German but 6 speak neither language.

   a   Draw a Venn diagram to show the information.
   b   What is the probability that a person chosen at random:
      i   speaks only German
      ii   speaks both foreign languages
      iii   speaks only one foreign language
      iv   does not speak French?

Grouped data

1996 Olympic Games – Men's Marathon
Top 100 finishers

Time (min)	132 –	137 –	139 –	142 –	146 –	150 –	157
Frequency	15	18	18	20	11	18	

1   Draw a histogram to show these times.

2   (Do **not** use the statistical function on your calculator to answer this question.)
Calculate an estimate of:
a   the mean time
b   the standard deviation of the times.

3   a   Draw a cumulative frequency curve for the men's marathon.
b   Estimate:
   i   the median time
   ii   the interquartile range of the times.
c   Estimate how many times were:
   i   less than 135 minutes
   ii   greater than 155 minutes
   iii   between 140 and 150 minutes.

1996 Olympic Games
Women's Marathon
Top 60 finishers

Time	Frequency
146 –	5
151 –	9
154 –	8
156 –	12
158 –	9
162 –	10
167 – 176	7

4   Draw a histogram to show these times.

5   Use your calculator to estimate:
a   the mean time
b   the standard deviation of the times.

6   a   Draw a cumulative frequency curve for the women's marathon.
b   Estimate:
   i   the median time
   ii   the interquartile range of the times.
c   Estimate how many times were:
   i   less than 150 minutes
   ii   greater than 165 minutes
   iii   between 150 and 160 minutes.

7   Use your answers to Questions **2**, **3**, **5**, and **6** to compare the marathon times for men and women.

1996 Olympic Games
GB Athletics Team

Age	Frequency	
	Track	Field
18 –	7	2
23 –	27	10
28 –	20	7
33 – 42	5	4
Totals	59	23

8   Draw a histogram to show the age distribution of:
a   track athletes   b   field athletes.

9   Explain why drawing frequency polygons on the same diagram would not give a fair comparison of the ages of track athletes and field athletes.

10   a   Use your calculator to estimate the mean and standard deviation for:
   i   track athletes   ii   field athletes.
b   Compare the two distributions.

1996 Olympic Games – Great Britain Team
Ages of Competitors at 20/7/96

22	21	29	18	26	16	23	23	28	31	26	29	27	20	27	20
20	24	19	23	21	24	25	18	21	20	21	23	26	20	21	19
21	31	30	24	27	31	27	23	30	35	27	25	23	22	27	36
27	24	20	23	27	27	26	30	35	23	30	24	29	24	24	31
31	26	23	19	29	29	27	24	32	32	25	23	24	21	38	39
28	25	32	31	27	31	24	21	30	32	24	29	38	29	34	22
29	23	24	29	32	24	40	30	24	21	23	27	31	22	23	29
35	31	24	24	22	32	23	29	27	30	27	26	21	27	29	26
23	21	22	25	27	32	26	26	28	29	22	25	37	25	18	22
29	35	34	32	30	25	29	28	27	35	25	28	34	29	29	28
23	27	22	27	34	35	30	30	41	37	40	31	27	26	35	31
33	38	42	35	36	40	36	29	20	16	22	16	26	23	21	29
29	27	27	23	28	25	34	30	27	28	30	23	33	20	33	26
26	29	30	29	29	25	28	27	25	24	28	31	32	27	25	26
26	31	23	23	21	30	20	32	28	35	31	28	24	29	24	27
24	30	27	28	27	26	28	29	34	22	27	32	26	24	27	20
27	22	29	28	31	26	24	25	28	30	34	27	24	30	21	30
21	29	21	27	27	28	48	19	34	47	31	36	25	29	28	29
21	27	22	28	31	26	23	25	19	29	31	30	25	32	24	29
28	28	25	29	30	26	29	34								

11   a   Group this age data using a class interval of 2.
b   Combine some of your classes at each end of the distribution.
c   Use your new groupings to draw a histogram.

12   a   The age data is listed at random. Choose a systematic sample of:
   i   20   ii   40   iii   80
b   For each of your random samples:
   i   group the data   ii   draw a histogram
c   Compare the shape of your distributions.

Solving equations graphically

1 Solve each pair of equations graphically.

  a $x + 4y = 6$
       $2x + 5y = 9$

  b $5x - 3y = 8$
       $3x + y = 2$

  c $5x + 7y = 29$
       $x + 3y = 9$

  d $3x + 2y = 15$
       $4x - 2y = 13$

  e $5x - 4y = 14$
       $3x + 2y = 4$

  f $3y + 2x = 2$
       $2y - 6x = {}^-17$

  g $4y + 2x = 23$
       $2y - 6x = 1$

  h $4x - 5y = 3$
       $2x + 3y = 18$

  i $2x + 3y = 16$
       $4x - y = 11$

  j $2x - 3y = {}^-2$
       $2x + 2y = 13$

2 Give the line of symmetry for each of these graphs.

  a $y = x^2 + 8$
  b $y = x^2 + 4x$
  c $y = x^2 - 8x$
  d $y = x^2 + 6x - 4$
  e $y = 12x - x^2$
  f $y = 5 - 8x - x^2$

3 For x: $4 \leqslant x \leqslant 4$ draw graphs of these curves on the same axes.

  a $y = x^2 - 2x - 5$
  b $y = 4x - x^2$

4 For x: $^-5 \leqslant x \leqslant 5$ draw graphs of these curves on the same axes.

  a $y = 2x^2 + 3x$
  b $y = 3x^2 - x$

5 For x: $^-8 \leqslant x \leqslant 6$ draw the graph of $y = x^2 + 3x - 5$.

  a   Use the graph to solve these equations.
     i $x^2 + 3x - 5 = 4$
     ii $x^2 + 3x - 5 = {}^-3$
     iii $x^2 + 3x - 5 = 12.5$

  b   What can you say about any values you read from the graph?

6 For values of x: $^-3 \leqslant x \leqslant 5$ draw the graph of $y = x^2 - 2.5$

  a   On the same axes draw the graph of $y = 1.5x$
  b   Use the graphs to solve the equation
         $x^2 - 2.5 = 1.5x$

7 Draw a suitable graph and solve the equation
         $(x - 4)^2 - 12 = 0$

8 For values of x from $^-2$ to 6 draw the graph of $y = 2x(x - 4) - 10$.

  Use the graph to solve $2x(x - 4) = 10$.

9 For x: $^-5 \leqslant x \leqslant 5$ draw the graph of $y = x^2 + 6x - 2$.

  a   By drawing an additional graph use the graph to solve $x^2 + 4x + 1 = x + 4$.
  b   Explain how you can use your graph to solve the equation $x^2 + x + 2 = 7 - 7x$.
  c   Find an approximate value for x that will satisfy $x^2 + x + 2 = 7 - 7x$.

10 On a pair of axes draw a graph of $y = \dfrac{6}{x} - 4$.
  Use x: $^-5 \leqslant x \leqslant 5$.

11 For x: $^-6 \leqslant x \leqslant 6$ draw the graph of
   $y = \dfrac{12}{x} + 8$.

  Give the equation of any asymptotes to the graph.

12 For x : $1 \leqslant x \leqslant 10$ draw the graph of
   $y = x + \dfrac{10}{x} - 12$.

  Use the graph to find approximate values for:

  a   the minimum value of y
  b x when $y = {}^-3.4$.

13 For values of x from $^-4$ to 5 draw the graph of $y = x^3 + 4$.

14 On the same axes draw the graphs of:

  a $y = x^3 + 5$
  b $y = 5 - x^3$

15 Draw the graph of $y = x^3 - 2x^2$ for values of x from $^-4$ to 4.

  a   Use the graph to solve $x^3 - 2x^2 = 0$.
  b   From the graph find an approximate value for x when $y = 10.4$.

16 Sketch and label these graphs.

  a $y = 5x + 2$
  b $y = x^2 - 6$
  c $y = x^3 + 1$

17 Show how completing the square helps to sketch the graph of $y = x^2 + 6x - 1$.

18 For the graph of $y = x^2 + 4x - 6$ give:

  a   the minimum value of y
  b   the point at which the minimum value of y occurs
  c   the intercept with the y-axis.
  d   Sketch the graph of $y = x^2 + 4x - 6$.

Trigonometric graphs

1 The radial lines on the diagram below are drawn at intervals of 30°.
The polar coordinates of A are (3, 30°).

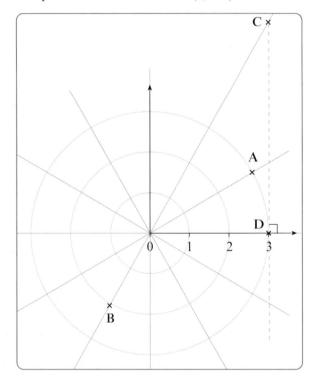

  a Give the polar coordinates of B and D.
  b Calculate the cartesian coordinates of points A and B.
  c The line CD is perpendicular to the polar axis.
     Calculate the polar coordinates of C.

2 a Make a table of values for $y = 4 \cos 20t$ for $t = 0, 1, 2, …, 20$.
  b Draw the graph of $y = 4 \cos 20t$ on axes with $0 \le t \le 20$ and $^-8 \le y \le 8$.
  c For what values of t is:
     i $y \le 0$ **ii** $y \le 2$?
  d What is the maximum value of y?
  e For what values of y is:
     i $y = 0$ **ii** $y = ^-2$?
  f **i** On the same axes sketch the graph of $y = 4 \cos 20t - 2$.
     ii Give the maximum and minimum value of $4 \cos 20t - 2$.

3 Solve each of these for $0° \le x \le 360°$.
Find two values of x such that:

  a $\cos x = 0.5$ **b** $\sin x = ^-0.5$
  c $\tan x = ^-1$ **d** $\sin x = \cos x$
  e $\cos x = \cos 205°$ **f** $\sin x = \sin 205°$
  g $\tan x = \tan 205°$ **h** $\sin x = \sin 105°$
  i $\cos x = \cos 105°$ **j** $\tan x = \tan 105°$

4 Solve each of these in the range $^-90 \le p \le 450$.
  a List all the values of p for which:
     i $\sin p = \sin 54°$ **ii** $\cos p = \cos 54°$
     iii $\tan p = \tan 54°$ **iv** $\sin p = \sin 154°$
     v $\cos p = \cos 154°$ **vi** $\tan p = \tan 154°$
  b Find all the solutions of these equations.
     i $\cos p = ^-\cos 62°$ **ii** $\sin p = ^-\sin 62°$
     iii $\sin p = 1$ **iv** $\cos p = 0$

5 Sketch each of these graphs for $0° \le x \le 360°$.
  a $y = \frac{1}{2} \cos x$ **b** $y = \frac{1}{2} \sin x$
  c $y = 5 \sin x$ **d** $y = \cos 3x$
  e $y = \sin x - 5$ **f** $y = 2 \cos x + 1$

6 Sketch each of these graphs for $^-90° \le x \le 540°$.
  a $y = \sin (x + 45°)$
  b $y = \cos (x - 90°)$

7 a On one pair of axes, with $0° \le x \le 360°$ draw the graphs of:
     i $y = \cos x$
     ii $y = \frac{1}{2} \sin x$.
  b Use your graphs to solve the equation:
     $\cos x = \frac{1}{2} \sin x$

8 Give the maximum and minimum value of y for each of these.
  a $y = 6 \cos x$ **b** $y = \sin x + 6$
  c $y = 8 \cos x$ **d** $y = \sin 2x$
  e $y = 3 \sin x + 6$ **f** $y = 2 \cos 3x - 4$

9 This is the graph of $y = a \sin bx + c$, where a, b and c are constants.

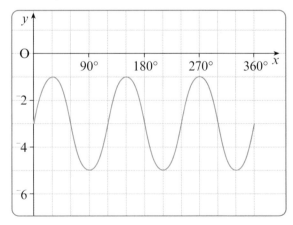

What are the values of a, b and c?

10 Solve each of these equations in the range $^-90° \le p \le 450°$.

  a $\sin p = \cos p$ **b** $\sin 2p = \sin 80°$
  c $\cos 3p = 0.5$ **d** $\tan 3p = 1$

Inequalities

1 Which of these numbers is not a possible value for t where $t \leqslant {}^-7$?
${}^-8, 4, 71, {}^-3.2, {}^-7.003, {}^-28.6, {}^-7, {}^-0.33$

2 What are the integer values for k, where

a $9 > k \geqslant 4$ **b** ${}^-3 \leqslant k \leqslant {}^-1$
c ${}^-5 \leqslant k < 1$ **d** ${}^-4 \geqslant k > {}^-7$
e ${}^-57 < k < {}^-56$ **f** $24 \leqslant k \leqslant 24$
g ${}^-14.2 \geqslant k > {}^-16$ **h** $6 > k > 0$
i $k^2 \leqslant 16$ **j** $9 < k^2 + 8$
k $12 - k^2 \geqslant 3$ **l** $4(k^2 + 3) \geqslant 3(2k^2 - 2)$?

3 Write two other inequalities in h which describe the same integer values as ${}^-2 < h < 2$.

4 Explain why these two inequalities are different types of inequality from each other.

> This chair is suitable for people with weights given by $5 \leqslant w \leqslant 15$, where w is their weight in stones.

> The waiters in a restaurant are given by $5 \leqslant w \leqslant 15$ where w is the number of waiters.

5 Draw graphs and label the regions described by these inequalities:

a $7 \leqslant x \leqslant 10$ **b** ${}^-4 \leqslant x < 1$
c ${}^-5 < x < {}^-2$ **d** $0 < x \leqslant 4$
e ${}^-1 \leqslant y < 3$ and $x \geqslant 4$
f $0 \leqslant x \leqslant 6$ and ${}^-6 < y < {}^-2$
g $y \geqslant x$ and $9 \geqslant x \geqslant 6$
h $2x + y < 10$ and $y \geqslant \frac{1}{2}x + 1$

6 What two inequalities describe the shaded region on this graph?

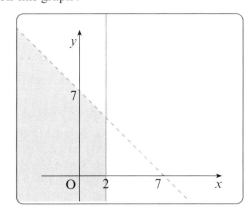

7 The conditions on x are given by the inequality ${}^-4 \leqslant x < 3$.
What is:

a the smallest possible value of x^2
b the largest possible value of x^2?

8 Solve the following inequalities.

a $3x \geqslant 27$ **b** $6t < {}^-42$
c $52 \geqslant 4p$ **d** $k^2 \leqslant 121$
e $1 + 3w < 7$ **f** $5q + 7 > 53.5$
g $19 \leqslant 3t - 5$ **h** $7 - 2h \geqslant 3$
i $4(3f - 2) < 28$ **j** $c^2 - 5 < 76$
k $36 \leqslant 3(2g + 3)$ **l** $3x + 5 > x - 1$
m $3j - 2 < 2j + 17$ **n** $5d + 20 \geqslant 6 - 2d$
o $24 - 8v > 6 - 4v$ **p** $2(x + 3) \leqslant x - 7$
q $5 - 3s > 5 + 3s$ **r** $9u + 6 \leqslant 7u$
s $5(4 - 3j) < 7j - 4$ **t** $5 + 2r^2 > 23$
u $2(3x^2 + 2) > 3(4x^2 - 3) + 1$

9 If the limits for x and y are given by $4 < x < 7$ and $7 < y < 9$, what can you say about the limits for:

a xy **b** $x + y$ **c** $\dfrac{y}{x}$?

10 Sam is planting an orchard with a mixture of apple bushes and pear trees. An apple bush needs an area of 16 m^2 and a pear tree needs 24 m^2. An apple bush costs £8 and a pear tree £10. She has £200 to spend and her orchard can have a maximum area of 432 m^2.
Sam wants at least half of her plants to be apple bushes but at least 6 must be pear trees.
Let a represent the number of apple bushes and p the number of pear trees.
This graph shows only some of the boundaries.

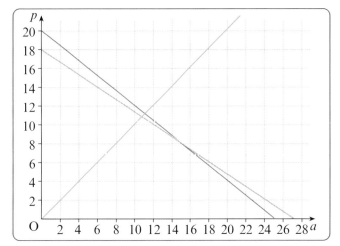

a Write inequalities for:
  i the land area   **ii** the cost of plants
  iii the number of pear trees.
b Explain why $p < a$.
c Draw the complete graph, label each line, and shade out all the regions not required.
d How many of each type gives the maximum total number of plants.
What is the total cost of these plants?

Working with percentages

1 Calculate, giving answers correct to 2 dp:

   a 38 as a percentage of 60

   b £14 as a percentage of £55

   c 68 as a percentage of 24

   d 1550 as a percentage of 2500.

2 Nina bought a secondhand bicycle for £45.
She later sold the bike for £58.
Calculate her percentage profit to 2 sf.

3 Give answers to each of these correct to 2 dp.

   a Increase 25 kg by 18%.

   b Increase 1400 km by 62%.

   c Increase 3560 miles by 4%.

   d Increase 1350 yards by 36%.

4 Last year one company sold 19.6 million CDs.
Next year they plan to increase sales by 18.5%.
How many CDs do they plan to sell next year?

5 Give your answers to these correct to 2 dp.

   a Decrease 485 ml by 12%.

   b Decrease £45.75 by 24%.

   c Decrease 65 mm by 65%.

   d Decrease 0.8 cm by 8%.

6 This year an arable farm used 12.4 tonnes of
herbicides. They plan to decrease the herbicides
used by 8.5% per year.
Calculate, to 2 sf, the herbicide they plan to be
using three years from now.

7 The price of each item is given ex.VAT.
Calculate the price including VAT at todays
standard rate, to the nearest penny.

   a crash helmet £185.85

   b cycle tyre £11.69

   c fishing rod £44.86

   d steam iron £21.75

   e microwave oven £268.55

   f VCR £159.99

   g personal CD player £135.38

   h CD £9.24

   i phone £49.99

   j multimedia PC £1499

8 A printer is advertised for £132 + VAT
Calculate the total price of the printer.

9 The VAT (at 17.5%) paid on a bill was £15.
Calculate the total for the bill.

10 Jamal has a maximum of £10 000 to spend on
building a garage. Calculate the maximum he can
spend ex.VAT.

11 Callum sees the same model TV advertised by two
shops in this way:

TV World	£199.99 inc. VAT
Price busters	£169.99 ex.VAT

   a From which shop would you advise Callum to
buy the TV?
Give reasons for your answer.

12 Calculate the simple interest charged, or paid, on
each of these:

   a £675 borrowed for 5 years at 12% pa

   b £12 400 borrowed for 2 years at 17% pa

   c £170 saved for 4 years at 3% pa

13 Rearrange the simple interest formula,
$I = P \times R \times T$, to make r the subject.

14 £1400 was saved at 3.6% simple interest.
The total interest paid was £378, for how long
was the saving?

15 Calculate the compound interest charged, or paid
on each of these:

   a £500 saved for 8 years at 6% pa

   b £1400 borrowed for 3 years at 19% pa

   c £250 saved for 12 years at 7.5% pa

   d £105 saved for 7 years at 3%

   e £12500 borrowed for 12 years at 16%

   f £32 saved for 13 years at 4%

   g £750 borrowed for 3 years at 21%

   h £3675 borrowed for 5 years at 17%

   i £125 saved for 9 years at 8%

   j £500 saved for 30 years at 4.5%.

16 Rearrange the compound interest formula to make
the time of the investment the subject.

17 These prices include VAT. Calculate each price
ex.VAT.

   a freezer £299.99   **b** CD £12.99

   c camera £44.99   **d** phone £9.99

   e climbing boots £75   **f** tent £89.95

   g kettle £26.99   **h** PC £129.99

   i calculator £18.99   **j** TV £139.99

18 Jo bought a ski jacket in a '15% off sale' for £85.45.
Calculate the pre-sale price of the jacket?

19 In 1995 Ferrykink made a profit of £3 600 000.
This was 14% more than the profit for 1994.
Calculate the profit made in 1994.

Circle properties

1 Draw any circle, and a chord AB.
  a Label:
    i the minor segment
    ii the major segment.
  A chord CD is such that the circle is divided into two segments that are the same size.
  b What can you say about the chord CD?

2

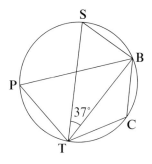

  a Name an angle in the minor segment.
  b Calculate the size of TBS. When TP̂B = 75°
     Explain your answer.

3 In the diagram PT is a chord and O the centre of the circle.

  Calculate the size of TP̂O.
  Give reasons for your answer.

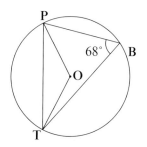

4 The circle has a centre O.
  a Calculate the size of PT̂B. Explain your answer.
  b What is the size of AĈB? Explain your answer.
  c Explain why AB̂P is 76°.

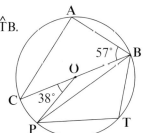

5 The circle has a centre O.
  a Explain why PÂT is 48°.
  b Calculate PĈT. Explain your answer.

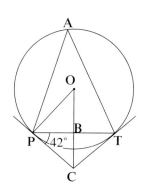

6 **a** Explain why TB̂P is 35°.
  b Calculate BP̂T. Give reasons for your answer.
  c Explain why AĈB is 73°.

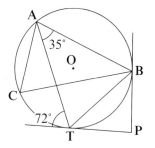

7 AC is a tangent to the circle with centre O. AC is 12.5 cm long and B is the midpoint.
  a If AE = 5 cm, calculate the length of EG to 1 dp.
  b If DF = 11.2 cm, calculate to 1 dp the length of CD.

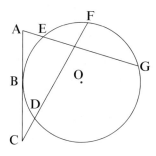

8 AC is a tangent to the circle with centre O. AC is 16.2 cm long and B is the midpoint.
  a If AD is 4 cm, and EF is 7.5 cm calculate the size of FD̂E to 2 sf.
  b Calculate the area of triangle FDE to 3 sf.

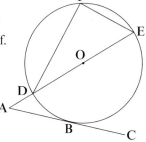

9 **a** Explain why EĈD = 31°.
  b Calculate the size of AB̂C. Explain your answer.
  c EÂB = 52° Give two different explanations to show this.

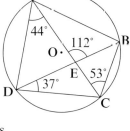

10 Show why an expression for DÂB is given as:

   $180 - a$

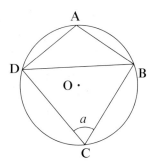

Working with angles

1 Calculate the area of each of these triangles:

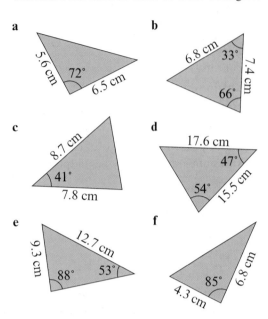

a 5.6 cm, 72°, 6.5 cm

b 6.8 cm, 33°, 66°, 7.4 cm

c 8.7 cm, 41°, 7.8 cm

d 17.6 cm, 47°, 54°, 15.5 cm

e 12.7 cm, 9.3 cm, 88°, 53°

f 85°, 4.3 cm, 6.8 cm

2 Triangle ABC has an area of 30.4 cm².

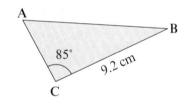

85°, 9.2 cm

Calculate the length of AC.

3 Use the sine rule to calculate ? in each of these triangles.

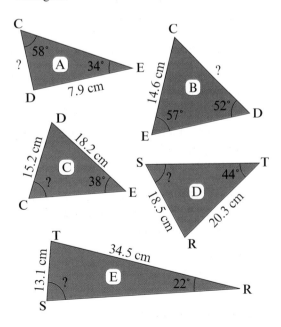

A: C, 58°, ?, 34°, E, D, 7.9 cm

B: C, 14.6 cm, ?, 57°, 52°, D, E

C: D, 18.2 cm, 15.2 cm, ?, 38°, E, C

D: S, ?, 44°, T, 18.5 cm, 20.3 cm, R

E: T, 13.1 cm, 34.5 cm, ?, 22°, R, S

4 Calculate the length of CD in each of these triangles:

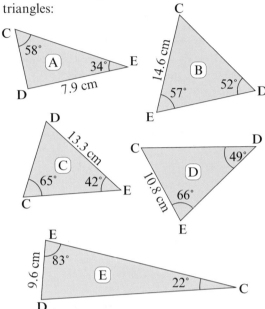

A: C, 58°, 34°, E, 7.9 cm, D

B: C, 14.6 cm, 57°, 52°, D, E

C: D, 13.3 cm, 65°, 42°, E, C

D: C, 49°, 10.8 cm, 66°, D, E

E: E, 9.6 cm, 83°, 22°, C, D

5 Calculate BAC in each of these triangles:

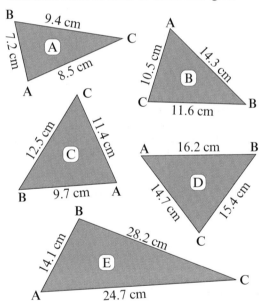

A: B, 9.4 cm, 7.2 cm, C, A, 8.5 cm

B: A, 14.3 cm, 10.5 cm, C, B, 11.6 cm

C: C, 12.5 cm, 11.4 cm, B, 9.7 cm, A

D: A, 16.2 cm, B, 14.7 cm, 15.4 cm, C

E: B, 14.1 cm, 28.2 cm, A, 24.7 cm, C

6 For triangle PQR, copy and complete the table.

Angle	p (cm)	q (cm)	r (cm)
$P = 54°$	**a**	7.3	8.5
$Q = 63°$	8.4	**b**	9.1
$R = 49°$	11.5	9.8	**c**
$P = 74°$	**d**	3.5	4.5
$Q = 57°$	37.5	**e**	31.8

Processing data

1

> ### Town Centre Survey
>
> **1** Do you come into the town centre often? ☐ Yes ☐ No
>
> **2** Do you agree that the town centre should be pedestrianised? ☐ Yes ☐ No
>
> **3** What do you think about buses? _____

    a Criticise each of these questions.
    b Write an improved question for each one.

2

> ### Body Matters
> Right-handed people are more likely to have a stronger left eye than right eye.

Design an experiment to test this hypothesis.

3   **a** Carry out your experiment.
    b Analyse the data you collect.

4   **a** Do you think the hypothesis is true or false?
    b Explain why.

5

> ### Body Matters
> Do right-handed people fold their arms differently to left-handed people?

Design an experiment to answer this question.

6   **a** Carry out your experiment.
    b Analyse the data you collect.
    c Interpret your results to answer the question.

7

Motorbikes – Size of Engine & Price

Engine size (cc)	250	900	600	125	650	900	500	750
Price (£)	4500	8100	6700	2400	5100	6700	3400	9200

    a Draw axes: horizontal 0 to 1300
                    vertical 0 to 12 000
    b Plot the motorbike data on your diagram.
    c Draw a line of best fit.
    d Describe any correlation between size of engine and price.

8 Estimate the price of a motorbike with engine size:
    a 800 cc   **b** 450 cc

9 Estimate the engine size of a motorbike costing:
    a £4000   **b** £6500

10 Extend the line of best fit on your scatter diagram to estimate:
    a the price of a motorbike with a 1000 cc engine
    b the engine size of a motorbike costing £10 000.

11 The GB Team for the 1996 Olympic Games had 123 female competitors, and 189 male competitors. Show how a stratified random sample of 60 competitors is chosen.

12 The ages of female and male competitors, listed at random, are:

> ⊙⊙⊙   **1996 Olympic Games – Great Britain Team Ages of 123 Female Competitors at 20/7/96**
>
> 21 26 16 23 31 27 20 20 24 24 18 23 26 21 31 24
> 27 20 23 27 23 24 29 24 24 31 26 23 29 32 23 24
> 38 28 32 31 31 24 21 30 38 29 22 24 32 40 30 31
> 23 32 29 27 21 27 23 27 25 25 22 35 29 28 25 28
> 34 35 30 37 31 26 35 35 36 16 16 33 20 33 26 26
> 29 30 29 29 25 28 27 25 24 28 31 32 26 31 23 30
> 20 28 31 28 24 29 30 27 27 29 22 29 28 30 27 28
> 47 25 29 27 28 31 26 31 29 28 34

> ⊙⊙⊙   **1996 Olympic Games – Great Britain Team Ages of 183 Male Competitors at 20/7/96**
>
> 22 29 18 23 28 26 29 27 20 19 23 21 25 21 20 21
> 20 21 19 30 31 27 23 30 35 27 25 23 22 27 36 27
> 24 27 26 30 35 30 31 19 29 27 24 32 25 21 39 25
> 27 32 24 29 34 29 23 29 24 24 21 23 27 22 29 35
> 31 24 24 22 23 30 27 26 29 26 21 22 25 32 26 26
> 28 29 22 37 18 29 34 32 30 25 27 35 29 29 28 23
> 27 22 27 34 30 41 40 27 31 33 38 42 36 40 29 20
> 22 26 23 21 29 29 27 27 23 28 25 34 30 27 28 30
> 23 27 25 26 23 21 32 35 24 27 24 28 26 28 34 22
> 27 32 26 24 27 20 27 28 31 26 24 25 30 34 27 24
> 30 21 21 29 21 27 48 19 34 31 36 28 29 21 22 23
> 25 18 29 30 25 32 24 28 25 29 30 26 29

    a Use your answer to Question **11** and choose a systematic sample from each group.
    b For the 60 competitors in your sample:
        i group the data   **ii** draw a histogram.

13 For your grouped data, calculate an estimate of:
    a the mean age
    b the standard deviation of the ages.

14   **a** Choose another stratified random sample of 60 competitors by allocating a number to each competitor in the group, and using a random number table.
    b **i** Group the data for your second sample using the same groups as in Question **12**
        ii Draw a histogram.

15 For your second sample, calculate an estimate of:
    a the mean age
    b the standard deviation of the ages.

16 Compare your two samples.

Exploring graphs

1 Convert the following:

    a 4.38 hours to hours and minutes

    b 12.76 hours to hours and minutes

    c 5 hours 16 minutes to hours

    d 8 hours 51 minutes to hours

    e 24 m s^{-1} to km h^{-1}

    f 16 m s^{-1} to mph

    g 58 mph to m s^{-1}

    h 152 km h^{-1} to m s^{-1}.

2 A bike travels 96 miles in $8\frac{1}{2}$ hours.
Calculate its average speed in mph.

3 How many miles does a car travelling at an average speed of 65 mph cover in 3 hours 45 minutes?

4 How long does it take Alison, walking at an average speed of $3\frac{1}{2}$ mph, to travel $8\frac{1}{2}$ miles?

5 Between traffic lights a car covered a distance of 132 metres in 9 seconds.
What was its average speed in mph?

6 A balloon drifting at 6 m s^{-1} travelled a total distance of 16.8 miles.
How long did this flight last?

7 How many metres would an arrow fly in 15 seconds at an average speed of 96 km h^{-1}?

8 This is a graph of the distance of a dog from its owner who sits still on a bench.

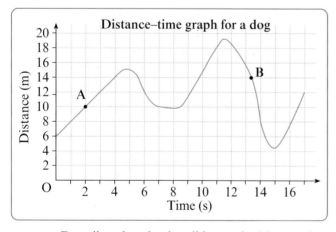

Distance–time graph for a dog

    a Describe what the dog did over the 16 seconds.

    b At what times was the dog 12 metres from its owner?

    c How far from the owner did the dog start?

    d When did the dog stop to sniff?

    e At what time was the dog moving fastest?

    f Estimate how fast the dog was running at:

      i point A   **ii** point B.

9 This graph shows the speed of Helen on her scooter as she pulls away after a junction.

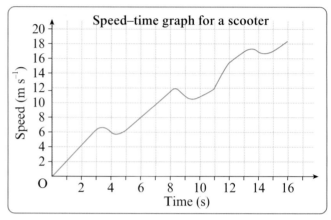

Speed–time graph for a scooter

    a What do you think the dips in the graph indicate Helen was doing?

    b Estimate Helen's acceleration:

      i after 6 seconds

      ii after 11 seconds.

    c Estimate how far Helen travelled in the first 2 seconds.

    d Use the trapezium rule with trapeziums of width 2 seconds to estimate the distance Helen travelled in 16 seconds.

    e What was Helen's average speed in mph?

    f Is it possible to tell from this graph if Helen was travelling in the same direction over the 16 seconds. Explain your answer.

10 This graph shows the flow rate of water from a gutter at the start of a storm.

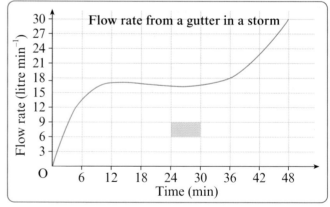

Flow rate from a gutter in a storm

    a What does area of the red rectangle represent?

    b **i** Use the Trapezium Rule to estimate the area under the graph between 0 and 48 minutes.

      ii What does this area represent?

    c Calculate an estimate of the average flow rate over the first 48 minutes.

Vectors

1

$$\mathbf{u} = \begin{pmatrix} ^-2 \\ 5 \end{pmatrix} \qquad \mathbf{v} = \begin{pmatrix} 1 \\ 4 \end{pmatrix} \qquad \mathbf{w} = \begin{pmatrix} 5 \\ 6 \end{pmatrix}$$

Write each of these vectors as a column vector, and draw it on a coordinate grid.

a 2u   **b** 3v   **c** ⁻2w   **d** v + w
e u + v   **f** 2w − 3v   **g** 2v − u   **h** 3w − 5v + 2u

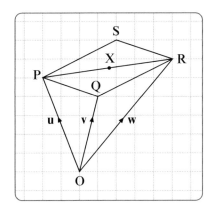

2 PQRS is a parallelogram.
Write each of these in terms of **u**, **v**, and **w**.

a $\overrightarrow{PQ}$ **b** $\overrightarrow{QR}$ **c** $\overrightarrow{SP}$ **d** $\overrightarrow{RS}$ **e** $\overrightarrow{OS}$

3

$$\mathbf{u} = \begin{pmatrix} ^-2 \\ 5 \end{pmatrix} \qquad \mathbf{v} = \begin{pmatrix} 1 \\ 4 \end{pmatrix} \qquad \mathbf{w} = \begin{pmatrix} 5 \\ 6 \end{pmatrix}$$

a Write each of your answers to Question **2** as a column vector.
b Use the diagram to check your answers.

4 Give the resultant vector for:

a $\overrightarrow{PQ} + \overrightarrow{QR}$ **b** $\overrightarrow{PS} + \overrightarrow{SR}$ **c** $\overrightarrow{PQ} + \overrightarrow{QR} + \overrightarrow{RS}$

5 What is special about the vector $\overrightarrow{RS} + \overrightarrow{SP} + \overrightarrow{PR}$?

6 Use your answers to Question **2** to give the resultant vectors in Question **4** in terms of **u**, **v**, and **w**.

7 Show that **v** − **u** is the negative vector of **u** − **v**:
a using a sketch
b using column vectors
c using algebra.

8 X is the midpoint of PR.
Prove that X is also the midpoint of QS.

9 These vectors include three pairs of parallel vectors.

   2v − 3u   6u + 4v   2u + 3v   6u − 9v

     3v − 2u   4v − 6u   ⁻3u − 2v

List each pair.

10

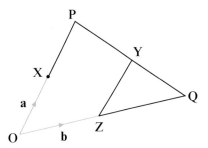

OPQ is a triangle.
X, Y, and Z are the midpoints of each of the sides.

a Give $\overrightarrow{PQ}$ in terms of **a** and **b**.

b Prove that ZY is parallel to OP and half its size.

11

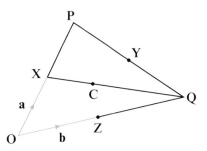

OPQ is a triangle.
X, Y, and Z are the midpoints of each of the sides.
The ratio XC : CQ is 1 : 2.

a Give these in terms of **a** and **b**.
   i $\overrightarrow{XQ}$ **ii** $\overrightarrow{XC}$
b Prove that P, C, and Z are collinear.
c Give the ratio PC : CZ
d Prove that O, C, and Y are collinear.
e What do your answers tell you about point C?

12

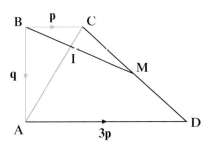

In this diagram, M is the midpoint of CD.
The ratio BI : IM is 2 : 3.

a Give these in terms of **p** and **q**.
   i $\overrightarrow{CD}$ **ii** $\overrightarrow{CM}$ **iii** $\overrightarrow{BI}$
b Prove that the ratio AI : IC is 4 : 1.

Transforming graphs

1 Functions f, g and h are defined so that:

$$f(x) = \frac{1}{x - 5}$$

$$g(x) = (x + 3)^2 - 5$$

$$h(x) = \frac{3}{x} + 4$$

a Calculate:
  i $f(6)$ **ii** $g(1)$ **iii** $h(2)$
  iv $f(^-3)$ **v** $g(^-3)$ **vi** $h(^-3)$

b Find values of x for which:
  i $f(x) = 0.1$ **ii** $g(x) = 4$ **iii** $h(x) = 7.75$

2 An experiment is carried out to investigate the bounciness of a ball. The ball is dropped from different heights and the maximum height of the rebound is measured.

The results are shown in the table below.

Drop height D (cm)	50	100	150	200
Rebound height R (cm)	46	92	139	180

a Draw a graph to show that R and D are linked by a formula of the form $R = aD + b$, where a and b are constants.

b Estimate the values of a and b.

c What do you think the rebound height will be when the drop height is 350 cm?

3 A small weight is dropped from the top of a building. Its position is recorded at intervals of 0.5 seconds using an electronic camera.

The results are shown in the table below, giving distance from ground d (m) and time taken t (seconds).

t	0	0.5	1	1.5	2	2.5	3
d	50.0	48.8	45.1	40.0	30.4	19.4	5.9

a Draw the graph of d against t^2.

b **i** Does your graph support the claim that d and t are connected by an equation of the form $d = pt^2 + q$?

  ii If it does, estimate the values of p and q.

4

x	0	2	4	6	8	10	12
y	$^-2.4$	$^-0.8$	4.2	11.7	23.1	37.5	55.0

a Draw a graph to show that x and y are linked by a formula of the form $y = mx^2 + n$, where m and n are constants.

b Estimate the values of m and n.

c Find the value of y when $x = 5$.

5 This is a sketch of the graph of $y = f(x)$ where $f(x) = x^2 - 6x + 10$.

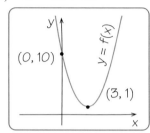

a Sketch graphs of:
  i $y = -f(x)$ **ii** $y = f(-x)$ **iii** $y = f(x) + 3$
  iv $y = f(x + 3)$ **v** $y = f(x - 2) + 1$

b Describe a transformation that maps $y = f(x)$ to each graph.

6 This is the graph of the function $y = g(x)$.

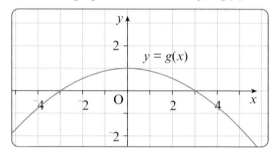

Sketch graphs of:
a $y = 2g(x)$ **b** $y = g(2x)$ **c** $y = g\left(\frac{1}{2}x\right)$

7 This is the graph of the function $y = k(x)$.

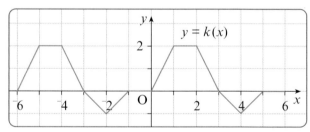

a For $^-3 \leq x \leq 3$, sketch graphs of:
  i $y = k(^-x)$ **ii** $y = k(2x)$ **iii** $y = k\left(\frac{1}{2}x\right)$
  iv $y = k\left(\frac{1}{3}x\right)$ **v** $y = \frac{1}{2}k(x)$ **vi** $y = 2k(x)$
  vii $y = k(x) + 3$ **viii** $y = k(x + 3)$
  ix $y = k(x - 2)$ **x** $y = k(x - 3) - 4$

b In terms of k, write the equation of the graph below.

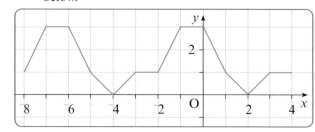

Formula sheet

In the GCSE examination you will be given a formula sheet like this one.
You should use it as an aid to memory, and it will be useful to become familiar with the information on the sheet.
The formula sheet is the same for all examining groups.

Area of triangle $= \frac{1}{2} \times$ Base $\times$ Height

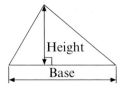

Area of parallelogram = Base $\times$ Height

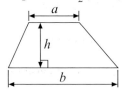

Area of trapezium $= \frac{1}{2}(a + b)h$

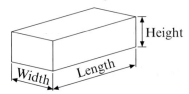

Volume of cuboid = Length $\times$ Width $\times$ Height

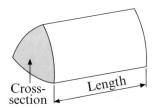

Volume of prism = Area of cross-section $\times$ Length

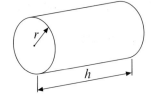

Volume of cylinder $= \pi r^2 h$
Curved surface of cylinder $= 2\pi rh$

Volume of a sphere $= \frac{4}{3}\pi r^3$
Surface area of a sphere $= 4\pi r^2$

Trigonometry

$\sin \theta = \dfrac{\text{opp}}{\text{hyp}}$

$\cos \theta = \dfrac{\text{adj}}{\text{hyp}}$

$\tan \theta = \dfrac{\text{opp}}{\text{adj}}$

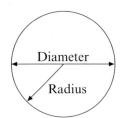

Circumference of circle $= \pi \times$ Diameter
$= 2 \times \pi \times$ Radius

Area of circle $= \pi \times$ (Radius)^2

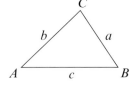

In any triangle ABC

Sine rule $\quad \dfrac{a}{\sin A} = \dfrac{b}{\sin B} = \dfrac{c}{\sin C}$

Cosine rule $\quad a^2 = b^2 + c^2 - 2bc \cos A$

$\cos A = \dfrac{b^2 + c^2 - a^2}{2bc}$

Area of triangle $= \frac{1}{2}ab \sin C$

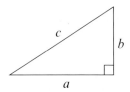

Volume of cone $= \frac{1}{3}\pi r^2 h$
Curved surface area of cone $= \pi rl$

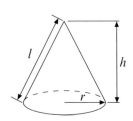

Pythagoras' theorem
$a^2 + b^2 = c^2$

The Quadratic Equation

The solutions of $ax^2 + bx + c = 0$
where $a \neq 0$, are given by

$$x = \frac{-b \pm \sqrt{(b^2 - 4ac)}}{2a}$$

Standard Deviation

Standard deviation for a set of numbers $x_1, x_2, ..., x_n$,
having a mean of x is given by

$$s = \frac{\Sigma(x - x)^2}{n} \quad \text{or} \quad s = \sqrt{\frac{\Sigma x^2}{n} - \left\{\frac{\Sigma x}{n}\right\}^2}$$

Number

N1
Units, conversions, and
compound measures

You are expected to
know approximate values
of the conversions below:

1 gallon = 4.546 litres
1 kilogram = 2.205 pounds
1 mile = 1.609 kilometres
1 inch = 25.4 mm
1 foot = 30.48 cm

You are also expected to
know the exact values for
these conversions:

1 foot = 12 inches
3 feet = 1 yard
1 pound = 16 ounces
1 stone = 14 pounds
1 gallon = 8 pints

N1.1 Given that 1 mile = 5280 feet:
Convert a speed of 50 mph to a speed in feet per second.

N1.2 A milk tank holds 25 000 litres when full.
The contents of the tank are emptied into a bottling plant.
To completely empty the tank, from full, takes 15 minutes 24 seconds.

  a Calculate how many litres per second flow from the tank.
  Give your answer to 2 dp.
  b How many gallons per minute is this?

N1.3 When Joel came back from New York, the exchange rate was:

  £1 = $1.55

He changed $425 to £ sterling.
The smallest amount the bank can give is a £1 coin.
How many pounds did he have in total?

N1.4 In a French supermarket Sylvie bought 400 g of pasta for 9.50 FF.

  a At this price, what would she pay for 1 kg of the pasta?
  b When Sylvie bought the 400 g of pasta the exchange rate
  was £1 = 7.60 FF.

Explain why the 400 g of pasta would cost £1.25 in sterling.

N1.5 A recipe asks for 12 ounces of flour but the scales only measure in grams.
Calculate the weight of flour in grams.

N1.6 The area of a tennis court is 261 square metres.
Convert this area into square feet.

N1.7 In France the petrol consumption of cars is given in the form
'x litres per 100 kilometres'.
Convert a consumption of 45 miles per gallon to litres per 100 km.

N1.8 In France a litre of milk cost 5.63 FF while, at the same time, in the UK
a pint of milk cost 31p. At that time the exchange rate was £1 = 9.12 FF.
In which country was milk cheaper and by how much, to the nearest
penny?

N1.9 In 1995 Fiona's height was 4 feet 10 inches..
By 1997 she had grown to 1.65 metres.

  a What was her height in feet and inches in 1997?
  b By how many centimetres had she grown in the two years?

N1.10 A hurricane is the description of a wind speed in excess of 32.7 metres
per second. Convert this speed to miles per hour.

N1.11 The pressure under a full-grown elephant's foot is about 15 000 kg per
square metre.
Convert this to a pressure into pounds per square inch.

N2
Estimation, accuracy
and bounds

N2.1 Iso-cool deodorant is sold in two sizes:
Regular, which contains 80 ml and Large, which contains 155 ml.

a The contents of the regular size is measured to the nearest 10 ml.
What is the smallest amount it can contain when unopened?

b The contents of the large size is measured to the nearest 5 ml.
What is the smallest amount it can contain when unopened?

N2.2 George always measures in imperial units.
He uses a tape marked in tenths of an inch.
He measures the width of a table as 27 inches (to the nearest inch).

a **i** What is the widest the table could be?
ii What is the narrowest the table could be?

b George wants to convert his measurements to millimetres:
i What is the widest the table could be?
ii What is the smallest the width of the table could be?

N2.3 The dimensions of this rectangle are given correct to 1 dp.

What are the upper and lower
bounds for the area of the
rectangle?

3.4 m

6.7 m

N2.4 In this triangle the labelled lengths are given to the nearest centimetre.

a Calculate the largest possible value
of angle BAC.

b Calculate the smallest possible value
of the length AB.

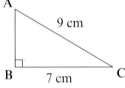

A

9 cm

B   7 cm   C

N2.5 A firm that makes biscuit tins uses tinned steel plate with the
following dimensions:

Length	420 mm (to the nearest mm)
Width	324 mm (to the nearest mm)
Thickness	0.16 mm (to the nearest 0.01 mm)

If a sheet with the minimum dimensions is used rather than one with
the maximum dimensions, what percentage saving in volume of steel is
achieved?

N2.6 To calculate the surface area of a cone of height h and base radius r,
Mike uses the formula:

$$A = \pi r(r + \sqrt{r^2 + h^2})$$

For a cone with a height of 28.73 cm and a base radius of 41.26 cm show,
by using suitable approximations, that the surface area is roughly 10 000
square centimetres.

> You must show enough
> working to convince
> someone that you did not
> use a calculator.

N2.7 A spherical basketball has a volume of 73 600 cm³, to the nearest 100 cm³.
What is the minimum internal diameter for the circular ring at the mouth
of the basketball net which will allow the ball to pass through?

N3

Types of number

N3.1 **a** List all the factors of 12.
b Which of these numbers is a multiple of 12?
16   288   300   432   612   724

N3.2 **a** Write 108 as a product of primes.
b Use your answer to part **a** to write 108^3 as a product of primes.

N3.3 **a** List the prime factors of:
i 555   **ii** 3171.
b Hence find the highest common factor of 555 and 3171.

N3.4 The winning numbers for the Lottery were given as below:
The numbers possible are from 1 to 49.

1st number   a square number between 20 and 30
2nd number   the ninth triangular number
3rd number   a multiple of 7, and a multiple of 5
4th number   the number of prime numbers between 10 and 20
5th number   the square root of 1369
6th number   the sixth multiple of 3
Bonus number   2 to the power of 3

a What are the six winning numbers?
b List all the factors of the bonus number.
c Which of the winning numbers is prime?
d **i** Find the sum of the six winning numbers.
    ii Write this sum in standard form.

N3.5 Explain why the recurring number $4.\dot{7}14\dot{2}$ is not irrational.

N3.6 **a** Which of the following numbers are irrational?

$$\sqrt{3\tfrac{1}{16}}   2+\sqrt{2}   \sqrt{2}\times\sqrt{3}   25^0+5+5^{-2}   5-\pi$$

b Write each of the rational numbers above in the form $\dfrac{a}{b}$
where a and b are integers and b is non-zero.

N3.7 Simplify the expression $\sqrt{24}\times\sqrt{21}$ as far as possible, leaving your answer in surd form.

N3.8 A circle of radius r fits exactly inside the square ABCD of side 2 metres.
Say if each of the following is rational or irrational giving your reasons in each case:
a the diameter of the circle
b the shaded area of the diagram
c the perimeter of the square
d the diagonal of the square AC.

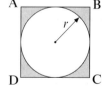

N3.9 Give a value for a, other than $a = 5$, to make the answer to $\sqrt{a}\times\sqrt{5}$
a irrational   **b** rational.

N3.10 What fraction is equivalent to the recurring number 0.45454545 … ?

N4
Fractions, decimals and
percentages

N4.1 In a test of memory, four students were given fifteen seconds to read from a list of numbers.

- Claire read out   75%   of the numbers
- Rob read out $\frac{3}{5}$ of the numbers
- Joel read out   0.625   of the numbers
- Nicole read out $\frac{7}{10}$ of the numbers

a **i** Which student read out most numbers?
ii Which student read out fewest numbers?
You must show, and explain, all your working.

There were 120 numbers in the list.

b How many numbers did Joel read out?
c How many more numbers did Claire read out than Rob?

N4.2 **a** Write $\frac{3}{8}$ as a decimal.

b Is $\frac{3}{8}$ larger or smaller than 0.4? Explain your answer.

c List these numbers in order, starting with the smallest.
$\frac{1}{2}$ 0.6 $\frac{1}{5}$ $\frac{3}{8}$ 0.085

d Which is larger: 0.805 or 0.85? Explain your answer.

N4.3 Ian packs and labels pizzas.
He starts his shift with a sheet of 1000 labels.
After working for an hour he has used 72 labels.

a **i** What fraction of the labels has Ian used after an hour?
ii Write this fraction in its lowest terms.

During the second hour Ian uses $\frac{1}{4}$ of the labels that are left over.

b How many labels does Ian use in the second hour?

During the third hour Ian uses $\frac{1}{2}$ of the labels that he has left.

c How many pizzas does Ian pack in the first three hours of his shift?

N4.4

> ## JETSTREAM   THE HOLIDAY AIRLINE
>
> Report for the year 1996
>
> 1996 was another year in which Jetstream increased its number of flights.
>
> There were a total of 2448 flights:
>
> $\frac{3}{8}$ of all flights were to Malaga
>
> $\frac{1}{6}$ of all flights were to Orlando
>
> $\frac{1}{4}$ of all flights were to Corfu
>
> $\frac{1}{12}$ of all flights were to Faro
>
> All other flights were to Malta

a How many Jetstream flights were there to each destination?
b What fraction of the flights were to Malta?

Jetstream say in their brochure:

> Over 35% of all our flights are to Malaga

c Are Jetstream right to claim this? Explain your answer.
d Roughly 15% of all Jetstream flights were to which destination?
Explain your answer.

N4.5 Lisa and Mario win a total of £1560 in a draw. They share the prize equally. Lisa invests her share, for five years, in an account that pays interest at 6.5% pa compound. Mario invests his share for the same length of time in an account that pays interest at 8% in the first year, and 5.75% pa compound for each of the following years.

Calculate the total in each of their accounts at the end of five years.

N4.6 In January 1994 Carla paid £179.99 for a mobile phone. She kept the phone for three years, and during that time the price of mobile phones was said to fall by an average of 48% per year. In January 1997 Carla replaced her phone with a new one. Using what she paid for her phone in 1994 as a guide, calculate what she can expect to pay for her new phone if it is similar to her old one. Give your answer correct to the nearest 50 pence.

N4.7 Schools can claim back any VAT they pay on items they purchase. The hockey team at Ashlands School replace their strip at a total cost of £910.04 which included VAT at 17.5%.

  a Calculate the ex-VAT price of the new strip to the nearest pound.
  b Calculate, to the nearest penny, the VAT the school can claim back.

N4.8 The world stocks of a species of fish were said in 1992 to be decreasing by an average of 8% each year. A headline in a newspaper suggested that in thirteen years the species of fish would be extinct.

  a Comment on the headline.
  b In 1992 the Fisheries Agency estimated that world stocks were a total of 2.3×10^5 tonnes.
     i When are stocks estimated to be less than 1.4×10^5 tonnes?
    ii Estimate world stocks in 2001.

N4.9 A sports stadium has seating for 65 000 people.
For the semifinals of a tournament the seats are priced in this way:

    20% of the seats £22.50
    18 200 seats £18
    11 050 seats £12.50
    30% of the seats £8.50
    the remaining seats .... NO CHARGE

  a   **i** For what percentage of the seats is no charge made?
     ii How many seats is this?
  b What percentage of seats are to be sold for £12.50?
  c Every seat in the stadium is full for the semifinal.
    How much, in total, is taken from ticket sales?

N4.10 A motorbike costs £9650 new.
The secondhand price guide describes how the value drops each year:
At the end of the first year the bike loses 16% of its value.
At the end of year 2 it loses 9% of its value at the start of that year.
At the end of year 3 it loses 7% of its value at the start of that year.
At the end of three years Tony says a bike has lost 32% of £9650.

  a Do you agree with Tony? Explain your answer.
  b At the end of three years, calculate what the value of a bike will be according to the price guide.

N4.11 Last year, Caterfare made a pre-tax profit of £136.4 million.
This year they forecast their pre-tax profits will be down by 4.7%.

Estimate the pre-tax profits of Caterfare for this year.

N4.12 Rick's car broke down on the motorway. The total bill for towing and repairs came to £435. Rick paid with his new credit card.

Rick decides that he will not use the card again until the £435 is paid off, and that he will pay £35 at the end of each month off his credit card bill.

The credit card company charges interest at 1.85% per month on the money that Rick owes them on the first day of the month.

a At the start of month 4, how much will Rick owe on his credit card?
b After how many months will Rick owe roughly £235?
Explain your answer.
c If Rick decides not to use the card again until he has cleared the bill for his car, in how many months do you expect that he will be using his credit card again?

N5
Indices and standard form

N5.1 Calculate the value of each of these giving your answer in standard form.
a $(25.8 \times 10^{-3}) \times (1.5 \times 10^{5})$ **b** $54\,000\,000\,000 \div 0.000\,108$
c $(6 \times 10^{-3}) \div (2.4 \times 10^{-6})$ **d** $(5 \times 10^{7}) - (5 \times 10^{5})$
e $(4 \times 10^{-4})\frac{1}{4}$

N5.2 The Moon has a mass of 7.343×10^{19} tonnes.
The Earth is said have a mass 81 times greater than the mass of the Moon.
Calculate the mass of the Earth. Give your answer in standard form.

In general you will not gain marks by simply copying your calculator display.

You must interpret the display and write it as a number in standard form.

N5.3 The area of the Earth's surface is given as 5.1×10^{10} km². Land covers roughly 30% of the Earth's surface.
a Roughly what area (in km²) of the Earth's surface is not land?
b The Pacific Ocean covers approximately $165\,250\,000$ km².
In standard form write the area of the Earth's surface covered by the Pacific Ocean.
c The ten largest oceans and seas in the world cover a total area of about $352\,100\,000$ km².
i Write this total area in standard form.
ii Roughly what fraction of this total is made up by the Pacific Ocean? Show your calculations.

N5.4 Evaluate the following.
a $16^{\frac{1}{4}}$ **b** 5^{-2}
c $3^{5} \times 5^{3}$ **d** $\frac{1}{3}^{\frac{1}{2}}$
e $27^{\frac{2}{3}}$ **f** $(\sqrt{3})^{3}$

N5.5 Find the value of x if:
a $3^{3x-18} = \frac{1}{27}$ **b** $16^{x} = 256$

N5.6 Simplify $(x^{4} \times y^{-6})^{\frac{1}{2}}$ giving your answer without negative indices.

N5.7 Estimates from the United Nations show that in the 1980s the population of the world increased from 4.45×10^9 to 5.292×10^9.

   a How many people does this increase represent?
Give your answer in standard form.

   b Roughly, what is this increase as a percentage?

N5.8 In 1991 UK manufacturers of sweets spent £8.834×10^7 on advertising. Advertising for tea was a quarter of this amount.

How much was spent in total on advertising tea and sweets?

N5.9 The diameter of the Earth is approximately 1.3×10^7 metres.

The volume V of a sphere is given by $V = \frac{4}{3}\pi r^3$, where r is its radius.

   a Estimate the volume of the Earth in cubic metres, giving your answer in standard form to 3 significant figures.

   b The Earth weighs about 6×10^{24} kg.
Estimate the Earth's density in kg per cubic metre.
Give your answer in standard form to 2 significant figures.

N6
Ratio and proportion

N6.1 The weights of two tins of baked beans are in the ratio $15:25$.

   a Write this ratio in its simplest terms.

The smaller tin contains 225 grams of beans.

   b Calculate the weight of beans in the larger tin.

   c Calculate the weight of beans in the smaller tin, as a percentage of the weight of beans in the larger tin.

N6.2 A salad dressing is made from three ingredients:
olive oil (V), malt vinegar (M), and raspberry wine vinegar (R), in the ratio:

$$\begin{array}{ccccc} V & : & M & : & R \\ 5 & : & 2 & : & 1 \end{array}$$

   a How much malt vinegar, is needed to mix with 350 ml of olive oil.

Rick is making 2 litres of this salad dressing.

   b How much of each ingredient does he need?

> Check that your answers give a total of 2 litres.

N6.3 The plan of a sports hall is drawn to a scale of $1:250$.

On the plan the length of the weights room is 9 cm.

   a In metres, what is the actual length of the weights room?

The fitness gym is 18 metres wide.

   b What measurement represents this width on the plan?

   c Roughly, what is this actual width in feet?

N6.4 This is a recipe for 25 sultana scones:

      500 g   S.R. flour
        25 g   baking powder
      250 g   butter
        25 g   caster sugar
      125 g   sultanas
      cold milk to mix

This recipe is changed to make just 5 scones.

   a What weight of sultanas was used for just 5 scones?

This recipe is changed to make 480 scones.

   b Give the weight of each ingredient, in kg, for this recipe.

N6.5   A Victorian field microscope enlarges lengths in the ratio $2:7$.
A woodlouse, 1.2 cm long, is looked at under this microscope.

How long will the woodlouse appear under the microscope?

N6.6   Students at Aselbury College organise a sponsored swim for charity.
They decide to donate the proceeds to charities in this ratio:

Famine aid   :   Disaster aid   :   Medical research   :   The homeless
    4   :   3   :   2   :   5

After the event they donated £147.21 to Disaster aid.

a   How much did they donate to Medical research?
b   What was the total raised by the sponsored swim?

The ratio of males to females who swam was $2:3$.

c   What fraction of those who swam were female?

N6.7 W varies directly as the positive square root of S.
W has a value of 18 when S is 36.

a   Write a formula connecting W and S.
b   Use your formula to calculate the value of W when S is 81.
c   Calculate the value of S when W is 30.

N6.8   When you throw a tennis ball into the air, the maximum height the ball
reaches, h, is in direct proportion to the square of the initial speed, s,
you throw it at.

a   If h is 4 metres when s is 10 metres per second, express h in terms of s.
b   Calculate the value of s when $h = 25$ metres.
c   If Liz throws a tennis ball up at twice the speed that Zoe does, what is
the ratio of the maximum heights the balls reach?

N6.9

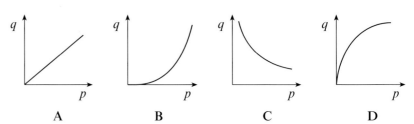

      A   B   C   D

a   Match each of these graphs with one of the following equations.

$$q = \frac{k}{p} \qquad q = kp^2 \qquad q = k\sqrt{p} \qquad q = kp$$

b   **i** Which of the graphs matches the values in the following table?

p	3.61	2.89	2.25	1.69
q	0.95	0.85	0.75	0.65

    ii Find an equation connecting p and q.
    iii Find the value of p when $q = 0.25$.

N6.10   The brightness of light, L, at a certain point is inversely proportional to
the square of the distance, d, of the point from the source of the light.

a   Express this relationship mathematically.
b   Calculate the ratio of the brightness of light 2 metres from a bulb to
the brightness of light 6 metres from the bulb.

N7
Miscellaneous

N7.1 Morag either runs or cycles to work. When she compares her average running speed with her average cycling speed, she finds the two average speeds are in the ratio:

$$1 : 2.5$$

It takes Morag 45 minutes to run to work.

a How long would you expect Morag to spend cycling to work?

Morag says that the journey to work is almost exactly 6 km.

b Using this distance, calculate her average cycling speed (in kph).

N7.2 The rainfall at an airport was measured (in mm) each day for a week. The records were given in this way:

Mon 4.2   Tue 3.5   Wed 0.4   Thurs 2.1   Fri 0   Sat 0   Sun 1.2

a Calculate the average daily rainfall:
   i in millimetres   **ii** in inches.

The runways have a total surface area of 4.2 km².

b Calculate the total volume of rain that fell on the runways over the week:
   i in litres   **ii** in gallons.

c In litres per hour, what was the average amount of rain that fell on the runways over the week?

Algebra

A1
Formulas

A1.1 One formula used to calculate velocity v is: $v = u + ft$

   a Calculate the value of v when $u = 0$, $f = 8$ and $t = 12$

   b Calculate the value of v when $u = 3.5$, $f = 15.6$ and $t = \frac{1}{4}$.

   c **i** Rearrange the formula to express t in terms of v, u, and f.

      ii Calculate t when $u = 6.2$, $v = 30.7$ and $f = 5$.

A1.2 Tradewinds is a mail-order firm that sells T-shirts for £6.99 each.
To every order they add £3.50 for postage and packing.

   a Write down a formula for the total cost, £C, of an order for n T-shirts.

   b Show how you use your formula to calculate the total cost for an order of 5 T-shirts.

A1.3 Trolleycraft's new supermarket trolley has 8 wheels.
Jenny uses Trolleycraft's formula to work out how many wheels to order:

$$w = 8t + 3600$$

where w is the total number of wheels to order and t is the number of trolleys they expect to sell.
Trolleycraft expect to sell 15 000 of these new trolleys.

   a Calculate the total number of wheels Jenny should order.

Jenny was on holiday, so Gary used the formula and ordered 28 200 wheels.

   b How many trolleys did Gary expect to sell?

A1.4 The power used by a light bulb can be calculated with this formula:
$P = IR^2$, where P is the power (in watts), R is the resistance (in ohms) and I is the current (in amps).

   a Calculate the value of P when $I = 8$ and $R = 60$.

   b Rearrange the formula to express I in terms of R and P.

A1.5 The formula for the volume V of a cone is: $V = \frac{1}{3}\pi r^2 h$,

where r is the radius of the base and h the perpendicular height.

   a Calculate the volume of a cone where $r = 4$ cm and $h = 12.5$ cm.

   b **i** Rearrange the formula to express r in terms of V and h.

      ii Calculate the value of r, to 1 dp, when $V = 50$ and $h = 25$.

A1.6 The diagram shows how boards in a fence are nailed together – with some nails just for decoration!
A single board needs 5 nails, two boards need 8 nails, three boards need 11 nails, and so on.

   a How many nails are needed for a fence of 15 boards?

   b **i** If b is the number of boards, and n the number of nails, write a formula for the total number of nails for any number of boards.

      ii Use your formula to calculate the number of nails needed for a fence with 1484 boards.

A1.7 Eco-hire use this formula to calculate the cost (£C) of car hire:

$$C = 12.50 + 0.18k + 35d$$

where k is the distance travelled in km and d is the number of days hire.
What is the total cost of 4 days hire when 1152 km was travelled?

A2
Solving linear
and simultaneous
linear equations

A2.1 Solve these equations:

a $5x + 3 = 12 - 2x$ **b** $3(x - 4) = 45 - 4x$ **c** $\frac{1}{2}x = 3.5$

d $5(y + 2) = 3(6 - y)$ **e** $\frac{3}{4}(6a - 30) = a$ **f** $4(1 - c) = 10$

A2.2 Pia is 5 years older than Sean.
If Pia is n years old, write an expression in n for Sean's age.

A2.3 A hockey club has d members. Three-eighths of its members are injured.

a Write an expression for the number of members who are not injured.
b 18 members have injuries, find a value for d.

A2.4 A picnic mug costs 8 pence and a plate costs 7 pence.

a Write an expression for the total cost in pence of n mugs.
b Jo bought y mugs and two more plates than mugs.
   i Write an expression for the number of plates bought.
   ii Write an expression for the total cost of the plates she bought.

Nick bought k mugs, and three more plates than mugs.
In total he paid 81 pence.

c Write an equation for the mugs and plates Nick bought.
d Solve your equation to find:
   i the number of mugs he bought
   ii the number of plates he bought.

A2.5 At the heritage tram centre, adult tickets are £6.
The charge for children is £3.50.
On 28 July 1990, n adult tickets were sold.
The number of child tickets sold was 228 more than the number for adults.

a Write an expression, in n, for the number of tickets sold at £3.50.
b Write an expression, in n, for the total paid for adult tickets.
c Write an expression, in n, for the total paid for tickets on 28 July 1990.

The total for ticket sales on 28 July 1990 was £24 947.00.

d Write an equation for the total ticket sales.
e Solve your equation to find:
   i the number of adult tickets sold on 28 July 1990
   ii the number of tickets sold at £3.50 on that day.

> As you are told that the
> total for the ticket sales was
> £24 947.00
> you can check your answer.

A2.6 **a** **i** Rewrite the equation $5(x + 8y) = 35$ to express x in terms of y.
   ii Solve your equation to find the value for x when $y = 7$.
b Solve the equation $5(p - 3) = 8(p - 6)$.

A2.7 I start with a number, k.
I double my number.

a Write an expression, in k, for the number I now have.

I start with k, treble it and subtract 5.

b Write an expression, in k, for the number I now have.

With one starting number k, when I double it, it gives exactly the same
answer as trebling it and subtracting 5.

c **i** Show this as an equation in k.
   ii Solve your equation to find this starting number.

A2.8 Liam sold 142 tickets for a show. This was p tickets at £4.50 and y at £6.

a Write two equations in p and y if he collected a total of £724.50.
b Solve your equations to find the number of each type of ticket sold.

A2.9 The plan shows a walkway around a tank at the sea-life centre.
Every edge of the walkway has a rail (but not over the way in or the way out !).

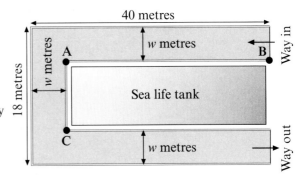

a Write an expression in *w* for the distance AB on the plan.
b Write an expression for the distance AC.
c Write an expression for the floor area of the walkway.
d Write an expression for the total length of rail used for the inside edge of the walkway.
e Write an expression in *w* for the total length of rail used for the walkway.

The total length of the inside and outside rails is 184 metres.

f **i** Write an equation in *w*, for the total length of rail used.
   ii Solve your equation and find the width *w* of the walkway.
   iii Calculate the floor area of the walkway.

A2.10 Wasim is a fencing contractor.
He has the contract for a post-and-rail fence around a car park.

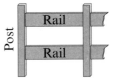

This table shows the number of rails needed for the number of posts used.

Number of posts	1	2	3	4
Number of rails	0	2	4	

a How many rails are needed with ten posts?

If *x* is the number of posts and *y* is the number of rails Wasim uses:

b Write down a formula that links *x* and *y*.
c Write your formula to express *x* in terms of *y*.

Wasim ordered 158 posts at the start of the job.

d How many rails should he have ordered for this number of posts?

The shape of the car park was changed and Wasim needed an extra 66 rails.

e How many extra posts did he need?

A2.11 Solve the simultaneous equations:

a $2x - y = 3$
  $3x + y = 5$

b $3w + 2t = 7$
  $2w + 2t = 5$

c $a - 3b = {}^-5$
  $4a + 2b = 8$

d $2p - t = 10$
  $5p + 2t = 7$

e $3y + 2a = 7$
  $4a + y = 9$

f $v + 5w = 95$
  $12v - 8w = 120$

A2.12 Jim has a part-time job stacking shelves in a supermarket.
In his pay packet last week he had £10 notes, £5 notes and £1 coins.
There were 4 fewer £5 notes than £10 notes.
There were 8 more £1 coins than £5 notes.

Jim had *n* £10 notes in his wage packet.

a Write an expression for the number of £5 notes in the packet.
b Jim had £96. How many £10 notes, £5 notes and £1 coins were there?

A2.13   Andy polishes cutlery. He is allowed 2 minutes 37 seconds to polish
3 forks and 5 knives. To polish five forks and 2 knives he is allowed
2 minutes 34 seconds.

    a   Write two equations for the time allowed to polish knives and forks.

    b   Solve your equations to find the time allowed to polish 4 knives and
a fork.

A2.14   A camp-site charges different fees for tents and caravans per night.
The first night the site was open there were 8 tents and 15 caravans, and a
total of £150.50 was collected in fees. The last night the site was open it
took a total of £273 in fees for 18 tents and 25 caravans.

    Write and solve two equations to find the fees charged per night for a
tent and for a caravan.

A2.15   A train from York to Scarborough had five coaches.
As the train left York, in the first coach there were 57 passengers, and
there were p passengers in each of the other coaches.

    a   Write an expression for the total number of passengers on the train.

    The conductor counted 301 passengers a few minutes after leaving York.

    b   Write an equation in p, and solve it, to give the number of passengers
in each coach.

    c   Factorise completely:

        i $9y^2 - 12y$ **ii** $4a^2 + 24a$ **iii** $125h + 50h^2$

    d   Solve the simultaneous equations:

$$3p - t = 6$$
$$4p + 4t = 16$$

A3
Quadratic and polynomial
equations

A3.1   Anna wants to solve the equation $x^2 + 4x = 20$, correct to 1 dp.

    First she tries $x = 4.0$, and finds the value of $x^2 + 4x$ to be 32.

    Try other values of x to find a solution to the equation $x^2 + 4x = 20$.
You must show all your working, and give your solution correct to 1 dp.

A3.2   A number w is the solution to the equation $w^3 = 40$.

    a   Between which two consecutive integer values must w lie?

    b   Use trial and improvement to find a value for w, correct to 1 dp.

A3.3   **a**   Find a value for c that solves the equation $c^3 - 4c = 105$.

    b   Explain the method you use and show any stages in your work.

    c   Find three solutions to the equation $c^3 - 4c = 0$.

A3.4   A number p is a solution to the equation $p^2 - 2p = 18$.

    a   Show that a solution to the equation lies between:

$$p = 5 \quad \text{and} \quad p = 6$$

    b   Use trial and improvement to find a solution to the
equation $p^2 - 2p = 18$.
Give the value for p correct to 1 dp.

A3.5   Use trial and improvement to solve the equation:

$$x^2 - 5x = 32$$

    Give your answer correct to 1 dp.

A3.6 Connor enters puzzle competitions to win prizes.
This is the latest puzzle.

> Two integers, both less than 100, are squared.
> When the squares are subtracted the answer is 1331.

Connor starts his working by writing this:
If the two numbers are k and m, then $k^2 - m^2 = 1331$.

He then uses trial and improvement. This is the start of his work:

Trial	k	m	k^2	m^2	$k^2 - m^2$	1331?
1	60	50	3600	2500	1100	Too small
2	62	50	3844	2500	1344	Too big

Rhian looked at trial 1 of Connor's work, and said that 50 and 60 could not possibly be correct, because of their last digits.

a Explain how, by just looking at the last digits, $60^2 - 50^2$ cannot be 1331.

b Either by continuing Connor's trials, or by another method of your own, find values for k and m such that:
$$k^2 - m^2 = 1331$$
If you use a method of your own, you must show all your working.

A3.7 Given that

> y is a decimal number to 1 dp, and
> $y^5 = 1307$ correct to the nearest whole number:

Find a suitable value for y, making sure you show all your working.

A3.8 A right-angled triangle is such that its base is 5 cm shorter than its hypotenuse, and its height is 40 cm shorter than its hypotenuse.
The triangle has an area of 750 cm^2 and the length of the hypotenuse is given as n cm.

a Show that an equation for the area of the triangle can be written as $n^2 - 45n = 1300$.

b Solve the equation to find a suitable value for n.

c Calculate the perimeter of the triangle.

A3.9 Explain why Alex could not solve the equation $2x^2 + 5x + 6 = 0$ using a trial-and-improvement method.

A3.10 **a** Show that the equation $1 + \dfrac{11}{x - 3} = x$ is equivalent to the equation $x^2 - 4x - 8 = 0$.

b Use the formula $x_{n+1} = 1 + \dfrac{11}{x_n - 3}$ to find a solution (to 1dp) to the equation $x^2 - 4x - 8 = 0$. Use a starting value of $x_1 = {}^-2$.

A3.11 An equation in x is given as $x(x + 2)(x - 2) = 16$.

a If a solution for x is given as $h < x < k$, where h and k are integers, find suitable values for h and k.

b Find a value for x correct to 1 dp.

A3.12 **a** Show that the equation $x^2 - x - 8 = 0$ is equivalent to $x = \sqrt{(x + 8)}$.

b Use the iterative formula $x_{n+1} = \sqrt{(x_n + 8)}$ to find a value for x, correct to 2 dp, that is a solution to $x^2 - x - 8 = 0$.

A4
Linear, quadratic and polynomial graphs

A4.1 **a** Give the equation of a line parallel to $y = 3x$.
  b Give the equation of a line a right-angles to $y = 3x$.
  c Give the equation of a line parallel to $y = \frac{1}{2} - 3x$ that passes through the point $(0, \ ^-2)$.
  d A linear equation is given as $x = \dfrac{y + 5}{3}$.

  Give this equation in the form $y = mx + c$.
  e Without drawing a graph, show that the point $(3, 4)$ lies on the line $y = 3x - 5$.

A4.2 When Gita keyed in the equation $y = \frac{3}{4}x + 2$ her calculator displayed this graph.

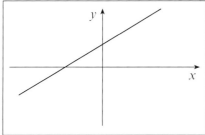

When Ian keyed in $4y = 3x + 8$, the graph looked the same as for Gita.

  a Show that Gita and Ian's equations are equivalent.
  b What is the gradient of the graph of $y + 3x = 4$?
  c Sketch the graph of $y = 3x - 4$.

A4.3 A standard and a longlife light bulb were both tested.
The standard bulb lasted for x days.
The longlife bulb lasted for y days.

  a The combined life of the two bulbs was 16 days.
    Explain why $x + y = 16$.
  b The longlife bulb lasted 5 days longer than the standard bulb.
    Write down a different equation that connects x and y.
  c Draw the graph of $x + y = 16$.
  d On the same axes draw the graph for your equation in part **b**.
  e Use your graphs to find the life of each type of bulb.

A4.4 **a** On a pair of axes draw the graph of $y = 3x + 5$.
    Use values of x from $^-3$ to 3.
  b On the same axes draw the graph of $y = 1 - x$.
  c Use your graphs to solve the simultaneous equations:
$$y = 3x + 5$$
$$y = 1 - x$$

A4.5 **a** Write the equation $4x = 6 + 3y$ in the form $y = mx + c$.
  b Draw the graph of $4x = 6 + 3y$ for x: $^-1 \leqslant x \leqslant 4$.
  c By drawing another suitable graph solve the simultaneous equations:
$$6 = 4x - 3y$$
$$4 = 2x - y$$

A4.6 By drawing two suitable linear graphs solve the simultaneous equations:
$$3x + 4y = 8$$
$$2x - 3y = 7$$

A4.7 Solve these simultaneous equations graphically.
$$2x + 3y = -8$$
$$3x - 4y = 5$$

A4.8   **a** On one pair of axes draw graphs of $2y = 3x - 4$ and $y = 5 - x$.
       Use values of x from $^-2$ to 4.

     b Use your graphs to solve the following pair of simultaneous equations:
$$2y = 3x - 4$$
$$y = 5 - x$$

     c Give the gradient of a line parallel to the line $2y = 3x - 4$.

     d Solve the equation $2x + 1 = ^-1.8$.

A4.9   This graph shows the charge for video repairs.

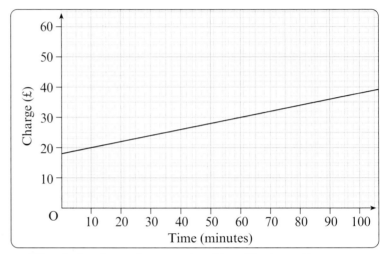

     a What is the charge for a repair taking 45 minutes?

     b What is the gradient of the straight-line graph?

     c What does the gradient of the line tell you about the charge?

     d Write down the equation of the line.

     e Ella decides that the most she can spend on repairing her video is £50.
        What is the maximum time that can be taken for this repair?

A4.10 **a** Draw a pair of axes with:
       values of x from 0 to 6 and values of y from 0 to 30.

     b Draw a graph of $y = x^2$ on these axes.

     c Use your graph to find an approximate value of x when $y = 12$.

     d Use trial and improvement to find a value of x for which $x^2 = 14$.
       Give your answer correct to 2 decimal places.

A4.11 **a** Draw a pair of axes with values of: x from $^-3$ to 3, and y from $^-3$ to 8.

     b Draw a graph of $y = x^2 - 2$.

     c From your graph give the two values of x when $y = 1$.

     d By drawing a suitable additional graph find approximate solutions to
       the equation $4x^2 - 8 = 4 + x$.

A4.12 **a** Draw the graph of $y = x^2 + 1$ for x: $^-4 \leqslant x \leqslant 5$.

     b By drawing a suitable tangent to the curve of $y = x^2 + 1$ find an
       approximate value for the gradient of the curve when $x = 2$.

A4.13   A designer is told that an arch-shape:

◆ has the equation $y = 8 - \dfrac{x^2}{2}$

and   ◆ has the y-axis as a line of symmetry.

a Draw a pair of axes with values of x from $^-4$ to 4, and y from 0 to 10.

b On your axes, draw a graph to show the complete arch-shape.

c Use your curve to estimate the value of y when $x = 2.5$.

d From your graph find two approximate values of x where $8 - \dfrac{x^2}{2} = 4$.

A4.14   **a** For values of x: $^-2 \leqslant x \leqslant 2$, draw the graphs of $y = x^3 + 1$ and $y = 2 - x^2$ on the same axes.

b Use your graph to find an approximate solution to the equation $x^3 + x^2 = 1$.

c On the same axes draw a graph of $y = x^2 + 2x - 3$. Use your graph to find approximate solutions to these equations:

i $2x(x + 2) = 5$
ii $x^2(x - 1) = 2x - 1$

A4.15   **a** For values of x such that x: $^-2 \leqslant x \leqslant 2$ draw the graph of $x^3 + x^2 - 4x - 4$.

b Estimate from the graph values of x, between $^-2$ and 2, that satisfy the equation $x^3 + x^2 - 4x - 3 = 0$.

c Draw a tangent to the graph at $x = 0.5$ and estimate the gradient of the curve at this point.

d By drawing the graph of $y = x^2 - 5$ on the same axes, estimate solutions to the equation $x^3 + 1 = 4x$.

A4.16   **a** For values of x between 0 and 10 draw the graph of $y = \dfrac{3 - x}{x}$.

b As x becomes increasingly large, explain what happens to the value of $\dfrac{3 - x}{x}$.

c By drawing an additional linear graph, find an approximate solution to the equation $x^2 - x = 3$.

A4.17   **a** On a pair of axes with values of x from zero to 10 draw the graph of $y = \dfrac{8}{x}$.

b On the same axes draw the graph of $y = 4x - x^2$.

i The equation $4x - x^2 = \dfrac{8}{x}$ has two solutions, only one of which is an integer value. Use your graphs to find the two solutions.

ii Calculate the non–integer solution correct to 2 dp.

c Estimate the gradient of the graph of $y = 4x - x^2$ at the point where $x = 1$.

A4.18   By drawing suitable graphs estimate a solution to the equation $\dfrac{2}{x} = x^2 + 2$.

A5
Inequalities, regions and
linear programming

A5.1 The school hockey team is planning a dance show to raise money for kit. Ticket sales must raise at least £420.

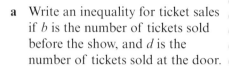

tickets: £3
(before the day of the show)

a Write an inequality for ticket sales if b is the number of tickets sold before the show, and d is the number of tickets sold at the door.

At the door
tickets: £4

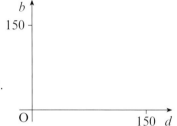

b On axes like these, draw the boundary line and shade out the region which does not meet the conditions for ticket sales.

The dance show will be in the sports hall. Safety rules allow an audience of only 150.

c Write an inequality with b and d to match the safety rules.
d On your graph shade out the region which does not meet the safety rules.
e If 46 tickets are sold before the show, what is the range of possible values for d?

A5.2 Write down all the whole number values of x, such that:

a $^-4 \leqslant x < 5$ **b** $1 \leqslant 2x - 5 < 10$ **c** $14x - 4x^2 > 0$

d $2 \geqslant x + 1 > ^-4$ **e** $9 \leqslant 3x + 4 < 22$ **f** $\dfrac{55}{x^2} > 4$

A5.3 Solve the inequalities:

a $2x - 3 > 13$ **b** $2(2x + 1) < 14$ **c** $13x + 5 < 7x + 3$
d $x^2 < 196$ **e** $9x + 4 > 15x + 16$ **f** $25 - x^2 < 16$
g $x^2 < 1$ **h** $2(3x - 2) < 11$ **i** $3 < x + 1 \leqslant 10$

A5.4 If p is an integer, write down the greatest value of p for which $5p + 4 < 21$.

A 5.5 Rearrange the inequality $5d - 4 < 12 + 2d$ into the form $d <$ a number.

A5.6 **a** Draw a pair of axes with values of x from 0 to 5, and y from 0 to 5.
b Shade in the single region which satisfies all these inequalities:

$$y > 2 \qquad 0 < x < 4 \qquad x + y > 5$$

A5.7 p is an integer such that $^-6 \leqslant p < 1$.
What is the smallest possible value of p^3?

A5.8 **a** What are the equations of lines AB and CD?

b List the three inequalities which define the shaded triangular region.

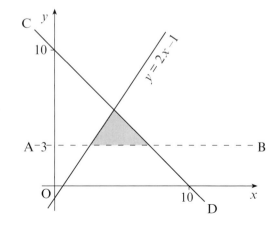

A5.9 Copy the graph and shade the region where the following inequalities are both true.

$y > x + 1$ and

$y < 4 - 2x$

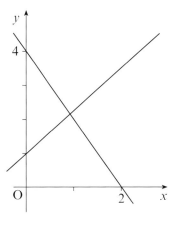

A5.10 On a set of axes label with a letter R the single region which satisfies all of these inequalities: $x > 5$, $y > 2$, $y < \frac{1}{2}x + 1$

A5.11 A village school is organising a fete to raise money. The fete will take place on a playground which has an area of 400 square metres.
Two types of stall will be allowed: charity stalls and dealer stalls.
Each charity stall is allowed 40 metres^2 and each dealer stall 20 metres^2.
The school makes £5 profit from each charity stall and £8 profit from each dealer stall.
The organisers want more dealer stalls than charity stalls.
Let c be the number of charity stalls and d the number of dealer stalls.

a Show that the inequality for the space available can be written as $2c + d \leq 20$.

b Write an inequality which compares the number of each type of stall.

c The school wants to make a profit of at least £80.
Write an inequalty involving c and d for the profit.

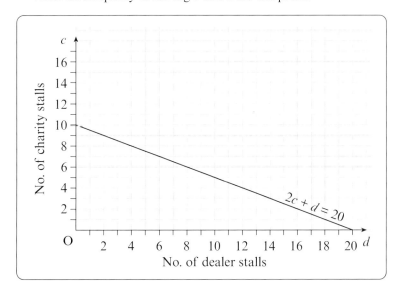

d The graph above shows the boundary for the space condition.
Copy the graph, show the other boundaries and shade out the regions which do not meet the conditions.

e What is the maximum value for the total number of stalls?
How many of each type is this?

f What is the maximum profit the school could make while satisfying all the conditions?

A6
Manipulation

A6.1 Given that $v = \frac{1}{2}$, $w = \frac{3}{4}$, $x = 3$ and $y = {}^-2$ evaluate:

a $\dfrac{v}{w}$ b wx^2 c $(v + w)^2$

d $\dfrac{v^2 + w}{x}$ e $x^3 - vy$

A6.2 Multiply out:

a $5x(2x - 3)$ b $4a(3x^2 + a - 1)$ c $(x - 2)^2$ d $a(a^2 - 2a + 3)$

A6.3 Expand and simplify:

a $(x + 3)(x + 2)$ b $(y + 1)(y - 2)$ c $(2x + 1)(x - 2)^2$
d $(5w + 2)(2w - 5)$ e $(c - 2)^3$ f $(x + 2)(2x - 3)(x - 1)$

A6.4 Use the formula $v = \dfrac{1}{r} + \dfrac{1}{t}$ to:

a calculate v when $r = 5$ and $t = 3$
b give the value of v as a decimal when $r = 8$ and $t = 5$.

A6.5 For the formula $v^2 = u^2 + 2fs$:

a calculate the value of v if $u = 12.5$, $f = 32$ and $s = 24.75$
b rearrange the formula so that u is the subject
c   i make s the subject of the formula
     ii calculate the value of s, when $f = 32$, $v = 252$ and $u = 248$.

A6.6 a Evaluate the formula $\sqrt{s} = ft^2$:

     i when $f = 32$ and $t = 5$ ii when $f = 32$ and $t = \frac{1}{2}$.

b Make f the subject of the formula.
c Make t the subject of the formula.
d   i Calculate a value for t when, $s = 256$, and $f = 32$.
     ii Iqbal said that when t is calculated from this formula, it always has
     two values. Do you agree? Explain your answer.

> When you are looking for rules, or writing formulas, it often helps to look at differences in sequences.

A6.7 Factorise each of these expressions completely:

a $vx + vy$ b $2x - 4y$ c $p^2 - 36$ d $y^2 - 18y + 45$
e $3ax^2 - 6ax$ f $h^2 + ht$ g $a^2b - b^2a$ h $6a^2 + 2a^2b$

A6.8 Factorise each of these expressions:

a $4a^2b - 6a^2b^2$ b $t^2 + 9t - 90$ c $2m^2 - m - 3$ d $p^2 - 13p + 36$
e $4h^2 - 11h - 3$ f $6x^2 - 10x - 4$ g $n^3 - 16n$ h $8b^3 - 72b$

A6.9 To calculate the focal length of a lens this formula is used: $\dfrac{1}{f} = \dfrac{1}{v} + \dfrac{1}{u}$

where f is the focal length, v is the distance from image to lens, and u is the distance from object to lens.

a Calculate the exact value of f when $v = 2$ and $u = 5$.
b Calculate f when $u = 0.1$ and $v = 2.5$.

A6.10 This logo is four rectangles (equal in size) around a square.

a Write and simplify an expression for the perimeter of the logo.
b Show that the area of the logo is given by $4w(w + 4) + 16$.

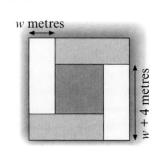

w metres

$w + 4$ metres

A7
Number patterns and sequences

A7.1 Jo is planning a design for paving slabs in a shopping centre.
Work on the scheme will start on day 1.
The numbers on the plan shows the day each slab is to be put in place. So:

4	3	2	1	2	3	4
4	3	2	2	2	3	4
4	3	3	3	3	3	4
4	4	4	4	4	4	4

on day 1   1 slab is placed
on day 2   5 slabs are placed
on day 3   9 slabs are placed.

This pattern continues to build up.

a Copy and complete this table, up to day 7.

Day number, d	1	2	3	4	5	6
Number of slabs, n	1	5	9			

b **i** Write a formula in n and d that can be used to calculate the number of slabs placed on any day.
   ii With your formula, calculate how many slabs are placed on day 41.

A7.2 This is part of a sequence P of whole numbers:

   ..., 2 , 4 , 8 , 16 , a , b , c , ...

a In sequence P, what are the values of a, b, and c?
b For the complete sequence P, are all numbers even? Explain.
c Write an expression for the nth term of sequence P.

This is part of another whole number sequence (R).

   0 , 1 , 3 , 7 , 15 , ... , ... , ... ,

d What are the next two terms of sequence R after 15?
e Write an expression for the nth term of sequence R.
f Calculate the 150th term of sequence R.

A7.3 When Forth CD opened every fourth customer was given a free CD.

a Which of these were given a free CD?

   Jenny   Raj   Ranjit   Dave   Iqubal   Mel
   50th   72nd   104th   138th   216th   550th

b Every 150th customer was given a free personal CD player.
The nth customer was the first one to have a free CD and CD player.
What was the value of n?

A7.4 The nth term of a sequence is given by the expression: $n(n + 1)^2$.

a List the first five terms of the sequence.

b Explain why every term in the sequence must be an even number.

A7.5 Some designs are made with pins and springs. They grow in a regular way.

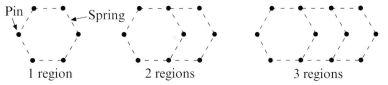

   1 region   2 regions   3 regions

a Complete the table for up to 8 regions.

b Write a general term in n for
   i the number of pins, p
   ii the number of springs, s.

Number of regions, n	1	2	3
Number of pins, p	6	9	12
Number of springs, s	6	10	14

c One design has 225 pins. How many springs does it have?
d Another design has 226 springs. How many pins does it have?

A7.6 The nth term of a sequence is given by:

$$a_{n+1} = 3a_n - 3a_n^2$$
$$a_1 = 0.2$$

Although you are asked to give each term to only 3 sf, make sure you keep the full values in your calculator as you go along.

a Calculate the first four terms giving each answer to 3 sf.
b As n becomes larger, the value of a_n approaches a limit. Between which two numbers, to 1 decimal place, is the limit situated (for example, between 0.3 and 0.4)?

A7.7 The fourth term of a sequence is 319.
The sequence is generated by $s_{n+1} = 4s_n + 3$.
What is the first term?

A7.8 Write an expression for the nth term in each of these sequences.

a 3, 7, 11, 15, ...
b 49, 48, 47, 46, 45, ...
c 5, 7, 9, 11, 13, ...
d 0, 3, 8, 15, ...
e 1, 8, 27, 64, ...
f 2, 6, 12, 20, 30, ...
g 9, 16, 23, 30, 37, 44, ...
h 1, 3, 7, 15, 31, 63, ...

A7.9 For each fractional sequence:

a list the next two terms.
b find an expression for the nth term.

A $\frac{1}{3}, \frac{2}{5}, \frac{3}{7}, \frac{4}{9}, \frac{5}{11}, \cdots$
B $\frac{2}{99}, \frac{4}{98}, \frac{6}{97}, \frac{8}{96}, \frac{10}{95}, \cdots$
C $\frac{1}{2}, \frac{8}{3}, \frac{27}{4}, \frac{64}{5}, \cdots$
D $\frac{1}{2}, \frac{2}{3}, \frac{3}{4}, \frac{4}{5}, \cdots$
E $\frac{2}{3}, \frac{4}{9}, \frac{8}{27}, \frac{16}{81}, \cdots$
F $\frac{59}{61}, \frac{56}{64}, \frac{51}{69}, \frac{44}{76}, \cdots$

A8
Functions and graphs

A8.1 **a** The diagram shows a sketch of $y = f(x)$. Copy the sketch and add a sketch of $y = f(x) - 3$ to your diagram.
b On your diagram sketch a graph of $y = f(x - 3)$.

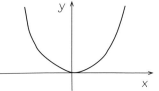

A8.2

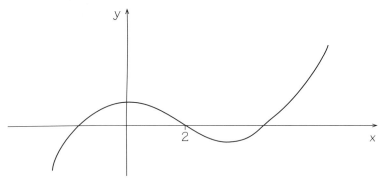

This is a sketch of the graph of $y = f(x)$ where $f(x) = (x + 1)(x - 2)(x - 5)$.

a Calculate the value of $f(0)$.
b On a pair of axes sketch a graph of $y = f(^-x)$.
c Describe a single transformation that will map the graph of $y = f(x)$ on to the graph of $y = f(^-x)$.
d Use your graph to suggest solutions to the equation $f(x) = f(^-x)$.

A8.3 **a** For values of x where $^-5 \leqslant x \leqslant 5$ draw the graph of $y = f(x)$
  when $f(x) = (x - 2)^2 + 6$.
  b On the same axes draw the graph of $y = x^2$.
  c Describe the transformation that will map the graph of
  $y = (x - 2)^2 + 6$ on to the graph of $y = x^2$.

A8.4 The graph of $y = 5x^2 - x^3$ is plotted on the axes below.

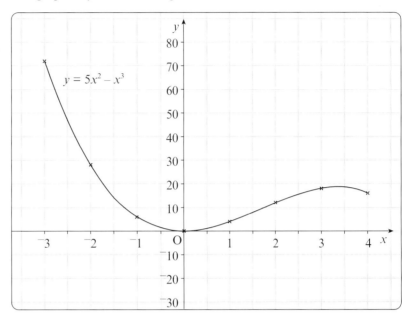

a Copy the axes and graph.
b Use your graph to find three approximate values of x that satisfy the
  equation $5x^2 - x^3 = 10$.
c **i** On your axes draw a reflection of your graph in the line $y = 0$.
  ii Give the equation of the image produced.
d **i** From your graph show that the equation $x^3 - 5x^2 + 9x + 18 = 0$
    has a solution for x, where $^-2 \leqslant x \leqslant ^-1$.
  ii Estimate one solution to the equation $x^3 - 5x^2 + 9x + 18 = 0$.
  iii Find a solution to $x^3 - 5x^2 + 9x + 18 = 0$ correct to 2 dp.

A8.5 **a** Sketch a graph of $y = \dfrac{2}{x}$.

  b On your diagram reflect the graph of $y = \dfrac{2}{x}$ in the line $x = 0$.

  c Give the equation of the image after reflection.

A8.6 **a** For values of x from $^-2$ to 5, draw the graph of $y = 2x^2 - x^3$.
  b Use the graph to find an approximate value of x that will satisfy
  the equation $2x^2 - x^3 = 10$.
  c Between $^-2$ and 5, the equation $n = 2x^2 - x^3$ has only one solution.
  Comment on the value of n.
  d **i** Sketch the reflection of $y = 2x^2 - x^3$ in the line $y = 0$.
  ii Give the equation of the image after reflection.

A8.7 The diagram shows a sketch of the graph of
  $y = f(x)$
  a Sketch the graph of $y = f\left(\dfrac{x}{2}\right)$.

  b Sketch the graph of $y = f(x - 1)$.

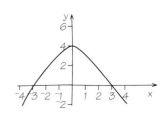

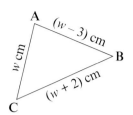

A9
Miscellaneous

A9.1 Triangle ABC has sides of: w cm, $(w + 2)$ cm, and $(w - 3)$ cm.

a Write and simplify an expression for the perimeter of ABC.

ABC has a perimeter of 41 cm.

b Find the length of each side of the triangle.

A9.2 **a** For triangle CDE, write an expression for the length of CE.

Misha and Greg work out a formula for the area A of triangle CDE.

Misha gives $A = \dfrac{m(6 + k)}{2}$

and Greg gives $A = 0.5\,km + 3\,m$.

b Which formula is correct? Explain your answer.

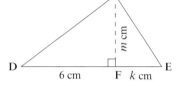

A9.3 The diagram shows a kite shape with one line of symmetry. Let A be its area.

Kim and Patrick both write a formula for the area of the kite.

Kim writes:

$A = 3x^2 - [ab + b(3x - a)]$

Patrick writes:

$A = 3x(x - b)$

a Show that these two formulas are equivalent.

b Find the area of the kite shape if $x = 8.4$ cm, $a = 5.6$ cm, and $b = 4.2$ cm.

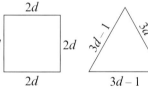

A9.4 The diagram shows a square of side $2d$, and an equilateral triangle of side $3d - 1$.

The two shapes have the same perimeter.

a Write and simplify an expression in d for the area of the triangle.

b The two shapes have the same perimeter. Write and solve an equation to find the dimensions of each shape.

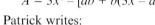

A9.5 You take part in a quiz.
You have no calculator, and nothing to write with.
The first question in the arithmetic round is: Work out $0.4 \times 700\,000$.

a **i** Explain a method you might use to work out the answer.
ii What is $0.4 \times 700\,000$?

b Factorise $na + nb$

c The second question in the round is:
Work out $(0.4 \times 560\,000) + (0.4 \times 140\,000)$
i Explain how your answers to parts **a** and **b** can help with the second question.
ii What is $(0.4 \times 2600) + (0.4 \times 1400)$?

A9.6 Salma chooses an integer value.
All she will say about it is that n represents the value.

a Explain why $2(n - 1)$ must be an even number.
b Explain why
n + one more than n + one less than n
gives an answer that must be a multiple of three.

A9.7 Two consecutive numbers are such that:

$$(3 \times \text{first number}) + (4 \times \text{second number}) = 172$$

    a Write and solve an equation to find the two numbers.
    b What are the common factors of the two numbers?
    c What is the LCM of the two numbers?
    d Multiply the two numbers, and give the answer in standard form.

A9.8   **a** Factorise $a^2 - 4b^2$.
    b Explain how this factorisation can help you calculate the value of:

$$12.5^2 - 5.5^2$$

    without using a calculator.

A9.9 You think of a whole number n, and tell Sian and Mina.

    Sian doubles your number and adds 3.
    Mina subtracts 4 from your number.

    a Write and simplify an expression for the answer A when Sian and Mina multiply their numbers..
    b If the answer A is zero, what can you say about the number chosen?
    c Show that $4n^3(n + 11) + 12(10n + 12) - 87n^2$ is an expression for A^2.

A9.10 Two groups of people went to the cinema:

    Group A. Two adults and five children. Their tickets cost £26 in total.
    Group B. Four adults and three children. Their tickets cost £31 in total.

    a Write two equations to represent this data.
    b Draw graphs of your equations on the same axes.
    c Use your graphs to find an approximate charge for an adult ticket, and for a child's ticket.
    d Solve your equations algebraically for accurate values for the ticket prices.

A9.11   **a** For values of x from zero to 10, draw the graph of $y = \dfrac{2 + x}{x}$.

    b Describe the value of y as the value of x becomes large.
    c Give the equations of two asymptotes to the graph of $y = \dfrac{2 + x}{x}$.

    d By drawing a suitable additional linear graph, use your graph to find an approximate solution to the equation $x(3x + 2) = 2(2 + x)$.

A9.12   **a** Solve the equation $2x^2 + 3x - 8 = 0$ giving solutions correct to 2 dp.
    b By drawing appropriate graphs show that $2x^2 + 3x - 8 = x^2 - 3x - 2$ has a solution where $0 \leqslant x \leqslant 1$.
    c Estimate this solution from the graph.
    d Find this solution correct to 2 dp using the formula for the solution of quadratic equations.

Shape, space and measures

S1
Angles and polygons

S1.1

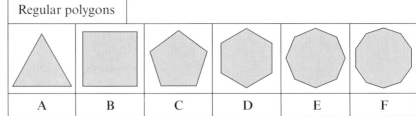

Regular polygons					
A	B	C	D	E	F

a Name each regular polygon in the table.
b For polygons A, B and C, give the sum of the interior angles.
c For polygons D, E and F give the size of one interior angle.
d **i** A regular heptagon has how many sides?
   ii Calculate the size of one interior angle of a regular heptagon.
e Calculate the size of an exterior angle of polygon F.
f Which of these polygons are shapes that will tessellate? Explain your answer.

S1.2 The diagram shows part of the roof frame of a building.
AR = RC = RT = PT = DP = AP
Angle ADT = 55°
Angle ABT = 38°

a What type of triangle is △ARP?
b Calculate angle PTR. Explain your working.

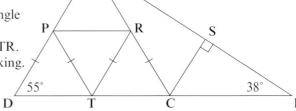

Sketch a diagram to work on. Label any angle or distance you know, or have calculated on your sketch.

When you are asked to explain or give reasons, it is important to do so clearly. In this way you will gain the maximum number of marks.

c Calculate angle CAS. Give reasons for your answer.

An identical frame is placed so that the quadrilateral ABWD is formed.

d What is the mathematical name of the quadrilateral:
   i ABWD
   ii ACWD
   iii PRCD?

e How many lines of symmetry has the shape:
   i ABWD
   ii ACWD
   iii PRCD?

f **i** What is the mathematical name for the shape PDXYCR?
   ii Is PDXYCR a regular shape? Explain your answer.

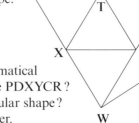

S1.3 A quadrilateral has angles of 54°, 37°, 40°, and k°.
Calculate the value of k.

S1.4 ABCDEFGHI, is a regular polygon.
K is the centre of the polygon.

a Calculate the value of *y* and the
value of *x*.
Explain your calculations.

b What can you say about the angles
KGE and GEK?
Give reasons for your statement.

c Calculate the size of angle GKE.
Explain your working.

GHIA and KGFE are both quadrilaterals.

d Is GHIA congruent to KGFE?
Explain your answer.

e **i** What is the sum of the interior angles of GHIA?
ii Calculate the size of angle AGH.

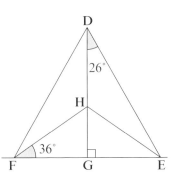

S1.5 The diagram shows a mast DG.
Wires from the mast are fixed at E and F.

FG = GE, and angle DGE = 90°.

a Calculate these angles and explain
your working:
i GĤF
ii HÊG
iii DÊH

b Give two reasons why FĤD = 126°.

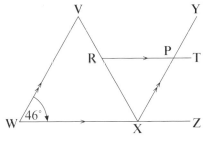

S1.6 A pentagon, PQRST, has angle P = angle R = 138°.
Also angle S = angle T = 111°.
It has one line of symmetry.

a Calculate the size of angle Q.

b Prove that PQ is parallel to RS.

c Show on a sketch any other sides which are parallel to each other.

S1.7 In this diagram RT is parallel to WZ, and WV is parallel to XY.
VW = WX, and ∠VWX is 46°.

a For each angle, calculate its
size, and explain your working.
i ∠WVX **ii** ∠YXZ
iii ∠VXY **iv** ∠XPR
v ∠YPT **vi** ∠TPX

b Explain why angle XRP is 67°.

c Is triangle PRX equilateral?
Give reasons for your answer.

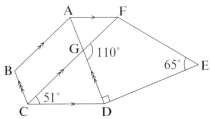

S1.8 In the diagram AF is parallel to CD, AB is parallel to FC and BC is
parallel to AD. ∠FCD = 51°,
∠FGD = 110°, ∠GDE = 90° and
∠FED = 65°.

Calculate the size of the following
angles showing your reasoning in
each case.

a ∠GFE   **b** ∠GAF
c ∠ABC

S2
Angles in circles

S2.1 In Diagram 1, AE, EB, FC and AC are straight lines. Angle FDE = 55° and angle FCA = 35°.

Calculate:

a angle DBC
b angle FED.

Diagram 1

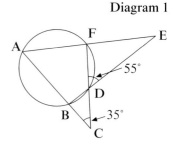

S2.2 In Diagram 2, A and B are the centres of two circles. GC is a tangent to both circles and meets them at points F and D. JH is a tangent to both circles. CH is a tangent to the circle with centre A.

a Prove that AB is a straight line.
b Prove that the line HJ bisects the line DF.
c Prove that angle DIF is a right angle.

Diagram 2

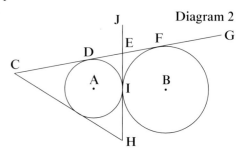

S2.3 In Diagram 3, FE is a tangent which meets the circle at C. $\angle DBC = 28°$ and $\angle BCE = 40°$. BC = BA.

Calculate the size of:

a $\angle CFD$
b $\angle CBA$
c $\angle BAD$.

Diagram 3

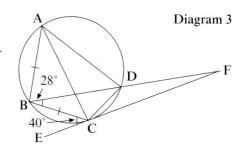

Build up your diagram so that it shows all the information you are given and have found.

You are expected to explain each stage you go through with mathematical reasons.

S2.4 In Diagram 4, EF is a tangent which meets the circle at D and point C is its centre. $\angle AGD = x°$ and $\angle BAD = y°$.

Express the following angles in terms of x and y. Simplify each expression as far as possible.

a $\angle ACD$ **b** $\angle BDE$
c $\angle ADB$ **d** $\angle ABD$

Diagram 4

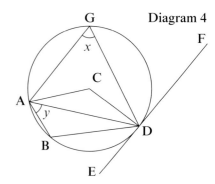

S2.5 In Diagram 5, BE and EG are tangents which meet the circle at points D and F. C is the centre of the circle. $\angle FDE = p°$ and $\angle AHD = q°$.

Express the following angles in terms of p and q.

a $\angle DHF$ **b** $\angle HDA$
c $\angle DFC$ **d** $\angle HFG$

Diagram 5

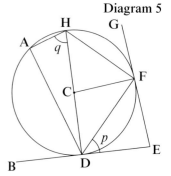

S3
Fixing position

S3.1 ABCD is a rectangle.

A is at (1, 4), B is at (3, ⁻2), and C is at (0, ⁻3).

a Give the coordinates of D.
b Give the coordinates of the point where the diagonals of ABCD intersect.
c Give the coordinates of the midpoint of AB.
d The rectangle is rotated 90° anticlockwise about the point A. Give the new coordinates of point B.

S3.2 The diagram represents a cuboid drawn on a 3-D grid.
The coordinates (x, y, z) of:

A are: (4, 0, 0)
C are: (0, 5, 3).

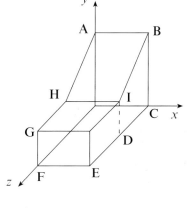

a Give the coordinates of:
   i B   **ii** D
b Give the coordinates of the midpoint of the line BD.
c Give the coordinates of the midpoint of the line DC.
d **i** Explain how you calculate the volume of this cuboid.
   ii If this cuboid is drawn on a one centimetre 3-D grid: Calculate the volume of the cuboid.

S3.3 Two points A and B are plotted on a 3-D grid marked in centimetres. A is the point (3, ⁻2, 5), and B is the point (3, ⁻2, 8).
What is the length AB?

S3.4 In the prism shown, these are some of the 3D coordinates:

H (0, 4, 6), E (5, 0, 12), A (0, 10, 0)

a What are the coordinates of each of these points?
   i F   **ii** C   **iii** B
   iv G   **v** D   **vi** I
b How many units long is the line CE?
c What angle does the plane AHIB make with the horizontal? Explain your reasons.

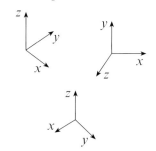

The x, y and z axes can be shown in many orientations, for example:

You need to remember that the coordinates are always given in the form (x, y, z) regardless of the spacial positioning of the axes.

S3.5 The L-shaped prism in the diagram has the following coordinates:

A (0, 4, 9), F (16, 8, 4), H(16, 0, 0).

a Give the coordinates of each of these points:
   i B   **ii** D
   iii G   **iv** C
b What is the volume of the prism in cubic units?

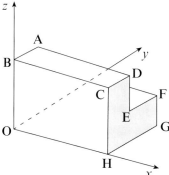

S4
Length, area and volume

S4.1 A washer is made by cutting a circle of metal from the centre of a metal disc.

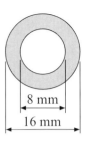

  a Calculate the shaded area of the washer.
  b Discs are cut from the centre of a strip of metal 25 metres long and 20 mm wide.
    i What is the largest number of discs that can be cut from one 25 metre strip?
    ii Calculate the total area of waste when washers are made from this strip.

S4.2 One of a set of childrens building blocks is an 8 cm cube with a hole drilled through it. The hole has a radius of 3 cm.

  a What is the volume of the block after the hole has been drilled?

  All of the surface area of the drilled block is to be painted.

  b Calculate the area to be painted on each block.

  c A litre of the paint to be used will cover 4 m². How many drilled blocks can be painted with 1 litre of this paint?

S4.3 A display sign at a garage is designed with a weight (the shaded part) at the bottom so it does not fall over in strong winds. The whole solid is basically a cone on top of a hemisphere. The diagram shows a section through the sign with the dimensions as given.

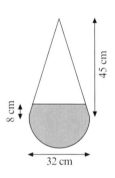

  a Calculate the volume of the whole solid.
  b Calculate the volume of the weight.

Problems like these on area and volume often use other aspects of mathematics such as Pythagoras' theorem, similar figures,
Area of $\Delta = \frac{1}{2} ab \sin C$,
and so on.

S4.4 A new park is to be made which is based on the position of an obelisk O. BC and AD are arcs of circles with centre O.

The bearings and distances of points from the obelisk are:

point A 045°, 90 metres
point B 052°, 30 metres
point C 128°, 30 metres
point D 135°, 90 metres.

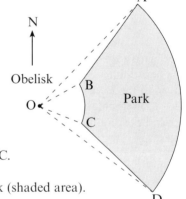

  a Calculate the angles
    i AOB   **ii** BOC.
  b Calculate the area of the sector OBC.
  c Calculate the area of triangle AOB.
  d Hence calculate the area of the park (shaded area).

S4.5 Three foam cubes have edges with lengths of 10 cm, 15 cm and 20 cm.

  a What would be the edge length of another cube which has the same volume as the total volume of the three above?
  b The cubes are stacked as a jewellery display stand which is then covered in velvet.
    What is the total surface area of the stack, excluding the bottom?

S4.6 A new brand of cheese comes shaped like a hexagonal prism of length 26 cm. The cross-section is a regular hexagon which measures 20 cm across the flats.

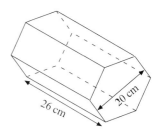

    a Calculate, showing all your working, the area of the cheese's cross-section.

    b What is the volume of the cheese?

The cheese is packed in a cuboidal box, as shown, so that it is a tight fit.

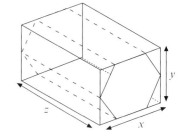

    c What are the dimensions x, y and z?

    d Calculate the volume of air in the box.

S4.7 The diagram shows a wire frame for a plastic refuse sack. The frame is made of three circles of wire and four straight wires welded together.

The top circle has a diameter of 45 cm, the middle circle a diameter of 40 cm, the bottom circle a diameter of 35 cm. The centres of the circles are 40 cm apart.

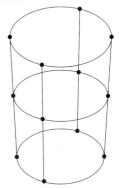

    a Calculate the total length of curved wire used.

    b Calculate the length of a straight wire.

    c Calculate the total length of wire used.

    d A plastic sack is placed in the frame. What is the capacity of the sack in cm³?

S4.8 A rectangular-based right pyramid container has the dimensions shown.

    a Calculate the perpendicular height of the pyramid.

    b Calculate its volume.

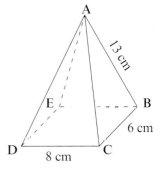

The pyramid is full of coloured liquid. This liquid is then poured into the cylinder shown which has a height of 10 cm and a curved surface area of 283 cm².

    c What is the radius of the cylinder?

    d What height will the liquid reach in the cylinder?

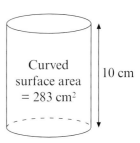

S4.9 In each of the expressions below, k and p both represent a length.
For each expression say if it represents an area, a length, or a volume.

a $3k$ **b** $2kp$ **c** $k^2(k + p)$ **d** $\frac{1}{k} \times p^3$

e Explain your answer to part **c**.

S4.10 All of the letters h, j, k, l and m represent lengths.
The letters are used in this set of expressions:

$$jk, \quad 0.75\pi h^2, \quad \pi k, \quad \tfrac{1}{2}\pi km, \quad \tfrac{1}{3}\pi m^2 l, \quad \sqrt{(k^2 + h^2)}$$

a Which of these expressions may represent area?
b Explain how you decide if an expression represents area.
c Which of the expressions represent a volume?
d Explain how you decide if an expression represents volume.

S4.11 This diagram shows a magazine storage box.
The letters represent lengths in centimetres.

This formula was given for the
volume of the box.

$$V = \frac{c(b + e)}{2}$$

Explain why this cannot be a formula
for a volume.

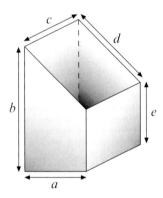

S4.12 The diagram shows a cross-section of a building
used as a velodrome.
The letters represent distances in metres.

An architect wants to estimate the area A
of the cross-section.

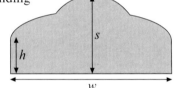

a The formula: $A = \frac{1}{5}(10h + 4s + w)$ is

suggested for this calculation.
Explain why this cannot be a formula for area.

b Three other formulas are suggested. They are:

$$A = \tfrac{1}{5} \times 10hsw \qquad A = \tfrac{1}{5}w(10h + 4s) \qquad A = \tfrac{1}{5}(w + 10h)$$

Which of these formulas might be a formula for area?
Explain your answer.

S4.13 Alex is a designer who works for a packaging company.
A supermarket asked for a box that was like a squashed cylinder.

The final design Alex decided on had lengths in centimetres labelled as:

$$b \qquad h \qquad \text{and} \qquad s$$

These expressions represent quantities that are part of Alex's design:

$$\pi bh \qquad \pi(b + s) \qquad \pi bhs \qquad \pi h(b + s)$$

a Which of these expressions might represent area?
b Which expression might be for volume?
Explain how you decided.

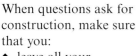

S5
Construction, loci and scale drawing

When questions ask for construction, make sure that you:
- leave all your construction lines visible
- do any drawing in pencil, so that mistakes can be erased
- do not erase any line, unless you have something to replace it with.

S5.1 On a grid mark the points P(2, 1) and R(5, 4).

   a On your grid mark any two points A and B, that are the same distance from both P and R.

   b Draw the locus of points that are the same distance from both P and R.

S5.2 The diagram shows two grooves in a stage floor, AB and CB, each 6 metres long.
A screen PR, 5 metres long, slides in the grooves.
When fully in use, the ends P and R are in groove AB.
For storage, P and R are in groove BC.

   a Construct an accurate diagram of the grooves. Use a scale of 1 : 200.

   b On your diagram draw the position of the screen when the end R is 3.5 m from A.

   c A point Q on the screen is 1 metre from the end P. Draw the locus of the point Q as the screen is moved from in use to its storage position.

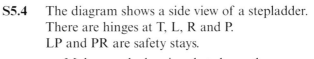

S5.3 The diagram shows a wheel of radius 1 cm that travels for 5 cm horizontally and then up a slope at an angle of elevation of 30°.
P is the centre of the wheel.

   a Draw the horizontal surface full size and **construct** the slope at an angle of 30°.

   b Draw the locus of the point P, as the wheel moves horizontally and then up the slope.

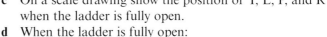

S5.4 The diagram shows a side view of a stepladder.
There are hinges at T, L, R and P.
LP and PR are safety stays.

   a Make a scale drawing that shows the position of T, L, P and R. Use a scale of 1 : 50.

   b Draw the locus of P as the ladder is opened and closed. Each leg moves by an equal amount.

When the ladder is fully open, LPR is horizontal.

   c On a scale drawing show the position of T, L, P, and R when the ladder is fully open.

   d When the ladder is fully open:
     i what is the angle at T?   **ii** how far below T is the hinge at P?

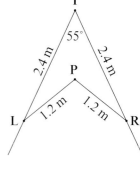

S5.5 Three towns A, B and C lie on the vertices of an equilateral triangle with sides of 8 km. A new superstore is to be sited equidistant from B and C and not more than 5 km from A.

   a Construct and label the triangle using a scale of 1 : 100 000.

   b Construct the locus of all points equidistant from towns B and C.

   c Show clearly the possible positions of the new superstore.

S5.6 The line AB, which is 10 cm long, forms a fixed side of the parallelogram ABCD. The sides AD and BC can vary in length.

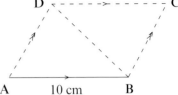

a Copy the line AB and draw the locus of point D which gives the parallelogram an area of 35 cm². Do not bother about points below AB.

b On the same diagram, draw the locus of point D which gives an angle of 90° to angle ADB.

c Shade in the region where the parallelogram has an area greater than 35 cm² **and** where angle ADC is less than 90°.

S5.7 The scale drawing below shows a hall with a power point at P and a new extension with no power points and a wooden floor.
An electric floor polisher is attached to point P with a lead and can reach up to 6 metres from it.

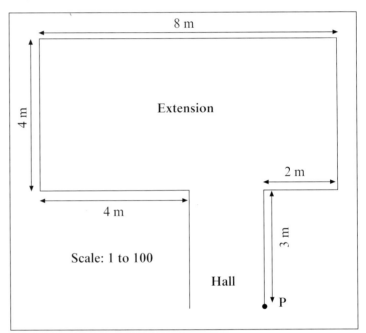

a Make a copy of the plan to the same scale.

b Shade the part of the extension floor which can be polished.

S5.8 The triangle ABC with sides of 3 cm, 4 cm and 5 cm is rolled clockwise along the line PQ.

With this type of rolling question try cutting/tearing out a template of the triangle and rolling that. It makes the problem much easier to visualise.

a Draw the triangle full size.

b Draw the triangle resting on different sides as it rolls along.

c Draw the locus of the point A as the triangle rolls through one complete revolution.

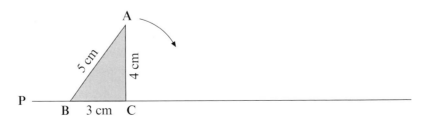

S6
Compound measures and graphs

S6.1 The 1996 Atlanta Olympic Marathon was won by Josia Thugwane of South Africa in a time of 2 hours 12 minutes 36 seconds (2:12:36).
The Olympic Marathon is run over:

26 miles 385 yards.

a Given that 1 kilometre = 0.6214 miles and that there are 1760 yards in a mile, calculate the marathon distance, in kilometres, correct to 1 dp.

b Calculate Josia's average speed over the course in km/h.

S6.2 The graph shows the journey of a bus and a taxi between Barnsley and Retford.

Barnsley to Retford is a distance of 60 km.

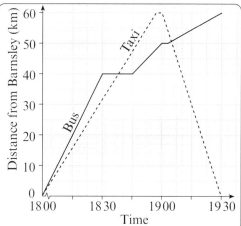

a When did the taxi pass the bus for the first time?

b At 18 45 how far from Retford was:
  i the bus
  ii the taxi?

c What was the average speed of the taxi between Barnsley and Retford?

d Describe the journey of the bus, in terms of distances, speeds and times.

e How long did the taxi spend in Retford before returning to Barnsley?

f The taxi driver sets a target to average 50 mph over a journey.
For the return trip, was he on target? Explain your answer.

S6.3 This graph shows the speed of a car over a 20-second interval.

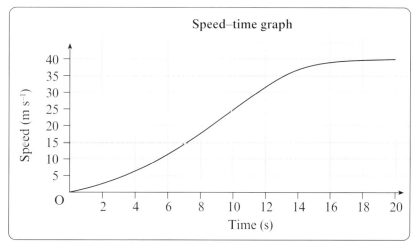

Speed–time graph

a Was there any point over the 20 seconds where the car was slowing down? Explain your answer.

b Estimate the acceleration of the car 8 seconds from the start.

c **i** Estimate the area under the graph for the interval $0 <$ Time <14.
  ii What does this area represent?

d Estimate the car's average speed over the first 14 seconds in km/h.

S6.4 The diagram below shows the cross-section of a river at Derpool measured at 4-metre intervals from the left bank.

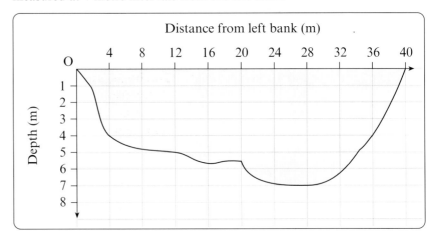

a Use the trapezium rule to calculate the cross-sectional area of the river to the nearest square metre.

b The water in the river is flowing at 0.25 metres per second. Calculate the time it would take (to the nearest second) for one million litres of water to pass the Derpool cross-section.

S6.5 The graph below shows the speeds of three runners A, B and C in a fixed distance athletics race. All three runners finished the race.

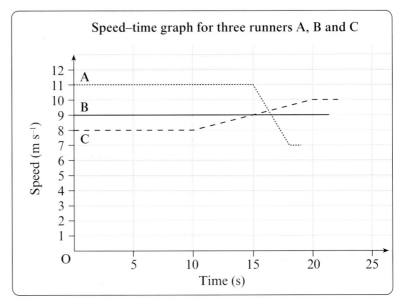

a Who won the race?
How can you tell?

b Over what distance was the race being run?
Explain your answer.

c How far had each person run over the first 15 seconds?

d What different strategy was being used by each runner?

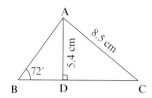

S7
Pythagoras and trigonometry

S7.1   In triangle ABC calculate the length of BC.

S7.2   This frame is made with 28 rods, each 18 cm long.

Calculate the direct distance between each pair of points.

a   A to Q
b   A to G
c   N to F
d   I to C
e   M to H
f   Q to G

Coordinates are used for each point on the frame.
For example: F is (0, 0, 0)   B is (18, 0, 0) and H is (0, 36, 0).

g   Complete these coordinates for P: (__ , 18, __)
h   Give the coordinates of Q.
i   Give the coordinates of M.

S7.3   When an aircraft takes off it climbs to its cruising height in two stages.
This diagram shows that for the first part of the climb, a ground distance of 15 miles was covered.

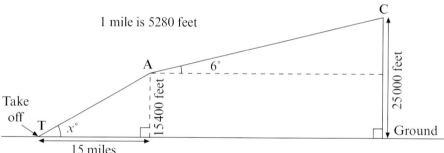

a   i   At first the aircraft climbs at $x°$ to the horizontal.
         (Give all calculator places.)

         Calculate the value of x.

    ii   Give your answer correct to the nearest degree.

b   i   For the second part, the climb is at 6° to the horizontal.
         Calculate the ground distance covered for this part of the climb.
    ii   Give your answer correct to the nearest 50 feet.

c   Give the total ground distance covered for the whole climb.

For each part of the question you must decide whether to work in feet or in miles, but avoid using both.

S7.4   The diagram shows a ladder placed between two sets of racks in a factory.
The ladder fixing is in the floor at P and reaches point B on one set of racks and point D on the other set.
Point B is 3.7 m from the floor.

a   Calculate the height of D above the floor.

b   Calculate angle BPD, the angle that the ladder turns through.

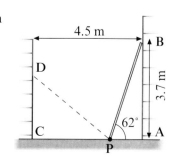

S7.5 The diagram shows the fishing boat Predator (P) and
two lights A and B marking wrecks.
A is 550 metres due north of B.

From P: the bearing of A is 058°, and
the bearing of B is 127°.

Calculate the distance:

a PA   **b** PB.

A second boat (R) is 600 metres from B.
The bearing of B from R is 212°.

c Calculate the distance of R from A.

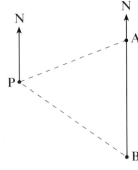

S7.6 The pilot of a rescue helicopter at point P sees a stationary dingy D.
The angle of depression to the dingy is 30°.

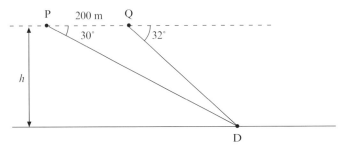

The pilot flies on 200 metres to point Q at the same altitude.
From Q the angle of depression to the dingy is now 32°.

Calculate the altitude *h* of the helicopter.

S7.7 The diagram shows a glass garden cloche in the shape of a right pyramid
with a square base with sides of 45 cm.
It is placed over plants and acts like a
mini greenhouse.

The lengths VB, VC, VD and VA are
all 50 cm.
Point E is on the base and directly
below point V.

a Calculate the length AC.
b Calculate the angle VAC.
c Calculate the height of the cloche.
d What angle does the plane VAD
make with the base ABCD?
e What volume of air does the cloche contain?

S7.8 A roof truss spans a distance of 8.2 metres and the pitches its sides are
35° and 42°. Calculate the height *h* of the truss.

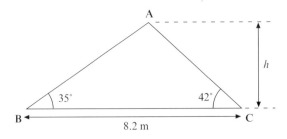

S7.9 A climbing frame in an adventure playground has a framework shaped like a tripod, where each leg is 2.4 metres long.

A net is later thrown over the frame.

A rope is tied round the frame by attaching it to the midpoint of each leg. This holds them together so that each leg forms an angle of 43° with the next leg.

Calculate the length of rope needed (ignore the rope used in the knots).

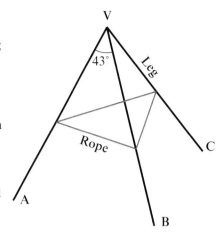

S7.10 The diagram shows a triangle DEC inside a larger one ABC. AD = 12 cm, DB = 14 cm and BC = 38 cm.

a Calculate the length AC to 1 dp.

b Calculate the area of triangle ABC.

c Show clearly why the length DE is approximately 10 cm.

d Calculate the length DE.

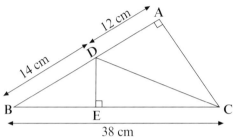

S7.11 A triangle ABC is constructed such that angle ABC = 52°, AC = 7 cm and BC = 8 cm.

Calculate the **two** possible values for the length BA.

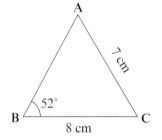

S7.12 The diagram shows a lighthouse, a buoy and a tanker.

From the lighthouse the bearing of the tanker is 130° and the bearing of the buoy is 220°.

The bearing of the buoy from the tanker is 265°.

The buoy is 3000 metres from the lighthouse.

a Calculate the distance of the buoy from the tanker.

The tanker heads directly towards the buoy at a speed of 15 knots.

b How far will it have sailed when it is at the point on its route which is closest to the lighthouse?

c After how many minutes will this be?

1 knot is a speed of 1 nautical mile per hour. 1 nautical mile is 1852 metres.

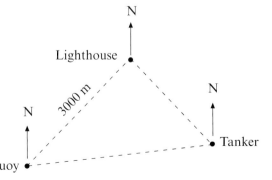

S8
Transformation

S8.1 Copy this grid, and the triangle ABC.

a Rotate ABC 180° about O. Label the image A′B′C′

b Rotate triangle ABC 90° clockwise about (2, ⁻1). Label the image A″B″C″

c Draw the image of ABC, after a translation with vector $\begin{pmatrix} ^-5 \\ 2 \end{pmatrix}$

Label the image A‴B‴C‴.

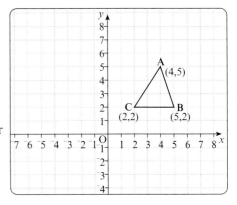

S8.2 Copy the grid and triangle ABC as for Question **S8.1**.

a Triangle ABC is reflected in the line $y = x$. Draw the reflection of ABC and label it A′B′C′.

b With B as the centre of enlargement, enlarge ABC by a scale factor of ⁺2. Label the image A″B″C″.

S8.3 a What single transformation will move the shape from position A to position B? The point (2, 1) is marked on the grid.

b The shape can be moved from position A to position B by combining two different transformations.

Give the two different transformations.

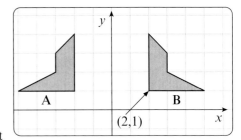

S8.4

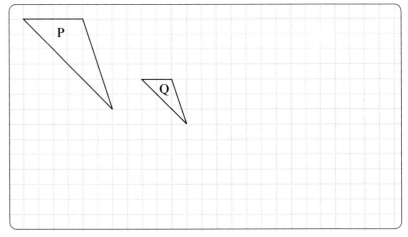

In this diagram, triangle Q is an enlargement of triangle P with centre of enlargement C.

a Copy the diagram on to squared paper.

b On your diagram, mark and label the centre of enlargement C.

c Give the scale factor of the enlargement.

d On the same diagram, draw an enlargement of triangle Q with centre C and scale factor ⁻1. Label the new triangle R.

e Describe fully a transformation, other than an enlargement, that maps triangle R on to triangle Q.

S9
Similarity and congruence

S9.1 Triangles NRC and WVY are similar.

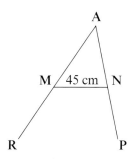

a What is the size of angle RNC?
Give reasons for your answer.

Dave calculates the distance VY to be 11.5 cm.

b Explain why Dave must be wrong.

c Calculate the distance VY.

S9.2 The diagram shows a stepladder used in a library. M and N are midpoints of the sides AR and AP.

a Explain why triangle ARP is similar to triangle AMN.

b Calculate the length of RP. Explain your working.

c Is triangle ARP an enlargement of △AMN? Explain your answer.

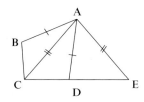

S9.3

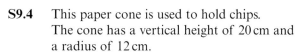

In the diagram, AB = AD and AC = AE, and angles BAD and CAE are equal.

a Show that triangles ABC and ADE are congruent.

b Show that AC bisects angle BCE.

S9.4 This paper cone is used to hold chips. The cone has a vertical height of 20 cm and a radius of 12 cm.

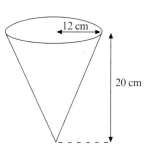

a Calculate the volume of the cone.

A mathematically similar cone has a vertical height of 24 cm.

b Calculate the volume of this larger cone.

S9.5 These two wooden blocks are similar.

The surface area of block X is 160 cm².
The surface area of block Y is 360 cm².

The volume of block X is 400 cm³.
Calculate the volume of block Y.

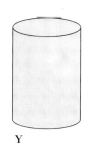

S10
Vectors

S10.1

PQRS is a parallelogram.

Write each of the following vectors in terms of **v** and **w**.

a $\overrightarrow{RS}$ **b** $\overrightarrow{PR}$ **c** $\overrightarrow{SQ}$

S10.2

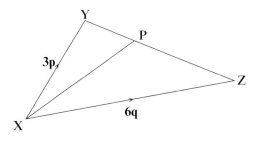

In this diagram, $YP = \frac{1}{2} \, YZ$.

Express each of these vectors in terms of **p** and **q**.

a $\overrightarrow{YZ}$ **b** $\overrightarrow{YP}$ **c** $\overrightarrow{XP}$

S10.3

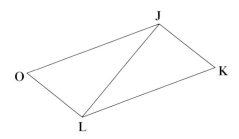

OJKL is a parallelogram.

$\overrightarrow{OJ} = 3\mathbf{x} + 4\mathbf{y}$ and $OL = 5\mathbf{x} - 2\mathbf{y}$.

a Give $\overrightarrow{JL}$ in terms of **x** and **y**.

b M is the point where $\overrightarrow{KM} = ^-2\mathbf{x} - 7\mathbf{y}$.

    Show that M lies on an extension of the line JL.

S10.4

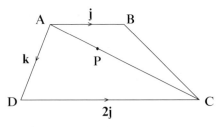

In this diagram, $AP = \frac{1}{3} \, AC$.

a Give each of these vectors in terms of **j** and **k**.

    i $\overrightarrow{BD}$ **ii** $\overrightarrow{AP}$ **iii** $\overrightarrow{CP}$

b Prove that the points B, P and D are collinear.

c Give the ratio BP : PD.

S11
Graphing trigonometric
functions

S11.1 **a** For $0° \leqslant x \leqslant 180°$ draw the graph of $y = 4 \sin x + 2$.
  b Use your graph to solve the equation $4 \sin x + 2 = 5.7$.
  c By drawing an additional suitable graph, on your axes, solve the equation $4 \sin x = \cos x + 3$

S11.2 **a** For $^-180° \leqslant x \leqslant 630°$ sketch the graph of $y = \cos x$.
  b Mark and label all angles shown by your sketch graph where $\cos x = 0.5$.

S11.3 **a** For $0° \leqslant x \leqslant 360$ draw the graph of $y = 2 \cos x + 1$.
  b Show on your graph that the equation $2 \cos x + 1 = 1.5$ has two solutions in the interval $0° \leqslant x \leqslant 360°$.
  c Use your graph to solve the equation $2 \cos x + 1 = 1.5$ for values of x between $0°$ and $360°$.

S11.4 **a** On the same axes sketch the graphs of $y = \frac{1}{2} \sin 3x$ and $y = \frac{1}{2} \cos 3x$. Take values of x such that $0° \leqslant x \leqslant 360°$.
  b **i** For $0° \leqslant x \leqslant 360°$, how many solutions are there to the equation $\frac{1}{2} \sin 3x = \frac{1}{2} \cos 3x$?
    ii Solve $\frac{1}{2} \sin 3x = \frac{1}{2} \cos 3x$ in the interval $0° \leqslant x \leqslant 360°$.

S11.5 **a** For $w: 0° \leqslant w \leqslant 90°$, and $k: 180° \leqslant k \leqslant 360°$. Draw a diagram to show w and k if $\tan w = \tan k$.
  b If $w = 42°$, find a value for k.

S11.6 **a** On a pair of axes draw the graph of $y = \sin x$, for values of x between $0°$ and $360°$.
  b The equation $\sin g = \sin 205°$ is satisfied by angle g. What is the value of g? (g is not $205°$).
  c **i** Show on your graph that the equation $\sin x = \frac{1}{4} \cos x$ has two solutions in the interval $0° \leqslant x \leqslant 360°$.
    ii Give approximate solutions to the equation $\sin x = \frac{1}{4} \cos x$.

S11.7 The height h metres of a fixed point P on a Ferris wheel, above a beam, after a time t seconds from the start of motion is given by the equation
$$h = 1 + 7.5 \sin (30t)°.$$
  a Draw a graph of h against t for $0 \leqslant t \leqslant 15$.
  b After approximately how many seconds is P level with the beam?
  c In the first 15 seconds, when was P a height of 4 metres above the beam?

S11.8 **a** For values of x from $0°$ to $360°$ draw the graph of $y = 3 \sin x$.
  b Use your graph to solve the equation $3 \sin x = 0.8$ in the interval where $0° \leqslant x \leqslant 360°$.
  c Find two approximate solutions to the equation $^-2 = 3 \sin x$.

S12
Miscellaneous

S12.1 The diagram shows a rectangle of paper with two folds, AB and CD.
The two folds cross at the point P so that:

AP = 10 cm and PB = 20 cm.

a Calculate the distance AE.
b Calculate the distance CP, giving your reasons.
c Calculate the distance AC.
d Calculate the size of angle ABE.
e Explain whether △ AEB and △ BDP are similar.

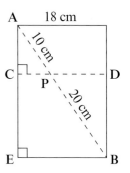

S12.2

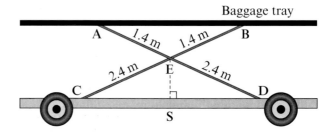

The diagram shows a baggage tray lift used for loading aircraft.
As the angle at E changes, the legs AD and BC move up or down.

The baggage tray is at its full height when angle AEB = 35°.

a At its full height what is the size of angle EDC?

A safety rod is fixed between E and S when the tray is at full height.
S is the midpoint of CD and angle ESD = 90°.

b Calculate the length of ES.
c Calculate the distance SD.
d Calculate the distance AB.
e When the tray is at full height, what is the perpendicular distance between the tray and CD?

S12.3 Draw a pair of axes with:

the x-axis from 0 to 12
the y-axis from 0 to 10.

a **i** Plot and label the following points:
A (0,0)   B (4, 10)   C (8, 10)   D (12, 0)
ii Join A to B, B to C, and C to D with straight lines.
b Draw straight lines to join:
i points A and C
ii points B and D.

Label the point where BD crosses AC as P.
From your diagram:

c List two triangles that are similar.
d List two triangle that are congruent.
e Calculate the area of triangle APD.
f Calculate the size of angle APD.

Handling data

D1
Probability

D1.1 Javed collected data on the faxes received by a company.
Every fax was for one of the following departments: UK Sales, Export Sales, Production.

UK Sales received half of all faxes.
Export Sales received one third of all faxes.
Production received all the other faxes.

Yesterday, two faxes were received before 7 am.

a Calculate the probability that:
  i the first fax was for UK Sales
  ii the first fax was for Production
  iii both faxes were for Export Sales.

b Calculate the probability that both faxes are:
either for Production or for Export Sales.

D1.2 A company made spinners to be given away with a games magazine.
The spinners were 5-sided, showing scores of 0, 1, 2, 3 and 4.
There was a fault in manufacture, and all the spinners were biased in the same way.
This table shows probabilities for the spinners:

Score	0	1	2	3	4
Probability	0.2	0.3	0.1	0.1	

a What is the probability of scoring 4 with one spinner?

b One of these biased spinners is spun 200 times.
Roughly how many times would you expect a score of 1?

c Two of these spinners are spun together 1000 times.
How many times would you expect to score a total of 3?

D1.3 Simon is fashion-conscious and likes to choose items of clothing that go together. When he dresses each morning he must decide whether to wear shorts or jeans, and whether to wear a T-shirt or polo shirt.

If he chooses jeans, the probability he wears a T-shirt is 0.7 and, if he chooses shorts, 0.3 is the probability that he wears a polo shirt.

In summer, 0.8 is the probability that he wears shorts.

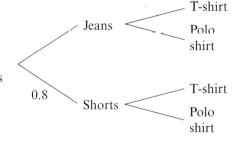

a Complete the tree diagram to show all the probabilities for summer.

b Calculate the probability that Simon wears a polo shirt on any particular day.

In winter Simon's shirt is covered, so it is an evens chance that he will wear either a T-shirt or polo shirt regardless of whether he wears shorts or jeans.
The probability that he wears jeans and a T-shirt is 0.45.

c What is the probability that Simon wears shorts in the winter?

D1.4 A bag contains 5 blue sweets and 4 red sweets.
Alison picks one sweet at random, notes its colour, then eats it.
Shane then picks another sweet and eats it.

   a Draw a tree diagram to show the situation and label the branches with the probabilities.

   b Calculate the probability that both Alison and Shane pick a blue sweet.

   c Find the probability that they pick sweets of the same colour.

Katy comes along and picks another sweet.

   d What is the probability that all three people pick blue?

Zoe and Sadiq then pick a sweet each.

   e What is the probability that all five people pick red sweets?

D1.5 A fox watches the entrance of a rabbit warren.
Rabbits either come out in different sized groups: singly, in pairs, in threes, and in fours.
The probability of different numbers of rabbits coming out in a group are:

Number of rabbits	1	2	3	4
Probability	0.4	0.1	0.2	

   a What is the probability that a group of three or more rabbits will emerge from the entrance?

   b If the fox watches while two groups of rabbits emerge, what is the probability that exactly three rabbits will have come out in that time?

D1.6 The probability that Amy watches BBC1 all evening is 0.3 if she does not know what programmes are on. The probability increases to 0.6 if she knows what's on.
If the probability that she knows what's on, on any night, is 0.9:

   a complete the tree diagram and show the probabilities

   b calculate the probability that Amy will watch BBC1 all night.

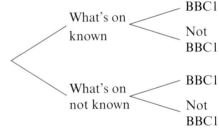

D1.7 Dawn throws a fair ten-sided dice eighty times and records the scores.

Score	0	1	2	3	4	5	6	7	8	9
Frequency	7	10	4	9	8	12	9	7	6	8

   a What was the relative frequency of a score of 8?

   b Find the relative frequency of a score greater than 3.

   c Dawn then programs a computer to simulate the throwing of the same fair dice 8 000 000 times.
What would you expect to be the number of times a score of 3 would be recorded? Explain your answer.

D2
Histograms and
frequency polygons

D2.1 Baxter Insurance asked each of its employees how long they took to travel in to work one morning.

This table shows the results of the survey.

Time (x minutes)	Frequency
$0 \leqslant x < 10$	33
$10 \leqslant x < 15$	36
$15 \leqslant x < 20$	47
$20 \leqslant x < 30$	84
$30 \leqslant x < 40$	49
$40 \leqslant x < 60$	56
$60 \leqslant x < 120$	96

Draw a histogram to represent the survey results.

D2.2 The Ritz Cinema carried out a survey to find out the ages of the audiences watching its films.
The age distribution of the audiences one Saturday are given in the table.

Age (years)	5 –	10 –	15 –	25 –	40 –	65 – 90
Frequency	27	38	43	57	55	35

Draw a histogram to show this distribution.

D2.3 The maternity ward at the Queen's Hospital recorded the weights of a sample of 60 new-born baby boys.

Weight (kg)	2.5 –	3.0 –	3.5 –	4.0 –	4.5 – 5.0
Frequency	5	13	21	15	6

a Give the mid-class value of the 2.5 kg class.
b Draw a frequency polygon to represent this data.
c Describe this distribution of weights.

D2.4 The following table shows the ages of the entries in the women's under-45 event at the Westbourne Open Tennis Championships.

Age group	18 20	21 – 25	26 – 30	31 – 44
Frequency	6	13	6	7

a Tony says the 18 – 20 age group has a class interval of 2 years.
　i Explain why Tony is wrong.
　ii Give the correct class interval of the 18 – 20 age group.
b What is the class interval of the 31 – 44 age group?
c Draw a histogram to represent the women's ages.
d This table shows the ages of the entries in the men's under-45 event.

Age group	18 – 20	21 – 25	26 – 34	35 – 39	40 – 44
Frequency	6	6	9	8	3

　i Explain why the mid-class value for the 21 – 25 group is 23.5 years.
　ii Give the mid-class value for the 26 – 34 age group.
　iii Draw a frequency polygon to show the men's age distribution.
　iv On the same diagram, draw a frequency polygon for the women.
　v Use the frequency polygons to compare the men's and women's ages.

D2.5 The marketing director of Baxter Insurance recorded the length of 100 telephone calls she made.

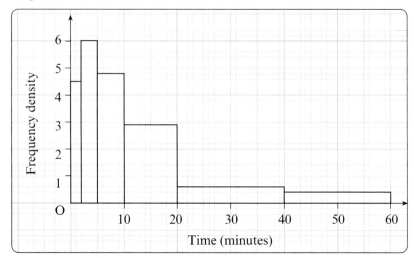

a She made 24 calls which lasted between five and ten minutes. How many calls lasted between 10 to 20 minutes?

b Make a table like this to show the number of calls in each class.

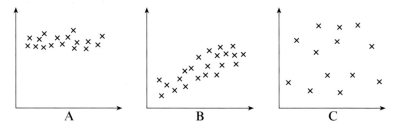

Time (t minutes)	$0 \leqslant t < 2$
Frequency	

D3

Scatter diagrams and correlation

D3.1 Scatter graphs A, B, and C describe different situations.

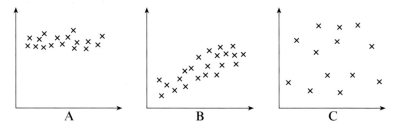

For each of these, say which graph might describe the situation. You might possibly state 'none of these'.

a the size of feet against age at which the driving test was passed

b height against age for children in a junior band

c height against boot size for members of a rugby club

d age against number of visits to a cinema in one year

e the age of adults compared with their height

f the number of tickets sold against how many days until a pop concert

Give reasons for your answers.

D3.2 Carlos carried out a survey of children between 7 and 15 years old. As part of the survey, age, height, weight, and shoe size were recorded.

a Sketch scatter graphs to show the most likely result of plotting:
   i age against shoe size
   ii height against weight
   iii shoe size against weight.

Carlos also collected data on fitness and drew a scatter diagram of height against fitness.

b **i** What correlation would you expect the graph to show?
   ii Give reasons for your answer.
   iii Sketch a possible scatter diagram for this type of data.

D3.3 The graph shows the results for a group of students who are studying French and Mathematics.

In each test there were a possible 30 marks.

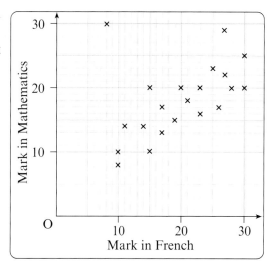

a Describe, in a sentence, what the graph tells you about the results.
b What correlation does the graph show?

Make a copy of the graph.

c On your copy of the graph, add a line of best fit (by inspection).

Iain is an average member of the group. He gained 18 marks in the French test, but was absent for the Mathematics test.

d Estimate what mark Iain might have gained in Mathematics. Give reasons to support your estimate.

Sofka is very good at Mathematics, but has only been studying French for a few months.

e Put a circle around the cross on your graph that could represent Sofka.

D3.4 A taxi driver recorded the time (*t* minutes), and distance (*d* km) for her twelve fares one day.

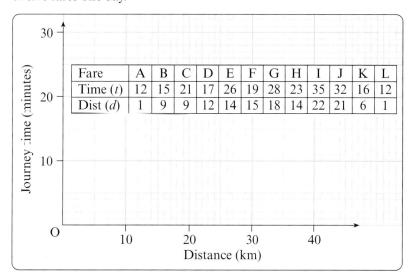

Fare	A	B	C	D	E	F	G	H	I	J	K	L
Time (*t*)	12	15	21	17	26	19	28	23	35	32	16	12
Dist (*d*)	1	9	9	12	14	15	18	14	22	21	6	1

a i Copy the axes as above.
  ii Draw a scatter diagram to show the information in the table.
b Describe the correlation shown by the scatter diagram.
c Add a line of best fit to your scatter diagram.

Her next fare is a journey of 18 km.

d From your diagram estimate how long this journey will take. Give reasons for your answer.

D4
Averages and measures
of spread

D4.1

Temperature (°C)	22	23	24	25	26	27	28	29	30	31
Number of days	4	3	4	2	6	3	5	1	2	1

The table shows the temperature at each midday, on a beach in August.

a What is the modal temperature?

b Find the median temperature.

c State the range for this distribution of temperatures.

d Calculate the mean temperature.
Give your answer correct to 1 dp.

D4.2 The table shows the
results of a survey (in 1990)
to find out how many
CDs teenagers buy
in a year.

a What is the modal class
for this distribution?

b Copy and complete
the table.

c **i** Calculate an estimate
of the mean number
of CDs bought in a
year by teenagers.

ii Explain why an exact value for the mean cannot be calculated.

Number of CDs	Frequency (f)	Midpoint (x)	fx
1 to 5	3		
6 to 10	8		
11 to 15	12		
16 to 20	10		
21 to 25	6		
26 to 30	1		

The survey was repeated in 1995, but the number of CDs were grouped
in this way: 1 to 10, 11 to 20, and 21 to 30.

An estimate was calculated for the mean number of CDs bought.

d Which estimated mean is likely to be more accurate, the 1990 or 1995?
Give reasons for your answer.

D4.3 A manufacturer of fuses tests them until they fail.
This table shows the failure times, to the nearest hour.

a Give the class
which contains the
median failure time.

b Calculate an estimate of
the mean failure time.
Give your answer to
the nearest minute.

c **i** Give a reason why
the mean failure time
is not the best average
to use when comparing
these fuses with a set
made by another company.

ii What might be a better average to use?
Explain your answer.

Failure time	Frequency of fuses	Midpoint
1 to 10	0	5
11 to 20	16	
21 to 30	12	
31 to 40	41	
41 to 50	8	
51 to 60	13	

D4.4 An ice-cream company is testing two machines that make choc-ices.

    a For machine A the weights, in grams, of a sample of choc-ices are:

        49   51   52   52   48   53   50   49   52   54

        Calculate the mean and standard deviation of this sample.

    b A sample from machine B has a mean weight of 52 grams and a standard deviation of 3.27 grams.
        Compare the samples from the two machines.

D4.5 A printing company has 8 employees. Their monthly salaries are:

        £1025 £1025 £1215 £1415 £1505 £1505 £1630 £1840

    a Calculate the mean and standard deviation of the monthly salaries.

    The management are considering two salary bonus schemes.

    b Scheme A gives all employees an extra £140 a month.
        What effect would this have on the mean and standard deviation of the monthly salaries?

    c Scheme B increases all salaries by 10%.
        What effect would this have on the mean and standard deviation of the monthly salaries?

    d If the employees were allowed to vote for one of the schemes, which scheme do you think would be the more popular?
        Explain your answer.

D4.6 From the Year 11 group at Valley School, 60 students achieved at least 2 GCSEs at grade C or above. The distribution is given in the table below.

Number of GCSEs	2	3	4	5	6	7	8
Number of students	3	6	8	11	17	9	6

    a Calculate the mean and standard deviation of this distribution.

    A mistake was made in recording the GCSE results and the correct distibution should have been as follows.

Number of GCSEs	2	3	4	5	6	7	8
Number of students	3	6	8	11	17	6	9

    b Without calculating the correct values, describe the effect this mistake has on the mean and standard deviation you calculated in part **a**.

D4.7 The table below shows the distribution of property values in Coalthorpe using the Council Tax bands.

Band	Property value (£000's)	Percentage	Midpoint
A	0 – 40	24	20
B	– 52	33	
C	– 68	21	
D	– 88	16	
E	– 120	6	

    a Calculate an estimate of the mean property value in Coalthorpe.
    b Calculate an estimate of the standard deviation of the values.

D5
Cumulative frequency

D5.1 Alison and James are professional snooker players. They practised daily before their last tournament and recorded the scores for 80 breaks.

This table shows Alison's break scores.

Break score (x)	$70 < x \leqslant 80$	$80 < x \leqslant 90$	$90 < x \leqslant 100$	$100 < x \leqslant 110$	$110 < x \leqslant 120$
Frequency	8	34	25	9	4

a Draw a cumulative frequency graph to show Alison's break scores.
b i Explain how you can use your graph to find Alison's median score.
   ii What is Alison's median break score?
c Give the interquartile range of her scores.

For his 80 break scores, James had a median score of 94, and an interquartile range of 14.

d Who was the more consistent player, Alison or James?
   Give reasons for your answer.

> Remember:
> cumulative frequency is shown along the vertical axis of a cumulative frequency graph.

D5.2 A consumer group tested a sample of eighty Super Cell batteries.
The life of a battery in a torch was recorded, in hours, in this table.

Life (hours)	450–	500–	550–	600–	650–	700–	750–	800–	850–
Frequency	5	7	14	20	0	14	11	7	2

a Draw up a cumulative frequency table for this data.
b Draw a cumulative frequency graph for the test results.
c Use your graph to estimate the number of Super Cell batteries which lasted more than 620 hours.
d Find the interquartile range for the data.
e Show on your graph the median life of a Super Cell battery.

In a second test eighty Mega Power batteries were tested.
The median life for a Mega Power battery was 560 hours, and the interquartile range of the Mega Power test data was 130 hours.

f Comment on the two types of battery tested.

D5.3 A survey asked people how many telephone calls they made in a week.
These are the results.

Number of calls	0 – 10	11 – 20	21 – 30	31 – 40	41 – 50	51 – 60	61 – 70	71 – 80
Number of people	8	15	26	21	4	2	0	9

a Draw a cumulative frequency table for the data.
b Draw a cumulative frequency graph to show the results of the survey.
c From your graph, estimate the median number of telephone calls made.

This headline was printed in a newspaper.

Survey shows we're hooked!

80% of people make more than 35 telephone calls a week

d Does this survey data support this headline?
   Give reasons for your answer.

D5.4 Melchester United Football Club are investigating the age distribution of their supporters. A sample of 200 supporters were asked their ages.

The ages ranged between 5 years and 70 years, and the lower and upper quartiles of the ages were 29 years and 44 years respectively.

a Draw a possible cumulative frequency curve for the sample.

b Use your curve to estimate the median age of the club's supporters.

c Use the curve to estimate how many supporters in the sample were aged between 18 and 35.

D5.5 During the month of June, the highest daily temperatures in Cape Town were recorded. The results are set out in the table below.

Temperature (°C)	0 –	10 –	15 –	18 –	21 –	26 –
Number of days	4	7	6	7	6	0

a Draw a cumulative frequency table for this data.

b Use your table to draw a cumulative frequency curve.

c Use the curve to estimate:
  i the median temperature
  ii the interquartile range of the temperatures.

The cumulative frequency curve for the highest daily temperatures in Durban in July is drawn below.

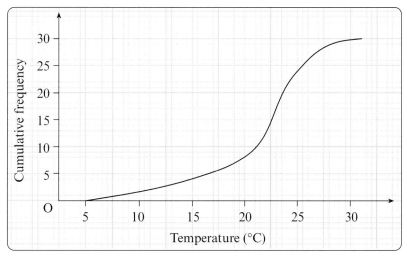

d Compare the spread of temperatures in Cape Town and Durban.

D6

Questionnaires and
sampling

D6.1 In a survey Ella asked three groups of 100 people this question:

Do you think we should build more canals?

These are the results:

Set A Yes 3   **Set B** Yes 88   **Set C** Yes 44
         No 97   No 12   No 56

The three groups of people she asked were:

  ◆ the Road Transport Federation
  ◆ people leaving a cinema
  ◆ the Canal Heritage Society.

a Match each set of results to a group of 100 people.

b Explain how you decided on your match.

c Which group do you think best shows public opinion? Give reasons for your answer.

D6.2 Imagine you want to find out the most popular flavour of crisps that are bought, and that you can ask 50 people.

a Design a data collection sheet for this information.

b Fill in your data collection sheet as if you had carried out the survey. (Invent replies for all 50 people asked.)

c Explain what the results of your survey show, and how this might help when ordering crisps for the school shop.

D6.3 In a soft drinks survey, students in years 10 and 11 were asked to comment on the soft drink they choose most often. These are the results.

		Orange juice	Milk	Fizzy drinks		
				Lemonade	Cola	Water
Year 10	F	15	7	21	40	15
	M	25	15	17	35	9
Year 11	F	21	9	18	34	22
	M	18	12	19	37	16

Lyn says that males (M) prefer fizzy drinks, and females (F) choose drinks that are not fizzy.

Does the data in the table support Lyn's view?
Explain your answer. Make sure you refer to years 10 and 11.

D6.4 A paper ran the following headline about teenagers and what they eat.

> **Has fruit had its chips?**
> 92 out of every 100 teenagers eat no fruit each day, but over half of them eat chips every day.

Is this true in your school?
List four questions you might ask to test this headline in your school.

D6.5 In a housing survey Ria and Mel wrote different questions to collect the same data.

Mel asked: "What type of house do you live in?"

Ria asked: Tick the box that describes the type of house you live in
Flat ☐ Semi-detached ☐ Detached ☐ Terrace ☐

a For each question:
  i give one advantage
  ii give one disadvantage

b How might you improve Ria's question?
Give reasons for your answer.

If, in the survey, you wanted to know the ages of the people questioned:

c **i** Give an example of two different types of question you could use.
  ii Which of the questions do you think is better? Explain why.

D6.6 Sanjay and Ruth are investigating how much money students at their school receive each week.
The number of students in each year group is given in the following table.

Year group	7	8	9	10	11
No. of students	202	187	173	179	159

Show how Sanjay and Ruth can choose a stratified random sample of 100 students for their investigation.

D6.7 Kim is carrying out a survey at her school on recycling.
The age and sex distribution of the 804 students in her school is:

Year group	Females	Males	Total
9	98	113	211
10	90	101	191
11	111	103	214
12	59	53	112
13	28	48	76

Kim takes a sample of 80 students.

a Explain why Kim should include different numbers of females and males from Year 9 in her sample.

b Calculate the number of females and males Kim should sample from each year group.

D7
Miscellaneous

D7.1 Jenny sells ice-cream on a beach.
The table shows the number of boxes of each flavour she orders for one week.

a Show this information as a pie chart.

This diagram shows the data in the table.

Vanilla	150
Strawberry	180
Choc Chip	60
Almond	0
Lemon	80
Lime	70

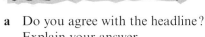

A   B   C   D   E

b Match each part of the diagram to a flavour from the table.

D7.2 This sales graph was printed in a paper with the headline:

Sales rocket between '93 and '96

a Do you agree with the headline? Explain your answer.

The graph has been drawn to mislead.

b Explain any misleading parts of the graph.

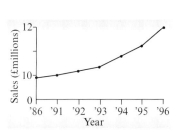

D7.3

Pupils spend hours every day watching television!

Jenny became fed up with headlines like this. She decided on a survey in her school. The question she asked was:

How many minutes did you spend watching TV last night?

These are the results:

45	75	100	120	80	55
180	145	90	90	5	135
60	25	120	180	150	25
90	60	75	150	145	0
120	135	45	60	60	0
180	75	90	120	150	30
150	0	60	90	105	0

a Draw a frequency table with a class interval of 30 minutes for this data. The first class should be:

0 minutes up to, but not including, 30 minutes.

b What is the modal class for this data?

c In which class is the median?

d Draw a cumulative frequency curve for this data.

e Estimate the number of pupils who watched TV for at least an hour.

f **i** With this data if you were asked the question:
"On average how long did these students spend watching TV?"
what would be your answer?

 ii Explain why you chose a particular average.

Jenny thinks the pupil group she asked are typical.

g If you asked a pupil at random, estimate the probability that they watched at least two hours TV last night.

D7.4 The pie chart shows the results of a survey into when people last visited a dentist.

In the report written with this pie chart was the comment:

"… only 4200 of those in the survey had been to the dentist this year …"

a How many people in total, are represented by this pie chart? Explain how you calculated this total.

b How many of those in the survey never visit the dentist?

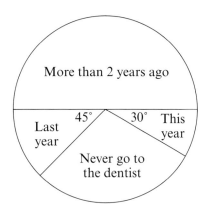

A television documentary about this report claimed that:

"… The report shows that three-quarters of those in the survey haven't been to the dentist in the last two years …"

c **i** With this data, is this a sensible claim to make?

 ii Give reasons for your answer.

d **i** Would you choose a pie chart, or a different diagram for this data?

 ii Give reasons for your answer.

D7.5 Terry is investigating the readability of books. For each book, he takes a sample of 100 sentences and records the number of words in each one.

For Book A, the distribution of words is as follows:

No. of words	Frequency
1 – 5	13
6 – 10	24
11 – 15	20
16 – 20	18
21 – 25	11
26 – 30	6
31 – 35	3
36 – 40	5

a Give the modal class.
b In which class does the median lie?
c Calculate an estimate of the mean number of words in a sentence.
d Copy and complete this cumulative frequency table for Book A.

No. of words	<1	<6	<11	<16	<21
Cumulative frequency					

e Use your table to draw a cumulative frequency curve.
f Use your curve to estimate:
   i the median number of words in a sentence
   ii the interquartile range.

Book B has a median number of words per sentence of 19, and an interquartile range of 9 words.

g Which book do you think is easier to read?
Explain your answer.

D7.6 Jo calculates that the mean number of points scored in 12 league games by the Wessex Warriors rugby league team is 33.5 exactly.

a How many points did the Wessex Warriors score in their 12 games?

At the start of the season, the Wessex Warriors' manager estimated the probabilities that the team would win, lose, or draw a game as:

Result	Win	Lose	Draw
Probability	0.6	0.3	0.1

b Calculate the probability that the Warriors:
   i won their first two league games,
   ii had one win and one draw in their first two games,
   iii did not lose any of their first three games.

The Warriors actually won 8 of their 12 league games.

c Did the team do better or worse than the manager expected?
Explain your answer.

Using and applying

U1
Last one in ?

Kate designs a new game for a school fete.

Any number of players can take part in each game.

At the beginning of each game, a circle of chairs is made, one chair for each player.

The chairs are numbered 1, 2, 3, 4, 5, ...

Each player sits on a chair.

This diagram shows a circle of chairs for 15 players:

Kate begins at chair 1.

To each player in turn she says, 'Stay, Go, Stay, Go ... ' and so on round the circle.

For 'Stay', the player stays on the chair; for 'Go', the player leaves.

This continues round and round the circle until only one player is left on a chair.

That person wins the game.

1 In a game where 15 players take part, which chair is the winning chair ?

2 Find a rule that gives the winning chair for any number of players.

U2
Number strips

For this pair of numbers on a strip of five squares ...

... the blank squares are filled so that each number is the sum of the two numbers on its left.

| 1 | 5 | | | |

| 1 | 5 | 6 | 11 | 17 |

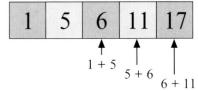

1 + 5
5 + 6
6 + 11

1 On a strip of five squares:

    a Find the number in the last square, if the numbers in the first two squares are 6 and 3.

    b Try different pairs of numbers in the first two squares.
Find a rule to calculate the last number from the first two numbers.
without calculating the numbers in between.

    c Investigate rules for longer strips.

2 **a** Find all the numbers in a strip of five squares with 5 as the first number and 16 as the last number.

    b Investigate methods to complete a strip when you know the first and last number.

U3
Triangles before the eyes

This diagram shows a growing pattern.

The pattern is based on equilateral triangles of:
Side 1, Side 2, Side 3, Side 4, ...

1   How many triangles can you identify in the triangle of side 4?

2   Find an expression for the number of triangles that can be identified in a triangle of side n.

3   In what size of triangle will it be possible to identify about a million triangles?

U4
Discs in place

These discs are placed alternately by colour.

What is the smallest number of moves you need to sort the discs in this way.

You must move the discs according to this rule:

   The position of any two discs can change only if the two discs are immediately next to each other.

1   Write an expression for the number of moves needed for n discs of each colour.

2   What if discs are placed in this order, and the same rule applies?

How many moves for n of each colour?

3   Investigate other starting arrangements with the same rules.

4   What if you introduce a third colour? fourth colour? ...?

5   What if you use a different rule?

⊗ ANSWERS

SECTION 1

Starting points

A1 **a** Any multiple of 40   **b** Any multiple of 36

A2 **a** 14   **b** 15   **c** 24   **d** 4

A3 **a** 1, 2, 3, 6   **b** 1, 5

A4 **a** 1   **b** 2   **c** 4   **d** 18

A5 It has only one factor.   **A6** 31, 37

A7 Any other even number will have at least three factors: 1, 2 and itself

B1 **a** $2^2 \times 5$ **b** $2^2 \times 3^2$ **c** $5 \times 7 \times 11$ **d** $2^3 \times 3^2 \times 7$

B2 **a** 2016   **b** 16335

C1 $\frac{8}{20}, \frac{12}{30}, \frac{6}{15}$ and $\frac{2}{5}$ **C3** **a** $\frac{3}{5}$ **b** $\frac{1}{6}$

D1 **a** $1\frac{1}{4}$ **b** $2\frac{2}{3}$ **c** $3\frac{1}{3}$ **d** 5

D2 **a** $\frac{18}{7}$ **b** $\frac{3}{2}$ **c** $\frac{37}{8}$ **d** $\frac{3}{1}$

E1 **a** $\frac{4}{5}$ **b** $\frac{1}{3}$

E2 **a** $\frac{2}{7}$ **b** $\frac{11}{15}$ **c** $\frac{2}{7}$ **d** $\frac{1}{2}$ **e** $\frac{15}{16}$ **f** $\frac{1}{12}$ **g** $\frac{5}{4}$ **h** $\frac{9}{5}$

E3 $\frac{4}{7}$ **F1** **a** $6x - 3$ **b** $4y + 8$ **c** $20 - 15a$ **d** $35b + 30$

Exercise 1.1

1 **a** 24   **b** 180

2 **c** For two prime numbers a and b:
   HCF = 1
   LCM = ab

3 **a**

Numbers	Product	HCF	LCM
12, 70	840	2	420
7, 24	168	1	168
4, 36	144	4	36
70, 110	7700	10	770

   b HCF $\times$ LCM = Product
   c LCM = 72

4 8, 160   16, 80   32, 40

5 31 July

6 $960\,\text{cm}^3$ (Edge lengths are 8 cm, 12 cm and 10 cm.)

7 **a** $2^2 \times 3 \times 7$
   b 1
   2
   3
   7
   2^2
   2×3
   2×7
   3×7
   $2^2 \times 3$
   $2^2 \times 7$
   $2 \times 3 \times 7$
   $2^2 \times 3 \times 7$
   c 12
   d 900 (27 factors)

Exercise 1.2

1 **a** $\frac{17}{20}$ **b** $3\frac{3}{4}$ **c** $1\frac{15}{16}$ **d** 4

2 **a** $\frac{5}{6}$ **b** $\frac{5}{16}$ **c** $\frac{8}{15}$ **d** $2\frac{1}{4}$

3 **a** 6   **b** 3   **c** 3   **d** 6

4 $\frac{10}{3} = 3\frac{1}{3}$

5 8

6 Assuming $a, b > 1$
   $\frac{1}{a} + \frac{1}{b} = \frac{a+b}{ab}$

   $ab \geqslant (a + b)$

   So $\frac{a+b}{ab} \leqslant 1$

7

	$\frac{n^5}{5}$	n	$\frac{n^3}{3}$	+
1		1		
2		10		
3		59		
4		228		
5		669		

8 **a** **i** $\frac{15}{16}$ **ii** $\frac{511}{512}$ **iii** $\frac{2^n - 1}{2^n}$ **9** $\frac{1}{4} + \frac{1}{28}$ **10** $\frac{1}{2} + \frac{1}{3} + \frac{1}{6}$

11 **b** Any pair x, y such that $y = 1 + \frac{y}{x}$ **12** $\frac{9273}{18546}$

Exercise 1.3

1 L   **2** P – S, Q – U, R – W and T – V

3 **a** $\frac{1}{3n}$ **b** $\frac{8}{x}$ **c** $\frac{a-b}{10}$ **d** $\frac{p}{2}$

   e $\frac{3m}{4n}$ **f** $\frac{v}{8}$ **g** $\frac{z}{15}$ **h** 2

4 **a** $\frac{x}{5} - \frac{2}{5} = \frac{x-2}{5}$ **b** $\frac{2}{m} \times \frac{n}{6} = \frac{n}{3m}$

   c $\frac{y}{x} + \frac{z}{x} = \frac{y+z}{x}$ **d** $\frac{6}{n} \div \frac{1}{n^2} = 6n$

   e $\frac{3t}{10} + \frac{2t}{10} = \frac{t}{2}$ **f** $\frac{2}{b+3} \div \frac{1}{b-2} = \frac{2(b-2)}{b+3}$

5 A – G, B – C, D – F and E – H

Exercise 1.4

1 **a** C   **b** $\frac{22}{3c}$

2 E – L, F – G, H – J and I – K

3 **a** $\frac{3m}{4}$ **b** $\frac{5p}{8}$ **c** $\frac{5q + 2r}{10}$ **d** $\frac{2s - st}{2t}$

   e $\frac{(4y - 5x)}{xy}$ **f** $\frac{17}{2f}$ **g** $\frac{2p + 2}{(p+3)(p-1)}$ **h** $\frac{z + 12}{z(z + 6)}$

4 **a** $\frac{8}{x} - \frac{5}{3x} = \frac{19}{3x}$ **b** $\frac{3}{x} + \frac{2}{(x+5)} = \frac{5(x+3)}{(x+5)}$

   c $\frac{^-3}{(x+1)} + \frac{3}{x} = \frac{3}{x(x+1)}$ **d** $\frac{1}{(x+1)} + \frac{2}{(x-2)} = \frac{3x}{(x+1)(x-2)}$

Exercise 1.5

1 **a** $\frac{9}{28}, \frac{9}{40}, \frac{9}{54}$ **c** Both the difference and product = $\frac{9}{n(n+3)}$

2 **b** Any pair of fractions of the form $\frac{1}{n}$ and $\frac{1}{(n+1)}$

3 $\frac{a}{n} - \frac{a}{(n+a)} = \frac{a}{n} \times \frac{a}{(n+a)}$

4 For two fractions $\frac{1}{a} + \frac{1}{b} = \frac{1}{a} \div \frac{1}{b}$ when $(b + a) = b^2$

5 **a** Fractions equivalent to 3
   b For a fraction $\frac{a}{b}$ add or multiply by the fraction $\frac{a}{(a-b)}$

   For example: $\frac{6}{2} + \frac{6}{4} = \frac{6}{2} \times \frac{6}{4}$

Exercise 1.6

1 **a**

1	$\frac{1}{2}$	$\frac{1}{3}$	$\frac{1}{4}$	$\frac{1}{5}$	$\frac{1}{6}$	$\frac{1}{7}$	$\frac{1}{8}$	$\frac{1}{9}$
$\frac{1}{2}$	$\frac{1}{6}$	$\frac{1}{12}$	$\frac{1}{20}$	$\frac{1}{30}$	$\frac{1}{42}$	$\frac{1}{56}$	$\frac{1}{72}$	
$\frac{1}{3}$	$\frac{1}{12}$	$\frac{1}{30}$	$\frac{1}{60}$	$\frac{1}{105}$	$\frac{1}{168}$	$\frac{1}{252}$		
$\frac{1}{4}$	$\frac{1}{20}$	$\frac{1}{60}$	$\frac{1}{140}$	$\frac{1}{280}$	$\frac{1}{504}$			
$\frac{1}{5}$	$\frac{1}{30}$	$\frac{1}{105}$	$\frac{1}{280}$	$\frac{1}{630}$				
$\frac{1}{6}$	$\frac{1}{42}$	$\frac{1}{168}$	$\frac{1}{504}$					
$\frac{1}{7}$	$\frac{1}{56}$	$\frac{1}{252}$						
$\frac{1}{8}$	$\frac{1}{72}$							
$\frac{1}{9}$								

2 $\frac{1}{8} - \frac{1}{9}$ and $\frac{1}{56} - \frac{1}{252}$

3 **a** $\frac{1}{110}$ **c** $\frac{1}{n} - \frac{1}{(n+1)} = \frac{1}{n(n+1)}$

4 $\frac{1k}{k(k+1)} - \frac{1}{(k+1)(k+2)} = \frac{2}{(k+1)(k+2)}$
   k, $k + 1$ and $k + 2$ are three consecutive numbers so at least one is an even number, so the numerator can be cancelled to 1.

End points

A1 **a** 21   **b** 630   **A2** 42 and 96   **A3** 20 posts

B1 **a** $\frac{5}{9}$ **b** $\frac{5}{18}$ **c** $\frac{7}{10}$ **B2** 1.2

B3 **a** $\frac{1}{2} + \frac{1}{6} = \frac{2}{3}$

$\frac{1}{2} + \frac{1}{6} + \frac{1}{12} = \frac{3}{4}$

$\frac{1}{2} + \frac{1}{6} + \frac{1}{12} + \frac{1}{20} = \frac{4}{5}$

$\frac{1}{2} + \frac{1}{6} + \frac{1}{12} + \frac{1}{20} + \frac{1}{30} = \frac{5}{6}$

b $\frac{8}{9}$

C1 **a** $\frac{x}{2}$ **b** $\frac{3}{4}$ **c** $3z$ **d** $\frac{3b + 7a}{ab}$ **e** $\frac{c + 5}{c(c + 1)}$ **f** $\frac{2d + 1}{(d + 6)(d - 5)}$

Section 2

Starting points

A1 **a** **i** reflex **ii** acute **iii** right
b **i** equilateral **ii** right–angled
c Triangles ABD, ADE

B1 **a** 60° **b** 300° **c** 45°

B2 **a** $a = 35°$ **b** $b = 35°$ **c** $c = 72.5°$

C1 $d = 116°$ $e = 116°$ $f = 64°$ $g = 64°$

D1 **1** trapezium
2 rectangle square
3 square rhombus
4 rectangle square parallelogram rhombus

E1 1080° **E2** 142° **E3** 129° **E4** **a** 1800° **b** 150°

Exercise 2.1

1 **b** $a = 74°$ $b = 53°$ $c = 53°$ $d = 74°$ $e = 53°$ $f = 53°$

2 $a = 62°$ $b = 120°$ $c = 117°$

Exercise 2.2

1 **a** Any five pairs from:
a, c and e $\qquad$ b, d and f
g, i and k $\qquad$ h, j and l
b Any three pairs from:
b with i or k $\qquad$ c with h
d with k $\qquad$ e with j or h
h with c or e $\qquad$ i with b
j with e $\qquad$ k with d or b

2 $a = 72°$ $b = 135°$ $c = 45°$

3 **d** **i** 65° **ii** 54° **iii** 61° **iv** 54° **v** 126° **vi** 61°

4 $a = 42°$ $\qquad$ $b = 77°$
$c = 61°$ $\qquad$ $p = 72°$
$q = 72°$ $\qquad$ $r = 72°$
$x = 68.5°$ $\qquad$ $y = 68.5°$
$z = 68.5°$

5 **a** **i** 52° **ii** 52° **iii** 52° **iv** 64°
b AB and DC are parallel
c trapezium
d It does not have 4 equal sides.

Exercise 2.3

1 **b** As the parallelogram is stretched:
◆ ABC does not change
◆ ABD becomes larger
◆ CBD becomes smaller.
c AMB becomes smaller.
d **i** obtuse **ii** right **ii** acute

2 **a** Statement 3
b Statements 1, 2 and 3

3 **a** ABC = 120° BCD = 90° CDA = 60° DAB = 90°
b **i** BCA, CDM, ADM **ii** ACD, ADC, ABD, CBD
c Right angle
d 2 from AD, CD and AC AB, BC AM, MC
e No **f** BD

Exercise 2.4

1 **b** **A** triangle or right-angled triangle
B quadrilateral or trapezium
C hexagon
D pentagon
E hexagon or regular hexagon
F triangle or equilateral triangle
G pentagon
H triangle or equilateral triangle
I hexagon

c **i** **A** 90°, 60°, 30°
B 120°, 120°, 60°, 60°
C 60°, 120°, 90°, 90°, 60°, 300°
D 120°, 120°, 120°, 90°, 90°
E 120°, 120°, 120°, 120°, 120°, 120°
F 60°, 60°, 60°
G 60°, 120°, 90°, 30°, 240°
H 60°, 60°, 60°
I 120° 120°, 60°, 300°, 30°, 90°

2 **a** Polygons A, G and I
b Cards 2, 5 and 6
c **i** Card 2 – Irregular
ii Card 6 – Only one obtuse angle
d Card 1
e 19 different 7–dot polygons

Exercise 2.5

1 **a** **i** Polygons B and I **ii** Cells d and g
b **i** 8 cells
ii Cell f – a regular polygon will always have at least one line
of symmetry

Exercise 2.6

2 **a** 144° **b** 360° is not a multiple of 144°.

3 360° is not a multiple of 135°.

4 **a** Yes **b** No

Exercise 2.7

1 **a** Polygon J – 2 Polygon K – 2 Polygon L – 1
b **i** Polygon K is a rhombus **ii** Polygon L is a rhombus
c $a = 108°$ $b = 36°$ $c = 72°$ $d = 144°$ $e = 108°$

2 **a** **i** parallelogram **ii** heptagon
b $a = 135°$ $b = 45°$ $c = 135°$ $d = 75°$ $e = 285°$ $f = 75°$ $g = 105°$

Exercise 2.8

1 **a** $a = 56°$ $b = 42°$ $c = 69°$ $d = 104°$ $e = 89°$
b $56 + 42 + 69 + 104 + 89 = 360$

2 **b** 30° **c** 150°

3 $e = 40°$ $f = 140°$ $g = 70°$ $h = 40°$

Exercise 2.9

1 **b** **ii** Exterior angle at B is 67.5° Exterior angle at D is 157.5°

2 **a** **i** AFC = 45° FAC = 67.5° ACF = 67.5°
ii Exterior angle at A is 112.5°
Exterior angle at C is 112.5°
Exterior angle at F is 135°
b 5 different triangles
c 45°, 67.5°, 90°, 112.5°, 135°, 157.5°

End points

A1 $a = 42°$ $b = 67°$ $c = 109°$

B1 **a** **i** Polygon C
ii Polygons B and E
b **A** rhombus **D** rectangle
B isosceles triangle **E** kite
C equilateral triangle

D1

Polygon	a Interior angles	b Exterior angles
B	120°	60°
	30°	150°
	30°	150°
E	90°	90°
	120°	60°
	90°	90°
	60°	120°

D2 45°

Section 3

Starting points

A1 C **A2** 4

B1 **a** $\frac{6p + 8}{p(p + 2)}$ **b** $\frac{4}{3}$ **c** $\frac{5}{p(p + 5)}$ **d** $\frac{10}{3}$

B2 A and F B and E D and H C and G

B3 **a** 3 **b** 2, 10

Exercise 3.1

1　　　**a**　　　　**b**
　A　$a(a + 5)$　　$a^2 + 5a$
　B　$b(b - 2)$　　$b^2 - 2b$
　C　$c(c - 5)$　　$c^2 - 6c$
　D　$d(12 - d)$　$12d - d^2$
　E　$4(8 + e)$　　$32 + 4e$
　F　$7(8 - f)$　　$56 - 7f$

2　　　**a**　　　　**b**
　P　$5(2p + 2)$　$10p + 10$
　Q　$4(3q - 2)$　$12q - 8$
　R　$r(2r + 2)$　$2r^2 + 2r$

3　A　$2a$　　B　b　　C　c　　D　$d + 3$　　E　$e + 2$

4　**a**　$4x + 12 = 4(x + 3)$　　**b**　$6p - 4 = 2(3p - 2)$　　**c**　$2a + 8 = 2(a + 4)$
　d　$10 - 5q = 5(2 - q)$　　**e**　$3t^2 - 4t = t(3t - 4)$　　**f**　$6s^2 + 7s = s(6s + 7)$

Exercise 3.2

1　**a**　$8b - 10$　**b**　$24 - 6x$　**c**　$3c - 12$　**d**　$11y - 15$　**e**　^-2a　**f**　$5a - 14 + 2b$

2　A and D

3　**a**　$5a + 5$　　**b**　$x + 15$　　**c**　$7a - 6$　　**d**　$11 - 4x$
　e　$3x - 23$　　**f**　$7x + 4$　　**g**　$x - 9$　　**h**　$17x + 4y$

Exercise 3.3

1　**a**　$6ab$　　**b**　$3pq$　　**c**　$20xy$　　**d**　$30pq$
　e　$2x^2$　　**f**　a^2b　　**g**　$2xy^2$　　**h**　$6a^2b$
　i　$6p^2q$　　**j**　a^5　　**k**　$6b^3$　　**l**　$10bc^3$

2　A and E　　B and F　　C and H　　G and I

3　**a**　$ab + 4a$　　**b**　$2mn + 3mp$　　**c**　$6xy + 4xz$　　**d**　$ac + c^2$
　e　$p^2 - pq$　　**f**　$4a^2 - 4ab$　　**g**　$2ab - 4ac$　　**h**　$6a^2 + 8ab$
　i　$8pq - 12p^2$　　**j**　$6p^2q + 4pq^2$　　**k**　$4x^2y - 8xy^2$
　l　$3x^3y - 3xy^3$

4　**a**　$2x^2 + x$　　**b**　$5ab + 4a$　　**c**　$x(x + 2)(x - 1)$　　**d**　$11a + 2b$
　e　$4p^2 + 6q$　　**f**　$6a$

5　C

6　**a**　$9a + 26b$　　**b**　$10x + 5y$　　**c**　^-7x　　**d**　$10x^2 + 3xy$　　**e**　$2a^2b$
　f　$3a^2b + 3ab - 2ab^2 + 2b^2$

7　**a**　$6a^2 - 6ab + 12b^2$　　**b**　$16x^2y + 20xy^2 - 6xy$　　**c**　$pq^2 - 4p^2q$
　d　$^-2m^2n - 8mn^2 + 12m^3$

8　**a**　$\dfrac{8x + 5}{(x + 1)(2x + 1)}$

　b　$\dfrac{x - 2}{(x + 2)(x + 1)}$

　c　$\dfrac{3x + 26}{(x - 3)(x + 4)}$

　d　$\dfrac{3x^2 + 10x - 4}{(x + 2)(x + 4)}$

Thinking ahead

A　Triangle 1:　Left circle, 24
　　　　　　　　Rectangle, 42
　　　　　　　　Right circle, 18

　　Triangle 2:　Left square, 14
　　　　　　　　Left circle, 70
　　　　　　　　Right circle, 30

B　Triangle 3:　Left circle, $15c$
　　　　　　　　Rectangle, $24 + 15c$
　　　　　　　　Right circle, 24

　　Triangle 4:　Left circle, $6pq$
　　　　　　　　Rectangle, $6pq + 8p^2$
　　　　　　　　Right circle, $8p^2$

　　Triangle 5:　Left circle, $2ab^2$
　　　　　　　　Rectangle, $2ab^2 + 4a^2b$
　　　　　　　　Right circle, $4a^2b$

C　Triangle 6:　Left square, $2x^2$
　　　　　　　　Right square, $3x$
　　　　　　　　Rectangle, $4x^2 + 6x$

　　Triangle 7:　Left square, $2b$
　　　　　　　　Right square, 3
　　　　　　　　Rectangle, $4b^2 + 6b$

　　Triangle 8:　Left square, $2a$
　　　　　　　　Right square, $3b$
　　　　　　　　Right circle, $10a + 15b$

Exercise 3.4

1　**a**　$2(x + 7)$　　**b**　$2(4x - 5y)$　　**c**　$x(5 + y)$　　**d**　$p(q + p)$
　e　$2d(3 + 2e)$　　**f**　$3a(2b + 3)$　　**g**　$2a(1 - 4b)$　　**h**　$3a(a + 4)$
　i　$5y(3x + 4z)$　　**j**　$ab(a + b)$　　**k**　$3cd(4c - 5)$　　**l**　$5y(5x^2 + 3z)$

2　Triangle L:　Left square, $2a$
　　　　　　　　Right square, 6
　　　　　　　　Right circle, $6a$

　　Triangle M:　Top square, b
　　　　　　　　Left square, b
　　　　　　　　Left circle, $2a^2$

3　**a**　b
　b　Triangle N:　Top square, b
　　　　　　　　Left square, 5
　　　　　　　　Right square, a

4　Triangle O:　Top square, c
　　　　　　　　Left square, c
　　　　　　　　Right square, 8
　　　　　　　　Right circle, $8c$

　　Triangle P:　Top square, 2
　　　　　　　　Left square, $2d$
　　　　　　　　Right square, $3b$
　　　　　　　　Right circle, $6b$

5　**a**　Triangle Q – two solutions from:

　　◆　Top square, 2
　　　　Left square, $2p^2$
　　　　Right square, $4pq$

　　◆　Top square, 4
　　　　Left square, p^2
　　　　Right square, $2pq$

　　◆　Top square, p
　　　　Left square, $4p$
　　　　Right square, $8q$

　　◆　Top square, $2p$
　　　　Left square, $2p$
　　　　Right square, $4q$

　　◆　Top square, $4p$
　　　　Left square, p
　　　　Right square, $2q$

　b　5 (excluding 1 in the top square)

6　3 (excluding 1 in the top square)

7　**a**　$5(x + 2y + 4)$　　**b**　$3(2a - 3b + 4c)$　　**c**　$x(2x + 3 + y)$
　d　$7(2x - 4y + 3z)$　　**e**　$2x(x + 4y + 3)$　　**f**　$ab(6b + 2a + 5)$

Thinking ahead

A　**a**　$1 : x^2$　　　$2 : 3x$　　　$3 : 2x$　　　$4 : 6$　　**b**　$x^2 + 5x + 6$

B　　　　**a**　　　　　　　**b**
　　P　$(2p + 4)(p + 3)$　　$2p^2 + 10p + 12$
　　Q　$(3q + 5)(2q + 3)$　　$6q^2 + 19q + 15$

C　**a**　B, C, E　　**b**　$n^2 - 2n - 8$

Exercise 3.5

1　C　　**2**　**a**　D

3　**a**　$a^2 + 4a + 3$　　**b**　$d^2 + 14d + 45$　　**c**　$3e^2 + 22e + 7$
　d　$10a^2 + 13a + 4$　　**e**　$6b^2 + 19b + 15$　　**f**　$6c^2 + 25c + 14$

4　**a**　$x^2 + 2x + 1$　　**b**　$x^2 + 4x + 4$　　**c**　$x^2 + 6x + 9$

5　Missing entries are: x^2, $4x$, ^-2x, 8, $x^2 - 6x + 8$

6　**a**　**i**　$(x + 3)^2 - 12x$ or $(x - 3)^2$　　**ii**　$x^2 - 6x + 9$
　b　**i**　$x^2 - 8x + 15$　　**ii**　$x^2 - 10x + 25$　　**iii**　$x^2 - 2xy + y^2$

7　Missing entries are: $6x^2$, ^-15x, $2x$, $^-5$, $6x^2 - 13x - 5$

8　**a**　$2z^2 + 3zt + t^2$　　**b**　$6k^2 + 17mk + 5m^2$　　**c**　$2c^2 + 17cd + 21d^2$
　d　$6p^2 + 13pq - 5q^2$　　**e**　$5f^2 - 8fg + 3g^2$　　**f**　$21w^2 - 4w - v^2$

9　A and I, B and F, C and H, D and G

10　**a**　$z^2 - t^2$　　**b**　$4k^2 - m^2$　　**c**　$4c^2 - 9d^2$　　**d**　$9p^2 - q^2$
　e　$25f^2 - 9g^2$　　**f**　$49w^2 - v^2$

11　M, N

12　**a**　**i**　$x^2 + 2x + 1$　　**ii**　$x^3 + 3x^2 + 3x + 1$
　　iii　$x^4 + 4x^3 + 6x^2 + 4x + 1$
　b　$x^6 + 6x^5 + 15x^4 + 20x^3 + 15x^2 + 6x + 1$

13　**a**　$a^3 + 3a^2 - 10a$　　**b**　$p^3 - 5p^2 - 2p + 24$　　**c**　$4q^3 - 22q^2 - 42q$
　d　$2x^3 + 13x^2 + 13x - 10$

Thinking ahead

A   **a**   Missing entries are: 6, 6, 6, 102, 103, 105, 6   **b**   They are all 6
   c $(n + 2)(n + 3) - n(n + 5)$

Exercise 3.6

1   **A**   **a**   Missing entries: 2, 2, 2   **b** $(n + 1)(n + 2) - n(n + 3)$ **c**   2
     B   **a**   Missing entries: 1, 1, 1   **b** $(n + 1)(n + 1) - n(n + 2)$ **c**   1
     C   **a**   Missing entries: 12, 12, 12   **b** $(n + 3)(n + 4) - n(n + 7)$ **c**   2

2   **a**   **D**   **i** 7   **ii** 6   **E**   **i** 3   **ii** 6   **F**   **i** 5   **ii** 20
   b   **i** $a + b = c$ **ii** ab

3   **A**   **a**   Missing entries: 4, 2, 0   **b** $(n + 1)(n + 1) - n(n + 2)$ **c** $6 - 2n$
     B   **a**   Missing entries: 7, 6, 5   **b** $(n + 2)(n + 4) - n(n + 7)$ **c** $8 - n$
     C   **a**   Missing entries: ⁻3, ⁻2, ⁻1   **b** $n(n + 5) - (n + 7)^2$ **c** $n - 4$

Exercise 3.7

1   **a** $(x + 7)(x + 1)$ **b** $(p + 8)(p + 1)$ **c** $(t + 9)(t + 1)$
   d $(m + 2)(m + 6)$ **e** $(n + 3)^2$ **f** $(a + 9)(a + 4)$

2   **a** 8   **b** 5   **c** 7   **d** 11   **e** $t + 3$ **f** $p - 8$

3 $(x - 1)(x + 4)$ **4** $(x - 2)(x - 4)$

5   **a** $(p + 3)(p - 1)$ **b** $(m + 5)(m - 2)$ **c** $(t - 5)(t + 1)$ **d** $(r - 7)(r + 4)$
   e $(x - 5)(x - 3)$ **f** $(n - 6)(n - 1)$ **g** $(t - 4)(t + 3)$ **h** $(b - 6)(b + 2)$
   i $(x + 6)(x - 2)$

6 $(x - 4)(x + 4)$

7   **a** $(t + 3)(t - 3)$ **b** $(r + 5)(r - 5)$ **c** $(4p + 1)(4p - 1)$
   d $(3x + 2)(3x - 2)$ **e** $(x + y)(x - y)$ **f** $(x + 3p)(x - 3p)$

8   A, C

Exercise 3.8

1 $(2x + 3)(x + 2)$

2   **a** $(3x - 1)(x - 3)$ **b** $(4y - 3)(y + 1)$ **c** $(4p + 1)(p - 3)$
   d $(4x + 3)(x - 1)$ **e** $(3x - 1)(x + 3)$ **f** $(3a + 1)(a + 3)$
   g $(5n - 1)(n - 2)$ **h** $(3x - 4)(x + 1)$ **i** $(3x - 1)(x - 1)$

3   **a**

Across	Down
2 $(2x + 1)(2x + 1)$	1 $(3x + 1)(3x - 1)$
4 $(x + 1)(x - 1)$	2 $(x - 1)(x - 1)$
5 $(3x - 5)(x + 1)$	3 $(2x + 1)(2x - 1)$
7 $(2x + 3)(2x + 1)$	4 $3(x - 1)$
8 $(5x + 1)(x - 1)$	5 $(3x + 2)(x + 2)$
10 $(x - 4)(x - 1)$	6 $(x + 1)(x - 5)$
13 $(x - 2)(x + 2)$	9 $(5x - 4)(x + 1)$
14 $(4x + 7)(x - 2)$	11 $(x - 7)(x + 2)$
	12 $(2x - 3)(2x + 3)$
	13 $(x - 7)(x + 7)$

4   **a** $a = 36, b = 6$ **b** $a = 6, b = 3$ **c** $a = 6, b = 1$ **d** $a = 4, b = 2$

5   **a** $3(x - 2)(x + 1)$ **b** $3(2x + 5)(x + 1)$ **c** $2(3x - 1)(x + 3)$
   d $7(2x + 1)(x - 2)$ **e** $3(x - 1)(x - 1)$ **f** $4(x - 1)(x + 1)$

6   **a** $n(n + 1)(n - 1)$

7   **a** $(x + y)(x + y)$ **b** $4(x + y)(x + y)$ **c** $(3x + 4y)(3x - 4y)$

Exercise 3.9

1   **a** $p + 1$ and $p + 2$ **b**   **i** $3p + 3$ **ii** $3(p + 3)$

2   **a**   **i** ⁻4   **ii** 0   **iii** 6   **iv** 14   **b** $(n + 3)(n - 2)$

3 $n^2 - 6n + 9 = (n - 3)^2$ and the square of any number is greater than or equal to zero.

4   **a**   **i**   Top: $y - 8$
         Bottom: $y + 8$
         Right: $y + 1$
         Left: $y - 1$
    ii $(y + 8)(y + 1) - (y - 8)(y - 1)$
   iii $(y + 8)(y + 1) - (y - 8)(y - 1)$
       $= (y^2 + 9y + 8) - (y^2 - 9y + 8)$
       $= 18y$
   b   **i**   Top: $y - n$
         Bottom: $y + n$
         Right: $y + 1$
         Left: $y - 1$
    ii $(y + n)(y + 1) - (y - n)(y - 1)$
       $= (y^2 + ny + y + n) - (y^2 - ny - y + n)$
       $= 2ny + 2y$
       $= 2(n + 1)y$
   iii   320

Exercise 3.10

1   **a** $(a + b)(a - b)$ **b**   **i** 9600   **ii** 2200

2   **a**   3, 5, 7, 9, 11, ...   **b**   A sequence of add numbers, starting at 3.
   c $(n + 1)^2 - n^2 = 2n + 1$ **d**   **i** 2467   **ii** 24 624 624 245

3   **a** $(n + 5)2 - n^2 = 10n + 25$ **b**   **i** 1255   **ii** 3045

Exercise 3.11

1   **a**   **i** $\frac{1}{2}$ **ii** $\frac{1}{3}$ **iii** $\frac{1}{4}$
   b   The fractions are all unit fractions and the denominators increase by 1.
   c   **i** $\frac{1}{n + 1}$

2   **a**   **i** $\frac{1}{n - 1}$ **ii** $\frac{n + 1}{n}$ **iii** $\frac{n}{2}$ **iv** $\frac{2n}{n - 3}$
   b   **i** $\frac{1}{49}$ **ii** $\frac{51}{50}$ **iii** 25   **iv** $\frac{100}{47}$

3   **a** $\frac{2(x^2 + 3) + x(x + 9)}{6} = \frac{(x + 1)(x + 2)}{2}$

End points

A1   **a** $22b + 16$ **b** $26b + 14$ **c** $10ab^2 + 4a^2b$ **d** $3x^2y - 7xy^2 - 37xy$

A2   C

A3   **a** $a^2 + 9a + 8$ **b** $b^2 + 8b + 16$ **c** $5c^2 + 17c + 6$
   d $d^2 + d - 2$ **e** $6e^2 - 5e - 50$ **f** $3f^2 - 23f + 14$

A4   **a** $5 \times 10 - 4 \times 8$ $6 \times 11 - 5 \times 9$ $7 \times 12 - 6 \times 10$
   b   66   **c** $(n + 1)(n + 6) - n(n + 4)$
   d $(n + 1)(n + 6) - n(n + 4) = 3n + 6 = 3(n + 2)$

B1   **a** $4(2p + q)$ **b** $6(a - 2b)$ **c** $a(a + b)$ **d** $m(7 + 3n)$
   e $2y(4x + 5)$ **f** $2a(2b + 3a)$ **g** $xy(3y - 5x)$ **h** $2pq(2 - 3p)$
   i $h(2g^2 - 5h)$

B2   **a** $(k - 2)(k + 7)$ **b** $(k - 2)(k - 7)$ **c** $(k + 14)(k - 1)$

B3   **a** $(x + 11)(x + 1)$ **b** $(x + 7)(x + 2)$ **c** $(x + 5)(x - 1)$
   d $(x + 3)(x - 2)$ **e** $(x - 5)(x + 4)$ **f** $(x - 3)(x - 2)$
   g $(x + 10)(x - 10)$ **h** $(2x - 5)(x - 3)$ **i** $(3x + 4)(3x - 4)$
   j $(5x - 1)(x + 1)$ **k** $(x - 2y)(x + 2y)$ **l** $(2x - y)(2x - y)$

B4   B and D, C and E   **B5**   **a** $\frac{x - 4}{3}$ **b** $x > 4$

SECTION 4

Starting Points

B1

	X	Y
a Mode	15 and 42	25
b Median	39.5	38
c Mean	42.5	48.8
d Range	69	93

C1   **a**   £340   **b**   £340   **c**   £314.89 (to 2 dp)

C2   The modal wage and median wage are not misleading averages.
     The mean wage *is* a misleading average because only 6 of the 9 wages
     are greater than it; the very small wage of £112 is the reason for this.

D2   Blue   **D4**   **a** 0   **b** 4   **D5**   **a** 1   **b** 0.9 (to 1 dp)

E1

	Red	Blue	Green	White	Silver	Black	Brown
a	21%	25%	8%	13%	8%	17%	8%
b	75°	90°	30°	45°	30°	60°	30°

F5   **a**   54%   **b**   35%   **c**   11%   **F6**   **a**   39%   **b**   33%   **c**   28%

Thinking ahead

A   **a** 7   **b** 8

Exercise 4.1

1   **a**   **ii** William 2.5 $(7 - 4.5)$ Bryony 2 $(7 - 5)$ Daniel 3 $(8 - 5)$
   b   Bryony, because the interquartile range of her scores is the lowest.

A

	Kate	Bob
Interquartile range	76.5 − 45.5	76 − 45
	= 31	= 31

Kate and Bob appear to be equally consistent.

Exercise 4.2

1   **a**   14.5
   b   Bob is more consistent than Kate because the mean deviation of his
      scores is lower.

2   **a**

	Zoe	Matt	Javed
Mean deviation	5.5	8.75	7.56

     i Zoe   **ii** Matt
   b   Zoe is the most consistent archer because her scores are the least
      spread out. Matt's scores show the most variation because his mean
      deviation is the greatest.

3   58

Exercise 4.3

1 a Zoe 6.60 (to 3 sf)   Matt 10.0 (to 3 sf)   Javed 8.56 (to 3 sf)
   b Zoe, Javed, Matt

2 a 17.2 (to 3 sf)
   b

	Kate	Bob
Mean deviation	15.5	14.5
Standard deviation	16.7	17.2

   c Bob has a higher standard deviation than Kate, but a lower mean deviation.
   d Bob's two lowest scores and two highest scores are further from the mean than Kate's.
   The distance from the mean of these extreme values has a greater effect on the standard deviation than the mean deviation because the deviations are squared.

3 a 53   **b i** 13.6 (to 3 sf)

4 a 42 54 60 72 90
   b Mean 63.6   Standard deviation 16.4 (to 3 sf)
   c The mean and standard deviation are both increased by 20%.

5 The mean is increased by 15, but the standard deviation is unchanged.

Exercise 4.4

1 a 1.55 (to 3 sf)
   b Bob's scores show less variation in Round 6, because the standard deviation is lower than in Round 7.

2 b Paula 2.7   Zoe 1.90 (to 3 sf)   Matt 2.49 (to 3 sf)
   c Zoe's scores have the smallest standard deviation because her scores with the larger frequencies are near her mean score.
   Paula's is much more inconsistent and her larger frequencies are at the extreme scores, so she has a much larger standard deviation than Zoe.
   Matt's scores with the larger frequencies are closer to his mean score than Paula's but further away than Zoe's, so the standard deviation of his scores is in between the other two.

Exercise 4.5

1 a Zeta 61   Carlo 57.5
   b Zeta 11.5 (to 3 sf)   Carlo 12.5 (to 3 sf)
   c Zeta's scores are higher than Matt's on average, and show less variation.

2

	Dean	Leah	Jack
Mean	5.8	5.4	4.8
Standard deviation	1.23	1.16	1.49

   Dean's scores are higher than Leah's and Jack's on average, but Leah is the most consistent.
   Jack has the lowest mean score, and his scores also show the most variation.

3 a

	Eliza	Sam
Median	4	4.5
Interquartile range	1	2.5
	(5 – 4)	(5.5 – 3)

   b Sam's scores are higher than Eliza's on average, but Eliza's scores show much less variation.

A a ii 7   **b ii** 8

Exercise 4.6

1 Lee   Faith   Tegan   Aqib
      5   6   4.5   7

2 a The median if halfway between the 40th value and the 41st value, i.e. halfway between 7 and 8.
   b The total frequency is 80: the lower quartile is between the 20th and 21st values (both 6); the upper quartile is between the 60th and 61st values (both 9); interquartile range equals 9–6.

A a X 38 Y 36 Z 38   **b** X 3.5 Y 4 Z 2.5

Exercise 4.8

1 c The distributions for restuarants X and Z are both bell–shaped and have the same range.
   Restaurant X, however, has smaller frequencies at the tails, and larger frequencies in the middle.

2 c Restuarant W: distribution is negatively skewed,
   Restuarant Y: distribution is positively skewed.

3 a i X 38.1 Y 36.1 Z 38.0 (all to 3 sf)
   b

Distribution	Averages
Negatively skewed	Mean < Median < Mode
Positively skewed	Mode < Median < Mean
Bell-shaped	Mean = Median = Mode

Exercise 4.9

3 A – the water wastage in 1997 is $\frac{1}{2}$ the wastage in 1995, but the diagram gives the impression the wastage is $\frac{1}{4}$ because the height and the width of the 1995 water drop have been halved.
   B – the vertical axis does not start at 0 which gives the impression that the water wastage of Mercia and Saxony is about 3 to 4 times that of Wyvern.

End Points

A1 a 65.5   **b** 8.75   **c** 11.5 (to 3 sf)

B1 Mean 60.5   Standard deviation 11.5 (to 3 sf)

C1 Mean 7.6   Standard deviation 1.49 (to 3 sf)

D1 a

	Robin	Tina
Mean	7.6	7.42
Standard deviation	1.49	1.30

   b Robin's scores are higher than Tina's on average, but Tina is the more consistent.

E1 a 8   **b** 2.5 (9 – 6.5)

G1 A – the vertical axis does not start at 0, which gives the impression that the amount of gas supplied by Flame is about 6 times that of Western and $2\frac{1}{2}$ times that of GasOil.
   B – the amount of gas supplied in 1997 is $2\frac{1}{2}$ times the amount supplied in 1996, but the diagram gives the impression it is much more than this because the height and the width of the 1996 flame have been increased $2\frac{1}{2}$ times.

SECTION 5

Starting points

A1 a 33, 39   **b** 30, 41   **A2** 31

A3 a …, 32, 38, 44   **b** …, 47, 65, 86   **c** …, 57, 83, 114

A4 a 6   **b** 79

B1 b 46 matches
   c

Pattern number (n)	Number of matches (m)
1	6
2	11
3	16
4	21
5	26

   d $m = 5n + 1$

Exercise 5.1

1

Pattern number (n)		Number of matches (m)
2	→	4
3	→	5
4	→	6
20	→	22
n	→	$n + 2$

2 a

Pattern number (n)		Number of matches (m)
1	→	4
2	→	8
3	→	12
4	→	16
5	→	20
6	→	24

   b $n \to 4n$ **c** 400 matches   **d** pattern 155   **e** pattern 124

Thinking ahead

A 301

Exercise 5.2

1 a $m = 2n + 1$ **b** 17 matches

2 a $m = 4n + 1$ **b** 161 matches   **c** Pattern 32

3 a $m = 6n - 2$ **b** 598 matches

4 b $m = 4n + 2$

5 a

50	→	249
n	→	$5n - 1$

   b

2	→	22
3	→	18
4	→	14
11	→	⁻14

   c

28	→	⁻75
p	→	$9 - 3p$

Thinking ahead
A **a** 19, 21   **b** 29   **c** 105

Exercise 5.3
1 Sequence A   **a** $3n + 3$ **b** 153
   Sequence B   **a** $5n - 4$ **b** 246
   Sequence C   **a** $10n + 3$ **b** 503
   Sequence D   **a** $8n - 6$ **b** 394

2 **b** $3n + 2$ **3** $n + 7$ **4** 1, $^-$2, $^-$5, $^-$8, $^-$11

5 **a** $22 - 2n$ **b** $32 - 10n$ **c** $1 - 2n$ **d** $15 - 5n$

Thinking ahead
A **b** 800 small squares

Exercise 5.4
1 **a** $n^2 + 1$ **b** $n^2 + n$ **c** n^2

2 $(n^2 + n) \div 2$, $n(n + 1) \div 2$ or equivalent

Exercise 5.5
A 402 (i.e. $n^2 + 2$)

1 **a** $u_n = 3n^2$ **b** 21675

2 **a** 35   **b** $n^2 - 1$

3 Sequence A   **a** 39, 52   **b** $n^2 + 3$
   Sequence B   **a** 144, 196   **b** $4n^2$
   Sequence C   **a** 41, 48   **b** $7n - 1$
   Sequence D   **a** 41, 54   **b** $n^2 + 5$
   Sequence E   **a** $-11, -24$ **b** $25 - n^2$
   Sequence F   **a** 11, 24   **b** $n^2 - 25$

4 **a** 284, 388   **b** $u_n = 8n^2 - 4$ **c** $u_{n+1} = 8n^2 + 16n + 4$

5 Sequence A   **a** $u_n = 2n^2 + 1$ **b** 201
   Sequence B   **a** $u_n = 3n^2 - 2$ **b** 298
   Sequence C   **a** $u_n = 7n^2 + 4$ **b** 704
   Sequence D   **a** $u_n = 5n^2 - 3$ **b** 497
   Sequence E   **a** $u_n = 2n^2 - 7$ **b** 193
   Sequence F   **a** $u_n = 3n^2 - 8$ **b** 292

6 **a** $u_n = 17 - 4n^2$ **b** $^-$1583

7 **a** 1, 6, 15, 28, 45, 66, 91   **b** $u_n = 2n^2 - n$ **c** 19900
   d $u_n = 4n^2 + 4n - 2$

Exercise 5.6
1 **a** 2^n **b** $2^n - 1$ **c** 2^{n-1} **d** 2^{n-3} **e** 3^{1-n} **f** 2^{-2n}

2 **a** $\dfrac{n}{100 - n}$ **b** $\dfrac{n^2}{2^{n+1}}$ **c** $\dfrac{3n}{n^3}$ **d** $\dfrac{n^2 + 1}{2^n + 1}$

3 **a** $u_n = 200 - 4^n$ **b** $u_n = 45 - n$

4 **b** $u_n = n(n - 2)$ or $u_n = n^2 - 2n$

5 **b** $u_n = \frac{1}{2}n(n + 1)$

Exercise 5.7
1 **a** 1, $^-$0.8, $^-$1.16, $^-$1.232, $^-$1.246   **b** 1, 24, 116, 484, 1956
   c 1, $^-$8, $^-$0.8, $^-$2.857, $^-$1.647   **d** 1, 1, 1, 1, 1

2 $h_4 = 4.7\dot{2}$ $h_6 = 4.644067\dot{7}98...$

3 u_n approaches 3 as n gets larger

4 **a** $p_6 = 1.324900445...$ **b** converges

5 $a_1 = 7$ **6** **a** 0.32   **b** limit = 0.5

End points
A1 **a** $m = 2n + 3$ **b** 495 matches

B1 Sequence A   **a** $n^2 + 1$ **b** 401
   Sequence B   **a** $n + 5$ **b** 25
   Sequence C   **a** $3n + 6$ **b** 66
   Sequence D   **a** $5n^2$ **b** 2000
   Sequence E   **a** $6 - n^2$ **b** $^-$394
   Sequence F   **a** $n^2 - 50$ **b** 350
   Sequence G   **a** $4n^2 - 5$ **b** 1595
   Sequence H   **a** $3n^2 + 1$ **b** 1201

B2 **a** 3^{n+2} **b** 2^{n+2} **c** $2^n + 2$ **d** $4^n - 3$

B3 **a** $\dfrac{2^n}{n^2 + 1}$ **b** $\dfrac{2n + 1}{3n^2}$

C1 **a** 4, 21, 446, 198921, ...   **b** diverges

C2 **a** $k_2 = ^-1.5$, $k_3 = ^-0.923076923...$ **b** Converges to limit of $^-$1

SKILLS BREAK 1
1 **a** 90 tiles (9 boxes)   **b** £24.10   **c** £20.51

2 **a** They will not tessellate.   **b** £1.47

3 **b** 1120 tiles   **c** 1176 tiles

4 **a** Regular hexagon   **b** 120 degrees   **d** 10 cm

5 **b** 198 tiles   **c** £332.48

6 The $2\frac{1}{2}$ litre size

7 £37   **8** £7.45

9 **a** Regular octagon   **b** 135 degrees   **c** 9.6 cm × 9.6 cm

13 **a** Yes   **b i** An increase per unit price   **ii** 5%

14 2.2 g   **15** **b** 442 cm²   **16** **c** 17%

SECTION 6

Starting points
A2 **a** No   **b** Yes   **c** Yes   **d** No

B1 F

B3 No, a quadrilateral is not a rigid shape like a triangle. The angles could be different.

C2 Isosceles

Exercise 6.1
3 **b** and **c** are almost identical.

Thinking ahead
A The length BC can either be about 9.3 cm or 1.7 cm.

Exercise 6.2
1 **a** $\triangle$ EBD, SAS   **b** $\triangle$ DCB, AAS   **c** $\triangle$ CDA, ASA
   d $\triangle$ AFD, SAS   **e** $\triangle$ FCB, RHS   **f** $\triangle$ AEC, SAS

2 **a** There are two different lengths that RQ could have, so the shapes are not necessarily congruent.

3 **a** congruent, SSS   **b** congruent, SAS   **c** not necessarily
   d congruent, RHS   **e** not necessarily   **f** congruent, AAS

Thinking ahead
A A, C and H

Exercise 6.3
2 60°, 30°

Thinking ahead
E **b** The locus cuts the line AB in half at right angles.

Exercise 6.4
1 **c** The distances are always equal.

3 **c** All three bisectors meet at one point.

4 **e** The bisectors all intersect at the centre of the circle.

Exercise 6.5
1 **a** 2 cm   **b** 20 metres

2 The distance from tap to tree will be about 35 metres

5 **b** about 12 km   **c** about 5 km

6 Two different quadrilaterals are possible, a convex and a concave one. The circle just touches all 4 sides of the convex quadrilateral.

Exercise 6.6
1 **d** The locus is a circle with diameter AB.

2 **e** Angle DCE is a right angle   **f** It is a right angled triangle

3 BGC, BGA, EGC, EGA, ECB, EAB

4 **a** AB = 28.6 metres   **b** AD = 20.2 metres

End points
B1 Both bisectors have the same gradient

C2 The three bisectors intersect at a point

D1 **a** congruent, SAS   **b** not necessarily   **c** not necessarily
   d congruent, SAS   **e** congruent, ASA   **f** congruent, RHS

SECTION 7

Starting points
A1 **a** $0.\dot{7}$ **b** $0.1\dot{2}\dot{3}$ **c** 4.56

A2 **a** 5.656565 ...   **b** 56.565656 ...   **c** 565.656565 ...

A3 **a** 0.25   **b** $0.\dot{3}$ **c** $0.5\dot{4}$ **d** $0.5\dot{6}$ **e** 0.375

B1   **a**   35   **b** 4^{-3}

B2   **a**   81   **b** $\frac{1}{9}$ **c**   1   **d** $\frac{1}{5}$

    e   512   **f**   36   **g** $\frac{4}{9}$ **h** $\frac{1}{16}$

C1   **a**   13   **b**   10   **c**   2.6   **d**   2.1

C2   **a**   3.5   **b**   10.2   **c**   2.6

C3   **a**   7   **b**   1.5   **c** $^-$10

C4   **a** $\frac{1}{5}$ **b** $\frac{7}{10}$ **c** $\frac{6}{5}$ or $1\frac{1}{5}$

Exercise 7.1

1   **a**   2   **b**   1.5   **c** $^-$1

2   A $(3\sqrt{8} = 2)$ D $(5\sqrt{32} = ^-2)$

3   **a** $\frac{3}{4}$ **b** $\frac{2}{3}$ **c** $\frac{1}{5}$

4   1.8

5   **a**   150.0625   **b**   3   **c** $^-$91.125

6   **a** $\sqrt[3]{6^4} = 6^2$ **b** $\sqrt[3]{2^6} = 2^2$ **c** $\sqrt[4]{5^8} = 5^2$

7   **a**   **i** $x = 4$ **b** $x = 6$

Exercise 7.2

1   **a** 6^5 **b** 5^4 **c** 7^8 **d** 3^1 or 3   **e** 2^{11} **f** 5^{-6}

2   **a** $7^3 \times 7^5 = 7^8$ **b** $4^0 \times 4^5 = 4^5$ **c** $3^{-4} \times 3^6 = 3^2$

    d $\frac{5^7}{5^{10}} = 5^{-3}$ **e** $\frac{2^5}{2^4} = 2$ **f** $(7^3)^5 = 7^{15}$

3   **a** x^8 **b** x^6 **c** x^{10} **d** x^2 **e** x^4 **f** x^{-2}

4   **a** $(t^3)^4 = t^{12}$ **b** $(q^5)^{-1} = q^{-5}$ **c** $(p^2)^{-4} = \frac{1}{p^8}$

5   **a**   5   **b** $^-$2   **c** $^-$1

6   **a** $a^2 \times a^4 = a^6$ **b** $a^{10} \div a^2 = a^8$ **c** $a^3 \div a^{12} = a^9$ **d** $(a^4)^3 = a^{12}$

7   **a** $x = 8$ **b** $x = 6$ **c** $x = 1$

8   **a** $2p$ **b** $\frac{6q^4}{5}$ **c** $2r^4$

Thinking ahead

A   **a** ± 5 **b**   9   **B**   2

Exercise 7.3

1   A and G   B and H   C and E   D and F

2   **a** ± 6 **b**   5   **c** ± 3 **d** $\pm\frac{1}{7}$ **e** $\frac{1}{2}$ **f**   1

3   **a** $\frac{2}{3}$ **b** $\frac{1}{3}$

4   A and E   B and G   C and F   D and H

5   A and F   B and H   C and D   E and G

6   A $\left(\frac{1}{4}\right)$

7   **a**   25   **b**   27   **c**   9   **d**   128   **e** $\frac{1}{8}$ **f** $\frac{1}{81}$

8   **a**   **i**   B, C, D   **ii**   A, B, C, D, F   **iii**   B, C, D, E

    b   Examples are: 4096, 531 441, 16 777 216

9   243   **10**   **a** $\frac{1}{27}$ **b**   9

Exercise 7.4

1   **a** $x = 3$ **b** $y = ^-1$ **c** $z = 2$ **d** $a = \frac{1}{5}$ or 0.2

    e $b = \frac{^-1}{3}$ **f** $c = ^-4$ **g** $p = \frac{5}{2}$ or 2.5   **h** $q = \frac{4}{3}$

    i $r = \frac{^-3}{4}$ or $^-$0.75

2

Across		Down	
2	61	1	10
3	1024	2	64
6	1331	3	16
8	27	4	243
		5	81
		6	17
		7	32

Thinking ahead

A   B and E

Exercise 7.5

1   **a**   B and E

2   **a**   Integer values: B, C, F, G and H

3   A and H   B and D   C and F   E and J   G and I

4   **a** $2\sqrt{10}$ **b** $\sqrt{21}$ **c**   3   **d**   8

    e $3\sqrt{5}$ **f**   45   **g** $11 + 4\sqrt{7}$ **h** $18 + 12\sqrt{2}$

    i $3 - 3\sqrt{2} + \sqrt{5} - \sqrt{10}$ **j**   2   **k** $33 + 6\sqrt{30}$ **l**   144

5   **a**   20 000 000 or 2×10^7 **b**   2   **c**   3

Exercise 7.6

1   **a** $\frac{5}{11}$ **b** $\frac{8}{9}$ **c**   43/111   **d** $\frac{2}{3}$ **e** $\frac{1}{33}$ **f** $\frac{3}{7}$

2   **a**   irrational   **b**   irrational   **c**   rational

    d   rational   **e**   irrational   **f**   rational

3 q

4   **a** $\frac{1}{15}$ **b** $5\frac{1}{15}$ or $\frac{76}{15}$ **c** $\frac{1}{6}$

    d $\frac{5}{6}$ **e** $\frac{23}{990}$ **f** $\frac{7}{300}$

Exercise 7.7

1   **a**   irrational   **b**   irrational   **c**   rational   **d**   irrational

    e   rational   **f**   rational   **g**   rational   **h**   irrational   **i**   rational

2   **a**   Examples are: 20, 45, 80 ...

    b   Any value except those in the above list.

3   **a**   irrational   **b**   irrational   **c**   rational   **d**   irrational

    e   irrational   **f**   rational

4   **a**   irrational   **b**   irrational   **c**   irrational   **d**   irrational

    e   rational   **f**   irrational

5   **a**   always irrational   **b**   could be rational or irrational

    c   always irrational

6   Examples are: $\sqrt{n}$, where $16 < n < 25$.

7   Examples are: $\frac{49}{16}, \frac{81}{25}, \frac{121}{36}$ ...

Exercise 7.8

1   **a** $5 + \sqrt{13}$ cm   **b**   **i**   XYZ   **ii**   PQR and XYZ

2   **a** $\sqrt{13}$ cm   **b**   **i** $\frac{1}{7}\sqrt{13}$ **ii** $\frac{6}{7}$ **iii** $\frac{1}{6}\sqrt{13}$

3   **a** $2\sqrt{2}$ m or $\sqrt{8}$ m   irrational

    b   8 m   rational

    c $\sqrt{8}\pi$ m   irrational

    d 2π m^2 irrational

4   **a**   **i**   16 cm   **ii** $4\sqrt{8}$ cm or $8\sqrt{2}$ cm   **b**   Square n where n is odd.

End points

A1   **a**   3   **b**   6   **c**   2

B1   **a** $2^4 \times 2^8 = 2^{12}$ **b** $\frac{3^4}{3^6} = \frac{1}{3^2}$ **c** $(7^2)^3 = 7^6$

B2   **a** $2x^7$ **b** x^4 **c** $81x^{12}$

C1   **a** ± 10 **b**   16   **c** $\frac{1}{8}$

C2   **a** $x = \frac{1}{3}$ **b** $x = ^-2$ **c** $x = ^-\frac{1}{4}$

D1   **a** $\sqrt{10}$ **b** $4\sqrt{2}$ **c**   63   **d** $1 - 2\sqrt{6}$

E1   **a** $\frac{3}{11}$

E2   **a**   irrational   **b**   rational   **c**   irrational   **d**   rational

    e   irrational   **f**   rational

E3   **a**   **i** $\sqrt{2}$ cm   **ii** $\sqrt{3}$ cm   **b**   Triangle 3   **c**   irrational

SECTION 8

Starting points

A1   **a**   23.47   **b**   4.16   **c**   142.86   **d**   12.30

A2   **a**   56.5   **b**   0.3   **c**   6.0   **d**   600.0

B1   **a**   150   **b**   16   **c**   3400   **d**   6.3   **e**   0.36   **f**   1 100 000

B2   **a**   30   **b**   200   **c**   0.05   **d**   500 000   **e**   100   **f**   0.000 09

C1   **a** 8^{10} **b** 6^2 **c** 10^{-2} **d** 10^{-2} **e** 4^{-10} **f** 10^2 **g** 5^8 **h** 6^{-12}

D1   **a** 3.45×10^5 **b** 4.17×10^{-3} **c** 4.297×10^1 or 4.297×10

    d 4×10^6 **e** 2.3×10^{-6} **f** 6.413234×10^3

D2   **a**   6740   **b**   0.000 15   **c**   652.41   **d**   0.000 000 2

Exercise 8.1

1   299.5 cm   **2**   **a**   15.65 cm   **b**   15.55 cm

3   **a**   7 750 000   **b**   7 650 000   **c**   7 650 000 $< L <$ 7 750 000

4 $0.165 < t < 0.175$

Exercise 8.2

1   **a**   755 g   **b**   745 g   **2**   **a**   46.2 cm   **b**   1.2 cm

3   **a** $132.4 < L < 134.9$ metres   **b**   42.89°

4   **a**   Upper 81.837 525, lower 81.642 525   **b**   Upper 39.02, lower 38.98

5   min 62.8875, max 64.5575 (range 1.67)

Exercise 8.3

All estimates based on rounding to 1sf

1   **a**   6000   **b**   24000   **c**   4 000 000   **d**   25 000

    e   750   **f**   100   **g**   250   **h**   30 000

2 a £18 000   **b** both rounded up, multiplication compounds the increases

3 120

5 a too large   **b** about right   **c** about right   **d** too small
e too small   **f** too big   **g** about right   **h** about right

7 When the numbers are of the same magnitude.

Exercise 8.4

1 a 17784   **b** 17.784   **2** 0.1035

3 a 8657.5   **b** 17.5741   **c** 0.201 526
d 1360   **e** 1.514 878 112   **f** 1682.106 888

4 $A = 300 \times 300 \times 0.4 = 36000\,cm^3$, $B = 50 \times 400 \times 1 = 20\,000\,cm^3$
$C = 3 \times 0.4 \times 70 = 84\,cm^3$ (65.8 is closer to 70 than 60)

5 About 0.4 cm

Exercise 8.5

1 a 67.725 848   **b** absolute error 0.017 352 43, error % 0.026 (to 3 dp)
c 6.3%

2 (To 2 sf)   **a** 0.60%   **b** 0.000 008 5%   **c** 0.53%   **d** 0.040%.
The Chinese one is most accurate (accurate to 6 dp).

3 a 5.077 105 433   **b i** $\dfrac{3 \times 10^3}{300 + 300}$ **ii** 5   **c** 1.52% (to 2 dp)

4 9.3%

Exercise 8.6

1 875   **2** 500 seconds

3 a speed 1.07×10^5, radius 1.50×10^8 **b** 8.808×10^3 hours, a year.

4 a 5×10^2: 9.6×10^{-5} **b** 0.048 m

5 a 7.32×10^{-23} **b** 1.366×10^{22}

6 4.373×10^{-2} minutes   **7** 6.74×10^1 m

8 a $5.3 \times 10^{14}\,m^2$ **b** 7.5×10^{-11} tonnes/m^2

End points

A1 a 6.75 cm   **b** 9.75 cm   **c** $338.6 \le$ volume (cm^3) ≤ 352.5
d 208.8766 cm^2

B1 a 300 000   **b** 3 000 000   **c** 0.000 05   **d** 100

C1 a 1458   **b** 1.2% (to 1 dp)   **D1** 1.296×10^4 tonnes

SECTION 9

Starting points

A1 a $y^2 + 8y + 15$ **b** $k^2 - k - 12$ **c** $n^2 - 6n - 27$ **d** $w^2 - 9w + 20$ **e** $v^2 - 64$

A2 a $2n^2 - 5n - 12$ **b** $3w^2 - 22w - 16$ **c** $12y^2 - 25y + 12$
d $4k^2 - 12k + 9$ **e** $3v^3 + v^2 - 9v - 3$

A3 a $2y^3 - 2y^2 - 12y$ **b** $3x^3 + 6x^2 + 3x$ **c** $x^3 + 3x^2 - 13x - 15$
d $4n^3 - 4n^2 - 5n + 3$ **e** $x^3 + 6x^2 + 12x + 8$ **f** $2k^3 + 6k^2 + 16k + 24$

B1 a $(y + 7)(y + 2)$ **b** $(k + 8)(k + 5)$ **c** $(x + 6)(x - 2)$
d $(w + 9)(w - 4)$ **e** $(y - 8)(x - 3)$ **f** $(y - 8)(y - 1)$
g $(p + 12)(p - 5)$ **h** $(b + 9)(b - 8)$ **i** $(x - 4)(x - 12)$
j $(n + 5)(n - 5)$ **k** $(y + 10)(y - 10)$ **l** $(a + b)(a - b)$
m $(2y + 6)(2y - 6)$ **n** $(4x + 6y)(4x - 6y)$ **o** $(10a + b^2)(10a - b^2)$

C1 a $y = -4.5$ **b** $y = 3.4$ **c** $x = 2$ **d** $x = 3$ **e** $x = 4$

C2 a $x - 2$ **b** $n - 0.375$ **c** $w - 21$ **d** $k = 2$ **e** $v = \frac{13}{6}$

C3 a $y = 8\frac{2}{3}$ **b** $u = 8$ **c** $k = 10$ **d** $h = 12$ **e** $a = 2$

C4 a $w = -7$ **b** $k = 3.5$ **c** $n = \frac{1}{8}$

D1 Length 15 cm   Width 9 cm   **D2** 20

D3 Bus A 53, bus B 44, bus C 50.

Exercise 9.1

A a £2.30   **b** £6.90
B a £4   **b** 96p   **c** 28p   **d** 68p

1 a $x = 6, y = 9$ **b** $x = 8, y = 1$ **c** $x = 6, y = 2$ **d** $x = 2, y = -1$
e $x = -2, y = 3$ **f** $x = 3, y = -4$

2 c $n = 10$ **d** $m = -1$

3 a $v = 2, w = 12$ **b** $w = 3, v = -1$ **c** $v = 3, w = -2$ **d** $v = 3, w = 2$
e $v = 3, w = -1$ **f** $v = 3, w = -2$ **g** $v = 2, w = -1$ **h** $v = 1, w = 3$
i $v = -1, w = 2$

Exercise 9.2

1 a $a = 10, b = 2$ **b** $a = 2, b = 5$ **c** $a = 4, b = -3$
d $a = -2, b = 8$ **e** $a = 3, b = 1$ **f** $a = 6, b = -4$
g $a = -2, b = -1$ **h** $a = 4, b = -2$ **i** $a = 3, b = -2$
j $a = 2, b = 1$ **k** $a = 2, b = -3$ **l** $b = 4, a = -1$

2 $k = 5, n = 10$ **3** $m = 6, n = 1$

4 a $x = 4, y = 2$ **b** $y = 5, x = 3$ **c** $x = 2, y = 1$
d $x = -1, y = 2$ **e** $x = 5, y = -1$ **f** $x = 7, y = -4$
g $x = -3, y = -2$ **h** $x = 3, y = -4$ **i** $y = -1, x = 2$
j $x = 3, y = -5$ **k** $x = -1, y = 2$ **l** $x = -2, y = 3$

Exercise 9.3

1 Adult £6.50, child £4   **2** Regular 16 g, jumbo 54 g

3 Small 63, large 26   **4** $13 \times$ £5 notes, $9 \times$ £10 notes

5 $123 \times 10p$, $257 \times 20p$ **6** One number 7, other number 5

7 $m = 4$, $c = -2$ **8** Standing 16 200, seated 12 300

9 a $m = 3, n = 8$ **b** $3x + y = 8$

10 a $a = 1, b = 3, c = -5$ **b** $y = x^2 + 3x - 5$

11 a $a = 2, b = -3, c = 1$ **b** $y = 2x^2 - 3x + 1$

12 a $a = 3, b = -1, c = -4$ **b** $y + x = 3x^2 - 4$

13 a Machine A 16.5 hours, machine B 8.5 hours   **14** $a = 8, b = 18$

Exercise 9.4

a $y = -4$ or $y = -1$ **b** $y = -6$ or $y = -3$ **c** $y = -8$ or $y = 3$
d $x = -7$ or $x = 1$ **e** $x = -9$ or $x = 4$ **f** $x = -9$ or $x = 7$
g $w = 11$ or $w = -4$ **h** $w = 15$ or $w = -7$ **i** $w = 16$ or $w = -7$
j $a = 3$ or $a = 5$ **k** $a = 7$ or $a = 5$ **l** $a = 5$ or $a = 6$
m $b = 5$ or $b = 2$ **n** $b = -28$ or $b = -3$ **o** $b = 15$ or $b = -2$
p $c = -12$ or $c = 5$ **q** $c = 9$ or $c = 5$ **r** $c = -15$ or $c = 3$
s $h = -15$ or $h = 14$ **t** $h = 21$ or $h = -19$ **u** $h = 3$ or $h = 14$
v $n = -15$ or $n = 12$ **w** $n = 7$ or $n = 8$ **x** $n = 17$ or $n = -8$

Exercise 9.5

1 a $y = 0$ or $y = -8$ **b** $y = 0$ or $y = 5$ **c** $y = 0$ or $y = 18$
d $h = \pm 10$ **e** $h = \pm 5$ **f** $h = \pm 9$

2 a $x = 0$ or $x = 12$ **b** $x = 0$ or $x = -79$ **c** $x = 0$ or $x = -\frac{1}{3}$
d $x = 0$ or $x = \frac{1}{4}$ **e** $x = \pm 13$ **f** $x = 0$ or $x = 1$
g $x = 0$ or $x = \frac{2}{5}$ **h** $x = 0$ or $x = -\frac{5}{4}$ **i** $x = 0$ or $x = -\frac{2}{7}$

Exercise 9.6

1 a $x = \frac{2}{3}$ or $x = -\frac{1}{4}$ **b** $x = \frac{5}{2}$ or $x = -\frac{1}{3}$ **c** $x = \frac{3}{2}$ or $x = -\frac{1}{2}$
d $x = -\frac{1}{5}$ or $x = \frac{1}{2}$ **e** $y = -\frac{4}{3}$ or $y = \frac{1}{3}$ **f** $y = \frac{2}{3}$ or $y = \frac{1}{2}$
g $h = \frac{1}{3}$ or $h = -\frac{2}{3}$ **h** $a = \frac{1}{7}$ or $a = 1$ **i** $a = -\frac{2}{3}$ or $a = \frac{1}{2}$
j $c = \frac{1}{5}$ or $c = 2$ **k** $c = \frac{1}{3}$ or $c = -3$ **l** $c = \frac{4}{3}$ or $c = 4$
m $c = 0$ or $c = 31$ **n** $w = \frac{2}{3}$ or $w = 2$ **o** $w = \frac{1}{6}$ or $w = 2$

2 a $x = 0$ or $x = \frac{1}{2}$ **b** $x = 0$ or $x = 3$ **c** $x = 0$ or $x = -\frac{1}{4}$
d $y = 0$ or $y = \frac{8}{5}$ **e** $y = 0$ or $y = \frac{1}{2}$ **f** $y = -\frac{1}{5}$ or $y = \frac{1}{5}$
g $k = \pm\frac{1}{4}$ **h** $k = 0$ or $k = 9$ **i** $k = 0$ or $k = 5$
j $w = 0$ or $w = 1$ **k** $w = \pm\frac{1}{3}$ **l** $w = 0$ or $w = \frac{4}{3}$
m $c = 0$ or $c = 31$ **n** $c = 0$ or $c = \frac{3}{7}$ **o** $c = \pm\frac{3}{4}$

Exercise 9.7

1 a $x = -2.35$ or $x = 0.85$ **b** $x = -1.55$ or $x = 0.80$
c $x = -4.19$ or $x = 1.19$ **d** $y = -4.30$ or $y = -0.70$
e $y = -3.35$ or $y = -0.15$ **f** $y = 1.46$ or $y = 0.14$
g $p = 1.43$ or $p = 0.23$ **h** $p = 1.71$ or $p = 0.29$
i $p = 1.62$ or $p = -0.62$ **j** $w = -1.85$ or $w = 1.35$
k $w = 1.81$ or $w = -1.47$ **l** $w = 0.72$ or $w = 0.28$
m $a = -1.82$ or $a = 0.82$ **n** $a = 1.09$ or $a = 0.92$
o $a = 1.13$ or $a = -0.88$ **p** $c = -1.11$ or $c = 0.11$
q $c = -1.46$ or $c = 0.14$ **r** $c = -1.16$ or $c = -0.12$
s $n = -2.35$ or $n = 0.85$ **t** $n = 5.54$ or $n = -0.54$
u $n = 4.37$ or $n = -1.37$

2 a $x = -2.27$ or $x = 1.27$ **b** $x = 2.18$ or $x = 0.15$
c $x = -1.80$ or $x = 0.55$

Exercise 9.8

1 b $x = -10.477$ or $x = 0.477$ **2** $b^2 < 4ac$ **3** $x = -8.36$ or $x = 0.36$

4 a $x = -12.16$ or $x = 0.16$ **b** $x = -7.12$ or $x = 1.12$
c $x = -14.07$ or $x = 0.07$ **d** $b^2 < 4ac$
e $b^2 < 4ac$ **f** $x = -7.16$ or $x = -0.84$

5 $x = -4.19$ or $x = 1.19$

6 a $x = -5.70$ or $x = 0.70$ **b** $x = -7.27$ or $x = 0.27$
c $x = -2.62$ or $x = -0.38$

Exercise 9.9

1 a $x = 9$ or $x = ^-4$ **b** $x = 12$ or $x = ^-5$
  c $x = 9$ or $x = ^-7$ **d** $y = ^-9$ or $y = 3$
  e $y = ^-4.79$ or $y = ^-1.88$ **f** $y = ^-6$ or $y = 1$
  g $w = 6.27$ or $w = ^-1.27$ **h** $w = ^-4.21$ or $w = 0.71$
  i $w = \pm\frac{1}{6}$ **j** $v = \pm\frac{1}{5}$
  k $v = 0$ or $v = \frac{5}{3}$ **l** $v = 0.57$ or $v = ^-2.19$
  m $a = ^-1.90$ or $a = 0.40$ **n** $a = 1.63$ or $a = ^-1.38$
  o $a = \pm\frac{1}{10}$

Exercise 9.10

1 a Length 28 cm, width 16 cm   **b** 32.25 cm   **2** 24 and 18
3 a 36 cm   **b** 972 cm²   **4** $\angle ABC = 37.61°$
5 $t = ^-14.72$ or $t = 2.72$ **6 a** Base 36 cm   height 27 cm   **b** 108 cm
7 a $w = 8.5$ **b** 50.14 cm   **c** 4.28°
8 50.5 and 54.5   **9 b** 54

Exercise 9.11

1 c $x = ^-12$ or $x = 7$ **2 c** $x = ^-11$ or $x = 5$
3 a $x = ^-14$ or $x = 4$ **b** $x = ^-12$ or $x = 9$ **c** $x = ^-14$ or $x = 12$
  d $x = ^-7$ or $x = 3$ **e** $x = ^-10$ or $x = 12$ **f** $x = ^-9$ or $x = 8$

Exercise 9.12

1 b $x = ^-12$ or $x = 5$
2 a $x = 7$ or $x = ^-3$ **b** $x = 12$ or $x = ^-4$ **c** $x = 16$ or $x = 15$

End points

A1 a $x = 3, y = ^-2$ **b** $x = ^-3, y = ^-1$ **B1** Adult £4.80 child £2.65
C1 a $x = ^-8$ or $x = 3$ **b** $x = 13$ or $x = ^-5$
  c $x = 12$ or $x = 3$ **d** $x = ^-3$ or $x = ^-2$
D1 a $x = ^-6.32$ or $x = 0.32$ **b** $x = 0.35$ or $x = 8.65$
  c $x = ^-2.69$ or $x = 0.19$
E $x = ^-5.54$ or $x = 0.54$ **F** Length 38 cm   width 15 cm
G a $x = ^-6$ or $x = 1$ **b** $x = 3$ or $x = 5$

SECTION 10

Starting points

A1 a $x = 3$ **b** $y = ^-1$ **C1 a** 90°   **b** (0, 1)   **F1 a** V, Y and Z

Thinking ahead

A c rotation of $^+90°$ about (1, 1)
  d i rotation 180° about (0, 1)
    ii reflection in $y = x - 1$
    iii rotation $^-90°$ about ($^-2, ^-1$)

Exercise 10.1

1 b G and H are in the same orientation but in different positions.
2 b J and K are exactly the same.
3 2 and 3 are commutative; 1 and 4 are commutative.

Exercise 10.2

1 b i rotation $^+90°$ about (1, 1)
    ii rotation 180° about (1, 2)
    iii reflection in $y = ^-x$

Exercise 10.3

1 a translation $\begin{pmatrix} 2 \\ 2 \end{pmatrix}$
  b rotation 180° about (2, 0)
  c rotation 180° about (3, 1)
2 a i reflection in $x = 5$
    ii reflection in $y = x$
    iii rotation 180° about (4, 1)

Exercise 10.4

1 b B
  c

Object	Image	SF	Centre
S	Y	2	(4, 8)
X	U	$\frac{1}{2}$	(12, 8)
E	A	2	(8, 8)
Q	W	$^-1$	(8, 6)

  d T and M are in different orientations.
  e i rotation $^-90°$ about (8, 8)
    ii enlargement SF $\frac{1}{2}$ with centre (8, 12)
    iii rotation 180° about (6, 8)

Exercise 10.5

2 b i rotation $^-90°$ about (4, 1)
    ii translation $\begin{pmatrix} 4 \\ 2 \end{pmatrix}$
    iii rotation of $^+90°$ about (2, 5)
  c i enlargement SF 2 with centre ($^-1, ^-2$)
    ii enlargement SF 2 centre ($^-5, ^-4$)
3 a enlargement SF $\frac{1}{2}$ with centre ($^-1, 0$)
  b enlargement SF $\frac{1}{2}$ with centre ($^-3, ^-2$)
5 c i enlargement SF $^-2$ with centre (0, 1)
    ii enlargement SF 2.25 with centre (0, 1)
  d i enlargement SF $^-\frac{1}{2}$ with centre (0, 1)
    ii enlargement SF $\frac{4}{9}$ with centre (0, 1)

Thinking ahead

A b Each pair of transformations maps the object on to itself.

Exercise 10.6

1 a translation $\begin{pmatrix} 1 \\ 2 \end{pmatrix}$
  b rotation $^+90°$ about (1, 0)
     or
    rotation $^-270°$ about (1, 0)
  c enlargement SF 0.5 with centre ($^-1, 2$)
2 a reflection in $y = ^-x$
  b All reflections are their own inverse.
3 c rotation 180° about (x, y)
     or
  enlargement SF $^-1$ with centre (x, y)

End points

A1 c i rotation of 180° about (0, $^-1$)
    ii rotation of $^+90°$ about (0, 0)
    iii translation of $\begin{pmatrix} 0 \\ 4 \end{pmatrix}$
  d i translation of $\begin{pmatrix} 0 \\ 4 \end{pmatrix}$
    ii reflection in $y = ^-3$
    iii rotation of 180° about (1, 0)
  e i rotation of $^-90°$ about (1, $^-1$)
    ii rotation of 180° about (0, $^-3$)
     or
  enlargement SF $^-1$ with centre (0, $^-3$)
B1 a enlargement SF 4 with centre (3, $^-1$)
  b rotation $^+270°$ about (0, 2)
     or
  rotation $^-90°$ about (0, 2)
  c translation $\begin{pmatrix} 0 \\ 3 \end{pmatrix}$
B2 reflection in $y = x + 1$

SKILLS BREAK 2

1 a 12 lines of symmetry   **b** 12
2 a 133 m² (nearest m²)   **b** 1805 cm² = 0.1805 m²
  c About 7.6 m³ (Note: diameter of window to centre of frame is 13.36 m)
3 a 45°   **b** 135°
4 a 29 cm (to 2sf)   **b** 595 cm² (to 3 sf)
5 1080 tons (or 1120 tons)
6 a 46 m   **b** 9° (to nearest degree)   **c** 2.5° (to 2 sf)
7 About 370 steps
8 0.05%
9 045°
10 a £7.43   **b** £1.49 cheaper
11 French 0.42, English 0.38
12

	French	English
Range	14	12
Mean	5	4.9
Mode	5	4
Median	2	4

Different answers are possible but must be justified.
13 a $\frac{1}{3}$ **b** $\frac{1}{6}$ **c i** $\frac{1}{3}$ **ii** $\frac{1}{2}$ **d** Profit
14 a Adult £99 child £89   **b** £277

Section 11

Starting points

A1 **a** $d = 5.5$ **b** $y = {}^{-}14$ **c** $x = 4$ **d** $p = 6$ **e** $\frac{17}{11}$

f $k = \frac{2}{3}$ **g** $n = 18$ **h** $g = {}^{-}11$

A2 **a** $c = \frac{15}{2}$ **b** $x = \frac{4}{5}$ **c** $x = 12$ **d** $v = {}^{-}2$ **e** $w = 1$

f $a = 4.4$ **g** $x = 6$ **h** $y = {}^{-}120$

B1 **a** $3(2bc - 5ax + by)$ **b** $6(3a^2 + 4b^2c)$

c $a(3ax - 5y^2 + 6b - c)$ **d** $ax(y - ax + xy - b)$

e $3cd(2c - 5b)$ **f** $4ax(2y^2 + 3b - 5a + 4)$

g $2a(2x + 3c) - b(2 + 3c)$ **h** $ab(4a - 3x) + 2x(4a - 3x)$

i $(2a - xy)(3x^2 + 2y)$ **j** $(2b - a)(abc - b^2cy)$

C1 **a** $x = \sqrt{(4a + 3)}$ **b** $x = \sqrt{\frac{(5c + 1)}{3}}$

c $x = (3a - 7)^2$ **d** $x = \frac{49}{a}$ **e** $x = \frac{16a^2}{25}$

Exercise 11.1

1 **a** £10.25 **b** **i** $n = \frac{C - 50}{15}$ **ii** 129 **c** 63

2 **a** 900° **b** **i** $n = \frac{S + 360}{180}$ **ii** 20

3 **a** **i** 55.924 m **ii** more (1.68%) **b** **i** $t = \frac{x - w}{wk}$ **ii** 30.5°

4 **a** 34 283 cm² **b** **i** $h = \frac{S - 2\pi r^2}{2\pi r}$ **ii** 17 cm

5 **a** $y = \frac{5x + 3}{6}$ **b** $y = \frac{2a + 12}{3}$ **c** $y = \frac{2a - 3x}{2}$

d $y = \frac{3a - 8}{6}$ **e** $y = \frac{x^2 + 6}{12}$ **f** $y = \frac{1 - 5a^2}{2}$

g $y = \frac{6a - p}{7}$ **h** $y = \frac{2x - 1}{x}$ **i** $y = \frac{6a - x^2}{8a}$

j $y = \frac{a + 6x}{3x}$ **k** $y = \frac{{}^{-}3c - x^2}{3c}$ **l** $y = \frac{10x^2 - 2}{x}$

m $y = \frac{p^2 - 3.5}{1.5a}$ **n** $y = \frac{3 - a}{ax}$ **o** $y = \frac{{}^{-}11 - 3a}{x^2}$

p $y = \frac{5 - a^2b}{2a^2}$ **q** $y = \frac{x^2 + 3a^2 - 4}{3a}$ **r** $y = \frac{at^2 - t^2 - 1}{at}$

s $y = \frac{t + 2 - 3dt}{adt}$ **t** $y = \frac{hr^2 - \pi d}{2h}$ **u** $y = \frac{ar^2 - 3\pi}{2a}$

Exercise 11.2

1 **a** 17.6 **b** $k = \frac{5p}{11}$ **c** $1.361\, kg$

2 **a** $h = \frac{2A}{b}$ **b** 80 cm

3 **a** 20°C **b** $F = \frac{9C + 150}{5}$ **c** 75.2°F

4 **a** $y = \frac{4z}{3}$ **b** $y = \frac{3m}{x}$ **c** $y = 2d - 4$ **d** $\frac{7d + 4h}{4}$

5 **a** 130.1 kph **b** $d = \frac{5st}{18}$ **c** $t = \frac{18d}{5s}$

6 **a** ${}^{-}24°$ **b** $h = 300G - 300I$ **c** 15000

7 16.2

8 **a** $\frac{5}{6}x$ **b** $\frac{3}{4 \sin 32°}$ **c** $3(4b + 5a)$

d $\frac{bt + a}{t}$ **e** $\frac{a^2}{b}$ **f** $\frac{c^2 - b}{4ab}$

g $\frac{3(1 - 4a)}{8}$ **h** $\frac{3 + 2c}{2c}$ **i** $\frac{\tan 50° - 3c}{6c}$

j $\frac{3 - 2y^2}{ay^2}$ **k** $\frac{10x + 3b - 15a}{3}$ **l** $\frac{\cos 3x - a \sin 2x}{2a \sin 2x}$

m $\frac{a - 3ay}{3y}$ **n** a **o** $\frac{1}{6}k^2(2c - 1)$ **p** $\frac{5a + 3}{3}$

q $\frac{3(1 + 2k - 12b)}{4(k - 6b)}$ **r** $\frac{\cos 135° + 2 \sin 65°}{\sin 65°}$ **s** $\frac{3d + 3}{ad}$

t $\frac{hr^2 - \pi d}{2h}$ **u** $\frac{a^2r - 3\pi}{2a}$

Exercise 11.3

1 **a** $w = \frac{(S - 2ab)}{2(a + b)}$ **b** $a = \frac{(S - 2bw)}{2(b + w)}$ **c** $b = 3.6$

2 **a** $w = \frac{2P}{(4 + \pi)}$ **b** 50 m

3 **a** **i** $b = \frac{V}{(ac - 2ad)}$ **ii** 14.5 cm **b** 12 cm

4 **a** $\frac{3ac}{4a - y}$ **b** $\frac{4x}{3 - 2a}$ **c** $\frac{2x - 5}{3x - a}$ **d** $\frac{4 - b^2}{a - c^2}$ **e** $\frac{15 - 2a^2}{3(a + 2)}$

f $\frac{3kx^2}{2 - k}$ **g** $\frac{8x}{3t - 4c}$ **h** $\frac{3x}{a - 5}$ **i** $\frac{3k + x^2}{1 + 2k}$ **j** $\frac{8y}{3 - 4a^2y}$

k $\frac{2}{3(6 - 2a - ax)}$ **l** $\frac{k}{2(3 - m^2 + n)}$ **m** $\frac{x}{a - 2f^3 - 1}$

n $4 \sin 42°$ **o** $\frac{3a}{ak - 1}$ **p** $y + 1$ **q** $\frac{5}{3a^2}(\tan 55° + bc)$

Exercise 11.4

1 About 9.5 seconds **2** **b** $u = 8.4$ **3** $r = \sqrt{(3v/\pi h)}$

4 $\sqrt[3]{\frac{3V}{4\pi}}$ **5** $\frac{s^2(s - a)(s - b) - A^2}{s(s - a)(s - c)}$

6 **a** $\sqrt{(y^2 - 3a + 4)}$ **b** $\sqrt{\frac{x - 3y}{2a}}$ **c** $\sqrt{\frac{y - 1}{x}}$ **d** $\sqrt{\frac{4 + x}{a}}$

e $\sqrt{\frac{2x + 5a}{a}}$ **f** $\sqrt[3]{\frac{3x + 2a}{2a}}$ **g** $\sqrt[3]{\frac{x - 1}{a}}$ **h** $\sqrt{\frac{c}{1 - 2a}}$ **i** $\frac{a^2 + 1}{3}$

j $2(2a^2 + 1)$ **k** $\sqrt{\frac{w^2 - 3}{a}}$ **l** $\frac{1}{\sqrt{c^2 - 1}}$ **m** $\sqrt{\frac{4a^2 - x^2y^2}{4}}$

n $\frac{r - a\pi^2}{\pi^2}$ **o** $\frac{k^2y}{4\pi^2}$ **p** $\frac{a + c + x}{2}$ **q** $\frac{(c - 4)(c - 2)}{2}$ **r** $\frac{x^2 + 4}{4}$

Exercise 11.5

1 82.5 m

2 **a** 121.5 cm³ **b** 64 cm³

3 **A** **a** 42 **b** ${}^{-}8$ **c** 6 **d** ${}^{-}14$ **e** 10.75 **f** ${}^{-}14.25$

B **a** 42 **b** 12 **c** 12 **d** 0 **e** 15.75 **f** 0.75

C **a** 47 **b** ${}^{-}193$ **c** ${}^{-}4$ **d** ${}^{-}16$ **e** 3.625 **f** ${}^{-}29.875$

D **a** 42 **b** 12 **c** 12 **d** 0 **e** 15.75 **f** 0.75

E **a** 42 **b** ${}^{-}28$ **c** 0 **d** ${}^{-}28$ **e** 5.75 **f** ${}^{-}29.25$

F **a** 96 **b** ${}^{-}64$ **c** 15 **d** 5 **e** ${}^{-}9.625$ **f** 4.125

4 **a** **i** $v = 31.1$ m/s **ii** $v = 21$ m/s

b **i** $u = 119.5$ m/s **ii** $u = 131.3$ m/s **iii** $u = 17$ m/s

5 **a** 1.098×10^2 m³ **b** $r = \sqrt[3]{\frac{3V}{4\pi}}$

End Points

A1 **a** $x = \frac{(5 - a)}{3}$ **b** $x = \frac{(a - 3)}{6}$ **c** $x = \frac{(5 - 2v)}{6}$

d $x = \frac{(3a - b)}{5y}$ **e** $x = \frac{(3 - bc)}{4}$

B1 **a** $v = \frac{4(a - x)}{3}$ **b** $v = \frac{(3a - 14)}{10}$ **c** $v = \frac{(2a + 3)}{3a^2}$

d $v = \frac{(4ax + 8y - 5)}{2}$ **e** $v = \frac{33a}{12}$ **f** $v = \frac{(c^2b - 3)}{2c^2}$

g $v = \frac{2wx}{(3w - x)}$

C1 **a** $c = \frac{(3 - ax^2)}{x}$ **b** $c = \frac{8x}{(b + y - 2a)}$

c $c = \frac{(2a^2 - b)}{(bx + 6a)}$ **d** $c = \frac{3 + 2a - a^2b}{b^2 - a^2}$

e $c = \frac{(9xw - 2)}{(1 + 9x^3)}$ **f** $c = \frac{(ax - 2)}{(a^2 + x - y^2 - 1)}$

D1 **a** $y = \dfrac{25}{x}$ **b** $y = a^2 + 2ax + x^2 - 1$ **c** $y = \dfrac{4}{(2x-1)^2}$

     d $y = \dfrac{ab^2}{9}$ **e** $y = \dfrac{(4a^2 - 25)}{4}$ **f** $y = \dfrac{4}{x^2 + a - b}$

     g $y = \sqrt{\dfrac{2b-3}{6}}$ **h** $y = \sqrt{\dfrac{3a - a^2}{15}}$ **i** $y = \sqrt[3]{\dfrac{2a+b}{5}}$

D1 $652\,\text{cm}^2$ **b** 8.5 c   **E2** 7.4

Section 12

Starting Points

D1 **a** $3:1$ **b** $1:3$

B1 **a** $4:1$ **b** $2:5:4$ **c** $9:12$
     $12:3$ $1:2\tfrac{1}{2}:2$ $3:4$
                              $6:8$

B2 $2:5$ $1:3:2$ $10:20$
     $10:25$ $3:9:6$ $2\tfrac{1}{2}:5$
     $1:2\tfrac{1}{2}$

B3 **a** $3:2$ **b** $2:3$ **c** $2:4:1$ **d** $10:1$ **e** $4:3:6$

C1 W and Y are in proportion
     X and Z are in proportion

D1 **a** **i** $\tfrac{5}{8}$ **ii** 0.625 **iii** 62.5%
   b **i** $1\tfrac{4}{5}$ **ii** 1.8 **iii** 180%
   c **i** $\tfrac{7}{12}$ **ii** $0.58\dot{3}$ **iii** 58.3%
   d **i** $1\tfrac{4}{11}$ **ii** $1.\dot{3}\dot{6}$ **iii** 136.36%
   e **i** $\tfrac{11}{18}$ **ii** $0.6\dot{1}$ **iii** 61.1%
   f **i** $\tfrac{17}{24}$ **ii** 0.7083 **iii** 70.83%

E1 **a** Amy £75, Ben £45, Zoe £30   **E2** **a** 75 min   **b** 90 min

F1 **a** EFG and JKL are similar so they must have the same angles.
   b L   **c** **i** LJ   **ii** GF

G1 **a** 0.5   **b** 4   **c** 0.3   **d** 0.75

Exercise 12.1

1 345 g caster sugar, 450 ml water, 75 g cocoa, 1800 ml chilled milk

2 **a** 60 g   **b** 75 ml
   c 300 g white sugar, 100 ml milk, 100 ml water, 50 g butter, 20 g cocoa

3 **a** 7 drops   **b** 2 egg whites (not 1.75 egg whites)

Exercise 12.2

1 **a** 315 ml   **b** 525 ml

2 **a** 250 kg   **b** **i** $2:1:9$ **ii** 2400 kg

3 **a** 800 cm (8 m)   **b** 9 cm

Exercise 12.3

1 **a** 2.5   **b** 12.75 cm   **c** **i** 1.2142857 ...   **ii** 1.2142857 ...
   d RXYZ is an enlargement of RSTU, so the shapes must be in proportion.

Exercise 12.4

1 **a** MNOP
   b All corresponding angles are equal and all ratios of lengths of corresponding sides are equal

2 **a** EFGH & MNOP ABCD & IJKL QRST & UVWX
   b $2:3$, $1:2$, $4:3$ respectively

Exercise 12.5

1 **a** 4.56 cm   **b** 4.2 cm

2 DF has been multiplied by the ratio greater than 1 instead of the ratio less than 1.

3 12.3 cm

4 **a** 1.6 cm
   b The angle at J is equal to the angle at M so JK and MN must be at the same angle to LM, and are therefore parallel to each other.

Exercise 12.6

1 **a** ABD and CAD are similar because they have the same angles: each triangle has a 90° angle and the angle D, so the third angles must also be the same.

   b **i** BA **ii** BD   **b** **i** 13.3 cm **ii** 10.6 cm

2 **a** **i** 1.5 **ii** 1.5
   b KMO and NML are similar because all ratios of lengths of corresponding sides are equal.
   c 3.9 cm

3 **a** DEF and GHF are similar because all ratios of lengths of corresponding sides are equal:
     $\dfrac{\text{DF}}{\text{GF}} = \dfrac{8}{5} = 1.6$ $\dfrac{\text{EF}}{\text{HF}} = \dfrac{4}{2.5} = 1.6$
   b 3.25 cm

4 DEF is in a different orientation to GHF.
   For example, if GHF was enlarged by a scale factor of ¯1.6, using F as the centre of enlargement, then the enlargement would need to be 'flipped-over' to give DEF.

Exercise 12.7

1 **b** The line passes through $(0,0)$ because 0×0.25 equals 0.
   c The constant and the gradient are the same value.
   d $h = 0.25b$

2 **a** $\dfrac{b}{h} = 4$ **b** $b = 4h$

3 **b** No: plotting a against b does not give a straight line.

4 **a**

	W	X	Y	Z
Height (h)	1	1.25	1.5	1.2
Area (A)	2	3.125	4.5	2.88

   c No: plotting A against h does not give a straight line.

5 **a**

	W	X	Y	Z
h^2	1	1.5625	2.25	1.44
A	2	3.125	4.5	2.88

   c Yes: plotting A against h^2 gives a straight line that, when extended, passes through $(0, 0)$.

6 **b** $h = 0.25b + 1.5$
   c

	A	B	C	D
$\dfrac{h}{b}$	0.625	0.5625	0.55	0.5

7 **a** **ii** No: plotting h against b does not give a straight line.
   b **ii**

	P	Q	R	S	T
$\dfrac{1}{b}$	0.3	0.25	0.2	0.16	0.125
h	2	1.5	1.2	1	0.75

     iii Yes: plotting h against $\dfrac{1}{b}$ gives a straight line that, when extended, passes through $(0, 0)$.

Exercise 12.8

1 **a**
     $\dfrac{h}{w}$
     A4 1.4142857 ...
     A3 1.41
     A2 1.4142857 ...
     A1 1.4158249 ...
     A0 1.4137931 ...
   b $\sqrt{2}$ is irrational.   **c** $h = \sqrt{2}w$

2 **a** $36\,\text{cm}^2$ **b** **i** $h = \dfrac{36}{w}$ **i** $wh = 36$ **iii** $w = \dfrac{36}{h}$

3 **a**

d	5	7	9	10	14
d^2	25	49	81	100	196
g	10	19.6	32.4	40	78.4

   b $g = 0.4d^2$

Exercise 12.9

1 **a** $m \propto \dfrac{1}{v}$ or $m = \dfrac{k}{v}$ **b** 54   **c** $m = \dfrac{54}{v}$ **d** 12
   e m doubles when v is halved.

2 **a** $s \propto \sqrt{q}$ or $s = k\sqrt{q}$ **b** $s = 7\sqrt{q}$ **c** 42

3 **a** $p = \dfrac{90}{t^2}$ **b** 10   **c** p is multiplied by 4 when t is halved.
   d $t = \sqrt{\dfrac{90}{p}}$ **e** 5

4 **a** $n \propto \dfrac{1}{d^2}$ or $n = \dfrac{k}{d^2}$ **b** 20 000   **c** $n = \dfrac{20\,000}{d^2}$
   d **i** 200 **ii** 102

5 **a** $A \propto d^2$ or $A = kd^2$ **b** 3.5   **c** $A = 3.5d^2$ **d** $1263.5\,\text{cm}^2$

6 **a** $t = 1.6\sqrt{h}$ **b** 11.3 seconds

7 a $f \propto \frac{1}{a}$ or $f = \frac{k}{a}$ **b** 42 **c** $f = \frac{42}{a}$ **d** 2.625 mm

8 a $r = \frac{4}{f^2}$ **b** 0.015625 or $\frac{1}{64}$ **c** 2

9 a $m = 3.2w^3$ **b** 86.4 cm³ **c** 1 : 8

End Points
A1 a i 375 g **ii** 10 tablespoons **b** 3 eggs
B1 EFGH and NOPQ
C1 a 2.5 cm **b** 5.6 cm
D1 a They have the same angles:

ΔROS   ΔTOU

R = T (alternate angles)
S = U (alternate angles)
O = O (corresponding angles)

b 5.4 cm
E1 a $s = 2.25\sqrt{h}$ **b** 22.5 seconds
E2 a $w = \frac{6}{q}$ **b** 0.6 **c** w halves when q is doubled. **d** 0.8

SECTION 13

Starting points
A1 a A C and F are prisms.
  b A cuboid, B triangular-based pyramid, C cylinder, D pentagonal-based pyramid, E octagonal-based pyramid, F hexagonal prism
B1 a 72 cm² **b** 84 cm² **c** 16 cm²
C1 4.5 cm² (to 2 sf)   **C2** 8.28 (to 2 dp)
D1 To 2dp: a volume 106.02 cm³, surface area 194.88 cm²
  b volume 38.88 cm³, surface area 96.12 cm² **c** volume 45.9 cm³, surface area 82.2 cm²
E1 To 2dp: volume 81.78 cm³, surface area 112.70 cm²

Exercise 13.1
1 a 559 cm² **b** 1716.5 cm²
2 To 2dp: **a** 3010.62 mm² **b** 1204.25 cm²
3 a 183.7 cm² (to 1dp) **b** more **c** 85.4 cm (to 1 dp)
4 a 154 mm × 136 mm **b** 504 mm² **c** 1380 mm²
  d 16288 mm² **e** $\frac{2}{9}$ (or 0.2223)
5 To 2dp: **a** 254.47 mm² **b** 763.41 mm² **c** 21%
6 a $\frac{1}{4}\pi x^2$ **b** $x^2(1 - \frac{1}{4}\pi)$ **c** $x^2(1 - \frac{\pi}{2})$

Exercise 13.2
(All answers to 2dp)
1 a 9.49 cm², 12.75 cm **b** 792.62 m², 143.33 cm
  c 600.24 cm², 104.62 cm **d** 113.14 m², 42.69 cm
2 a 395.84 cm² **b** 79.98 cm

Exercise 13.3
1 a 87.5 cm³ **b** 2.2 cm **2** 16.5 (to 1dp)
3 a 27.24 m³ **b i** 390 bags **ii** £1996.80
4 a 46.25 m² **b** 555 m³ **c** 435 m³ **d** 0.435 litres
5 a 603.2 cm² (to 2 dp)
6 7.1 cm (to 1dp)
7 a $8 \times 12 \times 10 = 960$ cm³ **b** about £600
8 a 42 029.7 cm² (to 1 dp) **b** 11 600 cm²
9 To 2 dp: **a** 30.16 cm² **b** 165.88 cm² **c** 578.20 cm² **d** 1633.8 cm²
10 To 2dp: **a** 13 266.29 m³ **b** 10 366.57 m²
11 To 2dp: **a** 1290.15 cm³ **b** 182 g
13 a $v = x(yz - \pi r^2)$ **b** $s = 2[x(y + z) + yz - \pi r(r - x)]$
14 $R = \frac{6V}{S}$

Exercise 13.4
1 a 300 cm³ **b** 75 ml **c** 170 g
2 c 575.532 cm² **d** 4.44% (to 2 dp) **e** 44.25 cm³ **f** 38.055 g
3 a 217 146 88.42 cm³ **b** 21 714.688 42 litres
4 To 2dp: **a** volume = 217.08 cm³, density = 1.07 g/cm²
  b volume = 649.27 cm³, density = 0.95 g/cm²

Exercise 13.5
1 a B and C **b** 1 **c** A
3 a i C,D **ii** A,B **b** A = 8, B = 1, C = 6, D = 2

Exercise 13.6
1 a 167.55 cm³ (to 2dp) **b** 135.3 cm² **c** 185.60 cm²
2 0.51 m³ **3 a** 41.57 cm² **b** 166.28 cm³
4 a B (A = 261.8 cm³, B = 523, 6 cm³)

Exercise 13.7
1 a (to 2dp) 3.14 cm² 12.57 cm² **b** 4
  c (to 2dp) 0.52 cm³, 4.19 cm³ **d** 8
2 a 34 cm **b** 19.1 cm or 191 mm
3 4.5×10^{10} km² **4** 24.8 cm (to 1dp)
5 To nearest integer: **a** 348 455 mm³ **b** 28 510 mm³
6 To nearest integer: **a** 707 cm² **b** 707 cm²

Exercise 13.8
1 To 2dp: **a** 25.55 cm³ **b** 75.99 cm²
2 51.48 cm (to 2dp) **3 a** 18.56 cm³ **b** 25%
4 a 115 m³ **b** 920 cm³ **d** 772.7 cm²
5 a 38.2 mm³ **b i** 1700.48 cm³ **ii** 1455.7 cm³
6 a $h - 6$ **b** $h = 9.6$ cm, 3.6 cm **c** 152.36 cm³ (to 2dp)
7 It depends on the size.

Exercise 13.9
A a A = 6 cm² B = 24 cm² **b** A = 1 cm³ B = 8 cm³ **c i** 1 : 4 **ii** 1 : 8
1 a 13.07 cm² (to 2dp) **b** 124.2 cm²
2 a 1 : 0.4 (or 1 : $\frac{2}{5}$) **b** 6.63 cm (to 2dp)
3 b 22.77 mm (to 2dp)
4 a 64 cm² **b** 3564 cm³ **c** 1.78 cm² (to 2dp)
  d 49 cm² **e** 39.11 cm³ (to 2dp) **f** 1056 cm³
5 4.76 m(to 2dp)
6 a 2 **b** $\frac{1}{4}$ **c** 8 **d** $\frac{1}{8}$ **e** $\frac{1}{2}$ **f** 4

Exercise 13.10
1 a length **b** volume **c** area
2 a $\frac{1}{2}lz(x+y)$ **3 a** $\pi(a + b)$ **b** πab
4 a area **b** length **c** length **d** volume **e** volume **f** area

End points
A1 73.86 cm² (to 2dp) **B1** 4
C1 a 3.848 m³ (to 3dp) **b** 14.02 m² **b** 3848 litres
D1 To 2dp: **a** 25.98 cm **b** 720.15 cm³ **E1** c, e, f

SECTION 14

Starting points
A1 a $\frac{3}{12} = \frac{1}{4}$ **b** $\frac{1}{12}$ **c** $\frac{2}{12} = \frac{1}{6}$
A2 a $\frac{5}{12}$ **b** $\frac{4}{12} = \frac{1}{3}$ **c** $\frac{8}{12} = \frac{2}{3}$ **d** $\frac{2}{12} = \frac{1}{6}$
  e 1 **f** 0
A4 a $\frac{2}{6} = \frac{1}{3}$ **b** $\frac{3}{6} = \frac{1}{2}$ **c** $\frac{5}{6}$ **B1** $\frac{1}{5}$ **B2** $\frac{5}{8}$

C1 a $\frac{3}{16}$ **b** $\frac{1}{4}$ **c** $\frac{4}{7}$ **d** $\frac{1}{12}$ **D1** 0.23
D2 a 0.77 **b** 0.16 **c** 0.55 **d** 0.44 **e** 0
D3 a and **c** **E1** $\frac{1}{6}$ **E2** $\frac{1}{3}$ **E3 b** $\frac{1}{4}$

Exercise 14.1
1 a AB, AC, AD, AE, BC, BD, BE, CD, CE, DE **c** 10 handshakes
2 b 15 handshakes
3 a

No. of people	1	2	3	4	5	6
No. of handshakes	0	1	3	6	10	15

  c 21 handshakes
4 a S1P, S1Z1, S1S2, S1Z2, PZ1, PS2, PZ2, Z1S2, Z1Z2, S2Z2
  b $\frac{1}{10}$ **c** $\frac{1}{5}$ **d** $\frac{9}{10}$ **e** $\frac{7}{10}$ **5** $\frac{3}{14}$

Exercise 14.2
1 a $\frac{25}{81}$ **b** $\frac{5}{18}$ **c** $\frac{2}{27}$ **d** $\frac{1}{12}$
2 a $\frac{5}{12}$ **b** $\frac{4}{11}$ **d** $\frac{7}{22}$ **e i** $\frac{1}{66}$ **ii** $\frac{1}{22}$ **iii** $\frac{19}{66}$

3 b $\frac{1}{6}$ **c** $\frac{5}{9}$ **d** $\frac{5}{6}$

4 a $\frac{1}{10}$ **b** 0 **c** $\frac{3}{10}$ **d** $\frac{3}{5}$

5 a 4, 1 – 1, 4 – 1, 3, 1 – 1, 1, 3 – 3, 1, 1 – 1, 1, 1, 1, 1

  b crossed out = bust, ticked = wins a prize

  d i $\frac{1}{252}$ **ii** $\frac{1}{4}$ **iii** $\frac{2}{9}$

  e Untrue – only about 48% chance   **f** About £160 profit

Exercise 14.3

1 b i 0.47 (to 2 sf) **ii** 0.43 (to 2 sf)

2 a 0.28 (to 2 sf) **b** 0.41 (to 2 sf) **c** 0.31 (to 2 sf)

3 0.016 (to 2 sf)

Exercise 14.4

1 a $\frac{4}{16}$ **b** $\frac{7}{16}$ **c** $\frac{11}{16}$ **2** $a + b = c$

3 a $\frac{5}{16}$ **b** $\frac{7}{16}$

4 b $\frac{10}{16}$ **c** 2 men have both an earring and a moustache

5 a $\frac{3}{16}$ **b** $\frac{4}{16}$ **c** $\frac{5}{16}$

Exercise 14.5

1 b No, since some necklace wearers also have fair hair.

2 a $\frac{11}{16}$ **b** $\frac{5}{16}$ **c** $\frac{5}{16}$ **d** $\frac{2}{16}$ **e** $\frac{4}{16}$

3 a $\frac{7}{16}$ **b** $\frac{12}{16}$ **c** $\frac{12}{16}$ **d** $\frac{9}{16}$

4 a Not exclusive – some girls may play both.

  b Exclusive – girls cannot be boys.

  c Exclusive – drivers are never passengers.

  d Not exclusive – some bus drivers could also be tall women.

  e Not exclusive – some dancers could also be mechanics.

Exercise 14.6

1 a 0.12 **b** 0.32 **c** 0.47 **d** 0.53 **e** 0.13

2 a 0.15 **b** 0.19 **c** 0.53

3 0.44   **4 a** The sets do not overlap. **b** 0.55 **c** 0.45

Exercise 14.7

1 b i $\frac{19}{44}$ **ii** $\frac{39}{44}$ **iii** $\frac{25}{44}$ **iv** $\frac{5}{44}$

  c Because there are 6 people in the intersection of C and E

2 b i $\frac{28}{200} = \frac{7}{50}$ **ii** $\frac{80}{200} = \frac{2}{5}$ **iii** $\frac{140}{200} = \frac{7}{10}$ **iv** $\frac{27}{200}$

End points

A1 a $\frac{3}{12}$ **c i** $\frac{7}{26}$ **ii** $\frac{25}{26}$ **B1 b** 0.35 (to 2 sf)

C1 a Exclusive – for dice, no multiple of 3 is also square.

  b Exclusive – no square number is also prime.

  c Not exclusive – 2 is both prime and even.

  d Not exclusive – 1 is both triangular and square.

D1 b i $\frac{16}{34} = \frac{8}{17}$ **ii** $\frac{28}{34} = \frac{14}{17}$ **iii** $\frac{3}{34}$

SECTION 15

Starting points

A1 a Median 70, Interquartile range 3

  b Median 70.5, Interquartile range 4

A2 Median 71, Interquartile range 3

B1 a Mean 69.85, Standard deviation 2.63 (to 3 sf)

C1 The 2nd round scores are one less on average.

  There is greater variation in the 1st round scores.

C2 b The 3rd and 4th round scores were two more on average.

  There is slightly greater variation in the 1st & 2nd round scores.

D1

64 – 66	67 – 69	70 – 72	73 – 75
a 3	11	17	9
b 2	11	19	8

D2 b 70 – 72 (for both rounds)

D3

64 – 65	66 – 67	68 – 69	70 – 71	72 – 73	74 – 75
1	2	11	14	6	6

E1 70.4   **E2** 70.4

Thinking ahead

A a 26.625 **b** 26.375

Exercise 15.1

1 b 70.4 and 2.61 (to 3 sf)

2 a Day 1 **i** 878 **ii** 80.1 (to 3 sf)

  Day 2 **i** 826 **ii** 127.4 (to 4 sf)

  b The scores on day 1 were higher on average.

  There is much greater variation in the day 2 scores.

Exercise 15.2

1 b The 700 – 799 class has a class interval that is twice as big as the other two classes.

Exercise 15.3

1 A continuous **B** discrete **C** continuous

2 If times were to be rounded down, then runners would appear to have run faster than they actually had run.

  If distances were to be rounded up, then throwers would appear to have thrown further than they actually had thrown.

3 a 24.5 years

  b The ages are given in complete years. If the ages had been given in years and months, then a more accurate mean age could have been calculated.

Exercise 15.4

2 b 19.75, 20.25, 20.75, 21.5   **c i** 20.125 m **ii** 0.504 m (to 3 sf)

3 b i 18.7 m (to 3 sf) **ii** 0.788 m (to 3 sf)

4 The men threw further on average by nearly 1.5 m.

  The amount of variation is greater in the women's distances.

5

0.12 –	0.14 –	0.15 –	0.16 –	0.17 –	0.18 –	0.19 –	0.21 –	0.27	Total
5	3	5	12	11	3	6	2		47

6 d Yes, because doubling the frequencies for the finals gives the same total frequency as the total frequency for the semifinals.

7 a Mean 0.169 s (to 3 sf) Standard deviation 0.0286 s (to 3 sf)

  b Mean 0.171 s (to 3 sf) Standard deviation 0.0283 s (to 3 sf)

8 a The hypothesis is probably false.

  b The mean reaction time in the finals was only two thousandths of a second faster than in the semifinals, and the variation in the times was almost identical.

Exercise 15.5

1 a

<700	<800	<850	<900	<950	<1000	<1100
0	8	18	31	39	47	50

2 a

<76	<80	<81	<82	<84	<87	<89
0	6	12	20	33	46	48

Exercise 15.6

1 a

<73	<75	<76	<77	<78	<80	<82
0	6	12	28	35	48	52

2 a about 77 m **b** about 2.5 m

3 The distances thrown in the javelin final were about 5 m further on average, and showed greater variation.

4 b about 840 points **b** about 180 points

5 a about 880 points **b** about 115 points

6 On average, the decathletes scored about 40 more points in each event on day 1. The amount of variation in the points scores was much greater on day 2.

7 d Median about 60.8 m Interquartile range about 4.4 m

Exercise 15.7

1 about 28 throws   **2** about 13 throws

3 b about 15 jumps

Exercise 15.8

3

Sample size	Mean (to 3 sf)	Standard deviation (to 3 sf)
25	36.6	13.0
50	35.0	12.6
100	33.7	10.7

4 As the sample size increases, the mean and standard deviation get closer to the values for the whole population.

End points

A2 b The total frequencies need to be about the same for the frequency polygons to give a fair comparison.

B1 a 63 m **b** 2.53 m (to 3 sf)

B2 Mean distance 63.0 m (to 3 sf)   Standard deviation 2.92 m (to 3 sf)

C1 **b** **i** about 7.95 m   **ii** about 0.50 m

C2 Median about 6.78 m   Interquartile range about 0.32 m

D1 The men jumped nearly 1.2 m further than the women on average. There was less variation in the women's jumps.

D2 The men and women threw the same distance on average. There was greater variation in the women's throws.

E1 **b** **i** about 14 throws   **ii** about 13 throws

SKILLS BREAK 3

1 **a** 1.2×10^{-4} m   **b** 2.79×10^{-3} m³

2 **a** 1866.106 cm³   **b** 76 tubes   **3** 3211 mm

4 **a** 5   **b** 10%   **5** **b** 4903 cm³   **d** $h = \dfrac{3c + \pi r^3}{\pi r^2}$

6 No: 6% of £3.75 = $22\frac{1}{2}$ p   **7** **c** 6.19 s and 11.81 s

8 Costs were coffee 75 p, tea 52 p   **9** $\frac{3}{8}n$ or $0.375n$

10 No: 8.7375 litres required   **12** **a** 131.42 cm³   **b** 122.5 cm²

SECTION 16

Starting points

A1 **a** 4, 3   **b** $\frac{1}{5}$, 8   **c** 0.8, 1.5   **d** $1\frac{1}{4}$, $1\frac{3}{4}$ **e** $-\frac{1}{4}$, 1   **f** 6, 0

  g 1, 0   **h** 0, 12

A2 $y = \frac{5}{2}x + 3$ **A3** $y = -x - 2$

B1a $y = \frac{3}{5}x + 3$ **b** $y = -\frac{5}{2}x + 4$ **c** $y = \frac{4}{3}x + 1$

  d $y = -\frac{3}{2}x + 2$ **e** $y = \frac{7}{2}x - \frac{1}{2}$ **f** $y = \frac{1}{3}x - 1$

  g $y = -2x + \frac{5}{4}$ **h** $y = -\frac{5}{4}x + \frac{3}{2}$ **i** $y = 4x - 2$

  j $y = \frac{9}{2}x + \frac{3}{2}$ **k** $y = -\frac{1}{10}x + \frac{4}{5}$ **l** $y = \frac{4}{9}x + \frac{4}{3}$

  m $y = -\frac{4}{3}x + 12$ **n** $y = \frac{5}{12}x - \frac{10}{3}$ **o** $y = \frac{3}{10}x + \frac{3}{10}$

  p $y = -\frac{1}{2}x + \frac{3}{4}$ **q** $y = 3x - 20$ **r** $y = 2x + \frac{24}{5}$

  s $y = -\frac{2}{9}x + \frac{2}{3}$ **t** $y = \frac{1}{2}x + \frac{9}{8}$

Exercise 16.1

1 **a** $x = -1, y = 2$ **b** $x = 1, y = 4$ **c** $x = -2, y = 2$

  d $x = 2, y = 3$ **e** $x = 1\frac{19}{37}, y = 5\frac{16}{37}$ **f** $x = 1, y = -1$

2 $x = -1, y = 4$ **3** **c** $x = 2, y = 1$ **4** **b** $x = \frac{22}{5}, y = \frac{14}{5}$

5 **a** $x + y = 63, x - 9 = 2y$ **b** 45 females, 18 males

6 **a** $y - 25 = 4x, x + y = 500$

  b **ii** 95 litres of Extra Virgin. 405 litres of Virgin oil

  c **i** $y - 40 = 6x$

  ii To 1dp: 65.7 litres of Extra Virgin, 434.3 litres of Virgin oil

7 **b** $x = 3, y = 5$ **8** $y = \frac{1}{2}x + 3$

Exercise 16.2

1 **a** $x = -1$ **b** $x = -1$ **2** **b** $x - 1.5$ **c** $y = x^3 - 3x - 8$

3 **b** When multiplied by $-\frac{1}{2}$ it gives the points where the graph intercepts the x-axis.

4 **a** $x = -2$, y intercept -3 **b** $x = \frac{1}{2}$, y intercept 2

  c $x = -2.5$, y intercept 0   **d** $x = 3$, y intercept 1

  e $x = -3$, y intercept -2 **f** $x = -4$, y intercept 3

  g $x = 0$, y intercept -7 **h** $x = 3$, y intercept 8

  h $x = 3\frac{1}{2}$, y intercept 5

Exercise 16.3

1 **a** $y = 10$ **b** solution at intersects   **c** $x \approx 2.2$ or $x \approx -7.2$

3 **a** Only one intersect for x: $-8 < x < 6$ **b** $x \approx 3.4$ **c** $x < -8.4$

4 **a** $x = 2$ or $x = 3$ **b** $x \approx 0.5$ or $x \approx 4.5$ **c** $x \approx -0.7$ or $x \approx 5.7$

5 **a** **i** $x = -1$ or $x = 5$ **ii** $x \approx -2.5$ or $x \approx 6.5$ **b** $x = 2$

6 **a** **ii** $x = 1$ or $x = 3$

7 **a** **i** $x \approx -5.8$ or $x \approx 0.8$ **ii** $x \approx -4.6$ or $x \approx -0.4$ **iii** $x \approx -5.8$ or $x \approx 0.8$

  b **i** $x \approx -3.3$ or $x \approx 0.3$ **ii** $x \approx -0.4$ or $x \approx 2.6$ **iii** $x \approx -3.4$ or $x \approx 0.4$

  c **i** $x \approx 0.6$ or $x \approx 4.6$ **ii** $x \approx 0.3$ or $x \approx 3.7$ **iii** $x = -0.2$ or $x = 4.2$

  d **i** $x \approx -1.8$ or $x \approx 0.3$ **ii** $x \approx -2.4$ or $x \approx 0.85$

  e **i** $x = 0$ or $x = 2.5$ **ii** $x \approx -0.35$ or $x \approx 2.85$

8 $x \approx -4.24$ or $x \approx 0.24$ **9** $x \approx 0.3$ or $x \approx 1.8$

11 **b** $x = -1$ or $x \approx 5.1$ **c** $x \approx -1.8$ or $x \approx 2.8$

12 **b** $x = 0.2$ or $x = -4.2$ **c** $x \approx -1.6$ or $x \approx 2.6$

13 **a** $y = 8 + x$ **b** $y = 4 - 4x$

14 **b** $x = 1$ or $x \approx -7$ **c** $x \approx 2.3$ or $x \approx 1.3$ **d** $x \approx -3.6$ or $x \approx -0.8$

15 **b** $x \approx -6.3$ or $x \approx 1.3$ **c** $x \approx -5.9$ or $x \approx 0.9$ **d** $x \approx -6.5$ or $x \approx 1.5$

  e $x = 2$ or $x = -2$ **f** $x = 0.7$

Exercise 16.4

1 **a** **ii** $x = 0$ and $y = 0$ **2** **b** $x = 0$ and $y = 3$

3 $x = 0$ and $y = -8$ **4** **b** asymptote $y = 2$

5 **a** **i** $x = 3$ or $x = -4$ **ii** $x \approx 5.2$ or $x \approx -2.2$ **iii** $x \approx 3.5$ or $x \approx -3.5$

7 **b** y approaches $-x$ **c** $x = 0$ and $y = -x$

9 **a** $y = \dfrac{8}{x} + x + 3$

Exercise 16.5

1 **i** $y \approx -3.1$ **ii** $x \approx 2.3$ or $x \approx 5.2$

2 **a** maximum ≈ 6.25 **b** $x = 0.5$ or $x = -3.4$

3 **a** maximum ≈ 15.25 **b** $x \approx -0.6$ or $x \approx -4.4$

  c $x = 1$ or $x \approx -3.8$ **d** **i** $x \approx -1.3$ or $x \approx -4.8$

  e **i** minimum ≈ 4.6 **ii** $x \approx 0.5$ or $x \approx -3.6$ **iii** $y = -7 - 2x$

4 **a** **i** minimum ≈ -3.7 **ii** $x \approx 3.8$ or $x \approx -0.8$

  c $-6 <$ minimum for $\frac{1}{2}(x^2 - 3x - 5)$, $y = -6$ is an asymptote to $y = \dfrac{4}{x} - 6$

5 **a** $x = 2$ **b** $x = 3$ is an asymptote to $y = \dfrac{2x}{(3 - x)}$

Exercise 16.6

2 **a** $x = -2$ or $x = 0$ **b** $x \approx -4.4$ or $x \approx -0.4$ or $x = 2.8$

  c **ii** $x = 0$ or $x = 4$

  d **iii** $x \approx -1.1$ or $x \approx 1.7$ or $x \approx 3.4$ **e** **iii** $y = 12.4$

3 **a** $x \approx 3.5$ **b** $x = 2$ or $x = -1$ **c** $n < -4$

4 **a** $y \approx 11$ **b** $x \approx 2.6$ **c** $x \approx 2.5$ **d** $x \approx -3.4$ or $x \approx -0.3$ or $x \approx 3.8$

5 **a** $x = -2$ or $x \approx 1$ or $x = 2$ **b** $y \approx 4.4$ **c** $x \approx -1.8$ or $x \approx 0.5$ or $x \approx 2.3$

6 **b** **i** $w \approx 4.4$ and $(w + 8) \approx 12.4$ **ii** $w \approx 1.8$ and $(w + 8) \approx 9.8$

  iii $w \approx 6.8$ and $(w + 8) \approx 14.8$

  c $A \approx 45$ cm²   **d** $w = 5.5$ (to 1dp)

7 **a** $w(2w - 4)$ **c** **i** $w \approx 5.3$ and $(2w - 4) \approx 6.6$

  c **ii** $w \approx 6.7$ and $(2w - 4) \approx 9.4$ **c** **iii** $w \approx 7.4$ and $(2w - 4) \approx 10.8$

  d $A \approx 40$ cm²   **e** 5.8cm by 7.6cm

Exercise 16.7

1 **a** $y = (x + 3)^2 - 11$ **b** $y = -11$ **c** $(0, -2)$

7 $y = x^2 + 6x + 5$ i.e. $a = 1, b = 6,$ and $c = 5$

End Points

A1 **a** $x = 2$ and $y = -1$ **b** $x = 3$ and $y = 1$

A2 Adult £5, child £3.50   **B1** $x = 2$

B2 **a** $x = 2$ or $y = -4$ **b** $x = 5$ or $x = -2$ **c** $x \approx -1.5$ or $x \approx 2.5$

  d $x = -2$ or $x = 3$

B3 **b** $x = -1.2$ or $x = 1.7$ **c** $x = \pm 1.7$ **d** $x = 0.5$ or -2

C2 $x = 0, y = 5$ **C3** $x = 0, y = 4$

D1 **a** -1.1 **b** 2.5, 5

D2 14.25   **b** 0.7, -5.7 **c** $-1.2, -4.2$

D3 **i** 5.2×11.2 **ii** 3.4×9.4 **c** 61.56 cm²   **d** 3.6

E5 $y = x^2 + 4x + 8, a = 1, b = 4, c = 8$

SECTION 17

Starting points

A1 **a** **i** $(2.60, 2.34)$ **ii** 3.05 cm²   **b** 75.4°

A2 110.11 cm²   **A3** **a** $\frac{4}{5}$ or 0.8   **b** $\frac{3}{5}$ or 0.6

B1 Estimates of: **a** 0.77   **b** 0.64

B2 Estimates of: **a** 23.6   **b** 66.4

B3 **a** 70°   **b** 42°   **c** 45°

Exercise 17.1

1 **a** 0.68   **b** 0.87   **c** 0.77   **d** 2.30   **e** 1.97   **f** 2.5

2 **a** **i** 3.86   **ii** 3.70   **iii** 3.19   **b** **i** 30°   **ii** 20°

Exercise 17.2

1 b (⁻17.32, 10)

2 b i 22.98 **ii** 19.28 **c** (⁻22.98, 19.28)

d i B (20, 70°)
C (30, 250°)
D (10, 320°)
ii B (6.84, 18.79)
C (⁻10.26, ⁻28.19)
D (7.66, ⁻6.43)

3 a (13, 225°) → (⁻9.19, ⁻9.19)
(40, 114°) → (⁻16.27, 36.54)
(25, 291°) → (8.96, ⁻23.34)
b (21.53, ⁻22.30) → (31, 314°)
(⁻16.19, 3.24) → (17, 169°)

4 a $r = \sqrt{(x^2 + y^2)}$ **b** $(r\cos\theta, r\sin\theta)$ **c** $(\cos\theta, \sin\theta)$

Exercise 17.3

1 232°

2 a 0.616 **b** ⁻0.788

4 a ⁻0.809 **b** 0.809 **c** ⁻0.809

5 a sin 53° → sin 127°
sin 233 → sin 307
cos 127° → cos 233°
b sin 53° = sin 127° ≈ 0.799
sin 233 = sin 307 ≈ ⁻0.799
cos 127° = cos 233° ≈ ⁻0.602

6 a 90° < θ < 270° **b** 180° < θ < 360°

7 a i cos (⁻90°) = 0 sin (⁻90°) = ⁻1
ii cos (⁻52°) = 0.616 sin (⁻52°) = ⁻0.788
b i ⁻306° **ii** ⁻260° **iii** ⁻160

8 b Three values from: ... ⁻270, 90, 450, 810, 1170, ...

Exercise 17.4

1
	Max	Min
a	1	⁻1
b	1	⁻1

2 30°, 150°

3 a i 320° **ii** 145°, 215° **iii** 252°, 288°
b i 64.2°, 115.8° **ii** 154.2°, 205.8°
c i 60° < x < 300° **ii** 210° < x < 330° **iii** 45°, 225° **iv** 45° < x < 225°

4 a Two values from: 420°, 660°, 780°, 1020°, ...
b One value from: ⁻60°, ⁻300°, ⁻420°, ⁻660°, ...

5 a One value from: 450°, 810°, 1170°, 1530°, ...
b One value from: ⁻270°, ⁻630°, ⁻990°, ⁻1350°, ...

6 a One value from: ... ⁻270°, 90°, 450°, 810°, ...
b One value from: ... ⁻90°, 270°, 630°, 990°, ...

7 A False, e.g. x = 150° gives sin (180° − 150°) = 0.5
but sin (180° + 150°) = ⁻0.5
C False, e.g. x = 30° gives sin 30° + sin 30° = 1
but sin (30° + 30°) = $\frac{\sqrt{3}}{2}$
D False, e.g. x = 30° gives cos 30° = $\frac{\sqrt{3}}{2}$
but cos (90° + 30°) = ⁻0.5

Exercise 17.5

1 a
t	0	10	20	30	40	50	60	70	80	90	100
h	9	4.5	⁻4.5	⁻9	⁻4.5	4.5	9	4.5	⁻4.5	⁻9	⁻4.5

c 9 mm **d i** 60 milliseconds **ii** 30 milliseconds
e 16 whole stitches

2 b Yes
c The needle on the second machine rises higher during sewing.

Exercise 17.6

1
		Max	Min
a	A	3	1
	B	2	⁻2
	C	1	⁻1

2
		Max	Min
b	i	⁻1	⁻3
	ii	3	⁻3
	iii	1	⁻1

3
	Max	Min
a	1	⁻1
b	5	⁻5
c	−3	⁻5
d	2	0
e	0	⁻4
f	5	⁻1

5
	a	b
A	$y = \cos ax$	a = 2
B	$y = \sin x + a$	a = 3
C	$y = \cos x + a$	a = ⁻1
D	$y = a \cos x$	a = 2
E	$y = a \sin x$	a = 4

6 a + c **9** A and C

Exercise 17.7

2 a i 45° **ii** 225° **b** 135°, 315°

4 a 50° **b** 230°, 410°

5 a 60°, 240° and 420° **b** ⁻25°, 155° and 335° **c** ⁻32°, 148° and 328°

6 a i 57.290 **ii** 114.589 **iii** 572.957 **iv** 5729.578
b i ⁻57.290 **ii** ⁻114.589 **iii** ⁻572.957 **iv** ⁻5729.578
d 630°

End points

A1 a (⁻1.50, 3.60) → (3.90, 112.62°)
(6.00, ⁻1.75) → (6.25, 343.74°)
(⁻0.60, ⁻0.80) → (1.00, 233.13°)
b (⁻2.63, 9.65)

B1 a 70°, 290° **b** 110°, 250° **c** 140°, 320° **d** 208°, 332°

B2 cos 41° = cos 319°, cos 139° = cos 221°, cos 131° = cos 229°

C2 B ($y = \cos x° + 2$)

SECTION 18

Starting points

A1 b 2, ⁻2, 1.634, $4\frac{3}{4}$

A2 a 5,6,7,8,9 **b** ⁻2, ⁻1, 0, 1, 2, 3 **c** 70, 69, 68
b ⁻4, ⁻5, ⁻6, ⁻7, ⁻8, ⁻9, ⁻10, ⁻11

A3 ⁻4 < h < 6

A4 Any two from ⁻3 ≤ g ≤ 1 ⁻3 ≤ g < 2 ⁻4 < g < 2 ⁻4 < g ≤ 1

A5 ⁻3 ≤ f ≤ 6 or ⁻3 ≤ f ≤ 7 or ⁻4 < f < 7

B2 ⁻2 ≤ x ≤ 6 and 3 < y ≤ 7

C3 x + y ≤ 8 or y ≤ 8 − x and y > $\frac{1}{2}$x

Exercise 18.1

1 a y < 7 **b** s ≤ 8 **c** p ≥ 6 **d** b > 3.5
e a ≤ ⁻8 **f** x > 8.4 **g** k ≤ $4\frac{2}{3}$ **h** a ≥ 7
i d < ⁻5 **j** a ≤ ⁻13

2 a a ≥ $\frac{11}{3}$ **b** k < 2.8 **c** x > ⁻9 **d** n ≥ 3.5
e q < ⁻0.8 **f** k > 2 **g** h < ⁻$\frac{1}{3}$ **h** c < 2.5
i h < $1\frac{1}{11}$ **j** p ≥ $2\frac{2}{7}$

3 a ⁻4 < x < 1 **b** ⁻2 < x < 5 **c** ⁻1 < x < 15 or 15 > x > ⁻1
d ⁻3 < x < ⁻1

Exercise 18.2

1 a d ≥ 6 or d ≤ ⁻6 **b** ⁻4.123 < g < 4.123 **c** ⁻7 ≤ a ≤ 7
d h > 4 or h < ⁻4 **e** t < ⁻4, t > 4 **f** ⁻2 ≤ c ≤ 2
g c ≥ 1 or c ≤ ⁻1 **h** f > 2 or f < ⁻2

2 a ⁻6, ⁻5, ⁻4, ⁻3, ⁻2, ⁻1, 0, 1, 2, 3, 4, 5, 6
b ⁻4, ⁻3, ⁻2, ⁻1, 0, 1, 2, 3, 4 **c** ⁻3, ⁻2, ⁻1, 0, 1, 2, 3
d ⁻2, ⁻1, 0, 1, 2 **e** ⁻2, ⁻1, 0, 1, 2 **f** ⁻1, 0, 1

3 Cannot have square of a number being negative

4 c has no solution **5** 1, 2, 3

Exercise 18.3

1 a On a dotted line since t + d < 20 not ≤ 20
b One cannot have 16.5 ducks and 2.5 turkeys.
c Substitute d = 13, t = 3 in 4t + 3d ≥ 50.
This gives 51 ≥ 50 which is true.
d £65

2 b v ≤ 7 and n ≤ 8
d 10 ferries (either 5 Neptunes and 5 Vikings or 6 Neptunes and 4 Vikings)

3 a i $4E + 5C \leq 60$ **ii** $7E + 3C \geq 42$
  b A is $7E + 3C = 42$, B is $4E + 5C = 60$
  c $C \geq \frac{1}{2}E$ or $E \leq 2C$

4 a A is $L = 4$, B is $W = 17$, C is $W = 8$, D is $L + W = 25$
  b $L \geq 4$ **c** $8 \leq W \leq 17$ **d** $L + W \leq 25$
  e 50 m **f** continuous rather than discrete data **g** 17 m

5 c Min 2, max 9 **d** min 3, max 12
  e min 10 (5 of each type), max 16

End points

A1 a ⁻1 **b** ⁻5, ⁻4, ⁻3, ⁻2, ⁻1, 0, 1, 2, 3 **c** 4, 5, 6, 7
  d ⁻56, ⁻57, ⁻58, ⁻59, **e** ⁻3, ⁻2, ⁻1, 0, 1, 2, 3 **f** ⁻3, ⁻2, ⁻1, 0, 1, 2, 3

B1 a $x \leq 6$ **b** $f > 3$ **c** $a \geq 12$ **d** $k > ⁻5$
  e $s \leq 4$ **f** $d > 1.5$ **g** $x < ⁻10$ or $x > 10$ **h** $⁻2 \leq x \leq 2$

D1 a $S > L$ **b i** $S + L \leq 200$ **ii** $4S + 5L \geq 720$ **iii** $S \leq 3L$
  d £899 takings (101 standard, 99 luxury)

SECTION 19

Starting points

A1 a 0.75, 75% **b** 0.625, 62.5% **c** 1.6, 160% **d** 1.25, 125%
  e 1.2, 120% **f** 0.65, 65% **g** 0.25, 25% **h** 3.167, 316.7%

B1 a 357.5 miles **b** £290 **c** 1587 **d** £116.20
  e 16.2 metres **f** £1.71 **g** 12.5 pence **h** 0.24 miles

C1 a 65% **b** 46.20% **c** 12.5% **d** 125% **e** 3% **C2** 14%

D1 a £13.60 **b** 5.6 mm **c** 1540 grams **d** 20 pence
  e i 50.7 mm **ii** 5.07 cm

Exercise 19.1

1 a 115% **b** 506 grams

2 a 413 kg **b** 518.52 **c** 5.49 m **d** £37 800 **e** £36.30
  f 30 186 tonnes **g** 3 815 000 litres **h** 0.69 cm

3 206 037 280 cars **4** 26 grams

5 a 311.6 kg **b** 303.68 km **c** 21.12 m **d** £290 680 **e** £18.36
  f 16 588 tonnes **g** 4 717 000 **h** 1.2 cm

6 1466 kg **7 a** 1125 cars

8 a 26 650 cars **b** 14 350 cars **9** 7644.3 kg

10 £22 471 **11** £1191 **12** £3 281 000

13 425.22 litres per minute ... a total of about 223.5 million litres per year

Exercise 19.2

1 a £18.80 **b** £51.99 **c** £217.38 **d** £22.80 **e** 85 pence
  f £432.89 **g** £307.85 **h** £28.85 **i** £10.99 **j** £221.72
  k 40 pence **l** 13 pence

2 a £287.88 **b** £42.88 **3** £34.50 **4** £31.90

Exercise 19.3

1 a £115.32 **b** £29.78 **c** £63.82 **d** £56 **e** £158.94 **f** £12.33
  g £42.54 **h** £680.83 **i** £84.25

2 a £57 **b** £11.40 **3** £24 **4** 500 grams **5** £55.70

6 £137 515 **7 a** 70 875 bulbs **b** 25 515 pearl bulbs **c** 16 : 9

8 a £20 384 **b** $p = \frac{63s}{83}$

9 147 428 **10 c** $= \frac{p}{1.175}$ (VAT at 17.5%)

Exercise 19.4

1 a £324 **b** £67.20 **c** £1350 **d** £10 200

2 a £5950 **b** £9450

3 £66 440 000 **4** 4.6%

Exercise 19.5

1 a £103.26 **b** £175.71 **c** £1217.61 **d** £1529.58 **e** £1030.32
  f £7015.63 **g** £197.32 **h** £2.23 **i** £14 428.07 **j** £56.95

2 a £1947.46 **b** £6947.46

3 9 years **4** £22 841 **5 a** 42 years **b** 9 years

Exercise 19.6

1 £5108.77 **2** £22 930.76

3 At end of 3 years: Celine £3105.74 Rhian £2936.50

4 £47 098.84 **5 a** 4.6% **b** 5.8%

6 a $T = p\left(1 + \frac{r}{100}\right)^n$

Exercise 19.7

1 £19.65

2 a £1184.60 **b** £24.68

3 a £267.39 **b** £8021.70

4 a £38 784.03 **b** £66.19 per m²

End Points

A1 556.8 km **A2** 426 ml **A3** £52.45 **A4** 39 200
A5 b 15 weeks **B1** £998.74 **B2** £485.03 **C1** £2.272 million
C2 38 0766 **D1** £74.03 **D2** 4.5% **E1** £12 836.47

SECTION 20

Starting points

A1 b PA = PB **c** Yes **e** APO = BPO **f** yes **h** OAP = OBP = 90°

Exercise 20.1

1 a AEC, and ADC **b** CAD, and CED **c** 58° **d** 41° **e** 41°

2 a 74° **b** 37° **c** 90° **d** 53° **e** 37°

3 a EFD **b** 284° **c** 38° **d** 52°

4 a 41° **b** 49° **d** 61°

5 a 18.51 (2dp) **b** 8.33 cm **c** 55.5 cm²

6 a i $10a$ **ii** $90° - 5a$ **b i** $10a + 27° + 180° + 43° = 360°$
  b ii CAD = 55°, DOC = 110°, ODC = 35°
  c OB = b / cos 47° **d** 125°

7 a i a **ii** b **iii** $2a$ **b** $180° - a - b$ **c** $180° - a$
  d $\frac{180° - a - 2b}{2}$ **e** $\frac{a}{2}$

8 a 63° **b** 49° **e** 5° **9** $73° + x$

Exercise 20.2

3 Squares and isosceles trapezia

4 b $v = 78°$, $w = 40°$, $x = 102°$, $y = 140°$ **6** 102°

7 a HEG = 36°, HFG = 144° **b** 72° **c** No

8 a i 67.5° **ii** 112.5° **iii** 127° **b** 106°

9 a i $\frac{v}{2}$ **ii** $90° - \frac{v}{2}$ **iii** $45° + \frac{v}{2}$

10 a 28° **b** 69° **11 a** 105° **b** Yes **c** 40°

End points

A1 a 54° **b** 61° **A2 a** EBD **b** CEA

B1 a 126° **b** 54° **C1** 62° **D1** 54° **D2** 72° **D3** 36°

E1 a TP = √(SC × CP) **b** SC = $\frac{\text{TP}^2}{\text{CP}}$ **c** 6 cm

F2 b $k = 20$ angles: 60°, 80°, 100°, 120°

SKILLS BREAK 4

1 1497 **2** About 35.5 people per boat

3 £295 800

4 a 58 000 m³ (to 2 sf) **b** About 500 000 tonnes (to 1 sf)

5 a 14 knots **b** 3 h 19 min **c** 1 h 29 min

6 a $C = \frac{5(F - 32)}{9}$ **b** 2.2°C **c** about 55% error

8 a 1170 **b** 3546 **9 a** 0.61 **b** 0.43 **c** 0.25

10 38% (to 2 sf) (Note: 499 out of 1316) **11** 70 000 tons

13 a Angle ABH = 58° (Alternate angles) + 14° (Angle sum of triangle)
      = 72°
  b 28.5 feet (to 2 sf) **c** 8.8 feet (to 2 sf)

14 a 20 000 00 **b** 21 800 00 **15** 11 people

SECTION 21

Starting points

A1 a i 060° **ii** 240° **iii** 240° **b** About 210° **c** 20 km

B1 b 36.1 km **C1** 56° **C2 a** 26 km **b** 15 km

D1 a i 30° **b** 102° **c** 78° **d** 45°

E1 b About 104° **E2 b** 117°, 63° **F1** 27° **F2** 5.1 cm

Exercise 21.1

1 a 4.9 cm² **b** 5.2 cm² **c** 5.1 cm² **d** 2.4 cm²

2 a 6 cm² **b i** 30°, 150° **c** 90°

3 a 46°, 134° **b** 15 cm²

4 a Max 3.45 cm Min 3.35 cm: **b** Max 3.9 cm² Min 3.6 cm²

5 a $\frac{1}{2}a^2\sin 60°$ **b i** $\frac{a}{3}$ **ii** $\frac{2}{3}$ **c i** $\frac{1}{2}$ **ii** $\frac{1}{3}$

   d $\frac{2}{9}$ **e i** $\frac{1}{3^n}$ **ii** $\frac{2}{3^n}$

Exercise 21.2

1 D

2 a $m = \dfrac{7.6 \times \sin 42°}{\sin 65°}$ **b** $\sin L = \dfrac{8.0 \times \sin 65°}{7.6}$

Exercise 21.3

1 b 5.3 cm **2 a** 4.2 cm **b** 5.0 cm **c** 3.6 cm

3 b 7.2 cm and 8 cm **4** 11.60 cm² **5 a** 48.5° **c** 3.2 cm

Exercise 21.4

1 a 29.4° **b** 47.5° **c** 34°

2 a 119.5 ° **b** 139.2 cm²

3 a 0.57073 … **b** 34.8° and 145.2°

4 b i 64.5° and 115.5° **ii** 51.7° and 128.3°

Exercise 21.5

1 a i $d^2 = e^2 + f^2 - 2ef\cos D$ **ii** $f^2 = e^2 + d^2 - 2de\cos F$ **b** 2 and 3

2 a $\cos E > 0$ **b** $\cos D = \cos 90° = 0$ **c** $\cos C < 0$

Exercise 21.6

2 a = 94.8° n = 6.79 cm n = 4.74 cm **3** 95.1° **4** 26.7 cm²

5 a i 108° **ii** 36° **iii** 72° **b** 6.5 cm **c** 16.9 cm **d** 12.4 cm²
   e 2 triangles

6 a Area 11.6 cm² Perimeter 23.3 cm **b** 7
   c ii Area 99.9 cm² **ii** Perimeter 45.6 cm

8 a 73.5 cm² **b** 30.90 cm

9 192 cm² **10 a** $\frac{1}{2}nr^2\sin\left(\dfrac{360°}{n}\right)$

   b
n	Area (to 2dp)
20	3.09
40	3.13
100	3.14
1000	3.14

11 9 cm

Exercise 21.7

1 a 036° **b** 128.0 km **c** 050.5°

2 a 323° **b i** 39.8 km **ii** 158.8° **c i** 14.44 km **ii** 19.17 km
   d 6.98

3 17.47 km **4 a** 4572.80 **b** 032°

5 8.016 km **6** 15.81 n. miles

Exercise 21.8

1 a 141.931° **b i** 43.01 m **ii** 30.23° **iii** 30.23°

2 a Jameston and Palter **b** 11.38 m (must be rounded down)

Exercise 21.9

1 a i D (4, 6, 0) **ii** G (4, 6, 3) **iii** A (0, 0, 3)
   c OC and GF **d** 5 **e iii** 7.81 cm **f** 22.59°

2 a i 7.21 cm **ii** (2, 3, 3) **b** 24 cm³ **c i** 4.69 cm **ii** 39.76°

Exercise 21.10

1 a 16.25 cm **b** 11.13 cm **c** 42.64 **d** 56.1° **f** 50.79°
   g 347.7 cm² **h** 329.84 cm³

3 a 10.67 cm³ **b** 45° **c** 5.66 cm **d** 60° **e** 13.87 cm²
   f 2.31 cm **g** 35.3°

4 a 4 cm³ **b** 7.82 cm² **c** 1.53 cm²

End Points

A1 a 8.19 cm **b** 8.10 cm **A2 a** 81.9° **b** 15.98 cm

B1 a 66.85° **b** 12.33 cm **c** 70.57 cm² **C1 a** 73° **b** 61.78°

C2 a 5.12 cm **b** 103.7° **D1** 5.39 km

D2 72.93 nautical miles (to 2dp) **E1** 281.50 m (to 2dp)

E2 75° (to 2sf) **F1** 86.69 cm (to 2dp)

SECTION 22

Starting Points

D1 a matches with Q **b** matches with R **c** matches with P

Exercise 22.1

1 a Different people are likely to have different ideas of what is meant by 'early' and 'late'

2 a The question leads people into giving the answer 'Yes'.

3 a The question could be answered in several different ways, e.g. 'on the sofa', 'in Australia', etc.

4 a Question 1 is a leading question; it leads people into giving the answer 'Yes'.
   Question 2 is not clear; different people are likely to have different ideas of what is meant by 'frequent'.
   Question 3 is ambiguous; the courts could be tennis, or squash, or badminton, etc.
   Question 4 has a poor list of choices, i.e. there is no box to tick to answer £2.

Exercise 22.3

1
	Yr 7	Yr 8	Yr 9	Yr 10	Yr 11	Total
Boys	14	15	17	15	15	76
Girls	16	16	15	13	14	74
Total	30	31	32	28	29	150

2 75 competitors 45 support staff.

3 a
	Competitors	Support Staff	Total
Male	45	32	77
Female	30	13	43
Total	75	45	120

   b Divide the total number of females by 500, and then multiply by the sample size of 75.

4 a 58.6 million

   b
England	N.Ireland	Scotland	Wales	Total
417 236	14 505	43 515	24 744	500 000

Exercise 22.4

1 c Negative **2 c** Positive

Exercise 22.5

1 Moderate negative correlation, i.e. people with higher incomes give a smaller percentage of their income to charity than people with lower incomes.

2 Strong negative correlation, i.e. house prices decrease the further towns are away from London.

3 Moderate positive correlation, i.e. the greater the pressure in the eye, the higher the refractive power of the lens.

Exercise 22.6

1 a about 90 miles **b** about 80 miles

2 a about £73 000 **b** about £85 000

3 a about 15 miles **b** about £110 000

5 b Moderate positive correlation, i.e. the longer the pregnancy, the heavier the baby is.
   c i about 273 days **ii** about 3.9 kg

6 No: doctors do not allow a pregnancy to continue after a certain number of days, because of the risk to the mother's health.

End Points

A1 a Question 1 is not clear: different people are likely to have different ideas of what is meant by 'local'.
   Question 2 is ambiguous: it could refer to the amount of traffic, or the type of traffic, etc.
   Question 3 is leading: it leads people into giving the answer 'Yes'.

C1
Belfast	Cardiff	Edinburgh	London	Total
846	825	1220	7109	10 000

D1 d Strong negative correlation, i.e. the larger the size of engine, the lower the number of miles to the gallon.

E1 a about 32 mpg **b** about 1.9 litres

E2 a about 18 mpg **b** about 4.7 litres

SECTION 23

Starting points
A1 41 minutes   **A2** 47 mph   **A3** 2 min 26 s

A4 a 31 mph (to 2 sf)   **b** 17 ms⁻¹ (to 2 sf)   **B1** 5200 cm²

B2 375 square units   **C1** Joe – D, Sally – B, Ravi – A, Charlie – C

C2 A and B   **C3** B and C   **C4** 9:45 am

C5 a 80 miles   **b** 135 miles   **c** 97 miles   **d** 120 miles

C6 1½ hours   **C7** C, 70 miles   **C8** 100 miles

C9 a 11:30 am and 3:05   **b** Passed in opposite direction

C10 9.3 mph   **C11** 30 mph   **C12** Faster (steeper gradient)

C13 a A   **b** just before 12 noon
   c Small variations of speed will not show up on the graph.

Exercise 23.1
1 about 71 km from Glasgow

2 a 6.8 kph (2 sf)   **b** Running, slow cycling, steam roller!

3 a 11:30 am   **b** 35.6 kph

4 Julie starts fast and slows down, Simon starts slowly and speeds up.

5 a 23.1 kph   **b** 23.1 kph

6 Julie fastest, then Ayesha, then Simon

7 a about 1:45   **b** about 10:30

8 a about 70 km   **b** about 90 km

9 about 12 noon   **10** about 70 km

Exercise 23.2
2 a about 11:15   **b** about 135 mph   **c** speeding fines maybe

Exercise 23.3
1 Gradient steeper   **2 a** Stationary   **b** constant speed

3 a The bike is stationary   **b** same gradient
   c Bikes did not reach such high speeds in second spurt.

Exercise 23.4
1 A, acceleration 0.9 m s⁻² C, deceleration 0.5 m s⁻²
   D, acceleration 0.2 m s⁻² E, acceleration 0.2 m s⁻²
   F, deceleration 0.8 m s⁻²

2 0   **3** Only **b** is true   **4 b** 5 m s⁻²

Exercise 23.5
A a 3 mph   **b** 6 miles   **c** 6 squares

B 11:30 am – 12:30 pm

C a 10.5 miles   **b** 10.5 squares

D a speed increasing   **b** about 2.5 squares   **c** 13 miles

1 a 2 hours   **b** A, G and N   **c** 60 km h⁻²   **d** 40 km h⁻²

2 225 km   **3** 460 km

4 a 4½ to 5½ hours   **b** about 100 km

5 b 292.5 miles   **c** 545 miles
   d i 52 mph   **ii** 9:30 to 2pm and 4pm to 5pm

Exercise 23.6
3 a The more trapeziums, the more accurate   **b** Too crude an estimate
   c Takes too long

4 b 2460 m   **c i** 20 s   **ii** 3040 m   **d** 515 m

5 about 570 m   **6** about 670 m

Exercise 23.7
1 a 30 litres   **b** about 1170 litres

2 a 12 miles   **b** about 450 miles   **c** about 28 mpg

3 b about 2500 m³

End points
A1 2 s, 4.5 s, 8.5 s, 15.5 s   **A2** 0 s and 7 s   **A3** 0 s and 16 s

A4 starting to decelerate   **B1** about 3 m s⁻² at A, about 5 m s⁻² at B

B2 about 17 m s⁻² at C   **B3** 3.5 s, 6.5 s and 13.5 s   **B4** at the start

C1 about 25 m   **C2** about 320 m   **C3** about 20 m s⁻¹

SECTION 24

Starting Points
B1 a $\begin{pmatrix} 5 \\ ^-1 \end{pmatrix}$ **b** $\begin{pmatrix} 1 \\ ^-2 \end{pmatrix}$ **c** $\begin{pmatrix} 1 \\ 4 \end{pmatrix}$

C1 a $4x - 2y = 2(2x - y)$ **b** $4x - 2y = ^-2(y - 2x)$
   c $9y - 3x = 3(x - 3y)$ **d** $9y - 3x = 3(3y - x)$

C2 a $\frac{1}{2}(2x + y)$ **b** $\frac{1}{3}(x - 3y)$ **c** $\frac{1}{2}(3x + y)$
   d $\frac{1}{3}(4x - y)$ **e** $\frac{2}{3}(x + y)$ **f** $\frac{2}{3}(2y - x)$

D1 a $3:1$ **b** $1:3$ **D2 a** $\frac{1}{4}$ **b** $\frac{3}{4}$

Exercise 24.1
2 a $\begin{pmatrix} ^-1 \\ 3 \end{pmatrix}$ **b** $\begin{pmatrix} 8 \\ 2 \end{pmatrix}$ **c** $\begin{pmatrix} 3 \\ 6 \end{pmatrix}$ **d** $\begin{pmatrix} 2 \\ 6 \end{pmatrix}$ **e** $\begin{pmatrix} 3 \\ 6 \end{pmatrix}$

3 $\begin{pmatrix} 5 \\ 4 \end{pmatrix}$ **4 b** $\begin{pmatrix} 5 \\ 4 \end{pmatrix}$ **6 a** $\begin{pmatrix} 5 \\ 1 \end{pmatrix}$

Exercise 24.2
2 a $\mathbf{p + r}$ **b** $\mathbf{p + 2q}$ **b** $^-\mathbf{p + 2q}$

Exercise 24.3
1 b $-(\mathbf{q - p}) = ^-\mathbf{q + p} = \mathbf{p} + ^-\mathbf{q} = \mathbf{p + q}$

4 $\mathbf{p - (q - r) = p - q + r}$ and $\mathbf{(p - q) - r = p - q - r}$

5 $\mathbf{r = 2p - q, \ s = 2q - p, \ t = ^-3p - q}$

6 c $\mathbf{2q - 6p = 2(q - 3p) = ^-2(3p - q)}$

7 $^-\mathbf{2p - q}$ and $\mathbf{2p + q}$, $\mathbf{2p - q}$ and $\mathbf{2q - 4p}$, $\mathbf{2p + 4q}$ and $\mathbf{p + 2q}$

8 a $\mathbf{2p, 2q, ^-2p, ^-2q}$ **b** $\mathbf{0}$

Exercise 24.4
1 a $2\mathbf{c - d}$ **b** $\overrightarrow{YX} = \overrightarrow{YQ} + \overrightarrow{QX} = 2\mathbf{c - d} + 2\mathbf{d - c} = \mathbf{c + d}$

2 a i $\overrightarrow{ED}$ **ii** $\overrightarrow{EG}$ **iii** $\overrightarrow{HE}$ **iv** $\overrightarrow{EG}$

3 a $\overrightarrow{FG} = \overrightarrow{FE} + \overrightarrow{ED} + \overrightarrow{DG} = ^-\mathbf{q} + ^-\mathbf{p} + 2\mathbf{q} = \mathbf{q - p}$
   b i $\overrightarrow{EZ} = \overrightarrow{EF} + \overrightarrow{FZ} = \mathbf{q} + \frac{1}{2}(\mathbf{q - p}) = \mathbf{q} + \frac{1}{2}\mathbf{q} - \frac{1}{2}\mathbf{p} = \frac{1}{2}(3\mathbf{q - p})$
   ii $\overrightarrow{DZ} = \frac{1}{2}(3\mathbf{q + p})$

Exercise 24.5
1 $\overrightarrow{QD} = \overrightarrow{QP} + \overrightarrow{PD}$ $\overrightarrow{QS} = \overrightarrow{QP} + \overrightarrow{PS}$
   $= ^-2\mathbf{c} + 3\mathbf{d} - \mathbf{c}$ $= ^-2\mathbf{c} + 2\mathbf{d}$
   $= 3\mathbf{d} - 3\mathbf{c}$ $= 2\mathbf{d} - 2\mathbf{c}$
   $= 3(\mathbf{d - c})$ $= 2(\mathbf{d - c})$

2 a i $\frac{2}{3}(\mathbf{p + q})$ **ii** $2\mathbf{q - p}$
   b $\overrightarrow{EH} = \overrightarrow{ED} + \overrightarrow{DH}$
   $= ^-\mathbf{p} + \frac{2}{3}(\mathbf{p + q})$
   $= ^-\mathbf{p} + \frac{2}{3}\mathbf{p} + \frac{2}{3}\mathbf{q}$
   $= \frac{1}{3}(2\mathbf{q - p})$
   $= \frac{1}{3}\overrightarrow{EG}$

3 a i $\mathbf{y - x}$ **ii** $\frac{1}{3}(\mathbf{y - x})$
   b $\overrightarrow{OM} = \overrightarrow{OJ} + \overrightarrow{OM}$ $\overrightarrow{OL} = \overrightarrow{OJ} + \overrightarrow{JK} + \overrightarrow{KL}$
   $= \mathbf{x} + 2\mathbf{y}$ $= \mathbf{x} + \mathbf{y} + \frac{1}{3}(\mathbf{y - x})$
             $= \mathbf{x} + \mathbf{y} + \frac{1}{3}\mathbf{y} - \frac{1}{3}\mathbf{x}$
             $= \frac{2}{3}\mathbf{x} + 1\frac{1}{3}\mathbf{y}$
             $= \frac{2}{3}(\mathbf{x} + 2\mathbf{y})$

Exercise 24.6
1 $\overrightarrow{NP} = \overrightarrow{NO} + \overrightarrow{OP}$ $\overrightarrow{VW} = \overrightarrow{VO} + \overrightarrow{OW}$
   $= ^-\mathbf{x} + \mathbf{y}$ $= ^-2\mathbf{x} + 2\mathbf{y}$
   $= \mathbf{y - x}$ $= 2\mathbf{y} - 2\mathbf{x}$
             $= 2(\mathbf{y - x})$

2 $\overrightarrow{IM} = \overrightarrow{IJ} + \overrightarrow{JM}$ $\overrightarrow{IL} = \overrightarrow{IH} + \overrightarrow{HL}$
   $= 3\mathbf{t} - 3\mathbf{s}$ $= ^-\mathbf{s} + \mathbf{t}$
   $= 3(\mathbf{t - s})$ $= \mathbf{t - s}$

3 a $\overrightarrow{OT} = 4\overrightarrow{OU}$ $\overrightarrow{US} = \overrightarrow{UO} + \overrightarrow{OS}$ $\overrightarrow{XW} = \overrightarrow{XO} + \overrightarrow{OU} + \overrightarrow{UW}$
   $= 4\mathbf{a}$ $= ^-\mathbf{a} + 2\mathbf{b}$ $= ^-\mathbf{b} + \mathbf{a} + \frac{1}{2}(2\mathbf{y} - \mathbf{a})$
             $= 2\mathbf{b} - \mathbf{a}$ $= ^-\mathbf{b} + \mathbf{a} + \mathbf{b} - \frac{1}{2}\mathbf{a}$
         $\overrightarrow{UW} = \frac{1}{2}(2\mathbf{b} - \mathbf{a})$ $= \frac{1}{2}\mathbf{a}$
   b $\overrightarrow{XW} = \frac{1}{2}\mathbf{a}$ $\overrightarrow{ST} = \overrightarrow{SO} + \overrightarrow{OT}$ $\overrightarrow{XV} = \overrightarrow{XS} + \overrightarrow{SV}$
             $= ^-2\mathbf{b} + 4\mathbf{a}$ $= \mathbf{b} + 2\mathbf{a} - \mathbf{b}$
             $= 4\mathbf{a} - 2\mathbf{b}$ $= 2\mathbf{a}$
         $\overrightarrow{SV} = 2\mathbf{a} - \mathbf{b}$

End Points
A1 a $\begin{pmatrix} 2 \\ 8 \end{pmatrix}$ **b** $\begin{pmatrix} 6 \\ 3 \end{pmatrix}$ **c** $\begin{pmatrix} 3 \\ 3 \end{pmatrix}$ **d** $\begin{pmatrix} 3 \\ 2 \end{pmatrix}$ **e** $\begin{pmatrix} 6 \\ 5 \end{pmatrix}$ **f** $\begin{pmatrix} 0 \\ 10 \end{pmatrix}$

B1 $3\mathbf{r} + \mathbf{s}$, $6\mathbf{r} + 2\mathbf{s}$ $3\mathbf{s} - \mathbf{r}$, $2\mathbf{r} - 6\mathbf{s}$

B2 $3\mathbf{t} - 6\mathbf{s} = 3(\mathbf{t} - 2\mathbf{s}) = {}^-3(2\mathbf{s} - \mathbf{t})$

C1 **a** $\overrightarrow{CD} = \overrightarrow{CB} + \overrightarrow{BA} + \overrightarrow{AD}$ **b** $\overrightarrow{CD} = {}^-\mathbf{p} + \mathbf{q} + 3\mathbf{p} = 2\mathbf{p} + \mathbf{q}$

C2 **a** $\overrightarrow{BM} = \overrightarrow{BC} + \overrightarrow{CM} = \mathbf{p} + \frac{1}{2}(2\mathbf{p} + \mathbf{q}) = \mathbf{p} + \mathbf{p} + \frac{1}{2}\mathbf{q}$

$= 2\mathbf{p} + \frac{1}{2}\mathbf{q} = \frac{1}{2}(4\mathbf{p} + \mathbf{q})$

b $\overrightarrow{AM} = \overrightarrow{AB} + \overrightarrow{BM} = {}^-\mathbf{q} + \frac{1}{2}(4\mathbf{p} + \mathbf{q})$

$= {}^-\mathbf{q} + 2\mathbf{p} + \frac{1}{2}\mathbf{q} = 2\mathbf{p} - \frac{1}{2}\mathbf{q} = \frac{1}{2}(4\mathbf{p} - \mathbf{q})$

D1 **a** **i** $\overrightarrow{RQ} = \overrightarrow{RO} + \overrightarrow{OQ}$

$= {}^-2\mathbf{a} + 2\mathbf{b}$

$= 2\mathbf{b} - 2\mathbf{a}$

$= 2(\mathbf{b} - \mathbf{a})$

ii $\overrightarrow{PQ} = \overrightarrow{PO} + \overrightarrow{OQ}$ $\overrightarrow{PG} = \frac{1}{2}\overrightarrow{PQ}$

$= {}^-2\mathbf{c} + 2\mathbf{b}$ $= \mathbf{b} - \mathbf{c}$

$= 2\mathbf{b} - 2\mathbf{c}$ $= 2(\mathbf{b} - \mathbf{c})$

b $\overrightarrow{EH} = \overrightarrow{ER} + \overrightarrow{RH}$ $\overrightarrow{FG} = \overrightarrow{FP} + \overrightarrow{PG}$

$= \overrightarrow{ER} + \frac{1}{2}\overrightarrow{RQ}$ $= \mathbf{c} + \mathbf{b} - \mathbf{c}$

$= \mathbf{a} + \mathbf{b} - \mathbf{a}$ $= \mathbf{b}$

$= \mathbf{b}$

c $\overrightarrow{EF} = \overrightarrow{EO} + \overrightarrow{OF}$ $\overrightarrow{HG} = \overrightarrow{HQ} + \overrightarrow{QG}$

$= {}^-\mathbf{a} + \mathbf{c}$ $= \frac{1}{2}\overrightarrow{RQ} + \frac{1}{2}\overrightarrow{QP}$

$= \mathbf{c} - \mathbf{a}$ $= (\mathbf{b} - \mathbf{a}) + (\mathbf{c} - \mathbf{b})$

$= \mathbf{c} - \mathbf{a}$

D2 **a** **i** $\overrightarrow{YM} = \overrightarrow{YX} + \overrightarrow{XM}$ $\overrightarrow{YW} = \frac{2}{3}\overrightarrow{YM}$ $\overrightarrow{YZ} = \overrightarrow{YX} + \overrightarrow{YX}$

$= {}^-2\mathbf{c} + \mathbf{d}$ $= \frac{2}{3}(\mathbf{d} - 2\mathbf{c})$ $= {}^-2\mathbf{c} + 2\mathbf{d}$

$= \mathbf{d} - 2\mathbf{c}$ $= 2(\mathbf{d} - \mathbf{c})$

b **i** $\overrightarrow{XN} = \overrightarrow{XY} + \overrightarrow{YN}$ $\overrightarrow{XW} = \overrightarrow{XY} + \overrightarrow{YW}$

$= \overrightarrow{XY} + \frac{1}{2}\overrightarrow{YZ}$ $= 2\mathbf{c} + \frac{2}{3}(\mathbf{d} - 2\mathbf{c})$

$= 2\mathbf{c} + \mathbf{d} - \mathbf{c}$ $= 2\mathbf{c} + \frac{2}{3}\mathbf{d} - \frac{4}{3}\mathbf{c}$

$= \mathbf{c} + \mathbf{d}$ $= \frac{2}{3}(\mathbf{c} + \mathbf{d})$

SECTION 25

Starting points

A1 **b** A linear $y = kx + c$, where k is about 0.4 and c is about 4
   B non-linear
   C linear $y = kx + c$, where k is about 6 and c is about 6

B2 $\begin{pmatrix} 6 \\ 5 \end{pmatrix}$

C1 **a** **i** 43 **ii** ${}^-2$ **iii** 13.75 **iv** ${}^-5$ **b** 0.75 (to 2 dp)

Exercise 25.1

1 A $y = kx^2 + p$ $k = 0.8$ $p = {}^-2$ $y = 0.8x^2 - 2$
   B $y = pq^x$ $p = 0.3$ $q = 2$ $y = 0.3 \times 2^x$
   C $y = kx^2$ $k = 1.6$ $y = 1.6x^2$
   D $y = k\sqrt{x}$ $k = 2.5$ $y = 2.5\sqrt{x}$
   E $y = qx^k$ $q = 0.1$ $k = 3$ $y = 0.1x^3$
   F $y = \dfrac{k}{x}$ $k = 0.5$ $y = \dfrac{0.5}{x}$ or $y = \dfrac{1}{2x}$

2 $p = 6$ $q = 1.8$ **3** $q = 4$ $k = 0.5$

Exercise 25.2

1 **b** It is approximately a straight line graph.
   c $d = kt^2 + p$, where k is about 4.9 and $p = 0$.
   d about 31 metres   **e** about 4.5 seconds

2 **b** $c = kr^2 + p$, where k is about 80 and p is about 65
   c about £1685

3 **b** The intercept is 0 and it is a straight line graph.
   c about 20   **d** about 155 seconds

4 **b** A $p \approx 642000$ C $q \approx 0.4$

Exercise 25.3

1 **a** $y = 2x - 2$ **b** $y = {}^-\frac{1}{2}x + 3$ **d** Reflect in $y = 0$

2 **b** **i** $y = {}^-2x + 1$ **ii** $y = 3x - 4$ **iii** $y = {}^-\frac{1}{2}x - 1$
   c $y = {}^-4x - 3$ or equivalent

3 $y = {}^-x - 8$ or equivalent

4 **b** **i** $y = {}^-x - 1$ **ii** $y = 2x - 3$ **iii** $y = \frac{1}{4}x + 1$
   c $y = 5x - 1$ or equivalent

5 **b** Vectors $\begin{pmatrix} p \\ q \end{pmatrix}$ such that $p - q = 6$

6 $y = 3x + (1 + w - 3v)$ **7** $y = kx + (l + b - ka)$

Exercise 25.4

2 **b** A translation $\begin{pmatrix} 2 \\ 0 \end{pmatrix}$ **3** Graph A   **4** **b** A translation $\begin{pmatrix} {}^-3 \\ 2 \end{pmatrix}$

5 Should be f$(x + 4) + 5$ for a vector $\begin{pmatrix} {}^-4 \\ 5 \end{pmatrix}$ or f$(x - 4) + 5$
   for a vector $\begin{pmatrix} 4 \\ 5 \end{pmatrix}$ for the graph $y = f(x - 4) + 5$

6 **b** **i** A reflection in $y = 0$ (x-axis)
      ii A reflection in $y = 0$ will always map $y = f(x)$ to $y = {}^-f(x)$

7 **b** A reflection in $x = 0$
   c A reflection in $x = 0$ will always map $y = f(x)$ to $y = f({}^-x)$

8 For all values of x, $({}^-x)^2 = x^2$ so g$(x) = g({}^-x)$

9 **a** Graph C   **b** Graph A

12   Graph
   a $y = f(x)$ D
   b $y = f(x + 5)$ A
   c $y = f(2x)$ B
   d $y = f(\frac{1}{2}x)$ E
   e $y = {}^-f(x) + 10$ F
   f $y = f(x - 3)$ C

Exercise 25.5

2 **b** A reflection in $y = 0$ or the x-axis
   c Two from: $x = {}^-2$, $x = 1$ and $x = 4$

3 **b** A translation $\begin{pmatrix} {}^-1 \\ 2 \end{pmatrix}$ **c** $x = 3$

4 **a** **i** 3.25 **ii** 0.8 **iii** 0.5

5 A $y = k(x + 1) - 2$ B $y = k(2x)$

End points

A1 $p = 8$ $q = 1.5$

B1 **b** **i** It's a straight line graph **ii** $a \approx 3.6$ $b \approx 6.1$ **c** About £14.10

C1 **b** $y = f(x - 1) - 2$

SKILLS BREAK 5

1 3.53 metres (to nearest cm) **2** 5.88×10^{21} tons

3 **a** 40080 km **b** 40100

4 **a** 1.09×10^{12} km³ (to 3 sf) **b** 5.4×10^9 tons/km³

5 **a** 0.2 m **b** 3600 mm **c** 20 400 00 revolutions (to 3 sf)

6 1830 days (to nearest day) **7** 0.61 m

8 approximately 188 m³

9 **a** 14.8 mph **b** About 6.5 metres per second

10 about 18 minutes **11** 5.6×10^3 **12** 2227 cm²

13 **a** 20.2 cm (to 3 sf) **b** 670 000 (to 3 sf) **c** 677 kg (3sf)

14 21.2 m² **15** $1 : 349$

16 **a** **i** $1 : 2277$ **ii** $1 : 569$ **b** a mere 2 ft tall

17 **a** 192 digits **a** 2277 digits **b** 8 digits/sec

18 56 days **19** **a** about 51° **b** 242 m **c** about 11 km/h

20 about 1 minute (54 s)

21 **a** 2.21 m³ **b** 2.5×10^4 m³

22 **a** 14 cans **b** 24 stories **c** 2.52 m

23 6.8 years **24** **a** 68 000 salamis (to 3 sf) **b** 22 500 00 rotations

25 $1 : 2$ (twice each letter!)

IN FOCUS 1

1 **a** 1 **b** 5 **c** 7 **d** 10 **e** 18 **f** 60

2 **a** $\frac{13}{36}$ **b** $1\frac{1}{6}$ **c** $\frac{7}{10}$ **d** $\frac{9}{10}$
   e $\frac{5}{8}$ **f** $1\frac{17}{18}$ **g** $4\frac{7}{24}$ **h** $\frac{31}{44}$ **i** $1\frac{5}{8}$

3 **a** $1\frac{2}{3}$ **b** $1\frac{1}{4}$ **c** $1\frac{1}{2}$ **d** 3
   e $5\frac{1}{15}$ **f** $\frac{4}{5}$ **g** $6\frac{17}{18}$ **h** $\frac{3}{50}$

4 **a** $3\frac{2}{3}$ **b** $1\frac{1}{9}$ **c** $\frac{3}{100}$ **d** $\frac{3}{10}$
   e $5\frac{1}{2}$ **f** $4\frac{1}{2}$

5 **a** $\frac{1}{3}$ **b** $\frac{25}{144}$ **c** $\frac{1}{3}$ **d** $\frac{1}{8}$
   e $4\frac{1}{2}$ **f** $\frac{4}{7}$

6 **a** $\frac{8}{7}$ **b** $\frac{15}{19}$ **c** $\frac{21}{16}$ **d** $\frac{10}{19}$

7 **a** $\frac{2}{3} = \frac{1}{2} + \frac{1}{6}$ **b** $\frac{1}{4} = \frac{1}{5} + \frac{1}{20}$
   c $\frac{1}{9} = \frac{1}{10} + \frac{1}{90}$

8 **a** Square A

$\frac{3}{2}$	$\frac{1}{3}$	$1\frac{1}{6}$
$\frac{2}{3}$	1	$1\frac{1}{3}$
$\frac{5}{6}$	$1\frac{2}{3}$	$\frac{1}{2}$

b Change $2\frac{1}{4}$ to $2\frac{7}{12}$

9 A and D, B and H, C and G, and F and I

10 **a** $\frac{4x}{9}$ **b** $\frac{2}{5}$ **c** $\frac{3}{x}$ **d** 21

e $\frac{3x}{10}$ **f** $\frac{10}{3x}$ **g** $\frac{7x+2y}{14}$ **h** $\frac{2x+12}{x(x+4)}$

i $\frac{x-2y}{4}$ **j** $\frac{5}{x-1}$ **k** $\frac{x-1}{x+2}$ **l** $\frac{y+2x}{xy}$

m $\frac{5x-4}{x(x-1)}$ **n** $\frac{y-x^2}{xy}$ **o** $\frac{x-1}{x+4}$ **p** $\frac{5x+7}{(x+1)(x+2)}$

q $\frac{5x-7}{(x-3)(x-1)}$ **r** $\frac{6}{x+3}$ **s** $\frac{x+4}{x(x+2)}$

t $\frac{6x-3}{(x-1)(x+2)}$ **u** $\frac{5y+x+11}{(x+1)(y+2)}$

11 **a** $\frac{6}{x}-\frac{3}{x-3}=\frac{3(x-6)}{x(x-3)}$

b $\square = 9$

IN FOCUS 2

1 **a** $b=47°$ $c=133°$ $d=47°$ $e=133°$
b $b=51.5°$ $c=128.5°$ $d=51.5°$ $e=128.5°$
c $a=11°$ $b=11°$ $c=169°$ $d=11°$

2 **a** 73°, 73° and 34° **b** isosceles **c** **i** 146° and 34° **ii** 73° and 107°
f **i** 90° **ii** 73° **iii** 73° **iv** 17° **v** 17°

4 $a=73°$ $b=46°$ $c=92°$ $d=120°$
$e=17°$ $f=72°$ $g=198°$ $h=275°$
$i=120°$ $j=60°$ $k=60°$ $l=60°$ $m=36°$

IN FOCUS 3

1 **a** m^2n^2 or $(mn)^2$ **b** $4p^2q$ **c** $18a^2b$
d a^3g^3 or $(ag)^3$ **e** $20p^3$ **f** $28a^3b$

2 **a** $24a-18b$ **b** $pn-p^2$ **c** s^2+st
d $6mn-6m^2$ **e** $5x^2+5xy$ **f** $4u^2+3u$
g $5pq+3pr$ **h** $12mn+21n^2$ **i** $27ab+9a^2$

3 **a** $2n+7m$ **b** $3a^2-a$ **c** $2b$ **d** $8x+2xy-2y$ **e** $4p+3q$
f $8p^2+2pq+5q^2$ **g** $4m^2+2mn-6n$ **h** $2x-2xy$

4 D

5 **a** $16x^2+4x$ **b** $13xy+30x^2$ **c** $6q-6p$ **d** $9a+6b$
e p^2-4p+6

6 **a** $\frac{8p+2}{(p+1)(p-1)}$ **b** $\frac{2p-2}{(p+4)(p+2)}$

c $\frac{9p+1}{(2p+1)(3p-2)}$ **d** $\frac{p+11}{6}$

7 **A** $2c+3$ **B** $3+4b$

8 **a** $p(7+3q)$ **b** $m(1+3n)$ **c** $4q(2p+1)$ **d** $3y(1-4x)$
e $2b(b+5)$ **f** $6b(3a+4c)$ **g** $xy(y-2)$ **h** $3ab(3a+2b)$
i $3mn(4m-3)$

9 **a** $w^2+8w+12$ **b** $y^2+14y+45$ **c** x^2-6x+9
d v^2-5v+6 **e** $b^2-8b+15$ **f** $2b^2-11b+15$
g h^2-25 **h** t^2-9

10 **a** $4w^2-9$ **b** $4p^2+4p+1$ **c** $15x^2+8x-12$ **d** $12g^2-43g+35$

11 **a** $(x+3)$ and $(x+4)$ **b** $(x+2)$ and $(x+6)$
c $(x+1)$ and $(x+6)$ **d** $(x+2)$ and $(x+3)$
e $(x+1)$ and $(x+12)$ **f** $(x+2)$ and $(x+4)$

12 **a** $(x+2)(x+2)$ **b** $(x+4)(x+5)$ **c** $(x+1)(x+6)$
d $(x+5)(x+4)$ **e** $(x+2)(x-3)$ **f** $(x-10)(x-1)$
g $(x+4)(x-2)$ **h** $(x-1)(x-2)$ **i** $(x-2)(x-2)$

13 **a** $\frac{3}{x+3}$ **b** $\frac{4}{x+6}$

14 **a** $(x+3)$ and $(x-2)$ **b** $(x+1)$ and $(x-3)$ **c** $(x-3)$ and $(x-2)$
d $(x+2)$ and $(x-2)$ **e** $(x+3)$ and $(x+2)$ **f** $(x+3)$ and $(x-3)$

15 **a** $(3x+4)(x+3)$ **b** $3(x-1)(x-4)$ **c** $(2x-1)(x-4)$
d $3(2x+1)(x-1)$ **e** $3x(x-2)$ **f** $(3x-5y)(3x+5y)$

16 **a** $p=8, q=4$ **b** $p=9, q=3$

17 **a** $\frac{7p-5}{(p-3)(p+1)}$ **b** $\frac{4-3a+3b}{2(a-b)^2}$ **c** $\frac{9a^2p}{2}$ **d** $\frac{6}{(p+1)(p-1)}$

18 **a** $(p+q)(p-q)$ **b** **iii** $p=75, q=74$

19 264 826 482 647 **20** $x+2$

IN FOCUS 4

1

	Dina	Cian	Joe
a Mean	64	63.5	64.25
b Mean deviation	4.57	5.33	5
c Standard deviation	6.05	6.16	5.74

2 Mean 49.25 Standard deviation 5.74
3 Mean 80 Standard deviation 7.56
4

	Sally	Gavin
Mean	6.17	6.5
Standard deviation	2.07	1.59

Gavin's scores are higher than Sally's on average, and also show less variation.

5

	Peggy	Toby	Sue
Median	6	5.5	7
Interquartile range	2	3	3.5

Sue's scores are the highest on average, but they also show the most variation. Peggy is the most consistent.

6 **a** P 36 Q 38 R 38.5 **b** P 3 Q 3.5 R 3

7 **b** Restuarant P: distribution is positively skewed,
Restuarant R: distribution is negatively skewed.

8 **A** The vertical axis does not start at 0: it gives the impression the growth rate in Year 4 is about 7 times the rate in Year 1.

B The number of videos sold in 1997 is 1.5 times the number sold in 1996, but the diagram gives the impression it is much more than this because the height *and* the width of the 1996 video have been increased 1.5 times

IN FOCUS 5

1

Sequence W	Sequence X	Sequence Y
b $a_n=2n+1$	**b** $a_n=4n$	**b** $a_n=12n-8$
c 21 matches	**c** 40 matches	**c** 112 matches

2 **a**

1	→	9
2	→	12
3	→	15
4	→	18
…		…
20	→	66
…		…
n	→	$3n+6$

b

1	→	3
2	→	⁻1
3	→	⁻5
4	→	⁻9
…		…
40	→	⁻153
…		…
n	→	$7-4n$

3 **a** $n \to 4n^2$

4 **A** $3n-2$ 88 **B** n^2+1 901
C $5n-3$ 147 **D** $3n^2$ 2700
E $12-n^2$ 888 **F** n^2-899 1
G n^2-2 898 **H** $3n^2-3$ 2695
I $2n^2+4$ 1804 **J** $7-2n^2$ ⁻1793

5 **a** 2^{n+3} **b** 2^n+3 **c** 2^{n-1} **d** $4-2^n$ **e** 3^{n-2} **f** $27-3^n$

6 **A** **a** $u_4=2205$ **b** diverges
B **a** $u_4=1$ **b** diverges
C **a** $u_4=2.2$ **b** converges (to limit of 2)
D **a** $u_4=5.014705882\ldots$ **b** converges (to limit of 5)

IN FOCUS 6

4 **a** not necessarily **b** congruent, AAS **c** not necessarily
d congruent, SSS **e** not necessarily **f** congruent, ASA

5 **c** The tent is outside the field and across a main road

IN FOCUS 7

1 **a** No **b** Yes **c** No **d** Yes **e** No **f** Yes
2 **a** 4 **b** 0.6 **c** ⁻3 **d** 1.1
3 **a** 2.5 **b** 1.6 **c** 2.2
4 **a** $\frac{1}{64}$ **b** $\frac{3}{5}$ **c** $\frac{1}{7}$

5 a 3.71293 **b** 4 **c** 9 **d** $^-$5.63 × 10^{-35}

6 a 4^8 **b** 3^{-1} **c** 2^0 **d** 2^{12} **e** 6^{-14} **f** 6^2 **g** 6^{-2} **h** 6^{-14}

7 a 3 **b** $^-$2 **c** $^-$1

8 a y^5 **b** y^{30} **c** $81y^8$ **d** $12y^7$ **e** y^1 **f** $2y^4$ or $2/y^4$ **g** $3y^6$
h $2y^{-2}$ or $2/y^2$ **i** $\frac{11}{10}$ or $1\frac{1}{10}$

9 A, D and H; C, E and G

10 a 7 **b** 9 **c** 3 **d** 7 **e** 1 **f** 5 **g** $\frac{1}{3}$
h $^-$4 **i** 2 **j** $\frac{1}{4}$ **k** $\frac{1}{6}$ **l** $^-\frac{1}{3}$ **m** 49 **n** 64
o 4 **p** 32 **q** 64 **r** 125 **s** 8 **t** 81 **u** 243
v 81 **w** $\frac{1}{16}$ **x** $\frac{1}{64}$ **y** $\frac{1}{27}$ **z** $\frac{1}{32768}$

11 a $x = 2$ **b** $x = ^-3$ **c** $x = \frac{1}{3}$ **d** $x = 6$ **e** $x = 1$ **f** $x = ^-1.5$
g $x = \frac{2}{3}$ **h** $x = \frac{3}{2}$ **i** 8 **j** $x = ^-2$ **k** $x = ^-\frac{2}{3}$ **l** $x = 1024$

12 a 6 **b** $\frac{1}{5}$ **c** $\sqrt{14}$ **d** 10 **e** $8 + 2\sqrt{15}$ **f** $5 - 2\sqrt{14}$ **g** $\sqrt{2}$
h $21 + 4\sqrt{5}$ **i** $2 - 6\sqrt{11}$

13 a $\frac{1}{3}$ **b** $\frac{4}{11}$ **c** $\frac{1}{99}$ **d** $\frac{14}{111}$ **e** $\frac{5}{9}$ **f** $\frac{1}{11}$
g $\frac{6}{7}$ **h** $\frac{3}{11}$

14 c Examples are: $\frac{16}{9}, \frac{25}{16}, \frac{36}{25}, \frac{49}{25} \cdots$

15 a irrational **b** irrational **c** rational **d** irrational **e** irrational
f irrational **g** irrational **h** irrational **i** rational

16 a i irrational **ii** rational **iii** rational **iv** irrational **v** irrational
b i irrational **ii** irrational **iii** rational

IN FOCUS 8

1 a 5.67 **b** 12.7 **c** 10 **d** 2140 **e** 15.78 **f** 93 748 000
g 16 **h** 500

2 a 40 000 **b** 200 **c** 240 **d** 250 000 **e** 350
f 0.000 75 **g** 120 000 **h** 40 000 **i** 280 000 **j** 90 000

3 a 1200 ; 1.4% (to 1dp) **b** 20 000 ; 9.8% (to 1dp)
c 20 ; 21.5% (to1dp) **d** 400 000 ; 26.9% (to 1dp)
e 16 ; 47.3%(to 1dp)

4 a 5.55 < boundary < 5.65 **b** 53.5 < boundary < 54.5
c 685 < boundary <695 **d** 56.3715 < boundary < 56.3725
e 64.995 < boundary < 65.005 **f** 95 < boundary < 105
g 99.5 < boundary < 100.5 **h** 159 950 < boundary < 160 050
i 12.85 < boundary < 12.95 **j** 15 995 000 < boundary < 16 005 000
k 999.995 < boundary < 1 000.005 **l** 7.000 05 < boundary < 7.000 15

5 a 31.6< perimeter (m) < 32 **b** 59.347 5 < area (m^2) < 60.937 5
c 623.15< cost (£) < 700.78

6 20.23 < speed (m/s) < 24.09

7 130.92 < volume (m^3) < 143.79 (to 2dp)

8 a $4.35 × 10^5$ **b** $1.2 × 10^7$ **c** $3.21 × 10^{-4}$
d $5.426745 × 10^1$ **e** $6.54 × 10^8$ **f** $6.54 × 10^{-2}$

9 a 5 230 **b** 0.000 001 5 **c** 0.109 4 **d** 0.03

10 a $1.579 014 × 10^5$ **b** $2.25 × 10^8$ **c** $1.0 × 10^{-7}$
d $7.289 876 5 × 10^{-4}$ **e** $6.48 × 10^{-4}$

IN FOCUS 9

1 a $x = 4.5$ **b** $x = 4$ **c** $x = ^-2.5$ **d** $x = 2$
e $x = 13$ **f** $x = 7.25$ **g** $x = ^-26$ **h** $x = 46$
i $x = 0.75$ **j** $x = 4$ **k** $x = ^-2.1\dot{6}$

2 long side 26 cm, short side 17 cm.

3 a $x^2 - 2x - 15$ **b** $2x^2 - 7x + 3$ **c** $8 + 2x - 15x^2$ **d** $^-4x^2 + 15x - 9$
e $x^2 - 16$ **f** $4x^2 - 9$ **g** $x^3 - 4x^2$ **h** $2x^3 + 6x^2 - 16x$
i $3x^4 + 15x^3 + 12x^2 - 3x$ **j** $x^3 + 9x^2 + 11x - 21$
k $^-15 - 22x + 10x^2 - x^3$ **l** $x^3 + 12x^2 + 17x - 60$ **m** $x^3 - 7x - 6$

4 a $x = 3, y = 1$ **b** $y = 1, x = 2$ **c** $x = 1, y = ^-1$ **d** $x = 3, y = ^-2$
e $x = ^-1, y = 2$ **f** $y = 2, x = ^-1$ **g** $y = 5, x = ^-3$ **h** $y = ^-8, x = ^-10$
i $x = ^-2, y = ^-3$ **j** $x = 4, y = ^-2$

5 5 and $^-4$ **6** five pound notes,37, ten pound notes 18.

7 scientific £8.45, graphical £12.95

8 5 pence coins 1778, 20 pence coins 472. **9** 165 small, 213 large.

10 a $x = ^-12$ or $x = 7$ **b** $x = 7$ or $x = 1$ **c** $x = ^-9$ or $x = 6$
d $x = 12$ or $x = 3$ **e** $x = 6$ or $x = ^-2$ **f** $x = 20$ or $x = ^-16$
g $x = 15$ or $x = ^-4$ **h** $x = 6$ or $x = 8$ **i** $x = ^-15$ or $x = 9$
j $x = 13$ or $x = 5$ **k** $x = 4$ or $x = 5$ **l** $x = 14$ or $x = 2$
m $x = 0$ or $x = 3$ **n** $x = ±8$ **o** $x = ±14$
p $x = ±100$ **q** $x = 3$ or $x = ^-\frac{1}{2}$ **r** $x = 2$ or $x = ^-5$
s $x = ^-1$ or $x = \frac{2}{3}$ **t** $x = 1$ or $x = ^-\frac{4}{3}$ **u** $x = ^-\frac{1}{2}$ or $x = \frac{2}{3}$
v $x = ^-6$ or $x = \frac{1}{6}$ **w** $x = \frac{1}{4}$ or $x = ^-2$ **x** $x = \frac{1}{2}$ or $x = ^-\frac{2}{3}$

11 a $x = 0.70$ or 4.30 **b** $x = 0.32$ or $x = ^-6.32$
c $x = ^-7.87$ or $x = ^-0.13$ **d** $x = 3.30$ or $x = ^-0.30$
e $x = ^-2.79$ or $x = 1.79$ **f** $x = ^-3.83$ or $x = 1.83$
g $x = ^-0.56$ or $x = 3.56$ **h** $x = ^-7.12$ or $x = 1.12$
i $x = 4.65$ or $x = ^-0.65$ **j** $x = 2.30$ or $x = ^-1.30$
k $x = ^-5.45$ or $x = ^-0.55$ **l** $x = ^-1.62$ or $x = 0.62$
m $x = ^-2.64$ or $x = 1.14$ **n** $x = ^-1.18$ or $x = 0.85$
o $x = 0.39$ or $x = ^-0.64$ **p** $x = ^-1.09$ or $x = 0.66$

12 a $x = ^-8$ or $x = 2$ **b** $x = 5$ or $x = 1$ **c** $x = 8$ or $x = ^-4$
b $x = ^-5$ or $x = 3$

IN FOCUS 10

3 b iii rotation $^+$90° about (1, 1)
or
rotation $^-$270° about (1, 1)
ii reflection in $x = 5$
c i rotation $^-$90° about (6, 2)
or
rotation $^+$270° about (6, 2)
ii reflection in $y = ^-x$
d i C **ii** F **iii** E
e rotation 180° about (4, $^-$1)
or
enlargement SF $^-$1 with centre (4, $^-$1)

4 b rotation 180° about (1, 0)
or
enlargement SF $^-$1 with centre (1, 0)
c i rotation of 180° about (4, 0)
ii rotation of $^-$90° about (3, 0)
iii translation of $\begin{pmatrix} 2 \\ 2 \end{pmatrix}$

5 b i translation of $\begin{pmatrix} ^-11 \\ ^-3 \end{pmatrix}$
ii rotation of 180° about (7.5, 1.5)
or
enlargement SF $^-$1 with centre (7.5, 1.5)
iii rotation of 180° about ($^-$0.5, 1.5)
or
enlargement SF ($^-$1 with centre ($^-$0.5, 1.5)

6 A reflection in any line.
A rotation of 180° about any point.
An enlargement SF $^-$1 with any centre.
Other possibles are:
an enlargement SF 1 with any centre
a translation of $\begin{pmatrix} 0 \\ 0 \end{pmatrix}$

IN FOCUS 11

1 a $\dfrac{4 - 5a}{3}$ **b** $\dfrac{5 - a}{2}$ **c** $\dfrac{3a - b}{6}$
d $\dfrac{2a + 1}{7}$ **e** $\dfrac{2 - 3a}{3}$ **f** $\dfrac{5 + 3a}{13}$
g $\dfrac{n + 3}{3a^2}$ **h** $\dfrac{1 - 5y}{ay}$ **i** $\dfrac{2 - y^2 - ay}{a}$
j $\dfrac{1 - 3\,ac^2 + ac^3}{bc^2}$ **k** $\dfrac{2bc + wy}{w}$ **l** $\dfrac{ab - 2an + cn}{a}$
m $\dfrac{b^2a - a^2b}{3b^2}$ **n** $\dfrac{a(\pi + 2)}{\pi y}$ **o** $\dfrac{5w - 1}{3w}$
p $\dfrac{2a^2 - 3a - 1}{2a}$ **q** $\dfrac{4}{a}$ **r** $\dfrac{6 - a}{7a}$
s $\dfrac{h - ab}{0.5c}$ **t** $\dfrac{w^2}{4}$

2 11 days

3 a £260.10 **b i** $t = \dfrac{c - 3n}{0.15}$ **ii** 850

 c i £21 **ii** 15 pence **iii** 120

4 a $3a + 6$ **b** $\dfrac{10(1 - x)}{3}$ **c** $\dfrac{a}{2}$ **d** $\dfrac{3x - 2}{4a}$

 e $\dfrac{a^2 - b}{6}$ **f** $\dfrac{2(5x + 9)}{3}$ **g** $\dfrac{2 + 3ax}{ax}$ **h** $\dfrac{5a}{6}$

 i $\dfrac{3 + x^2}{2x^2}$ **j** $\dfrac{3w - x^2}{3}$ **k** $\dfrac{a}{b \cos 30°}$ **l** $\dfrac{3x^2}{2a}$

 m $\dfrac{2(1 + 2a^2)}{3a^2}$ **n** $\dfrac{a + 1}{2}$ **o** $\dfrac{bc}{a}$ **p** $\dfrac{10a}{15 - b}$

 q $\dfrac{3}{\cos 30°}$ **r** $\dfrac{x + ab}{a}$ **s** $\dfrac{5x^2 - 3}{2}$ **t** $\dfrac{a + 1}{w}$

5 $n = \dfrac{a}{2b + c}$

6 a $\dfrac{3}{x - y}$ **b** $\dfrac{1}{t^2 - 3}$ **c** $\dfrac{c + 2}{3 - a}$ **d** $\dfrac{6 + a}{a + 4}$

 e $\dfrac{10}{6 - a^2}$ **f** $\dfrac{ab - 3}{2 - ab}$ **g** ^-x **h** $\dfrac{y - ax}{a - b^2}$

 i $\dfrac{2ay}{6a - 1}$ **j** $\dfrac{w}{\sin x + \sin y}$ **k** $\dfrac{4}{1 - 3w}$ **l** $\dfrac{1}{b(b - a^2)}$

 m $\dfrac{b - 1}{2c - a}$ **n** $\dfrac{b(3n + 2a)}{a - 3n}$ **o** $\dfrac{1}{bc - 3a}$

 p $\dfrac{2}{1 + 3a}$ **q** $\dfrac{4an - 1}{2}$ **r** $\dfrac{9b - c^2 n}{3ab}$ **s** $\dfrac{5a}{5y - 2}$ **t** $\dfrac{2}{1 - 2a^2}$

7 $\dfrac{S}{2r(h + r)}$ **8 a** $\dfrac{C + 50y}{1.85 + y}$ **b** £1.85

9 a $(1 + x)^2$ **b** $1 - 9a^2$ **c** $\dfrac{4x^2}{3}$ **d** $\dfrac{(a - b)^2 + 3}{2}$

 e $\dfrac{(a^2 + 1)^2}{9}$ **f** $\dfrac{(2x - 1)^2}{5}$ **g** $\dfrac{2\sqrt{3}x}{3}$ **h** $\dfrac{1}{(x + 3)^2}$

 i $\sqrt{(y^2 - 1)}$ **j** $\sqrt{\dfrac{ax - 1}{2}}$ **k** $\dfrac{2}{\sqrt{(3 + a)}}$ **l** $\sqrt{\dfrac{3x}{1 + y}}$

 m $\sqrt{\dfrac{ab}{b - a}}$ **n** $\sqrt{2}$ **o** $\dfrac{1}{\sqrt{a^2 + 1}}$

 p $\sqrt{\dfrac{1 + a^2 k}{a - k}}$ **q** $\dfrac{1}{\sqrt{3(2a - 1)}}$ **r** $\sqrt{(x + 2)}$

10 a $\sqrt{\dfrac{\pi R^2 - A}{\pi}}$ **b** 5 cm **11** $\dfrac{4a\pi^2}{t^2}$

IN FOCUS 12

1

	Icing sugar	Margarine	Plain chocolate	Flour
a	90 g	405 g	180 g	405 g
b	20 g	90 g	40 g	95 g

2 a 450 ml **b** 630 ml

3 a 2.9 cm **b** 1 : 3000

 c The total number of parts in the ratio 1 : 3000, i.e. 3001, has no meaning because the 1 and the 3000 are different types of quantity.

4 a 0.75 **b** 8.1 cm **b i** 0.703 **ii** 0.703

 d EFGH is an enlargement of JKLM, so the shapes must be in proportion.

5 EFGH and IJKL **6 a** 3.9 cm **b** 8.8 cm

7 a ABE and BDC are similar because they have the same angles: each triangle has a 90° angle and the angle in ABE at B is equal to the angle in BDC at D (alternate angles), so the third angles must also be the same.

 b i BD **ii** BC **c** 9.8 cm

8 a i 1.75 **ii** 1.75

 b MOP and MQN are similar because all ratios of lengths of corresponding sides are equal.

 c 0.5 cm

9 a $z \propto p^2$ or $z = kp^2$ **b** 0.6 **c** $z = 0.6p^2$ **d** 15

 e $p = \sqrt{\dfrac{z}{0.6}}$ or $p = \sqrt{\dfrac{10z}{6}}$ or $p = \sqrt{\dfrac{5z}{3}}$ **f** 12

10 a $l = \dfrac{36}{w^2}$ **b** 5.76 cm **c** 1.2 cm

IN FOCUS 13

1 A 2 B 5 **3 a** 3 **b** 9

4 To 2dp: **a** 19.83 cm **b** 5.30 cm **5** 82.47 cm^2

6 To 2dp: **a** 73.50 cm^2 **b** 35.82 cm

7 To 2dp: **a** 1539.38 cm^3 **b** 603.35 cm^2

8 To 2dp: **a** 209426.94 cm^3 **b** 18162.97 cm^2

9 13.68 cm (to 2dp)

10 a length **b** area **c** area **d** volume **e** length
 f area **g** none **h** volume **i** none **j** area
 k none **l** volume **m** area **n** volume **o** area
 p length

IN FOCUS 14

1 a $\frac{1}{6}$ **b** $\frac{2}{6} = \frac{1}{3}$ **c** $\frac{4}{6} = \frac{2}{3}$

2 a $\frac{4}{6} = \frac{2}{3}$ **b** $\frac{2}{6} = \frac{1}{3}$

3 a $\frac{2}{36} = \frac{1}{18}$ **b** $\frac{5}{36}$ **c** $\frac{10}{36} = \frac{5}{18}$ **d** $\frac{1}{36}$ **e** $\frac{31}{36}$

4 To 2dp: **a** 0.61 (2dp) **b** 0.84 **c** 0.77

5 a i $\frac{2}{9}$ **ii** $\frac{7}{54}$ **iii** $\frac{10}{27}$ **b i** $\frac{1}{12}$ **ii** $\frac{13}{18}$ **iii** $\frac{5}{18}$

 c $1 - \frac{2}{7} = \frac{5}{7}$ **d i** $\frac{1}{12}$ **ii** $\frac{25}{216}$

6 b i $\frac{51}{310}$ **ii** $\frac{1071}{2480}$ **iii** $\frac{819}{2480}$ **iv** $\frac{63}{248}$ **c i** $\frac{154}{1549}$ **ii** $\frac{755}{14384}$

7 To 2sf: **a i** 0.011 **ii** 0.12 **iii** 0.86
 To 2sf: **b i** 0.0018 **ii** 0.16 **iii** 0.012

8 b i $\frac{1}{5}$ **ii** $\frac{4}{15}$ **iii** $\frac{8}{15}$ **iv** $\frac{2}{5}$

IN FOCUS 15

2 a 143.1 min (to 4 sf) **b** 6.42 min (to 3 sf)

3 b i about 141.8 min **ii** about 9.3 min
 c i about 7 **ii** about 4 **iii** about 43

5 a 158.8 min (to 4 sf) **b** 6.58 min (to 3 sf)

6 b i about 157.2 min **ii** about 8.7 min
 c i about 4 **ii** about 11 **iii** about 34

9 The total frequencies need to be about the same for frequency polygons to give a fair comparison.

10 (These estimates use mid–class values of 20.5, 25.5, 30.5 and 38).
 a i Mean 27.7 (to 3 sf) Standard deviation 4.47 (to 3 sf)
 ii Mean 28.8 (to 3 sf) Standard deviation 5.13 (to 3 sf)
 b The track athletes are just over a year younger on average. There was greater variation in the ages of the field athletes.

11

Age	16–	18–	20–	22–	24–	26–	28–	30–	32–	34–	36–	38–	40–	42–	44–	46 – 48
Frequency	3	8	27	35	42	55	54	38	15	18	6	4	4	1	0	2

IN FOCUS 16

1 a $x = 2, y = 1$ **b** $x = 1, y = ^-1$ **c** $x = 3, y = 2$
 d $x = 4, y = 1\frac{1}{2}$ **e** $x = ^-2, y = ^-1$ **f** $x = ^-2\frac{1}{2}, y = ^-1$
 g $x = 1\frac{1}{2}, y = 5$ **h** $x = 4\frac{1}{2}, y = 3$ **i** $x = 3\frac{1}{2}, y = 3$
 j $x = 3\frac{1}{2}, y = ^-3$

2 a $x = 0$ **b** $x = ^-2$ **c** $x = 4$
 d $x = ^-3$ **e** $x = ^-6$ **f** $x = ^-4$

5 a i $x \approx ^-4.8$ or 1.8 **ii** $x \approx 0.5$ or $^-3.5$ **iii** $x \approx 2.9$ or $^-5.9$

6 b $x \approx 2.5$ or $^-1$ **7** $x \approx 0.5$ or 7.5 **8** $x \approx 5$ or $^-1$

9 a $x \approx 0.8$ or $^-3.8$ **c** 0.6 **11** $x = 0$ and $y = 8$

12 a $^-5.7$ **b** $x \approx 1.4$ and 7.2

15 a $x \approx 0$ and $x \approx 2$ **b** $x \approx 3.1$

18 a $^-10$ **b** $(^-2, 10)$ **c** $y = ^-6$

IN FOCUS 17

1 a B: (2, 240°) D: (3, 0°) **b** A: (2.60, 1.50) B: ($^-1$, $^-1.73$)
 c C: (6, 60°)

2 a

t	0	1	2	3	4	5	6	7	8	9	10
$4\cos 20t$	4	3.76	3.06	2	0.69	0.69	2	3.06	3.76	4	3.76

t	11	12	13	14	15	16	17	18	19	20
$4\cos 20t$	3.06	2	0.69	0.69	2	3.06	3.76	4	3.76	3.06

 c i $4.5 \leqslant t \leqslant 13.5$ **ii** $3 \leqslant t \leqslant 15$ **d** 4 **e i** 4.5, 13.5 **ii** 6, 12
 f ii Max: 2 Min: $^-6$

3 a 60°, 300°   **b** 210°, 330°   **c** 135°, 315°   **d** 45°, 225°
e 155°, 205°   **f** 205°, 335°   **g** 25°, 205°   **h** 75°, 105°
i 105°, 255°   **j** 105°, 285°

4 a i 54, 126, 414   **ii** ⁻54, 54, 306, 414   **iii** 54, 234, 414
    iv 26, 154, 386   **v** 154, 206   **vi** ⁻26, 154, 334
  b i 118, 242   **ii** ⁻62, 242, 298   **iii** 90, 450   **iv** ⁻90, 90, 270, 450

7 b 63°, 243° (to nearest degree)

8   Max   Min
  a   6   ⁻6
  b   7   5
  c   8   ⁻8
  d   1   ⁻1
  e   9   3
  f   ⁻2   ⁻6

9 $a = 2$ $b = 3$ $c = $⁻3

10 a ⁻45, 225, 405   **b** 40, 50, 220, 230
  c ⁻20, 20, 100, 140, 220, 260, 340, 380
  d ⁻45, 15, 75, 135, 195, 255, 315, 375, 435

IN FOCUS 18

1 4, 71, ⁻3.2, ⁻0.33

2 a 8, 7, 6, 5, 4   **b** ⁻3, ⁻2, −1   **c** ⁻5, ⁻4, ⁻3, ⁻2, ⁻1, 0
  d ⁻4, ⁻5, ⁻6   **e** none   **f** 24   **g** ⁻15   **h** 1, 2, 3, 4, 5
  i ⁻4, ⁻3, ⁻2, ⁻1, 0, 1, 2, 3, 4   **j** 0   **k** ⁻3, ⁻2, ⁻1, 0, 1, 2, 3
  l ⁻3, ⁻2, ⁻1, 0, 1, 2, 3

3 Any two from ⁻2 < h ≤ 1, ⁻1 ≤ h ≤ 1, ⁻1 ≤ h < 2

4 The weight is a continuous measure but the number of waiters is discrete

6 $x + y$ ≤ 7 (or $y = 7 − x$) and x ≤ 2   **7 a** 9   **b** 16

8 a x ≥ 3   **b** $t < $⁻7   **c** p ≤ 13   **d** ⁻11 ≤ k ≤ 11   **e** w < 2
  f q > 9.3   **g** t ≥ 8   **h** h ≤ 2   **i** f < 3   **j** ⁻9 < c < 9
  k g ≥ 4.5   **l** $x > $⁻3   **m** j < 19   **n** d ≥ ⁻2   **o** v < 4.5
  p x ≤ ⁻13   **q** s < 0   **r** u ≤ ⁻3   **s** j > 1.09
  t $r < $⁻3 or r > 3   **u** $\sqrt{2} < x < \sqrt{2}$

9 a 28 < xy < 63   **b** 11 < $x + y$ < 16   **c** 1 < $\frac{x}{y}$ ≤ 2$\frac{1}{4}$

10 a i $2a + 3p$ ≤ 54   **ii** $4a + 5p$ ≤ 100   **iii** p ≥ 6
  d 12 apples and 10 pears, £196

IN FOCUS 19

1 a 63.33..%   **b** 25.45...%   **c** 283 .33...%   **d** 62%   **2** 29%

3 a 29.5 kg   **b** 2268 km   **c** 3702.4 miles   **d** 1836 yards

4 232 260 00 CD's

5 a 426.8 ml   **b** £34.77   **c** 22.75 mm   **d** 0.736 cm

6 11 tonnes

7 a £218.37   **b** £13.74   **c** £52.71   **d** £25.56   **e** £315.55
  f £187.99   **g** £159.07   **h** £10.86   **i** £58.74   **j** £1761.33

8 £155.10   **9** £85.71

10 £8510.64   **11** £199.74 Pricebusters

12 a £405   **b** £4216   **c** £20.40

13 $\frac{I}{PT}$ **14** 7.5 years

15 a £296.92   **b** £959.22   **c** £345.22   **d** £24.14   **e** £61700.34
  f £21.28   **g** £578.67   **h** £4382.26   **i** £124.88   **j** £1372.66

17 a £255.31   **b** £11.06   **c** £38.29   **d** £8.50   **e** £63.83
  f £76.55   **g** £22.97   **h** £110.63   **i** £16.16   **j** £119.14

18 £100.53   **19** £3157894.74

IN FOCUS 20

1 b CD is a diameter   **2 b** 683°   **3** 22°

4 a 109° **b** 33°   **5 b** 96°   **6 b** 110°

7 a 2.8 cm   **b** 2.8 cm   **8 a** 37°   **b** 37.0 cm²   **9 b** 75°

IN FOCUS 21

1 Answers to 2dp:
  a 17.31 cm²   **b** 13.70 cm²   **c** 22.26 cm²
  d 99.76 cm²   **e** 37.16 cm²   **f** 14.56 cm²

2 6.63 cm(to 2dp)

3 Answers to 1dp:
  a 5.21°   **b** 15.54°   **c** 47.5°   **d** 49.7°   **e** 80.6°

4 Answers to 1dp.
  a 5.2 cm   **b** 15.5 cm   **c** 9.8 cm   **d** 25.4 cm   **e** 13.1 cm

5 Answers to 1dp.
  a 73.0°   **b** 53.1°   **c** 72.2°   **d** 59.6°   **e** 88.9°

6 Answers to 1dp.
  a 7.3 cm   **b** 9.2 cm   **c** 9.0 cm   **d** 4.9 cm   **e** 33.5 cm

IN FOCUS 22

1 a Question 1 is not clear; different people are likely to have different ideas of what is meant by 'often'
Question 2 is leading; it leads people into giving the answer 'Yes'
Question 3 is ambiguous; it could refer to the number of buses on the roads, or the comfort of buses, etc.

7 d Moderate positive correlation, i.e. the larger the size of engine, the higher the price

8 a about £7200   **b** about £4900

9 a about 320 cc   **b** about 690 cc

10 a about £8500   **b** about 1220 cc

11 Female   Male   Total
    24   36   60

IN FOCUS 23

1 a 4 h 23 min   **b** 12 h 46 min   **c** 5.27 h   **d** 8.85 h
  e 86.4 k h⁻¹   **f** 36 mph   **g** 26 ms⁻¹   **h** 42.2 ms⁻¹

2 11.3 mph   **3** 244 miles   **4** 2 h 26 min

5 32.8 mph

6 1 h 15 min   **7** 400 m

8 b 3s, 6s, 9s, 13.5s   **c** 6m   **d** between 7th and 8th second
  e after about 14 seconds   **f i** about 2 m s⁻¹   **ii** about 5 m s⁻¹

9 a changing gear   **b i** about 1.6 m s⁻²   **ii** about 2 m s⁻²
  c about 4 m   **d** about 160 m   **e** about 22 mph   **f** no

10 a a volume of 18 litres
  b i about 800 litres
    ii total volume of water in 48 minutes.
  c about 17 litres min⁻¹

IN FOCUS 24

1 a $\begin{pmatrix} ⁻4 \\ 10 \end{pmatrix}$ **b** $\begin{pmatrix} 3 \\ 12 \end{pmatrix}$ **c** $\begin{pmatrix} 10 \\ ⁻12 \end{pmatrix}$ **d** $\begin{pmatrix} 6 \\ 10 \end{pmatrix}$
  e $\begin{pmatrix} ⁻1 \\ 9 \end{pmatrix}$ **f** $\begin{pmatrix} 7 \\ 0 \end{pmatrix}$ **g** $\begin{pmatrix} 4 \\ 3 \end{pmatrix}$ **h** $\begin{pmatrix} 6 \\ 8 \end{pmatrix}$

2 a **v−u**   **b** **w−v**   **c** **v−w**   **d** **u−v**   **e** **u−v + w**

3 a $\begin{pmatrix} 3 \\ 1 \end{pmatrix}$ **b** $\begin{pmatrix} 4 \\ 2 \end{pmatrix}$ **c** $\begin{pmatrix} ⁻4 \\ 2 \end{pmatrix}$ **d** $\begin{pmatrix} 3 \\ 1 \end{pmatrix}$ **e** $\begin{pmatrix} 2 \\ 7 \end{pmatrix}$

4 a $\overrightarrow{PR}$ **b** $\overrightarrow{PR}$ **c** $\overrightarrow{PS}$

5 The vector is equal to 0.

6 a **w−u**   **b** **u−w**   **c** **w−v**

7 b **v − u** $= \begin{pmatrix} 1 \\ 4 \end{pmatrix} − \begin{pmatrix} 2 \\ 5 \end{pmatrix} = \begin{pmatrix} ⁻3 \\ ⁻1 \end{pmatrix}$

  u − v $= \begin{pmatrix} 2 \\ 5 \end{pmatrix} − \begin{pmatrix} 1 \\ 4 \end{pmatrix} = \begin{pmatrix} 3 \\ 1 \end{pmatrix} = ⁻\begin{pmatrix} ⁻3 \\ ⁻1 \end{pmatrix} = −(\mathbf{v−u})$

  c − (**u − v**) = − **u + v** = **v − u**

8 $\overrightarrow{QS} = \overrightarrow{QR} + \overrightarrow{RS}$ $\overrightarrow{QX} = \overrightarrow{QP} + \overrightarrow{PX}$
      = **w − v + u − v** $= \overrightarrow{QP} + \frac{1}{2}\overrightarrow{PR}$
      = **u − 2v + w**   = **u − v** + $\frac{1}{2}$(**w − u**)
                          = **u − v** + $\frac{1}{2}$**w** − $\frac{1}{2}$**u**
                          = $\frac{1}{2}$(**u − 2v + w**)

9 **2v − 3u, 4v − 6u**
  6u + 4v, − 3u − 2v
  6u − 9v, 3v − 2u

10 **a** $\vec{PQ} = \vec{PO} + \vec{OQ}$
$= \bar{2}\mathbf{a} + 2\mathbf{b}$
$= 2\mathbf{b} - 2\mathbf{a}$
$= 2(\mathbf{b} - \mathbf{a})$

b $\vec{OP} = 2\mathbf{a}$

$\vec{ZY} = \vec{ZQ} + \tfrac{1}{2}\vec{QP}$
$= \mathbf{b} + (\mathbf{a} - \mathbf{b})$
$= \mathbf{a}$

11 **a** **i** $\vec{XQ} = \vec{XO} + \vec{OQ}$
$= \bar{}\mathbf{a} + 2\mathbf{b}$
$= 2\mathbf{b} - \mathbf{a}$

ii $\vec{XC} = \tfrac{1}{3}\vec{XQ}$
$= \tfrac{1}{3}(2\mathbf{b} - \mathbf{a})$

b $\vec{PZ} = \vec{PO} + \vec{OZ}$
$= \bar{2}\mathbf{a} + \mathbf{b}$
$= \mathbf{b} - 2\mathbf{a}$

$\vec{PC} = \vec{PX} + \vec{XC}$
$= \bar{}\mathbf{a} + \tfrac{1}{3}(2\mathbf{b} - \mathbf{a})$
$= \bar{}\mathbf{a} + \tfrac{2}{3}\mathbf{b} - \tfrac{1}{3}\mathbf{a}$
$= \tfrac{2}{3}(\mathbf{b} - 2\mathbf{a})$

c 2:1

d $\vec{OY} = \vec{OP} + \vec{PY}$
$= \vec{OP} + \tfrac{1}{2}\vec{PQ}$
$= 2\mathbf{a} + \tfrac{1}{2}(2\mathbf{b} - 2\mathbf{a})$
$= 2\mathbf{a} + \mathbf{b} - \mathbf{a}$
$= \mathbf{a} + \mathbf{b}$

$\vec{OC} = \vec{OX} + \vec{XC}$
$= \mathbf{a} + \tfrac{1}{3}(2\mathbf{b} - \mathbf{a})$
$= \mathbf{a} + \tfrac{2}{3}\mathbf{b} - \tfrac{1}{3}\mathbf{a}$
$= \tfrac{2}{3}(\mathbf{a} + \mathbf{b})$

e The lines joining each vertex to the midpoint of the opposite side intersect at point C.

12 **a** **i** $\vec{CD} = \vec{CB} + \vec{BA} + \vec{AD}$
$= \mathbf{p} + \mathbf{q} + 3\mathbf{p}$
$= 2\mathbf{p} + \mathbf{q}$

ii $\vec{CM} = \tfrac{1}{2}\vec{CD}$
$= \tfrac{1}{2}(2\mathbf{p} + \mathbf{q})$

iii $\vec{BM} = \vec{BC} + \vec{CM}$
$= \mathbf{p} + \tfrac{1}{2}(2\mathbf{p} + \mathbf{q})$
$= \mathbf{p} + \mathbf{p} + \tfrac{1}{2}\mathbf{q}$
$= \tfrac{1}{2}(4\mathbf{p} + \mathbf{q})$

$\vec{BI} = \tfrac{2}{5}\vec{BM}$
$= \tfrac{2}{5}\tfrac{1}{2}(4\mathbf{p} + \mathbf{q})$
$= \tfrac{1}{5}(4\mathbf{p} + \mathbf{q})$

b $\vec{AC} = \vec{AB} + \vec{BC}$
$= \bar{}\mathbf{q} + \mathbf{p}$
$= \mathbf{p} - \mathbf{q}$

$\vec{AI} = \vec{AB} + \vec{BI}$
$= \bar{}\mathbf{q} + \tfrac{1}{5}(4\mathbf{p} + \mathbf{q})$
$= \bar{}\mathbf{q} + \tfrac{4}{5}\mathbf{p} + \tfrac{1}{5}\mathbf{q}$
$= \tfrac{4}{5}(\mathbf{p} - \mathbf{q})$

In focus 25

1 **a** **i** 1 **ii** 11 **iii** 5.5 **iv** 0.125 **v** $\bar{}5$ **vi** 3
b **i** 15 **ii** 0 **iii** 0.8

2 **b** $R = aD + b$ where $a \approx 0.9$ and $b \approx 0$ **c** about 315 cm

3 **b** **ii** $p \approx \bar{}5$ **q** ≈ 50

4 **b** $m \approx 0.4$ **n** ≈ 2.4 **c** about 7.6

5 **b** **i** A reflection in $y = 0$ **ii** A reflection in $x = 0$
iii A translation $\binom{0}{3}$ **iv** A translation $\binom{\bar{}3}{0}$ **v** A translation $\binom{2}{1}$

7 **h** $y = k(x + 2) + 1$

Exam-style questions

N1.1 $73\tfrac{1}{3}$ feet per second

N1.2 **a** 27.06 litres per second **b** 357.10 gallons per minute

N1.3 £274

N1.4 **a** 23.75 FF

N1.5 340 g (to 3sf)

N1.6 2809.38 sqft (to 2dp)

N1.7 6.28 litres per 100 km (to 2dp)

N1.8 Cheaper in GB by 4p per pint (or 7p per litre)

N1.9 **a** 5' 5" (to the nearest 1") **b** 17.68 cm

N1.10 73.16 mph (to 2dp)

N1.11 21.3 pounds per square inch (to 3sf)

N2.1 **a** 75 ml **b** 152.5 ml

N2.2 **a** **i** 27.5" **ii** 26.5"
b **i** 699 mm **ii** 673 mm (to the nearest mm)

N2.3 22.2775 m² < area < 23.2875 m²

N2.4 **a** 61.93° (to 2dp) **b** 4 cm

N2.5 6.57% (2dp)

N2.7 Diameter > 52.01 cm (2dp)

N3.1 **a** 1, 2, 3, 4, 6, 12 **b** 288, 300, 432, 612

N3.2 **a** $2^2 \times 3^3$ **b** $2^6 \times 3^9$

N3.3 **i** $3 \times 5 \times 37$ **ii** $3 \times 7 \times 151$ **b** 3

N3.4 **a** 25, 45, 35, 4, 37, 18, 8 **b** 1, 2, 4, 8 **c** 37
d **i** 164 **ii** 1.64×10^2

N3.5 $4.7142 = \frac{47138}{9999}$

N3.6 **a** $2 + \sqrt{2}, 5 - \pi$ **b** $\frac{7}{4}, \frac{8}{1}, \frac{151}{25}$

N3.7 $6 \times \sqrt{14}$

N3.8 **a** rational $= \frac{2}{1}$ **b** irrational ($4 - \pi$) **c** rational $= \frac{8}{1}$
d irrational ($2\sqrt{2}$)

N3.10 $\frac{5}{11}$

N4.1 **a** **i** Claire **ii** Rob **b** 75 **c** 18

N4.2 **a** 0.375 **b** smaller **c** 0.085, $\frac{1}{5}$, $\frac{3}{8}$, $\frac{1}{2}$, 0.6 **d** 0.85

N4.3 **a** **i** $\frac{72}{1000}$ **ii** $\frac{9}{125}$ **b** 232 **c** 652

N4.4 **a** Malaga 918, Orlando 408, Corfu 612, Faro 204, Malta 306
b $\frac{1}{8}$ **c** yes **d** Orlando

N4.5 Lisa £1068.67 Mario £1053.51

N4.6 £25.50

N4.7 **a** £774.50 **b** £135.54

N4.8 **b** **i** 6 years **ii** $1.09\,000 \times 10^5$ tonnes

N4.9 **a** **i** 5% **ii** 3250 **b** 17% **c** £923 975

N4.10 **a** Tony is wrong **b** £6860.11

N4.11 £129.9892 million

N4.12 **a** £359.16 **b** 7 months **c** 15 months

N5.1 **a** 3.87×10^3 **b** 5×10^{14} **c** 2.5×10^3
d 4.95×10^7 **e** 10^{-4}

N5.2 5.9478×10^{21}

N5.3 **a** 3.57×10^{10} km² **b** 1.6525×10^8 km²
c **i** 3.521×10^8 km² **ii** roughly $\frac{1}{2}$

N5.4 **a** 2 **b** $\frac{1}{25}$ **c** 30375 **d** $\frac{1}{\sqrt{3}}$ or 0.577 (to 3dp)
e 9 **f** $3\sqrt{3}$ or 5.196 (to 3dp)

N5.5 **a** $x = 5$ **b** $x = 2$

N5.6 $\frac{x^2}{y^3}$

N5.7 **a** 8.42×10^8 **b** roughly 19%

N5.8 $1.104\,25 \times 10^8$

N5.9 **a** 1.15×10^{21} **b** 5.2×10^3

N6.1 **a** 3 : 5 **b** 375 g **c** 60%

N6.2 **a** 140 ml
b olive oil 1250 ml, malt vinegar 500 ml
raspberry wine vinegar 250 ml

N6.3 **a** 22.5 m **b** 6 cm **c** about 60 ft

N6.4 **a** 25 g **b** flour 9.6 kg, baking powder 480 g,
butter 4.8 kg caster sugar 480 g, sultanas 2.4 kg

N6.5 4.2 cm

N6.6 **a** £98.14 **b** £686.98 **c** $\frac{3}{5}$

N6.7 **a** $W = 3\sqrt{S}$ **b** $W = 27$ **c** $S = 100$

N6.8 **a** $h = 0.04s^2$ **b** 25 m/s **c** 4 : 1

N6.9 **a** A is $q = kp$, B is $q = kp^2$, C is $q = \frac{k}{p}$, D is $q = k\sqrt{p}$
b **i** D **ii** $q = 0.5\sqrt{p}$ **iii** p = 0.25

N6.10 **a** $L \propto \frac{1}{d^2}$ **b** 9 : 1

N7.1 **a** 18 minutes **b** 20 km per hour

N7.2 **a** **i** 1.6 mm **ii** 0.064 of an inch
b **i** 4.788×10^7 litres **ii** 1.05×10^7 gallons
c 285 250 litres per hour

A1.1 **a** 96 **b** 7.4 **c i** $t = \dfrac{V - u}{f}$ **ii** 4.9

A1.2 **a** C = £6.99n + £3.50 **b** £38.45

A1.3 **a** 123 600 wheels **b** 3 075 trolleys

A1.4 **a** 3840 **b** I = $\dfrac{P}{R^2}$

A1.5 **a** 209 cm³ (to 3sf) **b i** r = $\sqrt{\dfrac{3v}{\pi h}}$ **ii** 1.4 cm

A1.6 **a** 47 nails **b i** $3b + 2 = n$ **ii** 4454

A1.7 £359.86

A2.1 **a** $1\frac{2}{7}$ **b** $8\frac{1}{7}$ **c** 7 **d** 1 **e** $6\frac{3}{7}$ **f** ⁻1.5

A2.2 $n - 5$

A2.3 **a** $\frac{5}{8}d$ **b** 48

A2.4 **a** $8n$ pence **b i** $y + 2$ **ii** $7(y + 2)$ pence
  c $15k + 21 = 81$ pence (or equivalent)
  d i 4 mugs **ii** 7 plates

A2.5 **a** $n + 228$ **b** £6n
  c £6n + £3.50 $(n + 228)$ (or equivalent)
  d £6n + £3.50 $(n + 228)$ = £24 947.00 (or equivalent)
  e i 2542 **ii** 2770

A2.6 **a i** $x = 7 - 8y$ **ii** $x = ⁻49$ **b** $p = 11$

A2.7 **a** $2k$ **b** $3k - 5$ **c i** $2k = 3k - 5$ **ii** $k = 5$

A2.8 **a** $p + y = 142$ and $4.5p + 6y = 724.5$ (£) (or equivalents)
  b 57 tickets costing £6 and 85 costing £4.50

A2.9 **a** $40 - w$ **b** $18 - 2w$ **c** $98w - 2w^2$
  d $98 - 4w$ **e** $196 - 4w$
  f i $196 - 4w = 184$ **ii** 3 m **iii** 276 m²

A2.10 **a** 18 rails **b** $2x - 2 = y$ (or equivalent)
  c $x = \dfrac{y}{2} + 1$ **d** 314 **e** 33

A2.11 **a** $x = 1.6, y = 0.2$ **b** $w = 2, t = 0.5$
  c $a = 1, b = 2$ **d** $p = 3, t = ⁻4$
  e $a = 2, y = 1$ **f** $v = 20, w = 15$

A2.12 **a** $n - 4$
  b 7 ten pound notes, 3 five pound notes, and 11 one pound coins.

A2.13 **a** $3f + 5k = 157$ (seconds). $5f + 2k = 154$ (seconds) or equivalent
  b 1 minute 32 seconds

A2.14 The fees were: tent £4.75, caravan £7.50

A2.15 57 passengers in the 1st coach and 61 in each of the other coaches

A3.1 2.9 or ⁻6.9

A3.2 **a** $3 < w < 4$ **b** $w = 3.4$ (to 1dp)

A3.3 **a** $c = 5$ **c** $c = 2$ or ⁻2 or 0

A3.4 **b** 5.4 or ⁻3.4

A3.5 8.7(to 1dp) or ⁻3.7(to 1dp)

A3.6 **b** $k = 66, m = 55$

A3.7 $y = 4.2$(to 1dp)

A3.8 **b** 65 cm **c** 150 cm

A3.9 $5^2 < 4 \times 2 \times 6$

A3.10 **b** ⁻1.5

A3.11 **a** $3 < x < 4$ **b** 3.0

A3.12 **b** 3.37

A4.1 **c** $y = ⁻3x - 2$ **d** $y = 3x - 5$

A4.2 **b** ⁻3

A4.3 **b** $y = x + 5$ or equivalent
  e standard, about $5\frac{1}{2}$ days; longlife, $10\frac{1}{2}$ days

A4.4 **c** $x = ⁻1, y = 2$

A4.5 **a** $y = \frac{4}{3}x - 2$ **b** $x = 3, y = 2$ (graphically)

A4.6 $x \approx 3, y \approx \frac{1}{3}$ (graphically)

A4.7 $x = ⁻1, y = ⁻2$ (graphically)

A4.8 **b** about $x = 2.75$ and $y = 2.25$ **c** 1.5 **d** $x = ⁻1.4$

A4.9 **a** about £27 **b** $\frac{1}{5}$
  d $y = \dfrac{x}{5}$ + £18 (or equivalent)
  e 160 minutes (2 hours 40 minutes)

A4.10 **c** about 3.5 **d** about 3.75

A4.11 **c** about 1.75 and ⁻1.75 **d** 1.9 and ⁻1.6 (graphically)

A4.12 **b** 4

A4.13 **c** 4.875 (graphically) **d** ⁺2.83, ⁻2.83 (graphically)

A4.14 **b** $x = 0.75$ (graphically)
  c i $x = 0.9$ (graphically) **ii** $x = ⁻1.2, 0.5$ and 1.8 (graphically)

A4.15 All graphical estimates
  b $x = ⁻0.75$ and 1.9 **c** ⁻2.2 **d** $x = 0.3$ and 1.9

A4.16 **b** The value of $\dfrac{3 - x}{x}$ approaches ⁻1 **c** ⁻2.3 (estimate)

A4.17 **c i** $x = 2$ and 3.2 **ii** 3.24 **d** 2

A4.18 $x = 0.8$

A5.1 **a** $3b + 4d > = 420$ **c** $b + d \leq 150$ **e** $70 \leq d \leq 104$

A5.2 **a** ⁻4, ⁻3, ⁻2, ⁻1, 0, 1, 2, 3, 4 **b** 3, 4, 5, 6, 7 **c** 1, 2, 3, 4, 5, 6
  d ⁻4, ⁻3, ⁻2, ⁻1, 0, 1 **e** 2, 3, 4, 5 **f** ⁻3, ⁻2, ⁻1, 0, 1, 2, 3

A5.3 **a** $x > 8$ **b** $x < 3$ **c** $x < ⁻\frac{1}{3}$ **d** ⁻14 < x < 14
  e $x < ⁻2$ **f** ⁻3 > x > ⁻3 **g** ⁻1 < x < 1 **h** $x < 2.5$
  i ⁻2 < x ⩽ 9

A5.4 3

A5.5 $d < 5\frac{1}{3}$

A5.7 ⁻216

A5.8 **a** $y = 3$ and $x + y = 10$ **b** $y > 3, x + y = < 10, y \geq 2x - 1$

A5.11 **b** $c < d$ **c** $5c + 8d \geq 80$
  e 13 stalls. 6 charity, 7 dealer stalls. **f** £86

A6.1 **a** $\frac{2}{3}$ **b** $6\frac{3}{4}$ **c** $1\frac{9}{16}$ **d** $\frac{1}{3}$ **e** 28

A6.2 **a** $10x^2 - 15x$ **b** $12ax^2 + 4a^2 - 4a$
  c $x^2 - 4x + 4$ **d** $a^3 - 2a^2 + 3a$

A6.3 **a** $x^2 + 5x + 6$ **b** $y^2 - y - 2$
  c $2x^3 - 7x^2 + 4x + 4$ **d** $10w^2 - 21w - 10$
  e $c^3 - 6c^2 + 12c - 8$ **f** $2x^3 - x^2 - 7x + 6$

A6.4 **a** $\frac{8}{15}$ **b** 0.325

A6.5 **a** 41.72 **b** $u = \sqrt{(u^2 - 2fs)}$
  c i $s = \dfrac{v^2 - u^2}{2f}$ **ii** 31.25

A6.6 **a i** $\sqrt{s} = 800$ **ii** $\sqrt{s} = 8$ **b** $f = \sqrt{\dfrac{s}{t^4}}$
  c $t = \sqrt[4]{\dfrac{s}{f^2}}$ **d i** ±0.707 (to 3dp)

A6.7 **a** $v(x + y)$ **b** $2(x - 2y)$ **c** $(p + 6)(p - 6)$
  d $(y - 3)(y - 15)$ **e** $3ax(x - 2)$ **f** $h(h + t)$
  g $ab(a - b)$ **h** $2a^2(3 + b)$

A6.8 **a** $2a^2b(2 - 3b)$ **b** $(t - 6)(t + 15)$ **c** $(2m - 3)(m + 1)$
  d $(p - 9)(p - 4)$ **e** $(4h + 1)(h - 3)$ **f** $(6x + 2)(x - 2)$
  g $n(n - 4)(n + 4)$ **h** $8b(b - 3)(b + 3)$

A6.9 **a** $1\frac{3}{7}$ **b** 0.096 (to 3dp)

A6.10 **a** $8w + 16$

A7.1 **b i** $n = 4d - 3$ **ii** 161

A7.2 **a** 32, 64, 128 **b** No **c** 2^{n-1}
  d 31, 63 **e** $2(n - 1) - 1$ **f** 7.136 238 454 × 10⁴⁴

A7.3 **a** Raj, Ranjit, Iqubal **b** 300th customer

A7.4 **a** 4, 18, 48, 100, 180

A7.5 **b i** $p = 3 + 3n$ **ii** $s = 2 + 4n$ **c** 298 **d** 171

A7.6 **a** 0.200, 0.480, 0.749, 0.564 **b** between 0.6 and 0.7

A7.7 4

A7.8 **a** $4n - 1$ **b** $50 - n$ **c** $2n + 3$ **d** $n^2 - 1$
  e n^3 **f** $n^2 + n$ **g** $7n + 2$ **h** $2^n - 1$

A7.9 A **a** $\frac{6}{13}, \frac{7}{15}$ **b** $\dfrac{n}{2n + 1}$

  B **a** $\frac{12}{94}, \frac{14}{93}$ **b** $\dfrac{2n}{100 - n}$

  C **a** $\frac{125}{6}, \frac{216}{7}$ **b** $\dfrac{n^2}{n + 1}$

  D **a** $\frac{5}{6}, \frac{6}{7}$ **b** $\dfrac{n}{n + 1}$

E   **a** $\frac{32}{243}, \frac{64}{729}$ **b** $\frac{2^n}{3^n}$

F   **a** $\frac{35}{85}, \frac{24}{96}$ **b** $\frac{60 - n^2}{60 + n^2}$

A8.2   **a**   10   **c**   Reflection in $y = 0$

A8.3   **c**   A translation of $\begin{pmatrix} 2 \\ 6 \end{pmatrix}$

A8.4   **b**   ⁻1.3, 1.8, 4.5 (approximate values)
      c   **ii** $y = x^3 - 5x$
      d   **ii**   ⁻1.2 (approximation)   **iii**   ⁻1.13

A8.5   **c** $y = -\dfrac{2}{x}$

A8.6   **b**   ⁻1.5 (approximation)   **c** $0 > n > 1.19$ **d**   **i** $y = x^3 - 2x^2$

A9.1   **a** $(3w - 1)$ cm   **b**   AC = 14 cm, BC = 16 cm, AB = 11 cm

A9.2   **a** $\sqrt{(m^2 + k^2)}$ **b**   both

A9.3   **b**   105.84 cm²

A9.4   **a** $\sqrt{\dfrac{3(9d^2 - 6d + 1)}{4}}$ **b**   square side 6 cm and triangle side 8 cm

A9.5   **a**   **ii**   280 000   **b** $n(a + b)$ **c**   **i**   1 600

A9.7   **a**   24 and 25   **b**   1   **c**   600   **b** 6×10^2

A9.8   **a** $(a - 2b)(a + 2b)$

A9.9   **a** $2n^2 - 5n - 12$ **b**   The number chosen was 4.

A9.10   **a** $2p + 5m = £26$, $4p + 3m = £31$ (or equivalent)   **d**   £5.50 and £3

A9.11   **b** y approaches ⁺1   **c**   asymptotes are $y = 1$ and $x = 0$
       d $x \approx $ ⁻1.2

A9.12   **a** $x = 1.39$ or $x = $ ⁻2.89   **d** $x = 0.87$

S1.1   **a**   A equilateral triangle   B square   C pentagon
       D hexagon   E octagon   F decagon
      b   A 180°   B 360°   C 540°
      c   D 120°   E 135°   F 144°
      d   **i**   7   **ii**   128.57° (to 2dp)
      e   36°
      f   equilateral triangles, squares and hexagons

S1.2   **a**   isosceles   **b**   70°   **c**   17°
      d   **i**   kite   **ii**   rhombus   **iii**   trapezium
      e   **i**   1   **ii**   2   **iii**   1
      f   **i**   hexagon   **ii**   no

S1.3   229°

S1.4   **a** $x = 40°$ and $y = 140°$ **b**   They are equal   **c**   80°   **d**   no
      e   **i**   360°   **ii**   angle AGH = 40°

S1.5   **a**   **i**   54°   **ii**   36°   **iii**   28°

S1.6   **a**   42°   **c**   Sketch to show QR // PT

S1.7   **a**   **i**   67°   **ii**   46°   **iii**   67°   **iv**   46°   **v**   46°   **vi**   134°
      b   ∠XRP = ∠RXW = 67°   **c**   No: ∠PRX = 67°

S1.8   **a**   95°   **b**   59°   **c**   110°

S2.1   **a**   90°   **b**   35°

S2.3   **a**   12°   **b**   100°   **c**   68°

S2.4   **a** $2x$ **b** y **c** $x - y$ **d** $180° - x$

S2.5   **a** p **b** $90° - q$ **c** $90° - p$ **d** $90° - p$

S3.1   **a**   (⁻2, 3)   **b** $(\frac{1}{2}, \frac{1}{2})$ **c**   (2, 1)   **d**   (7, 6)

S3.2   **a**   **i**   B(4,5,0)   **ii**   D(4,0,3)   **b**   (4, 2.5, 1.5)   **c**   (2, 2.5, 3)
      d   **ii**   60 cm³

S3.3   3 cm

S3.4   **a**   **i**   (0,0,12)   **ii**   (5,0,0)   **iii**   (5,10,0)
       iv   (0,4,12)   **v**   (5,0,6)   **vi**   (5,4,6)
      b   12 units   **c**   45°

S3.5   **a**   **i** (0,0,9)   **ii**   (16,4,9)   **iii**   (16,8,0)   **iv**   (16,0,9)
      b   832 units³

S4.1   **a**   150.8 mm²   **b**   **i**   1562 discs   **ii**   2644.6 cm²

S4.2   **a**   286 cm³ (to 3sf)   **b**   478.25 cm² (to 2dp)   **c**   83 cubes (to 2sf)

S4.3   **a**   20 642.36 cm³ (to 2dp)
      b   13936.59 (to 2dp)

S4.4   **a**   **i**   7°   **ii**   76°   **b**   596.90 m² (to 2dp)
      c   164.52 m² (to 2dp)   **d**   5764.82 m² (to 2dp)

S4.5   **a**   23.13 cm (to 2dp)   **b**   3 300 cm²

S4.6   **a**   346.4 cm²   **b**   9007 cm²
      c $x = 23.09$ cm (to 2dp), $y = 20$ cm, $z = 26$ cm
      d   3000 cm³ (to 4sf)

S4.7   **a**   376.99 cm (to 2dp)   **b**   80.16 cm (to 2dp)
      c   697.6 cm (to 1dp)   **d**   101054.6 cm³ (to 1dp)

S4.8   **a**   12 cm (to 2dp)   **b**   192 cm³ (to 2dp)
      c   4.50 cm (to 2dp) **d**   3.01 cm (to 1dp)

S4.9   **a**   length   **b**   area   **c**   volume   **d**   area

S4.10   **a** jk, $0.75\pi h^2$, $\frac{1}{2}\pi km$ **c** $\frac{1}{3}\pi m^2 l$

S4.12   **b** $A = \frac{1}{5}w(10h + 4s)$

S4.13   **a** πbh, $\pi h(b + s)$ **b** πbhs

S5.4   **d**   **i**   60°   **ii**   2.08 m (to 2dp)

S6.1   **a**   42.2 km   **b**   19.1 km/h (to 1dp)

S6.2   **a**   about 18.40 h   **b**   **i**   20 km   **ii**   about 13 km
      c   about 30 kph   **d**   about 10 mins
      f   yes: 120 km/h ≈ 74.6 mph

S6.3   **a**   no   **b**   3.3 m/s²   **c**   **i**   245   **ii**   metres (distance covered)
      d   63 km/h (60 km/h – 70 km/h)

S6.4   **a**   198 m²   **b**   20 seconds

S6.5   **a**   A (took less time)   **b**   200 m (9 m/s × 22 s = 198 m)
      c   A 165 m, B 135 m, C 122.5

S7.1   8.32 cm

S7.2   Answers **a** to **f** to 2dp
      a   56.92 cm   **b**   40.25 cm   **c**   25.46 cm
      d   44.09 cm   **e**   59.70 cm   **f**   31.18 cm
      g   P(18, 18, 18)   **h**   Q(18, 36, 18)   **i**   M(18, ⁻18, 18)

S7.3   **a**   **i**   11.003 541   **ii**   11° (to nearest degree)
      b   91 337.9 ft (to 1dp)   **ii**   91 350 ft
      c   (to 1dp) 170 537.9 ft (or 32.3 miles)

S7.4   **a**   3.34 m   **b**   65° (to 2 sf)

S7.5   **a**   470.50 m (to 2dp)   **b**   499.61 m (to 2dp)   **c**   320.61 m (to 2dp)

S7.6   1518.42 m (to 2dp)

S7.7   **a**   63.64 cm (to 2dp)   **b**   50.48° (to 2dp)   **c**   38.57 cm (to 2dp)
      d   59.74° (to 2dp)   **e**   26 102 cm³

S7.8   3.23 m

S7.9   2.639 m (to 3dp)

S7.10   **a**   26.7 cm   **b**   360.3 cm² (to 1dp)   **d**   10.2 cm (to 1dp)

S7.11   7.97 cm and 1.88 (to 2dp)

S7.12   **a**   4242.64 m (to 2dp)   **b**   2121.32 m   **c**   4.58 minutes

S8.3   **a**   a reflection in the y-axis
      b   several answers including: a reflection in $x = 2$ and a
       translation $\begin{pmatrix} 4 \\ 0 \end{pmatrix}$

S8.4   **c**   scale factor 0.5   **e**   rotation 180° centre C

S9.1   **a**   48°   **c**   10 cm

S9.2   **b**   90 cm   **c**   yes

S9.4   **a**   3015.93 cm³ (to 2dp)   **b**   5211.53 cm³ (to 2dp)

S9.5   1350 cm³ (allow for rounding)

S10.1   **a**   ⁻**v**   **b**   **w + v**   **c**   **v – w**

S10.2   **a** $6q - 3p$ **b** $3q - \frac{3}{2}p$ **c** $3q + \frac{3}{2}p$

S10.3   **a** $2x - 6y$

S10.4   **a**   **i** $\mathbf{k} - \mathbf{j}$ **ii** $\frac{1}{3}(\mathbf{k} + 2\mathbf{j})$ **iii** $\frac{2}{3}(2\mathbf{j} - \mathbf{k})$ **c**   1 : 2

S11.1   **b** $x \approx 68°$ and 112°   **c** $x \approx 60°$ and 147°

S11.2   **b**   ⁻60°, 60° 300° and 420° (marked on graph)

S11.3   **c** $x \approx 75°$ and 285°

S11.4   **b**   **i**   6   **ii** $x = 15°, 75°, 135°, 195°, 255°$ and 315°

S11.5   **b** $k = 222°$

S11.6   **b**   335°   **c**   **ii** $x \approx 15°$ and 195°

S11.7   **b**   after 6.2 s and 11.8 s (approx)
      c   after 5.2 s and 12.8 s (approx)

S11.8   **b**   15° and 165° (approx)   **c**   222° and 318° (approx)

S12.1   **a**   24 cm   **b**   6 cm   **c**   8 cm   **d**   53.13°

S12.2   **a**   72.5°   **b**   2.29 m   **c**   72 cm   **d**   84 cm   **e**   3.63 m

S12.3   **d**   BPA and CPD   **e**   45 square units   **f**   77.3°

D1.1 **a** i $\frac{1}{2}$ ii $\frac{1}{6}$ iii $\frac{1}{9}$ **b** $\frac{5}{18}$

D1.2 **a** 0.3 **b** 60 (approx) **c** 60

D1.3 **b** 0.3 **c** 0.1

D1.4 **b** $\frac{5}{18}$ **c** $\frac{4}{9}$ **d** $\frac{5}{42}$ **e** 0

D1.5 **a** 0.5 **b** 0.08

D1.6 **b** 0.57

D1.7 **a** $\frac{6}{80}$ or 0.075 **b** $\frac{50}{80}$ or 0.625 **c** approximately 800 000

D2.3 **a** 2.75 kg **c** bell-shaped

D2.4 **a** ii 3 years **b** 14 years **d** ii 30.5 years

D2.5 **a** 29

D3.1 **a** matches C **b** matches B **c** matches B
 d matches C **e** matches A **f** matches B

D3.2 **b** positive correlation

D3.3 **a** It shows a likely link between student attainment in
 Mathematics and French.
 b positive correlation

D3.4 **b** positive **d** 29 min

D4.1 **a** 26°C **b** 26°C **c** 9°C **d** 25.8°C (1dp)

D4.2 **a** 11 to 15

 b

Number of CD's	frequency	Mid-point	fx
1 to 5	3	3	9
6 to 10	8	8	64
11 to 15	12	13	156
16 to 20	10	18	180
21 to 25	6	23	138
26 to 30	1	28	28

 c i 14.375 CD's ii The data is only available in groups.
 d The 1990 mean is more likely to be accurate because a smaller
 class interval was used.

D4.3 **a** 31 to 40 **b** 34 minutes
 c i The extreme values in the distribution distort the mean.
 ii The median might be a better average as the extreme values
 will be ignored

D4.4 **a** Mean 51, standard deviation 1.84
 b B scores are higher on average, but are more inconsistent.

D4.5 **a** Mean £1395, standard deviation 270.20 (to 2dp)
 b Mean goes up by £140, standard deviation stays the same.
 c Mean goes up by 10%, standard deviation shows 10% wider
 spread.

D4.6 **a** Mean 5.4, standard deviation 1.62 (to 2dp)
 b Mean increases slightly, standard deviation shows greater
 variation.

D4.7 **a** mean £51.300 **b** standard deviation £23 259

D5.1 **b** ii about 88 **c** about 11
 d Alison (smaller interquartile range)

D5.2 **c** about 46 **d** about 200 **e** about 625
 f Megapower is the best (smaller range, higher median)

D5.3 **c** 27 or 28 calls (about 27.5)
 d No: only about 30% made more than 35 calls.

D5.4 **b** about 37 years **c** about 55 supporters

D5.5 **c** i about 14°C ii about 12°C
 d Durban – less widely spread (interquartile range is smaller)

D6.1 **a** set A Road Transport Federation, set B Canal Heritage Society,
 set C people leaving a cinema

D6.3 No: the data does not support Lyn's view.

D6.6

Year		7	8	9	10	11
No of students		22	21	19	20	18

D6.7 **a** Year 9 has more males than females.
 b

Year	Females	Males
9	10	11
10	9	10
11	11	10
12	6	5
13	3	5

D7.1 **b** A matches Lemon, B matches Vanilla, C matches Choc-Chip,
 D matches Strawberry, E matches Lime.

D7.2 **a** No: the sales axis does not start from 0.
 b The scale of the x-axis is not uniform.

D7.3 **b** from 60 up to but not including 90 minutes
 c from 90 up to but not including 120 minutes
 e about 31 people **g** $\frac{5}{21}$

D7.4 **a** 50 400 **b** 14 700 **c** i yes

D7.5 **a** 6 – 10 words **b** 11–15 words **c** 15.25 words
 d

<1	<6	<11	<16	<21	<26	<31	<36	<41
0	13	37	57	75	86	92	95	100

 f i 14 words ii 12/13
 g A – because B has more words per sentence and shows
 less variation.

D7.6 **a** 402 **b** i 0.36 ii 0.12 iii 0.343
 c slightly better. 7.2 wins expected